Twentieth
Century
America

Twentieth Century America

IRWIN UNGER

DEBI UNGER

ST. MARTIN'S PRESS   NEW YORK

Senior editor: Don Reisman
Development editor: Michael Weber
Project editor: Beverly Hinton
Text design: Leon Bolognese and Associates, Inc.
Graphics: Vantage Art
Photo researcher: Lynn Goldberg Biderman
Cover design: Darby Downey
Cover art: *Empire State* by Milton Bond. Jay Johnson, America's Folk Heritage Gallery, New York City.

Library of Congress Catalog Card Number: 88-63078

Manufactured in the United States of America.
43210
fedcba

For information, write:
St. Martin's Press, Inc.
175 Fifth Avenue
New York, NY 10010

ISBN: 0-312-03590-X (cloth)
ISBN: 0-312-00302-1 (paper)

Library of Congress Cataloging-in-Publication Data

Unger, Irwin.
    Twentieth-century America / Irwin Unger and Debi Unger.
        p.   cm.
    Includes bibliographies.
    ISBN 0-312-03590-X.— ISBN 0-312-00302-1 (pbk.)
    1. United States—Civilization—20th century.   I. Unger, Debi.
II. Title.
E1691.1.U54   1990   88-63078
973.9—dc20   CIP

To
Anthony, Brooke, Elizabeth, Miles and Jody, Paul and Eszter
and Layla
with love

Preface

As the twentieth century enters its final years, it calls out increasingly for review and interpretation. No doubt every century strikes those who have experienced it as a time of revolutionary change, but few periods, we believe, have encompassed such swift and often catastrophic transformation as have the years since 1900. Much of this process, of course, has been worldwide. Throughout the entire era, however, the United States has played a major role on the world stage. America's fate has been intertwined with virtually every important development taking place anywhere in the world.

And yet, the intimate and continuing connection between America's history and the history of the world in the twentieth century makes the story of the United States one that is distinctive from the stories of other nations. By the beginning of the century, the United States was already a world leader in technology and in the arts and styles of middle-class living, and its leadership in culture would be confirmed and reinforced when it also became a world political leader after 1945. The social, economic, and cultural history of the United States during this period, then, is the story of a nation that helped to "invent" the twentieth century for the rest of the world.

Although most instructors have long abandoned the notion that history is the story of rulers and elites, students still fear that their history courses will be dry recitations of politicians' names and the dates of treaties and Supreme Court decisions. *Twentieth-Century America* should change their minds. It deals not only with the political and diplomatic events of 1900 to 1990; it also describes intellectual, economic, social, cultural, demographic, and psychological change. It not only concerns presidents, judges, and senators; it also deals with painters, sports figures, movie stars, rock musicians, inventors, businesspeople, scientists, and journalists.

On the other hand, the text does not err by going to the opposite extreme. We believe that what elites believed and did, for good or ill, vitally affected virtually everyone. We have, accordingly, not ignored the political decision-making process and the political movements that helped transform American life. We have also tried to integrate the social-cultural story into the whole. With the exception of Chapter 2 on the new city, the events of daily life and the values, amusements, and customs of ordinary Americans are not kept separate but are incorporated into larger frameworks. The parts hang together, we believe, in *Twentieth-Century America*. (For instructors who do not wish to cover the entire twentieth century, St. Martin's Press publishes our *Postwar America: The United States since 1945,* which contains the last six chapters of this text.)

Every book is to some extent a cooperative effort—a text like this, inevitably, even more than most. We have reason to be grateful to many skilled and generous people for help in bringing *Twentieth-Century America* to completion. First, we would like to thank our editor at St. Martin's Press, Michael Weber. Michael's keenly attuned ear and remarkable knowledge of American history placed him far beyond the ordinary editor in his contribution to the final product. We would also like to thank St. Martin's senior editor Don Reisman and project editor Beverly Hinton. A number of scholars read the entire manuscript—or portions of it—and commented thereon. Among them were Professors Howard W. Allen of Southern Illinois University; Michael J. Brodhead of the University of Nevada, Reno; Leonard Dinnerstein of the University of Arizona; Henry C. Ferrell, Jr., of East Carolina University; Alonzo L. Hamby of Ohio University; Kenneth P. O'Brien of the State University of New York College at Brockport; Elizabeth I. Perry of Vanderbilt University; Peter L. Petersen of West Texas State University; Clifford H. Scott of Indiana University–Purdue University; Sarah Stage of the University of California, Riverside; and Hubert H. Wubben of Oregon State University. Their suggestions were extremely helpful, and they will find that many of them have been incorporated into the final text. Finally we would like to thank our agent, Gerrard McCauley, who helped to launch the book and has expedited the process of bringing it to a successful conclusion in a number of ways.

Irwin Unger
Debi Unger

Contents

MAPS AND CHARTS

Twentieth Century America

1
The
Nineties Watershed

The World's Columbian Exposition—the Chicago World's Fair—of 1893. (Library of Congress)

The Chicago World's Fair

One year late the United States celebrated the four hundredth anniversary of the discovery of the New World. The World's Columbian Exposition or Fair—the nation's official commemoration of Christopher Columbus's achievement—was held in 1893 on 700 acres near Chicago's lakefront. Reclaimed from sand and marshes, the ground was transformed into a fairyland of paths, trees, flowers, and gleaming white buildings by the skills of the country's finest architects, landscapers, and designers.

The Fair was representative of the decade. The 1890s were a watershed, a point in time when the old was dying and the new was struggling for birth. Stretching out behind was the isolated America of farms, villages, assured values, a population still predominantly of pre–American Revolution origins. Ahead was an imperial nation, a world leader, a country of factories and cities, a marketplace of contending ideas and values, with a cosmopolitan population drawn from every land on earth.

The World's Fair itself was a jumble of the past, the present, and the future. The scientific and technical exhibits displayed the best of what existed. Electricity Hall showed "the working of electrical apparatus in practical use," noted the official guide, and presented a "history of this science from its very inception, with models, and in some instances the actual appliances used by the early inventors." At the Transportation Building visitors could see "every mode of transportation, except the back of the mule and the foot of man." The amusements too were the most up-to-date. On the Midway, a broad street stretching the length of the Fair, was a giant Ferris wheel, 250 feet in diameter, from which one could view the entire 700 acres. This was a bibulous age, and the thirsty could buy beer, wine, and cocktails at a score of watering places. Also in the characteristic manner of the age, the Fair emphasized adults. Parents could deposit their small sons and daughters at the Children's Building, where they would be supervised by paid baby-sitters while their mothers and fathers took in the sights.

The Fair in many ways was also forward-looking. Reflecting the growing strength of the feminist movement, there was a Woman's Building, designed by Sophia G. Hayden, the first serious attempt to exhibit women's achievements in the arts, crafts, and literary realms from primitive times to the present. Housed at the Art Institute were displays looking toward, in the guidebook's words, a "new age in science, literature, education, government, jurisprudence, morals, charity, religion, and other departments." Some of the amusements also foreshadowed a new era. One of the Midway's chief attractions was Little Egypt, a naughty belly dancer whose popularity betokened a more permissive age following the public prudery of the recent past. An even more interesting feature of the Midway was an arcade where for a small price one could peer through a lens into a "kinetoscope," a device invented by that "wizard," Thomas A. Edison, and see a ninety-second show of figures moving as if they were alive.

Yet often, especially in its architecture, the Fair seemed to emphasize the past. The buildings, designed by the famous firm of Burnham and Root, were imitations of Greek and Roman temples. Painted white by spray guns, they gleamed in the bright summer air and delighted the hordes of visitors with their crisp classicism. But they were derivative throwbacks that did not reveal anything new or different about

American architecture. The Chicago architect Louis Sullivan, whose own Transportation Building, with its great Romanesque arch exotically ornamented, stood out from the rest, attacked the other structures as "bogus antique," and considered the Fair a bad influence on public taste. But even Sullivan's contribution looked to the past, although a different one from the others. His pioneer work in creating the modern office building still lay in the future.

Political Change

The Chicago World's Fair of 1893, then, caught the transitional nature of the decade. But it obviously could not reflect all the changes underway.

One of the most significant was the shift in the political environment. During the post–Civil War period, and especially in the 1880s, the two major American political parties had been of almost equal strength. Except for the periods 1889–91 and 1893–95, at no time between 1875 and 1897 did either party control both Congress and the presidency.

Politics as Sport

So evenly matched were the Democrats and the Republicans that national elections took on the qualities of exciting sporting events that brought the voters out in droves, if only to satisfy the competitive instinct.

Likening the politics of the Gilded Age—as the years from 1870 to 1900 are often called—to a game, a recreation, is not mere analogy. There were few legal holidays in these years and the workweek lasted through Saturday. Yet it was a rare employer who would interfere with the right of a free-born American male to exercise his civic rights. It is not surprising that political rallies became excuses to take the day off and enjoy oneself with friends and family.

Observers frequently noted the holiday atmosphere that surrounded these occasions. A reporter in 1876 described a political rally in Cambridge City, Indiana, with its "family parties in holiday attire" picnicking on the lawns, the "delegations . . . constantly arriving with music and banners; . . . troops of romping children, knots of rosy-cheeked girls, . . . young couples making love and eating luncheon at the same time. . . ." But the audience also paid close heed to the speeches. "As many people as can possibly hear pack in upon the seats rising amphitheater-like against a sloping hill, or make a thick ring around their margin," the reporter continued. "It is an attentive audience, quick to applaud a good point, and relishing keenly a funny story or witty remark."

Cultural Politics

The elements of play and competition were important in sustaining public interest in politics, but they do not explain party affiliations. Voters in those years were either Democrats or Republicans out of deep personal identification. Brand Whitlock, later mayor of Toledo, remembered that when he was growing up in Ohio the

Republican party was a "fundamental and self-evident thing." His family, neighbors, and friends considered Republicanism a "synonym for patriotism, another name for the nation." None of them could conceive that "any self-respecting person could be a Democrat."

During Whitlock's Ohio boyhood in the 1870s, views such as these were a legacy of Civil War loyalty to the Union. And in fact the Civil War and its accompanying issue of the place of African-Americans (blacks) in American political and social life was one of the chief political divisions in the 1890s and beyond. African-Americans themselves, although many had been disfranchised in the South after Reconstruction and few lived in the North, remained fiercely loyal to the party of Abraham Lincoln and emancipation. White southerners too were deeply influenced by the Civil War and its Reconstruction aftermath, but in the opposite direction: all but a handful—most living along the Appalachian spine where Civil War Unionism had been strong—were deeply committed Democrats. During the 1890s the leaders of the People's party—the Populists—for a time threatened to break the unity of the white Democratic South by appealing to white and black farmers alike. They made some gains, cutting into the dominance of the conservative "Bourbon" Democrats, those who wished to preserve white supremacy and elite planter-business rule. But they did not succeed in creating a true southern two-party system. In the end the "solid" Democratic South survived.

But political loyalties had other bases besides memories of the Civil War and the race issue. In the North, Republicanism ultimately derived from a view that the "Grand Old Party" (GOP) represented morality in politics as opposed to mere expediency. The great crusade against slavery was only a part of this moral stance. In addition Republicanism meant keeping the Sabbath as a holy day of rest, desisting from alcohol, and preserving the nonsectarian public schools. In each of these cases government must seek to protect and advance institutions and practices that reinforced a stable, godly community.

Republicanism made its strongest appeal to voters from a "pietistic" Protestant religious tradition that did not strictly separate the public from the private realms. Many old-stock native-born Americans north of Dixie belonged to these pietistic denominations—Methodist, Baptist, Congregationalist, and Presbyterian. Their numbers were particularly large, however, wherever people of New England ancestry were found: in rural New England itself, upstate New York, and in a broad band of the Midwest just south of the Great Lakes. People such as these—owing perhaps to their piety and sobriety—were often successful economically, forming the middle-class in many northern communities of mixed social origins. The effect of this circumstance was to associate Republicans with middle-class respectability in a special way.

Although most Republicans were of old-stock origins, more recent arrivals in the United States, including many Germans, Dutch, and Scandinavians, also voted for the GOP. But a common principle was at work here: as in the case of old-stock citizens, the loyalty to republicanism was strongest among those immigrants who belonged to the Protestant pietistic or "reformed" religious groups, where the emphasis was on personal conversion or regeneration rather than on religious practice and a set of clearly established beliefs.

In the North, apparently, the Democratic voters were mostly the rest—the nonpietists. Some of these people were native-born, and even of old stock. These included the nonchurched, those uninterested in religion or actively hostile to it. It also included Christians of the so-called liturgical faiths that emphasized ritual and ceremony and a prescribed credo rather than the necessity for personal conversion.

Some Lutherans belonged to this group, as did many Episcopalians. But the largest contingent consisted of Roman Catholics. A portion of the country's Catholic population could trace their ancestry to the colonial past; the overwhelming majority, however, were of relatively recent origin. The largest single group consisted of Irish-Americans who arrived in waves during the mid-nineteenth century and continued to come in large numbers after the Civil War. There were also many Germans from those parts of the *Vaterland* that had rejected Martin Luther and the other Protestant reformers. Since so many of the Catholic Irish and Germans were recent immigrants or the children of recent immigrants, their presence in the Democratic party gave it the appearance at times of being the party of the foreign-born. Their numbers also gave the Democrats a working-class cast, especially in the northern cities where most lived, since by and large they had not yet achieved the secure middle-class status of old-stock Americans.

In some ways the best descriptions of each major party in the Gilded Age were two epithets hurled by unfriendly critics. In 1884, during the course of the Grover Cleveland–James G. Blaine presidential race, a Presbyterian minister, the Reverend Samuel Burchard, called the Democratic party the party of "Rum, Romanism, and Rebellion," ticking off the party's major ethnic, religious, and sectional components. Some years before, Marcus Mills ("Brick") Pomeroy, a Democratic Wisconsin editor, blasted the Republicans as the "God and Morality" party. Although both remarks were derogatory, both also were accurate appraisals of the underlying loyalties that each party evoked.

Through much of the Gilded Age, especially in state and local elections, the parties struggled over cultural issues: parochial and foreign-language schools versus the nonsectarian "common school"; temperance laws versus the free production, sale, and consumption of liquor, beer, and wine; "blue laws" forbidding business, public sports, theatrical performances, and the like on Sunday versus the wide open "continental Sunday." These issues seldom reached the national level because the federal government of the day had little direct role to play in grass-roots social or educational matters. But eligible citizens generally established their party identities in response to local issues and voted for members of Congress or president accordingly.

Ideological Differences

Yet cultural differences are not sufficient to define the two major parties. There were also differences of principle and ideology, although these were often unclear and confused.

The Democrats, Jeffersonian in tradition and strongly southern, tended to support localism and states' rights as opposed to concentration of national power and authority in Washington. Most endorsed laissez-faire, a hands-off policy for government in relation to the economy. The Republicans, with roots in the Hamiltonian

Whiggism of the pre–Civil War period, accepted a more positive role for government, especially the federal government. In specific terms, the Republicans supported policies such as federal land grants to railroads to encourage construction of the transcontinent rail lines, high tariffs to protect American industry against foreign competition, and tight federal control of banks and money. The Democrats, opposed the land-grant policy, fought for freer trade to lower costs to consumers of foreign wares, and, especially in the South and West, favored a looser rein on money and banking. In each of these cases and others, however, the parties, whatever their primary principles, divided along sectional lines. The Democrats of Pennsylvania, the nation's premier iron and steel state, for example, were as protectionist as any Massachusetts Republican; the Republicans of Colorado, where silver mining was a major industry, were as opposed to national banks, "sound money," and the gold standard as any Georgia Democrat.

Taken together, although each party had certain central programmatic and ideological "tendencies," neither was "pure." Unlike their European counterparts, each represented a relatively broad umbrella under which voters of a wide range of views and principles could take shelter. To the despair of academics and dissenters, then as now elections often turned on candidates' personalities rather than party stands on specific issues.

Political Transition

Neither of the major parties during the 1870s and 1880s made an overt class appeal. Outside the South more Democrats certainly wore blue collars than white collars and more Republicans the reverse, but to have appealed to class loyalty would have risked uncomfortable social divisiveness and violated widely held pieties about American classlessness. Whatever the reasons, measured along a class axis, party allegiances overlapped substantially. This fact helps to explain the close party balance.

Then, in the West and the South long-smoldering rural and agrarian resentments over high interest rates, falling crop prices, railroad discrimination, and big business control of politics burst into flame. The resentment was in large part sectional, but it also took on class tones. Ignatius Donnelly, the Minnesota agrarian-intellectual and a founder of the People's (or Populist) party, declaimed about a nation fast dividing between "millionaires" and "tramps." The Populist platform of 1892 denounced "the great lords of plunder" and championed the oppressed "multitude." Although it is clear today that the Populists spoke largely for rural small business and the lower middle-class of the South and West against northeastern big business monopoly and the very rich, to many defenders of the status quo they seemed dangerous rabble-rousers determined to ally class against class and, if victorious, attack private property and undermine the established relations between rich and poor.

The Populists sought to win over the urban working-class, playing on the real discontent felt by blue-collar workers against long hours, low wages, hazardous and unhealthy working conditions, insecurity, and employer coercion. During the 1880s the Knights of Labor, organized in 1869, had expressed labor's desire for collective action to improve its lot. The Knights had peaked in 1885–86 with a membership of 700,000 and then, following the bomb-throwing incident at an anarchist rally in

Chicago (the Haymarket riot) and a failed strike against the Southwestern Railroad System, they declined. Thereafter the chief spokesman for labor was the American Federation of Labor (AFL), organized in 1886 by Samuel Gompers. Unlike the Knights, the AFL devoted most of its attention to skilled male workers, most of them native-born. Left out, either from bias or because they were more difficult to organize, were the industrial semiskilled, the foreign-born, African-American workers, and women. The AFL avoided politics and confined its efforts to improving its members' lot by collective bargaining with employers, with the strike as the ultimate weapon.

The Populist uprising failed. The Knights of Labor sent a delegation to the People's party organizing convention in St. Louis, but the Knights by then were in headlong decline. The AFL, on the upswing, refused to cooperate on the grounds that the Populists represented the nation's "employing farmers" and so had different interests from wage earners. Deprived of organized labor's enthusiastic support, the 1892 People party's presidential ticket of James B. Weaver of Iowa and James G. Field of Virginia received only one million votes out of twelve million cast, almost all in the deep South or the Plains and Mountain states. This was not an extraordinary performance, nor was the congressional election of 1894 any better. Neither of the two major parties as yet felt seriously challenged.

The Bryan-McKinley Campaign

In 1893 the stock market crashed, setting off a major depression. Unemployment soared; prices on the nation's farms, already low, plummeted. In the West and South many people blamed the gold standard; in the Northeast many blamed the agitation against the gold standard. The Democratic administration of Grover Cleveland further angered the West and South first by repealing the Sherman Silver Purchase Act that, sound money advocates believed, had precipitated the panic and then, to preserve the gold "reserve," by making a deal with J. P. Morgan and the international bankers. The rage of the nation's western and southern agrarians produced a revolt against northeastern "goldbugs" at the 1896 Democratic National Convention in Chicago and the surprise nomination for president of the thirty-six-year-old William Jennings Bryan, a former congressman from Nebraska.

The Republicans nominated William McKinley of Ohio. The Bryan-McKinley presidential race brought populist class resentment to the arena of major party conflict, frightening most of the major party leaders and deeply disturbing many middle-class voters. Bryan was a silverite who endorsed the western and southern demand for the free coinage of silver at the ratio to gold of sixteen to one. This was a way to end, he said, the domination of the rich over the poor, creditors over debtors, and the Northeast over the rest of the nation. He met formidable opposition within his own party. Many Democratic goldbugs defected. Some supported a separate National Democratic ticket; others voted for McKinley. Both they and their Republican equivalents considered Bryan and his followers radicals whose victory would threaten the stability of the capitalist order. They were, declared Theodore Roosevelt, "dangerous men, a menace to the nation."

Bryan hoped to sweep not only the West and South but also win the industrial workers of the eastern cities. Since the onset of the post-1893 depression, times had

Democrat William Jennings Bryan campaigning for president in 1896. (The Bettmann Archive)

gotten progressively harder and labor strife more bitter. In early 1894 "Coxey's Army" of unemployed workers had staged a march on Washington to demand federal intervention to provide jobs and restore prosperity. Soon after, a labor dispute at the Pullman Palace Car Company outside Chicago had precipitated a major railroad strike that brought federal intervention against the American Railroad Union led by Eugene V. Debs. With labor seething, Bryan had reason to believe that he might do well in the country's cities and industrial towns.

In fact he carried only the silver-mining Rocky Mountain states, the wheat-growing Great Plains, and the still solid South. He lost the Northeast, the older Midwest, and California and Oregon on the West Coast. In most places he did better in the rural areas than in the cities. (See Figure 1–1.)

Bryan had tried to create a new alliance of farmers, small-business people, and city workers—the "producing masses," in populist jargon. In fact he split the farmers between those who produced wheat and cotton for world markets (who voted for him) and those who produced pork, fruits and vegetables, and dairy products for domestic markets (who supported McKinley). He also drove many small-business people and industrial workers, especially in the Northeast, into the Republican camp. Such people were frightened off by what seemed to them divisive class appeals and, in the case of many wage earners, by the likelihood that free silver would raise consumer prices more effectively than it would employment. Bryan did modify the cultural dimensions of prevailing politics, but at the cost of converting many liturgical voters who formerly were Democrats into Republicans. This ended the close party balance that had existed since the end of the Civil War and made the Republicans the majority party. They would keep this ascendancy until the Great Depression and the New Deal of the 1930s.

The Bryan-McKinley campaign did, however, alter the political agenda. Although the currency issue, at least in its free silver form, would largely fade from politics, questions of wealth and poverty, concentrated economic power, the role of big business, and similar matters became focal points for political debate and discussion as never before.

Bryan also brought a new sectionalism into politics: West and South versus Northeast. By the mid-nineties the old North-South tensions, which had molded national politics since before the Civil War, ceased to matter much. On the Republican side the "Bloody Shirt" appeal that asked Union veterans to "vote as they shot" no longer could ensure loyalty to the party of Lincoln and emancipation except among the African-American minority who still retained the vote. Nor could Republican politicians work up much enthusiasm for continued baiting of the South. In 1889 a number of Republican senators had supported a federal elections bill (the Lodge

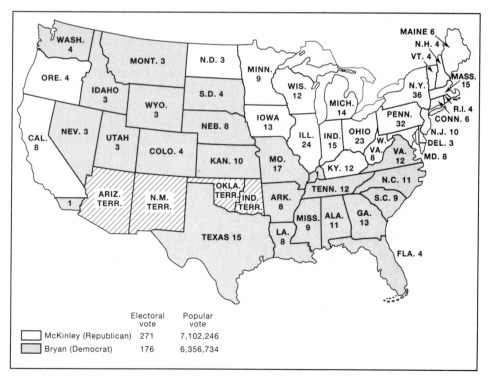

	Electoral vote	Popular vote
McKinley (Republican)	271	7,102,246
Bryan (Democrat)	176	6,356,734

Figure 1–1   The 1896 Presidential Election

Force bill) to ensure black voting rights in Dixie. The House passed the bill but the Senate did not. Even one of its supporters, Senator John Sherman of Ohio, denied any desire to "renew sectional excitement and controversy."

The Democrats, representing the defeated in 1865, remembered longer. The Democratic "solid South" would not be permanently breached for seventy-five years, yet the 1898 Spanish-American War helped to reconcile southerners to their Americanism and began the process that would make them today the country's most outspoken patriots.

Cultural Transition

In popular mythology the 1890s were the Gay Nineties, a time of new sophistication in the arts and popular culture, a time when Americans learned to enjoy themselves as never before, a carefree decade characterized by the high-kicking music hall soubrette in tights and bows, the barber shop quartet, and bawdy ballads. The myth is not false. The decade was fertile in the popular arts, and in many ways they were freer and more daring than during the stuffy years preceding.

Popular Music

The 1890s marked the appearance of some of the all-time favorite American pop tunes. Americans bought thousands of sheet music copies of "On the Banks of the Wabash," "Ta-Ra-Ra-Boom-De-Aye," and "While Strolling through the Park" to play on their parlor upright pianos. For a more raffish audience there was "Ragtime," a forerunner of jazz, stemming from the same urban Negro roots. Ragtime's earliest composers were African-American musicians in St. Louis, Memphis, and New Orleans. Its most successful practitioner was Scott Joplin, a classically trained black composer whose enormously successful "Maple Leaf Rag" of 1899 ushered in a ragtime fad that lasted until 1914. Ragtime seems innocent to us, but contemporary critics denounced it as "vulgar, filthy, and suggestive music." The critics' attacks made it all the more attractive to those young people, white as well as black, who sought to rebel against Victorian pieties.

Vaudeville and Burlesque

The 1890s was also the decade when vaudeville flourished. As an entertainment medium vaudeville went back to the traveling players of early modern times. By the 1880s, as developed and packaged by Tony Pastor, Edward Albee, and others, it had become a full-length variety show where for fifty cents to a dollar the audience could hear comedians, singers, and musical performers and watch animal acts, magicians, jugglers, and acrobats. Much of the humor was broad. Often it relied on ethnic stereotypes. Irish, Jews, Germans ("Dutch"), and African-Americans were all satirized and caricatured in ways that many contemporaries felt were funny—whatever the groups themselves may have thought.

Pastor was careful to keep vaudeville a family entertainment. He was only interested, he said, in "straight, clean variety shows." But another sort of live entertainment, geared to a male audience, also flourished in the 1890s in cities—burlesque. By recent standards 1890s burlesque was tame. Its emphasis even then was on the female form, but in those days the form was enclosed in close-fitting corsets and pink tights. The young women—usually beefy and blond—posed in pseudohistorical tableaux, sang comic songs, or performed in some mildly risqué skits. But as one contemporary critic noted, the girls "really had nothing to offer but their persons." After the triumph of Little Egypt at the Chicago World's Fair, many shows began to feature a belly dancer.

Motion Pictures

At the very end of the decade a new medium appeared, motion pictures. It would eventually eclipse vaudeville and become by far the most popular form of entertainment for the urban masses.

The title page of Scott Joplin's 1899 ragtime hit, "Maple Leaf Rag." (Culver Pictures)

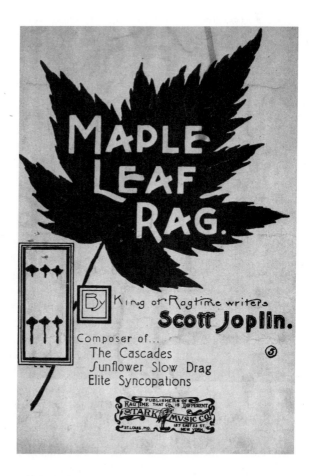

Soon after their introduction at the World's Fair, Edison's kinetoscopes were placed in storefront "parlors" throughout the country where for a few pennies customers could see a brief action sequence by peering through a peephole. So long as the moving film was confined to a box, however, profit was limited; only one person could watch at a time. The problem was solved by a contraption that threw images on a screen while moving a film strip through the device at a speed necessary to create the impression of motion. Edison bought the rights to one of the "projectors" and premiered his "vitascope" at Koster and Bial's vaudeville house in New York in 1896.

Motion pictures quickly became a standard part of many vaudeville performances, coming on at the end as a "chaser" between shows to get an earlier audience to leave while another took its seats. In 1900, when vaudeville performers around the country went on strike, the theater managers began to present full programs of motion pictures to keep the theaters open. This scheme proved successful beyond anyone's expectations. Not only did the owners survive the strike; they discovered that the public would pay to see the motion pictures. A new entertainment medium—and a new industry—had been launched.

Motion pictures ushered in a new era of mass entertainment. Here was a medium that could be enjoyed by audiences with little education and limited experience in life; viewers did not even have to understand English. Its nearest rival in these respects was baseball, but the "national sport" required some understanding of complex rules and a trip to a distant ballpark. The silent, flickering images of the "movies," with their childlike sketches of cavorting bathing beauties, prizefights, lovers kissing, and brief views of famous places, appealed to the lowest common denominator and were readily accessible. In 1905 two Pittsburgh impresarios established the "Nickelodeon," where customers paid five cents for admission. By 1908 thousands of nickelodeons were in operation, and movies had become the chief entertainment fare of millions of working-class Americans.

The Yellow Press

Although nothing could compete with the motion picture for "accessibility," the new *yellow press* ran a close second. The first successful penny newspaper was Benjamin Day's *New York Sun,* founded in 1833. In 1868 Charles A. Dana bought the *Sun* and transformed it into the modern American newspaper. Dana introduced the "human interest" story and filled his pages with gossip, crime, and scandal stories as well as amusing, sentimental, or pathetic pieces that captured the texture of everyday life. Yet despite Dana, the daily newspaper remained a vehicle for the educated middle class. Not until Joseph Pulitzer, publisher of the *St. Louis Post-Dispatch,* took over the *New York World* in the 1880s did the new journalism genre really find a mass audience.

Pulitzer was determined to make the declining *World* a winner. One way was to battle for "the people with earnest sincerity" and expose all "fraud and sham." The *World* advocated income and inheritance taxes, civil service reform, and better treatment of the immigrants who were pouring into New York. But popular causes,

Pulitzer knew, were not enough. The *World* must also entertain and amuse the masses of the city. To intrigue readers, Pulitzer launched a series of promotional schemes. The most famous of these was the dispatch of "girl-reporter" Nellie Bly on a trip around the world to beat the time of Phileas Fogg, Jules Verne's fictional hero of *Around the World in Eighty Days.* Nellie Bly won, making the circumnavigation in 72 days, 6 hours, 11 minutes, and 14 seconds from door to door.

Pulitzer's most successful scheme to capture the masses, however, was the comic strip. Although there had been several forerunners, it was Richard Outcault's "Yellow Kid," appearing as a feature of the *World's* new Sunday color section in early 1896, that marked the advent of newspaper "comics." The Kid was a preposterous-looking, bald, gap-toothed, tough street gamin who dressed for no discernible reason in a yellow flour sack and who talked a slum dialect of "deses," "dems," and "doses." The "Yellow Kid" does not seem very entertaining today. But in some oblique way it expressed the feelings of inarticulate turn-of-the-century city people and helped to push the *World's* circulation to one million readers by 1898.

Pulitzer's success brought William Randolph Hearst rushing into the field. Hearst was a Californian whose father had made a fortune in Nevada silver mining and then had acquired the *San Francisco Daily Examiner.* In 1887 he dropped out of Harvard and badgered his father into letting him take over the paper. By 1891, through zany promotional schemes, avid gossip mongering, and sensationalism, Hearst had made the *Examiner* the biggest daily on the Pacific Coast. But San Francisco seemed too small for a publisher with his ambitions. In 1895, with money pried from his now-widowed mother, Hearst bought the *New York Journal* and came to the metropolis resolved to beat Pulitzer at his own game.

One of Hearst's first moves was to steal Outcault and the "Yellow Kid" from his rival. Pulitzer soon got someone else to do the strip for the *World.* With both publications featuring the "Yellow Kid," a critic was quick to identify the new sort of newspaper as the "yellow press." Pulitzer then hired Outcault back to draw a new comic strip, "Buster Brown," about a young scamp and his dog that became even more popular with both parents and children than his first creation. What followed was a virtual comic-strip war with each of the press lords seeking to outdo the other with new characters in new situations to amuse the city working class and expand circulation.

Like Pulitzer, Hearst made his paper a defender of popular causes. The *Journal* attacked Consolidated Gas for its overcharges and forced it to lower its rates; it exposed the abysmal conditions under which many women worked in sweatshops; it agitated for the ten-hour work day; it campaigned for improved public schools. At the same time the *Journal,* like its rival, served up a daily diet of sex, crime, stunts, and human interest that intrigued the city's masses. At the end of the decade the Pulitzer-Hearst rivalry became a competition to stir up American outrage over Spain's treatment of Cuban revolutionaries seeking to oust Spain from one of its last remaining Western Hemisphere colonies. Correspondents for each paper looked for the latest outrages in Cuba to transmit to their editors. The war was pursued with brutal tactics by both sides, providing a steady stream of stories to make the blood of Americans boil. But occasionally the atrocities flagged. At such times, Hearst, especially, was happy to invent news to keep the pot boiling. By the time America entered the war in April 1898, both the *Journal* and *World* had achieved circulations of over one million.

Hearst used the yellow press to create a publishing empire that spanned a dozen cities and papers around the country. Other editors, including Frank Munsey and Edward Scripps, took up the yellow press formula. People of "good taste" did not approve of yellow journalism. Clergymen assailed Hearst and Pulitzer from their pulpits as purveyors of smut and sordid material. Literary clubs and librarians attacked the yellow press as both illiterate and "cheap." A more balanced critic, Lincoln Steffens, acknowledged that Hearst had championed many good causes. But if there was not "room . . . for a list of the good things Mr. Hearst has . . . tried to do," there also was not "room either for a list of the bad, the small things he has done; the scandals he has published, the individuals he has made to suffer beyond their deserts . . . . His papers 'appealed to the people'; yes, to their 'best interest,' and to their worst."

Literature

Serious fiction, especially the novel, took a new turn during the 1890s. By the 1870s a crop of young writers had appeared anxious to depict the world around them "realistically," without the sentimentality and sugarcoating that the previous age seemed to demand.

Realism

The realists favored the accurate depiction of life and manners. Fiction should avoid sugarcoating reality, making it prettier than it was. Their characters were not unusual men and women—princes, witches, pirates, artists, and eccentrics—but ordinary people—farmers, businesspeople, soldiers, homemakers. In the realists' novels and stories, people talk the way their kind actually do, whether slang and dialect or standard English. In their plots things do not happen that typical men and women do not encounter in daily life. They try to *report* life as it is actually lived.

The outstanding American realist was William Dean Howells, an Ohio-born newspaperman turned novelist who came east to edit the prestigious *Atlantic Monthly* after the Civil War. Howells's first works of fiction did not depart much from his contemporaries'. But then in *A Modern Instance* (1882), a study of married life, and *The Rise of Silas Lapham* (1885), a depiction of a self-made businessman, he introduced a new quality of portraiture drawn from recognizable life. During the 1890s Howells became more sensitive to the disparities of social life in America and wrote several novels that depicted the injustices of the existing economic order. In 1894, in imitation of Edward Bellamy's best-seller *Looking Backward,* he created a fictional socialist utopia in *A Traveller from Altruria.*

Naturalism

Although some of Howells's best work was written in the 1890s, he was already becoming dated by the transition decade. Newer authors, influenced by the French *naturalists,* especially Emile Zola, by scientific determinism, and by Darwinian notions of remorseless competition (discussed later in this chapter), were beginning to carve out a new approach to imaginative fiction.

The five novelists acknowledged as the core of the naturalist school were Hamlin Garland, Stephen Crane, Frank Norris, Jack London, and Theodore Dreiser. Each in his own way tried to go beyond what he perceived as the evasions of realism. The naturalists were not interested in the commonplace, however prevalent the commonplace was in life. They saw the world as a heartless interplay of deterministic forces in which men and women were mere objects, unable to control their own lives. The forces were economic or physical or biological, and they gripped—and usually crushed—their unheroic, passive characters in an irresistible embrace.

Garland The pioneer of the group was Hamlin Garland, a midwestern farmer's son who came east in the 1880s and fell under the influence of Howells. At the end of the decade Garland visited his family and friends in the Dakotas and was struck by the squalor and the agony of farm life. "Nature was as beautiful as ever," he reported in *Main-Travelled Roads* (1891), "but no splendor of cloud, no grace of sunset, could conceal the poverty of these people; on the contrary they brought out, with more intolerable poignancy, the gracelessness of these homes and the sordid quality of the mechanical daily routine of these lives." In a series of works through the 1890s (*Prairie Folks,* 1893; *Rose of Dutcher's Coolly,* 1895) he continued to portray the bleak life of farm folk.

Garland believed that his harsh description of rural America was truthful and honest; he called his approach "veritism." In a work of criticism, *Crumbling Idols* (1894), he sought to become the spokesman of a new group of younger writers who, like himself, were willing to depict the dark side of American life without fear of the Pollyanas. In fact, Garland, like the others, was selective in his subject matter and his interpretations: there were often other sides that were sunnier and more appealing. However influential, Garland's early works did not sell, and he eventually changed his line. He is remembered today largely for *A Son of the Middle Border* (1917), an account of his rural youth covered with a layer of saccharine nostalgia.

Crane Stephen Crane, one of the younger writers whom Garland sought to lead, wrote about urban, rather than rural, squalor and pain. Son of a New Jersey Methodist minister, Crane worked as a journalist and foreign correspondent for a number of years before trying his hand as an imaginative writer. His first novel, *Maggie* (1893), is about a poor girl living in New York's Bowery who is forced into prostitution and eventually commits suicide. Crane found it difficult to get his grim story accepted by a publisher. A far better work, *The Red Badge of Courage* (1895), describes the ordeal of a young soldier in his first battle during the Civil War and how he faces "the great death." Although in the end Henry Fleming lives, his story is not one of heroism on the model of the day but of survival, a much more modern concept of victory.

Crane's own life was untriumphant. He lived for long periods as an impoverished writer in New York's emerging bohemia. He drank too much, took drugs, and died of tuberculosis in 1900 at the age of twenty-nine.

Norris   Frank Norris was a Californian, educated at Berkeley, where he fell under the influence of Zola. In 1899 he published *McTeague,* the story of an unsuccessful San Francisco dentist and his wife, Trina, who are driven by greed and whose characters gradually deteriorate. McTeague's descent to the level of the brute culminates in his murder of Trina. In 1900 Norris conceived "an idea . . . big as all outdoors." He would write a trilogy of novels revolving about the epic of wheat: how it was produced, financed, and marketed for the hungry of the world. The first volume, *The Octopus* (1901), told of the struggle between California wheat growers and the Southern Pacific Railroad through the story of a single grower, Magnus Derrick. The confrontation eventually ends in tragedy. As usual with the naturalist writers, forces—human and natural—defeat even the best-intentioned men and women.

In the second volume of his series, *The Pit* (1903), Norris told about the Chicago grain exchange where brokers bought and sold wheat. Like *McTeague,* it describes the degeneration of personality under the pressure of avarice. The third projected volume, to be called *The Wolf,* was never written. Norris died in 1902 at the age of thirty-two.

London   Jack London, like Norris, was a Californian. Born into dire poverty, he learned about life along the Oakland waterfront while working as a seaman, a janitor, and a factory hand. His politics and personal philosophy came from both Karl Marx and the Social Darwinists through voracious reading at the public library. In 1897–98 London joined the gold rush to the Klondike, but returned as poor as he had gone. To earn money, he started to write about his Yukon experiences and published a collection of these stories, *The Son of the Wolf,* in 1900. Over the next few years he produced three novels—*The Call of the Wild* (1903), *The Sea Wolf* (1904), and *White Fang* (1906)—that marked him as a powerful storyteller in the new naturalistic mode.

In these and other works London combined a disgust for capitalist greed, a celebration of the primitive and amoral, and a sensitive feeling for nature. London was not always in control of this inconsistent material and his work often seems puerile. Despite his deficiencies as an author London became rich and famous. Late in life he retired to Sonoma County in California, where he began to build his dream house. In 1916, before it could be completed, he died of alcoholism.

Dreiser   Theodore Dreiser was probably the most influential and impressive of the naturalist writers who erupted on the scene in the 1890s. He was never a deft stylist; his prose is often crude and awkward. Yet his novels vibrate with more sheer power than those of all his colleagues. Much of Dreiser's long career falls well into the new century, but his first novel, *Sister Carrie* (1900), reflects the emerging naturalism of the nineties.

Dreiser was born the same year as Stephen Crane, 1871, to an immigrant German workman and an American-born Pennsylvania farm girl of German stock. He grew up in small towns in Indiana where the family experienced poverty, disappointment, and social ostracism. His father was a stern disciplinarian and a man obsessed with the pitfalls of unbridled sexuality. Dreiser's boyhood was inevitably beset by fears and doubts, many of them sexual.

One of the young man's formative experiences was his move to Chicago. Here he worked as a restaurant helper, a collector for an installment-plan furniture company, a laundry-wagon driver, and later a newspaper reporter. The contrasts between wealth and misery that he encountered stimulated his imagination. The city, he later wrote, "sang . . . and . . . I was singing with it."

Dreiser's first novel, *Sister Carrie,* is about a young small-town woman, Carrie Meeber, who comes to Chicago to help earn some money for her poor family. She finds work difficult to get and, discovering the value of her good looks, becomes the mistress of a glib traveling salesman, Charles Drouet. But Carrie finds that she can do better than Drouet and takes up with a prosperous saloonkeeper, George Hurstwood, who sacrifices his family and reputation to run off with her to New York. There Carrie carves a career for herself as an actress and in turn throws over the now unneeded Hurstwood. Hurstwood's personality falls apart.

The book's theme of the power of the sexual drives and their ability to destroy men and women was strong meat for the day. Doubleday & Page, which had signed the work, sought to back out of its contract. Ultimately the firm came out with a small edition of 1500 copies but failed to publicize it.

The book was greeted by a resounding silence. Not until it was reissued in 1907 was it widely noticed. Meanwhile, Dreiser had suffered a nervous breakdown and stopped writing. Following the novel's reissue, he recovered and went on to write a series of books over the next thirty-five years that brought to a culmination the naturalism of his youth. In works such as *Jennie Gerhardt* (1911), *The Financier* (1912), and *The Titan* (1914), he portrayed characters driven almost solely by their desires—for sexual fulfillment, for money, for power. Dreiser's world is a jungle where the strong triumph and the weak succumb. His most memorable work, *An American Tragedy* (1925), based on a real-life crime, recounts the fate of Clyde Griffiths, a young man without prospects who allows his pregnant girlfriend to drown so he can marry a well-connected young woman whose family can save him from poverty and obscurity. Clyde is tried and convicted of murder. The tragedy is "American" because Clyde's fate, in Dreiser's view, is the inevitable product of the fierce drives for status and wealth that blight American life.

Other Writers   Although art has a life of its own it is obviously influenced by the social and economic currents of its day. Kate Chopin was a novelist who spoke in the voice of the *new woman,* an emerging type of independent, well-educated, strong-minded woman, impatient with the restrictions and limitations imposed on her sex. In Chopin's novel *The Awakening* (1899), Edna Pontellier, wife of a New Orleans businessman and mother of two, finds her respectable life suffocating and in her quest for personal fulfillment casts it aside. In the end Edna dies by drowning, perhaps not the best endorsement of the new feminism.

Not all American authors of the turn-of-the-century followed the latest realist or naturalist literary fashions. Two of the finest were Henry James and Edith Wharton. Henry James wrote subtle, frequently overrefined, novels of manners revolving about sensitive young Americans confronting the more complex society and culture of Europe. He himself had difficulties achieving relationships with members of the opposite sex, but his heroines are strong-willed, competent women, unfazed by the restrictions imposed on them by the social proprieties of the day. Edith Wharton, a member of the old New York upper crust, wrote about the confrontation between a new vulgar plutocracy and the older mildewed elite. She disliked both, but her heroines, often copies of herself, are free-spirited members of the older aristocracy caught tragically between the two cultures.

Painting and Architecture

Americans did not lack for talented painters during the 1890s. Thomas Eakins, a Philadelphian trained in Paris and Spain, continued to paint in a realist style influenced by his profound knowledge of human anatomy, although his best works date from the 1870s and 1880s. Winslow Homer, a Bostonian who settled in Maine, spent the last decade of the century painting brilliant seascapes that capture the majesty and power of the marine aspect of nature. A painter who attracted little notice in his day but was acclaimed after his death was Albert Pinkham Ryder, a creator of brooding, mysterious scenes, that call out for symbolic interpretation. Mary Cassatt, a wealthy expatriate resident in Paris, absorbed the impressionism of her Parisian colleagues and gave it a special warmth and directness. In her own day she suffered the neglect of many women artists. Today she has come to be recognized as an important figure in the impressionist movement.

Although America had its talented painters during the 1890s, few were innovative. Not until the opening years of the new century would there be a distinctively American school of painting. In architecture, however, in that decade Americans made a major contribution to the world in the form of the skyscraper.

The Skyscraper

The skyscraper was a response to a number of special challenges created by the environment of the late nineteenth-century American city. By the end of the century land prices in major downtown areas were exorbitant by the standards of the day. The obvious way around this difficulty for those seeking abundant space was to build up. But a tall building had serious drawbacks. To bear the weight of many floors, foundations and lower walls had to be immensely thick. Besides the high cost entailed, this meant that much usable space would be wasted. And how were people, furniture, supplies, and so forth to be gotten conveniently to the top of, say, a twenty-story building?

The solutions were found by a number of architects, mostly working out of Chicago during the late 1880s and 1890s. These men combined the new technology of electricity with that of steel to create the modern skyscraper.

Instead of thick masonry walls to carry the weight, they devised the light but immensely strong steel frame. Walls in such buildings did not bear the weight; they were merely curtains to keep the elements out and the occupants in. To replace the stair, they used the fast electric elevator that could whisk people or freight from lobby to lofty building top in a matter of minutes.

The first steel-frame building on the new model was probably the Home

Insurance Building designed by William LeBaron Jenney in 1884–85. This structure and Jenney's later buildings took advantage of the new technology but only for practical ends. In appearance, they did not diverge from standard classical treatments of facades and other decorative characteristics. The man who saw that the new construction technique called for a different aesthetic expression was the architect of the Chicago World's Fair Transportation Building, Louis Henri Sullivan, a one-time employee of Jenney. While with the firm of Adler and Sullivan, he designed a number of structures, including the Wainwright Building in St. Louis (1890) and the Gage Building in Chicago (1898), that were the first true steel and curtain-wall buildings, although scarcely of modern skyscraper height. (The Wainwright Building was only twelve stories high.)

Sullivan's structures were not devoid of decoration. Indeed he was a master of

Steel-frame skyscrapers going up in Chicago early in the twentieth century. (The Bettmann Archive)

decorative detail. But the detail was subordinate to the building's *function.* Sullivan was something of a moralist who made honesty of architectural purpose into an ethical principle. "Form must follow function," he announced on frequent occasions, and structures that did not reveal their actual use—whether residential, commercial, governmental, or whatever—but sought to disguise themselves as Greek temples or Gothic churches were morally deficient. This vision was the basis for Sullivan's harsh attack on the classical Greco-Roman architecture of the Chicago World's Fair.

One architect who absorbed the Sullivanian ethic was a young man from Wisconsin, Frank Lloyd Wright. Wright worked for Adler and Sullivan during the 1890s and helped design Sullivan's Transportation Building for the 1893 Fair. Although he admired Sullivan's functionalism, he had little use for cities and in the course of his long life contributed little to the skyscraper form. In 1894 Wright set up for himself in Oak Park, Illinois, where he used functionalism as the design principle for private residences with clean horizontal lines suited to the flat midwestern prairies.

New Ideas

Shifts in politics, popular tastes and amusements, literature, and the visual arts were matched during the last decade of the nineteenth century by shifts in ideas and values.

Formalism

Most well-educated Americans during the years immediately following the Civil War viewed the world as a sort of mechanical contrivance. The universe was governed by laws that ultimately derived from God. The Lord had established these rules at the beginning, at the time when He created the earth, the sun, the planets, the stars and all living creatures. The universe now operated by these laws much as a clock was propelled by the wheels, springs, and gears forged by the clockmaker. Society too was a mechanism governed by fundamental laws. In the realm of social events, as in science, there were fixed principles. If we could discover these rules, we could understand how society worked, and this understanding in turn would guide us to correct social policy.

This way of thinking about society scholar Morton White has called *formalism.* Formalistic thinkers in law, economics, sociology, and philosophy derived basic principles and then drew inferences from them, much as one applied axioms to the solution of problems in geometry.

Whether in social or scientific thought, formalism was deductive, static, and tied to the past. In general it buttressed conservative social positions, attitudes that rejected political and economic change and favored the existing social order. It was a cast of mind appropriate to a world of mid-Victorian certitude, but it was by the 1870s already under powerful attack.

Darwinism

The chief source of the attack was *Darwinism,* the world view derived from the theories of Charles Darwin, the British naturalist who in 1859 astounded and disturbed the educated world with his book *The Origin of Species.* Darwin claimed that change was implicit in the biological world, that over the course of an immense period the competition among living creatures for survival had provided the impetus for change from simpler and more primitive to higher and more complex forms. The world was not a finished entity created in one blinding flash but a product of evolution, of slow change over time, a process that presumably was still not concluded.

The Origin of Species challenged simultaneously a flock of passionately held beliefs. It denied the Judeo-Christian story of the creation of the universe by God in six days, as expressed in Genesis, the first book of the Bible. Along with Darwin's later *Descent of Man,* it seemed to deny the semidivinity of humankind by connecting human beings to the animal world. It also challenged the mechanical view of the cosmos. Rather than a static clockwork device, repeating endlessly the same motions and processes, the universe seemed to resemble an organism that evolved over time.

In the social realm Darwinism lent itself to both conservative and liberal conclusions. Social conservatives in this era denounced government intervention in economic affairs to protect the weak and encourage greater social equality. Social progress, they insisted, could only come about if society allowed the laws of competition to operate without interference. Conservative *Social Darwinism,* as expounded by Herbert Spencer, a British philosopher, and William Graham Sumner, a Yale professor, endorsed unbridled economic competition. Only by allowing the principle of "survival of the fittest" (Spencer's phrase) to operate, could humankind forge ahead. Sumner issued essay after essay denouncing the "humanitarians, philanthropists, and reformers" who sought to protect the poor against their own incompetence, improvidence, and folly. Society, he insisted, must not try to guarantee equality of "results" but only equality of "chances." Government must pursue a totally hands-off policy if progress was to be made. In the end "the work of civilization" must be to increase or improve the "chances," not "redistribute the acquisitions which have been made between existing classes."

But there were also Social Darwinists who perceived a liberal lesson in Darwinism, who believed that the laws of evolution condoned overall social planning to decrease inequality and encourage a more benevolent society. According to Lester Frank Ward, *human* progress, at least, was not the result of dog-eat-dog. Civilization represented triumph *over* "the law of competition," not acquiesence in it. Foreshadowing the liberalism of the twentieth century, Ward advocated "the scientific control of the social forces by the collective mind of society for its own advantage."

Antiformalism

But it was above all its erosion of formalistic thinking that made Darwinism a force for social liberalism. The *antiformalist* social thinkers saw evolution as a powerful concept to refute rigid, conservative ways of thinking about society. By analogy with the natural realm as Darwin depicted it, in place of a static view of the social world they posed one in constant flux. Change, rather than persistence, characterized society. There were no fixed and unalterable social laws and public policy could not be deduced from first principles. Rather, each age, each era, could only chose its own course, one that was right for itself.

In the field of jurisprudence, the best exemplar of the new attitude was Oliver Wendell Holmes, Jr., a Boston Brahmin whose father and namesake was a prominent doctor and minor poet and essayist. In 1881 Holmes wrote *The Common Law,* in which he took direct issue with the standard view that law was deduced by judges from first principles.

> The felt necessities of the time, the prevalent moral and political theories, intuitions of public policy, avowed or unconscious, even the prejudices which judges share with their fellow men have a good deal more to do than the syllogism in determining the rules by which men should be governed.

In his 1897 speech "The Path of the Law," he sought to further demystify the law. "[T]he prophecies of what the courts will do in fact," he declared, "and nothing more pretentious, are what I mean by the law."

In the field of economic thought Holmes's views found their equivalent in the ideas of Thorstein Veblen, a dour, eccentric, nonconformist professor of economics at Stanford and other universities. Veblen had no patience with the standard economic models of the day, mostly derived from Adam Smith, David Ricardo, and their successors. These posited rational self-interest and the "invisible hand" of laissez-faire competition as the basic laws that guided economic events and built economic institutions. But like the supposed rules of jurisprudence, these laws did not come close to describing reality. The only way to understand what actually took place in business and the economy was to examine how economic institutions had evolved over time.

In his famous book *The Theory of the Leisure Class,* written in 1899, Veblen described modern capitalists as operating not by rational rules of profit maximizing but by considerations of status and prestige derived from a remote barbarian past. This explained such bizarre forms of behavior as "conspicuous consumption" and "conspicuous leisure," both designed to establish superiority over competitors, though both were counterproductive and costly. In this and later books Veblen helped establish the field of *institutional economics,* which sought to replace formalistic abstract principles with analysis of dynamic, changing historical processes as a way to understand how the economy really operated.

Religious Thought

By providing a powerful explanation for puzzling questions of human origins, Darwinism enormously increased the already powerful hold of science and its methodology on the minds of educated people and posed a serious challenge to Bible-oriented conservative Protestantism.

Traditionalists fought back with ridicule and contempt. Darwinism was the "bestial hypothesis" of human origins, charged one defender of orthodoxy. Those who repudiated the Bible were either "derationalized or demoralized, or both."

Those who accepted evolution's teachings were committing blasphemy, the religious conservatives said, and they would be punished for their sin.

But traditional Protestantism was under attack from several other quarters as well. If Darwinism challenged the Bible with an alternative explanation for human origins, the *higher criticism* took on God's revealed word directly by attacking orthodox belief in the supernatural elements of Christianity. The higher critics, armed with new linguistic, historical, and archaeological tools, denied miracles, questioned revelation, and—so their detractors held—reduced Christ to a human prophet and the Bible to a hodgepodge of myth, history, polemic, and ethical teachings, written by human beings over many centuries. The higher critics were mostly German, yet their views powerfully influenced the thinking of portions of the American Protestant clergy and laity alike. Even more accessible to Americans were the writings of the British thinkers Edward Tylor and James Frazer, who created a new field of comparative religion. Through Frazer's enormously popular 1890 work *The Golden Bough* thousands of Americans were introduced to the concept that Christianity was only one of many religions with equal claim to validity.

As the years passed and Darwinian ideas became more familiar, many clergymen and pious laypeople found it possible to reconcile their beliefs and the new views. In 1893 the New York Chautauqua, a popular lecture organization, noting the new atmosphere, without serious protest invited a Scottish scientist to give a series of talks on evolution to its mainstream audience. Yet the older views survived in many denominations, especially those that were rural based, and during the new century they became the core of a new religious *fundamentalism.*

Still another challenge to orthodoxy derived from the *Social Gospel* movement. Mainstream Protestantism of the Gilded Age emphasized personal salvation as the central concern of the good Christian. Achieving God's grace must be each individual's chief goal. By the 1800s, as Protestants tried to confront the new industrial era, some clergy came to believe that Christianity must shift its emphasis from the individual to the larger society. Christians must start "getting right" with their fellow men.

The first of the prominent Social Gospel preachers was Washington Gladden, a Congregational minister of Columbus, Ohio, whose *Applied Christianity* (1886) disseminated widely the Social Gospel ministers' views. Gladden believed that the churches could not be neutral in the struggles of the poor for a better life. He endorsed trade unions and the right to strike. He and many of his fellow Social Gospel spokesmen, also embraced the views of the higher critics regarding the human origins of Christianity and the Scriptures. The combination created in effect a Protestant *modernism* that would later confront a Protestant fundamentalism.

Under the influence of the Social Gospel idea many ministers and their congregations in the 1890s endorsed the *institutionalized church movement.* Abandoning their exclusive emphasis on spiritual concerns, these congregations sought to become community agencies with paid social workers, gymnasiums, athletic clubs, social halls, day nurseries, and sewing classes. In the next decade the combination of theological modernism and social liberalism would be embodied in the Federal Council of Churches of Christ in America, a union of liberal clergymen and Protestant laity.

Pragmatism

Evolutionary approaches had their influence even in the more abstract regions of thought. In the branch of philosophy known as *epistemology*—the study of how we know things—the result was *pragmatism,* a distinctive approach to the way to determine truth.

To the trio of men who officiated at the birth and development of pragmatism—Charles Peirce, William James (Henry's brother), and John Dewey—truth was not an absolute. What was true at one time was not true at another; what was valid for one set of circumstances was not valid for another. A true idea was not one that corresponded to some fixed, eternal standard. Truth was open, evolving, and unfinished. The final returns on truth would never be in.

How could one discover what was true given this indeterminacy? One could ask: What are the practical consequences of believing one thing true rather than another? As James at one point declared,

> Grant an idea or belief to be true, what concrete difference will its being true make in any one's actual life? How will the truth be realized? What experiences will be different from those which would obtain if the belief were false? What, in short, is the truth's cash value in experiential terms? *True ideas are those that we can assimilate, validate, corroborate and verify. False ideas are those we can not.*

Both Peirce and James were transitional figures who retained many of the old, individualistic notions of the nineteenth century. Dewey was a man of the new century. Born in Vermont, he took a doctoral degree at Johns Hopkins University in 1884 and went on to teach philosophy at the universities of Michigan, Minnesota, and Chicago. At the latter he directed the School of Education where he introduced new ideas in pedagogy at the experimental school.

Dewey believed that ideas must have practical utility; they must be at the service of society. This social approach he inserted into his educational philosophy. Young people, he insisted, "learned by doing." Rote knowledge was seldom retained because it had no use to the learner. But knowledge in connection with solving some interesting problem was firmly acquired. Dewey looked forward to a cooperative society to replace the dog-eat-dog attitude of his own day. He saw the schools as a way of encouraging such a society. They must become places where children not only learned economically useful skills but also learned to get along, to cooperate with one another in ways that suited the new integrated industrial society that was emerging. The principles Dewey developed in Chicago during the 1890s he carried to New York when he accepted an appointment at Columbia University in 1904. There they radiated out across the country in the form of *progressive education.*

The Nation's Outward Thrust

A final transition of the 1890s was the nation's abandonment of hemispheric isolation in favor of world-power status, a process that was not completed until after 1945.

Causes

Scholars have attributed the expansionist impulse that seized Americans in the 1890s to many things: economic drive, social anxiety, racism, emulation of the European great powers, a romantic notion of glory or adventure, Christian missionary zeal, and others. It is difficult to dismiss any of them.

One cause was the urge for adventure. By the mid-nineties the country had not been at war for an entire generation. The sons heard tales of the fathers' brave Civil War deeds and sacrifices and envied them the opportunities for heroism. Even those who had faced the struggles of the great war for the Union would find the Spanish-American War exhilarating. John Hay, who as a young man had been President Lincoln's personal secretary, called the 1898 Spanish conflict "a splendid little war."

At least as important was a growing sense that the United States, the world's richest nation, was still a nullity on the international scene. The country had been at best a regional power during the preceding fifty years, yet Americans had accepted this status without much protest. But matters now had changed. The country was no longer distracted by sectional conflict; it had filled in its boundaries and created its industrial superstructure and its railroad network. As the new century approached, there was a growing sense that new challenges were in order now that the old were gone. New worlds to conquer could be a metaphor; it could also be taken literally.

Economic forces also played an expansionist role. Not that the nation needed colonies for markets and investment outlets to preserve its social system, as Marxist scholars have claimed. Between the Civil War and 1897 American overseas investment rose from $75 million to a total of $685 million. The latter figure may appear large, but it was only 1 percent of the total value of capital investment. Even in the next three decades, when the role of the United States in international finance expanded enormously, U.S. foreign investment only amounted to 6 percent of total investment. It has been estimated that if there had not been a single American dollar invested abroad, the rate of return on U.S. capital would only have been under one percentage point lower than it was.

Nor were foreign markets necessary for American industry. Countries such as Great Britain, France, and Germany relied on foreign trade far more than did the United States, which had an enormous internal market of continental proportions. Moreover almost all of America's exports went to the developed, independent countries of Canada and Europe; very little was imported by African, Asian, or the more remote Latin American nations.

On the other hand, during the hard years of the 1890s businesspeople were fearful of economic decline and urged their government to help them by opening markets abroad to American goods. Meanwhile, politicians such as the handsome young Republican senator from Indiana, Albert Beveridge, talked about American factory overproduction and the "personal profit" that might come with colonies. The decade also experienced a mild panic over possible stagnation and growing social strife owing to the closing of the continental frontier. This view was encouraged by the writings of historian Frederick Jackson Turner, who in 1893 at the Chicago World's Fair announced that American democratic institutions and egalitarian values had come from the frontier experience and implied, now that the frontier was gone, that the United States would no longer be spared the social tensions of other industrial nations.

Navalism

However derived, the new expansionist mood was expressed in many ways. One was *navalism,* the urge to build a fleet equal to our proper role in the world.

In part this military revival was inevitable. During the Gilded Age, American military forces were ludicrous. In 1880 the United States Army had fewer than twenty-seven thousand officers and men. The American navy was described shortly before by the *Army and Navy Journal* as little more than a "heterogeneous collection of naval trash." These forces were insufficient to sustain the policies of even a middle-size power, and clearly something had to be done.

Starting in 1883 Congress began to appropriate funds for reconstructing the navy along modern lines. During the following decade navalism was fueled by the writings of Captain Alfred Thayer Mahan, a scholarly naval officer who taught at the newly established Naval War College in Newport, Rhode Island. In a series of books Mahan described how Britain had achieved greatness through her navy. In periodical articles he lamented the decline of the American fleet and raised the banner of naval revival. Mahan's writings infused new vigor into the navalism idea and helped guarantee that by the time the United States needed a modern fleet it would have one.

Navalism was a self-fulfilling prophecy. To run a modern navy required island coaling stations around the world, and these in turn became miniature colonies in distant places. The possession of a strong navy was also, in itself, a temptation to pursue an activist foreign policy. Although a symptom of a change in attitude, navalism was also an encouragement to change in itself.

Racism

Another inspiration for expansionism was the new Social Darwinism. Too much can be ascribed to Darwinism, perhaps, but it clearly did sanction the sense among the industrial nations of the world that they represented the culmination of the evolutionary process. Often this view had racial overtones. The rich peoples of northern Europe and English-speaking America represented, it implied, the fittest in the biological as well as the cultural sense. There was more than an echo of the Aryan supremacist notions of the Nazis in this. Although the death camps were a long way off, even during the 1880s and 1890s the racism of some Social Darwinists led them to justify the subjection of "lesser breeds" to the dominion of their superiors.

A Congregational minister was the chief purveyor of the racial argument for expansion. The Reverend Josiah Strong was a good Christian who wanted to encourage the growth abroad of missions to the heathen, but he couched his appeal in racist terms. His vision, as displayed in his best-selling book *Our Country* (1885), was of an all-conquering Anglo-Saxon race, one of "unequaled energy, with all the majesty of numbers and the might of wealth behind it." It would "move down upon Mexico, down upon Central and South America, out upon the islands of the sea." The

Anglo-Saxon people held in their hands "the destinies of mankind." The United States was fated to become "the home of this race, the principle seat of [its] power, the great center of [its] influence."

All told the concrete results of the upsurge in expansionism were not very great. In 1898 the United States went to war with Spain over Cuba largely in pursuit of humanitarian ends and perhaps to satisfy the long-frustrated sense of adventure. The war was a romp for the powerful United States. In a little more than six months and at the cost of 379 battle casualities and $250 million, it defeated Spain, freed Cuba from the harsh Spanish yoke, and acquired for itself Puerto Rico in the Caribbean and the Philippines in the Pacific. Along with Hawaii, annexed at virtually the same time, this constituted at best a very small empire compared to those of the European powers. Yet it did mark a departure from the prior continental focus of the United States and prepared the way for the great-power status that the country would assume in the next century.

The Population Watershed

The changes in a country's population—its size, location, and cultural characteristics—are an important aspect of its historical evolution. During the 1890s American population trends were unusual in several ways. Some of the special demographic characteristics of the decade were temporary breaks in the general trend line. But at least one marked a major transition from an old to a new overall pattern.

Population during the 1890s

By most measures of demographic change the transition decade of the 1890s represents a slowing down of processes long underway. In 1890 there were almost 63 million Americans, 13 million more than a decade before and an increase of more than 25 percent since 1880. The growth over the next ten years—that is, during the 1890s—was not as great. In 1900 the census recorded 75.9 million people, an increase of almost the same total number, 13 million, as in 1890, but now slightly under 21 percent. This decline in the growth rate followed the long-term trend of the nation's population. Yet the following decade showed a turn up. Between 1900 and 1910 the country would add 16 million people for an increase of more than 21 percent. In effect the 1890s represent a trough between two decades of higher population growth. The reason for this 1890s slowdown is not difficult to find. It is directly connected with the long post-1893 depression that affected so many other aspects of American life. The results did not derive from a decline in birthrates, however. American birthrates had been diminishing for at least two or three generations by 1890. Although economic considerations clearly affect how—and whether—men and women practice birth control and limit the size of their families, there is no evidence that the drop between 1890 and 1900 was faster than the general trend for the prosperous decades preceding and following. The explanation, then, is not the decline in the rate of natural increase—the excess of births over deaths—but the sharp drop in the number of immigrants entering the United States.

READING 1

The United States in 1900 and 1980 — A Comparison

	1900	1980
Total census population	75,994,575	226,545,805
Percent white	88	86
Percent black and other nonwhite	12	14
Percent of population living in urban areas	40	74
Percent of population living in rural areas	60	26
Median age of population	22.9	30.0
Percent 65 and older	4	11
Percent under 18	40	28
Life expectancy at birth	47.3	73.7
Percent of population 17-years-old graduating high school	6.3	71.4
Percent of population illiterate	10.7 (10-years-old and older)	0.5 (15-years-old and older)
Employment by sector as percent of total civilian labor force:		
agriculture	40	3
manufacturing	20	22
trade	14	20
services	6	29
Gross national product (1958 constant $)	76.9 billion	722.5 billion (1970 data)
Gross national product per capita (1958 constant $)	1,011	3,555 (1970 data)
Most valuable export	Unmanufactured cotton	Machinery
Most valuable import	Sugar	Petroleum and related products

	1900	**1980**
Merchandise trade balance $	+545 million	−25.5 billion
Civilian federal government employees	239,476	2,898,000
Active military personnel	125,923	2,051,000
Federal government budget surplus or deficit $	+46.4 thousand	−73.8 billion
Total national debt	$1.2 billion	$914 billion

Sources: Historical Statistics of the United States (Washington: U.S. Bureau of the Census, 1975) and *Statistical Abstract of the United States 1988* (Washington: U.S. Bureau of the Census, 1987).

The change was dramatic. In the decade 1880–89 some 5.3 million immigrants entered the country. In the period 1890–99 only 3.7 million came. Such people were indeed influenced by the state of the economy. Europeans kept in close touch with economic conditions in the United States through letters from compatriots who had gone before. They also read their newspapers closely for information about America. In most of the centers of emigration to the New World, the press kept close tabs on what was happening across the Atlantic because their readers were deeply concerned. Mary Antin, a Russian immigrant, wrote in 1899 that in her native country before she left, "America was in everybody's mouth. Businessmen talked of it over their accounts; the market women made up their quarrels that they might discuss it from stall to stall; . . . Children played at emigrating." The net effect of this flow of information was to make the size of the human stream crossing the Atlantic from east to west an excellent barometer of America's economic weather.

The economic slowdown of the 1890s affected internal migration patterns as well. For many decades the country's population had been moving westward. The hard times of the nineties did not end this process but slowed it substantially. Fewer Americans also left the farms and small towns to come to the cities. Urban population as a proportion of the total grew by almost 7 percent between 1880 and 1890. Between 1900 and 1910 the growth would be 6 percent. During the intervening decade of the 1890s it was only 4.6 percent, once again a decided trough. City growth had a number of dimensions—natural increase and foreign immigration as well as movement from rural to urban areas—but it is clear that here too scarce jobs and economic uncertainty made more Americans decide to stay put.

From "Old" to "New" Immigration

A more significant, and more permanent, change in the demographic flow across American borders was the shift in the major *sources* of immigration. By the end of the 1890s the bulk of the immigrants to America came not from northern and western

Europe, the origins of most newcomers since the beginnings of the American community, but from the more remote and culturally alien south and east of the continent. (See Figure 1–2.)

Several factors account for this change. In northern and western Europe those forces that had encouraged movement to the United States weakened. As Germany industrialized, fewer of its farm people had to leave for America to improve their lot. In Ireland, after a half-century of emigration and sharply falling birthrates, population pressure eased and reduced the impetus to leave the Auld Sod. British immigration dropped because a developed United States did not need the skills of the English, Scots, and Welsh as much as formerly. Would-be emigrés from the United Kingdom thereafter chose to go to the still undeveloped English-speaking colonies: Canada, Australia, New Zealand, and South Africa.

These shifts explain the decline of the influx from Europe's north and west. But how do we explain the rising tide from the south and east?

Certain common forces were at work in all of Europe's Mediterranean and Slavic regions. One was the growing linkage of these underdeveloped lands with the rest of the world. As ocean steamships increased in speed and comfort, as railroads replaced rutted trails, and as telegraph and postal services appeared, contact with America, and knowledge about it, improved. Soon the peasants and unskilled laborers of southern Italy; of the Hungarian and Slavic provinces of the Austro-Hungarian Empire; among

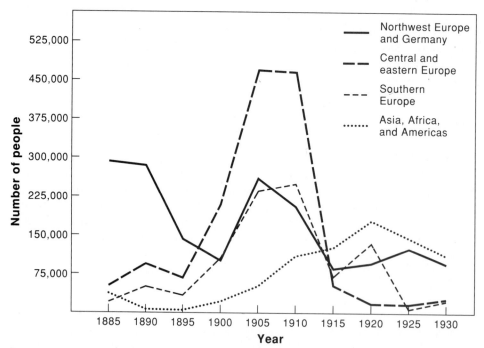

Figure 1–2 Immigration to the United States, 1885–1930

Source: *Historical Statistics of the United States* (Washington: U.S. Bureau of the Census, 1975), pp. 105–09.

the Poles, Ukrainians, Finns, Jews, and Baltic peoples of the Russian Empire; among the Greeks, Armenians, Serbs, Rumanians, Albanians, and Turks of the Balkans and the Ottoman Empire all began to recognize that America was a land of vast opportunity that was not impossibly remote and inaccessible.

This helps explain the effective "pull" of America in these newer regions. There was also a "push," or rather a number of pushes. One of these was the rapid rise in population that made it harder for peasants to acquire land or find jobs. In Italy between the early nineteenth century and the 1880s population growth rates increased almost four times. In Poland between 1870 and 1890 the number of people rose by two million. In Hungary, in the single decade of the 1880s, a similar increase took place. The only way these additional rural people could survive was by dividing land holdings into smaller and smaller plots. In Galicia, the Polish-speaking province of Austria-Hungary, there were 800,000 peasant plots smaller than seven acres by 1900. The effect of this process was to sharply reduce peasant incomes and diminish well-being.

At the same time, in areas where most of the land was initially owned by landlords, the forces of modernization displaced farm tenants and laborers. Landlords who discovered that there were large markets for grain in the growing cities of the industrializing countries introduced machines to replace labor. In Italy the lot of the rural population was worsened appreciably after Italian unification in 1871 by heavy taxes imposed by the northern controlled government on the lands of the country's southern portion, the Mezzogiorno.

Meanwhile modernization worsened conditions for southern and eastern European craft workers as well. By the last years of the century machine-made goods began to replace those produced by the wood-carvers, weavers, hatmakers, lace makers, and other skilled people of the countryside. The influx of factory products deprived rural folk of their livelihood or an important source of supplementary income.

Not all the forces behind the New Immigration were economic. Many of those leaving their homelands were in flight from persecution or tyranny, often both. Among the New Immigrant groups this was especially true of the Russian Jews and the Christian Greeks, Lebanese, and Armenians of Muslim Turkey. In both Russia and the Ottoman Empire legal barriers to advancement and, still worse, actual physical violence against the religious and ethnic minorities sent waves of emigrés fleeing the lands of their birth.

Not all who came stayed. By the 1890s, as a result of fierce competition among the steamship companies, transatlantic fares had fallen to as low as $15 to $25 dollars from ports such as Liverpool or Bremen, with another $5 or so required of each passenger for bedding, utensils, and personal articles. This amount entitled the emigrant to twelve or more days in steerage, a large undivided area below deck and usually close to the hot and noisy engines, where hundreds were packed together in a jumble of cots, rough tables and benches, and passengers' baggage. If the emigrants came from the Balkans or Russia they also had to add the cost of land travel to their total passage time and expense.

Despite the costs and the hardships this situation was far better than in the past, when emigrants came on excruciatingly slow sailing-ships, vessels even more crowded, unsanitary, and expensive. But speed and cheapness encouraged a large two-way traffic, mostly of young men who came to make money and then returned to Europe with a grubstake enabling them to buy land or start a business. Not all who came with this goal in mind achieved it. Many found it too difficult to save their money and returned defeated by bad luck, hard times, or ill health; others did well enough but decided that they would make America their home. Yet the return rate, especially among Greeks, southern Italians, and Slavs, was very high. In the entire period from 1880 to 1920, about 30 percent of all arrivals in the United States failed to stay in the country.

The New Immigration of the 1890s and after was not purely European. Although the Chinese were expressly excluded from coming to the United States by the 1882 Chinese Exclusion Act, some continued to trickle through. More numerous were the Japanese who came to what was then the independent kingdom of Hawaii during the late 1880s and early 1890s as contract laborers on the sugar plantations. In the 1890s some 26,000 also came to the West Coast of the continental United States, a harbinger of another 130,000 the following decade.

Much larger contingents came from neighbors to the north and to the south. The Canadian immigration was made up of both French- and English-speaking people. In the 1890s alone almost 100,000 French Canadians entered the United States to escape the poverty of Quebec and embrace the opportunity of New England. By 1900 there were almost half a million Canadians in that region. Meanwhile thousands of English-speaking Canadians crossed the border to take up land in the Plains states, a region with a better climate than their own harsh prairies.

"New" immigrants on their way across the Atlantic to America. Steerage quarters were below deck. (Library of Congress)

People of Mexican ancestry had lived in the United States ever since the acquisition of California and the Southwest following the Mexican War of 1846–48. Citizens of the Mexican Republic continued to drift across the border to California, Arizona, New Mexico, and Texas right through the remainder of the nineteenth century. By 1900 they still formed a relatively small group of newcomers compared to the flood from Europe. But it was a growing stream. In later years hundreds of thousands of Mexican laborers would cross the southern border to help construct and maintain the railroads, mine copper and silver, and do the back-breaking "stoop labor" in the vineyards and in the lettuce, cotton, and vegetable fields of the border region.

A Decade of Change

The new century would be built on the foundation of the 1890s. In that decade much that characterized the twentieth century first appeared: a new conflict-oriented politics, new popular mass media, naturalism in literature, modern architecture, and an imperial reach, the New Immigration.

One of the most imposing developments of the new century was the rise of a predominantly urban culture that politically and socially eclipsed the predominantly rural nation of the past. It is to this subject that we will now turn.

FOR FURTHER READING

A work on the Chicago World's Fair of 1893 that seeks to place the fair in the context of national cultural crisis is R. Reid Badger's *The Great Amerian Fair: The World's Columbian Exposition and American Culture* (1979). For a cultural interpretation of party politics in the Gilded Age see Paul Kleppner, *The Cross of Culture: A Social Analysis of Midwestern Politics* (1970) and Richard Jensen, *The Winning of the Midwest: Social and Political Conflict, 1888–1896* (1971). H. Wayne Morgan's *From Hayes to McKinley: National Party Politics, 1877–1896* (1969) treats the major parties in a traditional way. The best recent study of populism, although rather uncritical, is Lawrence Goodwyn's *Democratic Promise: The Populist Movement in America* (1976). The Bryan-McKinley campaign is compactly described in Paul Glad's *McKinley, Bryan and the People* (1964).

Works that deal with the popular culture of the turn-of-the-century include Albert F. McLean, Jr., *American Vaudeville as Ritual* (1965); Anthony Slide, *Early American Cinema* (1970); and the relevant chapters of Russel Nye's *The Unembarrassed Muse: The Popular Arts in America* (1970). The yellow press as well as the lives of his subjects are described in two biographies by William A. Swanberg, *Citizen Hearst* (1961) and *Pulitzer* (1967). Several standard treatments of the literature of the 1890s and beyond are Alfred Kazin's seminal *On Native Grounds* (1942) and Larzer Ziff's *The American 1890s: Life and Times of a Lost Generation* (1966). For the architecture of the period as well as much else see Lewis Mumford, *The Brown Decades, 1865–1895: A Study of the Arts in America* (1931). For the skyscraper the authoritative work is Carl W. Condit, *Rise of the Skyscraper* (1952).

Pragmatism and new kinds of social thought are dealt with in Morton G. White, *Social Thought in America: The Revolt against Formalism* (1957) and Paul Conkin, *Puritans and Pragmatists* (1968). The best treatment of the social dimension of Darwinism is Richard Hofstadter's *Social Darwinism in American Thought* (1955). Charles H. Hopkins's *The Rise of the Social Gospel in American Protestantism, 1865–1915* (1940) and Henry F. May's *Protestant Churches and Industrial America* (1949) are still the best works on Gilded Age religion.

For American expansion in the late nineteenth century see the two differing treatments of Ernest May, *Imperial Democracy: The Emergence of America* (1961) and Walter LaFeber, *The New Empire: American-Expansionism, 1860–1898* (1963).

The New Immigration of the period after 1880 is covered briefly but well in Alan Kraut, *The Huddled Masses: The Immigrant in American Society, 1880–1921* (1982).

2
The New City

Labor Day 1900 on Main Street, Buffalo, New York. (Library of Congress)

How Cities Grew

Until about 1920 more Americans lived on farms and in small towns than in cities and metropolitan areas. But by 1900 some 40 percent of the seventy-six million Americans already lived in areas classified by the Census Bureau as urban. (See Figure 2–1.) More important, the cities had already become the unchallenged foci of American political, economic, and cultural life, draining much of the vitality from the nation's rural regions. By 1900 "the city was not only here to stay, it had triumphed."

The Growth Process

Between 1890 and 1920 individual American cities grew at breakneck speed. In those years Chicago leaped from 1 million inhabitants to over 2.7 million; Washington from 190,000 to 438,000; Philadelphia from 1 million to 1.8 million; Atlanta from 66,000 to 201,000; Kansas City, Missouri, from 133,000 to 324,000. Los Angeles had the most spectacular increase of all: a tenfold gain from 50,000 to over 516,000.

The growth of individual cities and the increase in their total population do not fully measure the demographic shift from rural to urban. In 1910 the Census Bureau formulated the term *metropolitan district* to describe a central city of 200,000 persons or more surrounded by a region of smaller communities with a population density of 150 people per square mile. The new classification recognized that the influence of the big urban centers extended far beyond their city limits. By 1920, more than 28 million Americans—out of 105 million—lived in these immense metropolitan districts. Cities did not grow primarily by an excess of urban births over deaths. Although some natural increase occurred in the cities, it was not very large. City death rates, at least until about 1920, were high; city birthrates were low, far lower than rural birthrates. Most of the explosive growth of the urban centers was the result of successive incoming waves of outsiders, some from the nation's farms and villages and some from the farms, villages, and cities of Europe, Canada, Mexico, and Asia.

We have considered the shift of the foreign tidal wave from northern and western to southern and eastern Europe that began in the 1890s. This flood, although interrupted by World War I, continued right through the early 1920s when restrictive legislation (see Figure 1–1) began to choke it off. The peak decade of foreign immigration to the United States was 1900 to 1910, when almost 6.3 million of the Old World's "huddled masses" poured into the country. Some of these people went to the rural areas. Some Italians took up truck gardening in thinly settled spaces adjacent to the large cities; others worked in the vineyards of California. Greeks and Basques from Spain became sheepherders in the Mountain states. Many Japanese worked as agricultural laborers in Hawaii. Mexicans worked on farms in Texas, the Southwest, and California. But these cases were exceptional. Well over 80 percent of the Italians, Jews, and Slavs—the core of the New Immigration—chose to make the cities their home.

The movement from the American rural countryside to the cities is not as well documented statistically. We do not know how many millions of native American farm and small-town people came to the cities. Some figures are suggestive, however. In

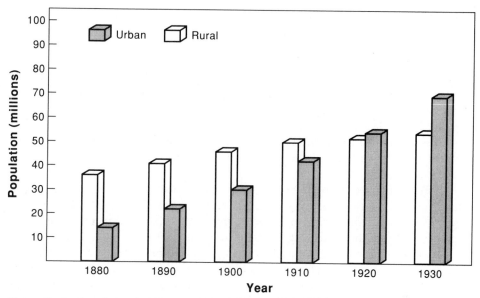

Figure 2–1   Population in Urban and Rural Areas, 1880–1930

Source: *Historical Statistics of the United States* (Washington: U.S. Bureau of the Census, 1975), pp. 11–12.

1920 about 20 percent of the population of Chicago, St. Louis, Detroit, Cincinnati, and Jersey City were native-born people from out of state, and the proportions in Los Angeles, Kansas City, Washington, Seattle, Portland, and Denver were in the 40 to 50 percent range. All told, according to scholar Blake McKelvey, eleven million native-born city dwellers in 1910 were transplanted rural and village people.

One element of urban growth often ignored was annexation. Many cities added to their population by absorbing communities previously outside their legal boundaries. Between 1890 and 1920 Atlanta increased its size from 9 to 27 square miles, Baltimore from 30 to 79, Boston from 39 to 44, Chicago from 178 to 199, Los Angeles from 29 to 364, Seattle from 13 to 68, and New York from 44 to 299.

The annexation process, so common through the 1920s, has practically ceased. Today, those who live in suburban communities consider the cities troublesome and expensive places to avoid. Today most of the country's cities are surrounded by an iron ring of satellite communities sealed off from the cities' social and financial problems.

From 1890 to 1920, however, annexation was often attractive. People took pride in being part of a vibrant and go-ahead place such as Chicago, Los Angeles, or New York. The cities also offered services that smaller communities could not match. Hyde Park's voters approved annexation to Chicago because they wanted better fire protection and lower gas rates. The citizens of Kensington and Germantown hoped to share in Philadelphia's world-famous water system. The big cities had superior transportation systems, better police protection, and even better schools, in those days, than smaller towns. This relative ease of annexation preserved the cities' tax bases and enabled them to provide the capital improvements and the day-to-day services that made city life manageable. That it has practically ceased in the older parts of the country in our day is one critical reason why American cities find it so hard to solve their problems.

Why People Came

The question of why people came to the cities in this period has no simple answer. The influx of the foreign-born can be understood by recalling why they came to the United States in general: jobs, freedom, toleration. But that explanation is not enough. Before 1860 most immigrants went to the rural areas; after about 1880 their destinations were far more often urban. Clearly the reason for the change lies in the shift between the earlier and later periods in economic advantage between city and country, factory and farm.

Changing relative economic opportunity also explains the influx of native-born country people. During the late nineteenth century agriculture was depressed, with prices falling and farm foreclosures increasing. After 1900 farm prices and incomes started to rise, but the increasing efficiency of farm machinery limited the need for farm labor. At the same time a paradoxical surge in land prices made it more difficult for a young man to start out as a farmer. One group deeply affected by industrial change was young farm women. The growing flood of manufactured consumer goods made their food preparation, sewing, and baking services less vital to their parents. Off they went to the cities to earn some cash.

Associated with these economic and technological forces were those of demography: farm birthrates remained higher than those of the cities, creating a surplus of human beings in the rural regions.

But the absence of economic opportunity was not the only force pushing people, especially young people, from the rural areas and pulling them to the cities. Rural men and women were repelled by the boredom and the physical and cultural isolation of life in the country, and they were drawn by the vivacity, color, and sociability of the city. In explaining its own popularity in the nation's farms and small towns, *Good Housekeeping* observed that rural women, "in many, many cases were pining for neighbors, for domestic help, for pretty clothes, for schools, music, art, . . . when the magazines came in." Hamlin Garland, the Iowa farm boy who helped found the naturalist school of fiction during the 1890s, caught the drabness of rural life in an account of a train trip west from his adopted city home. Garland observed,

> the farther I got from Chicago the more depressing the landscape became. . . . [M]y pity grew more intense as I passed from northwest Iowa into southern Dakota. The houses bare as boxes dropped on the treeless plains, the barbed-wire fences running at right angles, and the towns mere assemblages of flimsy wooden sheds . . . produced in me the effect of an almost hopeless and sterile poverty.

The City Environment

However depressing their original rural homes, newcomers to the early twentieth-century city often encountered less attractive and comfortable physical conditions than they had anticipated. Providing housing, water, power, sanitary services, and transportation for city dwellers was immensely expensive in time, energy, and money and few cities managed it without painful delays and serious missteps.

Housing

One of the first tasks of the new arrival in the big city was to find a place to live. It was often daunting, even for the relatively affluent.

By the closing years of the old century, few urbanites could afford the detached private house with backyard and front lawn their predecessors had enjoyed, and few such houses were being constructed in the city itself. The problem was land prices. These had soared since earlier years when city population was less dense and land close in had not yet reached an enormous premium.

The solution for middle-class families in some cities was the "French flat." These were apartment buildings of five or six floors, usually with the latest amenities —elevators, kitchens, bathrooms, large windows, and electricity. The first such structure was probably the Stuyvesant Apartment House built in 1869 on New York's Eighteenth Street. At first these flats were regarded suspiciously as some sort of immoral French fashion. By the end of the century they had become the norm in many large cities. In Boston, where the standard version was a "three-decker" of three floor-through apartments, "miles of middle class apartment houses . . . marched out . . . in every direction." By 1885, an observer announced, Chicago was experiencing a "flat fever."

The apartment house was a vast improvement over the boarding house arrangement that had been common for young middle-class urban families before the Civil War. Families now had their own private kitchens and dining spaces and could take meals together. They also had their own living rooms for family relaxation. For those who could afford them, the new flats helped restore some of the cohesion of rural family living. On the other hand, because they were expensive and necessarily limited in space, they placed a premium on family limitation. Apartment living undoubtedly reinforced the incentives to keep families small that had long operated in America, especially among the native-born.

The poor could not afford the new, luxury apartments, of course, and had to find other kinds of housing. Many newcomers, especially foreign immigrants, were single males who ended up boarding with compatriots who had some space to rent. This was usually a temporary arrangement, until the young man brought over his wife or parents. At that point the family sought its own apartment.

The quest was often disappointing. With the cities growing so fast landlords and developers had powerful incentives to provide dwelling space for arrivals. Yet they faced the constraints of high land and building costs. One solution was to carve up the large private houses of the departing rich into rabbit warrens of small apartments. Another was to construct shacks in the yards behind the older private dwellings. But these expedients were not enough, and developers were soon throwing up whole blocks of new tenements as cheaply as possible.

Each large city developed its own characteristic style of tenement. In Boston the wooden three-decker, with its cracked paint and sagging floors was typical.

New York City's Lower East Side of Manhattan, home to thousands of Jews and other immigrants from eastern Europe in the early 1900s. (The Bettmann Archive)

Philadelphia's housing for the poor was the "horizontal tenement," or the shack in the rear of an older private house. New York, the most congested of the major cities, with land prices higher than anywhere else, threw up thousands of jerry-built, narrow-fronted four-to six-story dwellings. These covered virtually all of the 25-by-100-foot lot, leaving no room for windows except at front and back. Nor did they have internal plumbing. Tenants were forced to use the common privy in the narrow, 10-foot space behind each building.

New York's extreme congestion made its housing problems worse than those of other cities. In other communities even immigrants, once they had established themselves economically, found it possible to become homeowners. In some cities, some groups had particularly high rates of homeownership. In Cleveland, for example, a majority of both Italians and Slovaks owned their own homes after 1910. Many immigrant families perceived homeownership as equivalent to landownership and were willing to borrow heavily to buy houses, forgoing expensive investments like higher education to do so. Still, city housing for the working class remained a major problem through the early 1900s and remains a problem today.

Jobs

After a home, the next thing a newcomer to the city had to find was a job. Fortunately the cities during this era were expanding their economic bases at a rapid clip.

City economies were not all the same. Some cities—Washington, D.C., the state capitals—were primarily administrative and governmental centers. There most of the jobs required reasonable levels of education and often "pull," because merit systems for public employees were still not universal.

Some cities were primarily devoted to manufacturing. A few were one-industry towns. Steel, for example, created Gary, Indiana; Birmingham, Alabama; and Johnstown, Pennsylvania. The electrical industry accounted for much of the growth of Schenectady, New York. But most manufacturing cities, especially the larger ones, were home to several major industries. In addition to steel Pittsburgh had an important glass industry. Chicago in 1900 had six major industries providing thousands of jobs: meat-packing, metal fabrication and machine tools, men's clothing, iron and steel, agricultural machinery, and railroad cars.

Almost all the biggest cities were heavily committed to manufacturing, but invariably they were commercial, financial, and educational centers as well. Chicago, besides being "hog butcher to the world," was the home of the "wheat pit," where most of the world's grain was traded, and was a railroad center through which most of the nation's east-west passenger and freight traffic moved. New York had important clothing, tobacco, and other industries, but its distinctive enterprises were printing and publishing, entertainment, foreign trade, and finance. Most big cities were wholesale centers where warehouses stocked lines of products needed by storekeepers and merchants in smaller communities.

Every large city was also a major retail center where millions of city people and many from the surrounding region bought their necessities as well as their finery. By 1900 the major city outlet for better consumer goods was the department store, invented in France but soon adopted by American merchants for its efficiency, its attraction for women shoppers, and its cheap labor costs.

Department stores were major employers of women. Women were paid less than men; in the 1890s they worked a ten-hour day for about six dollars a week. They also were more flexible than men in accepting the rapid-fire marketing changes that came in this period. Finally, they had greater rapport with the predominantly female clientele who patronized the stores. Few women rose to department-store managerial jobs. In the 1860s Margaret Getchell, the superintendent of Macy's in New York, was one of the few woman business executives in the whole country. Virtually all the women employees were confined to the sales force, which constituted the great majority of department-store workers.

Although economic expansion created millions of jobs, newcomers to the cities still had to find them. Family members or friends who had arrived earlier could be helpful. In fact the signal to come to the city was often a letter from a friend or relative that a job was available.

Immigrants were helped by fellow countrymen. This explains in part why individuals of one nationality were often concentrated in a given trade or occupation—Italians in the construction industry, Jews in the garment trades, Greeks in the candy and restaurant business, Slavs in the steel mills, and so on. Another explanation is the skills the immigrants brought with them. For example, many Jews had worked as tailors in Russia and Poland, and it was only natural that they use their skills in the garment industry in New York, Chicago, and Rochester.

Among some immigrant groups the job providers were middlemen who served as agents for employers. Among the Italians, for example, labor brokers called *padrones* operated in both Italy and the United States as intermediaries in the transatlantic job market. The padrones, who spoke both English and Italian, could communicate with immigrant workers and employers alike. They found jobs for their compatriots and helped ease their adjustment to American life. But they often exacted a high price for their services: *padrones* often took their clients' pay directly from the boss and kept a large percentage for themselves. They accepted fees from prospective employers but then did not deliver the jobs promised. Fortunately, the system did not outlast the growing maturity of the Italian immigrant community. By 1920 it was virtually dead.

When we consider the American city of the early twentieth century, we often see only the people at the bottom of the economic ladder. Our focus is understandable. Their plight arouses our sympathies, and they were, of course, the most numerous. But the cities also attracted many educated people and people with high-level skills. These men and women quickly joined the middle and upper layers of urban society.

A small proportion of the skilled were European immigrants. Every group of newcomers included a certain number of educated men and women—journalists, lawyers, doctors, businesspeople, teachers, actors, clergy—who came to serve their compatriots. Every immigrant district had restaurants and grocery stores run by immigrant small-business people who catered to the special tastes of their compatriots. Immigrant doctors usually flourished because they spoke the immigrants' language. Immigrant lawyers helped with the legal problems of their compatriots, and they were usually the first members of each immigrant community to enter politics. There was also, usually, a leaven of skilled immigrant machinists, printers, cabinetmakers, carpenters, and others who commanded good wages in the United States.

A larger proportion of native-born newcomers than foreigners were apt to be skilled and educated. The cities attracted the young, the capable, and the ambitious who could not find outlets for their talents in rural America. Young men and women interested in the theater, journalism, academic life, the law, science, and the arts often had no choice but to go to the big cities for both training and an appreciative audience. Many of course did not succeed; some returned home defeated. But most stayed on and found some sort of niche in the middle-class professional world.

Even to those whose only qualification was literacy, the city afforded expanded opportunity. As noted, cities were not only industrial centers; they were also commercial, educational, financial, and governmental hubs. City offices needed thousands of office workers to handle the paperwork of a modern business society. Many thousands of young women joined the office forces of banks, trading houses, and manufacturing firms to type the letters, file the documents, and do the bookkeeping. Many women also found jobs teaching in the expanding city schools that educated the newcomers. As mentioned, young native-born women also worked as salespeople in the retail establishments of the city. This new white-collar class, although frequently underpaid women, formed a layer above the unskilled blue-collar class of day laborers, factory workers, and domestic servants, most of whom were immigrants.

Transportation

Urbanites, then as now, needed ways to get to work and to move around. By about 1850 most of the larger American cities had ceased to be "walking cities" where transportation could be accomplished on foot. By the Civil War most had acquired horse-drawn streetcars moving on rails down the middle of the major traffic arteries. Then in the 1890s came the much faster, cleaner, and more efficient electric trolley. (See the photograph opening this chapter.) By 1902 over two billion passengers annually were being transported countrywide over 22,000 miles of track at an average speed of 10 to 12 miles per hour. This increase in velocity cut commuting time within the cities and thinned out central city populations. Developers quickly followed the trolley lines into the countryside, throwing up housing along the trolley routes to accommodate city dwellers anxious to escape the congestion and high costs of the older neighborhoods.

For most cities the electric streetcar remained the chief mode of transportation until the 1930s when it was replaced by the gasoline- or diesel-powered bus. But for the biggest cities, with their enormous volume of passengers and crushing street-level congestion, they were not enough. Two cities—New York and Chicago—adopted the elevated railroad raised on pillars high above city traffic to solve the problem. But the "el" was noisy and dirty and created blight along its right of way. In 1897, Boston, imitating several European cities, placed its electrified trains underground. The "subway" was soon taken up by New York (1903) and Philadelphia (1908).

City Sanitation and Health

By the opening years of the twentieth century, many of the physical problems of an earlier city era were on the way to being solved. By 1900 many streets, hitherto dirt tracks, had been paved with either asphalt or macadam made from crushed stone mixed with an oil binder and set on a graded foundation. Their cleaning, however, remained a problem. Although the trolley car had superseded the horsecar, there were still twenty million horses depositing vast amounts of liquid and solid waste on the streets and providing sustenance for clouds of flies in turn-of-the-century American cities. Sick and dead horses, abandoned by their owners, also befouled the streets.

Some relief came early in the new century with the arrival of the automobile. Between 1900 and 1915, the number of automobiles increased from eight thousand to two million. Automobiles, time would show, had their own pollution potential, but their first effect was to improve the sanitation and hygiene of the cities.

Science and engineering also came to the rescue. As early as the 1870s sanitation expert George Waring had asserted that disease could be spread by the "exhalations of decomposing matter in dungheaps, pigsties, privy vaults, cellars, cess-pools, drains and sewers." During the following decades Waring's intuitions were confirmed by the germ theory of disease as developed and demonstrated by Louis Pasteur and Robert Koch in Europe.

In the 1880s Waring achieved eminence as the designer of sewer systems for a number of major American cities, and in the 1890s he was appointed head of the New York Department of Street Cleaning. A skillful publicist, Waring made clean streets a major reform cause. His men would blitz a filthy empty lot or street, and then he would distribute "before and after" photographs to the newspapers. Waring dressed the sanitation-department workers in white uniforms and paraded them through the city pushing garbage carts and carrying brooms, while the commissioner himself led the procession on horseback.

Clean water had also begun to arrive by about 1900. Some cities faced a problem of merely meeting their burgeoning population's quantitative needs. New York early in the century was forced to extend its aqueduct system to water sources a hundred miles away. Los Angeles, blessed—or afflicted—with a dry climate, cast about desperately to find water for its thirsty citizens and became involved in a dramatic battle over water rights with the farmers and ranchers of the Owens Valley clear across the state. After much legal maneuvering, the federal government ruled in favor of the city and against the interests of a "few settlers" in the Owens Valley. In 1908 construction began on a 233-mile aqueduct that would solve the city's water problems for many years.

Besides quantity, there was the even more serious problem of quality. By the opening years of the century, it was evident that pure water was a necessity for the health of city people. Boston, with clean filtered water, had a death rate of 3.5 per ten thousand inhabitants. Philadelphia, with unfiltered water, had almost twice as many deaths. Unfortunately, the Philadelphia case was more typical. In 1900 only 6 percent of city people—1.8 million—were receiving filtered water through their taps. Progress was relatively fast thereafter. By 1910 the percentage was twice as great, and the number was 10 million. In 1920 almost every sizable American city had an abundant supply of potable water.

The growing public awareness of bacterial and viral disease encouraged improvement in municipal health programs. Between 1900 and 1907 cities with populations of over fifty thousand increased their public-health spending by 600 percent. Many cities began to require vaccination against smallpox for their schoolchildren and compelled commercial dairies to pasteurize their milk. There was a large expansion of municipally run hospitals as well as university-affiliated and religious "voluntary" hospitals. By 1910 there were 164 municipal hospitals and 574 public dispensaries. To improve health "delivery," especially to the poor, at the turn-of-the-century, New York social worker Lillian Wald introduced the visiting-nurse system near her Henry Street settlement house on New York's Lower East Side. At this time, moreover, urban school systems began to provide medical inspection programs for children.

The overall effect of these measures and programs was to bring down death rates dramatically, especially for infectious diseases. In 1900 the annual death rate in Massachusetts, a state with the best mortality statistics, was about 22 per

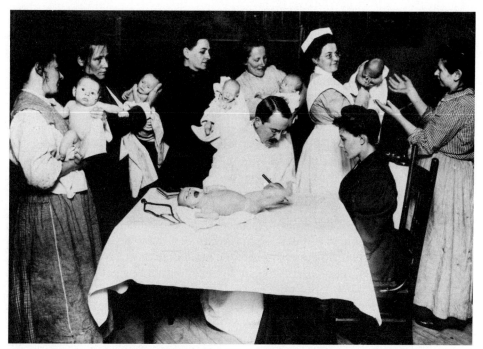

Infants being examined at a Chicago Infant Welfare Society office, c. 1910. (Chicago Historical Society)

thousand people. By 1925 it had fallen to 12.5. Since Massachusetts was over four-fifths urban, it is clear that the improvement was primarily in the longevity of city dwellers.

Fire and Crime

Fire had been a hazard in big cities at least from the reign of Roman emperor Nero on. In the colonial era and in the early nineteenth century, American cities had relied on volunteers to rush to the scene of conflagrations to work the pumping machines and the bucket brigades. The men were untrained and often incompetent; many were more interested in carousing and politicking than preventing disaster.

The great Chicago fire of 1871 and its near-equal in Boston a year later made city officials aware of the need for professional fire departments. Shortly afterward, city councils voted the necessary appropriations. Fortunately, new technology also came to the rescue. In the 1870s came the electric fire-alarm signal box and the automatic fire-sprinkler system. In the following decade chemical fire engines and steam-powered pumping engines arrived. Cities also began to require that new buildings, especially office structures and factories, be constructed of fire-resistant materials such as concrete, asbestos, steel, brick, and terra cotta. By 1900 American cities had far more effective firefighting forces than earlier in the century and were ahead of their European counterparts. Although Chicago was one-third the size of London, its fire department was as large as the British city's and had more horses and steam-powered pumping engines.

Crime has always been a major city problem. Crowded with the poor, the alien, the disaffected, the anonymous, and the indifferent, cities are nurseries of antisocial behavior. Fast-growing communities like American cities at the beginning of the twentieth century were especially conducive to crime. Thousands of newcomers were both unfamiliar with city life and with America. The cities were also arenas of contending cultural values where one person's crime was another person's custom. Finally, the cities flaunted great wealth while simultaneously consigning thousands to poverty. Such forces inevitably produced both temptations and frustrations and created the environment in which crimes against persons and property flourished.

Every generation of Americans is convinced that crime is getting worse, and those who lived at the end of the nineteenth century were no different. American cities around 1900 were almost certainly less crime ridden than they are today, but the figures seemed alarming. In the early 1880s the number of murders and homicides in the country had been reported as 1266, or about 25 per million people. By 1890 this had risen to 4300, or 68.5 per million; by 1898 the figure was 7840, or 107.2 per million. But murder was only the most spectacular crime that cities were prey to. Robbery and burglary, assault, riot, and similar felonies abounded. Police forces, magistrates, and citizens, then as now, also had to contend with thousands of "victimless" crimes involving moral infractions, violations of Sunday closing laws, and disregard of ordinances against gambling and "blood sports" (bare-knuckle boxing and cockfighting).

Explanations for the shocking crime figures varied. Social reformers tended to blame the existence of poverty and the inequalities of wealth. A few observers saw the American crime problem as the heritage of the unruly frontier tradition. Most contemporary experts placed the blame, as one said, "on unhealthy urban growth, unrestricted immigration, the saloon, and the maladjusted Negro."

Then as now the cities' chief weapon against crime was the police. Professional police forces had come to American cities during the early nineteenth century. By 1900 they were universal. Unfortunately, they were not very effective. Poorly paid and poorly educated, the city police often were corrupt and brutal. In a society where there was an enormous gap between what people professed and what they were willing to pay for, the temptation to payoffs was irresistible. Many big-city police accepted bribes from saloonkeepers, madames, pimps, gamblers, and illegal sports sponsors to look the other way at lawbreaking.

The public periodically lost patience with police corruption. In 1894 the Reverend Charles Parkhurst and the New York Society for the Prevention of Crime forced a legislative inquiry, known as the Lexow Commission, into New York City police misdeeds. The commission found that police appointments in New York were not based on skill or merit but were sold by politicians, and that police officials collected "protection" money from gamblers, saloonkeepers, and brothel owners, and took a percentage of profits from pickpockets and streetwalkers.

The revelations of the Lexow Commission so repelled the New York public that it elected a reform mayor, William Strong, who promptly chose Theodore Roosevelt as police commissioner. Roosevelt tried to get the mess under control, but in 1897 the corrupt Tammany political machine regained control of the mayor's office and ended the brief spasm of public virtue.

City Government

The agency responsible for many of the accomplishments—and for most of the failings—of cities in the early twentieth century was the city government. By 1900 city government was becoming more honest and effective, but it remained a highly flawed institution of the American republic.

The City Machine

The *machine* was the predominant political agency in most American cities at the end of the nineteenth century. It was an informal political mechanism designed to bypass the unwieldy and ineffective formal institutions of city government to get critically needed things accomplished.

Cities, as we have seen, required transit lines, pure water, health and sanitation facilities, fire and police protection, and a host of other services and capital improvements. These needs were urgent in communities expanding at breakneck speed in the half-century following the Civil War. Yet responsibility for meeting many of these needs was fragmented. For example, in 1911 the Cleveland city council found it had no authority to control the subsurface of public highways or regulate the architectural appearance of buildings fronting public highways. Nor could it require the isolation of tuberculosis patients or exclude noisy or unsanitary animals such as chickens and dogs from the city limits. In New York, the Board of Education was an autonomous body not responsible to the city government; the governor of the state chose the police and fire commissioners and the commissioners of Central Park without any say by the mayor. This situation, common in many states, reflected a rural-dominated state legislature's Jeffersonian distrust of the big cities. However explainable or even valid, the result was a power vacuum that made the pressing needs of the cities difficult to meet.

City government also lacked the means to deal with the social problems that beset the hordes of people, many poor and ignorant, who were newly arrived in the cities. Immigrants in particular were exposed to a harsh social environment marked at best by indifference, at worst by prejudice and hostility. They craved entertainment, but often could not afford it. The churches sought to ease their lot; immigrant national societies dispensed advice and money; and reformers and social workers provided programs and facilities. But all told, the private agencies could make little inroad into the enormous mountain of need, misery, and restlessness. Today *welfare* is largely the province of government—federal, state, and city. At the turn-of-the-century, however, there was no formal provision for government action in most of these areas, and the urban poor were the losers.

Into this double vacuum stepped the machine to accomplish what the formal political institutions could not. At its head was the "boss." The boss at times was the mayor or some other elected official. More often he held no office or only some sinecure without much formal power. His agents were the ward captains ("ward heelers" to their enemies) along with elected and appointed officials and loyal followers all mobilized to win elections and manage city affairs.

In some cities the machines called themselves Republican; most were nominally Democratic. But party affiliation was generally irrelevant. They were seldom concerned with the fate of the national party and in fact were often at war with the national leaders. Tammany Hall, the venerable New York Democratic machine, for example, bitterly feuded with Samuel Tilden, Grover Cleveland, Woodrow Wilson, and Franklin Roosevelt, the party's chief national leaders between 1876 and 1945.

The machines were moved by greed and fueled by patronage. The boss and his henchmen controlled jobs on the city payroll, and, in the absence of city job merit systems, they could distribute them at will. They also controlled franchises—for streetcar lines, electric lighting and gas companies, private water companies, and garbage-collection firms. They awarded lucrative contracts for various city services and for city construction. Finally, they were responsible for enforcing laws that many people did not want—Sunday closing laws, antigambling laws, and laws against vice. Almost anything within the power of the boss to do, or to refrain from doing, was for sale to the highest bidder and ultimately could be transformed into wealth for the machine's top leaders.

The machine's methods were unscrupulous. To stay in power, no shady trick was inadmissible. At election times, machine foot soldiers voted more than once, sometimes using the name of a dead voter or one long gone from the city. The Chicago machine was notorious for its cemetery vote. Or the machine stationed bullies at the polling stations to drive off known opponents or detain them in jail until after the election. The machines bought votes outright for five dollars or a pint of whiskey. When they could not find enough legitimate voters in the community, they imported floaters from other jurisdictions or naturalized noneligible foreigners in massive numbers just before elections. If all else failed, they invented voters. In Philadelphia, the opponents of the Republican machine charged it with casting the ballots of dogs, children, and fictional persons.

There is no question that the machines were corrupt, venal, and, at times, brutal. Yet they were not merely city pathologies. They also accomplished many of the things that, as we have seen, the formal institutions of government could not or would not. In Chicago, boss William Lorimer expedited the process of franchising streetcar lines and extending the city's gas lines to many new customers. Abe Ruef's intervention ended delays in bringing telephone lines to San Francisco. Cincinnati boss George Cox undertook extensive street-paving and sewer-construction projects, launched a $6 million waterworks program, built a professional police force, upgraded the fire department, and extended the city parks. And yet he managed to keep the tax rate low!

The boss and the machine also helped fill the welfare gap that left the city poor so badly exposed. The reason was not humanitarian, although bosses and ward heelers were at times compassionate. Rather, the reason was votes. Voting the dead, the noncitizen, the floater, or the fictitious was all very well. But at best, ballot box stuffing and the rest were only makeshifts. It was far better to win the actual support of the voters, and this could best be accomplished by making the machine a cornucopia of benefits to the city's poor and vulnerable.

READING 2

A Day in the Life
of a Tammany Hall Boss

George Washington Plunkitt was a Lower East Side ward captain for Tammany Hall, the Democratic political machine that dominated New York City for many years. In 1905 newspaperman William Riordan published Plunkitt of Tammany Hall, *a book purporting to contain Plunkitt's own reflections along with Riordan's knowledgeable account of his activities. In the following excerpt Riordan describes one of Plunkitt's days.*

2 A.M.: Aroused from sleep by the ringing of his doorbell; went to the door and found a bartender, who asked him to go to the police station and bail out a saloon-keeper who had been arrested for violating the excise law. Furnished bail and returned to bed at three o'clock.

6 A.M.: Awakened by fire engines passing his house. Hastened to the scene of the fire, according to the custom of the Tammany district leaders, to give assistance to the fire sufferers, if needed. Met several of his election district captains who are always under orders to look out for fires, which are considered great vote-getters. Found several tenants who had been burned out, took them to a hotel, supplied them with clothes, fed them, and arranged temporary quarters for them until they could rent and furnish new apartments.

8:30 A.M.: Went to the police court to look after his constituents. Found six "drunks." Secured the discharge of four by a timely word with the judge, and paid the fines of two.

9 A.M.: Appeared in the Municipal District Court. Directed one of his district captains to act as counsel for a widow against whom dispossess proceedings had been instituted and obtained an extension of time. Paid the rent of a poor family about to be dispossessed and gave them a dollar for food.

11 A.M.: At home again. Found four men waiting for him. One had been discharged by the Metropolitan Railway Company for neglect of duty, and wanted the district leader to fix things. Another wanted a job on the road. The third sought a place on the Subway and the fourth, a plumber, was looking for work with the Consolidated Gas Company. The district leader spent nearly three hours fixing things for the four men, and succeeded in each case.

3 P.M.: Attended the funeral of an Italian as far as the ferry. Hurried back to make his appearance at the funeral of a Hebrew constituent. Went conspicuously to the front both in the Catholic church and the synagogue, and later attended the Hebrew confirmation ceremonies in the synagogue.

continued

7 P.M.: Went to district headquarters and presided over a meeting of election district captains. Each captain submitted a list of all the voters in his district, reported on their attitude toward Tammany, suggested who might be won over and how they could be won, told who were in need, and who were in trouble of any kind and the best way to reach them. District leader took notes and gave orders.

8 P.M.: Went to a church fair. Took chances on everything, bought ice cream for the young girls and the children. Kissed the little ones, flattered their mothers and took their fathers out for something down at the corner.

9 P.M.: At the clubhouse again. Spent $10 on tickets for a church excursion and promised a subscription for a new church bell. Bought tickets for a baseball game to be played by two nines from his district. Listened to the complaints of a dozen pushcart peddlers who said they were persecuted by the police and assured them he would go to Police Headquarters in the morning and see about it.

10:30 P.M.: Attended a Hebrew wedding reception and dance. Had previously sent a handsome wedding present to the bride.

12 P.M.: In bed.

That is the actual record of one day in the life of Plunkitt. He does some of the same things every day, but his life is not so monotonous as to be wearisome.

Source: William L. Riordan (ed.), *Plunkitt of Tammany Hall* (New York: McClure, Phillips, and Company, 1905).

The range of benefits dispensed by the machines was broad. The machine helped immigrants get jobs. As reformer Jane Addams noted, "an Italian laborer wants a job more than anything else, and quite simply votes for the man who promises him one." The machines dispensed temporary jobs like shoveling snow in winter or permanent jobs such as positions in the sanitation department or the police force. Even teachers' jobs were often patronage appointments awarded for favors done for the machine. The machines also provided recreation. Tammany Hall's annual steamboat outings on the Hudson River were famous.

The machines often intervened for the city poor in their dealings with the law. They gave free legal aid and advice and helped to get voters out of minor scrapes. The boss and the ward heelers were usually tolerant of legal transgressions involving vice and victimless crimes. And why not? After all, the machine received large amounts of protection money from bordellos, gambling parlors, and saloons.

The machine also was sensitive to the emotional and psychological needs of the voters. Although many of the bosses and their lieutenants were Irish, they were usually tolerant of the newcomers from southern and eastern Europe who poured into the cities after 1890 and cultivated them and their children. This meant honoring their religious observances and family ceremonies, no matter how unfamiliar, and giving recognition to their talented young.

The Reformers

Whatever useful functions and services the machines performed, they dismayed and angered many citizens. Periodically reformers sought to break their hold on city government and replace them with honest and frugal leaders like themselves.

The reformers were often ineffectual people with a limited view of what the cities and their citizens needed. Many good government people ("goo-goos" to their opponents) were old-stock, middle- and upper-class men and women with little empathy for immigrants and the cities' working folk. At times, their outrage at the machines' dishonesty seemed to derive more from the high taxes the machines imposed to cover their costs than from moral considerations. To such goo-goos, good government was identical with cheap government that spared their own pocketbooks.

When the machines overdid their thievery, the resulting scandal would sometimes appall even their loyalists. The reformers would seize the chance to "turn the rascals out" and for a time would run the city government on honest principles. This generally meant frugal principles as well, which in turn not only cut out the graft and corruption but also the make-work jobs, the free gifts of food and clothes at Christmas, the summer outings, and much else besides.

Reformers of this kind often distrusted working-class voters. After all, it was their votes that had kept the machine in power. The solution was to reduce the power of elected officials and replace them by nonelected experts who would run the cities on scientific principles.

Reformers such as these, who emphasized *structural* change and frugality, seldom stayed in office very long. Once the spasm of virtue that had expelled the rascals subsided, the public turned once more to the familiar machine. As New York boss Richard Crocker told journalist Lincoln Steffens, "Our people could not stand the rotten police corruption. They'll be back in the next election; they can't stand reform either."

During the 1890s the structural–good-government reformers organized the National Municipal League to publicize and promote their views. In 1899 this group drew up a model city charter, which they touted as a cure for bad city government. They also endorsed the commission system and the city manager system. Both of these sought to eliminate party politics as the fuel for city government and to replace it with a nonpartisan system run by experts. The reformers, in advertising their schemes, frequently noted that there was no Democratic or Republican way to collect the city's garbage. Both plans were widely employed during the twentieth century, especially in smaller cities.

There was another type of municipal reformer, the *social* reformer, not moved solely by a desire for efficiency or economy. Melvin Holli, a prominent urban historian, describes the social reform movement as "humanistic and empirical," unwilling to impose "middle-class morality and patrician values upon the masses."

The structural–good-government types generally lacked the popular touch. One reason for their short tenures in office was their inability to win the public's affection. Their socially oriented colleagues were different. Reform mayors Tom Johnson and Newton Baker of Cleveland, Samuel ("Golden Rule") Jones and Brand Whitlock of Toledo, Hazen Pingree of Detroit, and Mark Phagan of Jersey City were warmhearted men with the common touch. Although most had started as successful businessmen, they quickly established alliances with the city's poor and fought their battles against privileged business groups indifferent to their workers or the public.

Reform Mayors   Hazen Pingree, a self-made shoe manufacturer, was initially a Republican conservative who ran for mayor of Detroit in 1889 to beat the machine. Once in office he set to work in the standard "goo-goo" manner to fire the crooks, cut out the financial fat, and increase the efficiency of city services.

But he soon discovered that much of the city's corruption derived from its business interests. His growing antagonism to the selfish business elite alienated many of Pingree's upper-class supporters. At the same time, however, he won the enthusiastic support of Detroit's Polish and German ethnic population, who kept him in office for eight years.

During that period, Pingree rebuilt the sewer system; constructed parks, schools, and a free public bath; forced down gas, telephone, and streetcar rates; established a municipal lighting plant; initiated a work-relief program for the unemployed; and imposed taxes on business firms that had long evaded their fair share.

Toledo's Samuel ("Golden Rule") Jones was another businessman. In his Toldeo factory, Jones sought to treat his workers by the golden rule of doing to others as one would have them do to you. Jones's employees enjoyed an eight-hour day with one week of paid vacation annually. They received a yearly Christmas bonus and were beneficiaries of a health-insurance scheme.

In 1897 Jones, elected mayor by a narrow margin, set about trying to bring to the citizens of Toledo the same benevolent regime he had conferred on his own employees. He established free night schools and kindergartens, built playgrounds, opened a lodging house for tramps, introduced the merit system into city hiring, raised the wages of city workers from $1 to $1.50 per day, and fought the street railway companies. He also tried to end capital punishment in Ohio.

Tom Johnson, like the other two, was a self-made millionaire who ran successfully for mayor of Cleveland in 1901. Unlike Pingree and Jones, Johnson was a social-conscience reformer from the outset. Once in office, he established a municipal lighting plant that reduced the city's electric costs by over a third and initiated municipal meat-and-dairy inspection schemes, a model building code, and a city-run sanitation service. He succeeded in lowering the city transit fare to three cents, although he failed in a long-fought battle to acquire for Cleveland outright ownership of the city transit system. In the words of a contemporary, Johnson made Cleveland "the best governed city in America," but the task exacted a toll. In 1911 he died while still in office, his health broken by his labors and his fortune dissipated.

At the left end of the municipal reform spectrum were Milwaukee's two socialist mayors, Emil Seidel (1910–1912) and Daniel Hoan (1916–1940). Both fought for a wide range of municipal programs to benefit the city's working-class. Between them the two instituted factory- and housing-inspection systems, established a city-run employment office, raised wages and lowered working hours for city employees, established free musical concerts, and built new parks and recreational facilities. Both men pushed hard for municipal ownership of transit lines and public utilities—a program that the more radical socialists dismissed contemptuously as "sewer socialism"—but found that the state's refusal to grant Milwaukee liberal home rule made this almost impossible to achieve.

The upsurge of municipal reform between 1890 and 1917 did not end machine rule. Some cities never experienced a strong reform impulse. In many that did, it proved shortlived. Machine rule continued as a fact of American urban life well into our own century and is not entirely dead today. If any force can be said to have destroyed the machine, it was the appearance of the welfare state after 1932 that took out of the bosses' hands the power to confer benefits on the poor and gave it to the federal bureaucracy. "Died of Welfare" might well be the epitaph on the tombstone of the American city machine.

City Life

To the millions pouring into the cities in the last years of the old century and the first years of the new, as well as to those already there, life was complicated, often hard, and always interesting.

Family

The crucible of city life was the family. But there was no single, typical urban family. Families varied according to class, ethnicity, and race. And of course we must allow for the diversity of all human institutions and the unpredictability of all human behavior.

White, native-born middle-class families tended to be small—smaller than either rural, immigrant, African-American, or working-class families. The middle-class consisted of strivers who placed a high premium on success and material comfort. It was expensive to raise and educate children in the city. City apartments were small, food costs were high, and children could not easily contribute, as they did on the farm, to the family's income. A large family in the city meant too great a sacrifice of material comfort. Urbanization was not the primary cause of falling birthrates, but city families did have fewer children than rural ones.

Another factor that made urban families smaller than country ones was the absence from the family circle of anyone but parents and children. It was not easy in the city apartment or tenement to take in grandparents or other family members. Moderately extended families were possible in the farmstead, but in the cities the nuclear family of parents and children was the almost invariable rule.

Middle-class city families were also less male-dominated. On the farm, husbands worked nearby and could firmly exercise the authority over wife and children that the patriarchal values of the day endorsed. In the new city environment, however, men seldom worked at home. Most had to commute to distant offices where they spent long hours each day, six days a week. With the family breadwinner absent much of the time, the mother inevitably became the central influence on the children's early moral and intellectual upbringing. The major financial decisions continued to be made, no doubt, by the men, but women's "sphere" expanded.

The smaller families of urbanites also freed women from many home responsi-bilities and permitted outside activities on a new scale. Formerly, only rich women, with their servants and governesses, found themselves with idle time to devote to self-cultivation or public service. Now they were joined by their middle-class sisters who, with fewer children to raise, had more time to devote to activities unconnected with the family.

As a result, a flood of civic-minded women's clubs replaced the older literary societies that had studied the poetry of Dante or the plays of Shakespeare. The latter had filled the leisure time of an earlier generation of middle-class women. The new clubs devoted their time to social and moral uplift and reform, especially in areas involving women and children. Many were affiliated with the General Federation of Women's Clubs. The membership of the federation was fifty thousand in 1898; by 1914 it was well past a million.

It would be a mistake to see middle-class parents, the fathers always away and the mothers anxious to go to their club meetings, as indifferent and unloving. Richard Sennett's study of middle-class families in late nineteenth-century Chicago shows that children found the family a haven in a difficult, competitive world, and resisted leaving home for as long as possible.

The picture we get of white, native-born working-class families is somewhat different from the one just described. Clearly, working-class families were larger, a phenomenon that was probably related to the lower expectations of blue-collar parents for their children. One could have more children if one was not obliged to keep them in school for advanced education. It was also undoubtedly connected to differences in knowledge of birth-control methods. These differences were signifi-cant. When Margaret Sanger, a fiery young radical trained as a nurse, came to the Lower East Side in 1912 to help poor women, she was appalled to find that many knew no other birth-control method than self-induced abortion. Thereafter, Sanger dedicated herself to the cause of disseminating contraception information, in the process offending the guardians of traditional morals. In 1914 she was indicted for sending "obscene" matter through the mails under the 1873 Comstock Act. Sanger won her case, and in 1916 she established a birth-control clinic in Brooklyn, the first of many. She continued to be attacked by social conservatives but refused to be deterred.

It is tempting to assume that the squalid housing conditions and the economic deprivation that often afflicted working-class urban families undermined family life. Reformers such as Jacob Riis, whose classic *How the Other Half Lives* (1890) is the first good description of the urban poor, often warned that life in the tenements would destroy "the home" if the worst conditions were not alleviated. Yet modern scholars see no sign of such an effect. Herbert Gutman's study of Paterson, New Jersey, in the 1880s shows that a majority of households were intact. It is time, he concludes, "to discard the notion that . . . industrialization caused little more than cultural breakdown and anomie."

Although the city did not destroy the white, native-born family, it did subject it to strains. The competitiveness of city life for young middle-class males, as we have noted, was severe. For working-class boys and girls there were temptations to turn to crime or prostitution to make the promise of American life a little more certain. It is clear that child labor, forced on working-class parents by inadequate income, was morally dangerous. Newsboys, for example, who hawked the penny press on city streets, were often without supervision and were easily drawn into petty crime and immorality.

Divorce may not be the best measure of family dissatisfaction and internal stress. It may only reflect the way a particular generation is able to express them. Yet, it is suggestive that the number of divorces soared between 1900 and 1920 from 55,000 to over 167,000, an increase of 300 percent during a period when the total population increased by only 25 percent. During that twenty-year period, the proportion of marriages that ended in divorce rose from one in twelve to one in nine. Most of these legal dissolutions were of middle-class marriages; then, as now, the poor chose the cheaper option of abandonment.

The city environment placed heavier burdens on African-American and immigrant families than it did on white families. Black migrants to the cities found jobs more difficult to get and hold than whites; they encountered severe hostility; they were forced to accept the housing leavings even immigrants would not take—and they paid more for them. Yet, recent studies show that the African-American family survived in the northern ghettos that began to expand after 1890 and even grew more cohesive. Like other migrants to the American urban-industrial environment from 1890 to 1920, blacks used the family as an effective crutch for the readjustment process.

To the foreign-born, the American industrial city compelled a triple adjustment all at once: to the United States, to the city, and to industrial society. Yet the evidence here, too, is that the family survived the strain. Virginia Yans, in her study of Italian immigrant families in Buffalo, concludes that "even as different members entered industrial America's work force, the immigrant family remained remarkably untouched."

That does not mean, however, that it was not altered. In eastern Europe many families did approximate the extended family of traditional societies. Such complex families seldom survived the transatlantic passage and generally reverted to the nuclear sort. And there were other results as well. In Europe, even more than America, the father was the head of the household. Children born in America learned a more democratic family pattern. Even more significantly, English-speaking, educated, native-born children often had advantages over foreign-born, sometimes illiterate, parents. When parents had to depend on their offspring for guidance around a strange city and a strange land, it was difficult for them to maintain their authority intact.

Immigrant groups in America did not fare equally well economically and socially, and it is often said that the differences are connected to distinctive family values. Italian families, for example, instilled in their offspring, especially their sons, a strong sense that they must always place loyalty to family first. Italian men were urged to choose work that would not disrupt their traditional family ties. As a consequence, Italian-Americans remained in construction work, gardening and horticulture, and the clothing business, occupations that did not require much formal education or confer high status. When these flourished, the individuals flourished, but they did not move past the family.

Jewish families emphasized the individual more, and they also placed a higher value on formal education. Young Jewish men were not pressured to stay in traditional

Jewish occupations, although many inevitably did. Through the channel of education, they were expected to move, if possible, beyond their parents into law, medicine, science, and the other learned professions. As a whole, they were remarkably successful, yet the Jewish family paid a price. As sons—and later daughters—went off into the higher reaches of professional life, a large gap in understanding and empathy opened up between the first immigrant generation and their upwardly mobile children.

City Schools

American education in these years underwent a remarkable upgrading. In 1870 the typical American could claim only four years of schooling. He or she was literate, but possessed only the most elementary knowledge of the "three R's"—reading, 'riting, and 'rithmetic. Schools were especially poor in the South where they were seriously underfunded and segregated by race besides. Most rural schools remained small, one-room affairs, where, amid a noisy babble and a barrage of spitballs and paper clips, the teacher had to deal simultaneously with little children who were barely toilet trained and restless, awkward adolescents. Even in the cities, however, the schools were small, ungraded, and limited in their offerings. Most teaching consisted of rote recitations, the regurgitation of names and facts memorized out of some outdated textbook.

Matters improved through the opening years of the twentieth century. In 1890 the outlay for schools nationally was $146 million. This grew to $230 million by 1900 and reached $525 million by 1913.

Much of the money spent went to the cities. Curricula expanded to include art, music, hygiene, and other subjects previously ignored. City schools vastly improved their physical plant. Gymnasiums, art rooms, laboratories, auditoriums, and play-grounds all became standard features of the best urban schools. The cities also lengthened their school year. From a national average of 143 days in 1898, the school year by 1914 had grown to 160, with the big cities mainly responsible for the increase.

Relatively little of the enlarged education outlays went into salaries. At the turn-of-the-century, the typical rural or small-town schoolteacher received $38 a month. This sum rose to $66 by 1914. The cities paid more, yet teaching even in the metropolises was never remunerative enough to attract many men. At one time teachers, especially in the high schools, had been predominantly male. By 1900 the men were mostly gone, replaced by well-educated women happy to take even the stingy salaries the school boards paid.

One of the most significant new educational trends was the appearance of the public high school. During the previous century most secondary schools had been private academies preparing their male students for college and their famale students for middle-class gentility. By the end of the century the growth of commerce, banking, accounting, office work, and education itself, much of it urban-centered, had created the need for a large corps of young people with clerical, writing, and other skills.

The cities responded by establishing a host of public high schools. These were not compulsory, but they were usually free. In 1870 there were 500 high schools, almost

A high school typing class, 1910. (Library of Congress)

all private, in the entire nation; they were attended by 2 percent of children of high-school age. In 1915 there were 11,600 high schools, with 20 percent of all high-school age children enrolled.

An important function of the city school systems was the assimilation of the immigrant. There were a few cultural pluralists like Professor Horace Kallen of Columbia University, who celebrated a diverse society in which each ethnic group's contribution to the overall American mix would remain intact. There were also many traditionalists who despaired of any possibility of the immigrants' incorporation into American life and favored exclusion of the "mongrel hordes." In the mid-1890s a group of Boston blue bloods organized the Immigration Restriction League to work for a literacy test designed to limit the number of newcomers from eastern and southern Europe. Congress passed literacy bills several times, but the president each time vetoed the measure.

But most native-born Americans opposed both the culturally lumpy society envisaged by Kallen and the totally closed door. Intead they wished to remake the foreign-born to their own predominantly Protestant, Anglo-Saxon specifications. The job, they assumed, could be accomplished primarily by the public-school system. As one Boston school official noted, the city schools would "train up all the children within its jurisdiction to be intelligent, virtuous, patriotic American citizens."

Immigrants often resisted this enforced assimilation through the school system. They wanted their children to become good Americans, but they deplored their loss of contact with their cultural and religious pasts. Many Catholic immigrants viewed the public schools, despite their supposedly nonsectarian character, as bastions of Protestantism, and they fought to establish their own parochial school system. In 1884 a Catholic Plenary Council meeting in Baltimore declared that all Catholic parishes in the United States must establish elementary schools for Catholic children to preserve their religious heritage. By 1903 there were nearly four thousand parochial elementary schools teaching one million students; there were several hundred Catholic high schools as well. The cost of this system was enormous, straining severely the limited resources of groups still new to the American environment and still poor.

Resistance to cultural coercion took many less formal forms. Foreign-born children often resisted, by inattention and misbehavior, the "American" lady in front of the room who looked so different from their own mothers. Many dropped out as soon as they could go to work. Some teachers in turn failed to respect their students' customs or heritage and sometimes found it difficult to disguise their dislike for the alien children who sat before them.

Yet schools frequently worked well. Immigrant children acquired English, got some idea of American values and ideology, and learned the history of their adopted country. They also picked up some of the middle-class ideas of hygiene and health and acquired work habits that would prove valuable in later life. Not all immigrants resisted the schools' assimilation and "uplift" process. Mary Antin, a Russian-Jewish girl who came with her family to Boston in 1894, wrote of her father's yearning for his children's acceptance into American life. Mr. Antin brought his children to school, she later wrote, "as if it were an act of consecration," his way of "taking possession of America." Mary herself gloried in the process of becoming a patriotic American. She had sat "rigid with attention" in her Boston school as her teacher read the story of the American Revolution. As she learned how America had achieved its independence, "what was meant by *my country*" dawned on her. She too was an American!

The Settlement House

An important agent of working-class and immigrant education and assimilation was the city *settlement house*. Run by idealistic college-educated men and women anxious to help alleviate the suffering of the poor and make their adjustment to city life less painful, settlement houses began to pop up in the larger cities during the 1880s.

By 1920 hundreds of settlements existed in almost every large city in the land. Two, Hull House in Chicago, run by Jane Addams, and the Henry Street Settlement in New York, run by Lillian Wald, established especially enviable reputations for innovative work with immigrants and served as important sources of reform ideas for what would become the progressive movement.

The settlements competed with the bosses in meeting the physical needs of the urban poor and providing help with jobs. They also fought the machines as corrupt and manipulative of the poor. Jane Addams, especially, allied herself with the urban reformers to fight the Chicago machine. But much of what they did was educational. Settlements held classes in English, American history, and citizenship to speed the assimilation process. They also taught classes in child care, personal hygiene, meal preparation, cooking, and other subjects designed to transmit to immigrant women the latest knowledge in the field or inform them how Americans did things. Although the settlement workers were usually more sensitive to immigrants' feelings and tried to avoid condescension, they did not always succeed. Some immigrants avoided the settlement houses as alien places where they were expected to become something they were not. (For more on the work of the settlement houses, see the next chapter.)

However painful the assimilation process, it was the price paid by immigrants to gain acceptance. Native-born Americans demanded that immigrants abandon the look, the speech, the customs, and the habits of the Old Country. The means of admission to the American dream would always be a large dose of assimilation.

Urban Leisure

Early twentieth-century cities were not only places to work; they were also places to play. Although workdays were long and vacations few, men and women always had some leisure and sought ways to fill it amusingly and profitably in the urban environment.

Participation Sports

When most Americans lived in the country, the opportunity for healthy recreation was almost limitless. Rural people had no trouble finding the space and time for fishing, hunting, walking, riding, sleighing, swimming, ice skating, and so forth. City life changed this. Many cities had failed to hold on to public land or to make provisions for acquiring it. New York, Washington, Boston, Philadelphia, San Francisco, and some other big cities had extensive park systems, but many others did not. Playgrounds were even rarer. Urbanites in most communities lived amid block after block of tenements or commercial buildings without open areas for recreation.

In the 1890s the safety bicycle with its two equal-size wheels enabled many urbanites to escape to the country during their day off. The Sunday bicycle excursion soon became a national craze, and ministers were soon complaining that the new fad was depriving them of their congregations on the Lord's day. The bicycle craze had two unexpected results. One was the movement for better roads. Started by the bicyclists, it gained momentum after the turn-of-the-century when automobile enthusiasts added their voices to the chorus. The other was a form of female liberation. Women had not been left out of the bicycle fad. Inventors had accommodated their needs with the drop frame that did not interfere with female skirts. Yet even the drop-frame machine did not permit the bustles and tight-laced corsets of the day. The effect was to force a reconsideration of what a "lady" was allowed to wear. As a contemporary writer remarked, "no woman would dare venture on the street with a skirt that stopped above her ankles and leggings that reached obviously to her knees. . . . [But the bicycle] has given to all American womankind the liberty of dress which the reformers have been sighing [for] for generations."

The electric streetcar provided another opportunity to escape the city. To drum up riders on Sundays and holidays, streetcar companies constructed amusement parks at the end of their routes. Outside of Boston there was Paragon Park; San Francisco had the Chutes; Philadelphia, Willow Grove; Chicago, White City; New York, Coney Island. Patrons were drawn to these parks by their Ferris wheels, merry-go-rounds, roller coasters, and shoot-the-shoots. They could also picnic and play games in the open fields, dance at the bandstands, listen to live concerts, and even attend theatrical performances. Families, clubs, and couples patronized the amusement parks by the thousands during the spring and summer months.

Children did not need to leave the cities' boundaries to enjoy the out-of-doors. They often made do very well with street games that relied on chalk to lay out boundaries or broomsticks to serve as bats. Urban children were inventive at adapting or actually creating a host of games that could be played on city streets. Some of these, such as—Hide-and-Seek and skipping rope survive today, while others, such as buck-buck, Johnny-on-the-pony, and ring-a-lievo have since disappeared.

By the late 1890s city reformers began to tackle the problem of providing open recreational space for children and adults alike. In the 1880s Boston opened the "first local recreation ground" equipped with a running track, field house, and trained attendants. In 1898 the city designated twenty city school yards for after-school play by children. The next year New York followed suit. In 1906, as part of the general impulse toward "improvement" of American life, a group of civic-minded reformers organized

Early twentieth-century bicyclists out for a spin. (The Bettmann Archive)

the Playground and Recreation Association of America to further encourage the playground movement and integrate the efforts of local playground societies. By 1915, a total of 432 cities maintained 3300 playgrounds with hundreds of men and women to staff them.

Spectator Sports

But the difficulty of finding adequate space, or perhaps the sheer craving for ease among people who worked hard physically, ultimately fostered the growth of commercial spectator sports. Easily in the lead was the "national sport," baseball.

Baseball Baseball was the descendant of several English games, all involving a bat, ball, and bases, that had been played in America as far back as the eighteenth century. Initially, the rules of play were improvised as were the teams and the schedule of games. At first baseball was the sport of gentlemen. The New York Knickerbockers wore white shirts, blue pants, and straw hats and celebrated each game with a formal dinner for players and guests. The game soon became more democratic, with "mechanics," laborers, and craftsmen forming their own teams. The Knickerbockers attempted to serve as arbiters of the game's play and rules, but the common folk rejected this role.

The Civil War accelerated the game's spread. Many Union and Confederate soldiers saw baseball played for the first time in the military camps, enjoyed it, and carried their enthusiasm back home after the war ended. In the immediate postwar period, newspaper writers created further interest by their colorful reports and by emphasizing the game's interesting statistics. In 1872, the magazine *Sports and Games* for the first time called baseball "the national game of the United States."

Meanwhile baseball was becoming increasingly commercialized. As early as 1858 team managers had begun to charge admission to see the game. In 1862 a Brooklyn promoter built a fenced-in field with a graded diamond and a clubhouse. But true professionalism came only in 1869 when the managers of the Cincinnati Red Stockings hired a team of professional players and sent them on a tour. They won every game they played.

Scores of clubs soon began to imitate the Red Stockings, and in 1871 ten teams formed a professional league. It soon collapsed, however, and in 1876 was replaced by the modern National League. The American League came early in the new century, and in 1903 the leaders of each league played one another in the first World Series. With 100,000 fans watching the eight games, the American League's Boston Red Sox beat the National League's Pittsburgh Pirates. Attendance at professional baseball games continued to climb, and at the 1913 World Series, where the Philadelphia Athletics beat the New York Giants four games to one, 151,000 spectators paid gate receipts of $336,000.

Like most other sports, baseball was an avenue to fame and success for young men from every walk of life and from almost every ethnic group. Most professional players at first bore Anglo-Saxon, Irish, or German names. By the 1920s Italian and Hispanic names began to creep in. One group, however, was excluded from major league baseball. By agreement among the leagues and the teams, African-American players were exiled to separate black leagues where salaries were low, equipment and ballparks shabby, and attendance, though enthusiastic, small. Despite the handicaps, African-American baseball was a lively and vigorous sport. Andrew ("Rube") Foster, a talented pitcher who managed the black Chicago American Giants, was able to boost attendance by arranging exhibition games between African-American teams and major league teams. By the early 1920s there were two black leagues, the National Negro Baseball League and the Eastern League. Teams such as the Chicago Giants, the Kansas City Monarchs, and the St. Louis Stars provided some outlet for black athletes, but they never provided the rewards of fame and money that the players deserved.

Boxing The urban sport that was least segregated racially was prizefighting. Boxing was frowned on by many middle-class people as brutal, and in many cities it was officially banned. But it was vastly popular, especially among working-class men, and many who could not attend a major match read about it avidly in their newspapers. One English visitor to the United States in the 1890s was shocked by the contrast of twelve columns devoted to a championship boxing match in his morning paper to only one, and that inside, to the death of the poet John Greenleaf Whittier.

During the 1880s and early 1890s the dominant figure in the prizefight ring was John L. Sullivan, the "Strong Boy of Boston." Sullivan's defeat of Jake Kilrain in a ferocious seventy-five–round, bare-knuckle bout in New Orleans brought him $20,000 in prize money and a diamond-encrusted belt donated by *The Police Gazette*. Sullivan became a local hero. When he returned to his native city, his fans packed the Boston Theater to do him honor, and the city's mayor and aldermen proudly occupied seats on the stage.

Far more than any other sport, boxing brought out ethnic loyalties—and prejudices. Sullivan's success thrilled his fellow Irish-Americans, and when John L. went down to defeat before liquor and "Gentleman Jim" Corbett in 1892, it was a blow to Irish-American pride.

Although at first excluded from championship contention, by the opening years of the new century even African-Americans found a niche in prizefighting. In 1908 Jack Johnson won the world heavyweight championship by defeating Tommy Burns in Sidney, Australia, and then, in 1910, he confirmed his title by beating James Jeffries, a white American boxer in Reno, Nevada. Like Sullivan, Johnson evoked the pride of his people. But he also aroused the hostility of the white public who sought a "white hope" to knock him off his pedestal. Dislike of Johnson was reinforced by his "consorting" with white women, and in 1913 he was tried for "abducting" his third wife, who was white. Johnson fled abroad to avoid prison, but in 1915 he fought Jess Willard, a white man, for the championship in Havana, Cuba; in a controversial decision, Johnson lost the match.

Other Sports Americans had other sports to distract them from the cares of daily life and fill their limited leisure time. For example, horseracing was popular in many cities. By the opening years of the new century, however, reformers who rightly believed that it encouraged gambling had begun to clamp down on racetrack betting. Some racing enthusiasts sold their horses; others transferred their activities to Europe.

They soon found ways to evade the antibetting laws, and it proved possible to continue "to improve the breed."

Football in these years was still an amateur college game most closely followed by the educated middle class, although it had begun to attract much working-class interest. The game had already developed some of its more dubious characteristics. Increasingly colleges awarded scholarships and conferred other benefits on top-ranking high-school players to induce them to come, justifying the accusation that the game was being professionalized. The introduction of close-formation plays made injuries, and even deaths, common. In 1903 forty-four young men died of football accidents. So serious was the outcry that in 1906 the major colleges formed the National Collegiate Athletic Association and adopted new rules—the forward pass, the ten-yard down, the onside kick, and the separation of rush lines—that promised to reduce the mayhem.

The reforms did not succeed, yet college football's popularity did not suffer. By 1914 attendance at some of the big games was as high as fifty thousand, inducing many schools to draw up plans for massive new stadiums. By this time football could be justified by college administrators as essential to building alumni support and subsidizing the intramural—and the less popular intercollegiate—sports programs.

The Arts

Sports were a mass attraction, but the cities were also the centers of high culture, the arts that pleased a well-educated and influential minority of the American people. To those Americans who were devotees of classical music, opera, painting, and the theater, either as audience or performers, the cities were powerful magnets. Hundreds, perhaps thousands, of talented young men and women annually came to the nation's largest cities to be close to the performing arts.

Music

America had no major composers in the classical tradition in the early twentieth century. It did not even have a large contingent of first-rate conductors, singers, or instrumentalists. But both the educated elite and many of the foreign-born, provided an appreciative audience for the work of European masters, and they were willing to pay for the best performers that Europe could supply. Although progress toward improving the musical sophistication of Americans was slow, it was perceptible. During these years the three symphony orchestras of the nineteenth century—in New York, Chicago, and Boston—were joined by Philadelphia, Minneapolis, New Orleans, and Seattle. The Metropolitan Opera in New York flourished as it never had before. Most of the players and conductors were foreign-born, but a few American conservatories had begun to train talented native-born performers.

Painting

The early twentieth-century city fostered something closer to an indigenous American school of painting. The so-called *ashcan school* of Robert Henri, Everett

Shinn, George Luks, John Sloan, William Glackens, and Maurice Prendergast originated in Philadelphia during the 1890s. Most of these young men had been newspaper illustrators whose pens provided the visual images to accompany news stories. When it became possible to print photographs in the daily press, they turned to painting, but their subject matter remained much the same as before—prizefights, cityscapes, and urban people at work and play. Their technique continued to have a rough illustrator quality; when combined with their focus on commonplace subject matter, it led their critics from the genteel "beaux arts" tradition of pretty technique and uplifting subject matter to sneer at them as the "ashcan school." They themselves viewed their work as democratic, consistent with the emerging urban culture of the masses.

At the beginning of the new century these Philadelphians moved one by one to New York, the country's cultural metropolis, where they were joined by a number of local artists. In 1904, six of the group held a show at the National Arts Club that one critic described as "an outlook where nature is seen under her most lugubrious mood, where joyousness never enters . . . and where unhealthiness prevails to an alarming extent." Excluded by the conservative National Academy of Design from its prestigious exhibitions, in 1908 eight of the group held their own showing at the MacBeth Gallery in New York; it attracted large crowds but gained few sales.

"The Eight," as the group was called, did not stay together for very long, but they helped inspire young realist American painters such as George Bellows, Jerome Myers, and Edward Hopper. They also helped break down the wall of gentility that surrounded American painting and prepared the way for the still more avant-garde postimpressionists who were revolutionizing the visual arts in Europe.

In 1913 The Eight and the more radical modernists sponsored an exhibition of the best new European and American work at New York's Sixty-ninth Regiment Armory. The American section made little splash. But the European exhibit of Fernand Léger, Georges Braque, Pablo Picasso, Paul Cézanne, Vincent van Gogh, Paul Gauguin, and the still more radical cubists who abandoned all attempt at representation was a shocking eye-opener. The sensation of the show was Marcel Duchamp's *Nude Descending a Staircase, No. 2,* a composition of closely overlapping outlines, like a set of stop-time photographs, which was merely suggestive of its theme.

Seventy thousand people came to see the exhibition in New York. Most went away puzzled or contemptuous. Critics had a field day at the modernists' expense. One of Duchamp's detractors called his picture "an explosion in a shingle factory." Yet there were many, expecially among the professional artists, who recognized that they had seen the future of visual art. One of the viewers, Hutchins Hapgood, recalled the show "as I would a great fire, an earthquake, or a political revolution; as a series of shattering events—shattering for the purposes of re-creation."

Theater

American theater began to find its voice in the early years of the new century. Until then the best of the stage had usually been the tours of British companies performing the English classics. American playwrights such as David Belasco, Bronson Howard, and Edward Harrigan were often skilled plot developers or clever satirists of ethnic and social types, but none of them was capable of doing justice to universal themes. In their hands the stage played to the lowest common denominator and was a medium of popular entertainment rather than an art form.

Matters began to change early in the century with the appearance of various *little theater* companies run by people who disdained the commercial stage as symbolized by New York's Broadway. In several cities between 1900 and 1912, these men and women began producing works by serious European dramatists who they believed had important things to say to modern audiences.

In 1915 a little theater group of young men and women from New York's Greenwich Village began to present experimental new plays at Provincetown on Cape Cod. The following summer, calling themselves the Provincetown Players, they staged a work by an unknown young man named Eugene O'Neill. That fall, on their return to New York, the group opened the Provincetown Playhouse in a converted stable in Greenwich Village. There, during the 1920s, they would produce almost all of the young playwright's works— including *Bound East for Cardiff, The Emperor Jones,* and *Anna Christie*— and in the process help create a new American theater.

Greenwich Village

Greenwich Village on Manhattan's Lower West Side was the seedbed of much of the new, more serious and radical sensibility in theater, literature, and art. A shabby, once-elegant district, its rents were attractively low. The community, moreover, resembled Paris more than a typical American city. For both reasons, the placed proved a magnet for creative young men and women fleeing the nation's small towns and starting careers in journalism, literature, theater, or one of the other arts.

At the center of the Village's creative vortex was Mabel Dodge, a rich bohemian who lived on one of the community's better streets and made her apartment the exciting center for the avant-garde in painting, sculpture, politics, and ideas. Here gathered people such as Margaret Sanger, the scandalous leader of the birth-control movement; journalist-reformer Hutchins Hapgood; "Big Bill" Haywood, leader of the radical Industrial Workers of the World (IWW), a radical union dedicated to replacing the capitalist wage system with labor cooperatives; the young novelist from Chicago, Floyd Dell; John Reed, a radical journalist from Portland, Oregon; the muckraker Lincoln Steffens; and Walter Lippmann, the brilliant young Harvard graduate who would become the dean of American journalism and adviser to presidents.

The habitués of the Dodge salon and the residents of the small apartment that dotted the Village were self-conscious bohemians whose lives were counterstatements to those of most Americans. Their views and styles foreshadowed those of more recent dissenters. Village women were feminists who believed in equal careers for themselves and despised the sexual repression of women in the heartland. Villagers were tolerant of homosexuality. They were often political radicals, and during the violent mill worker strikes in Lawrence and Paterson in 1912 conducted by Haywood's IWW, they threw their support to the workers. They even foreshadowed the hippies of the 1960s when Mabel Dodge held a psychedelic party in her apartment to test the effects of peyote buttons. Several of the guests had "bad trips," and a doctor had to be called.

Mabel Dodge, whose apartment in New York City's Greenwich Village became a center for the avant garde in the early years of the twentieth century. (The Bettmann Archive)

The formation of Greenwich Village marked the creation of an American intelligentsia, a subculture of artists and intellectuals whose influence radiated outward from lower Manhattan to influence urban, literate people everywhere in the country. Another such movement—in the Concord-Boston area two decades before the Civil War—had affected the course of American values and ideas and even politics. The new intelligentsia would do so once again.

The New City

Between 1890 and 1920 the city became the physical and cultural focus of American life. For the first time more Americans came to live in cities than on farms and in villages. In those years too the cities of the United States, more than ever before, drew the talented and able of the world into their orbits.

Early twentieth-century cities were not perfect places to live. They were abrasive, crime-ridden, dirty, cramped, and lonely. Yet by 1920 they were beginning to solve many of their worst problems. By that time the cities had acquired improved transit, sanitation, pure water, and fire and police protection services. A flock of compassionate reform mayors showed that local government could be improved. The building of playgrounds and the opening of amusement parks provided new outlets for exercise and entertainment. The cities' cultural amenities began to be upgraded with the advent of better schools and more museums, orchestras, and art galleries. The cities did not become utopias; they never would. But we can see that during the first few decades of this century, they became for a time eminently livable communities.

FOR FURTHER READING

The place to start for understanding the American city during the past century is Blake McKelvey, *The Urbanization of America, 1860–1915* (1963). Roy Lubove's *The Progressives and the Slums: Tenement House Reform in New York City, 1890–1917* (1964) places the period's urban housing problem in the context of the reform movement. A popular history of one department store is by Lloyd Wendt and Herman Kogan, *Give the Lady What She Wants! Marshall Field and Company* (1952). Urban transportation and early suburbanization are dealt with in Sam Bass Warner, Jr.'s *Streetcar Suburbs: The Process of Growth in Boston, 1870–1900* (1962). The garbage problem, or an early version of it, is described in Martin V. Melosi's *Garbage in the Cities: Refuse, Reform, and the Environment, 1880–1980* (1981). On the matter of clean water, see Nelson Blake, *Water for the Cities* (1956). The police provisions for one city, Boston, is treated by Roger Lane in *Policing the City: Boston 1822–1885* (1967).

The literature on the city machine in this period is voluminous. Some of the best works are: Seymour Mandelbaum, *Boss Tweed's New York* (1965); Zane Miller, *Boss Cox's Cincinnati* (1968); and Joel Tarr, *A Study in Boss Politics: William Lorimer of Chicago* (1971). Urban reformers and their achievements are described in Melvin Holli, *Reform in Detroit: Hazen S. Pingree and Urban Politics* (1969) and James B. Crooks, *Politics and Progress: The Rise of Urban Progressivism in Baltimore, 1895–1911* (1968).

Two new studies that deal with the quality of urban life in these years are: David Nasaw, *Children of the City At Work and Play* (1986) and Gunther Barth, *City People: The Rise of Modern City Culture in Nineteenth Century America* (1980). City families and their problems are dealt with in Richard Sennett, *Families Against the City: Middle Class Homes of Chicago, 1872–1890* (1970) and William O'Neill, *Divorce in the Progressive Era* (1967). City schools are the subject of David Tyack, *The One Best System: A History of American Urban Education* (1974) and Robert Carlson, *The Quest for Conformity: Americanization through Education* (1975). The standard work on the settlement movement is Allen Davis's *Spearheads for Reform: The Social Settlements and the Progressive Movement, 1890–1914* (1967). For sports in the early twentieth-century city, see the appropriate chapters of Foster Rhea Dulles, *A History of Recreation: America Learns to Play* (1965). For an interesting study of working-class leisure, consult Roy Rosenzweig, *Eight Hours for What We Will: Workers and Leisure in an Industrial City, 1870–1920* (1983).

On the ashcan school, the Armory show, and beyond, see Milton W. Brown, *American Painting from the Armory Show to the Depression* (1955). The Greenwich Village scene and the emergence of twentieth-century bohemia are depicted in Henry F. May, *The End of American Innocence, 1912–1917* (1959).

3
The Progressive Persuasion

The cover of the January 1903 *McClure's Magazine*, a leading forum of the progressive movement. The issue contained an influential article by Lincoln Steffens on corruption in Minneapolis. (Culver Pictures)

The New Political Era

The dawn of a new political era in the United States roughly coincided with the beginning of the new century. Many Americans active during the years 1900 to 1917 believed that they were passing through an exciting, promising, and innovative political epoch. A political scientist announced, "One of the most inspiring movements in human history is now in progress." When journalists, reformers, and reflective public figures later wrote about their experiences in this period, they remembered how a "progressive" mood had brought millions of citizens together in a movement to preserve and improve the quality of American life.

The Progressive Spectrum

Most recent scholars tend to emphasize one aspect of the complex entity we call *progressivism* to the exclusion of the others. At their hands progressivism becomes *solely* a Christian crusade, *solely* a drive for efficiency, *solely* a middle-class effort at self-protection, *solely* an attempt by enlightened businesspeople to head off radicalism, or *solely* an outgrowth of women's discontents. In truth, the concept of progressivism turns out to be curiously elusive. Even contemporaries disagreed about what it was and who or what was behind it. In fact, progressivism was a complex force in American life, bewildering in its variety and apparent contradictions. Few progressives, even in the political realm, were interested in universal reform, although most agreed that the old version of laissez-faire no longer served the needs of the American people and had to be adjusted in some way. Many believed that inefficiency and waste were what was wrong with the nation and that a regime of experts and engineers could put most of it right. Many progressives did indeed seem motivated primarily by a Protestant Christian vision of a heavenly kingdom on earth. These earnest men and women suffered for the children, for the poor, for the handicapped, for the afflicted, and the exploited. Still others saw themselves as the victims of political and economic forces that they could no longer control and sought to establish instruments for taming these forces. At the top there were indeed a few powerful businessmen who feared the possibility of revolution and encouraged more moderate change to preserve most of the existing system. The progressive movement probably encompassed a majority of the nation's politically alert and effective citizens—middle- and working-class, North and South, rural and urban—leaving out only the truly rich (and not all of these), those deeply conservative by temperament, and the minority who favored extreme, radical social change.

Causes of the Progressive Impulse

To reach such a large segment of the public, desire for change, dissatisfaction with the present, and fear of the future must have been widespread. Why were they? To understand the public mood we must review briefly the nation's recent past.

By the opening years of the new century the hard times of the 1890s had departed. On the farms, prices had begun to rise for the first time in over a generation. Urban people were also prosperous through much of the 1900 to 1917 period. Real wages for nonfarm workers rose substantially in the years 1900 to 1917. During the first decade of the new century per capita gross national product rose at the unusually rapid pace of almost 3 percent a year.

Yet economic grievances had not disappeared. Farmers might have been better off than during the nineties, but many remained in difficult straits. Tenancy continued to exist in the rural South and in fact got worse. Thirty-eight percent of all Texas farmers had been tenants in 1880; in 1910 more than 53 percent were tenants. Problems that still perplexed agriculture were the high cost of mortgages and credit, the arbitrary charges of the railroads, and the wild swings of prices. According to the journalist Charles Edward Russell, despite the farmers' "toil, skill, care, fortitude, and privations they had nothing to show except the bare fact of an existence kept by a hand-to-hand fight against adversity." Under the circumstances many rural Americans continued to accept Populist ideas that the nation was increasingly falling under the dominion of powerful business and financial combinations.

A majority of urban people during the Bryan-McKinley campaign of 1896, as we have seen, had rejected these ideas. They had not felt with the same force the economic squeeze of the last years of the century and so were not receptive to Populism. But as the new century began a number of things started to happen—or so it seemed—that altered their perceptions.

Business Consolidation

First there was business consolidation. Businesspeople have never liked competition and whenever and wherever possible they have colluded to prevent it. Early in American industrial history when transportation costs were high, it was possible for a local firm to impose a virtual monopoly in some community simply because it was too expensive for its customers to buy from a distant competitor. The advent of the canals and then the railroads slashed transportation costs and made it possible for efficient firms to penetrate the formerly isolated markets of competitors. As companies developed national markets for their products, they encountered national competition. This development initially helped reduce prices to consumers. Some of the price decline of the generation following the Civil War may well have been due to completion of the nation's vast railroad network, a development that brought remaining isolated regions, with high costs, into a competitive, low-cost national market.

But what benefited consumers did not necessarily benefit producers. Farmers, of course, were the chief losers by the falling prices of the late nineteenth century. But lower prices caused problems for business too. Among the railroads themselves, for example, competition for passengers between New York and Chicago at one point drove down fares to no more than a dollar. No one could make a profit at such a level. Net earnings of the New York Central per ton mile dropped from ninety-nine cents in 1869 to forty-six cents in 1872. Competition in steel was even more remorseless. Andrew Carnegie, by virtue of constant cost cutting and the steady growth of the steel market was able to slash the cost of a ton of steel from $65 to $20, leading one of his competitors to complain that such "unreasonable competition was childish and against public policy."

Business leaders tried many different approaches to end the "cutthroat" competition that efficient transportation had encouraged. One scheme was "pooling" whereby producers of a particular line of goods or suppliers of particular services agreed to fix market shares and to desist from price-cutting to undercut other firms and improve their relative standing. Another scheme was the "trust." Under this arrangement stockholders in several firms transferred all their property to a board of trustees and received in return certificates of trust. Thereafter the trustees ran the combined firms as one. Trusts were declared illegal as restraints on trade by various state courts during the 1880s and 1890s. In 1890 the Sherman Antitrust Act placed the federal government in direct opposition to "every contract, combination in the form of trust or otherwise, or conspiracy in restraint of trade or commerce among the several States or with foreign nations." But although trusts in the narrow sense were now outlawed, *trust* became a generic term for any large business combination.

Despite the state courts and the Sherman Act, the impulse toward business combination could not be checked. In 1889 the state of New Jersey legalized the "holding company," which allowed a corporation to buy control of other corporations, paying its own stock in exchange. In 1896 the law was amended to allow holding companies headquartered in New Jersey to control corporations chartered anywhere else. Thus they could legally operate any place in the United States. The holding company soon became the favorite device for business consolidation.

The business merger movement was delayed by the hard times following the panic of 1893 and by uncertainty over the Sherman Act. Then in the 1895 decision *U.S. v. E. C. Knight Co.* the Supreme Court declared that only mergers that directly restrained foreign or interstate *commerce* were illegal; no amount of manufacturing consolidation as such violated the law. With the Sherman Act thus emasculated, the legal way was cleared, and after the return of prosperity, the merger movement took off. Between 1898 and the end of 1903, a total of 234 industrial consolidations with a combined capitalization of $6 billion had been completed. The largest of these by far was the United States Steel Corporation, created in 1901 by combining the Carnegie Steel Company and eight other competing firms under the auspices of the investment banking firm led by J. P. Morgan. The new U.S. Steel was the world's first billion-dollar corporation.

Consumer Vulnerability

Although it is not certain that the merger movement resulted in higher prices for consumers, it was clearly perceived as an attack on consumers. In 1902 the Industrial Commission, a government agency, declared in no uncertain terms that combinations had "exerted an appreciable power over prices, and in practically all cases . . . [had] increased the margin between raw materials and finished products." That same year a series of articles by Charles Edward Russell explained that the reason why the public's "steaks and . . . roasts cost more than they did a short time ago" was collusion among members of the "Beef Trust."

The public's sense that it was being held for ransom by the trusts was confirmed by the price trends after 1896. Prices that had been declining ever since the end of the Civil War began to rise abruptly toward the end of the 1890s. Thereafter, through the years preceding World War I, they rose at a modest but steady rate. By 1914 average prices were almost 40 percent higher than in 1898. Whatever the reasons for this trend, to the consuming public it appeared that the "high cost of living" was an evil that must be laid at the door of the big businesses of the day.

Closely related to the mergers in the public mind was the *tariff.* Ever since the Civil War, business had been able to induce Congress to raise the duties on imports that sheltered American producers from foreign competitors. In itself this arrangement raised prices for consumers. But it also seemed to reinforce the trusts. The high tariff, in the opinion of many, was the "mother of trusts," and so operated to amplify the price-inflating potential of the business consolidations.

Urbanization increased the proportion of Americans who felt exposed to the economic power of larger business aggregations. City dwellers were even more vulnerable than rural people to the decisions made in the corporate offices of the giant firms. There were many small-business people who found that they could not compete with the more efficient business giants. Local butchers, for example, who once slaughtered their own cattle and hogs, found themselves reduced to retailers of beef and pork shipped to them by the big packers of Chicago. Although they fought back by warning consumers of the health hazards of the Beef Trust's product, they failed to stop the loss of business. Small oil refiners found themselves being forced to the wall by the Standard Oil Company, John D. Rockefeller's giant Cleveland-based refining combine. Many small-business men prized their autonomy and feared being demoted to the level of salaried employees. Mayor Hazen Pingree told the Chicago Conference on Trusts that when businesses consolidated, the small producers "become cogs and little wheels in a great complicated machine." If something were not done, "the middle class of which I speak will lose their sense of independence."

Most city people were not small producers, but all were *consumers,* and this status exposed them as never before to the economic exploitation of powerful others. Urbanites, unlike their country cousins, depended on streetcar and railroad corporations to get them to their jobs; they depended on food processors and packagers for most of their daily food; they relied on power and light companies for their illumination and on gas companies for their cooking fuel. They produced little for themselves; almost everything they consumed came to them through a long chain of anonymous middlemen who could not be policed or controlled and had unlimited power to deceive, defraud, and gouge. And almost no city dweller seemed to be exempt—neither rich nor poor, neither immigrant nor native-born American.

Worker Insecurity

Another source of the progressive impulse was the striving of working people for security. During the closing years of the last century American wage earners had experienced waves of severe unemployment. During the depression of the 1870s joblessness had climbed to 10 percent of the labor force. During the mid-1890s it reached almost 7 percent. At no time during the first two decades of the twentieth century did workers experience comparable rates, yet thousands looked unsuccessfully for work between 1907 and 1908 and again between 1913 and 1914.

Business downturns were not the only forces that made the lot of American workers uncertain. As early as 1900 doctors and scientists had begun to understand the effects of industrial pollutants on workers' health, but little had been done to curb the factory and mine practices that caused them. Thousands of industrial workers suffered from industrial diseases caused by coal dust, arsenic, phosphorus, and lead. Chronic illness often made such men and women unemployable. Furthermore, the incidence of industrial accidents was appalling. Thousands were maimed by the machines they worked on. The railroads were particularly unsafe. It was estimated that in 1907 alone over 4500 workers were killed in railroad accidents, over 12 a day on the average.

There was also the problem of the long, exhausting workweek. In 1890 the average workweek for industry was 60 hours; by 1914 it had only declined to 55.2 hours. For workers in especially demanding or exhausting trades the long hours were hazards to health and safety.

A worker sickened or maimed on the job was usually thrown into the ranks of the unemployed and unemployable. Employers seldom had any legal responsibility to them. Even if the accident or illness was the employer's fault, the only recourse the employee had was to sue for compensation. Assuming he or she could afford the costs, the likelihood of winning was not great. The plaintiff had to prove that the employer himself, not merely another worker, had been negligent.

Workers also faced the problem of coping with old age. Working men and women tried to provide for the time when they could no longer work by putting aside savings. Many succeeded. At the end of a long working life, those who survived its rigors often had accumulated a bank account or owned their own homes, or both. Still another form of "old-age insurance" was a large number of children, preferably sons, to take care of parents in their declining years. Yet for various reasons—improvidence or bad luck—many older working people found themselves, after years of hard work, without adequate incomes to sustain them through their final years.

Worker Minorities

Particular groups within the labor force were especially vulnerable during these years. By a wide margin, most African-Americans lived in the South; few were part of the industrial labor force. As late as 1900, a total of 86 percent of all African-American workers were employed either in agriculture or domestic service.

There were several reasons for this employment pattern. African-American workers were undoubtedly less skilled, on the whole, than white workers. More importantly they were the victims of prejudice on the part of employers and nonblack employees. Employers usually preferred white immigrants from Europe to their black fellow Americans, and white workers often would not work beside blacks. On occasion, however, northern factory owners *did* hire African-American workers—as strikebreakers. But invariably, as soon as the strike ended, they were let go. It was often said that African-American workers were "the last to be hired and the first to be fired."

Women were another labor-force minority. In 1870 there were 3.75 million women employed full-time for wages in the United States, about 15 percent of all wage earners. By 1910 women workers numbered about 8 million, some 20 percent of the labor force. Many of these women were salesclerks, teachers, nurses, stenographers, typists, and other white-collar workers. Yet at the end of this period most women workers remained domestic servants—housemaids, laundresses, governesses, and charwomen. And most of these workers were unmarried, younger women. In 1900 some 44 percent of all working women were single, and another 32 percent were divorced or widowed. Only 6 percent of the female labor force in 1900 consisted of married women.

Whichever category they belonged to, working women were seldom the most fortunate American workers. There is some evidence that where women worked at jobs identical to men's, they received comparable wages. But this situation was rare. Far fewer women were managers and professionals than men, in part owing to youth and lesser skills, but also because of simple prejudice, and their wages reflected this job distribution. Women also tended to be concentrated in industries such as textiles, boots and shoes, and food processing, where both capital investment per worker and worker productivity were low. These industries had to pay lower wages than most. It is true that only a minority of working women in these years supported themselves or their families solely by their own efforts. But for the many widows and divorced or deserted women who did, these low wages were a severe hardship.

Child Labor

Children represented an even more exposed group of workers. In 1910 an extraordinary one-quarter of all children between the ages of ten and fourteen were employed full-time in the United States. Of course, these children were not self-supporting. Rather, almost all were living at home and earning money to supplement the incomes of their parents. The largest proportion, it seems, were employed on the family farm or in the family business, and we must assume that they were treated considerately. Yet the lot of many other child workers was unenviable. Some worked at mining and slate picking—heavy, physically demanding jobs that exceeded their strength. Others were employed long hours in the South's cotton mills at a few pennies a day.

Plutocracy

The public feared not only the economic power of big business but also its political power. The liberal tradition has long held that the worst government is a *plutocracy,* or rule by wealth. Ever since the era of Thomas Jefferson the power of concentrated wealth has been deemed by many Americans a danger to free government. The Jeffersonian tradition was reinforced by the Jacksonians' attack on the "monster" Second Bank of the United States in the 1830s and the Populists' condemnation of the "money power" in the 1890s.

The common indictment of business's political influence had many particulars. The railroad companies, through their free pass system, bribed legislators and other

Young boys employed as coal miners in the early 1900s. (Library of Congress)

politicians. Large business firms maintained lobbyists at the state capitals and in Washington who saw to it that the legislatures and Congress passed laws they wanted and defeated those they opposed. Many of the legislators and members of congress were themselves rich industrialists or bankers who placed the interests of their businesses before those of their constituents.

During the early years of the new century public fears often centered on the investment banking houses that had masterminded many of the business consolidations of the era. As part of the merger process these firms—Kuhn, Loeb and Company; Kidder, Peabody; J. P. Morgan and Company; and others—often placed one of their officers on the board of directors of the new combination. Although the arrangements were intended to reassure stockholders that the new corporations would be soundly managed, critics saw them as a way by which the bankers had gained control of a large part of the American economy. In 1912–1913 a Congressional committee under Representative Arsène Pujo of Louisiana would investigate the "money trust" and conclude that there was indeed a danger to free government in the concentration of economic power at the financial top.

The Muckrakers

Reform movements are colorful, controversial, and exciting events, and they attract media attention the way flowers attract bees. Once under way, the press often sustains and expands such movements by providing free publicity. The media are the eyes and ears of the public, providing the information that enables it to judge the meaning of the many events outside the personal ken of most individuals. In this role, the media may even instigate the wave of discontent or concern that creates a reform movement.

The connection between reform and publicity was never so close as during the Progressive Era. Many of the political, economic, and social abuses that the progressives would deplore and seek to remedy occurred out of sight of the average citizen and could only have aroused indignation when exposed to the fierce glare of publicity. The reform agenda no doubt was instigated in part by ills that everyone could readily see. But much of it derived from the exposés of hidden evils undertaken by journalists called the *muckrakers.*

The term "muckraker" was affixed to the exposé writers of the day by President Theodore Roosevelt in 1906 in a fit of annoyance at their negativism. Roosevelt told the Gridiron Club of Washington that all too often reporters, like a character in John Bunyan's *Pilgrim's Progress,* "raked the mud of society and never looked up." Although Roosevelt may not have liked the perpetual carping of the exposé journalists, muckraker Lincoln Steffens told the president that they had helped create both him and the movement he led.

Muckraking had its roots in the investigative journalism of the metropolitan press during the 1880s and 1890s, but the exposés of editors such as Joseph Pulitzer never enjoyed a national audience. Then came the cheap weekly magazine, made possible by fast new presses and photoengraving. Selling at ten cents a copy, these magazines were instantly successful among middle-class urban readers. Frank Munsey's *Munsey's Magazine,* the first of these publications, soon attracted a host of imitators.

The new weekly magazine was an insatiable consumer of material. Editors needed a steady flow of punchy, fast-paced articles to fill its pages. This was a challenge that Samuel S. McClure, a peppery Indianan, was happy to take on. McClure was an aggressive and enterprising editor who, one wit declared, would have paid well for "a snappy life of Christ." He had a nose for writing talent, and his magazine, *McClure's,* was a primary outlet for some of the ablest journalists of the day.

One of his star authors was Ida Tarbell, a young woman from Pennsylvania, and in 1901 he assigned her the task of doing a series of articles about the Standard Oil Company. The series was well under way when *McClure's* now-famous issue of January 1903 (see the illustration opening this chapter) appeared with one of the Tarbell articles, another on municipal corruption by Lincoln Steffens, titled "The Shame of Minneapolis," and one on labor union abuses, "The Right to Work," by Ray Stannard Baker. The three pieces were accompanied by McClure's own editorial, which tied them together with the common theme of the growing contempt for law in America.

The issue was a sellout, and McClure quickly recognized that he had found a winning formula. The public was receptive to the new exposé journalism and cried for more information on the misdeeds of people in high and influential places. Before long a pack of other magazines, including *Collier's, Cosmopolitan, Everybody's Magazine,* and *American Magazine,* were in hot pursuit of the malefactors, grafters, and exploiters.

Nothing was sacred to the muckrakers. Tarbell and Steffens continued their work on municipal corruption and the ruthless practices of Standard Oil. Baker went on to deal with the injustices of racial discrimination against blacks and the abuses of railroads. David Graham Phillips wrote a sensational series in *Cosmopolitan* on the corrupt alliance of business and politics in the United States Senate. John Spargo, Edwin Markham, and others exposed the evils of child labor. The life insurance industry's fraudulent practices were revealed in Burton J. Hendrick's "Story of Life Insurance," and the frauds and deceptions of the patent medicine industry came under attack by Samuel Hopkins Adams in a *Collier's* series.

Muckrakers not only wrote magazine articles; they also wrote novels. In *Coniston* and *Mr. Crewe's Career,* Winston Churchill (not the British political leader) described the corrupt alliance of businessmen, politicians, and lawyers in the state capitals. Brand Whitlock, in *The Thirteenth District* and *In the Heart of Fool,* wrote a fictional treatment on the same theme. Robert Herrick's *Memoirs of an American Citizen* examined the mind of a corrupt and self-deceived businessman. Theodore Dreiser's *The Titan* and *The Financier* indicted the shady operations of traction magnate Charles Yerkes.

The most famous of the muckraking novels was Upton Sinclair's *The Jungle.* Sinclair, a novelist and writer, became a socialist in 1902 after reading the works of Karl Marx, Pyotr Kropotkin, and other European radical theorists. In 1905 the editor of a socialist journal paid Sinclair to write an exposé of wage slavery, and he accepted. Sinclair went to Chicago, the site of recent labor troubles, and spent some weeks looking into the meat-packing industry. His purpose, he later wrote, was to "set forth the breaking of human hearts by a system which exploits the labor of men and women for profits." Rather incidentally, however, Sinclair described how the meat-packers disguised spoiled meat with dyes and chemicals and how workers sometimes fell into the boiling fat-rending vats and were incorporated into the lard sold in stores.

The Jungle appeared in book form in 1906 and was an instant sensation, selling 25,000 copies in the first six weeks of publication. Unfortunately, in Sinclair's view, its success was for the wrong reason. He had intended to arouse sympathy for labor but instead had aroused anger against the meat-packers. "I aimed at the public's heart," he lamented, "and by accident I hit it in the stomach."

The New Republic Writers

The muckrakers were vivid, they were exciting, and they were engaging. But they were not always fair, and they were seldom thoughtful. There was, however, another group of writers who supplied much of the analysis and long perspective that the others lacked.

READING 3

Consumers and the Meat-Packing Industry

In 1906 the novelist Upton Sinclair wrote an exposé of the Chicago meat-packing industry intended primarily to arouse sympathy for the packing-house workers. The middle-class public, however, found his descriptions of the unsanitary conditions in the plants more riveting. In the end Sinclair's novel did far more to encourage consumer protection legislation than the Socialist transformation that he espoused.

Here is Sinclair's stomach-turning indictment of the process that put meat products on the tables of millions of Americans in the early part of this century. The story is told through the eyes of a fictional immigrant family that worked in the packinghouses.

With one member trimming beef in a cannery, and another working in a sausage factory, the family had a first-hand knowledge of the great majority of Packingtown [the meatpacking area of Chicago] swindles. For it was the custom, as they found, whenever meat was so spoiled that it could not be used for anything else, either to can it or else to chop it up into sausage. With what had been told them by Jonas[1] . . . . they could . . . read a new and grim meaning into that old Packingtown jest—that they used everything of the pig except the squeal.

Jonas had told them how the meat that was taken out of the pickle would often be found sour, and how they would rub it up with soda to take away the smell, and sell it to be eaten on free-lunch counters; also of all the miracles of chemistry which they performed, giving to any sort of meat, fresh or salted, whole or chopped, any color and any flavor and any odor they chose. In the pickling of hams they had an ingenious apparatus, by which they saved time and increased the capacity of the plant—a machine consisting of a hollow needle attached to a pump; by plunging this needle into the meat and working with his foot a man could fill a ham with pickle in a few seconds. And yet, in spite of this, there would be hams found spoiled, some of them with an odor so bad that a man could hardly bear to be in the room with them. To pump into these the packers had a second and much stronger pickle which destroyed the odor—a process known to the workers as "giving them thirty per cent." Also, after the hams had been smoked, there would be found some that had gone to the bad. Formerly these had been sold as "Number Three Grade," but later on some ingenious person had hit upon a new device, and

---

[1]Jonas was the brother-in-law of Jurgis Rudkus, the hero of *The Jungle*. He was a Lithuanian who worked at Durham's.

now they would extract the bone, about which the bad part generally lay, and insert in the hole a white-hot iron. After this invention there was no longer Number One, Two and Three Grade—there was only Number One Grade. . . .

It was only when the whole ham was spoiled that it came into the department of Elzbieta.[2] Cut up by the two-thousand-revolutions-a-minute flyers, and mixed with half a ton of other meat, no odor that was ever in a ham could make any difference. There was never the least attention paid to what was cut up for sausage; there would come all the way back from Europe old sausage that had been rejected and that was moldy and white—it would be dosed with borax and glycerine, and dumped into the hoppers, and made over again for home consumption. There would be meat that had tumbled out on the floor, in the dirt and sawdust, where the workers had tramped and spit uncounted billions of consumption [tuberculosis] germs. There would be the meat stored in great piles in rooms; and the water from leaky roofs would drip over it, and thousands of rats would race about on it. It was too dark in these storage places to see well, but a man could run his hand over these piles of meat and sweep off handfuls of dried dung of rats. These rats were nuisances, and the packers would put poisoned bread out for them; they would die and then rats, bread, and meat would go into the hoppers together. . . . Under the system of rigid economy which the packers enforced, there were some jobs which it only paid to do once in a long time, and among these was the cleaning out of the waste-barrels. Every spring they did it, and in the barrels would be dirt and rust and old nails and stale water—and cart load after cart load of it would be taken up and dumped into the hoppers with fresh meat, and sent out to the public's breakfast. Some of it they would make into "smoked" sausage—but as the smoking took time, and was therefore expensive, they would call upon their chemistry department and preserve it with borax and color it with gelatine to make it brown. All of their sausage came out of the same bowl, but when they came to wrap it they would stamp some of it "special," and for this they would charge two cents more a pound.

---

[2]Elzbieta was Jurgis' step mother-in-law, another Lithuanian who worked in the meat-packing plant.
Source: Upton Sinclair, The Jungle (New York: Airmont, 1965). pp. 128–29. Copyright 1905, 1906, 1933, 1946 by Upton Sinclair.

One of these was Herbert Croly, a journalist from a family with a tradition of "advanced" social thinking who was himself strongly influenced by William D. Lloyd's attack on Rockefeller, *Wealth against Commonwealth* (1894). In 1909 Croly took time off from journalism to write *The Promise of American Life,* a book that actually changed people's minds.

The work tackled the new problems of twentieth-century America. Croly believed it necessary for the United States to challenge poverty and social injustice, now made worse by industrialism and big business, with "official national action" that would marshaling federal power in an aggressive way. The Jeffersonian tradition of individualism, antiauthoritarianism, and localism no longer made any sense in an era when capitalists had become "too wealthy and powerful for their official standing in American life" and when the gap between rich and poor was growing. Hamiltonian activism must supersede this outdated philosophy, which was better suited to a world of small farmers. Americans must now accept purposeful and activist government that would avoid the "programme of international socialism," but engage in "reconstructive policy" to check the tycoons and make wealth less unequal. A few contemporaries believed Croly's "nationalism" to be near-socialism, but it was actually a foreshadowing of the modern welfare state.

Although it contained more than a trace of elitism, *The Promise of American Life* had a surprising impact. It impressed the educated public and was an instant publishing success. Soon after it appeared, the young ex-president, Theodore Roosevelt for the moment politically unemployed, read it and was deeply impressed by its message. It would influence his thinking when he returned to the political arena.

Another susceptible man was Willard Straight, a former Morgan banker who became bored with high finance and sought to make amends for his former sins by bankrolling a new liberal publication. In 1913 Straight and his wife met Croly and agreed to back a new progressive magazine with Croly as editor-in-chief.

The New Republic quickly became a major source of advanced progressive ideas. Its other two editors were Walter Weyl, a former settlement worker and an expert on wages-and-hours legislation, and Walter Lippmann, a young intellectual just arrived in New York from Harvard.

Lippmann was a child genius who had already flirted with socialism. By the time he arrived at *The New Republic* offices in Manhattan, he had also absorbed the new ideas associated with Viennese doctor Sigmund Freud and sought to make these politically and socially relevant. In *A Preface to Politics* Lippmann took issue with mainstream progressive moralism with its puritan cast. A good society, he said, would tap the creative instinctual energies of "vice, love, lust, and religion" to produce a more livable world. This was not the progressivism of *Emporia Gazette* editor William Allen White or of Sam McClure, but it spoke to the bohemians and the advanced thinkers in Greenwich village and helped recruit them to progressive causes.

Under its troika of editors *The New Republic* became the voice of the advanced progressives, not just in politics, but also in art, music, theater, and social thought. According to intellectual historian Henry May, by embracing the ideas of the magazine's editors, the young progressive intelligentsia "said good-by to equalitarianism, the agrarian past and the simple formulas of moral reform."

The Progressive Movement

Sometime after 1900 the attitudes, policies, perceptions, and goals just described became embodied in a movement called *progressivism*. It would dominate American political life for a decade and leave a legacy of modern liberalism.

Neighborhood Progressivism

The progressive movement started in the neighborhoods and the cities, spread to the states, and then finally penetrated national politics at the highest level.

The germs of neighborhood progressivism were often planted by the settlement houses discussed in Chapter 2. They were the "spearheads for reform," in the words of historian Allen Davis. Settlement workers were not just interested in dispensing knowledge, skills, and American practices or providing slum dwellers with recreational and community facilities; they were also social reformers who sought to bend basic institutions to fit their image of a more benevolent, rational, egalitarian society.

Many of the leading settlement workers, as we have seen, were well-educated middle-class women seeking a sense of purpose. Their stay in the settlements was sometimes brief, and many soon went on to other activities. Others, however, such as Jane Addams, Lillian Wald, Vida Scudder, Florence Kelley, and Mary Simkhovitch —along with their male equivalents—made the settlements or the new profession of *social work* their life occupations.

It was difficult for men and women such as these, living and working among the urban poor, not to lose their lofty do-good attitudes and come to understand the feelings and accept the values of the poor. Many came to realize that only legislation could provide the protection and security needed by society's weaker members.

The settlement people pushed legislation for the poor on every level. Settlement-house workers, or settlement "alumni," fought for better housing for the poor. Lawrence Veiller, formerly of New York's University Settlement, was the key figure in the writing of the city's tenement house code of 1901. The settlement-house workers were early activists in the playground movement. In Chicago, the first city playground was the work of Hull House workers. They also fought for city zoning laws to help improve neighborhoods by protecting them from the encroachment of noisome industries. At times the settlement workers found the city machines their greatest obstacle; when they did, they had no qualms about taking on the bosses. Much of the settlement workers' most valuable efforts were investigatory. Hull House workers made careful maps of Chicago neighborhoods to pinpoint the location of all ethnic groups. The Pittsburgh Survey of 1909–1914, whose purpose was to discover as much as possible of how the people of the city lived, was organized by settlement workers or former ones.

Since much of what most concerned the social justice settlement workers could only be tackled at the state level, they often transferred their reformist attention to the state capitals. There they fought for laws to limit child labor, to protect women workers from harsh labor conditions, and to provide insurance compensation for wage earners killed, injured, or made ill on the job. Florence Kelley, a Hull House alumna, was the author of the 1903 Illinois child labor law. When in 1908 Oregon's ten-hour law for working women was challenged in the Supreme Court, Kelley and Josephine Goldmark prepared the arguments and data used by the law's defender, Louis D. Brandeis. The innovative brief presented by the defendants, eschewing narrow legalisms and focusing on sociological data, was called the "Brandeis brief," although Goldmark was at least equally responsible for it. It carried the day with the

Supreme Court in *Muller* v. *Oregon* (1908), a decision upholding the right of a state to limit the working hours of women.

The Progressives and Labor

The local progressives were also active in the trade union movement. Trade unions were still weak in the United States in the early years of the new century. The American Federation of Labor (AFL), led by the Dutch-Jewish former cigar maker Samuel Gompers, had by 1904 succeeded in organizing only 1.7 million American wage earners out of over 18 million nonfarm workers. The great majority of these members, moreover, were skilled, native-born, male, white workers, the very ones who needed protection least. Outside the privileged circle were the masses of unskilled and semiskilled factory workers. Many of these were immigrants and many were women.

Progressives became involved in efforts to organize the semiskilled and unskilled factory workers in a number of cities, especially New York where the garment industry employed thousands of Jewish and Italian workers making ready-made clothing. Conditions in the garment shops were often abysmal. In the lofts where young women made shirtwaists, for example, "the air was stifling . . . and odiferous with sewer gases." The young workers, "as they bent over their work," reported one observer, "formed a picture of physical suffering that I certainly had never seen before." In March 1911, at the Triangle Shirtwaist Company, 141 young women died in a fire that raced through a factory loft in lower Manhattan. To prevent theft of material, the factory doors had been nailed shut. Many of the young victims leaped ten stories to their death to escape the inferno.

Fifteen months earlier the Triangle Shirtwaist Company had been one of many struck by 18,000 women workers protesting low wages, exhausting hours, and poor safety conditions. The predominantly male International Ladies Garment Workers Union had supported the young women. Help had also come from the Women's Trade Union League (WTUL), composed of middle-class women progressives, some of them members of prominent Social Register families. The WTUL leaders joined the strikers on their picket lines, came to rallies as observers to keep the police from using strong-arm tactics, ran the union headquarters, and raised money to offset lost wages and to bail strikers out of jail. A number of the middle-class women got themselves arrested for disorderly conduct and in the process brought the strikers much favorable publicity.

Progressives were also prominent in other strikes. Progressivism was reformist, rather than radical, in its basic thrust. Yet at the edge it shaded off into socialism and even anarchism. Especially among the artists, painters, journalists, and intellectuals of the Village there existed a stylish leftism growing out of contempt for the values of the bourgeoisie. The progressive intelligentsia lionized radical leaders, such as Bill Haywood and Elizabeth Gurley Flynn, and flirted with revolution. This commitment brought them into the camp of the proletariat in 1913 when Haywood's Industrial Workers of the World led a strike of the mill workers in Paterson, New Jersey.

Sweatshops were not confined to the garment industry. This photo, taken by reformer Jacob Riis, shows cigar makers at work. Riis reported that the work was "seventeen hours a day—seven days a week, at thirteen cents an hour—for two workers!" (The Bettmann Archive)

Progressivism in the States

The first state to fall under the progressive banner was Wisconsin, where the spark plug for change was the compact, dynamic young reformer, Robert M. La Follette. Born in tiny Primrose, Wisconsin, in 1855, La Follette had gone to the state university and become a lawyer. With the help of his brilliant wife, Belle, who was also a lawyer, he had won two terms in Congress as a Republican. In 1896 he decided to run for governor but was defeated by the opposition of the state Republican boss, Philetus Sawyer. Again, in 1898, Sawyer's opposition denied him the party nomination.

It is likely that much of La Follette's argument with the state Republican party regulars at this point was merely a conflict of ambitions. All through the Midwest, toward the end of the 1890s, state party factionalism was widespread. The losers in these internal party battles were often driven to insurgency by their inability to work the levers of power as they wished.

Yet it is also clear that their insurgency took advantage of a grass-roots movement of unease and discontent among the voters. In Wisconsin the mood battened on long-standing farm grievances over railroad rates and the unchecked influence of the large corporations on the legislature. It also drew strength from city voters' anger at utility rates and the fact that the lighting and gas companies had escaped their fair share of taxation. La Follette made these attitudes his own and used them effectively against the Sawyerites. In 1900, after his third try, he won the Republican nomination and then the governorship.

During La Follette's first gubernatorial term he earned the nickname "Fighting Bob" for his stubborn fight with the standpat legislature over railroad rate regulation and the direct primary for political nominations. In this struggle he was defeated. He ran for governor again in 1902 by appealing to the voters "to save Wisconsin's good name from. . . corporation knaves." By now the progressive mood was more pervasive among the electorate, and La Follette won votes from both parties and from all ethnic sectors of the electorate.

During his second term La Follette developed the "Wisconsin Idea" that put "mind to service in the cause of the public good." The governor created a "brains trust" out of the talented academics and thinkers at the state university in Madison and set them to work investigating problems, drawing up reports, and recommending legislation. Armed with this material, the governor pressured the reluctant legislators into cooperation.

By the time La Follette was elected to the United States Senate in 1905, he had extracted from the legislature a state primary law, a railroad tax law, and a measure establishing a commission to regulate railroad rates. Under his progressive successors Wisconsin also adopted the "initiative," allowing voters to bypass the legislature and introduce new laws directly, and the "referendum," allowing them to confirm or reject new laws. It also established a public utility commission to set rates for gas and power consumers, a workmen's compensation insurance scheme to reduce the cost of job accidents, and a board of public affairs to protect the state's vital natural resources from corporate exploiters.

Western states had similar leaders and similar programs. In Oregon there was former Populist, William U'Ren, a Wisconsin-born lawyer who, although he never held high office, was responsible for a rash of state direct democracy laws, such as the secret Australian ballot, the initiative and referendum, a corrupt practices act, and the "recall," which allowed citizens to remove corrupt officials from office before their terms expired. In California, Hiram Johnson, a Republican attorney who established his reputation by prosecuting the Ruef machine in San Francisco, went to the statehouse in 1911 and helped enact a flock of progressive laws including, as the centerpiece, one empowering the state railroad commission to impose rates and terms of service on the all-powerful Southern Pacific Railroad.

The eastern states too had their versions of progressivism. In New Jersey Democratic Governor Woodrow Wilson, the former president of Princeton University, between 1911 and 1912 enacted a strong public utilities law, a workmen's compensation act, a number of corporation-control measures, and a presidential primary law. A similar program came out of the administration of Republican Governor Charles Evans Hughes in New York from 1906 to 1910.

Many states in the Northeast and West attacked head-on the problems of society's weaker members. During these years thirty-two states enacted laws limiting the hours of child labor or prohibiting it entirely, fifteen passed laws establishing minimum wages, and thirty fixed workers' maximum hours. Unfortunately, from the reformers' perspective, the courts often struck down such labor legislation as violations of the right of free contract and the excessive enlargement of state power. In some states the reformers endorsed health and unemployment insurance, although fearing the courts' conservatism, they did not push these very hard.

Southern Progressivism

In 1913 *McClure's* published an article, "What Wilson Is Up Against" by George Kibee Turner, predicting that the southern conservatives in Congress were sure to fight the newly elected and progressive president, Woodrow Wilson. Yet there was a progressive movement in the South too, based on an alliance of former Populists and some of the more forward-looking business groups in the region's cities.

In Dixie, as in other parts of the country, antimonopoly, anticorporation attitudes were often at the heart of progressivism. But southern progressivism was given a special twist by regionalism. The big corporations were not only arbitrary and dangerous; they were also *Yankee* corporations located in the North, and they were draining the wealth of the southern people.

Typical of southern progressives were Jeff Davis (no relation to the Confederate leader). As Arkansas state attorney general during the 1890s, Davis had initiated over one hundred suits against insurance companies alone and dozens of others against oil companies, tobacco firms, and freight-express corporations for monopolistic practices and price-fixing. In 1901 he became governor and expanded these attacks. Davis felt a special affinity for the state's poor white farmers and was sometimes called "the Karl Marx for hillbillies."

Arkansas was not alone. In Georgia, Governor Hoke Smith enacted legislation abolishing railroad passes and a measure regulating railroad securities. Alabama's Braxton Bragg Comer, a planter, banker, and cotton manufacturer, launched a campaign against the railroads and forced them to lower their rates.

The South was, moreover, not a negative force in national progressivism. All the southern governors endorsed the progressive proposal for a federal income tax amendment and pushed their legislatures to ratify it. Southern members of Congress even supported efforts in Congress to limit child labor, although almost all the southern textile mills used children extensively to keep labor costs down.

Progressives and African-Americans

The progressives' concern for the downtrodden was weakest in the areas of race and nationality. Many progressive leaders—like conservatives—accepted explicitly the superiority of the white race, especially its north European portion, to all others.

They were often as skeptical of the New Immigrants from southern and eastern Europe as the conservatives and, like them, pressed for immigration restriction. Southern progressives were generally strong supporters of the "color line," no matter how much they favored lower tariffs, the income tax, and corporation regulation.

Indeed, the early years of the twentieth century, when progressivism became the political style, was a time of general retreat for southern African-Americans. In state after state, white supremacists erected ever higher walls of legal segregation around successive spheres of daily life. Although the *Jim Crow* process had begun during the Reconstruction era, it accelerated between 1890 and 1920. By the end of the period, state and local laws divided schools, parks, cemeteries, trains and trolley cars, comfort stations, theaters, and much else into a superior white and an inferior black version or section. At the same time African-Americans were pushed steadily out of trades formerly open to them. Under progressive governors, state legislatures enacted

This horrible scene shows the lynching of two African-Americans in Indiana early in this century. (Magnum)

laws—poll taxes and the all-white political primary—that almost obliterated the last traces of black voting in the section.

These years also saw an upsurge in racial violence as a brutal and terrifying system of southern social control. Although lynching was declining in the nation as a whole and although at times its victims were white, it continued in the South as a way of keeping African-Americans in their place. In 1900, some 100 blacks were lynched in the South; by 1914 the total for the new century had reached 1100. Race riots too were a feature of southern life in these years. In Atlanta in 1906, following sensational newspaper stories of black assaults on white women, white mobs attacked African-Americans on the city streets. Several days later they looted and burned the houses of blacks and fired rifles at black citizens. The city virtually closed down for a week.

But the racism of the period was not confined to the South. Although there was little legal segregation in the North, there was a great deal of bigotry and many informal limitations on African-American equality. Housing was in effect segregated; restaurants and hotels, despite antisegregation laws, often refused African-American patrons. In the North too there was a pattern of violence. One of the worst race riots of the period occurred in 1908 in Springfield, Illinois, Abraham Lincoln's hometown, when a white mob attacked black people and black-owned businesses to avenge the supposed assault by a black man on a white woman. Almost one hundred people were injured and six were killed. It took 5000 militiamen to restore order.

One of the more unfortunate expressions of race prejudice involved the president of the United States himself. Theodore Roosevelt was not the most bigoted American official by a long shot. Early in his first administration he invited the head of Tuskegee Institute, the African-American leader Booker T. Washington, to have lunch in the White House. The visit raised a storm of protest among white southerners, prompting the president to tell his good friend Senator Henry Cabot Lodge that the outcry only confirmed the "continued existence of that combination of Bourbon intellect and intolerant truculence of spirit . . . which brought on the Civil War."

Yet in 1906 Roosevelt showed that he was by no means free of racial intolerance. In August some soldiers of the African-American Twenty-fifth Infantry Regiment stationed near Brownsville, Texas, resentful of their treatment by local whites, shot up the town, killing one white man and wounding two others. Attempts to bring the culprits to justice were frustrated by the refusal of the entire regiment to cooperate with the investigators. The army inspector general then recommended that all the men of the Twenty-fifth be dishonorably discharged, although the unit included some of the most highly decorated soldiers in the American army. With the approval of the president, Secretary of War William Howard Taft complied.

The outcry was furious. African-American leaders denounced Roosevelt, hitherto a man they admired. The discharge, wrote one black journalist, had destroyed Roosevelt's standing with black Americans. "Jefferson Davis is more honored today than Theodore Roosevelt. Benedict Arnold would have a monument erected to his name sooner than Theodore Roosevelt." Republican Senator Joseph Foraker of Ohio succeeded in getting the Senate to investigate the incident, and in the end some of the discharged men were reinstated. Not until 1972, however, did Congress rescind the dishonorable dismissal of the rest.

African-American leaders did not take erosion of the limited gains of their people since Reconstruction lying down. During the previous twenty years the acknowledged leader of black Americans had been Booker T. Washington, Roosevelt's White House lunch guest. Born into slavery, Washington had been elevated by whites to the African-American leadership position when, at the 1895 Atlanta Cotton States and International Exposition, he had promised that black southerners would accept social segregation and political disfranchisement if they were given economic opportunity. Southern white leaders, happy to accept racial peace in exchange for conceding very little, eagerly embraced the "Atlanta Compromise." Thereafter Washington became the favored spokesman for the African-American community and the chief conduit for white patronage and funds to black causes and black institutions.

In truth, Washington's acquiescence must not be glibly condemned. It was a difficult time for African-Americans. They had been abandoned by their former political friends, had lost the vote, and were economically weak. Perhaps the Atlanta Compromise was the best bargain that could be struck. But by the beginning of the new century a new group of college-educated, northern-born black ministers, journalists, academics, and professionals began to challenge Washington's leadership.

Foremost of this group was W. E. B. Du Bois, a Massachusetts native who had received a Ph.D. in history at Harvard in 1896. After Harvard, Du Bois had taught at several black colleges and had achieved prominence through his sociological studies of African-American communities.

Du Bois considered Washington's approach a sellout of the black people in America, and in 1905 he and others of like mind met at Niagara Falls, Canada, and drew up a platform that rejected the Atlanta Compromise. The new militants demanded universal manhood suffrage, freedom of speech in racial matters, the abolition of all "caste restrictions based . . . on race and color," educational opportunity for all people commensurate with their abilities, and respect for human brotherhood and for the dignity of labor. They incorporated themselves as the "Niagara Movement" and met for several years thereafter to consider the plight of African-Americans and suggest remedies.

In 1909, following the tragic Springfield race riot, Du Bois and several of the Niagara militants joined with concerned white progressives to organize the National Association for the Advancement of Colored People (NAACP). The call to the meeting was written by Oswald Garrison Villard, grandson of the famous abolitionist William Lloyd Garrison, and many white liberals—including Jane Addams, John Dewey, Henry Moskowitz, Lincoln Steffens, and Mary White Ovington—attended. Although Washington was invited to the organizing session, he declined on the grounds that he was more interested in "progressive constructive work" for his race than in "agitation and criticism." In 1910 the NAACP was formally organized. Initially its officers were mostly white, but Du Bois was chosen to be the organization's director of publicity and research and the editor of its publication, *Crisis*.

Over the next few years the NAACP devoted its energies largely to educational work and to legal challenges of disfranchisement and segregation laws. By 1921 it had established a hundred branches in cities all over the country and had become the major African-American defense organization in the United States.

Progressives and Women

Women supplied much of the energy that infused progressivism. As we have seen, many of the most prominent settlement-house social progressives were women. By the early part of the new century, moreover, the women's club movement was being swept along by the reform wave. In 1904 Sarah Platt Decker of Colorado, president of the General Federation of Women's Clubs, made it clear that for club women the traditional "literary tea" focus was a thing of the past. "Ladies," Decker told her colleagues, "you have chosen me your leader. Well, I have an important piece of news to give you. Dante is dead. He has been dead for several centuries and I think it is time we dropped the study of his inferno and turned our attention to our own."

During these years women's groups took particular interest in temperance reform. Today we tend to associate antiliquor efforts with political and social conservatism. But in the early twentieth century, groups such as the Women's Christian Temperance Union (WCTU) and the predominantly male Anti-Saloon League were reform organizations that not only perceived alcoholism as a serious social evil but also worked for other kinds of social improvement. Under the leadership of Frances Willard, for example, the WCTU worked for labor reform, improved health facilities, kindergartens for young children, and even women's suffrage. One of Willard's favorite nontemperance causes was the movement to destroy "white slavery," the traffic of young women forced into prostitution by madams and procurers.

The most significant concern of women reformers, however, was the suffrage issue. A few women had been working for the enfranchisement of women ever since the 1840s. During the Reconstruction era, when Congress struggled with the question of citizenship for the recently freed African-Americans, feminists had acquiesced in putting black suffrage first.

During the Gilded Age, however, the struggle to get women the vote resumed, with two organizations—the American Woman Suffrage Association (AWSA) and the National Woman Suffrage Association (NWSA)—both working toward this end. AWSA, the older organization, was also the larger and the more conservative of the two. It accepted male members and supported the Republican party. It also supported a state-by-state approach to woman's suffrage. NWSA, run by Elizabeth Cady Stanton and Susan B. Anthony, was smaller, but endorsed a broad range of social goals beyond women's enfranchisement and advocated a federal constitutional amendment to give all women the vote at once. In 1890 the two bodies merged as the National American Woman Suffrage Association (NAWSA) and pursued its campaign for the vote on both the national and the state fronts using the tactics of education and quiet lobbying.

During the early twentieth century, under the new leadership of Carrie Chapman Catt and Anna Howard Shaw, NAWSA's membership soared from 13,000 in 1893 to 75,000 in 1910. By this time its core issue, woman suffrage, had became an integral part of the advanced progressive agenda. Yet progress was slow. In 1890 Wyoming gave women the vote, Colorado followed in 1893, Idaho and Utah in 1896, and Washington and California in 1910.

This piecemeal process did not satisfy a new group of impatient activists led by Alice Paul, a young Quaker who had become familiar with the militant tactics practiced

A New York City parade for women's suffrage in 1912. (The Bettmann Archive)

by English suffragists who chained themselves to lamp posts, went on hunger strikes, and attacked the party in power. In 1915 Paul and her followers seceded from NAWSA. The following year they formed the National Woman's Party and, as a goad to action, sought to defeat the Democrats in the 1916 congressional elections. In 1917 the Paul group aroused wide public sympathy when the police arrested many of them for picketing the White House.

By this time the cause was all but won. With the nation at war, many argued, the cooperation of all groups, including women, was essential. Besides, if World War I was really a struggle to "make the world safe for democracy," what better place to start than at home? On January 10, 1918, under President Woodrow Wilson's goading, the House of Representatives finally passed a women's suffrage constitutional amendment. The Senate complied in June 1919. On August 26, 1920, the thirty-sixth state ratified the Nineteenth Amendment, making it the law of the land. Women finally had the vote.

The Progressive Persuasion

By the opening years of the century, then, a powerful movement for reform was gathering momentum. The reformers and their supporters were derived from virtually all sectors of society: farmers and urbanites, working people and the middle-class, men and women, North and South, and black and white. The reform mood invaded both major parties (and would, in addition, generate a powerful third party that briefly challenged the other two). Its ideology borrowed from the Jeffersonian tradition of the independent citizen battling against concentrated wealth and power, but it added the notion of a strong federal government to protect the weak and control the strong. It drew from the Populists' solicitude for the rural "producing masses" and appended concern for the city consumer.

First manifest in the cities and the states, progressivism would finally reach Washington in the person of the twenty-sixth president of the United States, Theodore Roosevelt.

FOR FURTHER READING

Scholars have disagreed over the essential nature of progressivism. Gabriel Kolko, a man of the political left, argues in *The Triumph of Conservatism: A Reinterpretation of American History, 1900–1916* (1967) that progressivism was big business' attempt to ward off fundamental social and economic change; Samuel Hays in *Conservation and the Gospel of Efficiency: The Progressive Conservation Movement, 1890–1920* (1959) emphasizes the technocratic side of the movement. John Buenker, in *Urban Liberalism and Progressive Reform* (1973), sees the progressives as, in part, people of working-class background and sympathies; George Mowry in *The California Progressives* (1951) identifies the progressive impulse with the status anxieties of the middle class; and David Thelen in *The New Citizenship: Origins of Progressivism in Wisconsin, 1885–1900* (1972) detects an important consumer-fear component, as do Irwin Unger and Debi Unger in *The Vulnerable Years: The United States, 1896–1917* (1977).

The best work on business consolidation during the Progressive Era is Alfred Chandler's *The Visible Hand: The Managerial Revolution in American Business* (1977). For a specific consumer issue see James Harvey Young, *The Toadstool Millionaires: A Social History of Patent Medicines in America before Regulation* (1961). The circumstances of labor during these years are described in Irving Yellowitz, *Labor and the Progressive Movement in New York State, 1896–1916* (1965) and David Brody, *Steelworkers in America: The Nonunion Era* (1960).

State studies of progressive politics worth reading include Richard Abrams, *Conservatism in a Progressive Era: Massachusetts Politics, 1900–1912* (1964); Robert Maxwell, *La Follette and the Rise of the Progressives in Wisconsin* (1956); and Richard L. McCormick, *From Realignment to Reform: Political Change in New York State, 1893–1910* (1981). For southern progressivism see Jack Temple Kirby, *Darkness at the Dawning: Race and Reform in the Progressive South* (1972) and Sheldon Hackney, *Populism to Progressivism in Alabama* (1969).

The subject of blacks in the Progressive Era is dealt with in Frederick Broderick, *W. E. B. Du Bois: Negro Leader in a Time of Crisis* (1959); August Meier, *Negro Thought in America, 1880–1915: Racial Ideologies in the Age of Booker T. Washington* (1963); and Louis Harlan, *Booker T. Washington: The Making of a Black Leader, 1865–1901* (1975) and his second volume, *Booker T. Washington: The Wizard of Tuskegee, 1901–1915* (1983).

The role of women during the Progressive Era is described in Eleanor Flexner, *Century of Struggle: The Woman's Rights Movement in the United States* (1959); Aileen Kraditor, *The Ideas of the Woman Suffrage Movement, 1890–1920* (1965); and William O'Neill, *Everyone Was Brave: The Rise and Fall of Feminism in America* (1969). The best account of Margaret Sanger's turbulent life is Madeline Gray, *Margaret Sanger: A Biography of the Champion of Birth Control* (1980).

4
Progressivism in Action

Theodore Roosevelt, president of the United States from 1901 to 1909, brought progressivism into the White House. (The Bettmann Archive)

Roosevelt and Progressivism

Theodore Roosevelt did not invent progressivism. In fact there were those in the progressive camp who felt that he did the cause more harm than good. Yet without the incomparable "TR" much of the verve, the drama, and the excitement that progressivism generated would have been absent and the movement would have fallen short of what it actually accomplished.

TR

Theodore Roosevelt was an unusual man with a two-sided personality. His father was a prominent, civic-minded New York businessman of old, elite "Knickerbocker" lineage, his mother a Georgia belle whose family had supported the Confederacy. Roosevelt seems to have derived his sense of social responsibility from the first and his love of action from the second.

A sickly lad who overcame asthma and bodily frailty by a self-imposed program of physical fitness, Roosevelt would always be an advocate of the strenuous outdoor life and a lover of nature. Yet at the same time he was a cultivated man who wrote definitive histories of the westward movement and the naval War of 1812.

After graduation from Harvard in 1880 Roosevelt turned to politics, an unusual move for a young gentleman in an era when the country's political life seemed notoriously corrupt and opportunistic. In one term as Republican member of the New York state legislature, Roosevelt made his mark as a reformer, a defender of labor, and a zestful headline getter.

In 1886 after trying his hand at ranching in the Dakotas, he ran unsuccessfully for mayor of New York. In 1889, for his support of President Benjamin Harrison's winning ticket, he was appointed United States civil service commissioner. Roosevelt quickly made himself at home in Washington, becoming part of the high-toned circle of John Hay and Henry Adams, men who combined literary interests with a fascination with politics.

In 1895 Roosevelt returned to New York to become president of the Board of Police Commissioners in the reform administration of Mayor William Strong. Although he accomplished little of consequence, he brought the glare of publicity to the city's illegal saloons, corrupt police, and shameless prostitution by his late-night prowlings through the city's "Tenderloin" district in the company of the journalist Jacob Riis. In 1897 he returned to Washington as assistant secretary of the navy in the McKinley administration.

An aggressive nationalist who believed in America's destiny as a great power, Roosevelt used his office to project the nation's influence abroad. During the winter of 1898, in the absence of Secretary John D. Long, he ordered Commodore George Dewey to keep his Asiatic squadron in Hong Kong ready for war with Spain. When hostilities broke out, Dewey was ready to sail for Manila and easily defeated the Spanish fleet.

Roosevelt refused to stay at his navy desk. Instead, as second in command of the "Rough Riders," a regiment of western cowboys and eastern college men that he helped raise, he went off to Cuba. Roosevelt and his men fought in the battle of San Juan Hill and helped bring the war with Spain to a quick conclusion. He returned to the United States a genuine war hero, a status scarcely injured by his book describing his role in Cuba.

In the fall of 1898, shortly after returning from Cuba, Roosevelt was elected governor of New York with the reluctant acquiescence of the state Republican boss, Thomas Platt. Two years of Roosevelt in Albany was enough for Platt. The former Rough Rider was too incorruptible to suit Platt, and when the opportunity presented itself in 1900, he kicked Roosevelt upstairs as McKinley's vice presidential running mate. After the ticket's victory, Roosevelt resigned himself to oblivion—the usual fate of vice presidents—but then was rescued by McKinley's assassination in September 1901. A few days later he was sworn in as the twenty-sixth president of the United States; at forty-three the youngest man ever to hold the job.

Roosevelt's presidency, if not the most constructive on record, was surely the most exhilarating. As president "Teddy's" powers of self-dramatization did not desert him. TR was always a presence. William Allen White, the Kansas reformer-editor, noted that "when he came into a room, he changed all the relations in the room because . . . all minds and hearts turned to him." Roosevelt took immense pleasure in life. White reported that "he took joy in everything he did, in hunting, camping, in ranching, in politics, in reforming the police or the civil service." He brought a constant stream of journalists, sportsmen, artists, poets, statesmen, and cowboys to the White House and all reported on the gusto, the warmth, and the stimulation of the president's conversation, manner, and family relations.

Although he scarcely created the progressive movement, TR amplified it and disseminated it. He used the presidency as a "bully pulpit" to spread his views. He gave "young men in their twenties, thirties, and early forties," White declared, "a quickening sense of the inequities, injustice, and fundamental wrong of the political and economic overlay on our democracy." "Roosevelt bit me," White summed it up, "and I went mad."

Roosevelt's First Term

But much of this lay in the future. At first the new president seemed a cautious man. Succeeding to the presidency through the death of one's predecessor was not the best way to arrive at the highest office in the land. None of the four previous vice presidents who had occupied the White House had been successful; not one had even been renominated. Roosevelt knew that the conservative Republicans (the "Old Guard") who dominated both Congress and the leadership of the Republican party distrusted him. Senator Mark Hanna of Ohio, the Republican national chairman, considered him a "damned cowboy," and had declared in 1900 when Roosevelt's name was first mentioned for the vice presidential nomination, "Don't you realize that there's only one life between that madman and the White House?" Now that his worst fears had been realized, Hanna warned the new president, "Go slow."

Roosevelt was inclined to take Hanna's advice. Although a reformer as governor of New York, he distrusted the uninformed masses as much as he disliked the new plutocrats and the Republican Old Guard bosses. Besides, the reform impulse welling up in the cities and the states had not yet reached Washington. In the Senate a small group of powerful Republicans, all rich and closely connected to large corporations, controlled legislative affairs. Besides Hanna there was Rhode Island's Nelson Aldrich, friend of Wall Street and John D. Rockefeller's son-in-law; John Spooner of Wisconsin, "chief of the corporation lobbyists"; William Allison of Iowa, a master party manipulator; Matthew Quay of Pennsylvania, the long-time state Republican boss, and his New York equivalent, Tom Platt; and Ohio's Joseph Foraker, whose questionable ties to Standard Oil led to his resignation from the Senate in 1908. The House was dominated, after 1902, by Speaker Joseph G. Cannon of Illinois, a coarse-speaking, whiskey-drinking poker player, who always needed the spittoon close at hand. As an archconservative Cannon chose men to important committee appointments only when certain that they opposed what he as an Old Guard stalwart considered "class and local legislation."

Roosevelt was so unsure of himself and so sensitive to the conservative bias of Congress in these early months that he sent a draft of his first annual congressional message to Hanna for approval. To reassure the business community, he had already publicly promised not to alter McKinley's economic policies and had kept all of his predecessor's cabinet. (Two men who had resigned were replaced with equally conservative appointees.) The message of December 1901 endorsed the existing high Dingley tariff rates, expressed at least mild approval of large corporations as natural phenomena, asked for an educational test for future immigrants and a subsidized merchant marine, and, predictably, denounced anarchists and assassins. The *New York Post* declared that the message contained no "fireworks" and could have been written "by a man of sixty, trained in conservative habits."

Yet a closer look at the message reveals much of TR's future progressive course. It noted, for example, that the country needed to take stronger measures to conserve its forests and preserve its resources. It suggested some tariff reductions through reciprocal agreements with Cuba and the Philippines. Roosevelt was also afraid that the trusts might reveal "tendencies harmful to the general welfare," and pro- posed a new cabinet-level Department of Commerce and Labor that would, among other things, have the power to investigate and publicize corporate earnings and protect the rights of working men and women. He also asked for a revision of the 1887 Interstate Commerce Act to make it a more effective guarantor of equal treatment of shippers.

The Trusts

TR's attitude toward the trust problem, a major concern of the progressive era, was never fully satisfactory to the most advanced of his colleagues. He was never critical of great moneyed concentrations as such, but opposed only what he considered the "malefactors of great wealth," that is, those who used their wealth in antisocial ways. He also denied that he opposed trusts in themselves. What he could not abide was the lawlessness, irresponsibility, and arrogance of many large business corporations. When they abused their massive power, they were no better than those other enemies of democracy, the Socialists and the Populists. The country, he proclaimed, could "no more tolerate the wrong committed in the name of property, than wrong committed against property." Roosevelt never believed that the good old days of free competition could be restored through government break up of the large firms. In fact large-scale enterprise was probably efficient. If concentration of economic power had bad effects, then let the government step in and regulate rather than destroy the large corporations.

Despite this skepticism of "trust busting" one of the president's earliest acts was to prosecute the Northern Securities Company under the near-defunct Sherman Antitrust Act of 1890. This company was the creation of J. P. Morgan, E. H. Harriman, James J. Hill, the Rockefellers, and the firm of Kuhn, Loeb—some of the nation's largest railroad barons and financial tycoons—and brought together in one firm the three major northwestern railroads: the Northern Pacific; the Great Northern; and the Chicago, Burlington, and Quincy. Its purpose was to eliminate competition in the Northwest at the expense, presumably, of the shippers, the region's farmers and manufacturers. That the organizers' lawyers could even contemplate the merger was testimony to the Supreme Court's crippling of the Sherman Act in the 1895 E. C. Knight decision.

We can see that the Northern Securities case involved the very actions by "malefactors of wealth" that TR could not abide: irresponsible behavior that would harm the public. Yet Roosevelt startled the public as well as the Old Guard leaders and the tycoons when his attorney general, Philander Knox, filed suit under the Sherman Act on March 10, 1902, for dissolution of the Northern Securities Company.

When J. P. Morgan learned of the president's action, he immediately went to Washington to try to remedy the situation. "If we have done anything wrong," he told Roosevelt, "send your man [the attorney general] to my man and they can fix it up." This revealed precisely the attitude that TR detested: the government of the United States in Morgan's view was simply a rival power that could be brought to terms if the right approach were taken. "That can't be done," TR replied. Knox added that the suit was not intended to "fix up" illegal mergers but to stop them.

The federal court upheld the government's case: the Northern Securities merger was illegal. In 1904 the Supreme Court confirmed the decision by five to four. The Sherman Act, seemingly a dead letter, was now restored to life to the public's great applause.

Roosevelt moved against other large business combinations when he believed they were harmful. In 1902 he instituted a suit against Armour and Company, the so-called Beef Trust, for colluding to raise consumers' prices for dressed beef and pork and keep prices low for farmers' cattle and hogs. Over the next six years, TR used the antitrust laws sparingly but well against forty-four other corporations including such concerns as the American Tobacco Company, the Standard Oil Company, the New Haven Railroad, and the DuPont Corporation.

TR's antitrust activities relied on laws already on the books. But Congress helped him with some additional legislation. In February 1903 it established the new Department of Commerce and Labor with a Bureau of Corporations to collect and publicize information about corporations. That same month it passed the Elkins Act giving to the Interstate Commerce Commission stronger powers over rebates granted by railroads to large shippers. Firms that deviated from their published rates could be charged with a misdemeanor. The federal courts could also issue injunctions to suspend such charges.

Roosevelt and Labor

TR's qualified antipathy to big business was matched by his qualified sympathy for organized labor. As an enlightened member of the nation's elite with a family tradition of noblesse oblige, he felt compassion toward working people as a class. He also understood why labor unions were necessary. "One of us," he wrote in his autobiography, "can deal in our private lives with the grocer and the butcher or the carpenter or the chicken raiser, or if we are the grocer or the carpenter or butcher or chicken raiser, we can deal with our customers, because *we are all of about the same size.*" But in a "rich and complex society" individuals were "dwarfed" by the rich corporations and could not "deal with them on terms of equality." Under the circumstances individuals had the right to "act . . . in their own self-defense through private combinations, such as farmers' associations and trade unions."

Despite these views, as governor of New York Roosevelt had used the state militia to help break a strike of underpaid laborers working on the Croton Dam. As president, his attitude toward labor unions would be put to the test during the anthracite coal strike of May 1902.

The strike came after months of struggle between the anthracite-coal miners of the United Mine Workers (UMW) and the conservative mine operators over labor's demands for an eight-hour day, a wage increase related to the weight of coal mined, and union recognition. When the mine owners refused to consider these demands, John Mitchell, the UMW's moderate head, ordered fifty thousand miners to leave their jobs, shutting down the major source of home heating fuel for the East Coast.

The strike continued through the summer and into the fall without settlement. The mine owners, led by George Baer of the Reading Railroad, refused to negotiate, confident that with winter coming the public would support their position. But Baer and his colleagues were their own worst enemies. At one point Baer outraged the public by his haughty observation that the "rights and interests of the laboring man will be protected and cared for not by the labor agitators, but by the Christian men to whom God has given the control of the property rights of the country."

Roosevelt proposed face-to-face negotiations between the miners and the owners. The owners refused. They would not "deal with the outlaws," who, they claimed, had been responsible for violence and murder in the coalfields. The owners' contemptuous response angered TR, and he threatened to send federal troops to seize the mines. Baer and his colleagues denounced the scheme as state socialism, but finally yielded and agreed that if the miners returned to work they would accept a federal arbitration commission consisting of an army engineer, a coal operator, a federal judge, and an "eminent sociologist" to decide on the miners' demands.

Roosevelt chose as the eminent sociologist E. E. Clarke, president of the Railway Conductors Union, thus giving the union a voice. Yet the decision handed down in

March 1903 was mixed. There would be a wage increase and a reduction in work hours but neither union recognition nor a change in the way coal was weighed to calculate wages.

The settlement satisfied the union. It also pleased the president. TR called it a *square deal* for labor and capital and used the phrase to characterize his administration overall. The most significant result of the strike, however, was that it established a precedent for presidential leadership in labor disputes that affected the public interest.

Roosevelt and Conservation

One item on the progressive agenda mentioned in TR's first annual message was conservation. Since the Civil War era much of the public domain had slipped away from government ownership into the hands of private interests. In part the process had been desirable. Rich agricultural land had been transformed into thousands of small farms throughout the Plains and Mountain regions. But much of the forest area, waterpower sites, mineral deposits, oil fields, and grazing lands had been snatched up by speculators and commercial exploiters on terms that failed to benefit the public and with results that did not take into account the nation's future needs. By the end of the nineteenth century a few Americans began to worry that their country had been reckless with its natural endowment and to insist that something be done to stop the waste. They were called *conservationists*.

Roosevelt's concern for conservation stemmed from his love of nature and his years on his Dakota ranch. As governor of New York he had begun a program to preserve the state's forests, wild life, and natural beauty. His conservationist leanings were strongly reinforced by his friendship with Gifford Pinchot, a wealthy Pennsylvanian who had trained himself in European scientific forestry methods and returned to the United States determined to apply them to America's natural heritage.

Even before Roosevelt became president, Pinchot and his fellow conservationists had induced Congress to pass the Forest Management Act (1897) and gotten the federal government to set aside several vast forest reserves and create several new national parks (Glacier, Mt. Rainier, Grand Canyon). In 1898 Pinchot was appointed head of the new Forest Service in the Department of Interior.

Pinchot made his agency into a missionary society where young men from Harvard and Yale became proselytizers for the conservationist faith. By the end of Roosevelt's presidency conservation had become a major reform movement taken up by the American Civic Association, the General Federation of Women's Clubs, and even the Daughters of the American Revolution.

Pinchot's friendship with Roosevelt made a powerful partnership for conservation. Among the president's earliest acts was the transfer, on Pinchot's advice, of the Forest Service to the Department of Agriculture, where conservation was more warmly supported than in the Interior Department. In December 1901 TR requested that congress create a national forest reserve in the Appalachians to match the reserves in the West. In 1908 he held a White House conservation conference of federal officials and state governors that helped publicize the conservation movement.

TR in Yosemite National Park in 1904. (The Bettmann Archive)

Mainstream conservation had its critics both to the left and the right. Preservationists such as John Muir, the members of California's Sierra club, and many women's conservation groups considered the nation's natural endowment a source of spiritual and aesthetic delight that must be kept pristine for those who wished to commune with nature. They had little patience with those conservationists, such as Pinchot and Roosevelt, who believed that resources were there to be used commercially, although frugally and scientifically. To the more conservative conservationists, the preservationists often seemed to be moralistic "nature lovers." At times the two groups battled fiercely. The differences came to a head in the struggle over the Hetch-Hetchy Valley, which Muir and members of the Sierra Club wished to annex to Yosemite National Park and which the city of San Francisco coveted for a reservoir. Pinchot and Roosevelt sided with the city. The issue became so bitter that Muir was not invited to the 1908 White House conservation conference.

On the far right were those who did not accept conservation at all. Opponents of the conservation movement included ranchers, timber companies, mining companies, and western commercial groups in general. A few of the large resource firms saw the value of conserving forests and mineral reserves for future exploitation; many, however, simply wanted to maximize present profits, with no thought of later years. Ranchers, for their part, wanted maximum access to federal grasslands without worrying about overgrazing. Many westerners saw conservation as an eastern-imposed limitation on western growth. Western governors often objected to federal control of local resources. Rather than being set aside in federal preserves, they argued, western lands should be turned over to the states.

Despite the opposition both within his administration and without, by the time Roosevelt left office the conservation movement had made remarkable headway. In 1901 the forest reserve included 46 million acres in 41 reserves; by 1909 it had grown to 150 million acres in 159 reserves. In addition Roosevelt had withdrawn from private hands the right to purchase 1.5 million acres of waterpower sites and 80 million acres of mineral lands from the federal domain. More important, an enormous constituency had been created for the idea that the country's resources were not infinite and had to be preserved for later generations.

Roosevelt's Second Term

To no one's surprise in 1904 Roosevelt won his party's nomination for a full term by acclamation. The Republican convention in Chicago also nominated a wealthy conservative senator from Indiana, Charles W. Fairbanks, as his running mate. The Democrats at St. Louis, having nominated William Jennings Bryan twice before (1896 and 1900) and seen him defeated both times, turned to the lackluster Judge Alton B. Parker of New York, representative of the party's conservative eastern wing, and chose as their vice presidential candidate the rich senator, Henry G. Davis of West Virginia.

The campaign itself was unmemorable. Despite the moderate liberalism of TR's first term most of the nation's prosperous middle class and businesspeople favored him over his opponent. As the Republican *New York Sun* noted, "we prefer the impulsive candidate of the party of conservatism to the conservative candidate of the party which the business interests regard as permanently and dangerously impulsive." On election day Roosevelt and Fairchild resoundingly beat Parker and Davis with 56 percent of the popular vote to the Democrats' 37.7 percent, and 336 electoral votes to the Democrats' 140. As TR told his wife, his presidency was now "no longer a political accident."

Roosevelt announced to the nation in his December 1904 Congressional message that he would be moving in a more progressive direction during his second term. Half the message was devoted to proposals for new economic and social legislation. For the District of Columbia, where there was no constitutional question that Congress directly ruled, he proposed slum clearance, factory inspection, school attendance, child labor, and juvenile court legislation. These measures could serve as examples for the states to follow. He also proposed limits on the workday of railroad workers and railroad safety legislation, and recommended new railroad rate regulation to tighten the Elkins Act.

Railroad Regulation

Congress did little to implement the president's suggestions for Washington, D.C., but it did give him a somewhat tougher railroad regulatory law, the Hepburn Act. The

House version of the Hepburn bill gave the Interstate Commerce Commission (ICC) power to fix rates, not merely to pass judgment on them after they were set; outlawed free passes and free tickets; and gave the ICC access to railroad corporations' books so that it could evaluate the fairness of railroad rate increases. While pending in the more conservative Senate, this bill came under withering attack from both extremes. The railroads called "citizens' meetings" packed with their supporters that dutifully passed resolutions against railroad rate reform. They bombarded Dakota wheat farmers and Kentucky tobacco growers with warnings that the bill would lower the prices of their crops. Railroad officials recognized that they could not avoid some sort of additional regulation, but hoped to retain judicial review of all ICC decisions which in the past had often delayed or reversed unfriendly action. From the other side advanced progressives like Senator Robert La Follette of Wisconsin attacked the administration's proposal as too weak. The courts must not be allowed to delay or overrule ICC decisions and the commission must be given the power to assess the real value of the railroads' physical assets so it could determine a fair rate of return.

Breaking a venerable tradition that freshmen Senators were to be seen but not heard, Fighting Bob tried to win over the Senate to his side by an impassioned speech. His colleagues responded with rude inattention, paper shuffling, and loud talking when he declaimed that "the welfare of all the people as consumers should be the supreme consideration of the government." The results were predictable: the Senate rejected his amendments forty to twenty-seven.

As finally passed, the Hepburn Act of 1906 was a compromise measure. It enlarged the ICC from five to seven members and gave it authority over sleeping car and express companies as well as conventional railroad activities. It also placed oil pipelines, ferry companies, and toll bridge firms under ICC jurisdiction. The new law gave the commission the right to fix rates, but then made its decisions subject to judicial review. It sharply curbed the railroads' pass-dispensing practices and forbade them to carry their own products free of charge.

Consumer Protection

The Hepburn Act was designed primarily to protect shippers. Two other laws of 1906—the Pure Food and Drug Act and the Meat Inspection Act—were aimed directly at consumers.

Americans, then as now, reached for a pill or medicine bottle whenever they felt a physical twinge. And a horde of quacks were more than happy to meet their needs. There were literally hundreds of "patent medicines" on the market that promised instant symptomatic relief or permanent glowing health. One product claimed to cure "General Debility, Mental and Physical Depression, Imbecility, Confused Ideas, Hysteria, General Irritability, Restlessness and Sleeplessness at Night, Absence of Muscular Efficiency, Loss of Appetite, Dyspepsia, Emaciation, Low Spirits, Disorganization or Paralysis of the Organs of Generation, And, in fact, all the concomitants of a Nervous and Debilitated state of the system." Even when they did not fulfill their promises these wonders sometimes produced a state of well-being. Several contained 45 percent grain alcohol—as much as whiskey; others contained cocaine or opium.

Fraudulent products like this one, misleadingly advertised, were one of the major targets of the Pure Food and Drug Act, which was passed in 1906. (The Bettmann Archive)

Without a doubt such preparations produced a glow that covered up the aches and pains of the user effectively. They also created a flock of unwitting alcoholics and drug addicts.

In part American consumers were themselves responsible for their victimization by the patent medicine purveyors. But they could not be blamed for their exploitation by the meat-packers and food processors. Private citizens could not tell what adulterants were being put into their canned or packaged food. They could not detect preservatives used by the meat-packers to disguise the bad odor or repellent appearance of spoiled beef and pork. They could not tell that they were consuming concentrated fruit-flavored sugar rather than jam, or peeled turnips in syrup rather than canned peaches.

For years Dr. Harvey Wiley, chief of the Agriculture Department's Bureau of Chemistry, had denounced the abuses and deceptions of the food canners, meat-packers, and patent medicine manufacturers and demanded that they be forced by law to be honest. "What we want," he wrote, "is that the farmer may get an honest market and the innocent consumer may get what he thinks he is buying." Wiley was an effective publicist of the consumer protection movement. His "poison squad"—twelve Department of Agriculture volunteers who agreed to serve as guinea pigs, consuming a wide range of food products and drugs to test their effects—caught the imagination of the public.

Meanwhile the momentum for federal regulation was building. Early in 1905 a British medical journal published four articles on the abysmal sanitary conditions in the Chicago stockyards that concluded that American meat was basically unhealthy, a "menace" to those who ate it. In October *Collier's* began to publish Samuel Hopkins Adams's sensational muckraking articles on patent medicines. The following February Upton Sinclair's *The Jungle,* dramatizing the same conclusions as the British medical report, appeared in book form. Clearly the issue's time had come.

In November 1905, Roosevelt recommended a law "to regulate interstate commerce in misbranded and adulterated foods, drinks, and drugs" so as to "secure the health and welfare of the consuming public." A month later Senator Weldon B. Heyburn introduced a pure food and drug act into the Senate. The Heyburn measure was attacked by Senator Nelson Aldrich and his conservative colleagues and stripped of its provision forbidding false advertising. In the House the friends of the patent medicine lobby rallied to defeat the bill. "The federal government," one Georgia representative argued, "was not created for the purpose of cutting your toe nails or corns." Another member proclaimed that "millions of women . . ." understood more about "good victuals and good eating" than "Dr. Wiley and all his apothecary shop." In the end, Representative James Mann of Illinois guided the bill through the shoals, and it passed the House on June 23, 1906.

The Pure Food and Drug Act was a relatively weak measure. Its chief weapon against fraud was disclosure. It required that manufacturers label their products honestly. If a particular medicine contained alcohol, chloral hydrate, opiates, and other dangerous substances, the presence and the amount had to be stated on the package. The labels also could not contain "any statement, design, or device" that was "false or misleading in any particular." The measure provided the public with information it could use to protect itself, but it did not permit the government to forbid the sale of any drug preparation. Still it was a breakthrough that established the precedent for all later federal consumer protection legislation.

The Meat Inspection Act became law on the same day as the Drug Act. The bill had passed the Senate under the sponsorship of Albert Beveridge of Indiana without difficulty but had been held up in the House by Representative James Wadsworth of New York, a good friend of the packers. At this point Roosevelt intervened. TR had been disturbed by the Sinclair novel, and he had sent several officials to look into its charges. Their report had confirmed almost everything that Sinclair described, and now TR told Wadsworth that if the bill continued to be stalled he would release the report. Meat sales at home and abroad had already dropped and the meat-packers and their friends in Congress were panicked by the thought of further damaging disclosures. Faced with the president's threat, opposition to the Beveridge bill quickly collapsed and the measure, with modifications, passed.

The Meat Inspection Act of 1906, like the Pure food and Drug Act, was a weaker law than the reformers wanted. It required government approval of the meat-packing industry's sanitary arrangements. The costs of inspection, however, were placed on the government's shoulders, rather than the packers'; government inspectors were denied totally free access to the packing plants; and the packers were not required to label cans for prepared meat products. Yet once again a precedent had been set for an expansion of federal responsibility in an area of life where millions of Americans were vulnerable to the effects of irresponsible private power.

The Panic of 1907

Roosevelt's relations with the business community worsened as his second term drew to a close. In December 1906 the president had called for stiffer regulation of all business, not just the railroads. When, in the following months, the prices of stocks and other securities fell, the business community blamed TR. "I would hate to tell you whom I think you ought to go to for an explanation for all this," barked E. H. Harriman to the press when his Union Pacific shares plummeted 25 points. The president responded in kind. In August he charged that his business opponents were trying to create a financial panic "so that they may enjoy unmolested the fruits of their own evil doing."

The financial troubles of 1907 were primarily a downswing of the normal business cycle worsened by structural weaknesses in the banking and monetary systems. But whatever the cause, by September industrial production had slumped badly, and large New York banks that held the deposits of the smaller country banks were finding it difficult to meet their obligations. On October 23 the Knickerbocker Trust Company of New York suspended payments after handing out $8 million in one day to frightened depositors. Runs on other banks and trust companies quickly followed. The panic was on!

Roosevelt rushed back from vacation and instructed Secretary of the Treasury George B. Cortelyou to deposit $35 million of government funds in the New York banks to help them pay their creditors. Even more important, J. P. Morgan and members of the New York Clearing House pledged to lend besieged banks large sums of money. One of Morgan's deals during the panic period would haunt Roosevelt for years. To keep an important New York brokerage house from collapsing and adding to the panic's momentum, Morgan proposed that his U.S. Steel Company be allowed to buy the firm's $5 million holdings in the Tennessee Coal and Iron Company. This would add to U.S. Steel's already formidable monopoly power in the industry and no doubt be a violation of the antitrust laws. What Morgan wanted was for the president to approve the purchase for the sake of easing the financial crisis. Roosevelt agreed. By January 1908 after further Treasury actions to ease the money market, the panic subsided.

Although relatively few people were seriously hurt by the financial crisis and the brief business downturn that followed, the 1907 panic triggered a serious inquiry into the weaknesses of the country's financial structure and launched an attempt to remedy the problem. In May 1908 Congress passed the Aldrich-Vreeland Act establishing the National Monetary Commission headed by Senator Aldrich to recommend changes in the country's banking laws. It also authorized national banks to issue temporarily up to $500 million worth of additional bank notes in times of crisis to meet the needs of creditors. The Aldrich Commission report, finally submitted in 1912, made recommendations that were eventually incorporated into the 1913 Federal Reserve Act.

The Election of 1908

Roosevelt's second term was now coming to an end and he wanted to continue in office. Only fifty-years-old he was in the prime of life and full of energy. He admitted privately that he would make "no pretense that I am glad to be relived of my official duties." Unfortunately, in an impulse moment on the evening of the 1905 election, he had declared that "under no circumstances" would he "be a candidate . . . or accept another nomination" for public office, and he did not see how he could break his promise.

But TR did not intend to be excluded from playing a political role in 1908. Two years before the end of his term he had decided who his successor would be: William Howard Taft, his secretary of war, one of his closest supporters and friends during his second term. Although he had never held elective office, Taft had demonstrated his administrative ability as governor of the Philippines and seemed to have a strong commitment to reform. As Taft wrote in 1907, "Mr. Roosevelt's views were mine long before I knew Mr. Roosevelt at all."

Once having made his decision, TR used his powerful influence to secure the results he wanted. By the time the 1908 Republican convention met in Chicago, Taft had enough delegates to win on the first ballot. The Republican platform endorsed conservation and stricter enforcement of the antitrust laws. It also promised tariff revision, understood by most observers as downward revision of rates, but sufficiently ambiguous to avoid offending the manufacturers.

The Democrats at their convention in Denver turned for the third time to Bryan, with Indianan John W. Kern as candidate for vice president, and a platform condemning monopolies and pledging unequivocally for lower tariff duties. The Democrats also adopted a plank condemning the use of court orders (injunctions) in labor disputes, a growing practice that hurt organized labor and had been loudly condemned by AFL leader Samuel Gompers and others.

Bryan campaigned as vigorously as ever, claimed that *he,* not Taft, was TR's legitimate progressive successor. Taft proved a lackluster campaigner, revealing his lethargy and colorlessness. He also made clear that, although TR's own choice, he was less progressive than the outgoing president. He was "more safely to be trusted" with the presidency than the radical Bryan, he assured the voters at one point.

On election day Taft won with 7.7 million popular votes to Bryan's 6.4 million, and 321 electoral votes to Bryan's 162. Although the Republicans kept control of both houses of congress, they lost many seats to the Democrats. By itself this spelled trouble ahead. But it would soon become clear that another difficulty was the shift in Republican ranks. Many of the new Republican members were men of the most advanced progressive stamp. They would not take kindly to a leader who was slower to act on the reform agenda than TR himself.

The Taft Years

In his inaugural address Taft pledged to follow in TR's footsteps. He would be untrue to himself, to his promises, and to the party platform, he declared, if he did not

President Taft golfing. (Library of Congress)

support and expand the reforms his "distinguished predecessor" had undertaken. But in a matter of months the new president had alienated almost all of TR's friends and supporters and had become the ally of the Republican Old Guard.

To some extent the split was inevitable. Taft had none of the exuberance and vitality of TR. He was indolent, physically ungainly (he weighed over 300 pounds), and intellectually conservative; he possessed the contemplative disposition of a judge rather than the dramatic and activist personality of a political leader. Such a dull and ponderous man could not help but disappoint those raised on a heady diet of the vivid, rambunctious, and delightful TR.

The Ballinger-Pinchot Affair

Taft was also inept. He somehow managed to attack every progressive sacred cow even when he did not intend to. Nowhere is this failing better illustrated than in his battle with Gifford Pinchot.

The new president's appointment as secretary of the interior to replace Roosevelt's James Garfield (the son of the president of the same name), was Richard

Ballinger, a Seattle lawyer closely tied to the Northwest's mining and lumber interests. Garfield had worked closely with chief forester Gifford Pinchot, but one of Ballinger's first acts in office was to reverse TR's policy of withdrawing federally owned mineral lands and timberlands from private entry. Especially worrisome to Pinchot and the conservationists was Ballinger's scheme, revealed by Louis Glavis, a disgruntled former Interior Department employee, to allow a Morgan-Guggenheim syndicate to exploit valuable Alaska coal lands.

Pinchot protested to the president, but Taft sided with his cabinet adviser. Pinchot then wrote a series of magazine and newspaper articles and gave several speeches denouncing the deal and by implication his own Interior Department chief.

Throughout 1909 the controversy raged with all the conservationists and most of TR's partisans siding with Pinchot. Pinchot knew that he was jeopardizing his job as chief forester, but believed it important to publicize the Morgan-Guggenheim steal in every way possible even if this meant being fired. The president, although he considered Pinchot "a socialist and a spiritualist . . . capable of any extreme act," hoped to avoid a showdown.

Pinchot finally forced Taft's hand. In January 1910 he wrote a letter to Jonathan Dolliver, chairman of the Senate Agriculture and Forestry Committee, defending several officials who had denounced Ballinger. The letter violated a government rule that no official could communicate with congress without going through channels. The enraged president now had no choice and fired his disobedient chief forester. Pinchot had what he wanted.

The issue was now a full-blown scandal, and Congress appointed a joint committee stacked with progressives to investigate. The hearings went on for four months with Boston lawyer Louis Brandeis brilliantly defending the conservationists' case. By the time the hearings ended, the liberal public had concluded that the president was an ally of the "interests" and an opponent of his predecessor's political philosophy. The first step had been taken to a Taft-Roosevelt confrontation.

The Payne-Aldrich Tariff

The progressive Republicans' disillusionment with Taft ballooned when the president mismanaged the tariff revision promised by the 1908 party platform.

By 1909 the public was thoroughly disgusted with the "mother of trusts," as they called the existing high Dingley tariff. In April the House, under the leadership of Sereno Payne of New York, yielded to this feeling and passed a tariff revision bill moderately lowering existing duties. In the Senate Aldrich took charge of the measure and had the Payne bill amended almost out of recognition. In the bill submitted to the full Senate by Aldrich's committee, the House schedules on textiles, iron and steel, and lumber were all raised; most of the "free list" of products in the House bill was cut out as well as a provision for a federal inheritance tax to offset the expected loss of revenue.

The Aldrich bill outraged the progressive leaders in the Senate. By now the upper house had acquired a formidable contingent of midwestern liberals, including La Follette, Dolliver, Beveridge, Joseph Bristow of Kansas, Moses Clapp of Minnesota, and

Albert Cummins of Iowa. These Republican "insurgents" rallied to stop the Aldrich bill in defiance of the Republican leadership.

Dividing up the various schedules among themselves, they mastered the complexities of the bill. When the appropriate section of the measure came up for debate, each in turn rose to attack it. For three months, during the fierce heat of Washington's summer, they carried on the debate. In the past tariff struggles had generally been between competing groups of producers—manufacturers, merchants, and farmers. Now the opponents of high duties sounded the note of consumer protection. Under the tariff's influence, charged La Follette, "competition has been driven from the field. Hence there is shoddy in everything we wear and adulteration in everything we eat." Beveridge conceded that high duties served to protect American workers against the low wages of Europe, but it was now "high concern to . . . the prosperity of our people as a whole that a just and equal consideration should be shown the consuming public." A few defenders of the Aldrich bill rejected the insurgents' argument. Henry Cabot Lodge of Massachusetts noted that most Americans were both producers and consumers at the same time. But the insurgents succeeded in making consumers and their concerns the focus of the tariff issue debate.

In the end the anti-Aldrich bill forces were unsuccessful and the measure that was sent to the president for his signature was essentially the one that Aldrich's committee had originally submitted. It did not lower the Dingley rates; it actually raised many.

Taft had promised La Follette that if the bill that reached his desk did not substantially lower existing duties he would veto it. He reneged. The president was easily influenced by men such as Aldrich, and the Rhode Island senator had convinced him that the Payne-Aldrich tariff represented a realistic attempt to head off still more strongly protectionist legislation. Besides, the president did not know how to deal with Congress. His judicious temperament, unlike Roosevelt's, made him reluctant to appeal to the public over the heads of the Senate leadership. By now, moreover, Taft was fed up with the insurgents for rocking the political boat and was privately calling them "self-centered," "self-absorbed," "forward," "demagogues," and even "pretty stupid."

The president's unwillingness to help their campaign to defeat the Payne-Aldrich tariff by itself infuriated the Republican insurgents. But the final blow was yet to come. At the signing ceremony, the president called the bill "a sincere effort . . . to make a downward revision." Six weeks later at Winona, Minnesota, Taft praised the Payne-Aldrich bill as "the best tariff measure the Republican party has ever passed." There could now be no question: Taft had allied himself with the enemy.

Progressive Victories

The congressional progressives could claim some victories during the Taft administration's first two years. In 1910 they succeeded in passing the Mann-Elkins Act extending the supervision of the Interstate Commerce Commission to telephone, telegraph, cable, and wireless companies and giving the ICC additional powers to suspend railroad rate increases. Also in 1910 Congress passed the Mann Act, prohibiting the "white slave" trade—the interstate transportation of women for immoral purposes, an evil that had long concerned women's advocates and defenders of "social purity." During that year Congress also created the postal savings system, providing a safe haven at the U.S. post offices for the small sums put aside by ordinary savers.

The insurgents were also able to limit the powers of the conservative Speaker of the House, the profane Joseph Cannon. At the opening of the congressional session in March 1910, the House progressives, led by the young Republican George Norris of Nebraska, stripped the Speaker of his power to appoint the members of the House Rules Committee. They would have preferred to end Cannon's power to stop progressive legislation entirely by ousting him as Speaker, but that did not prove possible.

In their efforts to change the nation's political direction the progressives were not always at odds with the president. Taft preferred trying progressive cases to making progressive laws. He aggressively prosecuted the trusts and, in fact, during his four years the government launched more antitrust suits than during TR's seven. Yet in the end even here the president proved timid, drawing back when the business community began to complain that the prosecutions were undermining investors' confidence.

Taft versus Roosevelt

Soon after his successor's inauguration TR and his son Kermit had sailed off to Africa for a happy interlude of hunting big game. For an entire year the two killed lions, elephants, and zebras with abandon and combined their extended safari with two trips through Europe where the ex-president was treated as a world hero by reigning monarchs and commoners alike. During his year abroad TR was kept informed of Taft's transgressions against his sponsor's policies and friends by Pinchot, Dolliver, and William Allen White. Although Taft wrote to TR to explain his actions. Roosevelt returned home in June 1910 at the very least skeptical of Taft's loyalty to the progressive cause and to his own record of accomplishment.

Over the next few months relations between the two men worsened. During the summer, delegations of prominent progressives made pilgrimages to the Roosevelt estate at Oyster Bay, Long Island, to talk over the political situation. During these sessions they filled TR's ears with Taft's failings and hinted broadly that Roosevelt would receive their support if he decided to resume active politics. During the fall, TR set off on a speaking tour of the West in support of progressive Republican candidates in the state and congressional elections. It proved to be a triumphal procession. Wherever his train stopped, crowds of flag-carrying people appeared in their Sunday best and demanded that he speak. At his hotel in Fargo, North Dakota, a hundred little girls were waiting for him, each with a teddy bear in her arms. No one who craved the limelight like Roosevelt could help but find the attention intoxicating.

During this trip TR laid out to his listeners much of what would become known as the *New Nationalism*. Borrowing from Herbert Croly, TR proclaimed a more positive federal government than any national politician in the past. At Ossawatomie, Kansas, he announced that the new political philosophy put "the national need before sectional and personal advantage." The person who held that "every human right is secondary to his profit, must now give way to the advocate of human welfare, who rightly maintain[ed] that every man holds his property subject to the general rights of the community." Specifically it committed the country to eliminating the power of money from politics, a reduced tariff, graduated income and inheritance taxes, direct popular primaries for selecting candidates for office, and using national resources to benefit the public.

The midterm elections of 1910 were a repudiation of the Republican Old Guard. In the East, where they controlled the party machinery, they lost badly to progressive Democrats. In one of these contests, Woodrow Wilson, president of Princeton University, defeated a regular Republican for the governorship of New Jersey. In the West, where the insurgents were in the saddle, the party did well.

The results were a powerful lesson to TR and others. In Wisconsin they stirred the presidential ambitions of La Follette. When he returned to Washington in December, Fighting Bob helped organize the National Progressive Republican League (NPRL). The league would fight to secure progressive legislation in the states, especially the "direct democracy" of primaries and the initiative and referendum. This would be the preliminary to defeating Taft in 1912 and, incidentally, to winning La Follette the party nomination. Many prominent progressives joined the NPRL, but not TR. Roosevelt saw the organization as a tool of La Follette's own presidential bid and was skeptical of direct democracy in any case.

By the fall of 1911 the La Follette campaign to unseat Taft and secure the Republican nomination for himself was well underway. In mid-October the NPRL convened a progressive Republican convention in Chicago and endorsed La Follette unanimously. During the remainder of 1911 the Wisconsin senator campaigned to keep his name before the public and head off any attempt by TR to force himself into the nomination race. He did not succeed. On January 16, TR wrote publisher Frank Munsey that he would accept the Republican presidential nomination if it appeared to be a public draft rather than an act of personal ambition.

La Follette was not willing to concede, but then, in early February, he destroyed his chances by an after-dinner speech before the Periodical Publishers Association in Philadelphia. He had not eaten all day and just before he rose to speak he had taken a shot of whiskey to calm his nerves. It was late and his overstuffed listeners wanted to go home. Knowing he was before a hostile audience La Follette responded in kind, at points shaking his fingers at inattentive listeners. He also repeated himself, stretching out the talk to over two hours. By the time he finished, many of the audience had concluded that the senator had suffered a nervous breakdown, and the occasion was so reported in the press the next day.

Thereafter much of La Follette's progressive support slipped away. Early in February TR's letter to Munsey was published. Later that month he responded directly to contrived letters from several Republican governors urging him to run. "I will accept the nomination for President if is tendered me," he wrote, "and I will adhere to this decision until the convention has expressed a preference." During the spring, in the western states where the presidential primary had been adopted, TR won most of the delegates with La Follette a poor second and Taft behind both.

The Election of 1912

The Republicans   The June Republican convention in Chicago was a battle for the soul of the party. Both sides were prepared to fight, not only for candidates Taft or Roosevelt, but also for standpat conservatism or a complete reorientation of the GOP. Breaking with tradition, candidate Roosevelt came to Chicago, exhibiting his usual exuberant good spirits, "snapping his teeth, batting his eyes," and claiming that he felt "as strong as a bull moose." The president remained in Washington, now temporarily a quiet political backwater, contentedly playing golf. But the Old Guard leaders were at the Coliseum with a solid block of machine-elected delegates, including many southerners who represented scarcely any real Republican constituency, confident that they would win.

And they were right. Most of the Roosevelt delegations were contested, and when disputes were referred to the credentials committee, TR's supporters were almost invariably thrown out. Attempts to carry the day by enthusiastic demonstrations failed. At one point the TR people put on a fifty-two minute session of music, chanting, and parades. The Taft delegates sat grim faced and unmoved.

On Saturday, June 22 the convention formally renominated Taft. Immediately after, the Roosevelt forces, led by Senator Hiram Johnson of California, Gifford Pinchot, and others, marched out of the hall to the jeers of those who remained. The conservatives then renominated the ailing James Sherman as Taft's running mate, adopted a party platform, and adjourned.

The night before, foreseeing defeat, the Republican progressives had agreed to launch a third party. Meeting at Orchestra Hall, they formally resolved to create the Progressive Party of America and hold a nominating convention in August.

The Democrats   A few days following the debacle at Chicago, the Democrats held their convention in Baltimore. The front-runners were the Speaker of the House, James Beauchamp ("Champ") Clark of Missouri, a man with liberal credentials, and the tall, ascetic-looking governor of New Jersey, Thomas Woodrow Wilson. The controlling figure at the convention was Bryan, suspicious of Clark because of his supposed Wall Street connections. It would take forty-six ballots before Wilson won. With Thomas Marshall of Indiana as his running mate and a platform calling for drastic tariff cuts and the end of monopolies, the convention adjourned.

The Progressives   On August 5 two thousand men and women assembled at Chicago to provide a platform and candidates for the Progressive party, soon labeled "Bull Moose" after Roosevelt's earlier remark. The delegates included some old disgruntled politicians, and more of the new progressive officeholders, mostly from the Midwest and far West. It also included hundreds of reformers who had never attended a major party convention before. Conspicuous among the latter were "women doctors, women lawyers, women teachers, college professors, middle-aged leaders of civic movements, or rich young girls who had gone in for settlement work."

The atmosphere at Chicago was that of a revival meeting. On the first day Beveridge gave the keynote address calling for "social brotherhood as against savage

Woodrow Wilson campaigning in 1912. (The Bettmann Archive)

individualism," and "a broader liberty and a fuller justice." He finished with the words
"mine eyes have seen the glory of the coming of the Lord," echoed by the delegates'
singing of the "Battle Hymn of the Republic." The following day TR gave his
"Confession of Faith" concluding with the rousing battle cry, "We stand at
Armageddon and we battle for the Lord."

The delegates nominated Roosevelt and Hiram Johnson and adopted a platform
that foreshadowed much of the later welfare state. (See Reading 4.) Not until the days
of the New Deal would a party with some chance of success at the polls propose a
political program as bold. After endorsing the platform, the delegates sang a hymn and
adjourned.

The Campaign   The campaign that followed was one of the more significant in our
history. The public would have a sharper choice in 1912 than it would have for twenty

READING 4

The Progressive Party Platform of 1912

The most liberal expression of the progressive mood was the 1912 platform of the Progressive party. This document projected a role for government in the lives of ordinary Americans that was only attained half a century after its adoption. The platform reflected the "social" progressivism of the maverick politicians, social workers, academics, and activist women who came to Chicago in August 1912 to nominate Theodore Roosevelt on the Progressive, or Bull Moose, third-party ticket.

The conscience of the people, in a time of grave national problems, has called into being a new party, born of the nation's sense of justice. We of the Progressive party here dedicate ourselves to the fulfillment of the duty laid upon us by our fathers to maintain the government of the people, by the people and for the people whose foundations they laid. . . .

The Old Parties

Political parties exist to secure responsible government and to execute the will of the people.

From these great tasks both of the old parties have turned aside. Instead of instruments to promote the general welfare, they have become the tools of corrupt interests which use them impartially to serve their selfish purposes. Behind the ostensible government sits enthroned an invisible government owing no allegiance and acknowledging no responsibility to the people.

To destroy this invisible government, to dissolve the unholy alliance between corrupt business and corrupt politics is the first task of the statesmanship of the day.

The deliberate betrayal of its trust by the Republican party, the fatal incapacity of the Democratic party to deal with the new issues of the new time, have compelled the people to forge a new instrument of government through which to give effect to their will in laws and institutions.

Unhampered by tradition, uncorrupted by power, undismayed by the magnitude of the task, the new party offers itself as the instrument of the people to sweep away old abuses, to build a new and nobler commonwealth. . . .

The Rule of the People

. . . In particular, the party declares for direct primaries for the nomination of State and National officers, for nation-wide preferential primaries for candidates for the presidency; for the direct election of United States Senators by the people; and we urge on the States the policy of the short ballot, with responsibility to the people secured by the initiative, referendum and recall. . . .

Equal Suffrage

The Progressive party, believing that no people can justly claim to be a true democracy which denies political rights on account of sex, pledges itself to the task of securing equal suffrage to men and women alike.

Corrupt Practices

We pledge our party to legislation that will compel strict limitation to all campaign contributions and expenditures, and detailed publicity of both before as well as after primaries and elections. . . .

The Courts

The progressive party demands such restriction of the power of the courts as shall leave to the people the ultimate authority to determine fundamental questions of social welfare and public policy. . . .

Administration of Justice

. . . We believe that the issuance of injunctions in cases arising out of labor disputes should be prohibited when such injunctions would not apply when no labor disputes existed. . . .

Social and Industrial Justice

The supreme duty of the Nation is the conservation of human resources through an enlightened measure of social and industrial justice. We pledge ourselves to work unceasingly in State and Nation for:

Effective legislation looking to the prevention of industrial accidents, occupational diseases, overwork, involuntary unemployment, and other injurious effects incident to modern industry;

The fixing of minimum safety and health standards for the various occupations, and the exercise of the public authority of State and Nation, including the Federal Control over interstate commerce, and the taxing power, to maintain such standards;

The prohibition of child labor;

Minimum wage standards for working women, to provide a "living wage" in all industrial occupations;

The general prohibition of night work for women and the establishment of an eight hour day for women and young persons;

One day's rest in seven for all wage workers;

The eight hour day in continuous twenty-four-hour industries; . . .

Publicity as to wages, hours and conditions of labor; full reports upon industrial accidents and diseases, and the opening to public inspection of all tallies, weights, measures and check systems on labor products;

Standards of compensation for death by industrial accident and injury and trade disease which will transfer the burden of lost earnings from the families of working people to the industry, and thus to the community;

The protection of home life against the hazards of sickness, irregular employment and old age through the adoption of a system of social insurance adapted to American use;

The development of the creative labor power of America by lifting the last load of illiteracy from American youth and establishing continuation schools for industrial education under public control and encouraging agricultural education and demonstration in rural schools;

The establishment of industrial research laboratories to put the methods and discoveries of science at the service of American producers;

We favor the organization of the workers, men and women, as a means of protecting their interests and of promoting their progress. . . .

Currency

. . . The issue of currency is fundamentally a Government function and the system should have as basic principles soundness and elasticity. The control should be lodged with the Government and should be protected from domination or manipulation by Wall Street or any special interests. . . .

Conservation

. . . We believe that the remaining forests, coal and oil lands, water powers and other natural resources still in State or National control (except agricultural lands) are more likely to be wisely conserved and utilized for the general welfare if held in the public hands.

In order that consumers and producers, managers and workmen, now and hereafter, need not pay toll to private monopolies of power and raw material, we demand that such resources shall be retained by the State or Nation, and opened to immediate use under laws which will encourage development and make to the people a moderate return for benefits conferred. . . .

Source: Henry Steel Commager (ed.), *Documents of American History* (New York: Appleton-Century-Crofts, 1963), 7th ed., vol. II, pp 73–75.

more years. Taft clearly represented the past, the days before the progressive era when wealthy insiders made most of the political decisions for the nation. Roosevelt and Wilson were both progressives, but of different types. TR's new Nationalism was a fusion of Hamiltonian centralism with welfare state liberalism. Government should serve as the ultimate protector of the public against the uncertainties of life and the irresponsible power of selfish private interests. Wilson's *New Freedom,* strongly influenced by Louis Brandeis, was much more Jeffersonian, as suited a man with southern Democratic roots. Its chief thrust was that the public's interest would best be served if the old competition of small producers could be restored. Break up the big business combinations but do not substitute for them an equally big, oppressive government. TR would refer to the New Freedom as "rural Toryism" better suited to a simpler, bygone age than the complex present.

Another candidate in the field was the socialist Eugene V. Debs. Socialism had benefited from the whole shift left of the nation's political spectrum since 1900. Many of the advanced progressive reformers were secret—and not-so-secret—socialists. Christian socialism was a force among the liberal social gospel Protestant clergy. Many municipal reformers had found the socialist message compelling. The socialists had been further reinforced since 1900 by thousands of immigrants from Eastern Europe who had learned their hatred of bourgeois society by observing its excesses in Austria, Germany, or Russia. Debs himself was a eloquent speaker whose pleas for social justice for the downtrodden won the hearts of thousands.

The Socialist platform in 1912 attacked capitalism and called for nationalizing all the major means of production and distribution. This was standard socialist doctrine. In addition, however, it demanded many of the things that the advanced progressives favored: a shorter work week, an end to child labor, minimum wages, old-age pensions and social insurance, a steeply graduated income tax, women's suffrage, direct election of the president and of all judges by popular vote.

The election's outcome was predictable. Almost from the outset it was clear that Taft was an also-ran and the contest would be between TR and Wilson. Here the governor of New Jersey had the edge. Although the public loved TR, many advanced progressives were suspicious of his newfound militancy. Others were equally suspicious of his alliance with George W. Perkins, a rich former associate of J. P. Morgan selected as Bull Moose adviser on business and as party fund-raiser. Wilson had the added advantage of traditional Democratic support, especially in the South. The results were a Wilson electoral college landslide. The Democratic ticket took 435 electoral votes to TR's 88 and Taft's pathetic 8. The popular vote was much closer, however. Wilson would be a minority president with 6.3 million votes to his opponents' combined 8.5 million (TR, 4.1 million; Taft, 3.5 million; and Debs, 0.9 million). Viewed another way, the election was a triumph for the reform impulse in American politics. Over 11 million of the 14.8 million votes cast (that is the combined votes for Wilson, Roosevelt, and Debs) represented a mandate for some sort of major political change. (See Figure 4–1.)

Wilson's New Freedom

The new president was a remarkably able man. Son of a Presbyterian minister Wilson spent most of his youth in the South and then, after Princeton and a brief flirtation with the law, went to Johns Hopkins University for a doctoral degree in history. In 1891 he returned to Princeton as professor of jurisprudence and political economy. In 1902 he became the university's president.

As head of Princeton Wilson exhibited some of his best and worst personality traits. He fought successfully to reduce Princeton's social and athletic focus, introduced a series of major educational reforms, and brought many distinguished scholars to the campus. Yet his stubborn and self-righteous campaign for his concept of the graduate college resulted in his defeat at the hands of Dean Andrew West, who

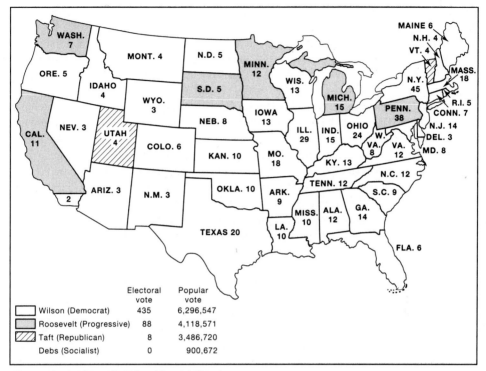

Figure 4–1 *The 1912 Presidential Election*

favored a different scheme. In 1910 Wilson was rescued from his academic difficulties by the Democratic bosses of New Jersey who thought he would serve usefully as a figurehead governor and offered him the party nomination. He won the election, and to the surprise of the public and the dismay of the bosses he brought the state an effective and progressive administration.

As president of the United States Wilson was determined to make changes. His reading of American history had convinced him that there was a serious flaw in the leadership system of the country. In his published doctoral dissertation, *Congressional Government,* he had endorsed the British system of parliamentary rule. But then Roosevelt's success in the White House had convinced him that for America presidential leadership was best after all and he resolved to emulate TR. He made his intentions clear from the outset when he called Congress into special session the day following his inauguration to consider tariff revision. When Congress assembled he broke precedent, established since Jefferson's day, and appeared before a joint session to deliver his message personally.

Tariff Reform

The Underwood tariff that finally emerged from Congress was the joint work of Wilson and Oscar Underwood of Alabama, chairman of the House Ways and Means Committee. Overall, the new tariff was the first major reduction in tariff rates since the beginning of Republican ascendancy fifty years before. Agricultural machinery that farmer's needed and a host of consumers' goods—food, clothing, and shoes—were put on the free list or taxed very lightly. It was anticipated that the government would lose $100 million by the rate reductions and to offset this loss as well as to shift some of the burden of taxation to the rich, congress passed the first income tax law under the terms of the new Sixteenth Amendment.

The Underwood bill passed the House without difficulty. The Senate proved less cooperative. Wilson feared that the upper chamber would once again make a mockery of a House tariff measure and used all his personal and official persuasive powers with senators. Still the lobbyists for manufacturing and producer groups who swarmed through Washington during the spring of 1913 threatened to overturn his work. On May 26 the president issued a public statement attacking the lobbyists and appealing to the public over the heads of the senators. A Senate investigation that followed Wilson's charges against the lobbyists and their influence demonstrated the truth of his claims and broke the Senate logjam. On June 26, by a vote of forty-seven to thirty-seven, the Senate approved the Underwood bill.

The Underwood tariff was greeted as a victory of the people over the "interests." "This is no tariff by log-rolling, by manipulation, by intrigue, by bribery," wrote the editor of *The New York World*. "It was dictated by no conspiracy between corrupt business and corrupt politics." The new tariff law was also perceived as a great triumph for Wilson's leadership. Its passage, another editor wrote, had raised Wilson "at a single stage from the man of promise to the man of achievement." In truth, there is no way of telling what the law might have accomplished. In less than a year the world would be plunged into war and all international trade would be severely disrupted.

The Federal Reserve Act

Next on the Democratic agenda after tariff reform was monetary and banking reform.

There was much to change if the country was to have a financial system adequate to its needs. One problem was the absence of a "lender of last resort" who could provide the commercial banks with infusions of credit during times of shortages. This role was especially critical during liquidity crises such as the 1907 panic, when everyone wanted cash and no one had any to lend except at exorbitant interest rates. There was also the lack of seasonal flexibility in the money supply. Both at the Christmas shopping period and the fall harvest months money was hard to get, while at other times the banks outside New York were so replete with cash that they lent it to the New York call-loan market where it invariably fueled dangerous stock market speculation.

Even the bankers accepted the inadequacy of the existing decentralized and chaotic national banking system and proposed as an alternative a single centralized National Reserve Association run by the commercial bankers that resembled the early nineteenth-century Bank of the United States. The association would issue the country's paper money, lend to the commercial banks, and hold the deposits of the federal government.

The bankers' proposal displeased most progressives, especially those with rural roots. They believed the banking system was already overconcentrated in New York and that Wall Street financiers exerted excessive power over the financial fate of the entire country. They also disliked the idea of private banks continuing to issue the bulk of the nation's money, deplored the absence from the bankers' proposal of any provision for cheap agricultural credit, and wanted any new banking bill to prohibit interlocking directorates that, as the Pujo committee had revealed (see Chapter 3), gave bankers extraordinary influence over the nation's business affairs. Wilson agreed with most of the agrarians' views and put his shoulder behind them.

Ultimately the law that appeared as the Federal Reserve Act of 1913 was a package of compromises. There would be twelve regional federal reserve banks, each in charge of a reserve district and subject to only weak overall supervision by a Federal Reserve Board located in Washington. The board would be appointed by the president with the advice and consent of the Senate, but each regional federal reserve bank would be headed by a private banker. The system thus was a hybrid of public and private.

The federal reserve banks would issue a new currency in federal reserve notes. These could be varied in amount through "open market operations"—buying and selling government securities, and through "rediscounting" of individual banks' commercial paper, lending them money with their own customers' IOUs as collateral. Through such means the new currency and credit system could be made to fluctuate with seasonal needs, meet the pressures of periodic financial crises, and regulate the long-term swings of the business cycle. Time would show that the measure had serious flaws, but the Federal Reserve Act of 1913 became the bedrock of the country's present central banking system.

Wilson and Antitrust

Wilson's New Freedom had at its heart the promise to protect the consumer and preserve democracy by restoring economic competition. In effect, the president had placed antitrust at the center of his program.

Wilson rejected the concept of an all-powerful government body that would tell business what to do. Instead, he favored prohibiting specific practices and then guaranteeing enforcement. A man of Jeffersonian antecedents, Wilson considered this approach more compatible with American tradition.

Wilson's antitrust concept was incorporated into two separate measures—the Federal Trade Commission Act and the Clayton Antitrust Act, both of 1914. The first law created a Federal Trade Commission (FTC), a five-person body charged primarily with the task of publicizing the activities of business and granted the authority to issue cease and desist orders, subject to judicial review, forbidding certain business practices. The Clayton Antitrust Act prohibited a number of practices designed to reduce competition, including interlocking business directorates and price discrimination that tended to create monopoly. Officials of corporations violating antitrust statutes could be held individually responsible for their firms' misdeeds.

Besides its antitrust aspects the Clayton Act sought to protect organized labor. To prevent the courts' and the government's misuse of the antitrust statutes both farmers' cooperatives and labor unions were exempted specifically from their jurisdiction. To further satisfy the trade union movement, the law limited the use of court injunctions against strikes except in cases where there was serious danger of irreparable injury to property. It also made strikes, peaceful picketing, and boycotts legal under federal law. Samuel Gompers, head of the AFL hailed the measure as labor's Magna Carta.

The Final Burst

Passage of the Clayton Antitrust and Federal Trade Commission acts virtually exhausted the Wilson administration's reform zeal. In part this merely reflected a general weakening of the reform impulse in early 1914 in response to a sharp downturn in the business cycle. Conservative Republicans blamed the economic slump on the Underwood tariff and the unfriendly attitude toward business implied in the new antitrust laws. The administration denied the charge, but to the chagrin of the more advanced progressives, Wilson was soon working hard to conciliate and reassure the business community.

There would be one more burst of reform, however, before the war raging in Europe shut down the entire progressive enterprise. The fuel would be political realities.

As the election of 1916 approached, Wilson faced a party in disarray. His preparedness program (see Chapter 5) had antagonized Bryan and most of the party progressives. The administration might hope for support from former Bull Moosers, especially if TR refused to run on the Progressive ticket for a second time, but Wilson's shift to the right after 1914 had offended many of them. The Democrats had won in 1912 only because the Republicans had split; they could not count on this happening again. Clearly something had to be done to reestablish the party's progressive credentials if it hoped to avoid returning to its also-ran status.

The first step in rehabilitating the administration's standing with the liberals was Wilson's nomination of Boston labor lawyer Louis Brandeis to the Supreme Court. Progressives like La Follette cheered the move. The conservative judicial and legal community, however, rallied against it, propelled in part by dismay at Brandeis's legal liberalism and in part by ingrained antisemitism. In the end the appointment was confirmed, and Brandeis went on to a distinguished career on the nation's highest court.

During the rest of 1916 there followed a barrage of measures that went beyond the president's limited New Freedom type of reform to help build the foundation for the welfare state. In July came the Federal Farm Loan Act providing farmers with cheap credit through twelve federal farm loan banks. The following month Congress passed the Warehouse Act permitting farmers to bring crops to bonded warehouses and get receipts in return. These could then be used as collateral for loans. Wilson also supported the Kern-McGillicuddy Act, establishing a workman's compensation system for federal employees, and the Keating-Owen child labor bill, forbidding sale of goods made by child labor in interstate commerce. The Adamson Act, in September, provided for an eight-hour day and time-and-a-half pay for workers on interstate railroads. As the historian Arthur S. Link notes, by the fall of 1916, the Democrats had "enacted almost every important plank in the Progressive [Bull Moose] platform of 1912."

Progressive Achievements

As we shall see in the next chapter, Wilson won reelection, but that was the last gasp of the progressive movement. In a matter of months the country would be at war, and much of the energy that had gone into changing America would be dissipated by the enterprise of killing Germans.

In many ways the accomplishments of the progressive years would prove less impressive with passing time. The courts would eviscerate the anti-injunction provision of the Clayton Act and strike down the Keating-Owen Act. During the following decade the regulatory commissions fell increasingly under the control of the industries they were charged with regulating. Direct democracy proved no panacea for undue influence by the wealthy and powerful on the course of legislation. Progressive consumer protection legislation ended the most scandalous abuses in the prepared food and patent medicine industries, but each of the measures had to be supplemented in later years to protect the public's health. Indeed almost every battle fought and seemingly won by the progressive crusaders would have to be refought.

Yet we must not be too skeptical. The progressives of the early twentieth century were the the first political group to understand that cities and a national market had created new challenges and new dangers, and they were the first group to tackle these problems within the framework of acceptable American values. However imperfect, theirs was no mean achievement.

FOR FURTHER READING

Students interested in Theodore Roosevelt are fortunate to have several readable biographies to consult. Among the best are Henry Pringle's wry *Theodore Roosevelt: A Biography* (1931); William Harbaugh's more sober *Power and Responsibility: The Life and Times of Theodore Roosevelt* (1961); and John Blum's specialized, but adept, study *The Republican Roosevelt* (1954). All the progressive presidents, including *both* Roosevelts, are described, and compared, in Blum's *The Progressive Presidents: Theodore Roosevelt, Woodrow Wilson, Franklin D. Roosevelt, and Lyndon B. Johnson* (1980). On TR and the trusts the student should consult Edwin Roswenc, *Roosevelt, Wilson and Trusts* (1950). For TR and labor, at one crucial point, see Robert J. Cornell, *The Anthracite Coal Strike of 1902* (1957). Conservation and the Ballinger-Pinchot affair are dealt with in James L. Penick, Jr., *Progressive Politics and Conservation: The Ballinger-Pinchot Affair* (1968) and Elmo Richardson, *The Politics of Conservation, 1897–1913* (1962). On the Pure Food and Drug Act see James Harvey Young, noted in the bibliography for Chapter 3, and also Oscar E. Anderson, Jr., *The Health of a Nation: Harvey W. Wiley and the Fight for Pure Food* (1958). For TR and the Brownsville Affair see Ann J. Lane, *The Brownsville Affair: National Crisis and Black Reaction* (1971).

The best biography of Taft, although too long, is Henry Pringle's two-volume, *The Life and Times of William Howard Taft: A Biography* (1939). For Taft's allies and supporters see Norman Wilensky, *Conservatives in the Progressive Era: The Taft Republicans of 1912* (1965). On the

Payne-Aldrich tariff and the Republican insurgents see Claude M. Bowers's old, but exciting, *Beveridge and the Progressive Era* (1932). Two more recent works on the Republican insurgents are more balanced, but less readable: John Braeman, *Albert J. Beveridge: American Nationalist (1971)* and Richard Lowitt, *George W. Norris: The Making of a Progressive, 1861–1912* (1963). The election of 1912 is covered by Amos R. E. Pinchot, *History of the Progressive Party, 1912–1916* (1958) and George Mowry, *Theodore Roosevelt and the Progressive Movement* (1946). Wilson's new freedom, and much else, is adeptly handled in Arthur Link's *Woodrow Wilson and the Progressive Era, 1910–1917* (1954).

5
Foreign Affairs through World War I

The "Great White Fleet," which President Theodore Roosevelt sent around the world in 1907–08. (The Bettmann Archive)

Foreign Policy under Roosevelt

The problems evoked by growth, complexity, wealth, and power that deeply influenced the course of domestic politics between 1900 and 1920 also affected America's relations with other countries. America did not become the world superpower it is today in those years, but during the administrations of Roosevelt, Taft, and Wilson, it took a giant step along the road that led to world-power status.

TR and the World

Roosevelt was a man temperamentally unfitted for leaving things alone. He suffered from motion sickness in both his private and his public life. The writer-historian Henry Adams, who knew him well, called him "pure act."

TR's activism extended far beyond the boundaries of his own country to encompass the world. At many points it was indistinguishable from bellicosity. William James noted that TR "gushes over war as the ideal condition of human society, for the manly strenuousness which it involves, and treats peace as a condition of blubberlike and swollen ignobility, fit only for huckstering weaklings."

Although seemingly obsessed with action, Roosevelt was a cosmopolitan and worldly man. As a child and youth he traveled abroad with his family. He had lived in Paris and Rome and studied German while staying with a family in Dresden. These contacts and experiences gave Roosevelt an ease in dealing with foreign rulers and diplomats unusual for Americans of the day. Yet TR deplored formality, even in diplomatic exchanges, and often communicated with ambassadors and visiting foreign statesmen during breakneck hikes through Washington's Rock Creek Park, while leaping over stone walls and streams.

During the 1890s TR had been a central figure in that small group of young Americans who deplored their country's diplomatic insignificance and favored a "large policy" of expanded American influence especially in the Caribbean and the Far East. Part of this attitude was the conviction that Americans were a superior people. This view not only influenced the literate elite; it was also widespread among ordinary Americans. As Mr. Dooley, Finley Peter Dunne's fictional philosophical Irish saloonkeeper remarked, "We're a gr-reat people. We ar-re that. An th' best iv it is, we know we ar-re." Although based on a reading of the country's democratic history, it also had racial overtones. Roosevelt was no crude "Nordic supremacist," but by and large he believed the Anglo-Saxon peoples superior to all others and somehow destined to rule the rest. However presumptuous, this was not simply self-seeking. It implied American duties as well as American rights, for a superior nation owed it to inferior ones to transmit democratic values and impose honest, efficient, and humane administration.

The Panama Canal

One of the first manifestations of Roosevelt's aggressive foreign policy was his handling of a Central American canal to connect the Atlantic and Pacific oceans.

For centuries such a project had been the dream of statesmen, merchants, and engineers, for it promised to correct a geographic mistake that mandated an immensely long sea voyage around Cape Horn to connect Atlantic with Pacific ports. In 1850 the United States and Great Britain had negotiated the Clayton-Bulwer Treaty in which the two countries agreed that any Central American canal would be jointly controlled, equally accessible to all users, and unfortified. Fifty years later, after the United States had acquired a small Caribbean and Asian empire, few Americans wished to remain tied to Britain's apron strings. Britain in the meantime, fearing the growing power of the aggressive German empire, sought improved relations with the United States. In 1901, after an initial impasse, the two countries agreed, in the second Hay-Pauncefote Treaty, to modify the Clayton-Bulwer agreement to permit the United States to build a canal alone and to fortify and defend it against enemies in time of war but to keep it open to all nations in peacetime and to charge equal tolls to all users.

Meanwhile, beginning in the 1880s, a private French company under the direction of Ferdinand de Lesseps, builder of the successful Suez Canal, had been pouring money into the construction of an interocean canal at Panama, where the ribbon of land connecting North and South America is narrowest. Almost $300 million was disbursed to scratch a channel through the jungles and mountains of the isthmus before the project went bankrupt, ruining thousands of French investors and creating a malodorous scandal.

Even before Roosevelt came to office, both an American firm interested in Nicaraguan route and the successor to the French company had hired lobbyists to induce Congress and other federal officials to accept their route and buy their assets. The two chief agents for the New Panama Canal Company were American lawyer William Nelson Cromwell and the Frenchman Philippe Bunau-Varilla, a major company stockholder. Cromwell's approach was direct: in 1900 he contributed $60,000 to the Republican presidential campaign fund. Bunau-Varilla mounted a propaganda barrage touting the route through Panama as the most direct, most practical, and cheapest—and one not subject, as the Nicaraguan, to the hazards of volcanic eruption.

In June 1902 Congress passed the Spooner Amendment authorizing Roosevelt to buy the assets of the New Panama Canal Company for $40 million and to acquire in perpetuity from Colombia, which then owned the province of Panama, a right-of-way across the isthmus. If Colombia agreed to these stipulations within a reasonable time, the canal would be built in Panama. If not, then the canal would be located in Nicaragua.

In January 1903 Secretary of State John Hay negotiated a treaty with the Colombian chargé in Washington, Tomás Herrán, promising his country a $10 million lump sum and $250,000 annually in return for a ninety-nine-year lease of a strip of Panamanian territory 3 miles wide on either side of the proposed canal. The Colombians, however, refused to ratify the Hay-Herran Convention on the grounds that the Americans had used undue pressure and had no right to sovereignty over any part of Colombia. Furthermore, the concession was worth at least $25 million.

Roosevelt might have turned to Nicaragua at this point, but the action of the Colombians had gotten his dander up. The people in Bogotá were "blackmailers," "bandits," and "contemptible little creatures," he shouted. They must not be allowed to hold up "one of the future highways of civilization." At one point he considered building the canal at Panama under an umbrella of American guns, but then decided that the plan presented to him by Cromwell and Bunau-Varilla to foment a revolution in Panama was a better idea.

In mid-October 1903 Bunau-Varilla met with a group of Panamanians anxious to secure the province's independence and paid them $100,000 to be used for bribes and to pay the costs of a proclamation of independence and a new constitution. Soon after, he visited Washington and extracted assurances from Hay and Roosevelt that American naval forces would intervene if the Colombians attempted to put down a revolt. On November 3, 1903, the day after the U.S.S. *Nashville* reached Panama, the rebels seized power from the local authorities, helped by a liberal distribution of New Panama Company gold to Colombian officials and Colombian troops. News reached Washington of the results in Panama a few days later and within hours the American government had recognized the new regime with Bunau-Varilla, a French citizen, as the new republic's foreign minister.

Several days after this the United States and the Republic of Panama negotiated the Hay–Bunau-Varilla Treaty granting full sovereignty to the United States over a 10-mile-wide "canal zone" in return for $10 million in gold plus $250,000 each year beginning nine years after ratification. Eventually the United States also signed over $40 million to the Morgan bank for the New Panama Canal Company. To this day it is not certain who ultimately got the $40 million.

The Building of the Canal   James Bryce, the British student of America, called the Panama Canal "the greatest liberty man has ever taken with nature." And in many ways it was—until our own era. Thirty-five thousand men worked for ten years cutting through the mountainous backbone of the isthmus and building mammoth lakes to provide water to fill the channel. The Canal commissioners moved millions of tons of earth and constructed enormous locks run by electric motors that alternately raised and lowered giant vessels hundreds of feet during movement from one ocean to the other. The cost was enormous for its day: $375 million.

Besides moving earth it was necessary to solve the horrendous health problems of working in the tropics. Fortunately by this time medical science had established that the mosquito was the carrier of the deadly malaria and yellow fever organisms. In 1904 the army dispatched Colonel William Gorgas, who conquered yellow fever in Havana after the Spanish-American War, to Panama to deal with the tropical diseases that had done so much to defeat the French. Gorgas and his team went on to clean up Panama's cities and eliminate malaria and yellow fever. Their work saved thousands of lives and, in fact, made the gigantic engineering feat possible.

The canal opened in 1914. Plans had been made for a major celebration; it was not to be. In August, the world exploded in the Great War, and the festivities were canceled. In the end, a cement carrier, the *Cristobal*, was the first ship to go completely through the Canal, to a perfunctory ceremony. Yet the giant enterprise had been successful and in later years would generate millions of dollars in tolls while enormously expediting world commerce. It also left behind a legacy of

One of the locks of the Panama Canal under construction.   (The Bettmann Archive)

Colombian resentment for which in 1921 the United States paid $25 million in compensation.

Roosevelt and the Caribbean

With the interocean canal underway, Roosevelt directed his attention to building up the navy. "It is contemptible for a nation. . . ," he announced, "to take positions which are ridiculous if unsupported by potential force, and then refuse to supply this force." Under his urging, in 1905, Congress provided funds for ten battleships, four armored cruisers, and a collection of other vessels. By 1909 the United States was the second-ranking naval power, behind Great Britain. Between 1907 and 1908 Roosevelt dispatched a flotilla of American battleships, the "Great White Fleet," to ports on virtually every continent to demonstrate America's new naval might. (See the photograph opening this chapter.)

Roosevelt, like many other Americans, considered the Caribbean an American lake, and did not hesitate to throw the country's weight around in that region. In 1901, as the price of ending the postwar American military occupation of their newly freed country, the Cubans agreed to the Platt Amendment pledging Cuba to enter into no agreement that would impair its sovereignty; never to incur financial obligations beyond its ability to pay; to allow the United States to intervene in Cuba to maintain law and order; and to lease or sell to the United States a naval coaling station on Cuban soil. The Platt Amendment in effect made Cuba a semiprotectorate of the United States.

America's Caribbean concerns went beyond Cuba. Most of the countries in the region were weak and unstable states, often unable to defend foreign residents against disorder or meet their debt obligations. These lapses often angered the European powers. In 1902, for example, Venezuela defaulted on its debts to Britain and Germany, and both nations imposed a blockade of its ports.

Although the United States did not intervene in this case, Roosevelt felt he could not allow Caribbean republics to continue to act irresponsibly while hiding behind the shield of the United States. In December 1904, following a debt default and threatened foreign intervention in the Dominican Republic, he announced his "Corollary" to the Monroe Doctrine. "Chronic wrongdoing," he stated,

> may in [Latin] America, as elsewhere, ultimately require intervention by some civilized nation, and in the Western Hemisphere the adherence of the United States to the Monroe Doctrine may force the United States, however reluctantly, in flagrant cases of such wrongdoing or impotence, to the exercise of an international police power.

On the basis of the Roosevelt Corollary, TR forced the Dominicans to accept American supervision of their national finances to guarantee honest tax collection and reduction of the Dominican debt. This was the first of many instances where in effect the Roosevelt Corollary would be applied to protect American interests at the expense of Latin American sovereignty. (See Figure 5–1.)

Roosevelt and the Far East

Roosevelt inherited the *Open Door* policy in the Far East from his predecessor, but he quickly made it his own. The Open Door was America's way to deal with the disintegration of China while avoiding the complexities, the moral perplexities, and the inconveniences incurred by the other powers. Other nations—Germany, Russia, Japan, and France—had long been taking advantage of China's turmoil under the Manchu rulers to annex pieces of the Celestial Empire and carve out spheres of exclusive economic influence for themselves. China's defeat in the Sino-Japanese War (1894–95) made the colonial powers even bolder. By the closing years of the nineteenth century it looked as if China would shortly fall under the total colonial dominion of the modern industrial nations, including Japan.

In both Britain and America there were defenders of China who admired Chinese civilization and deeply sympathized with the plight of the Chinese people. Leaders in both countries, moreover, viewed the other powers' predatory policies as likely to create rivalries and threaten their other far eastern interests. The two forces together—one charitable, the other self-serving—combined to produce the Open Door Policy, announced by Secretary of State John Hay in the fall of 1899 in a note to

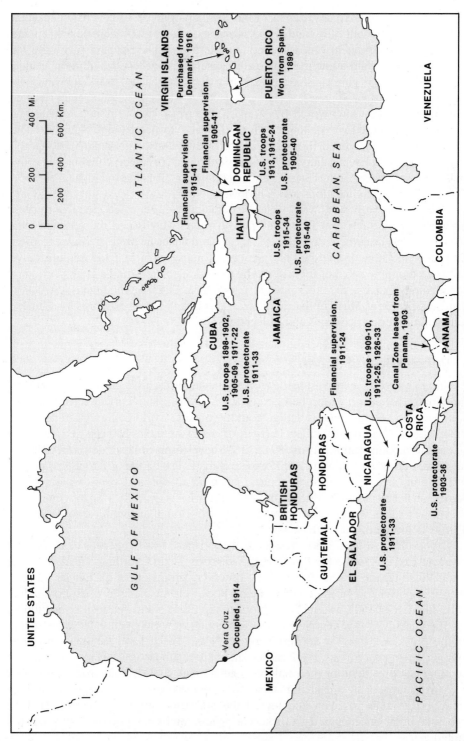

Figure 5–1   The United States in the Caribbean, 1898–1941

the governments of Germany, Russia, France, Britain, Italy, and Japan. The note took the form of a statement of hope that the addressed powers would agree to compete fairly with one another in China and not attempt to garner exclusive privileges for themselves and would allow the Chinese themselves to collect the imperial duties. Although the powers gave evasive answers, Hay declared that acceptance of the Open Door was "final and definitive."

One year later China would be plunged into chaos by the Boxer Rebellion, a bloody uprising aimed at expelling the "foreign devils" from the Celestial Empire. The anti-Western Boxers forced thousands of Europeans and Americans to flee to the safety of the Western legations in Beijing (Peking). To rescue their citizens, the powers, including the United States, sent 20,000 troops. This international army soon lifted the siege of the legations and put down the uprising.

Fearing that the powers would use the occasion to nullify the Open Door policy and wrest Chinese territory from the Manchu rulers, Hay issued the second Open Door note. This document declared that the United States favored "permanent safety and peace" in China and wished to "preserve Chinese territorial and administrative entity." In the same spirit of friendship, the United States returned a large portion of the indemnity that, like the other powers, it took from China for the Boxer destruction of life and property. Much of the money was earmarked for scholarships for Chinese students in American colleges and universities.

Roosevelt and Japan

America's growing interest in the Far East inevitably focused attention on relations with Japan. That island nation had been forced to abandon its policy of intellectual, diplomatic, and commercial isolation from the outside world by the American naval commander Commodore Matthew Perry in 1854 and thereafter had charged ahead on the road to modernization. From 1894 to 1896 a westernized Japan defeated China in war, seized Formosa (Taiwan) and Korea, and made itself a major far eastern power with a large army and a modern navy. Japanese troops had been a part of the international rescue force during the Boxer uprising. In 1902, Japan's emerging great-power status was comfirmed by a treaty with Britain allying the two nations in defense of the status quo in East Asia.

Roosevelt liked Japan and considered the Japanese less dangerous to China and American interests in the Far East than the Russians. Japan's startling defeat of Russia in the Russo-Japanese War of 1904–05, however, promised to tilt the far eastern balance of power too far the other way, and Roosevelt was pleased when both sides, in the summer of 1905, asked him to mediate the dispute and end further hostilities.

The resulting peace negotiations at Portsmouth, New Hampshire, were a triumph for the president; in 1906 Roosevelt won a Nobel Peace Prize for expediting the Russo-Japanese peace treaty. But it caused difficulties with Japan. The Japanese blamed the American president for their failure to get a financial indemnity from Russia and to secure control of all of Sakhalin Island. News of the peace terms tripped off violent anti-American riots in Japan and forced the authorities in Tokyo to put the U.S. Embassy under armed guard to protect it against mobs disappointed with Japan's limited gains.

Soon new troubles between the two nations erupted. For some years Japanese had been coming to Hawaii and the American West Coast as immigrants. Like the Chinese before them, they encountered racial prejudice and fears that they would undermine the American worker's living standards. The Japanese response to the Portsmouth Treaty now made matters worse. Soon the nation's more irresponsible newspapers, especially the Hearst press, were warning of a "Yellow Peril" across the Pacific, threatening the United States and its white civilization.

In the fall of 1906 the San Francisco Board of Education set off an international crisis by ordering the segregation of the city's Japanese children in a separate school. The Japanese government called the order a deliberate insult to the Japanese people and demanded that it be retracted. Roosevelt dispatched Secretary of Labor and Commerce Oscar Straus to California to investigate and concluded from the inspection that the order had, indeed, been a mistake. Yet the president had no control over the actions of the San Francisco school board and could do nothing to change the policy. In his December 1906 message to Congress, however, he called the segregation policy a "wicked absurdity," and hinted that if it were not changed he would consider strong measures. This mollified the Japanese but created a great outcry in California.

The issue was temporarily resolved when Roosevelt finally realized that the problem was not the schools but the steady flow of Japanese immigrants into California. By promising to screen out many of the Japanese, TR got the school board to rescind the segregation order. Between 1907 and 1908 Roosevelt negotiated a "Gentlemen's Agreement" with Japan. The Japanese government would not issue passports to Japanese manual workers who competed with American wage earners; the American government would not insult Japan by barring Japanese immigration completely, as it had Chinese in the 1880s.

One final attempt during the Roosevelt years to settle differences between Japan and America only produced later trouble. Roosevelt wanted to obtain Japanese acceptance of the Open Door policy, and to this end he negotiated the Root-Takahira Agreement of 1908. This document asserted that the two governments would support the status quo in the Pacific and the Open Door in China and that each would respect the Pacific possessions of the other. Roosevelt believed he had strengthened the integrity of China, but Japan claimed that the agreement endorsed its recent moves into China's loosely held Manchurian province. In effect Roosevelt had unintentionally weakened China and encouraged the territorial ambitions of Japan.

Taft and Dollar Diplomacy

For all its faults Roosevelt's vision of America's world role had its attractive aspects. His successor William Howard Taft, however, seemed incapable of viewing the world except as an economic opportunity for the United States. His foreign policy is often referred to as *Dollar Diplomacy*.

Manchurian Railroads

Both Taft and his secretary of state, Philander Knox, were lawyers, not diplomats, and neither knew much about foreign policy. Both sought to use the State Department to further American investment opportunities abroad and in the process made serious mistakes in their handling of international affairs. Their first error was to think that they could bolster the Open Door and Chinese sovereignty and at the same time advance the economic interests of American business.

In 1909 Knox tried to strengthen Chinese autonomy by securing an international loan so China could buy up all the foreign-owned railroads in Manchuria, its remote northern province. Russia and Japan, in particular, viewed the Manchurian railroads as the essential instruments of their economic penetration into north China, and Knox's efforts threatened both nations. Rather than enhancing Chinese independence, it brought together its chief adversaries in an even firmer agreement than before to divide Manchuria between them.

Knox's next move was to try to force the Chinese to accept American participation in an international consortium to build railroads in China proper. American financiers, however, were never very interested in the railroad scheme and went along with their government reluctantly. When Woodrow Wilson became president in 1913, he abandoned official American support and the bankers withdrew from the consortium.

Taft and Latin America

In Nicaragua Dollar Diplomacy showed its least attractive face. That country was ruled after 1893 by a ruthless strongman, José Santos Zelaya, who sought to extend his country's interests throughout Central America and believed the United States a major impediment to his goals. Zelaya tried to cancel a mining concession awarded to some Pittsburgh financiers and soon brought American wrath down on his head. Before long the United States was actively fomenting a revolution in Nicaragua. At the end of 1909 Zelaya resigned and fled the country. An extended period of disorder followed in Nicaragua, climaxing with the dispatch of American marines in 1912. Meanwhile, American capital poured into the country making it virtually an economic extension of the United States.

Wilson and the World

Woodrow Wilson was a much more perceptive and sensitive diplomatist than his predecessors. Of course he placed what he perceived as the nation's interests before other considerations, but he conceived of those interests in broader terms than either Roosevelt or Taft. As befitted the son of a minister, he had an idealistic vision of a world order governed by international law, of free exchange among nations, and of the right of subjugated peoples to national expression. The Wilson vision, however, was often naive and did not reckon with the complex and often brutal realities of international relations. It was also parochial. Wilson's world view was made in

America. It was of the world reconstructed on an American model of liberal capitalism, a model not shared by all people, everywhere.

Wilson's foreign policy, moreover, was at times not moral so much as moralistic. The president often sounded preachy and self-righteous, qualities that foreigners found offensive. Furthermore, he was stubborn. Throughout his life, Wilson had exhibited a pattern of digging in his heels when opposed and insisting on his way although the heavens threatened to fall.

Secretary of State Bryan

Wilson selected William Jennings Bryan as his secretary of state in payment for his support at the Baltimore Democratic convention. But the Nebraska Democrat proved to be a congenial choice. Like Wilson, he believed in America's mission to do good in the world and to serve as a model of international righteousness. Ironically, at times this attitude led to intrusions into other nations' affairs that foreigners found obnoxious and hypocritical.

One of Bryan's earliest and most characteristic actions was negotiating a series of treaties by which the signers agreed to submit disputes to investigatory commissions before resorting to war. Thirty of these "cooling off" treaties were signed including agreements with Great Britain, France, and Italy, although not with Germany. As realists pointed out, these were essentially meaningless; they deterred no one. Yet Bryan was always proud of this achievement. Bryan also withdrew State Department support from the Chinese railroad consortium favored by Taft and insisted that the United States abide by the equal treatment clause in the Hay-Pauncefote Treaty, although in 1912 Congress had exempted American vessels sailing from coast to coast from paying tolls. Wilson asked Congress to end the favoritism. After a hard fight he succeeded.

However sensitive to moral considerations in other parts of the world, Bryan and his chief were less scrupulous when it came to the Americas. Both men believed that they were acting for honorable ends, but the result was a policy of intervening in the affairs of the United States' neighbors to the south, which left a legacy of deep resentment.

By 1914 American intervention in the Caribbean–Central America area had become an almost annual event. In that year the Bryan-Chomorro Treaty, guaranteeing America's perpetual right to build another isthmian canal in Nicaragua in exchange for $3 million, virtually reduced that country to permanent dependency status. In 1915 U.S. marines landed in Haiti after a mob had hacked to pieces President Vilbrun Sam, a bloodthirsty tyrant, during the course of a revolt. The marines remained in charge of Haiti for several years. In 1916 marines landed in the Dominican Republic to put down the disorder that had followed an uprising against President Juan Jiménez. By the end of the year this operation had become a full-scale occupation of the country that continued until 1924.

Troubles in Mexico

Mexico was proof of the dangers of Wilsonian meddling in Latin American affairs. There in 1911 a revolution had toppled Porfirio Díaz, the strongman who had ruled for over thirty-five years. Díaz had brought his country stability and attracted a flood of foreign capital, including American investments in petroleum, copper, silver, and other metals. Foreign investment created a prosperous middle class of businessmen, ranchers, and professionals, although the country's vast mestizo and Indian majority remained submerged in poverty and illiteracy.

Díaz's overthrow was followed by near chaos. The dictator's first successor was an unstable visionary named Francisco Madero, who believed in invisible spirits. In February 1913 Madero was overthrown by General Victoriano Huerta, a brutal militarist, who promptly had his predecessor murdered.

Wilson came into office soon after and had to respond to the bloody events south of the border. Declaring in private that he would "not recognize a government of butchers," he recalled the American ambassador and refused to send another. Shortly after, he announced a policy of nonrecognition of governments that did not follow "orderly processes of just government based upon law, . . . [but] upon arbitrary or irregular force." Violating American diplomatic principles going back to Thomas Jefferson's day, Wilson, in effect, was passing judgment on the legality of other governments. It was a formula for trouble.

If Wilson expected to restrain Huerta, he was mistaken. In October 1913 Huerta threw 110 members of the Mexican parliament into jail and established a full-fledged military dictatorship. Wilson quickly moved to isolate Huerta diplomatically and was able to get the British to withdraw their support. "I am going to teach the South American republics [*sic*] to elect good men," he told the British representative in Washington.

When diplomatic pressure failed to topple Huerta, Wilson decided to support Huerta's new enemies: Venustiano Carranza, leader of the Constitutionalists, and Pancho Villa, a military chieftain, both of whom pledged to carry forward Madero's policies. In February 1914 Wilson lifted an embargo on arms shipments to Mexico, hoping that this would help Huerta's enemies.

Wilson soon reaped the harvest of his interventionism. In April 1914 some American sailors ashore in Tampico, Mexico, to pick up supplies for their ship stationed off the coast, were arrested by the Huertistas. Although they were soon released, the sailors' hotheaded commander, Admiral Henry T. Mayo, demanded the Mexicans apologize for the insult with a twenty-one gun salute of the American flag within twenty-four hours. Wilson agreed with Mayo's action but extended the time limit to a week.

Meanwhile word reached Washington that a German ship was about to land arms for Huerta at Vera Cruz. Wilson ordered the navy to occupy the city to prevent the arms from reaching the strongman. For three days American sailors and marines fought Huerta's troops on the streets of the city with casualties on both sides. Full-scale war with Mexico seemed certain.

Wilson had unintentionally put himself in a difficult position. If war came it would not be popular. Church groups, labor leaders, anti-imperialists, and even bankers were expressing dismay. Fortunately, the president was rescued by an offer by Argentina, Brazil, and Chile—the "ABC powers"—to mediate the dispute. Wilson gratefully accepted.

Pancho Villa and his forces in 1914.   (The Bettmann Archive)

The mediation commission met at Niagara Falls, Canada, for six months to consider Mexican problems. The delay enabled Wilson to withdraw American troops from Vera Cruz and increase his support of Carranza. In July Huerta finally resigned, leaving Carranza in control of Mexico City. But before long Carranza and Villa were at each other's throats, and Emiliano Zapata, an agrarian radical, entered the fray as a third party in the rivalry for control of Mexico.

Villa resented American support of Carranza and tried to bring the United States and the Carranza government to blows. In early 1916 he held up a Mexican train and massacred sixteen American mining engineers aboard. Soon after, he sent a raiding party across the border into New Mexico, and burned the town of Columbus, killing seventeen Americans. Wilson now ordered the army under General John J. Pershing to chase Villa into Mexico. Carranza approved the incursion, but the Mexicans did not like this violation of Mexican sovereignty. Mexican-American relations soon reached the breaking point once more. In February 1917 Wilson finally ordered Pershing back to his American base. Villa remained unpunished.

The next month the Mexican Congress officially installed Carranza as president of the republic and promulgated a new, liberal constitution. Wilson now extended full legal recognition of the Carranza government and sent a new ambassador to Mexico City. The crisis was over, but problems between the two nations would not be settled for another decade.

Wilson and the War in Europe

Wilson had ordered Pershing back across the border because the United States was on
the verge of joining the war that had been raging in Europe and around the world
since the late summer of 1914.

World War I (the "Great War") pitted the Central Powers—Germany and
Austria-Hungary, joined later by Bulgaria and the Ottoman Empire (Turkey)—against
the Triple Entente (the Allies), composed of Great Britain, France, Serbia, and Russia,
and joined subsequently by Italy and several smaller nations. (See Figure 5–2.) Its
trigger had been the August 1914 assassination by a pro-Serbian nationalist of
Archduke Franz Ferdinand, heir to the Austro-Hungarian throne. Egged on by its
German ally, Austria, determined to end Serbian nationalism's divisive effects on its
multinational empire, had attacked Serbia. The Serbs appealed to their Slavic big
brother Russia, which soon declared war on Austria, pulling in its ally, France.
Germany came to the aid of Austria and attacked France through Belgium, a nation
whose neutrality had been assured by international treaty in the 1830s. Germany's
violation of Belgian neutrality brought Britain into the fray on the side of France and

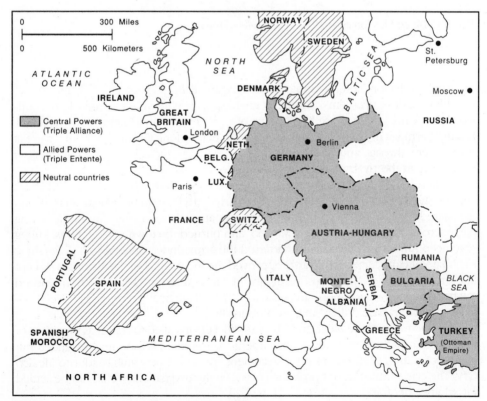

Figure 5–2   European Alliances in World War I

Russia. By early November the Allies and the Central Powers—and all their colonial dependencies—were locked in a worldwide struggle, the fiercest and most costly humanity had ever seen.

American Attitudes

The assassination of the Austrian archduke had caused scarcely a ripple in America. The event seemed remote, and the American press at first paid little attention to what seemed merely another Balkan crisis, one of many.

The snowballing big-power confrontation that followed attracted far more attention, of course, but many Americans continued to treat the events in Europe as distant, of no great concern to themselves or their nation. Most endorsed Wilson's neutrality proclamation of August 4, 1914, which declared that "the United States must be neutral in fact as well as in name, . . . impartial in thought as well as in action."

The mood of indifference and impartiality did not last very long. Americans had too much of an emotional stake in the events transpiring across the Atlantic. Millions of Americans were recent immigrants from Europe and retained loyalties that derived from their origins. Recent arrivals from Britain, France, and later Italy favored victory for the Allies. Many German-Americans cheered for the *Vaterland*. Recent immigrants also carried with them ancient animosities. Many Irish-Americans, for example, despised Britain, the oppressor of their homeland, and hoped to see her defeated. Jewish and Polish refugees from the czar's repressive regime had no reason to wish Russia victorious. The subjugated nationalities of Austria-Hungary, such as the Czechs, and those of Turkey, such as the Armenians, could only hope that defeat of the Central Powers would liberate their compatriots and bring self-rule.

And even among old-stock Americans there were barely submerged allegiances and affinities. Among some academics respect for German scholarship and culture was strong. Many midwestern farmers disliked British bankers. But these attitudes could scarcely match the affection for Britain. The American business and professional elite was strongly infused with Anglophilia, love of things British. They admired British manners, literature, and institutions and, to some degree, sought to imitate them in the United States.

Few Americans were more Anglophile than the president of the United States. Wilson profoundly admired British political institutions and in his first book, *Congressional Government,* expressed his preference for the parliamentary system over the American version of democracy. From the onset of hostilities, despite his pronouncements about neutrality, the president favored Allied victory. In August 1914 he told his brother-in-law that in the event of a German victory the "United States, itself, will have to become a military nation, for Germany will push her conquests into South America, if not actually into the United States."

Here Wilson was touching on an attitude that would deeply affect German-American relations between 1914 and 1917. Many informed Americans were suspicious of Germany's international ambitions. In recent decades imperial Germany had become a saber-rattling expansionist state with a powerful army, a world-class navy, and overseas colonies. Germany's militarism, especially its naval-building program, threatened Britain, which toward the end of the century had sought alliances in Europe to check Germany. The German danger also forced the British to turn to the United States, and in the twenty years preceding 1914 there had developed an informal *rapprochement* between the two countries marked by mutual concessions and international support. Britain acceded to America's goals in the Caribbean region. In return the United States, almost alone among the powers, avoided criticism of British actions against the Boers in South Africa during the Boer War of 1899–1902. Wilson's move to rescind the Panama Canal tolls exemption for American ships at Britain's behest was another sign of the change. By 1914 American policymakers had come to believe that outside the Western Hemisphere the status quo depended on continued preeminence of British imperial power. If Germany won, many influential Americans felt, the United States itself might be in danger.

Pro-Ally feeling was also a product of German conduct during the war itself. The kaiser's government was not the bestial tyranny of the later Nazis, but it *was* militaristic and indifferent to liberal, humane values. When Germany was criticized for violating the treaty preserving Belgian neutrality, German Chancellor Bethmann-Hollweg responded that the treaty was only a "scrap of paper." The occupation of most of small Belgium that followed further tarnished the German image. The Belgians defied the German authorities and some engaged in guerrilla attacks on German troops. In retaliation, the Germans executed hundreds of Belgian civilians and burned the Louvain University library. British propagandists made the most of German harshness and in fact blew it up to exaggerated proportions.

Neutral Rights

However strongly they endorsed one side or the other, most Americans hoped at first to stay out of the war. But they also demanded respect for America's rights as a neutral nation, and it was this issue that ultimately made peace impossible.

Americans had always insisted on an interpretation of international law that gave wide latitude for neutrals to trade in time of war. Except for contraband—goods such as guns and ammunition directly employed for fighting—this interpretation required that commodities carried aboard neutral vessels be allowed free shipment to belligerents. ("Free ships make free goods.") Blockades of enemy ports were allowable, but these had to be enforced by patrolling naval vessels that could stop and inspect neutral ships for contraband while protecting the lives of civilians and neutral citizens aboard them. They could not be mere "paper blockades"—declarations that a given enemy area was off-limits to neutral ships—for this would subject neutrals to extreme uncertainty and arbitrary attack.

If the war had been short, perhaps the United States could have made the belligerents accept its definitions of neutral rights. But after a series of spectacular German advances through Belgium and into northeastern France, the British and French forces stopped the German military steamroller. By early 1915 stalemate had developed on the western front, marked by bitter trench war—long periods of anxious inactivity punctuated by furious attacks in which thousands of men lost their lives charging massed artillery and deadly machine guns for gains of a few hundred yards.

By mid-1915 neither the Allies nor the Central Powers had much patience with America's assertion of neutral rights. The British by this time had declared a paper blockade of all German ports on the North Sea. They soon extended the contraband list to virtually everything, including food, that could remotely be of help to the enemy. They laid mines along major sailing routes forcing all neutral vessels to enter British ports to get safe sailing directions.

The Germans did not remain idle. Britain was an island nation that had relied for generations on foreign sources for food and raw materials and would soon become dependent on foreign arms and munitions as well. It was highly vulnerable to a naval blockade itself. Although Germany had challenged British naval suprem-acy before 1914, once hostilities began, the German surface fleet remained bottled up in the North Sea. This meant that any German counterblockade had to rely on the U-boat, a small, thin-skinned submarine that could easily evade the British navy and escape to the open sea. But such a vessel could not follow the normal rules of war that applied to surface cruisers: stopping vessels suspected of carrying contraband, providing for the safety of the crew and passengers, and towing captured civilian vessels into port for confiscation. The U-boat was only effective if it fired its torpedoes without warning, disregarding the safety of passengers and crew. In effect, the only way the Germans could counter the Allied blockade was by waging war against innocent civilians, tactics that could not help but outrage world—and especially American—opinion.

In February 1915 the German government announced that it would shortly begin unrestricted U-boat warfare against all enemy vessels found in a broad zone around the British Isles. Although the announcement exempted neutral vessels from the operation, Secretary of State Bryan replied that the Germans would be held to "strict accountability" for any American losses incurred.

Bryan was the most sincerely neutral high American official. He believed that Americans who traveled or shipped their goods on belligerent vessels should do so at their own risk; the American government should not protect them. Wilson disagreed. A major principle was at stake, "Once accept a single abatement of right," he declared, "and many other humiliations would certainly follow, and the whole fine fabric of international law might crumble under out hands piece by piece." This conclusion would have fateful consequences.

In May 1915, shortly after the strict accountability note was issued, a German submarine torpedoed and sank the British passenger liner *Lusitania* off the Irish coast. Almost 1200 lives, 128 of them American, were lost. Although the German Embassy in Washington had placed notices in the American press warning people to avoid traveling on belligerent ships, Americans were outraged. Editorials denounced the attack as "criminal," "bestial," "uncivilized," and "barbarous." "The torpedo that sank the *Lusitania*," declared the *Nation*, "also sank Germany in the opinion of mankind."

Wilson shot off a strong note of protest to the German government demanding a virtual end to submarine warfare against unarmed merchant vessels. In another note, he came close to threatening war if the Germans did not comply. Bryan wanted the president to soften his tone and when Wilson refused, Bryan resigned. He was succeeded by Robert Lansing, a man far more pro-British.

Left, the British liner *Lusitania* leaves New York on what proved to be its last voyage. Right, the warning Germany placed in American newspapers. (Both: The Bettmann Archive)

Meanwhile the German government dithered, unwilling to cripple its naval effort against Allied shipping but also reluctant to drive the United States into the Allies' arms. Then in August the British liner *Arabic* was sunk with the loss of two more American lives. Wilson was prepared to break relations with the German government, but on September 1 it issued the "*Arabic* Pledge" that "liners," would "not be sunk by our submarines without warning and without safety of the lives of noncombatants, provided that the liners do not try to escape or offer resistance."

Many loose strings remained. The German government had not yet apologized for the *Lusitania* attack or addressed itself to the issue of merchant vessels that did not carry passengers. But for the moment the crisis subsided.

The Battle for American Opinion

During the summer of 1915 the propaganda war reached a climax as both sides struggled to influence American opinion decisively. The Central Powers, despite help from Irish-American and German-American groups, had no expectation of winning America's active support; American neutrality seemed quite sufficient. The Allies could hope for more. Strong American help seemed possible, and even short of active military participation it could be decisive.

British propaganda sought to preserve the Allies' use of America as an arsenal and, if possible, actually bring the United States into the war. In the struggle for American minds the British and French had many advantages. The Allies controlled the Atlantic cables that brought most of the war news to the American newspaper reading public. They also could count on the similarity of political and social systems to encourage sympathy. The British, of course, spoke the same language as Americans both literally and figuratively. They understood American public opinion and usually managed to make the right appeal. One of their most effective instruments was the 1915 report by the respected former ambassador to Washington, James Bryce, about German atrocities in Belgium. This exaggerated document depicted the Germans as bestial "Huns" who had gone on a rampage of murder, rape, and destruction in the conquered country. Such a people and nation clearly deserved the condemnation of the whole civilized world.

The Germans could never match the British understanding of the American mind, but their effort to counteract the Allied propaganda barrage was marked by unnecessary ineptitude. For one thing they combined the drive to sway American opinion with feeble attempts to sabotage American industry. German agents planted bombs in factories producing war matériel for the Allies. They tried to foment strikes in munitions factories. Most of these operations were known to American intelligence through British agents planted in the German Embassy in Washington. The information was passed along to the American government and then published in the press to a great public outcry.

The most spectacular revelations of German misdeeds leaked when Dr. Heinrich Albert, a German agent, accidentally left his briefcase on the New York El while being trailed by an American intelligence agent. The material was handed over to Treasury Secretary William McAdoo, who gave it to the *New York World*.

At one time critics of American entrance into World War I charged that economic factors critically influenced American opinion. These factors should not be entirely dismissed.

Almost from the outset the British and French had been buying vast quantities of supplies in America. Initially they paid cash by liquidating their holdings of American government and commercial securities. As early as September 1914, however, Allied purchasing agents asked J. P. Morgan and Company to negotiate loans for them. At first the American government disapproved. Bryan refused to condone a $100 million loan to France as contrary to "the true spirit of neutrality," and the bankers backed off. By mid-1915 the administration had reconsidered, and the bankers were soon extending credit wholesale to the Allies. In addition many Americans bought Allied war bonds. These private loans continued after America's entrance into the war and were then supplemented by billions of dollars of government loans. By 1919, the combined Allied debt to American private citizens and the American government would total over $11 billion.

To some critics these loans made American foreign policy captive to the success of the Allies. As Allied war orders poured in, they argue, the American economy, in the doldrums in 1914, quickly recovered. Reluctant to prick the prosperity bubble and fearful that Allied defeat would endanger the vast American investment, the administration in effect made Americans partners with the Allies. Part of a larger arraignment that indicted all "the merchants of death"—the munitions makers and manufacturers as well as the financiers—this was a "devil theory" of the war's origins that found a congenial audience among American isolationists when endorsed by the Nye Committee of Congress in the 1930s.

But the truth is that the loans were more the *effect* of pro-Ally sentiment than the *cause*. Most of the country's bankers and business leaders were Anglophiles who needed no encouragement from profits to favor the Allies. The Wilson administration was also pro-Ally; Bryan was one of the few completely neutral officials of consequence in Washington. The administration could have withheld American loans to force the British and French to respect neutral trading rights, but their refusal to do so derived from their reluctance to impede the Allied cause rather than from fear of hurting the American economy if the loans were not forthcoming.

Peace versus War

The battle between outsiders over Americans' minds paralleled the struggle among Americans themselves over peace or war. In 1914 the European socialist parties had abandoned the cause of international working-class solidarity and heeded the call of patriotism. In all the belligerent countries socialist members of parliament voted for war appropriations. In the process they destroyed the world socialist organization, the Second International. American socialists, however, refused to abandon the traditional socialist skepticism of capitalist wars. These wars, they held, were over competing imperialist claims in which the world proletariat had no real stake. Besides the socialists, the American opponents of war included the Quakers, members of other traditional "peace churches," secular pacifists, and some progressives. To the progressives, even to those who were not outright pacifists, militarism was anathema, associated in their minds with bankers, big business, the armor-plate monopoly, and imperialism.

There was also a war party, and it was headed by none other than Theodore Roosevelt. TR seemed even more belligerent as an ordinary citizen than as president. He and his colleagues worked through the National Security League and the American Rights Committee, groups that made "preparedness" their slogan, although "intervention" might have been a more honest one. The preparedness proponents demanded that the United States arm itself for war on the ostensible grounds that such preparation would prevent actual conflict.

At first Wilson opposed the preparedness campaign, but after the *Lusitania* sinking he recognized that it must be appeased. In July 1915 he asked his war and navy secretaries to prepare beefed-up military budgets and informed Congress that he intended to submit requests for new military appropriations.

The plan as revealed in November called for $500 million for the navy, a larger army, and a new defense force of 400,000 soldiers to replace the national guard. In Congress and the country at large the plan was bitterly fought by many of the progressives, including Bryan, La Follette, Oswald Garrison Villard, and Jane Addams. The progressives almost succeeded in defeating it in Congress despite a presidential speaking tour through the isolationist Midwest designed to change public opinion. In the end Wilson got much less than he wanted for both the army and the navy, and the country would pay the price after April 1917.

Further Difficulties

For some months after the *Arabic* Pledge German-American relations superficially improved. Yet Wilson remained deeply suspicious of German intentions and feared that a diplomatic break over the *Lusitania* might still be unavoidable.

During this period Colonel Edward M. House, Wilson's close friend and adviser, concluded that the time had come to force the belligerents to make peace with no gains for either side. In January 1915 House had gone to Europe on a similar mission, but the effort had failed. In October the colonel prodded the president into trying once more, this time with the promise of American intervention on the side of the Allies if the Germans refused to negotiate. With the president's approval, House wrote British Foreign Minister Sir Edward Grey that "if the Central Powers were still obdurate, it would probably be necessary for us to join the Allies and force the issue." It was Wilson who had inserted the word "probably."

House visited Europe in January 1916 to speak to both sides. He could not budge either. He reported these discouraging results back to his chief but did not tell Wilson he had promised the French that if the Allies appeared to be "losing ground" the United States would "intervene." House later claimed that he only meant diplomatic intervention, but this does not seem credible.

In any event, a German-American crisis was averted when, in February, the kaiser's government finally expressed regret for the loss of American life in the *Lusitania* sinking and agreed to pay an indemnity. The Germans refused to concede the illegality of the attack, however, since that would have denied them the use of the submarine weapon. Yet the apology and reparations were enough for the moment to satisfy the American government.

Then, on March 24, a German submarine torpedoed and sank the French channel steamer *Sussex* with eighty casualties. On April 18 Wilson denounced German attacks on all shipping as "utterly incompatible with the principles of humanity . . . [and] the long-established and incontrovertible rights of neutrals." If Germany did not cease its attacks on unarmed merchant and passenger ships, the United States would break diplomatic relations. Although the German generals and admirals demanded rejection of this note, in the end the kaiser made the decision to give in to Wilson, and on May 4 the German government gave the *Sussex* Pledge: hereafter submarine commanders would observe the rules of search and visit before sinking merchant vessels both inside and outside the war zone around Britain and France. But the U-boat captains would abide by this rule only if the United States in turn forced the British to abide by international law in their blockade tactics. Most Americans, despite the qualifier, hailed the *Sussex* Pledge with relief. The crisis eased.

But as one end of the Allied-Central Powers see-saw went up, the other went down. During the months following the *Sussex* Pledge, relations with Britain worsened. At the end of April 1916 the British brutally crushed the Easter Rebellion mounted in Dublin by Irish nationalists with the help of the Germans. In August they hanged the Irish leader, Sir Roger Casement, and several of his followers. Irish-Americans were predictably outraged, but even pro-British Americans were shocked. "The Dublin executions have done more to drive Americans back to isolation," wrote *The New Republic*, "than any other event since the war began."

Matters were made still worse by the July publication by the British of a "black-list" of almost ninety American firms charged with helping the Central Powers. No British subject would be allowed to do business with these firms in any way. The president threatened to send an ultimatum to London but in the end settled for a milder protest.

The Election of 1916

By now a presidential election was fast approaching and peace or war promised to be a major issue. The Democrats, as we have seen (Chapter 4), were initially divided, with many angry at the president for his limited vision of progressive possibilities. Other Democrats, including Bryan and Champ Clark, considered Wilson's support of preparedness too great a concession to the war party. Another problem for the Democrats was that there would not in all likelihood be a separate Progressive party ticket to draw off votes from the Republicans, and even if there were, Roosevelt, having deserted the party he helped found, would not be its candidate. As we saw, Wilson's response was to launch a second wave of progressive legislation to keep the liberals on his side.

The campaign, however, ultimately turned on the war or peace issue. Wilson won easy renomination, despite the Democratic grumbling. The Republicans nominated Supreme Court Justice Charles Evans Hughes, the former progressive governor of New York. Both conventions showed a deep yearning for peace, the delegates cheering propeace speeches and propeace platform planks.

During the campaign the Democrats paraded as the party of peace and progress. The president reminded the independent progressives of how much his party had done to further the decade-long reform movement, and they flocked to the Democratic banner. Virtually all who had gone with the Bull Moose in 1912 chose the donkey over the elephant in 1916. Wilson also charged that the Republicans were the war party and that the election of Hughes would mean American intervention in Mexico and Europe. "I am not expecting this country to get into war," he told visitors to his summer home at Shadow Lawn, New Jersey. Everywhere the Democrats used the slogan, "He Kept Us Out of War!" and attacked the Republicans, especially Roosevelt, as warmongers.

Meanwhile the Hughes campaign floundered. Despite his progressive record as governor, Hughes became identified with the Republican Old Guard. He was also embarrassed by the support of German-Americans who considered him more friendly to the fatherland than Wilson. Wilson capitalized on this association by denouncing "hyphenate" voters—foreign-born citizens who were supposedly more loyal to their native lands than to their adopted country. To top it all, Hughes blundered badly in California by failing to meet with progressive Republican governor Hiram Johnson when both men were at the same hotel.

Yet the results were in doubt till the very end. The early returns on election night showed that Hughes had swept the East. Wilson went to bed at ten convinced that he would not be president come March 5. But then the western returns began to narrow the gap and in the end pushed Wilson over the top by a tiny electoral majority of 23 and a popular majority of 700,000. Observers noted that he might have lost California and the election if Hughes had not snubbed Hiram Johnson, but scholars are more inclined to credit Wilson's victory to the peace appeal and the final burst of progressive legislation that nailed down the support of former Bull Moosers.

The Break with Germany

During the weeks following the election, the British attempted to force neutral shippers to accept new admiralty rules that severely hurt trade. The American government once more protested. But in the meantime a series of sinkings by German submarines stretched the *Sussex* Pledge to its limits.

In December the Germans launched a peace offensive with terms so outrageous that there was no possibility the Allies would accept them. Simultaneously they took the plunge and authorized unrestricted shoot-on-sight submarine warfare against all shipping—military or civilian, Allied or neutral—if engaged in trade with enemies of the Central Powers. The German leaders knew this would probably bring the United States into the war, but they had concluded that America was already doing as much for the Allies as possible and formal hostilities would make little difference.

The announcement of unrestricted submarine warfare was not made until January 31, however; meanwhile Wilson had gone before Congress to talk about his hopes for the future world. The president called for "a peace without victory," the equality of all nations, freedom of the seas, and world disarmament—all guaranteed by a League of Nations. The speech, although by a leader of a nation still neutral, sent a surge of hope through many war-weary hearts in Europe.

A week later came the announcement of unrestricted U-boat warfare. After February 1, the kaiser's government announced, German submarines would sink without warning all ships, Allied and neutral, found in specified zones around Great Britain, France, and Italy and in the eastern Mediterranean. One American passenger ship would be allowed to travel between New York and Britain each week if it carried no contraband and was conspicuously marked.

On February 3 Wilson announced to a joint session of Congress that the United States had broken diplomatic relations with Germany. He expressed a desire, however, to avoid outright hostilities with the German government. Then on February 25 Wilson received news from London that goaded him into action. On that day Ambassador Walter Hines Page transmitted a note intercepted by the British from German Foreign Secretary Alfred Zimmermann to the German minister in Mexico. The minister was to propose to the Mexican government that if the United States and Germany went to war, Germany and Mexico would establish an alliance. Mexico would declare war on the United States and in the event of victory would receive back "the lost territories" of Texas, New Mexico, and Arizona. Mexico would also invite Japan to join the alliance.

The day after receipt of the Zimmermann telegram Wilson asked Congress for authority to arm American merchant ships and for undefined additional power to protect them against attack. Most congressmen were willing to grant Wilson the authority he requested, but a small group of midwestern isolationists, including La

Follette and George W. Norris (a Republican from Nebraska), refused to comply. Wilson then released the Zimmermann telegram to the newspapers in hopes of rallying public opinion behind the ship-arming bill. The House quickly gave him what he wanted, but the La Follette–Norris group in the Senate—called by the president "a little group of willful men"—filibustered the bill to death.

Frustrated by Congress, Wilson proceeded to arm American merchant ships on his own executive authority. Overt acts of war by Germany were not long in coming. On March 18 German submarines sank three American merchant vessels without warning with heavy loss of life.

The Great War for Democracy

On April 2, at 8:30 in the evening, President Wilson appeared before a special joint session of Congress and read his message calling for a declaration of war against Germany. Germany's contempt for American rights, he told the legislators, allowed him no other course. Wilson put the blame for war squarely on the submarine policy of Germany, especially on the unrestricted attacks begun on February 1. Yet the United States, he declared, would not be fighting for itself alone. We fight, he said, for all mankind, for "the vindication of right, of human right," against "autocratic governments backed by organized force." The struggle ahead promised to be a "fiery trial," but "the right" was "more precious than peace." The United States would be fighting "for democracy, for the right of those who submit to authority to have a voice in their own Government, for the rights and liberties of small nations, for a universal dominion of rights by a concert of free peoples as shall bring peace and safety to all nations and make the world itself free at last."

On April 4 the Senate voted for war 82 to 6; two days later the House concurred 373 to 50. The United States was now a belligerent in the most colossal war the world had ever known.

America's entrance into World War I made a crucial difference, a fact recognized by the cheering crowds in London, Paris, and Rome. Over 4.7 million men—and a few thousand women—entered the armed forces, and over 2 million were sent to France. About 1.4 million Americans saw active service against the Germans on the western front, and their addition of new blood alongside war-weary French and British forces helped tip the battlefield balance. The American navy also played a vital role, helping to rout the U-boats and guaranteeing safe delivery of millions of soldiers and vast quantities of vital freight to the front lines. America's entrance also had a powerful psychological effect. It restored Allied confidence and persuaded many Germans that victory was no longer possible.

Military Mobilization

The enormous American presence in France by the summer of 1918 was an impressive accomplishment. No one had foreseen it, not even the Allies. At first it had not seemed necessary for the administration to commit masses of American soldiers to the combat zone. But by the fall of 1917, after the revolution in Russia against the czar and the near collapse of the Italian front against Austria, Wilson concluded it would be necessary to send a major American Expeditionary Force (AEF) to France.

The nation did not rely on volunteers but, as in the Civil War, turned to a draft to raise the needed manpower. This time, however, the administration of the draft act (the Selective Service Act of 1917) was more democratic than fifty years before. All men twenty-one to thirty years old were ordered to appear at one of 4000 polling places to register on June 7. Each man was given a number. Six weeks later in the first of a series of lotteries these numbers were randomly drawn to determine in what order the men would be inducted after they passed medical examinations. Exemptions or deferments were awarded by local draft boards, composed of "neighbors and friends," for humanitarian reasons or because the registrant was needed by some vital war industry. Inevitably, there were injustices, yet compared with the Civil War draft that allowed men to buy their way out or find a substitute, the selection process seemed fair.

The draftees—along with the many volunteers—were sent off to thirty-two different camps for orientation and training. Each was given $25 a month, half of which had to be allotted to his wife and children if the enlisted man had any. Although low by civilian standards, the pay made American soldiers the richest in the world.

The American "doughboys" (the word apparently derives from the buttons on the soldiers' uniforms, which resembled dough cakes) were cosseted in other ways, too. Their spiritual needs were attended to by hundreds of military chaplains. The government also sought to protect them from the temptations of military life. Prodded by the prohibitionist lobby, the War Department closed saloons and liquor stores close to army posts and training camps. It also forced local authorities to shut down red light districts where prostitutes plied their trade. In September 1917 Secretary of the Navy Josephus Daniels compelled the mayor of New Orleans to close Storyville, the city's vice district. This act not only dispersed the prostitutes and the madames, it also scattered the jazz musicians who played in the bordellos, disseminating their music to new communities where it quickly took root.

The War Department under Newton Baker, the warmhearted former progressive mayor of Cleveland, was not an efficient agency. Baker's administration of the soldier-training process was a success, but he was slow to get rid of squabbling, incompetent bureaucrats. The War Department's chaos seriously held up supplies.

The Navy Department under Daniels, who was assisted by the young New York politician Franklin Roosevelt, was better run. A woman's rights champion, Daniels organized female service branches, the "yeomanettes" and the "marinettes." He also forced the admirals to surrender the idea of fleet actions against the Germans and to see that the navy's first task was to guarantee the arrival in France of the AEF and the enormous mass of matériel and supplies needed to support it.

For a time it seemed as if the war at sea would go against the Allies. In 1917 German U-boats sank almost 6.3 million tons of Allied shipping; had these losses continued it would have been disastrous. To meet the U-boat threat, the Americans adopted the convoy system of destroyer escorts to accompany slow merchant ships and troop ships to help ensure their safe arrival at British and French ports. The convoy system cut Allied-U.S. losses drastically.

Marshaling Resources

The gigantic military effort required an organization of resources unprecedented in the country's history. Secretary of the Treasury William McAdoo had to raise $24 billion to pay America's direct costs and another $11.2 billion for wartime and immediate postwar loans to the Allies. With the typical federal budget during peacetime running at less than $750 million annually, sums such as these seemed extraordinary.

McAdoo was equal to the task. The Treasury was able to raise taxes, which yielded almost $9 billion. Much of the increase came from a new income tax permitted by the Sixteenth Amendment adopted in 1913. The rest of the budget—two-thirds of the whole—was met by borrowing. McAdoo sought to tap the savings and income of ordinary citizens. Through posters, advertisements, and mass rallies the Treasury urged citizens to buy government bonds. Political leaders and show-business celebrities exhorted the public to invest its money to defeat the awful Hun. McAdoo mobilized the children of America by offering twenty-five "thrift stamps" that could eventually be converted into bonds. The Treasury hoped to soak up excess purchasing power created by war industries and at the same time arouse the public's patriotic fervor. It succeeded better at the second than at the first; consumer prices rose some 40 percent between 1917 and 1918. Yet the job was accomplished.

Herbert Hoover, a millionaire mining engineer who had administered American war relief to the hungry people of German-occupied Belgium, took charge of the food program. Under the Lever Act of August 1917 Hoover was given a broad range of powers to control the production, marketing, and conservation of food. But the food administrator chose to launch a voluntary effort under the slogan: "Food Will Win the War—Don't Waste It." Hoover and his aides propagandized for the "clean dinner plate." They proclaimed wheatless and meatless days. They promulgated twelve rules for restaurants meals, including bread only after the first course, sugar served only in cubes, a half ounce of butter per diner, and only one kind of meat. The Hoover office supplied farm journals with slogans and space-fillers: "Food Is Sacred. To Waste It Is Sinful"; "Wheatless Days in America Make Sleepless Nights in Germany"; "Serve Beans By All Means." Besides conserving, Hoover tried to increase output. His Grain Corporation bought up all wheat produced at record high prices and so encouraged farmers to increase their acreage. In 1918, despite climatic difficulties, the wheat crop soared from 640 million bushels to over 920 million.

McAdoo's and Hoover's efforts had consequences beyond the war effort. Both employed new techniques of public relations and accustomed Americans to a marketing approach that was commercially used, and abused, in the following years. McAdoo's bond sales also familiarized ordinary Americans with investments in securities, and Hoover's propaganda introduced many homemakers to good nutrition practices and improved the American diet.

But more important than food and finance were ships, arms, and munitions, and here American performance was mediocre. The fault lay not in the inadequacy of the American economy, but in the failure to start rearming in 1915 or 1916 and the lack of an overall war production plan.

Patriotic businessmen descended on Washington in droves as soon as war was

This poster was part of Herbert Hoover's program during World War I to increase food production. (Herbert Hoover Presidential Library)

HELPING HOOVER IN OUR U. S. SCHOOL GARDEN

declared offering to work for a "dollar a year" to get war matériel moving to the battlefront. Many were taken on but until the spring of 1918 they worked at cross-purposes, often competing for scarce labor and raw materials.

The shipbuilding program, essential to offset U-boat losses, was not a conspicuous success. After precious months of delay it was placed in the charge of steel magnate Charles M. Schwab, head of the Fleet Corporation. Schwab built several hundred new shipyards, including the mammoth Hog Island facility near Philadelphia that employed 34,000 workers. He planned to launch a ship every other day from Hog Island, but unfortunately the first vessel did not leave the ways until August 5, 1918. Three months later the war ended. The Allies in the end found the shipping they needed, but much of it came from confiscating German vessels stranded in the United States by the war and by renting or purchasing neutral tonnage, rather than from new construction.

Most other industrial products needed for the troops, such as planes, tanks, vehicles, artillery, rifles, shells, powder, and many other items, were also produced in quantities that were too little and too late. Not until March 1918 did Wilson, a man with little administrative ability himself, appoint a director of the War Industries Board to coordinate the industrial push. The president chose Bernard Baruch, a Wall Street speculator and major Democratic financial contributor, and he proved more adept at public relations and self-advertisement than at getting the goods flowing. Baruch had to struggle with the army over procurement and had little time to bring order and method into the production of war matériel before the fighting stopped.

The army did acquire enough rifles and machine guns, but the country could never supply its artillery needs, and the AEF fought largely with French cannon. Tank production was another fiasco. Not until the summer of 1918 did the Ford Motor Company begin to produce six-ton American tanks and none ever got to France. The re-cord with planes was almost equally dismal. Two American engineers designed an excellent airplane engine, but the commander of the AEF, John Pershing, could not make up his mind what sort of air force he wanted, and the Liberty engine kept being redesigned to suit his whims. All told, 4300 of these engines went overseas, but few were installed in American-built planes. In fact only a thousand or so of these planes were shipped to France. American pilots relied on the British and the French for equipment.

The Home Front

The war was a period of buoyant prosperity for most Americans. The draft created an acute labor shortage that pushed up real wages very rapidly and greatly increased the power of the unions. Despite this additional muscle, under the leadership of Samuel Gompers the unions exercised restraint, and there were few serious labor stoppages. Because so much of the government's expenditures were paid for by borrowing, prices, as we saw, rose sharply. These increases helped offset wage gains, but they encouraged farmers to expand production and increase vital food and fiber output.

Women and African-Americans

The wartime labor shortage benefited women and African-Americans. Many women were drawn into the labor force to work in the factories and shipyards. After the fighting ceased most of these left the job market. But the war experience made more women familiar with working outside the home and helped move the country further along the path to the modern dual-sex labor force.

The war affected African-Americans in many ways. Labor shortages accompanied by the precipitous drop of European immigration opened new work opportunities for black people. Between 300,000 and 400,000 African-Americans moved from the rural South to Chicago, Cleveland, Pittsburgh, Philadelphia, and other northern industrial cities. Wearing faded wash dresses and overalls, lugging sacks and cardboard suitcases, and carrying squawking chickens and pigs in crates or underarm, these internal, native-born "immigrants" were even more unprepared for life in the big industrial cities than the eastern Europeans who had poured through Ellis Island during the previous generation. The African-American northern press tried to help these newcomers cope with life in their new communities, but many of them were illiterate and could not absorb the message.

Employers of African-American industrial workers were happy to have them, but few other white northerners welcomed the newcomers. In 1917 East St. Louis was the scene of a bloody race riot fueled by resentment of African-American workers at a war factory. Forty blacks died. In the summer of 1918 a total of twenty-three blacks and fifteen whites lost their lives in another riot in Chicago. The Germans used the wave of brutal racism to stir up antiwar sentiment among African-Americans, but however justified black grievances were, the propaganda effort failed.

Over 360,000 African-Americans served in the nation's armed forces during the war. But they did not serve as equals. The military branches were racially segregated, like so many other sectors of American life. In the training camps, especially in the South, black enlisted men were treated badly by white officers. Off base they were often mistreated by white civilians. In Houston, Texas, a police raid on a soldier dice game led to a riot during which four policemen died. Thirteen black soldiers were hanged. At first the army made no provision to train African-American officers, but under the prodding of the NAACP it opened a black officer-training camp near Des Moines. All told, only 1,200 African-Americans received commissions, about one-sixth their proportionate number.

The policy of discrimination followed black troops overseas. The army tried to use black soldiers exclusively as laborers. The NAACP objected, and again under its prodding the army established several all-black combat divisions, which it then used badly. Nevertheless several African-American units acquitted themselves with distinction.

Intolerance

The treatment of African-Americans was only part of the upwelling of intolerance and bigotry on the home front. The war unleashed a wave of intellectual intolerance and fanatical conformism that had been largely absent during the progressive years. Although in some ways its antithesis, these attitudes nevertheless borrowed the progressives' crusading zeal and acceptance of big government.

Wilson was in part responsible for the intolerance that burst forth. The president had never been easy with people who opposed him, and now that he had brought America into a momentous struggle for the future of mankind, he could brook no disagreement. At a Flag Day ceremony he declared that "force, force to the utmost; force without stint or limit," must be used against both the foreign and domestic enemies of the United States. Those disloyal to the country must be cast down "in the dust."

This harsh response was incorporated into four measures passed by Congress during 1917 and 1918. The first, the Espionage Act (1917), imposed severe penalties on those convicted of aiding the enemy, obstructing military recruiting, or causing anyone to refuse duty in the armed forces. It also empowered the postmaster general to exclude from the mails publications found treasonable or seditious. The Trading with the Enemy Act (1917) allowed the president to establish censorship of publications and letters from abroad and of the foreign-language press in the United States. The Sedition Act (1918) forbade "printing, writing, or publishing any disloyal, profane, scurrilous, or abusive language" about the government or the armed forces. The Alien Act (1918) allowed the government to deport alien radicals who advocated violent overthrow of the government or assassination of public officials.

Armed with this formidable arsenal of repressive weapons, Postmaster General Albert Burleson and other federal officials declared war against dissenters. Burleson rescinded the mailing privileges of the socialist papers the *New York Call,* the *Milwaukee Leader,* and *The Masses.* Under the Espionage Act the government sentenced socialist leader Victor Berger to twenty years in prison and Eugene V. Debs, the perennial Socialist candidate for president, to ten years in jail for supposedly discouraging men from registering for the draft. Federal authorities also arrested, tried, and convicted 200 members of the Industrial Workers of the World. State and local authorities also clamped down on radicals and suspected traitors. In Minnesota the Republican governor ordered the head of the gadfly Nonpartisan League, Arthur Townley, indicted for sedition. In Los Angeles a liberal minister was sent to jail and fined $1200 for declaring that he preferred the ideas of radicals to those of the local Merchants and Manufacturers' Association. In February 1918 the Montana legislature passed a sedition act even harsher than the federal government's.

The intolerance went beyond laws and repressive officials. Everywhere vigilantes took action against suspected radicals or antiwar proponents. Accused disloyalists were beaten and insulted. Citizens of Germany or Austria living in the United States were abused and many were threatened with expulsion. Almost everything German came under unthinking attack. Superpatriot organizations such as the National Security League and the American Defense Society demanded that German—and all languages other than English—be forbidden on the streets and excluded from the schools. Oscar Ameringer, a German-born socialist editor, later described the "sweetless, wheatless, meatless, heatless and perfectly brainless days," when people "broke Beethoven's records, boycotted Wagner's music, burned German books, painted German Lutheran churches," and hanged a German Mennonite preacher in Illinois.

The Creel Committee

Much of the hysteria was a product of George Creel's Committee on Public Information, organized by the government soon after the war declaration to mobilize public opinion and fire up morale for the days of struggle to follow. Creel was a progressive editor from Denver who believed that truth was the best antidote to antiwar or anti-American feelings. Creel's committee mobilized the talents of 75,000 amateur orators to deliver four-minute talks on why the country was fighting (for democracy), what the enemy was like (bestial), and how to help the war effort (by working hard, conserving food, and not spreading rumors). It recruited scholars to defend the Allied cause and attack the enemy. It mobilized artists to draw recruiting posters, it beat the drums for food conservation, and it warned citizens to keep the enemy from learning military secrets. Creel was opposed to the irresponsible spreading of anti-German propaganda, but his committee helped foment some of the brutal intolerance of the war period.

The War Front

Fifty-three thousand Americans died in battle in World War I, 204,000 were wounded, and another 63,000 soldiers died from disease. These human costs were a tiny fraction of the losses sustained by Russia, France, Great Britain, Germany, and Austria-Hungary, each of which lost a million men or more. Yet the American militlary contribution, as noted, was critical to Allied victory.

Wilson had appointed John J. ("Blackjack") Pershing, leader of the effort against Pancho Villa, as commander of the American Expeditionary Force. Pershing arrived in France in June 1917, followed soon after by a small detachment of American troops from the regular army. The British and French commanders demanded that the untried Americans be distributed in units among their own men to fill gaps, but Pershing refused. The AEF, he insisted, would not be an auxiliary force for the Allies; it would be a distinct and separate command under its own officers.

Pershing's views prevailed and the American military performed in France as a distinct enterprise. It was a mixed performance. The AEF appeared on the scene when Allied morale was at a nadir. Britain and France had been fighting a frustrating and demoralizing trench war against a stubborn and skilled enemy. There had been many attempts to end the stalemate on the western front—including the first use of tanks and poison gas—but nothing had worked. Thousands of men had died in fruitless attacks on impregnable positions. To make matters worse, in March 1917 the czar's government in Russia was overthrown by a revolution. Then in November the radical Bolsheviks seized power from the Russian liberals and in early 1918 negotiated a humiliating peace with Germany. It now seemed likely that Germany would be able to transfer millions of men from the Russian front to the west to break the military impasse.

The first real test of American military prowess came in March 1918 when the Germans, reinforced by divisions from the Russian front, attacked the British at St.-Quentin and pushed a deep salient to within fifty miles of Paris. They soon shifted their attack southward to the region held by the French. The weary *poilus* threatened to crack until the American First Division was rushed into the line at Cantigny and stopped the Germans from breaking through. It was at Cantigny that the Germans learned that the raw American soldiers were brave and resourceful. It was a sobering experience.

The next important American engagement took place at Château-Thierry in June when the still-attacking Germans once again threatened to break through to Paris. The Americans sought to plug the hole with the Fourth Brigade of marines and the Second Army Division. At Belleau Wood the soldiers and marines walked singing into enemy fire and suffered thousands of casualties. But they stopped the German advance.

By mid-July the Allies and the Americans were themselves on the offensive with the Americans supplying much of the punch. The Allied-American Aisne-Marne offensive lasted for two weeks and pushed the Germans back decisively. In his memoirs German commander Erich Ludendorff described August 8 as the day when Germany lost the war. The reduction of the German-held St.-Mihiel salient in

READING 5

A Firsthand Account of War

Belleau Wood in June 1918 was the first major World War I battle fought primarily by American troops. The brunt of the German spring drive to break through to Paris and win the war fell on the marines attached to the U.S. First Army Division. The account below of a few hours of mayhem was written by Elton E. ("Slim") Mackin, a private in the Fifth Marine Regiment who, like most of his comrades, had never seen battle before.

The garish flare of a star-shell, blasting the deep gloom, brought into relief a file of replacements cautiously groping their way along the front opposite Torcy, and gave to each his first view of No Man's Land [the area between the opposing trenches] at night.

In the blinding light every man froze in his tracks. Rigid, their figures merged with the shadows of the wood that no enemy eye might detect movement among them. Since early dark these green troops had been making their way toward the firing line. Now, with night half gone, they were filtering through the trees along the crest of a ridge to take position in that thin line of shallow trenches and fox-holes which constituted the only barrier between Paris and the German drive. . . .

[At dawn] a distant gun barked and immediately after came a screaming roar followed by a flash—an explosion. There was a spatter of falling fragments among the trees, and somewhere near at hand, an anguished voice cried out in pain. As though by signal, entire batteries took up the chorus—the clatter of a machine gun—another—and the rising tide of sound merged into a crescendo that stifled thought and, for a moment, paralyzed all motion. Shrapnel rained upon the ridge. A running figure dashed along the line with a yell to take cover. Men sought shelter behind half-finished mounds of earth and hugged the ground. Whole trees crashed down as heavy shells shook and jarred the earth. . . . There were cries for "First aid, First aid," and other cries—wordless, terrible cries of men in agony.

Figures moved between the inexperienced men. Someone crouched at Slim's face and the voice of Sergeant McCabe came yelling at his ear, "Fix bayonets—fix bayonets—an' watch that goddam wheat!"

"Are they coming?" Slim managed to make himself heard; from a throat which seemed to choke the words in his breast.

"Yeah, when this barrage lifts, they'll come—and in numbers, Bud. Shoot low, and be ready to go meet them if they get too close."

His words penetrated Slim's consciousness like a sentence of doom.

Further speech was beyond him. His pet horror—the prospect of using a bayonet, of seeing enemy bayonets in action—appalled him. The very thought, the threat, made him weak.

"Don't turn yellow and try to run, because if you do and the Germans don't kill you, I will." With that the Sergeant left him.

Fascinated, Slim watched the sergeant's progress down the line. He marveled that anyone could walk through such a hail of steel. He expected to see the man go down with every step. . . .

Someone near at hand cried: "Here they come," and Slim's attention went to his immediate front. Out there beyond mid-field, figures took shape—a long double line of fighting men formed a wave of advancing infantry. Behind, at the far edge, another took shape, and even as he watched, a third wave debouched from a distant line of wood to join the advance. Three massed lines of bayonets reflected the first rays of a red sun peeping over the horizon.

Somehow the excitement which Slim had imagined would mark a battle scene was lacking. His own line was quiet now—too quiet; one could feel a mounting strain, a tension. The entire scene reminded him more of a maneuver, a sham battle, than the actual beginning of a fight. Word had passed: "Hold your fire!" The distant waves came nearer. Out in front, khaki clad figures emerged from a low thicket and fell back with unhurried steps, the men glancing over their shoulders. Someone shouted: "The outpost is in!"

Came a rapping burst of fire from a Hotchkiss gun close by. A gap opened in a gray-clad wave. Rifles began to crack, and, as the gap closed and the attack came on, the volume of fire increased to a pulsing roar.

Slim lay spellbound. His emotions were a mixture of fear, horror and appreciation of a spectacle undreamed of in all his little experience. The merging roar of rifle and machine gun fire gave rise to a feeling of elation—a thrill—a mounting hysteria, which drew him higher and higher from behind his protecting pile of earth to better see the panorama of courage and death depicted on that awful field before him.

Unheeded, shells burst nearby, their splinters keening round like angry hornets. Bits of bark spun off the trees and twigs and leaves came drifting down, but these were sensed, almost unnoticed. Rapt vision could not leave that scene in front.

Experimentally, his rifle raised to cover one of those forms. They were so like the silhouette targets of the rifle range at, say, six hundred yards. When glimpsed through the small aperture of a peep-sight they were nearly identical in outline, the breast-high figures of men, head and shoulders rising above the flood of waving grain through which they came. The difference was that these targets bobbed and swung along with the rise and fall of the terrain and were, or so it seemed, in never-ending numbers.

In fancy, all the German army was coming there. Here was a pageant of men at war, but with actors who did not behave like the story men of the older wars. Nothing was to be seen of the brave clash of bold spirits. No waving flags nor battle cries. Just a trudging mass of modern soldiery, closing in on another group of fellows who, for the most part, waited patiently to test in each the teaching of the trade—"Kill or be killed!"

Somehow the three enemy waves had merged into one and yet it was no stronger than the one had been before. Gaps opened in the surging rank and closed again but not so rapidly as at first. The line thinned, and thinned again, while the air was wild with sound of gunfire.

A fear that was almost panic gripped Slim's throat. The range was shorter now—too short. With its lessening his panic fear fought for mastery over reason. The urge was to flee, to get away. This was impossible—unreal. That thin line must go back. "Damn it, why wouldn't it go back?"

A cold bleak anger rose. It would go back! "Kill or be killed!" And here was the tool of his trade, a fitting of wood and metal. It came up, to snug in comfort like the arm of a pal. Its smooth stock caressed from shoulder to cheek-bone. Habit? Training! Target—the half drawn breath—a finger pressure—recoil.

Target? No. A man, a breast-high silhouette in dirty gray, under a dome of hat. He staggered and seemed to sag, suddenly, wearily, so close that one could see the shock of dumb surprise. A hand flung out, instinctive, to ease the fall; then, the figure settled, limp, at rest, pillowed in broken grain.

What had been a wave of fighting Germans became a broken outline—groups—individuals. Some still fell, some fled, while others dropped their arms to plead in fearsome stricken voices.

Most firing fell away, though here and there the most hardened killers shot men as they ran.

Victors rose. There were readjustments, shouts, commands. Stretchers passed, carried by willing prisoners. "Dig in! You—and you. Get ammunition, quickly now!"

"They'll be back again."

"Back?"

"Sure! They want this hill. Lucky we broke up that flank attack early."

An elated comrade, drunk with excitement, dropped down beside Slim. A cigarette changed hands.

"Light? Well, we sure stopped 'em 'at time, Son, didn't we?"

"Gee, I was scared at first. Did you see——?"

Slow puffs, a nod, an empty word or two. The elated one passed on.

The warm sun of a June morning poured on the now quiet wood. Its heat soothed and rested. Slim turned a bit to let his glance sweep the field. His look paused to note a sodden bundle of gray, among others. His wandering eye was caught by the gleam of a single empty cartridge among the drying clods of his little breastwork. Its brazen shine peered back, unblinking, accusing, reflecting a bit of the life-giving sun.

Slim turned face down, his head pillowed in the crook of his arm. He feigned sleep—. One can always dream. . . .

Source: ". . . And Suddenly He Didn't Want to Die" by Elton E. Mackin. From *American Heritage,* vol. 31 (February/March 1980), pp. 52–56. © 1980 American Heritage Publishing Company. Reprinted courtesy of Mrs. Marie Sage.

mid-September was an all-American operation. The American troops under Pershing performed well, taking 16,000 prisoners and 443 guns.

The Meuse-Argonne offensive launched soon after marked the end of the war. On September 26 a half-million American troops of the First Army attacked the three lines of barbwired German trenches between Verdun and Sedan and met fierce opposition. During the seven weeks of fighting through mud and constant rain, 26,000 Americans died and another 95,000 were wounded. The American cemetery at Romagné contains 16,000 graves of American young men. But gradually the Germans were pushed back, losing many prisoners and almost 900 big guns. (See Figure 5–3.)

The Armistice

By early October 1918 the German military acknowledged in private that the war was lost. Already beset with acute shortages of bread, meat, cloth, soap, and shoes, the

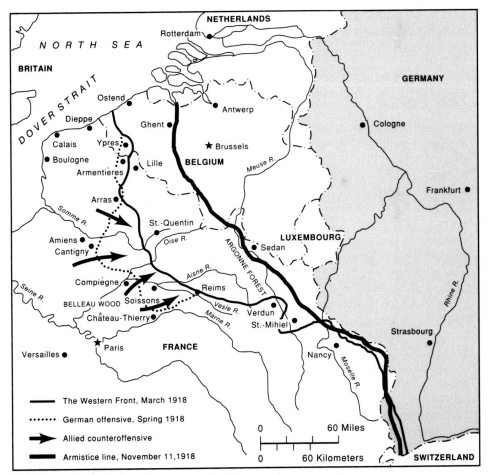

Figure 5–3   World War I: The Western Front, 1918

German civilian population soon caught the mood of despair. But they were also buoyed by hope. On January 8, Wilson had announced in his Fourteen Points the basis for a moderate peace. The points included a group of provisions intended to establish a juster world order: a peace treaty arrived at in the full glare of publicity, freedom of the seas, removal of international trade barriers, arm reductions, a fair adjustment of colonial claims, and a League of Nations. It also included several clauses to accommodate the territorial and nationalistic demands of the Poles, Italians, Serbs, and the subjugated peoples of the Austro-Hungarian Empire, and others to undo German territorial conquests, either recent or past. All told, the Fourteen Points seemed a generous basis for peace, one that the Germans could accept without shame or fear.

On October 5 the German chancellor addressed the Reichstag proposing an immediate armistice with the Fourteen Points as the basis for peace, and soon after he contacted Wilson. Meanwhile, the German military leaders proclaimed a constitutional monarchy, with a new liberal constitution. At the end of the month when the diehard head of the German navy ordered the fleet to sea, the sailors revolted. On November 9 the kaiser abdicated and fled to lifelong exile in neutral Holland. By this time Turkey had surrendered to the British and a disintegrating Austria-Hungary had ceased to fight. On November 11 at 11 A.M. the guns fell silent along the western front. The war was over.

The Peace

The war was won, but it remained to be seen whether the peace would be too. Most Americans had limited goals in November 1918. They had confronted and defeated an international bully who used atrocious weapons against innocent civilians and had violated America's rights as a neutral. That was enough. Few Americans had peace goals beyond being left alone.

But this attitude did not take into account realities. The United States could not expect to withdraw totally from Europe's political affairs. Most of the old rivalries, resentments, and fears remained, and the war had created new ones. It was foolish to expect Europe to settle down peaceably and spare the United States future difficulties. Wilson understood this, as did other well-informed people at home and abroad. Unfortunately many ordinary Americans wanted nothing more to do with Europe's problems.

Versailles

By the time of the Armistice Wilson's relations with America's allies were not good. The United States never formally joined the Allies, but fought the war as an "associated" power. During the war Wilson conducted a separate American foreign policy and had announced the Fourteen Points without consulting Britain, France, or Italy. As the end of the war approached, he hoped to take control of the peacemaking process and impose his will (which he equated with America's will) on the European nations, victors and vanquished alike. The president's vision was of a peace that would avoid rewards and punishments and so prevent future war-making resentments. In the spring of 1918, speaking off-the-record, he declared he intended to tell the delegates to the peace conference that "we come here asking *nothing for ourselves* and we are here to see *you get nothing.*"

In retrospect Wilson's "peace without victory" seems wise and farseeing. It was, however, unrealistic given the desires of Britain, France, Italy, and the other Allies to make the Germans pay for the war and advance their own interests. More legitimate, although equally incompatible with Wilson's goals, was France's desire for security against any future German attack. To make matters worse, Wilson mismanaged his part in the peace conference at Versailles, near Paris, and seriously damaged his cause.

His first mistake was going to Paris in person. There was little precedent for a president in office to leave the country, yet Wilson wished to be at the scene of the great events that would reshape the world and could not resist. With little capacity for warm human relations, he would often rub the other chief negotiators—France's Georges Clemenceau, Britain's David Lloyd George, and Italy's Vittorio Orlando—the wrong way. Wilson also chose a mediocre group of diplomats to accompany him and at the same time neglected to appoint an influential Republican to the delegation, although he would need the support of Republican senators for any peace treaty he came back with. His final mistake was to ask for a Democratic mandate in the November 1918 congressional elections. The voters returned Republican majorities in both houses, which seemed to repudiate the administration and give heart to his enemies. Wilson could now expect his political opponents to attack his policies unmercifully.

Wilson's arrival in Europe set off a wave of adulation. The American president symbolized the young, idealistic American nation. As foretold by the Fourteen Points, he represented a brave new world of peace and justice to replace the old balance of power diplomacy that had led the world to disaster. In Paris two million cheering people lined the Champs-Elysées as Wilson passed in an open car with French President Raymond Poincaré. In Milan banners proclaimed him the Savior of Humanity, Cavalier of Humanity, and the God of Peace. People kissed the places on programs and documents where he had signed his name.

The leaders of the Allied nations were less impressed by the American president. To these urbane and sophisticated men he seemed cold and distant as well as naive and self-righteous. Yet they were forced to go along with much that the American leader proposed.

First on Wilson's agenda was the League of Nations, a body representing the world's nations designed to resolve international disputes short of war. Wilson served as chairman of the committee to draft the League Covenant and it embodied many of the ideas of the Fourteen Points. At the heart of the covenant was the pledge by all member nations that they would "respect and preserve as against external aggression the territorial integrity and existing political independence of all members of the League." Nations would bring disputes to the League and abide by the decisions it reached. Those that refused to comply could be subject to economic and even military sanctions by the League members. The covenant also endorsed disarmament, open diplomacy, and a mandate system for European colonies that looked eventually to independence for colonial peoples.

Wilson was proud of his handiwork and believed that it would end the scourge of war. But he did not reckon with the hard facts. He had brought with him to Europe a group of young men organized as the "Inquiry" committee by Colonel House before the Armistice to provide information about Europe's complex economic, political, and social conflicts. But these experts could not tell Wilson how to overcome the fears and desires of the European leaders. The most serious impediment to Wilson's peace without victory idea was France's need for security against a future German threat. Wilson believed the League would be sufficient to prevent future German aggression against France, but the French preferred a permanently weakened Germany and, if possible, an American security guarantee. Wilson was willing to give Clemenceau the assurances he wanted, but in the end the Treaty of Guarantee he negotiated never made it past the United States Senate.

The French, however, did succeed in humbling and weakening Germany. Under the Treaty of Versailles the Germans were forced to reduce their army and navy to a minimal level, return Alsace-Lorraine to France, place the Saar region under League of Nations control for fifteen years, permanently demilitarize the Rhineland adjacent to France, agree to accept the decision of a reparations commission to determine German financial responsibility to the nations it had attacked, and accept blame for having started the war. Wilson considered these terms vindictive, but again hoped that the League would ultimately set things right. Even more important many Germans themselves deeply resented these terms. They called it a *diktat* (dictation) imposed on them by sheer force and resolved to repudiate it as soon as possible.

One important problem left unresolved by the peace conference was Russia. In the wake of the war's economic and political devastation many expected the Bolshevik Revolution to spread to Germany, Poland, the Balkans, and perhaps even to western Europe. The Bolsheviks sought to encourage the process by a propaganda campaign among workers and discontented intellectuals. Meanwhile Russia itself became a battleground between the Bolsheviks (the "Reds") and the counterrevolutionary monarchists (the "Whites").

The Allies and the United States did not ignore the struggle. Soon after the Bolshevik surrender to Germany they had sent troops to Russia's Murmansk-Archangel region and Siberia to try to keep Russia in the fight and to help check the dangerous virus of Bolshevism. The United States had joined both military expeditions largely to oblige the British and French. The American troops were soon removed.

Little if anything was done explicitly about the Reds at Versailles, although some attempt was made to contact the new Bolshevik leaders and draw them into the peace process. Some scholars believe that the Bolsheviks were an important hidden presence. The Bolshevik threat to Europe's stability, they say, lurked in the back of Wilson's mind and influenced his thinking. The new world order as defined at Vesailles, was, in effect, Wilson's liberal capitalist alternative to Red revolution.

The Fight for the Treaty

In February 1919, after presenting the League Covenant to the Peace Conference, Wilson returned home to sign some legislation and inform the American public in person about the work at Versailles. He arrived in the United States to find that the opposition was already laying down a barrage against the League and other provisions of the still-evolving peace treaty.

This opposition came from several sources. In the Senate his adversaries were mostly Republicans who disliked the president and wanted to embarrass him and his party. This group was led by Henry Cabot Lodge, the Massachusetts Republican who headed the Foreign Relations Committee. During Wilson's trip to France Lodge had induced a group of thirty-nine senators and senators-elect to sign a round-robin statement denouncing the League *"in the form now proposed"* and demanding that under no circumstances should the League Covenant be made part of the peace treaty.

Republican opposition was more than crude partisanship. Several of the League's Republican opponents had sincere reservations about America's permanent involvement in Europe's affairs. Some, such as Senator William Borah of Idaho, had resisted entrance into the war and now felt that the League would commit the United States to responsibilities that were not vital to its interests. "[W]e should stay out of European and Asiatic affairs," declared Borah. "I do not think we can have here a great powerful, independent, self-governing Republic and do anything else."

Opposition to the League and the evolving treaty also came from various "hyphenate" groups. Many German-Americans deplored the harsh terms imposed on their fatherland. Irish-Americans were unhappy that the peace treaty did not address

A pro–League of Nations cartoon during the debate over the Treaty of Versailles. (Library of Congress)

REFUSING TO GIVE THE LADY A SEAT.

the cause of an independent Ireland. Italian-Americans felt that the treaty ignored Italy's claims to territory along the Adriatic coast.

But perhaps the greatest impediment of all was the sheer weariness of the American people. For the best part of twenty years they had been living in an atmosphere of high dedication to change and progress. They had been conducting a permanent crusade, first to smite the malefactors of great wealth and then to disarm and punish the Hun. They were tired and wanted to shuck causes and return to the peace and quiet of private lives and the cultivation of personal gardens. To many of these people, the League seemed just another high-minded venture that could only disturb the nation's calm.

But public opinion was by no means totally hostile to the treaty. A solid bloc of Americans, including some of the old progressives, were as inspired by the vision of a new international order based on collective security as was Wilson himself. Many, however, were uneasy about the possible loss of American sovereignity to a supernational body and wanted reassurances that America would retain its freedom of action. Hoping to accommodate such moderates, Wilson squeezed several major concessions from the European leaders when he returned to Paris in April. The rights of the United States under the Monroe Doctrine would remain intact; American internal concerns would be exempt from League interference; and the United States could withdraw from the League any time it wished.

Back home once again in July Wilson formally presented the completed Versailles Treaty with the embedded League of Nations Covenant to the Senate for approval. The president worked hard to influence the ratification process, meeting frequently with Senate leaders to answer their questions and defend the treaty provisions. These meetings proved stiff. Wilson seemed too much the college professor lecturing naive freshmen. Recognizing that he was making little headway, he decided to take the League cause to the people in a major speaking tour.

The decision was unwise. Wilson was not well. For years he had suffered from some sort of vascular disease and may have experienced a series of small strokes. The western tour of twenty-two days that began on September 6 took him 8000 miles. He made thirty speeches defending the treaty and the League of Nations, often in halls where the acoustics were so bad that he had to shout to be heard. His health worsened, and after his address in Pueblo, Colorado, he collapsed and the tour was canceled.

On October 2, after he returned to Washington, he experienced a massive stroke that paralyzed the left side of his body and impaired his vision. For a while it seemed that he would not survive, but after lying for five or six weeks flat on his back, he was able to work for brief periods. Until his death in 1924, however, he remained an invalid.

For the duration of his term Wilson's leadership was severely impaired. For many weeks he was isolated from all visitors by his physician and his wife. Edith Wilson insisted on screening all communications, and for nearly six months she functioned almost as a surrogate chief executive.

During this period Wilson's judgment deteriorated. He refused to see the British ambassador, who wished to help him with passage of the treaty. He broke with Colonel House, his closest adviser and a man he had long considered indispensible. He dismissed his secretary of state, Robert Lansing, for no good reason.

More seriously he mishandled the treaty fight. Even at this point Wilson could have mustered a two-thirds majority for the treaty if he had used a conciliatory approach to his adversaries. Although he profoundly disliked the president, Lodge was not one of the "irreconcilables" such as Borah or Hiram Johnson and would have gone along with a League with "reservations" that protected American sovereignty. But now, more than ever, Wilson was certain that he was right and his opponents wrong, and he refused to budge. When, in November, the Senate voted for the first time on the treaty, he opposed the amendments containing reservations proposed by Lodge and the Foreign Relations Committee, and his supporters in the Senate joined with the irreconcilables to vote the amended treaty down. Immediately after this the irreconcilables and reservationists joined to defeat Wilson's unamended version. In February 1920 the treaty's supporters made another attempt to pass it with reservations, but Wilson again refused to release his Senate supporters and once more the treaty failed to receive the two-thirds vote needed for passage.

The Election of 1920: An Era Ends

Eventually the United States signed separate peace treaties officially ending hostilities with the Central Powers. Although several attempts were made to reconsider the League, they all failed and the United States never joined.

Meanwhile the election of 1920 administered the *coup de grace* to the progressive era. The election was held at a time when the public had lost faith in the administration and the Democratic party, and there was little chance that the ticket of Governor James M. Cox of Ohio and the former assistant secretary of the navy, Franklin Roosevelt, would win.

The Democratic candidates remained essentially true to the Wilsonian heritage. They supported the League of Nations and talked of a new burst of reform. But their position was a losing one. The president was an unpopular figure who epitomized all those trumpet calls to battle of the past that the public wanted to forget.

The Republicans were astute enough to see that their campaign must be essentially a negative one. Their candidates, Senator Warren G. Harding of Ohio and Governor Calvin Coolidge of Massachusetts, were mediocre men who stood for little except what Harding called "normalcy." This meant retreating from "heroism," "revolution," "experiment," and "agitation," and returning to "healing," "restoration," "equipoise," and "adjustment." The Republicans did not campaign directly against Cox and Roosevelt. Their target was the ailing invalid in the White House. "Mr. Wilson, and his dynasty, his heirs and assigns, or anybody that is his, anybody who with bent knee has served his purpose," declared Senator Lodge, "must be driven from all control of the government and all influence in it."

Two new constitutional amendments promised to change the political climate in 1920: the Eighteenth, prohibiting the manufacture, sale, and transportation of intoxicating liquors; and the Nineteenth, giving women the vote. The first eventually did; prohibition would divide the country politically and culturally during the coming decade although it had little affect in 1920. The second did not; women voters generally divided the same way men did.

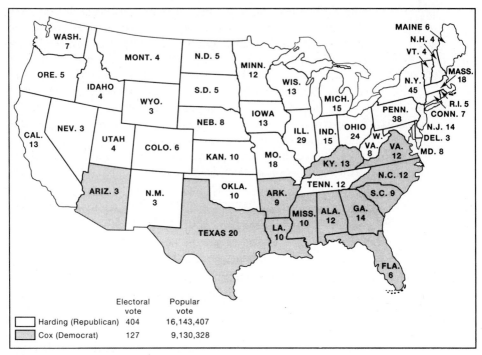

Figure 5-4   The 1920 Presidential Election

The results on election day were predictable. (See Figure 5–4.) Cox and Roosevelt received 9 million popular and 127 electoral votes to Harding and Coolidge's 16 milliion and 404. It was a landslide for normalcy, and normalcy of a certain sort was what it brought to America.

FOR FURTHER READING

On TR and foreign policy see the highly critical work by Howard K. Beale, *Theodore Roosevelt and the Rise of America to World Power* (1956). Also see Raymond Esthus, *Theodore Roosevelt and International Rivalries* (1970). On Panama the most readable work is David McCullough, *The Path Between the Seas: The Creation of the Panama Canal* (1977). U.S. policy in the Caribbean in these early years of the twentieth century is described in Dana Munro, *Intervention and Dollar Diplomacy in the Caribbean, 1900–1921* (1964). Charles Neu's *An Uncertain Friendship: Theodore Roosevelt and Japan, 1906–1909* (1967) handles its subject well. Also see Eugene P. Trani, *The Treaty of Portsmouth: Adventure in American Diplomacy* (1969). Jerry Israel's *Progressivism and the Open Door: America and China, 1905–1921* (1971) is the best recent work on the subject. Also see Paul Varg, *Making of a Myth: The United States and China, 1879–1912* (1968) and on the same subject the eager student will want to read Thomas McCormick's *China Market: America's Quest for Informal Empire* (1967). Wilsonian foreign policy in the large is treated in Edward H. Buehrig, *Woodrow Wilson and the Balance of Power* (1955). Wilson's policies toward Mexico are described in Robert E. Quirk, *An Affair of Honor: Woodrow Wilson and the Occupation of Veracruz* (1962) and in Clarence E. Clendenen, *The United States and Pancho Villa* (1961).

On the convoluted subject of Wilson and American entrance into World War I, the best sources are three books by Arthur Link, Wilson's modern biographer, *Wilson: The Struggle for Neutrality, 1914–1915* (1960); *Wilson: Confusions and Crises, 1915–1916* (1964); and *Wilson: Campaigns for Progressivism and Peace, 1916–1917* (1965). Also see Ross Gregory, *The Origins of American Intervention in the First World War* (1971). A work that looks closely into German motives during the U-boat and neutral rights controversies with the United States is Ernest May's *The World War and American Isolation, 1914–1917* (1959). TR and the preparedness movement are described in Hermann Hagedorn, *The Bugle that Woke America* (1940). A portion of the propaganda struggle for the American mind is described in Kevin O'Keefe, *A Thousand Deadlines: The New York City Press and the World War, 1914–1917* (1972). Barbara Tuchman has written a fascinating history of the Zimmerman telegram in *The Zimmerman Telegram* (1958).

The best recent treatment of Wilson as war president is Robert Ferrell's, *Woodrow Wilson and World War I, 1917–1921* (1985). For overall U.S. military strategy in World War I see Edward M. Coffman, *The War to End All Wars: The American Military Experience in World War I* (1968) and Frank Freidel, *Over There: The Story of America's First Great Overseas Crusade* (1964). A work on the wartime home front in general is Allen Churchill, *Over Here: An Informal Re-Creation of the Home Front in World War I* (1968). Robert D. Cuff, in *The War Industries Board: Business-Government Relations During World War I* (1973), has written the definitive study of wartime economic mobilization. But also see Daniel R. Beaver, *Newton D. Baker and the American War Effort, 1917–1919* (1966). Wartime labor is described in Frank L. Grubbs, Jr., *The Struggle for Labor Loyalty: Gompers, The A.F. of L., and the Pacifists, 1917–1920* (1968).

Much has been written about World War I intolerance. For the opponents of the war and their treatment see Horace Peterson and Gilbert Fite, *Opponents of War, 1917–1918* (1957). Also see Harry N. Scheiber, *The Wilson Administration and Civil Liberties, 1917–1921* (1960) and the pertinent sections of Nick Salvatore, *Eugene V. Debs: Citizen and Socialist* (1982). On wartime racial intolerance and best work is Elliott Rudwick's *Race Riot at East St. Louis, July 2, 1917* (1964). The treatment of German-Americans is described in Frederick Luebke, *Bonds of Loyalty: German-Americans and World War I* (1974).

The American propaganda campaign at home and abroad is treated eulogistically in George Creel's own account *How We Advertised America: The First Telling of the Amazing Story of the Committee on Public Information That Carried the Gospel of Americanism to Every Corner of the Globe* (1920). Less positive is George T. Blakey's *Historians and the Homefront: American Propagandists for the Great War* (1970).

Versailles is covered in Thomas A. Bailey, *Wilson and the Lost Peace* (1944), a book written in part to exhort Americans to avoid a similar lost peace in the 1940s. N. Gordon Levin's *Woodrow Wilson and World Politics* (1968) seeks to place the peace conference in the setting of fears of Bolshevik revolution. The domestic battle over the League of Nations is dealt with in Thomas Bailey's companion volume *Woodrow Wilson and the Great Betrayal* (1945) and Ralph A. Stone, *The Irreconcilables: The Fight Against the League of Nations* (1970). The definitive biography of Henry Cabot Lodge is John Garraty's *Henry Cabot Lodge: A Biography* (1953).

6
The Twenties:
The "New Era"

Hollywood stars Agnes Ayres and Rudolph Valentino in *The Sheik,* a hit movie of the 1920's. (The Bettmann Archive)

Normalcy

Warren G. Harding may not have been much of a grammarian, but he was not a bad prophet. In politics—and in several other areas of American life—*normalcy* became the prevailing mood of the middle-class public.

As Harding used the term, normalcy meant a retreat from the faultfinding and the zeal to improve institutions that had characterized the preceding twenty years. The new president had detected the fatigue of the American public after two decades of crusades, causes, and reforms and understood their desire to retreat to private pleasures and satisfactions. He intended to give them what they wanted.

Harding and his Republican successors tried to reverse the reform current of the progressive period. The Republican *New Era* was not a time of unrelieved political reaction. Various liberal bodies, such as women's organizations, church groups, and unions, continued to push a reform agenda. A "farm bloc" contingent in Congress, composed of southerners and westerners, opposed the probusiness bias of the Republican majority. In several state houses progressive governors, such as New York's Alfred E. Smith, continued to push legislation favorable to slum dwellers and working people. Some of the Roosevelt-Taft-Wilson progressives who emphasized efficiency survived the war. In the Harding administration and its New Era successors there were men such as Herbert Hoover and Charles Evans Hughes who had roots in the prewar progressive drive to rationalize governmental and economic processes and eliminate waste. As Harding's and then Calvin Coolidge's secretary of commerce, Hoover made his department the agency for eliminating production duplication and collecting data on business activities. He also strongly favored improvements in labor's conditions where it encouraged efficiency.

Yet those who attempt to absolve the twenties from the charge of political reaction go too far. The farm bloc did contain a few leaders—Senators George Norris and Robert La Follette, for example—who continued to deplore the influence of concentrated wealth in American society and hoped for a more egalitarian social order. But most of its members were primarily defenders of one economic pressure group—agriculture—against others and possessed no larger vision of a democratic society. Hoover and his colleagues also had a more limited view of social improvement than their prewar predecessors. Hoover was a humanitarian, but his sympathies could be called forth, it seemed, far more readily by natural disaster and war than by the more problematic ills of an imperfect social order.

All told, there was a distinct change in the political climate between the century's first two decades and its third. The new political mood was friendly toward business. Most progressives regarded big business as an enemy of the public, a dangerous force in the economy and the country's political life. Harding and the Republican leadership clearly did not. In his first message to Congress the new president asked for a higher tariff and lower taxes, federal subsidies to the American merchant marine, a national budget system, and a greatly expanded federal highway network, all measures to stimulate business expansion. Harding was not indifferent to the well-being of the ordinary citizen. But the New Era that the Republicans proclaimed was expected to benefit the masses by prosperity that began at the economic summit and trickled down to those below.

A Pro-business Climate

During the administrations of the three New Era Republican presidents—Warren G. Harding, Calvin Coolidge, and Herbert Hoover—the government shifted its concerns from labor and the consuming public to business.

Business and businesspeople were direct beneficiaries of enormous government favors during the twenties. Harding's request for tariff reform eventually became law as the Fordney-McCumber tariff of 1922, a measure that raised duties sharply on both agricultural and industrial imports.

Businesspeople benefited even more from the tax policies of Secretary of the Treasury Andrew Mellon, chief financial adviser to all three of the New Era Republican presidents. A wispy little man from Pittsburgh who wore a black suit and smoked long, thin cheroots, Mellon had made his millions by backing the Hall process for making aluminum and became interested in politics when mere money-making lost its charms. He never ceased to respect business and business people, however, and insisted that "government . . . be run on business principles." Mellon believed that the high wartime taxes remaining in force were throttling industry and holding back the economy's advance. As Treasury secretary he fought to slash corporation taxes, excess profit taxes, and the steep rates on the upper levels of personal income taxes. The remaining progressives and the farm bloc resisted his efforts to remove the burdens on business and the prosperous, but by 1925 they had capitulated. Thereafter the nation was saddled with a regressive tax system that mocked the hopes of those reformers who had supported the Sixteenth (income tax) Amendment as a way of reducing inequalities of income and wealth.

Big business did not win every battle during the twenties; the besieged liberals could still strike back. One of their biggest victories was the rescue of Muscle-Shoals, a wartime federal hydroelectric project on the Tennessee River, from sale to private business. After 1918 businesspeople were able to buy most government-built war plants for a song, but in the case of Muscle-shoals, they encountered the intrepid Senator Norris of Nebraska. Norris envisioned Muscle-Shoals as the nucleus of a government-operated regional development scheme. Such a project could convert the whole vast Tennessee Valley from a neglected rural slum to a region of well-cultivated farms, prosperous towns, and thriving factories, all based on cheap electric power from moving water. Norris failed during the twenties to induce the federal government to carry out his scheme of planned regional development, but his efforts planted the seed of the New Deal's innovative Tennessee Valley Authority.

As the lot of business improved, that of labor declined. Even before Harding's election, the Supreme Court, by a five to four decision in *Hammer* v. *Dagenhart* (1918), had declared unconstitutional the Keating-Owen Child Labor Act of 1916. In 1923 the Court considered the case of a District of Columbia minimum wage law for women and in *Adkins* v. *Children's Hospital* decided that it violated the workers' freedom and hence was void. The most telling blow against the social legislation of the progressives, however, was a set of Supreme court decisions that nullified the provisions of the Clayton Antitrust Act exempting unions from prosecution and injunctions. These had been hailed as "labor's Magna Carta" by Samuel Gompers. Organized labor was now once more at the mercy of hostile courts and district attorneys.

Labor Unrest

The executive branch proved equally unfriendly to organized labor. During the war the Wilson administration had endorsed unions in the interests of industrial peace. Union membership had burgeoned, and by 1920 over five million wage earners out of twenty-two million people in the nonfarm labor force, about 20 percent of the total, were union members. Four-fifths of this number—about four million—belonged to unions affiliated with the American Federation of Labor (AFL).

The immediate postwar period proved devastating to organized labor. During the war, as part of its bargain with the government, labor had desisted from strikes. By the time of the Armistice stored up frustrations and irritations were ready to boil over.

State militia arriving for duty during the Seattle, Washington, general strike of February 1919. (UPI/Bettmann Newsphotos)

In Seattle, then a near-frontier town where the militant Industrial Workers of the World (IWW) were a powerful presence, class resentments were intense. In February 1919 labor leaders called a general strike to shut the city down.

The strike threat terrified many of Seattle's middle class. The General Strike Committee promised to ensure continuance of fire protection, milk and mail deliveries, and heat and light services, but everything else would stop. Some of the labor groups had traditional trade union goals—union recognition, wage benefits, and the like. But the IWW and several other radical groups seemed determined to create some sort of revolutionary apocalypse and in their pronouncements raised the specter of class warfare with blood flowing in the streets. After dark on February 5, the strike's eve, "numerous Seattle families sat behind closed doors . . . cleaning rifles, shotguns and pistols," fearing the worst.

The next day the city came to a halt; only vehicles carrying signs saying "Exempted by the General Strike Committee" moved through the streets. The paralysis lasted only one day. On Friday the state militia appeared and set up machine guns at major intersections. Mayor Ole Hanson now demanded that the strike be called off, and after a day or two the workers drifted back to their jobs. The radicals had mistimed the revolution.

The Seattle general strike proved a disaster to labor. Nothing even close to revolution had occurred, but the strike badly frightened the American middle-class public and reinforced the linkage in people's minds between trade unionism and social revolution. The city of Seattle itself developed a reputation for labor extremism and for two decades was shunned by industry.

Conservative antiunion opinion was further strengthened during the fall of 1919 when the Boston city police went on strike. The police were badly paid and to increase their bargaining power with the city had organized a police union and joined the AFL. The police commissioner fired the ringleaders of the union movement. On September 9 the police struck. The city, conservatives said, was now at the mercy of the criminal element.

Then-governor Calvin Coolidge intervened. A dour, laconic, and colorless bureaucrat little known outside Massachusetts, Coolidge called in the National Guard and restored order. He achieved instantaneous national fame by tersely replying to a protest telegram from AFL president Samuel Gompers: "There can be no right to strike against the public safety by anybody, anywhere, anytime."

The third of the labor-shattering upheavals of 1919 was the steel strike. Many American steelworkers slaved in ferocious heat twelve hours a day, seven days a week. The mill owners insisted that they paid their men well and spent large sums on health clinics and safety devices. But they were fiercely antiunion, considering any attempt at establishing collective bargaining for the workers grounds for instant dismissal. Elbert Gary, head of U.S. Steel, the industry's largest firm, loftily declared, "We do not deal with labor unions."

Gary's opposition did not deter strike organizer William Z. Foster. A militant AFL leader who came to the steel towns in mid-1919 fresh from his success the previous year in organizing 200,000 packinghouse workers, Foster quietly formed a network of local union bodies. On September 19, acting on the steel union's orders, more than 350,000 steelworkers walked out in ten states and fifty towns.

Despite the resistance of the mill owners and the local politicians who backed them, the strike dragged on for three months. The owners brought in black strikebreakers and guarded them against the fury of the predominantly white strikers with private police and state troopers. In early November the skilled workers lost heart and returned to work. The bulk of the unskilled held out for two more months, although many were forced to brave the winter elements in tents when they were evicted from company housing. Finally in January, after 109 days, the strikers capitulated. They had won nothing, and the trauma of the defeat would delay further union-organizing efforts in steel for over a decade.

There were other major strikes later in the decade. In 1920 and again in 1922 the railroad workers walked out. In both cases the federal attorney general used court injunctions to hog-tie the strikers and force them back to work. All through the decade bloody labor battles occurred in the soft-coal fields of West Virginia, Illinois, and Kentucky between the United Mine Workers lead by the tough, eloquent John L. Lewis, and the mine operators. In 1926 the Communist party led a strike against the textile mill owners in Passaic, New Jersey, that lasted for over a year. From the early 1920s on, bitter strikes broke out periodically in the southern Piedmont area whence much of the cotton textile industry had moved from New England in pursuit of cheaper labor and cheaper power. The southern mill workers, mostly transplanted white tenant farmers, were poorly paid and lived in squalid company towns and company-owned housing. Unused to the ways of industry and unions, they nonetheless learned quickly from union organizers, many of them northern radicals, who filled the gap when the AFL proved too timid to challenge the South's traditional labor conservatism. Yet in the end the strikes at Gastonia, North Carolina, and other Piedmont communities were lost, like so many others of the decade, leaving workers unprotected from the free market.

The Shift to the Right

The failures of organized labor were an aspect of the general conservative ideological drift that characterized the 1920s. The rightward shift had several sources. In part it was an offshoot of the decade's general flight from social commitment and retreat to privatism. It was also an understandable reaction to excesses, both of word and deed, by an extreme left ignorant of American realities and convinced that revolution was not far off. But it was also encouraged by the deliberate scare campaign of excitable or cynical high-placed conservatives. Without this latter effort neither of the two former factors could have induced the spasm of fear and political intolerance that gripped the nation.

Red Scare

Actually it was President Wilson's attorney general, A. Mitchell Palmer, who set off the decade-long campaign against "Reds." By this time the American left was highly fragmented. The Bolshevik, or *Soviet* ("workers' council"), Revolution in November 1918 had split the socialists of Europe and the United States into two warring camps, a right element committed to democracy and skeptical of Bolshevik behavior, and a left that endorsed the Bolshevik "dictatorship of the proletariat" and slavishly supported Moscow's foreign policy. In late 1919 at the Socialist party convention in Chicago, the two wings had come to blows with the right expelling the left. The leftists soon after formed the Communist party of the United States.

Meanwhile the wartime repression in the United States, the Russian Revolution, and the chaos of postwar Europe had revived anarchist extremism; this was soon manifested by the anarchist trademark: bombs. In April 1919 a number of prominent conservative leaders received bombs in the mail. At the end of the month the New York post office intercepted explosives in sixteen packages addressed to J. P. Morgan, John D. Rockefeller, and other prominent men. During the spring there were other bomb threats and attacks, culminating in a huge explosion outside Attorney General Palmer's Washington home that blew up the perpetrator and scattered his anarchist pamphlets. A year later, 34 innocent clerks, messengers, and typists were killed and more than 200 injured when a mine hidden in a wagon at the corner of Broad and Wall streets in the New York financial district erupted in a giant blast.

It was in this tense and fearful atmosphere that Palmer, the "fighting Quaker," went to work. With a $500,000 appropriation from Congress, Palmer created an intelligence division within the Justice Department to investigate radicalism. To head the new agency he chose a young Washingtonian named J. Edgar Hoover, who believed that America faced the "most terrible menace of danger" and compared the times with the Dark Ages when Europe was overrun by "barbarian hordes."

Determined to "ship or shoot" anyone suspected of subversive activities, Palmer authorized a series of raids on radical centers all over the country. He also ordered the deportation to Russia of over two hundred radical leaders, although in most cases there was no evidence that they had violated any law. On December 21 several hundred alien radicals departed for Europe on an old army transport nicknamed the "Soviet Ark."

One week later, on New Year's Day 1920, the Justice Department raided Communist party offices around the country. This time, everyone present, for whatever reason, was carted off to jail. Federal agents seized every piece of suspicious printed matter; they even took the pictures on the wall. In Boston they took a sign that said "No Smoking" in undecipherable Cyrillic letters.

This operation netted between 4000 and 6000 people in thirty-three different cities. The suspects were kept in jail for weeks, mostly in filthy congested cells. In violation of their civil liberties they were held without being charged with specific crimes. In the end all that the raids produced were three small guns and no explosives. The courts soon released most of the prisoners for lack of evidence.

Sacco and Vanzetti

The public finally lost patience with Palmer. But one more venture connected with his anti-Red campaign would have momentous consequences. The authorities traced the pamphlets found outside the Palmer house at the time of the bomb blast to the Brooklyn printshop of two Italian anarchists. These men were promptly arrested and held incommunicado. Hoping to avoid the fate of the arrested men, the Boston circle of anarchists sent several members to round up incriminating anarchist literature. Two of these—Nicola Sacco and Bartolomeo Vanzetti—were intercepted by the police, questioned and searched. They were armed, and although they denied that they were anarchists, their true beliefs soon came out along with the information that both had evaded draft registration during the war. Soon after they were also accused of responsibility for a payroll robbery in South Braintree, Massachusetts, where $15,000 had been stolen and two guards shot to death.

By this time, although the panic of the immediate postwar period had abated, antiradical opinion continued to be widespread. Sacco and Vanzetti were tried for robbery and murder before a blatantly biased judge and sentenced to death. While their appeals wended their way through the courts, a Sacco and Vanzetti defense committee composed of liberal intellectuals and radicals sought to make the case into a test of American justice and civil liberties. At its height in early 1927 the Sacco-Vanzetti case became an international cause célèbre with one side convinced the two men were indeed anarchist monsters who deserved the severest punishment, and the other certain that they were martyrs to intolerance or to the brutality of a hypocritical capitalist class or both. On August 22, 1927, after the last appeals had been exhausted, Sacco and Vanzetti were electrocuted at Charlestown prison.

The angry split in public opinion persisted to the very end. Five days after the execution 50,000 men and women wearing red armbands set out in a funeral procession from Boston's Scollay Square to the anarchists' gravesites. Few made the complete journey. Club-wielding mounted police, infuriated by the outpouring of sympathy, rode into the marchers and scattered them before they could reach the cemetery.

The Two Nations: Twenties Culture

The novelist John Dos Passos at one point in the Sacco-Vanzetti controversy remarked that the opposing sides were "two nations." Dos Passos was referring to the political and ideological divisions in the country, but his observation could also have been applied to many other aspects of American life.

In fact it is not too much to say that throughout the 1920s a two-sided battle raged through the nation over what America should be. On one side were traditional Americans of old-stock, small-town, pious and conservative Protestant background who yearned for the more homogeneous, law-abiding, and reverent society of the past. On the other, was a newer America of big city sophisticates, religious liberals or nonbelievers, and newer-stock people outside the native Protestant small-town tradition. During the 1920s these two loosely defined groups engaged in a culture battle along a broad front of issues.

Intellectuals

American intellectuals in the 1920s were a community at odds with their society. This adversary relationship had occurred before—and would soon occur again—but the war added a dimension of disillusionment that exaggerated the intellectuals' response. Men such as Ernest Hemingway, John Dos Passos, E. E. Cummings, and William Faulkner returned from the war angry at the prewar pieties and hypocrisies that had sent so many brave young men to die. Only Hemingway had actually served much time at the front, but all perceived the war as an indictment of the civilization that had caused it. In novels such as Hemingway's *The Sun Also Rises,* Dos Passos's *Three Soldiers,* Cummings's *Enormous Room,* and Faulkner's *Soldier's Pay,* these members of the *lost generation* portrayed ordinary men and women struggling vainly and bravely to salvage some happiness and dignity from the holocaust created in the name of honor and country.

But war-inspired disillusionment was only one source of the writers' and intellectuals' skepticism. The predominant probusiness, self-congratulatory national mood offended the twenties intellectuals as similar attitudes would offend their successors. To the men and women who wrote the books, Americans seemed callow, materialistic, and philistine. Harold Stearns, in his influential critical anthology *Civilization in the United States,* noted that "the most . . . pathetic fact in the social life of America is emotional and aesthetic starvation." The critic and essayist H. L. Mencken took pleasure in insulting what he called the "booboisie" and challenging their attitudes and behavior. A popular feature of his magazine, *American Mercury,* was an "Americana" section made up of inanities and crudities culled from the nation's press that Mencken saw as characteristic of American life. Mencken delighted in the role of gadfly and skeptic. He defended prostitution and suggested abolishing the public school system. German in ancestry, he insisted all Anglo-Saxons were cowards. "Love," he declared at one point, "is the delusion that one woman differs from another." Mencken's cynicism and amused contempt for his nation's predominant culture were poses widely imitated by urban sophisticates who sought to distance themselves from the reigning values of the era.

The special target of many American writers of the period were the small towns they had themselves originally come from. Sherwood Anderson, in *Winesburg, Ohio,* condemned the sexual depravity and hypocrisy that he perceived behind the bland surface of a small Ohio community. Even more successful was Sinclair Lewis's *Mainstreet,* an account of how Carol Kennicott, a sensitive and cultivated young woman, was destroyed by the physical ugliness, banality, stifling conventionality, and basic dishonesty of life in Gopher Prairie, Minnesota. Lewis's next novel, *Babbitt,* transferred the indictment of middle-class American life to the larger community of Zenith, a middle-size city in the heartland. Its hero, George Babbitt, is a well-meaning, but conformist and limited, small-business man sustained by the hollow values of material success, boosterism, and contrived optimism. Babbitt, for all his failings, is a vivid character whose name quickly became the tag for every tasteless, middle-class conformist.

Another target for the sophisticates of the decade was traditional religion. Mencken ridiculed the clergy. Every minister, he said, was a fraud and should be carefully watched especially when young girls or boys were present. Sinclair Lewis depicted an evangelical minister in his 1927 novel *Elmer Gantry* as a raving hypocrite. At the same time conservative Protestantism was under fire from the more liberal denominations that accepted the Social Gospel and religious modernism. The conservatives in turn recognized the attitudes of the intellectuals and resented them.

Greater Sexual Freedom

The favorite target of the antagonistic intellectuals, however, was the supposed sexual repressiveness of mainstream America. The dirty secret of Anderson's *Winesburg, Ohio*'s citizens is sex. All its inhabitants are diminished by the sexual hypocrisies of the small Ohio town. But while the new novelists decried the Victorian social values of the day, in fact many were able to escape for the first time from their heavy hand. In the literary marketplace sex sold. James Branch Cabell's *Jurgen,* a novel about an amoral egotist whose amorous adventures take place in a fantasy land, became a sensation, although for a while it was banned by the authorities. Anita Loos's *Gentlemen Prefer Blondes* was a thinly disguised tribute to successful prostitution. Less explicitly sexual, but still celebrating the quest for sensation, were the novels and short stories of F. Scott Fitzgerald, a handsome Princetonian of Irish-Catholic heritage. In 1920 Fitzgerald became the bard of "flaming youth" and of the "Jazz Age" with his novel *This Side of Paradise.* Most of Fitzgerald's other novels, *The Beautiful and Damned, The Great Gatsby,* and *Tender Is the Night,* were commercial failures, but his many short stories and still more his own extravagant, hedonistic, and often alcoholic personal life epitomized the liberation of his generation from the constraints of the era. To women, especially college-educated women, the poet Edna St. Vincent Millay filled a similar niche. Her life as a bohemian free spirit intrigued many, and her famous lines, "My candle burns at both ends;/It will not last the night;/But ah, my foes, and oh my friends—/It gives a lovely light!" became a kind of emblem of the sexually liberated twenties woman.

The insistence on greater freedom in sexual matters of the twenties writers and intellectuals capped a trend that went back at least to the 1890s. During the early years of the century it was abetted by the experience of the Greenwich Village new bohemia. During the twenties, avant-garde writers, artists, and intellectuals continued to pour into the Village, making it more than ever the headquarters of the country's social nonconformists, cultural innovators, and radical dissenters. Millay, the critic Edmund Wilson, the novelist Floyd Dell, the playwright Eugene O'Neill, and a host of other creative men and women lived and partied in the Village and both absorbed and contributed to its reputation for free expression and "free love."

The sexual liberalism was also reinforced by contact with Europe. For many of these same people Paris—where the American dollar went much further than before the war—seemed an even more attractive haven than the Village. Hundreds of American writers, painters, musicians, and intellectuals (including Hemingway, Gertrude Stein, Fitzgerald, the poet Ezra Pound, and others) drifted into and out of the pleasure-loving expatriate community on the Paris Left Bank. Stein, a trained doctor who had given up medicine for literature, ran a famous Paris salon where high-powered American expatriates and visitors could mix with the avant-garde artists and intellectuals of France and Europe.

For those who prided themselves on being at the cutting edge of thought, the new

God was Sigmund Freud, the Viennese doctor who "discovered" the unconscious and in the process founded the psychoanalytic movement. Many of the avant-garde writers sought to incorporate Freudian insights into their work. O'Neill's plays *Desire Under the Elms* and *Strange Interlude* dealt with Freudian themes. William Faulkner used Freudian "stream of consciousness" narration in his 1929 novel *The Sound and the Fury.*

Freud had many things to say about the nature of the human mind, but what most impressed the intellectual and literary communities was his view that most mental illness came from the suppression of sexual urges. In various popularized and diluted forms these views reinforced the drift to more liberal attitudes toward the "libido," to use the Freudian term for the sex drive.

Flappers

Writers and thinkers helped alter the sexual sensibilities of their time, but the changes had social roots as well.

American women were a powerful force for moral change during the 1920s. In the years before 1917, as we have seen, American women had already entered politics and public life as reformers, social workers, and political activists. During the war even working-class women had taken on new public roles selling bonds, collecting scarce materials for the war effort, and delivering speeches to pump up morale. By creating labor shortages, the war also drew many women who might have stayed at home into factories and offices. In 1920 the feminist drives of the previous decades culminated in the Nineteenth Amendment to the Constitution, guaranteeing women the vote.

Greater participation in jobs and enterprise outside the home in itself would have loosened the traditional limitations on female sexual expression. As their independence and self-confidence grew, inevitably many women would have begun to demand the same social freedom as men. But besides these factors the war had shaken traditional moral beliefs more directly. Millions of young soldiers, confronted with the prospect of death or dismemberment, had taken their last flings, despite the effort of the moralists to protect their virtue by shutting down saloons and red-light districts adjacent to army camps. To ease tensions, many soldiers began to smoke cigarettes for the first time. Many had their first sexual experiences. And frequently these were with "good girls," who were urged by patriots to be "nice to the boys in uniform"—and often were to a fault, in the eyes of traditional moralists. The new attitudes, added to trends already underway in the 1890s, helped shape the *new woman.*

Economic change also sparked social evolution. During the 1920s many more women worked for wages than before and many more worked in occupations that required some skill. The number of female domestics declined in the twenties, but the number of female clerks, typists, salespeople, beauticians, and professionals increased. Many of the professional careers that women pursued were the lower paying ones, such as social worker and schoolteacher. But there was also a considerable increase in the number of women doctors, psychologists, college professors, and scientists.

More women professionals implies an increase in women's college enrollments. And so it was. By 1930 almost 44 percent of all college students were women. Before the war a large proportion of female college students had attended all-women schools such as Barnard, Wellesley, Bryn Mawr, and Vassar. Now a majority were found at the state universities. Here "Betty Co-ed" came in contact with young men on an unchaperoned basis in unprecedented numbers. The new circumstances led to new courtship relations between the sexes. "Dating" with a succession of partners, many casual, replaced the prewar formal "calling" by an interested young man on a young woman at her home, as a way of finding a mate. Linked with dating was the automobile, an arrangement that also encouraged freer sexual contact. Betty Co-ed was a trendsetter. Many of the new college customs filtered down to younger women and women from lower middle-class and working-class backgrounds.

All these social currents converged to produce the *flapper*. This type of young woman announced her presence by her appearance—short skirt, silk stockings, heavy makeup, and short, bobbed hair. Even more distinctive was her behavior. She was assertive and outspoken. She smoked, drank, danced the Charleston, "petted," and, sometimes, "went all the way."

In some ways the flapper was an extreme case. Especially in rural areas young women continued to conform to older ways. But the flapper was a model widely imitated by the young. All over the country skirts rose, hair shortened, traditional morals loosened. Through the later work of Alfred Kinsey and his associates on

Young people enjoying the more relaxed social and sexual mores of the 1920s. (The Bettmann Archive/BBC Hulton)

human sexuality, we know that the twenties was a sexual watershed for women. The Kinsey researchers discovered that twice as many young women of that decade as their mothers of twenty years before had had premarital sexual experiences.

The Media

The popular media helped to undermine traditional moral values. The twenties saw the birth of the tabloid, a small-format newspaper convenient for reading on the streetcar or subway and even more sensational than the yellow journals of the prewar period.

The movie industry took advantage of the new market for daring and suggestive material, although by the standards of our own day it was almost prudish. Before the war the sentimental tearjerker and the slam-bang action movie had been Hollywood's staples. Now they were joined by the torrid romance and the salacious exposé. Movies in the early twenties had titles such as *Her Purchase Price, A Shocking Night, The Joy Girl,* and *Forbidden Fruit.* Their producers promised their audiences kisses "where heart and soul and sense in concert move, and the blood is lava, and the pulse a blaze." The new movie idols were not the sweet, asexual Mary Pickfords or the clean-cut cowboy Tom Mixes; the big Hollywood stars were now Clara Bow, the "It" Girl, and Rudolph Valentino, the smoldering passionate "sheik." (See the illustration opening this chapter.) Even the historical and Biblical epics of Cecil B. deMille managed to insert a dollop of sex in the form of a heroine's revealing bath, a Roman orgy, or a slave girl's exotic dance.

One new medium that retained the innocence of the past was radio. Made technically possible by the vacuum tube, invented by Lee De Forest in 1906, its popular triumph was assured by the commercial drive of the decade.

During the war the government had restricted private broadcasting to prevent transmission of information to the enemy. After the ban was lifted, radio took off. At first radio stations were staffed by, and catered to, a handful of hobbyists who were satisfied with broadcasting and hearing almost any sound over the air waves. Then in November 1920 the first commercial station, KDKA of Pittsburgh, began to broadcast programs paid for by advertisers. Within a year there were eight more commercial stations, and by the end of 1923, 500 more. In 1926 the Radio Corporation of America (RCA) formed the first network linking nineteen stations. The next year the Columbia Broadcasting System (CBS) formed a second network. The audience for radio soon exploded. In 1923 General Electric sold eleven million receivers. By mid-decade radio was no longer a fad; it was a major entertainment and information medium that would transform the patterns of daily life.

Radio fare was inevitably wholesome. Anything that came willy-nilly into every home at the twist of a dial by a child or an adolescent had to be. To prevent any mishaps, however, the federal government, which was called in initially to prevent chaos from overlapping and interfering broadcast bands, ended up regulating the industry.

The Radio Act of 1927 did not impose government ownership of the broadcasting industry, the policy adopted in most of Europe. Guided by the pervasive business philosophy of the day, the 1927 measure handed control of the stations to government-licensed private operators who could use their frequencies, subject to minimal public interest requirements, to broadcast material that would attract commercial sponsors.

Under these terms anything that offended conventional moral standards was outlawed, but nothing very positive was required. The result was the the public was treated to a flood of light popular entertainment punctuated with a little high culture such as symphonic music or the classical opera. Among the more popular broadcasts of the decade were dance band music from city hotels, sports events, political speeches, and programs of popular songs by Rudy Vallee, Kate Smith, and Bing Crosby. In 1929 two white men, Freeman Gosden and Charles Correll, began a comedy series featuring the antics of two black men and a cast of other black characters. "Amos and Andy" became a spectacular hit and provided a model for the "sitcom" that would dominate the airwaves long past the heyday of radio.

Counterattack

To the millions of Americans from the country's rural and small-town regions the changes ushered in by the twenties were often distressing. New people, new kinds of behavior, and new ideas were challenging traditional customs and values. The city and city folk had always ridiculed the country and country people, but the new media now made it difficult to insulate the small town against the intrusion of the metropolis. Radio, for example, confronted the village world with sophistication in the popular arts and culture that it could not match. How many small-town musical groups must have lost their audience when people in Gopher Prairie could listen to Paul Whiteman or Rudy Vallee "coming live" from Chicago or New York?

The movies were even more intrusive. Young people, especially, watched Clara Bow or Rudolph Valentino and yearned to imitate their ways and their lives. One young man told a survey researcher of the day, "It was directly through the movies that I learned to kiss a girl on her ears, neck, and cheeks, as well as her mouth." The young man felt that the movies had expanded his horizons; his parents probably felt that they had corrupted his morals.

The seeming immorality of the media produced a reaction in traditional America. During the twenties numerous local "watch and ward" societies assumed the job of condemning "immoral" books and theatrical performances. Often their narrowness merely served to create demand for the condemned works and their opponents took advantage of the reaction. When the Boston censors banned an issue of Mencken's *American Mercury,* Mencken came north and on Boston Common offered the magazine to the secretary of the New England Watch and Ward society. He was promptly arrested. Mencken hoped to have a good time at the expense of the censors. The judge spoiled the fun by dismissing the case.

More serious was the reaction to movie immorality. The issue was not merely the content of movies; it was also the private lives of movie stars and movie industry people generally. In the opening years of the decade a series of sex scandals had rocked the industry. In 1922 the guardians of public morals, taking advantage of public dismay, succeeded in establishing the Motion Picture Producers and Distributors Association (MPPDA) to police the industry.

Under the leadership of "czar" Will Hays, postmaster general in Harding's cabinet and Presbyterian elder, the MPPDA (the "Hays Office") promulgated a set of rules for what the movies could show. Men and women, even though married, could not be depicted in the same bed. Kisses could not last more than a prescribed number of seconds. Cursing was forbidden so that even the vilest reprobates were limited to "dang" and "darn." A wide range of subject matter was also enjoined: movies could not touch on the themes of homosexuality, abortion, incest, drugs, or interracial sex. They could depict villainy, of course, but only if in the end it was punished. The net effect was to remove the movies even further from real life than in the past and confirm their role as pure escapism.

Controlling Immigration

Traditional America's fear of the new in ideas and behavior extended to people. Concern for the diluting effect of foreign immigration on American society, as we have seen, existed during the Gilded Age and in fact goes back to the colonial era. During the 1890s its focus was on the New Immigration of Slavs, Italians, Jews, Greeks, and other southern and eastern Europeans, most of whom seemed further from the culture of Protestant, Anglo-Saxon America than the northern Europeans of the pre–Civil War era.

Before World War I defenders of traditional America had fought the new immigration by demanding literacy tests for those admitted to the United States, a requirement that promised to exclude many people from the newer areas. Cleveland, Taft, and Wilson had all vetoed such bills on the grounds that the ability to read and write was not a proper test of "personal fitness." Not until 1917, during the height of wartime xenophobia, was Congress able to pass a literacy test law over the president's veto.

The new law accomplished less than expected. During the war European immigration had plummeted. But then in 1919 it rose abruptly. In that year over 430,000 refugees from Europe's devastation and poverty entered Ellis Island; the following year the number soared to over 800,000. As before the war most of these people were from Poland, Russia, Italy, and the Balkans.

The surge of new immigration set off a wave of concern that outdid anything of the past. This time the immigration restrictionists could count on the fear of Bolshevism, identified in the minds of many Americans with immigrants from eastern Europe. It could also draw on an epidemic of pseudoscientific writings on race by Madison Grant, Lothrop Stoddard, and others that glorified the European "Nordics" and disparaged the "lesser" "Alpines" and "Mediterraneans." Stoddard's 1920s book, *The Rising Tide of Color,* warned Americans not to "pollute" the racial heritage of the Nordic stock by merging with the lesser peoples of Europe. The ideas of Grant and Stoddard were popularized in Kenneth Roberts's series of *Saturday Evening Post* articles that concluded that a continuing deluge of eastern and southern Europeans would produce "a hybrid race of people as worthless and futile as the good-for-nothing mongrels of Central and Southeastern Europe."

Many of the restrictionist writers played particularly on age-old anti-Jewish feelings in the Christian community that expressed itself not only in efforts to limit immigration but also in strict college-admissions quotas and the exclusion of Jews from certain resort hotels, "restricted" residential neighborhoods, many business firms, law and medicine, college teaching, and private clubs.

Despite opposition from liberals, representatives of the recent immigrant community, and industrialists still interested in cheap labor the restrictionist impulse was successful. In May 1921 Congress passed the first "quota law," limiting immigration to the United States to 3 percent of each nationality present in the country in 1910, with no more than a total of 357,000 in any one year. But this was only a stopgap. In May 1924 it passed the Johnson-Reed Act (also called the National Origins Act) limiting the total number of European immigrants to 164,000, to be drawn from each country by a formula that made the quotas from southern and eastern Europe almost nominal. Instead of using 1910, the new baseline would be 1890, before most of the new immigrants had arrived in the United States. Moreover, only 2 percent of each nationality present in the baseline year would now be allowed to enter the country. Although the measure exempted Canada and the Latin American countries from the quota system, it cut the number of immigrants during the remainder of the decade to under 300,000 annually. After three centuries the era of free immigration to America was over.

The Ku Klux Klan

The effort of traditional America to push back the tide of change took its most extreme and deplorable form in the revived Ku Klux Klan.

The first Ku Klux Klan had been organized during post–Civil War Reconstruction as an instrument to keep blacks in their place and restore control of southern state governments to conservative white rule. Klansmen had terrorized blacks and their carpetbag and scalawag white sponsors. Their violent tactics had brought the Republican administration of Ulysses Grant down on their heads. By the early 1870s federal prosecution had destroyed the first Klan, although not the white supremacist mood it expressed.

In 1915 D. W. Griffith's path-breaking film *Birth of a Nation* inspired William J. Simmons, a former Methodist minister turned fraternal order promoter, to create a successor to the Klan of fifty years before. The Griffith movie had depicted the old Klan as a chivalrous organization dedicated to defending southern white womanhood against depraved blacks and gracious southern society against venal northern whites.

Simmons hoped to take advantage of the revived popularity of the Klan to create a new fraternal order that he as grand wizard could control and profit from. The new Klan was fitted up with an elaborate secret ritual, white sheeted-and-hooded costumes, and assorted paraphernalia. These items could be sold by a national headquarters and, along with membership dues, Simmons hoped these sales would provide a steady flow of money into his own pocket.

Unfortunately 1915 was a little too early and the new Klan a little too unfocused for it to take off as Simmons had hoped; in 1920 it still had only 2000 members. Then Simmons happened on two accomplished hucksters, Edward Young Clarke and Elizabeth Tyler, who catapulted the organization to national prominence.

A Ku Klux Klan rally in Kansas. (Kansas State Historical Society, Topeka)

Clarke and Tyler hired an army of "kleagles," to sell memberships in the Klan. Each kleagle collected a ten-dollar initiation fee. He kept four dollars of this amount and Clarke and Tyler another four dollars, leaving two dollars for the national organization, which earned additional money by selling pamphlets, regalia, and other Klan articles to the chapters and individual members. By the end of 1921 the two hucksters had signed up a million Klansmen.

Their success was not solely the result of energy and effective organization. The pair knew how to take advantage of the racial, cultural, and religious resentments that had surfaced since the war. In California kleagles played on the hostility to the Japanese. In Texas they told "Anglos" that the Klan would keep Mexican-Americans in their place. In the New York area they harvested the pervasive antisemitism and the hostility toward the foreign-born. In the south it was the prejudice against blacks, especially the more independent black war veterans, that induced people to fork out their ten-dollar fee. In all parts of the country anti-Catholicism was an important component of the Klan appeal.

The Klan also played on traditional Americans' resentment of the new urban morality. In Oklahoma City a vigilante "whipping squad" of eighteen Klansmen punished people who violated the traditional moral code. In Houston the Klan had a woman accused of bigamy whipped and tarred and feathered. A similar sentence was imposed on a doctor who performed abortions and on a shopkeeper accused of price gouging. In Louisiana a wife beater was stripped naked and then tarred and feathered. People who drank to excess, "stepped out" on their spouses, or refused to work suffered similar fates at the hands of Klan enforcers of old-fashioned morality. The Klan at times even resorted to murder to stop outspoken enemies.

READING 6

The Purposes of the Ku Klux Klan

During the cultural conflict of the 1920s traditional America at its most extreme was represented by the Ku Klux Klan. During the Reconstruction era the Klan had been an instrument of white supremacy and had helped "redeem" the South from "carpetbag"-"scalawag"-black rule. By 1871 federal prosecution for its violence and intimidation had virtually wiped the Klan out. In 1915 it revived and after World War I expanded north as a fraternal organization. In its new guise it devoted its energies to limiting the power and influence of blacks, Catholics, and Jews in American life and to protecting traditional small-town moral values against the corrupting influence of the new forces and habits of an urbanizing society. The following excerpt comes from the Klansman's Manual *of 1925.*

Objects and Purposes (Article II, The Constitution)

I. Mobilization

This is [the Klan's] primary purpose: "To unite white male persons, native-born, Gentile citizens of the United States of America, who owe no allegiance of any nature or degree to any foreign government, nation, institution, sect, ruler, person, or people; whose morals are good; whose reputations and vocations are respectable; whose habits are exemplary; who are of sound minds and eighteen years or more of age, under a common oath into a brotherhood of strict regulations."

II. Cultural

The Knights of the Ku Klux Klan is a movement devoting itself to the needed task of developing a genuine spirit of American patriotism. Klansmen are to be examples of pure patriotism. They are to organize the patriotic sentiment of native-born white, Protestant Americans for the defense of distinctively American institutions. Klansmen are dedicated to the principle that America shall be made American through the promulgation of American doctrines, the dissemination of American ideals, the creation of wholesome American sentiment, the preservation of American institutions.

III. Fraternal

The movement is designed to create a real brotherhood among men who are akin in race, belief, spirit, character, interest, and purpose. The teachings of the order indicate very clearly the attitude and conduct that make for real expression of brotherhood, or, "the practice of Klannishness."

IV. Beneficent

"To relieve the injured and the oppressed; to succor the suffering and unfortunate, especially widows and orphans."

The supreme pattern for all true Klansmen is their Criterion of Character, Jesus Christ, "who went about doing good." The movement accepts the full Christian program of unselfish helpfulness, and will seek to carry it on in the manner commanded by the one Master of Men, Christ Jesus.

V. Protective

1. *The Home.* *"To shield the sanctity of the home."* The American home is fundamental to all that is best in life, in society, in church, and in the nation. It is the most sacred of human institutions. Its sanctity is to be preserved, its interests are to be safeguarded, and its well-being is to be promoted. Every influence that seeks to disrupt the home must itself be destroyed. The Knights of the Ku Klux Klan would protect the home by promoting whatever would make for its stability, its betterment, its safety, and its inviolability.

2. *Womanhood.* The Knights of the Ku Klux Klan declares that it is committed to "the sacred duty of protecting womanhood"; and announces that one of its purposes is "to shield . . . the chastity of womanhood."

The degradation of women is a violation of the sacredness of human personality, a sin against the race, a crime against society, a menace to our country, and a prostitution of all that is best, and noblest, and highest in life. No race, or society, or country, can rise higher than its womanhood.

3. *The Helpless.* "To protect the weak, the innocent, and the defenseless from the indignities, wrongs, and outrages of the lawless, the violent, and the brutal."

Children, the disabled, and other helpless ones are to know the protective, sheltering arms of the Klan.

4. *American Interests.* "To protect and defend the Constitution of the United States of America, and all laws passed in conformity thereto, and to protect the states and the people thereof from all invasion of their right from any source whatsoever."

VI. Racial

"To maintain forever white supremacy." "To maintain forever the God-given supremacy of the white race."

Every Klansman has unqualifiedly affirmed that he will "faithfully strive for the eternal maintenance of white supremacy."

Not every Klansman was an intolerant bigot. In addition to those attracted by Klan racism and social prejudice, there were those who joined because they craved association. To these people the Klan was indeed a lodge not unlike the Elks or Masons.

Many of the Klan's victims fought back. Catholic workers broke up Klan parades and beat up Klan marchers. In Perth Amboy, New Jersey, a mob of 6000 people, mostly Catholics and Jews, descended on a Klan gathering and, despite the police, drove the white-sheeted crowd away with stones and clubs. More peaceful but probably more effective responses were the slashing 1921 *New York World* articles describing Klan activities and excesses.

Yet for a time the Klan continued to grow, sustained by the deep-seated fears and resentments of mainstream America. Under the leadership of Hiram Evans, who ousted Simmons from control in 1922, the Klan entered politics, becoming a major political force in the South and many places in the North. Even many decent men found membership in the Klan indispensable for political advancement. In 1922 the Klan unseated a Jewish member of Congress from Indiana and elected a pro-Klan United States senator. That same year a Klansman was elected governor of Oklahoma. Scores of local and state officials and candidates were happy to win the Klan's endorsement. And Klan influence even extended to national politics. At the 1924 Democratic national convention in New York's Madison Square Garden a solid Klan contingent prevented the Democrats from adopting an official anti-Klan resolution and kept the Catholic governor of New York, Al Smith, from getting the party's presidential nomination.

This was the Klan's high-water mark. Soon after the 1924 election David C. Stephenson, head of the powerful Indiana Klan, was accused of kidnapping and raping Madge Oberholzer, a state employee who escaped his unwelcome attentions only by taking her own life. Stephenson was sentenced to life imprisonment and when the Klan-supported governor refused to pardon him he "sang," revealing the corrupt relations between the Klan and scores of Indiana officials. Its reputation as the defender of traditional morality destroyed, the Klan quickly declined, to revive only in a later day.

The Fundamentalist Impulse

The major forces in American Protestantism before the war had been modernism and the Social Gospel movement. The first had enjoined Christians to come to terms with modern biblical scholarship and modern science; the second had preached the necessity of placing social change before personal salvation. (See Chapter 1.) After 1918 the nation witnessed a major revival of traditional Protestantism that was highly critical of both recent trends.

The traditionalists were called *fundamentalists* after a set of pamphlets issued in 1910 prescribing the five "fundamental" beliefs of orthodox Protestantism: the Bible's infallibility, Christ's virgin birth, His atonement for humankind's sins, the Resurrection, and the Second Coming. Fundamentalism was especially strong in the South and among Baptists, although the Methodists and Presbyterians also had fundamentalist wings.

During the twenties no cause mustered as much fundamentalist energy as the attack on evolution. Darwin's work, as we saw (see Chapter 1), denied the Biblical account of the creation and blurred humankind's distinction from the "brute creation." It deeply offended those who considered the Bible the exact word of God, and during the twenties fundamentalist Protestant ministers and pious lay people, such as the venerable Democratic leader, William Jennings Bryan, mounted a campaign to exclude the theory of evolution from the curricula of state-supported schools.

In 1924 the state of Tennessee passed a measure (the Butler law) making it "unlawful for any teacher in any of the . . . public schools of the state . . . to teach any theory that denies the story of the Divine Creation of man as taught in the Bible, and to teach instead that man has descended from a lower order of animals." A short item describing passage of the law appeared in the *New York Times* and was called to the attention of the American Civil Liberties Union (ACLU), an organization formed originally to defend free speech against government suppression during the war.

The ACLU was interested in a case to test the constitutionality of the antievolution act, but was unable to find a defendant who would deliberately violate the law. Then in Dayton, Tennessee, a small town north of Chattanooga, John Scopes, a bespectacled, young high-school science teacher, agreed to challenge the Butler law by teaching evolution. Scopes was indicted, and the ACLU had its case.

The "monkey trial" that followed at Dayton was a confrontation in miniature of the two Americas. Defending Scopes was the ACLU and some of the most prominent liberal lawyers in the country, including Clarence Darrow, the country's most controversial legal maverick and a professional agnostic. On the other side were the state's lawyers backed by Bryan, who had been added to beef up the prosecution. Dayton took on a carnival atmosphere as hundreds of reporters and spectators descended on the community in July 1925 to observe the happenings and join in the fun. Enterprising businesspeople hawked banners and sold cold drinks to the crowds milling around the town courthouse.

For a time it looked as if nothing much would be decided except whether Scopes had technically violated the law. The prosecution defeated every effort by the defense to have the case transferred to the federal courts and the law challenged as a violation of the constitutional right of free speech. The defense also was unable to call expert witnesses to defend the truth of evolution. But then Darrow managed to get Bryan on the stand as an expert witness for the Bible. The confrontation was at hand. Now, Darrow thought, he could "show up Fundamentalism . . . [and] prevent bigots and ignoramuses from controlling the education system of the United States." For his part, Bryan was ready to "protect the word of God against the greatest atheist and agnostic in the United States."

Darrow demolished Bryan, forcing him to reveal his inadequate knowledge of both science and the Bible and catching him in contradictions. Bryan's hedging even alienated his supporters and harmed the fundamentalist cause. On the other hand the case also revealed Darrow as an arrogant and smart-alecky man lacking in compassion and understanding of people unlike himself.

In the end the case settled little. Scopes was convicted and fined $100. On appeal, the Tennessee Supreme Court upheld the antievolution law, but then set aside the conviction on a technicality. The Butler Act and five other similar state statutes remained on the books, but were not thereafter enforced. Scopes went on to become a distinguished geologist. Bryan died days after the trial and was buried at Arlington National Cemetery. His tombstone reads "He Kept the Faith."

Prohibition

No issue divided the two Americas more decisively than *prohibition,* the attempt to stop drinking by forbidding the production, sale, and transportation of alcoholic beverages. The defenders of prohibition, called "drys," saw their cause as a "noble experiment" that if successful might eliminate the vast social evil of drunkenness and shape a more virtuous nation. Originating in the prewar progressive impulse to improve society, by the 1920s the prohibition movement would become more closely identified with the rural, fundamentalist attempt to control the immoral city and its immigrant, Catholic, and black inhabitants. Prohibition's opponents, called "wets," saw the issue in a very different light. The noble experiment, they said, was an attempt by moralists and pious Protestant busybodies to impose their puritan values on people who had the right to enjoy their harmless habits. "Reduced to its essential," wrote Mencken in his usual intemperate way, prohibition "is no more than a legal realization of the Methodist's hatred of the civilized man."

The bone of contention between the two sides was the Eighteenth Amendment to the Constitution, ratified in 1919, and the Volstead Act, its enabling legislation. The Volstead law specified as alcoholic beverages any drink containing more than one half of one percent alcohol. It exempted from the ban alcohol to be used for medicinal purposes or in religious ceremonies. The act also prescribed stiff punishments for violation of the law and placed its administration under a commissioner of prohibition in the Bureau of Internal Revenue.

The law would have been difficult to enforce under the best of circumstances. But forbidding even beer and light wine turned many moderate supporters against it, and in much of the Northeast and Midwest state and local officials refused to enforce the federal law. The federal government might have done its own enforcement, but this would have required thousands of agents, millions of dollars, and exceptional ruthlessness. Few Americans were willing to pay the price. At no time did the federal Prohibition Bureau ever have the money to employ more than 2900 agents, and many of these were either corrupt or inefficient.

Although the law probably reduced the incidence of alcoholism, it made drinking respectable among middle-class people by investing it with the lure of the forbidden. It now became "the thing to do." Women had played a large part in the fight for the Eighteenth Amendment, and in fact many of the most illustrious women social reformers had begun their work in the temperance movement. But in the rebellious twenties women, especially younger ones, were among the new recruits to drinking. In the past bars and saloons were frequented almost entirely by men. Now sophisticated women flocked to the illegal nightclubs and speakeasies that prohibition had spawned.

Americans developed extraordinary ingenuity in evading the law. Thousands made their own wine from grapes and other fruit or concocted "home brew" from grain. Others secured prescriptions from doctors attesting to their need for medicinal whiskey. Illinois records in 1922 showed that almost 2.3 million people got prescriptions filled for whiskey, gin, and other alcoholic "medicines." The amount of "sacramental" wine consumed by otherwise religiously indifferent Christians and Jews surged to remarkable levels.

Most drinkers, however, turned to bootleggers to supply their illegal needs. These entrepreneurs brought liquor in from Canada, the West Indies, and Europe by truck and ship and sold it to trusted and favored customers. They also supplied the speakeasies, the new illegal version of the saloon, with their whiskey and wine. Prohibition created a whole underground economy run by mobsters who were quick to profit from the split between what the law prescribed and what many Americans actually desired. Although organized crime had existed before, prohibition enormously advanced its growth and created a whole new criminal world dominated by men such as Al Capone, Dion O'Bannion, "Dutch" Schultz, and others. Respectable citizens patronized the mob either directly or in roundabout ways, but they were appalled by the mob's violence against those who stood in its way and by its ability to frustrate the legal authorities. By the end of the decade to most Americans' regret, prohibition had made the "gangster" a social type characteristic of the era and the American scene.

The African-American Migration North

As late as 1910 only 10 percent of the nation's African-American population lived outside the former slave states. There they were denied the franchise, excluded by Jim Crow laws from decent educational facilities and adequate public and private services, and subjected to a system of harsh intimidation and economic discrimination.

Many would have left the South to escape these conditions if they had been able to find decent jobs in the North. But northern white employers preferred European immigrants and would not hire blacks, except as strikebreakers. Then came the war, which cut off European labor sources, and employers abruptly changed their minds. A mass black exodus from the South's cotton and tobacco fields was soon underway. The immigration restriction laws, by cutting off a traditional source of cheap industrial labor, sustained the migration northward during the twenties. By 1930 approximately 2.3 million of the country's African-American citizens resided in the North and West, over a quarter of the total.

Most of the new arrivals were drawn to the big cities, with New York, Chicago, and Detroit attracting the largest number. There they worked largely at menial jobs in the mills, at the construction sites, and in white people's homes. African-Americans settled in segregated slum communities, not from choice but because middle-class whites were able to prevent their spread into their neighborhoods. The tight segregation pattern made for awesome congestion. African-American ghetto residents were packed into cut-up apartments meant for far fewer people. Landlords gave little attention to maintenance but, owing to the acute housing shortage in the ghetto, were able to charge blacks much higher rents than whites (although blacks normally earned far less in wages). This disparity between means and needs gave rise to the ghetto "rent party." A black family, faced with eviction for nonpayment of rent, would sell tickets to a gala in its apartment and offer food and liquor at a profit. If all went well, the proceeds would keep the landlord at bay for another month.

At times African-Americans encountered violence in the northern cities. In 1919 there were race riots in Charleston, South Carolina; Longview, Texas; Washington,

D.C.; Omaha, Nebraska; and Chicago. Scores of people, mostly blacks, were killed and hundreds hurt; property damage reached many thousands of dollars.

Marcus Garvey

Some urban African-Americans found refuge from the distressing circumstances of their new lives in the Universal Negro Improvement Association (UNIA) of Marcus Garvey. Garvey was a Jamaican who had come to the United States in 1916 and soon after organized the UNIA to spread the message of African-American separateness and black racial pride. A black skin was not a mark of inferiority, Garvey told the African-American newcomers to the big cities. On the contrary, black people had been responsible for the civilizations of ancient Egypt and Greece. African-Americans should never expect to be integrated into white American society. Instead they should establish their own parallel institutions and go their separate way. This philosophy led Garvey and his followers to establish a Negro Factories Corporation, a Black Star ocean-shipping line, and other black-run enterprises as well as separate African-American fraternal organizations.

By 1922 Garvey and the UNIA had approximately one million followers in such cities as New York, Chicago, Philadelphia, Detroit, Pittsburgh, Cleveland, and Cincinnati. Many of these people had invested their meager savings in his Black Star Line and other Garvey business ventures. That year, believing that his African-American separatism would please white racists, Garvey tried to make an alliance with

Marcus Garvey, leader of the Universal Negro Improvement Association, sitting in the left rear of his limousine. (Springer/Bettmann Film Archive)

the revived Ku Klux Klan. When the news leaked out, Garvey's enemies among African-American integrationist moderates of the NAACP attacked him fiercely. The blunder stirred up latent anti–West Indian sentiment with the American-born black community and led to mass defections.

The following year the federal government indicted Garvey for using the mails to defraud by selling stock in his Black Star Line. The government's case was weak, but Garvey was convicted and sentenced to a surprising five-year term by Judge Julian Mack, a member of the NAACP. Garveyism in organized form quickly disappeared, but the mood of African-American pride and separatism survived to resurface in the 1960s.

The Harlem Renaissance

Garveyism appealed primarily to poor, ill-educated African-American newcomers to the big cities. But the cities also drew the talented and the brilliant of the race. During the 1920s Harlem, in New York's upper Manhattan, became the center of an extraordinary intellectual, literary, and artistic outpouring called the *Harlem Renaissance.*

The Harlem Renaissance was the creation of African-American intellectuals and writers, some northern-born, some from Dixie, and some from the Caribbean. Alain Locke, head of Howard University's philosophy department, was a Rhodes Scholar who edited the magazine *Opportunity,* the publication of the National Urban League (an organization devoted to helping African-Americans adjust to life in the northern cities). Locke announced the cultural flowering of Harlem in *The New Negro* (1925) and did much to publicize it. The heart of the renaissance, however, was the work of poets such as Countee Cullen, Claude McKay, and Langston Hughes and novelists such as James Weldon Johnson and Jean Toomer. Each of these writers considered himself a *new Negro,* a proud being no longer willing to wait patiently for justice, but determined to assert his rights. Wrote McKay,

> If we must die, let it not be like hogs
> Hunted and penned in an inglorious spot,
> While round us bark the mad and hungry dogs,
> Making their mock at our accursed lot.

Toomer, in his remarkable novel *Cane,* seeks the roots of African-American identity and, although himself an urban man, finds it in the rural American South. McKay and Cullen discovered a different answer to the same quest. Although men of high Western culture, they found black identity in the supposed "primitivism" of Africa. Their views foreshadowed later black intellectuals' sense of separation from the European heritage.

The creators of the Harlem Renaissance were primarily writers, but there were also talented painters among them such as Henry Tanner and Meta Warrick as well as sculptors such as Richmond Barthe. The movement attracted a following among certain whites, most notably Carl Van Vechten, a writer, literary critic, and art patron who brought the talented Harlemites to the attention of a wider public and helped to create an audience for their works. Indeed for a time, Harlem with its performers and artists became a mecca for white dilettantes seeking out excitement from contact with an "exotic" culture and a forbidden race.

New Era Politics

The twenties was a Republican decade. Harding's landslide in 1920 was exceeded by that of Coolidge four years later. In 1928 the Republican victory was not as great proportionately, but it was still decisive. During the period, moreover, the Republicans retained control of both houses of Congress. Meanwhile, the Democrats, their voting strength split between a Catholic urban following and the "solid," predominantly fundamentalist south, were a prime victim of the cultural chasm that ran through the nation.

The Harding Administration

Harding's administration was marked by corruption of classic proportions. Our picture of the twenty-ninth president is of a genial, generous, but mediocre and morally lax man pushed, some say, by his wife, the redoubtable Florence King Harding, into aiming beyond his true capacity. The picture may be exaggerated; recent scholars give him better grades than their predecessors. But it is clear that his background as editor of a small-town Ohio newspaper did not prepare him adequately for the role of president of the United States.

Harding's greatest weakness was his confusion of personal loyalty and congeniality with political competence. Some of his choices for office were excellent ones. Everyone praised the selection of Charles Evans Hughes as secretary of state, Herbert Hoover as secretary of commerce, and Henry C. Wallace as secretary of agriculture. Secretary of Treasury Andrew Mellon, however feeble his social sympathies, was also an experienced financier and well regarded in the business community.

But many of the president's appointments were shoddy. Harry Daugherty, his attorney general, was a cheap political fixer whose only qualification was that he was Harding's old crony from the Ohio days, a man in whose presence Harding could relax and let down his hair. Daugherty brought Jess Smith and a flock of other Ohio fixers with him to Washington and the "Ohio gang" hangout on K Street became a political exchange where pardons, appointments, immunities, and other favors in the attorney general's power were swapped for cash.

The new secretary of interior, Albert Fall of New Mexico, was a former Texas marshal, prospector, and Rough Rider who looked every inch the upright western rancher. But he was venal and corrupt. Fall induced Navy Secretary Edwin Denby to transfer control of the Elk Hills naval oil reserve in California and the Teapot Dome reserve in Wyoming to the Interior Department. In exchange for thousands of dollars in bribes he then leased the reserves, intended to serve the nation in time of war, to two oil operators, Edward Doheny and Harry Sinclair.

Equally bad choices were Charles Forbes as head of the Veterans Bureau and Thomas Miller as Alien Property Custodian. Forbes took bribes for Veterans

Administration (VA) hospital contracts and got kickbacks from businesspeople who were allowed to buy supposedly surplus VA supplies for a song. Miller was paid off to sell at a giant discount a German-owned metals company that was sequestered by the government during the war.

Harding, although no moral paragon, did not himself profit from any of this and was upset when rumors began to reach him that some of his close friends had betrayed his trust. One story survives about a visitor to the White House one day discovering the president with his hands around Forbes's throat shouting, "You yellow rat! You double-crossing bastard!" Whether true or not, Harding allowed Forbes to resign and did not press charges.

The president was spared the full disclosure of his errors by dying in office while on a trip to the West Coast. He had been allowed by his doctors to undertake the tour on the understanding that he would relax. But he turned the trip into a political campaign tour that included making up to five speeches a day. In San Francisco Harding suffered a heart attack and died several days later.

Silent Cal and the 1924 Election

Harding's successor, Calvin Coolidge, was probably no more competent and certainly less amiable and generous than his predecessor. (Alice Roosevelt Longworth said that he seemed to have been "weaned on a pickle.") He was also a man of greater dignity and sounder moral principles. Coolidge helped clean the Augean stables at the Veterans Administration and the Alien Property office, fired Daugherty, and vigorously prosecuted the Teapot Dome culprits. Although both stingy and lazy he brought a higher tone to the White House, and his well-spoken wife, Grace, was one of the nation's most attractive first ladies.

Coolidge ran for a full term in 1924 and swamped John W. Davis, a Wall Street lawyer who had received the Democratic nomination only after the convention deadlocked between a southern and western wing behind the dry and Protestant William McAdoo and the midwestern and northeastern wing that favored the wet and Catholic Al Smith, governor of New York. Besides their disunity and lackluster candidate, the Democrats were handicapped by the third-party candidacy of the aging Robert La Follette, running on a ticket endorsed by dissident farmer-labor groups. The results were not surprising. Coolidge receive 15.7 million popular votes to Davis's 8.4 and La Follette's 4.8.

Coolidge's administration was marked more by negatives than positives. He opposed the McNary-Haugen scheme to achieve higher farm prices through federal purchases of surplus crops to be paid for by a special fee on farmers. Strongly pushed by the farm bloc in Congress, the McNary-Haugen bill passed in 1927, but was vetoed by Coolidge on the grounds that it amounted to price-fixing. Coolidge also vetoed a veterans bonus bill granting an endowment policy to each veteran proportionate to the individual's length of service. The principle on this would not be collectable for twenty years, but the veteran in the meantime could borrow a quarter of the eventual value. Congress overrode the president's veto.

In July 1927 the president went to the Black Hills of South Dakota for his vacation. It was the usual joyless Coolidge occasion. He fished in the local streams while wearing white gloves; his aides baited his hook and removed the catch. It was on this occasion that "Silent Cal" was induced to dress up as an Indian. The picture of the nation's dour chief executive with a feathered Indian warbonnet on his head appeared in every paper in the country to the public's great amusement.

But there was one serious bit of business on the trip. At a press conference at the Rapid City High School, the president lined the newspaper reporters up and as they filed by him handed each a strip of paper. The paper contained the words: "I do not choose to run for President in nineteen twenty-eight." There was a moment of stunned silence and then a mad rush to find the nearest telephone. Silent Cal was good copy to the end!

The 1928 Election

As the 1928 election approached, each of the two major parties had clear front-runners. Al Smith could not be denied the Democratic nomination this time. The Klan had passed its peak, and although anti-Catholic feelings remained strong, the New York governor seemed far preferable to another dud like Davis. Among the Republicans, Secretary of Commerce Herbert Hoover was far ahead as the presidential season began. Although stiff and humorless, Hoover seemed a man of high principle, a great humanitarian, and a skilled and effective administrator. Both men won their

President Coolidge wearing a Sioux headdress. (The Bettmann Archive)

respective party nominations and went on the fight a campaign that revealed as have few others the cultural seams in American society.

From the beginning Smith's campaign labored under severe handicaps. The country was exuberantly prosperous in 1928 and many Americans were certain that the Republican party was somehow responsible for it all. Besides, Hoover, "the great engineer," was also genuinely popular. Equally important were Smith's many apparent drawbacks. The Democratic candidate seemed the more limited, provincial man. A former Tammany protégé and product of "the sidewalks of New York," Smith lacked any understanding of the problems of western and southern farmers and any familiarity with foreign affairs.

More important to many voters was Smith's Catholicism. No Catholic had ever received a major party presidential nomination, and in the view of many Protestant citizens none ever should. Anti-Catholic bigotry went back to the beginning of the American community and been reinforced over the years by the successive waves of Irish, Italian, and Slavic immigration that broke over the nation from the 1840s onward. Many Protestants believed that a Catholic president would be beholden to the Pope and the Catholic hierarchy. He would be burdened by "a dual allegiance," wrote one critic, and be unable to decide issues in the best interest of the United States should the Church take an opposing position. Moreover, Smith was a wet who would be certain to undermine the noble experiment.

Smith tried to arouse the public's sense of fair play and respect for liberty of conscience. He called his critics bigots, denied his subordination to the Pope, and asserted his firm support for the secular public schools and for the separation of church and state. But nothing availed. The Republicans worked the prosperity issue openly and effectively. Republican campaign workers handed out copper medallions on street corners inscribed: "The Hoover Lucky Pocket Piece—Good for four years of prosperity." Hoover himself proclaimed that "the poorhouse is vanishing from among us . . . and we shall soon . . . be in sight of the day when poverty will be banished from this nation." At the grass-roots level the Republicans also loudly banged the anti-Catholic drum. Methodist Bishop James Cannon traveled widely through the West and South organizing anti-Smith committees. Just before the election the *Commercial Appeal* of strongly Protestant Memphis carried an advertisement headed "Vote as You Pray."

The results surprised no one. Although many thousands of Catholic voters came out to support their coreligionist, their contribution was more than offset by losses elsewhere. Like most Democrats before him, Smith carried the big cities. He also carried heavily Catholic Massachusetts and Rhode Island. But he did not carry a single normally Republican midwestern or western state and he lost heavily in the South where, for the first time since Reconstruction, Texas, Virginia, Florida, and North Carolina went Republican. It used to be said that Smith's campaign, although it failed, was a turning point for the Democrats and that it launched them on the course that would make them the normal majority party during the half-century that followed. More recent scholarship denies it this role: Smith did not make the cities Democratic; they already were. In fact he divided the Democrats and eroded their traditional southern base. It was the advent of the New Deal after 1932 that produced the turnabout that ended Republican predominance for almost half a century.

Herbert Hoover

Hoover's administration promised a new day for all Americans. His appointments included such first-rate men as Henry L. Stimson as secretary of state, President Ray Lyman Wilbur of Stanford University as secretary of the interior, Charles Evans Hughes as the new chief justice of the Supreme Court. He reappointed Andrew Mellon to the Treasury and then replaced him in 1932 with another capable banker, Ogden Mills. The Great Engineer also introduced new order into the affairs of the executive branch of government. *The New Republic* reported of his early months that he "does not run away from his troubles; he feels competent to solve them, and acts in most cases with a promptness and decision which have not been seen in the White House since Mr. Wilson's early days."

However good an administrator, Hoover was not a deft politician. Even before the 1929 economic collapse roiled the political waters, he found Congress hard to deal with. He and the legislators fought over agricultural relief and over the tariff and neither got their way. Congress failed to get a new version of a farm subsidy scheme, called the "export debenture" plan, past the president's veto. It had to settle for the Agricultural Marketing Act (1929), establishing a Federal Farm Board with a fund of $500 million to remove surplus crops temporarily from the market. The president, on the other hand, was unable to stop the protectionists on Capitol Hill from passing the Hawley-Smoot tariff (1930), which raised tariff rates to an all-time high, despite the warning of 1000 members of the American Economic Association that it would hurt the economy severely. Hoover signed the bill reluctantly.

Despite his difficulties Hoover's presidency might have gone down as one of the nation's more successful ones. But by the time he signed the Hawley-Smoot bill, the prosperous Republican New Era had ended. For the remaining months and years of his term Hoover would be forced to battle with the most severe economic crisis in the country's experience (see the next chapter). However unfairly, history would not be kind to his endeavors, and the American people would remember him as one of the great presidential failures.

Republican Foreign Policy

It once was said that the United States withdrew into deep isolation after its failure to join the League of Nations in 1920 and largely ignored the rest of the world. We now recognize that this was not true. At the same time we must not exaggerate American involvement in world affairs during the 1920s. The United States refused to accept responsibility for keeping the peace in Europe through guarantees of collective security and refused to accept the obligations that its new postwar economic power imposed on it.

Pacific Problems

During the 1920s Americans seemed more willing to take an active role in the Pacific than in Europe. Across the great ocean to the west it confronted a touchy and dissatisfied Japan, which was convinced that the United States was determined to keep it from achieving the place in the sun that it deserved. Japanese-American relations, seldom very good, were further strained at the Versailles Peace Conference. There Wilson kept the League Covenant from adopting a Japanese-sponsored resolution affirming the equality of all races, and managed to limit Japanese claims to former German Pacific colonies and to territory in China. Soon after Japan, the United States, and Great Britain found themselves engaged in a major naval armaments race that threatened to become dangerous.

To head off the confrontation, in August 1921 Secretary of State Hughes issued an invitation to eight powers with interests in the Pacific basin—Japan, Great Britain, France, China, Italy, Belgium, Portugal, and the Netherlands—to meet in Washington in November to discuss their differences. The Washington Naval Conference proved a stunning short-term success. Hughes's suggestions produced the Five Power Naval Treaty whereby the United States, Japan, Great Britain, France, and Italy agreed to abandon the construction of all battleships for ten years. Battleship tonnage was limited to an amount that would give Britain and the United States equality, Japan three-fifths their amount, and the two smaller naval powers, a little more than half Japan's. In addition the three largest Pacific naval powers agreed not to further fortify their Pacific island possessions.

The conference also produced the Four Power Treaty pledging the United States, Britain, Japan, and France to respect each other's possessions in the Pacific and to seek peaceful settlement of disputes in the Pacific area. A Nine Power Treaty, signed by all the attending nations, promised to uphold the American Open Door policy of respecting the sovereignty and independence of China.

The Washington Conference seemed more successful to contemporaries than it does today. None of the agreements to resolve Pacific disputes were effective. Although it placed limitations on battleships, it failed to limit aircraft carriers and, there-fore, simply displaced the naval race. Its provision relegating Japan to a three-fifths ratio of capital ships with the United States and Great Britain hurt Japanese sensibilities.

Japan's resentment of the United States was reinforced in 1924 when Congress adopted a measure specifically excluding all Japanese immigration to the United States. Until this point under the Gentlemen's Agreement of 1908 the Japanese had denied exit visas to unskilled laborers to accommodate American fears of cheap Asian labor competition. The Japanese action had avoided American exclusion and preserved Japanese pride. But now Congress insisted on treating the Japanese as it had the Chinese—as inferiors, forbidden as a nationality to emigrate and "ineligible to citizenship." The 1924 bill produced a storm of indignation among the sensitive Japanese. It was an "outrageous enactment," they declared, and should be met by a boycott of American products. The matter eventually blew over, but Japanese-American relations had been badly damaged and would only get much worse before they got better.

Latin America

During the 1920s and 1930s the United States improved its relations with its Latin American neighbors. In 1924 it removed its marines from the Dominican Republic, allowing the Dominicans to manage their own affairs for the first time in a decade. In 1933 it ended the military occupation of Nicaragua.

Most important was the settlement of outstanding differences with Mexico. These had sharpened during the mid-twenties, when president Plutarco Calles bitterly attacked the Catholic Church and threatened to limit American oil holdings in Mexico to fifty-year leases. Fortunately, despite outraged Catholic and business opinion at home, President Coolidge chose to negotiate and sent an emissary, the banker Dwight Morrow, to Mexico. A man of great charm and warmth, Morrow proved to be an effective diplomat. As a gesture of friendship, he arranged to have his son-in-law, the world-famous trans-Atlantic aviator Charles Lindbergh, fly to Mexico City and accept the plaudits of the Mexican people. Morrow got the Mexicans to tone down their anti-Catholic campaign and to compromise on the oil-land titles. Mexican-American relations quickly improved.

Europe and World Peace

The conspicuous failure of Republican twenties foreign policy was its disregard of collective security efforts in Europe. The internationalists of the Wilson era continued to agitate for U.S. membership in the League of Nations after 1920 but without success. Nevertheless the country participated in a nonmember capacity in a number of League international conferences on social issues and even stationed several permanent representatives in Geneva, the League's world headquarters. Proponents of world cooperation for peace came closer to getting the United States to join the World Court. In the end, however, American reservations about accepting World Court decisions as binding in international disputes involving American interests undermined the effort.

That Americans were not totally indifferent to collective actions for peace was made clear by that peculiar agreement known as the Kellogg-Briand Pact, signed in 1928. This document pledged each signing nation to renounce war "as an instrument of national policy in their relations to one another." Ultimately ratified by all the great powers it was an empty gesture that had no effect when conditions in Europe once again threatened the peace of the world. Yet the signature of the United States suggested that even Americans recognized the value of some collective action to ensure world peace.

The New Era

As Americans looked back at the twenties from the vantage of later decades, they often expressed regret at its passing. To many people it seemed a time of carefree zaniness— of flappers and Model Ts, of flagpole sitters and speakeasies, of Betty Co-ed and Village bohemians, of Fitzgerald and Millay. And it *was* all of these things. But it was also an era of bitter cultural strife and ugly racial, intellectual, and political intolerance, a time when middle-class Americans, understandably tired of crusades, retreated to an excessive privatism and let social problems pile up. But when Americans remembered the twenties, they recalled above all its prosperity. Especially from the decade that followed this would be the most vivid image, because seven months after Hoover's inauguration, New Era prosperity collapsed with a roar that echoed around the globe. The world was plunged into the greatest depression in modern history.

FOR FURTHER READING

The twenties has evoked some of the most colorful historical writing we have. For a delightful, although dated, overview see Frederick Lewis Allen's classic *Only Yesterday: An Informal History of the Nineteen Twenties* (1931). Also see William Leuchtenberg's *The Perils of Prosperity, 1914–1932* (1958). The decade's business climate and economy are described in James Prothro, *Dollar Decade: Business Ideas in the 1920's* (1954) and George Soule, *Prosperity Decade: From War to Depression, 1917–1929* (1947). The student can learn about labor's lot in the period from Irving Bernstein, *The Lean Years: The American Worker, 1920–1933* (1960) and David Brody, *Labor in Crisis: The Steel Strike of 1919* (1965). Antiradical activities are described in Robert K. Murray, *Red Scare, 1919–1920* (1955) and William Preston, Jr., *Aliens and Dissenters: Federal Suppression of Radicals, 1903–1933* (1963). Francis Russell's *Tragedy in Dedham: The Sacco-Vanzetti Case* (1962) seeks to reevaluate the forensic evidence to determine guilt for the actual commission of the crime.

American literature during the twenties can best be understood through the works of the writers themselves. But literary biography is the next best approach. Some good ones include Carlos Baker, *Ernest Hemingway* (1969); Mark Schorer, *Sinclair Lewis: An American Life* (1961); Linda Wagner, *Dos Passos: Artist As American* (1979); William Manchester, *Disturber of the Peace: H. L. Mencken* (1951); and Arthur Mizener on Fitzgerald, *The Far Side of Paradise* (1951). Also see again Alfred Kazin, *On Native Grounds* (1942). For the literary and intellectual expatriates see Malcom Cowley's *Exile's Return* (1934). On Greenwich Village in the 1920s consult Caroline Ware, *Greenwich Village* (1935).

For women during the twenties see Susan D. Becker, *The Origins of the Equal Rights Amendment: Feminism Between the Wars* (1981) and J. Stanley Lemons, *The Woman Citizen: Social Feminism in the 1920's* (1973). A first-rate study of college youth in the twenties is Paula Fass's *The Damned and the Beautiful: American Youth in the 1920s* (1977). Every student of 1920s society should read the classic contemporary study by Robert and Helen Lynd, *Middletown: A Study of Contemporary American Culture* (1929).

On the movies and Hollywood in this period see David Robinson, *Hollywood in the Twenties* (1968). Radio's early years are recounted in the first volume of Eric Barnouw's two-volume *A History of Broadcasting in the United States* (1965).

The counterattack of traditional America against the forces of modernism is described in a number of volumes. See Norman Furniss, *The Fundamentalist Controversy, 1918–1931* (1954), for the conservative Protestant reaction. For the Scopes trial see Ray Ginger, *Six Days or Forever? Tennessee v. John Thomas Scopes* (1958). The Klan of the 1920s is treated in Kenneth Jackson's *The Ku Klux Klan in the City, 1915–1930* (1967). The immigration restriction movement of the twenties is covered by John Higham, *Strangers in the Land* (1967).

There are several good books on 1920s prohibition. See Andrew Sinclair, *Prohibition: Era of Excess* (1962) and Joseph R. Gusfield, *Symbolic Crusade: Status Politics and the American Temperance Movement* (1963).

On African-Americans in the twenties North see Nathan Huggins, *Harlem Renaissance* (1971); Gilbert Osofsky, *Harlem: The Making of a Ghetto, 1890–1930* (1966); and E. David Cronon, *Black Moses: The Story of Marcus Garvey and the Universal Negro Improvement Association* (1955).

The politics of the 1920s can be understood through the following works: David Burner's *fine book The Politics of Provincialism: The Democratic Party in Transition, 1918–1932* (1967); Robert K. Murray, *The Harding Era: Warren G. Harding and His Administration* (1969); Donald R. McCoy, *Calvin Coolidge: The Quiet President* (1967); David Burner, *Herbert Hoover: A Public Life* (1979); Burl Noggle, *Teapot Dome: Oil and Politics in the 1920s* (1962); Francis Russell, *The Shadow of Blooming Grove: Warren G. Harding and His Times* (1968); and Edmund Moore, *A Catholic Runs for President, 1928* (1956).

The farm bloc is covered by Theodore Saloutos and John D. Hicks, *Agricultural Discontent in the Middle West, 1900–1939* (1951). For Republican foreign policy during the 1920s see Lewis Ethan Ellis, *Republican Foreign Policy, 1921–1933* (1968). The Washington Naval Conference is dealt with by Thomas Buckley in *The United States and the Washington Conference, 1921–1922* (1970).

7
The
Great Depression

A typical Great Depression scene: bread being distributed to the destitute. (The Bettmann Archive)

The Twenties Boom

The prosperity that collapsed with a resounding crash in October 1929 seemed unassailable to most middle-class Americans during the 1920s. Yet there were serious structural weaknesses in the twenties economy that in retrospect explain the disaster that would follow.

There is little question that in aggregate terms the 1920s was a period of remarkable economic growth. Between 1919 and 1929 total GNP grew from $84 billion to $103 billion, about 2 percent a year, faster than during the previous decade. Per capita income rose from an annual average of $517 between 1909 and 1918 to $612 during the next ten years. Real average earnings (taking into account price changes) had increased some 32 percent during the first two decades of the century. In the twenties alone they grew by 23 percent.

The prosperity was uneven—as it always is. Farmers, especially those of the Midwest and South, did not share in the boom. Between 1899 and 1914 agriculture had recovered from the bad times of the late nineteenth century. The war further swelled farm income. Higher prices and government encouragement led farmers to borrow money to invest in new tractors and harvesters and put new acreage into production. Good times continued into 1920 while devastated Europe called on America for food and fiber. Then, as Europe recovered and began to meet its own agricultural needs, farm prices slumped, and with them farm income. Unable to meet the debts incurred during the wartime expansion, many farmers went bankrupt. Between the years 1921 to 1924 and 1926 to 1929 forced sales of farms for nonpayment of taxes and to pay defaulted debts increased from twelve to twenty-one per thousand farmers. Some recovery of farm prices took place after 1925, but they never equaled the flush period of 1914 to 1921. Critics would argue that farmers had no right to expect prices and markets to be as good as the war years and that farmers in any case were always dissatisfied. Yet through most of the twenties the nation's farmers felt aggrieved that prosperity had passed them by and their discontent would fuel the aggressive congressional farm bloc.

But farmers were not the only losers during the decade. In New England the textile industry went into decline. Like agriculture, coal mining and other extractive industries had been pumped up by wartime need and deflated after 1919. Facing new competition from a growing network of hard-surfaced, long-distance highways and the trucks and passenger cars that rolled over them, the railroads also went into decline. Workers in these older industries lost jobs. Some middle-class groups also lost ground during the decade. Small merchants, particularly drugstore owners and grocers, faced by the expanding chain stores, went bankrupt in droves. Investors in the nation's vast interurban trolley system, constructed early in the century, were also hard hit and abandoned most of their operations when the lines proved unable to cope with competition from the private automobile.

Some important groups, then, were skipped over when the nation's economy surged during the 1920s. This fact should register as a growing disparity between rich and poor. And undoubtedly to an unemployed Massachusetts textile worker or a jobless Illinois miner, it must have seemed that the rich were indeed getting richer and the poor poorer. But in fact the share of total yearly income going to the richest 5 percent of American families was not increasing during the decade. Their share remained the same. On the other hand figures make it clear that the inequality of the past was getting no better: during the decade the richest 5 percent received 30 percent of the nation's income.

But however unequal the gains, the advance in absolute living standards of most Americans during the decade was real. In 1920, 35 percent of American households had electric lights; in 1930, 68 percent. In 1920, 20 percent of American families had inside flush toilets; in 1930, 51 percent. In 1920, 8 percent of American households owned washing machines; by 1930 it was 24 percent. Automobile ownership in this same decade went from 26 to 60 percent of all American families. Nor were these gains paid for by harder labor. During the 1920s the length of the average work week, although still long by comparison with today, declined by close to 10 percent.

Increased Productivity

The prosperity of the 1920s had many sources. One key element was the increased productivity of the American worker. During the decade the increase in output per man hour grew at the rate of 2.5 percent each year, a pace greater than all but the unusual years immediately following the Civil War. Not that Joe or Jane Factory Worker suddenly became dynamos of energy; rather, new technology, new machinery, and new ways of organizing production made their work more efficient.

The new technology that sparked the productivity leap was broadly distributed. In steel, chemicals, and textiles new products, new machines, and new processes pushed up the output per worker. Much of the decade's new technology was based on the adoption of electricity and the electric motor to bring power to the workplace. Technical innovation in turn was accelerated by the rationalizing of scientific research. Until the twenties technological innovation had usually been hit or miss, emerging from the practical experience of industrialists, foremen, and workers. The Edison Laboratory in New Jersey, established in 1876, had been the first important research laboratory and its successful creation of the phonograph, movie projector, and electric light bulb had set an example of what a deliberate focus on invention could achieve. By the twenties many large business firms had established research laboratories manned by university-trained scientists and these were at the cutting edge of new-product development.

Still another element in productivity rise was the improvement in skill level of the work force. The nation's outlay on education during the decade grew from 1.17 percent of the gross national product to 2.22 percent. Most of this increase went to high-school education. During the 1920s the proportion of the country's seventeen-year-olds who were high-school graduates increased from 16.8 to 29 percent of the total. College degrees awarded soared from 53,000 in 1920 to 140,000 in 1930. Meanwhile, on the production line, the increasing application of "scientific management" techniques developed before the war by Frederick W. Taylor, Frank B. Gilbreth, and others reduced workers' waste effort and motion.

The most vivid expression of the new technology and the new ways of managing

The automobile assembly line symbolized the new industrial technology of the pre-Depression period. This picture was taken on May 26, 1927. (The Bettmann Archive)

it was the moving assembly line, borrowed from the packinghouse system of dismembering and dressing animal carcasses and introduced into heavy industry by Henry Ford at his giant River Rouge automobile factory in 1914. At River Rouge the line moved at a steady 6 feet a minute while workers added parts or performed other operations on the advancing car chassis. Within two years the time it took to produce the basic Model T Ford car dropped from twelve hours to ninety minutes. There was an equivalent drop in price. In 1929 a Ford automobile cost under $400, a drop of 80 percent from 1909.

Ford, of course, had no monopoly on the assembly line; it was quickly adopted by other manufacturers of cars and other large and expensive products, bringing their prices down sharply as well. Meanwhile, in other areas of the economy—petroleum, chemicals, glass, tires, steel, tobacco products, and other items—new machines and new ways to organize output had similar results.

Mass Consumption

Ford's assembly line was more than a production technique. Henry Ford epitomized a new economic philosophy. Rather than trying to get as much money as possible for each item produced, Ford cut costs ruthlessly and made the product affordable by everyone. Even at the lower profit, mass consumption would make money for producers. Another part of the equation was higher wages, for only if

American workers were well paid could they afford even cheap automobiles and other items. In 1914 Ford had offered workers at his Detroit plant the then unheard of factory wage of five dollars a day and, although his carry-through did not equal his promise, his high-wage policy became a twenties ideal.

And ultimately Ford was right. Productivity growth during the twenties could make a difference only because there were enormous simultaneous increases in consumer demand. The growth of per capita income during the early years of the century topped off by the surge of the war period, brought many more Americans into the ranks of middle-class consumers, people with "discretionary" income, dollars not earmarked for food, clothing, and shelter. Most of the expensive gadgets— automobiles, radios, washing machines, electric toasters, and other appliances—that manufacturers offered during the twenties had been invented earlier. But generally only a small group of rich families could afford them. Now, millions of Americans joined the market for such items. Millions could also now pay for new services—at beauty parlors, bakeries, movie houses.

Manufacturers did not rely solely on cash customers, however. The consumer "durables" that the public now sought were both expensive and long-lived. These characteristics made them suitable for credit buying. Indeed only if credit were readily available could many people at the marginal-income end afford to buy them at all. Recognizing this reality, in 1919 two automobile entrepreneurs, William C. Durant and John J. Raskob, organized the General Motors (GM) Acceptance Corporation to finance installment buying of GM cars. The other car companies soon followed, and by 1927 two-thirds of all automobiles were purchased "on time." The scheme soon spread to the furniture, electrical appliance, sewing machine, and piano businesses. By 1929 total consumer debt outstanding had reached $7 billion. The United States had become a society where "buy now, pay later" (some said "buy now, pay never") was the guiding consumer principle.

The consumer boom of the twenties was stimulated primarily by the real convenience or pleasure derived from the new durables and services. Every society that has achieved the same level of income as 1920s America has followed the same road to mass consumption—unless the public has been held back by state coercion. The new wants came naturally, as it were, but in the twenties nothing was left to chance. Throughout the decade advertisers deluged the public with propaganda they hoped would stimulate dormant wants. It was during the twenties that the advertising industry under the leadership of Chicagoan Albert Lasker shifted from the unimagi-native selling of space in newspapers to catchy, often flamboyant multimedia campaigns to create new product images, arouse human interest, and attract attention to one product as opposed to another. "You furnish the girl; we furnish the home," promised one furniture store ad campaign. Such campaigns seemed to increase the market share of firms that used them and success brought prosperity. Advertising, which had been a small business with outlays of $400 million before the war, by 1929 had become a major industry with expenditures of $2.6 billion.

Investment

A final component of twenties prosperity was investment. The enormous increase in consumer demand stimulated a major boom in the capital goods industries, those that provided the new plant and equipment necessary to supply the public's wants. The public's insatiable desire for automobiles required ever larger outlays for machine tools, factory space, stamping machines, and so forth. The needs of the automobile also stimulated the glass, steel, petroleum, and rubber industries and created whole new businesses such as gas stations, auto-supply stores, and motels. The automobile also activated a network of intercity highways financed under the 1916 Federal Highways Act on a matching basis by state and federal governments. Billions were laid out for hard-surfaced highways for the first time. In fact it has been said that the 1920s highway-building program in the United States was one of the greatest public-works projects in history. One effect was to stimulate the cement and asphalt industries and to provide the American people with the best long-distance highway system in the world. By the end of the decade it became possible for an ordinary citizen, not just a daredevil sports enthusiast, to cross the United States, from coast to coast by car. The automobile and the improved highway system also encouraged suburban growth and so stimulated the construction industry.

Nor was the automobile the only enterprise that called forth large-scale capital outlays. Each of the industries it drew on in turn had to invest to keep up with automobile demand. And we must not forget the entirely new industries—radios and electrical appliances, for example—that also required large capital expenditures.

Sources of Weakness

The twenties economy, however buoyant and productive, was not, as we saw, without serious flaws. These would eventually undermine prosperity and turn good times into the worst depression in modern history.

Pockets of Poverty

One source of weakness was the uneven nature of prosperity. Although income disparities were not growing, neither were they diminishing. Poverty had not been banished in America. At the end of the decade there were still many Americans who were unable—credit buying notwithstanding—to become players in the consumer durables game. Many unskilled workers could not buy automobiles or washing machines or, in fact, purchase much more than the bare essentials of life for themselves and their families. In the northern cities such people were often immigrants or blacks. In the South they included both black and white sharecroppers and textile mill workers. Many midwestern farmers too were excluded from the mass consumption economy.

The effect of this remaining poverty was to narrow the total market for the products of industry and the new services economy. This in turn meant that *their* stimulating effect was smaller than it might have otherwise been. If more people had had the means to buy cars, refrigerators, and the rest, the boom might have lasted that much longer. As it was, by 1927 or 1928 the growth rate of demand for many consumer durables had begun to slacken, although not the absolute amount. To keen observers it seemed clear that the economic climate was about to change.

The International Economy

The international economy was another source of economic weakness. America entered the twenties era as the financial center of the Western world. After 1918 London's Threadneedle Street took a secondary position to New York's Wall Street as the major source of investment funds for capital-poor nations.

The shift in economic power was related to the enormous costs of the war and the Allied war debt to the United States. Besides the money extended by the United States to Britain, France, Italy, Belgium, and the other European associates during the war itself, the United States had made relief loans after the armistice to these nations and others and allowed them to buy on credit surplus U.S. supplies left in Europe at the war's end. With accumulated interest these loans amounted to over $20 billion by mid-decade.

These were a dead weight on the international economy. In retrospect it is easy to see that the United States probably should have written off the debts of its former allies. But while it did cut the Italian debt and lowered interest rates on the French, it refused to forego the bulk of the sums owed. President Coolidge spoke for most Americans when he responded to debt cancellation suggestions from Britain with the remark, "They hired the money, didn't they." However stressed, the British, French, and Italians were able to pay the United States because they could count on German reparations, assessed by the post-Versailles Reparations Commission at $33 billion. So long as Germany was able and willing to recompense the victorious Allied nations for its role in the war, part of this money could be used to reimburse the United States.

For several years the complicated shift of debts proved manageable. Under the Dawes (1924) and the Young (1929) plans Germany was able to get the Allies to scale down and spread out its reparations debt. For a time, although resentful, it paid the former Allies, who in turn paid "Uncle Shylock," as the British and French called the United States, referring to Shakespeare's character in *Merchant of Venice* who demanded his creditor's pound of flesh. But the system only worked briefly during the mid-1920s when Germany was prosperous and American bankers proved willing to lend Germany money without stint. Under this arrangement American dollars were transferred to the Germans, who then gave it to the British and the French, who then gave it back to the United States. In effect, Americans were indirectly paying themselves the money that foreigners owed them.

America's new creditor position was a measure of its strength and desirable in many ways, but it imposed obligations. When Britain had been the world's great creditor nation, it had opened its markets to foreign goods by a policy of free trade. Nations that owed Britain money—funds borrowed to build their railroads or factories—knew they could pay the interest and principle by selling freely to Britain. America, unfortunately, wanted to eat its cake and have it too. During the 1920s American businesspeople demanded protection against foreign competition and, as we have seen, in 1922 and again in 1930 Congress obliged them with tariff bills raising ever higher the wall of exclusion. Its debtors now faced the difficult problem of paying the United States without easy access to American buyers for their exports.

Under the circumstances foreign trade was carried on a river of American-lent dollars. If the high tariff kept foreigners from selling easily in the American market, they could buy American goods only on the cuff. Fortunately American bankers did not hesitate to lend generously to other nations, and in fact during the mid- and later-twenties they scoured the world for cities, counties, and countries that wanted to borrow. At one point there were over thirty American banks competing for the right to lend money to the city of Budapest and sixteen scrambling to finance Belgrade.

So long as the loans were forthcoming, international trade flourished. But what if the borrowers became disinclined or unable to pay and the loans dried up? Would foreign trade survive? Clearly the international economy was a fragile structure that could at the slightest sign of downturn or loss of banker confidence come crashing down. And if foreign trade collapsed, the market for billions of dollars of American goods abroad would be wiped out.

Dependence on Durable Goods

Still another weakness was related to the very core of the new postwar American economy: much of the market was in durable goods. Of course these are the very items that an affluent society wants and their relative availability is the measure of a society's prosperity. But such an economy is also more vulnerable to changes in prospects and expectations than one based on the necessities. Even when their incomes are threatened, families must pay rent, buy food, and replace clothing. But they do not have to buy a car or a radio. Nor do they have to replace one they already have very frequently because they are, after all, *durable* goods. Thus in a modern mass consumption society income is greater than in simpler economies, but so are the likelihood of sharp swings in economic activity and the contrast between peaks and valleys.

Today, after the experience of the bleak thirties, rich market societies have learned to cope with their vulnerability by an array of public policies. Modern capitalist nations now provide insurance for the unemployed, pensions for the aged, welfare for the chronically poor, and government investment to replace lagging private investment. But none of these safeguards existed in 1920s America. In the freewheeling economy of the twenties the highest peak could quickly turn into the deepest valley.

Speculation

A major weakness of the twenties economy was the speculative fever that gripped a large part of the public and the business community. Americans have never been averse to getting rich quick, but during the twenties it seemed that everyone was on the make, anxious to arrange deals that could make them millionaires overnight. Many people were duped by such swindlers as Charles Ponzi, a Boston businessman who promised to make vast profits for any investor who lent him money to speculate in foreign currencies. By using the funds of later investors to pay returns to earlier ones, Ponzi was able to impress the gullible. For a while the money poured in, but inevitably such "Ponzi schemes" failed. When in mid-1920 new investors grew scarce, down came the whole flimsy structure. Ponzi was indicted and sent to jail.

Scarcely less unsound was the investment craze in Florida land a few years later. Until World War I the site of present-day Miami was a mangrove swamp. Then real estate promoter Carl Fisher drained and cleared the land, erected seawalls, and built a causeway connecting the mainland to an offshore barrier island with wide beaches. By 1924 he and his partners were selling lots in Miami for $20,000 or more.

Similar promotions were launched up and down both Florida coasts, setting off a speculative craze reminiscent of land booms on the western frontier during the previous century. Prices soared. One northerner who bought a stretch of West Palm Beach for a song before the boom sold it for $800,000 in 1923. By 1925 the tract was worth $4 million.

Promoters of Florida real estate advertised widely and induced thousands of northerners to visit the new Eldorado. Once there they were talked into buying "options" to lots for a small down payment. These could then be sold to someone else for a profit. And how could the scheme fail? In new affluent America everyone would want to take a winter vacation in Florida; thousands would eventually retire there. If you had enough capital, there were millions to be made on the deal! The public rushed to speculate. "In cities and towns," a contemporary journalist reported, "men sold out their small shops, disposed of their homes, quit their jobs, . . . all fevered by dreams of easy wealth."

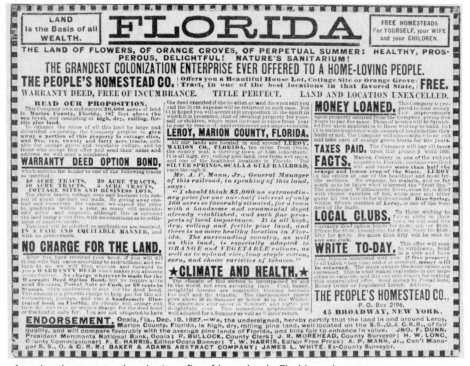

An advertisement touting the benefits of investing in Florida real estate. (Culver Pictures)

In reality the basic idea was valid: Florida would eventually become one of the fastest growing states of the Union and land prices would zoom. But this would not happen until after World War II; the land boom of the mid-1920s was premature. In any case no community could grow fast enough to support the decade's overblown expectations for land price rises. By early 1926 the visitors had begun to become sparse and profits on options began to slip. Then on September 18 a 130-mile-an-hour hurricane roared in from the Gulf and struck Miami. Hundreds of boats were smashed, 40,000 people lost their homes, and 100 people died. Several thousand-ton ships were lifted out of Biscayne Bay and deposited on the city's streets. The boom collapsed, leaving thousands poorer but wiser.

The lessons of the Florida land boom did not carry over into other areas, however. During the twenties far too many Americans caught the get-rich-quick fever. Prosperity appeared limitless, and it seemed almost shameful not to seize the golden chance.

The materialism of the decade even invaded religion. The dean of the University of Chicago Divinity School proclaimed that a man could make more money if he asked God's help in his business. A writer on religion asserted that Exodus provided insights into risks and liabilities. The best-seller from 1925 to 1926 was *The Man Nobody Knows* by Bruce Barton, a pious advertising executive who glorified Jesus as a successful businessman. He had "picked up twelve men from the bottom ranks of business," Barton wrote, "and forged them into an organization that conquered the world."

At times it seemed religion itself had become big business. In Los Angeles, revivalist and faith healer Aimee Semple McPherson, an ex-carnival barker, attracted thousands of displaced midwesterners and easterners seeking spiritual comfort to her "religious productions" featuring choral music, scenery, and dramatizations. Within five years after arriving in Los Angeles in 1921 with $100 in cash and a wreck of an automobile, McPherson had turned her Foursquare Gospel ministry into a giant commercial and personal success. By 1926 her Angelus Temple, a $1.5 million structure, had a payroll of $7000 a week, and McPherson had become one of the most honored and admired persons in the community.

With the ministers and the deans of religion so certain that God smiled on getting rich, how could any mere layperson argue!

The Big Bull Market

In this atmosphere it was inevitable that the stock market would become a magnet for affluent Americans with money to risk. Wall Street had always been the focus of speculation, of course, but stock gambling was further stimulated by the speculative spirit of the decade. It was also encouraged by the wartime liberty loans that had accustomed many Americans to investment in securities. As the decade advanced, the hope of instant wealth without working drew thousands into Wall Street's dangerous web.

At first buying stock was a sound business practice. Until mid-decade, stock prices were low and corporate profits and dividends guaranteed a good return. It made sense for an investor to buy a piece of the nation's prosperity. But by mid-1927 the speculative motive began to take over. Investors found that they could buy stocks on "margin," paying no more than 10 percent down, and by using the stock as collateral borrow the rest from brokers who in turn could borrow cheaply from the banks.

In this way a small amount of capital could be turned into a very large profit—if stock prices went up. If they fell, however, the broker could ask the stock buyer for more money (margin) to cover his loan, often forcing the speculator to sell out. If more investors had bought stock with their own money they could have held out when prices fell. Under the existing scheme, a moderate decline of the market could easily be amplified into a catastrophic collapse.

As 1928 turned into 1929, the economy itself was in a mild slump. Sales of durables had begun to fall off owing to the inevitable saturation of the market, and inventories had begun to pile up on manufacturers' and dealers' shelves. Yet these shifts did not deter the speculators. So avid were they for stocks to buy that brokers and bankers organized "investment trusts" that issued their own stock and used the proceeds to buy other shares. This scheme presumably enabled investors to diversify their holdings and so protect themselves from sharp declines in any given issue. Actually, the investment trusts merely assured further instability in the market once prospects clouded.

But for a while all was well. The deluge of speculators' money had produced a runaway "bull market" on Wall Street by early 1928. With every speculator expecting to become rich, for a time everyone did. Stock prices rose over 60 percent between December 1927 and September 1929, and many Americans experienced a rush of exhilaration as they contemplated their large paper profits. To many people it looked as if the country had discovered a surefire formula for affluence. "Half the people I knew," recalled historian-diplomat Claude Bowers, were "living in a fool's paradise, were joyously anticipating riches through the magic of the stock market." People riding the New York subway "who had previously preferred the highly spiced tabloids" were now reading the financial section of *The New York Times.*

Of course no one has ever found the correct formula for instant wealth. Many sophisticated businesspeople understood that the bull market was built on air and would have to come down. Some noticed danger signals of rising unemployment and continued farm distress. But those who warned publicly of an approaching recession were dismissed as pessimists who, if not careful, would be responsible for making true their dire predications. Such gloominess, noted one New York banker, "was more to be feared than Bolshevism."

The Great Crash

We do not know why the stock market crashed in the fall of 1929. The Federal Reserve Bank of New York, which could have choked off the cheap credit that was fueling the speculation, surely deserves some blame. The Bank feared it might trigger a panic and so refused to tighten money. But somehow bad financial and economic news from home and abroad began to filter through to the speculators and during the early fall of 1929 the market was hit by a series of brief slumps followed by rallies.

Variety reports the stock market crash. (The Bettmann Archive)

Monday, October 21 was a bad day even for glamour stocks such as RCA, GM, and U.S. Steel, but panic held off until "Black Thursday," October 24. The Exchange opened that morning with the knowledgeable traders certain that disaster was at hand. They were right. When the opening bell sounded, millions of stocks were offered for sale with few takers at any reasonable price. Brokers screamed for buyers, but there were none. In the visitors' gallery hysteria reigned, and the police had to clear it of people to prevent trouble. Hoping to stem the panic, as J. P. Morgan had done in 1907, a group of the largest New York bankers hastily organized a buying pool. For a while the news that they were supporting the market checked the slide. But only through the weekend. Then, on Monday, October 28, the bottom fell out. This time no one was willing to stand in the way of the avalanche, and it roared out of control.

Crash Becomes Depression

Except for a few brief rallies the stock market continued to fall for the next three years. By 1933, 75 percent of the total value of the country's stock securities—some $90 billion—had been wiped out.

By itself the stock collapse would have affected economic output and employment. Just.the way twenties prosperity was supposed to trickle down, so did disaster. Millions of the most affluent Americans no longer felt able to buy the expensive cars, furs, furniture, and vacations they normally did. But it also affected business investment. The collapse of confidence in the future brought down the investment rate catastrophically. No investors in their right mind would risk their money on a new factory or expensive piece of equipment when the likelihood of profit seemed nearly zero.

During the months following October 1929 the Federal Reserve Board might have made investment less risky by lowering interest rates. After the stock market crash of December 1987 this was just the course the "Fed" took, and it was effective. But after a brief flirtation with easy money, its 1929 predecessor, believing a major economic "correction" a healthy development, reversed direction and, by making money tight, further discouraged investment and consumption spending. Even President Hoover would describe the Fed as "a weak reed for a nation to lean on in time of trouble."

Now began a remorseless downward spiral of the economy. Consumers sought to tighten their belts all across the country. They could not easily dispense with food and clothing, but they could postpone buying cars, radios, and the other durables. The output of wheat and corn held up, but the volume of durables sales sank to levels not seen since the decade's beginning. Most severely hurt of all was the industry that produced the most durable product of all, housing. During the months following October 1929 the construction industry took a nosedive, falling to levels of activity not seen in the century. Millions of construction, automobile, appliance, and service workers soon lost their jobs.

By 1930 the unemployment rate had reached 9 percent; by 1931, 16 percent. In 1932, 24 percent of the labor force, almost twelve million workers, were jobless, the highest on record. (See Figure 7–1.) Had there been a system of social insurance in place, some of the blow would have been absorbed. But, as we saw, unlike most Western European countries, the United States had none. As an Englishman had observed before the crash, America's "social organization is right back in the Victorian

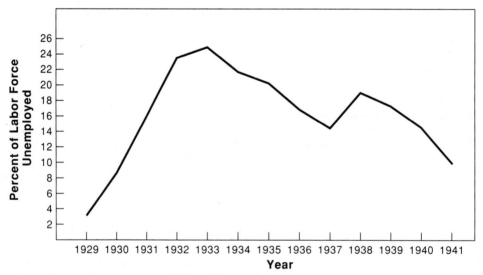

Figure 7–1   Unemployment, 1929–1941

Source: *Historical Statistics of the United States* (Washington: U.S. Bureau of Census, 1975), pp. 134–35.

Age. . . . She has no pensions for her old people; no medical benefits for her workers; no unemployment insurance for any trade." Now when people lost their jobs and exhausted their small savings; buying, except for necessities, stopped. Without jobs millions more left the ranks of durables consumers and set in motion still another round of layoffs.

The collapse of foreign trade further hurt the economy. Because it had been sustained primarily by American loans to customers abroad, it was unusually sensitive to business expectations. Once their confidence was shaken, American bankers refused to renew their foreign loans, and Europeans stopped buying American goods. Aggravating the difficulty was the high 1930 Hawley-Smoot tariff. Foreign governments retaliated against the American tariff by their own versions of protection. Before long foreign trade had virtually collapsed, converting the American downturn into a worldwide depression.

The Government's Response

As the economy slid into the abyss, most Americans were at a loss for a correct response. The conventional wisdom favored laissez-faire: let things alone. The government neither could nor should intervene directly in the private economy; it must be allowed to find its own equilibrium by sharp and thorough deflation. The business cycle was normal; the economic slump would probably be brief and recovery would soon follow. Although they would have shied away from the bluntness of his words, many educated Americans would have accepted Treasury Secretary Andrew Mellon's formula for handling the collapse: "Liquidate labor, liquidate stocks, liquidate the farmers, liquidate real estate. It will purge the rottenness out of the system. . . . Values will be adjusted and enterprising people will pick up the wreck from less competent people."

President Hoover was never as much of a laissez-fairist as his treasury secretary. A month following the stock market crash he held a series of meetings with business leaders at the White House and secured their promise to hold the line on wages to prevent a further drop in consumer spending. They agreed—if labor would desist from strikes and higher wage demands. The American Federation of Labor soon gave the required assurances. Businesspeople kept their bargain for some months, but they could not resist employment cutbacks, and by 1931 they were forced to abandon the wage floor as well.

The White House conferences, however, sought only voluntary restraints; even a believer in laissez-faire might have condoned them. Yet Hoover's record on government intervention to salvage the economy was mixed. In 1930 the president sought lower taxes to encourage business investment and consumer spending and called on local governments and public utilities to accelerate capital outlays for public facilities. He also increased the federal public-works budget and launched the dam-building project that eventually became Nevada's Hoover Dam.

Hoover's most constructive measure was a proposal, made in December 1931, for a government lending agency that would raise money by issuing tax-exempt bonds and then lend it directly to businesses in dire straits. Heeding his suggestion, in early 1932 Congress established the Reconstruction Finance Corporation (RFC) with a capital of $500 million and the power to borrow $2 billion more. Under its head, Charles G. Dawes, the RFC had granted $1.2 billion in loans to insurance companies, agricultural credit corporations, and other financial bodies within six months.

Nor was this all. The president endorsed a credit expansion act and a measure (the Federal Home Loan Bank Act) to ease the pressure on homeowners by expanding the resources of building and loan associations, savings banks, and insurance companies.

But there is another side to the coin. When the Congress elected in 1930 (with a Democratic House majority) convened, Hoover resisted its efforts to increase federal spending to give the economy a shot in the arm. In early 1931 he vetoed a $2 billion public-works bill introduced by New York Democratic Senator Robert Wagner, with the remark that "never before" had anyone made "so dangerous a suggestion." Most damaging to his historical reputation was his resistance to direct federal aid to the indigent and the unemployed.

The Problem of Relief

By 1931 millions of men and women were jobless and without income. Most tried desperately to stay afloat. Before all money drained away, some started small businesses, seldom with success. Especially pathetic were the hundreds of street-corner apple vendors who appeared in 1931 with stock supplied by the International Apple Shippers Association, a farm marketing group anxious to sell off its surplus fruit.

Families drew on their savings until they were gone. They cashed in life insurance, they pawned rings and other jewelry, and they borrowed from relatives and friends. When these sources finally failed, they turned to charity. Private charitable groups, religious and secular, set up soup kitchens and distributed free food. City and state governments did the same and provided some relief money to families.

But the relief burden far exceeded the means available to both private agencies and local governments. Never before had such a large proportion of the community been in need. Private funds were soon exhausted, and local and state governments, their tax revenues far below normal owing to economic slowdown, found themselves on the edge of bankruptcy. Many in fact were so strapped for funds that they could not maintain normal services. Thousands of public employees were laid off; other thousands suffered sharp wage cuts or were paid in IOUs redeemable at some future date.

The only institution that could carry the vast weight of the needy was the federal government, for it alone had the power to borrow in unlimited amounts to pay the bill. But Hoover opposed federal outlays for relief, primarily because he believed it would establish the dangerous precedent of federal handouts to the poor. He did set up several agencies to encourage private charity groups and help make their programs more efficient, but these accomplished almost nothing. Hoover did not even favor indirect federal relief. When Senators La Follette and Edward P. Costigan of Colorado proposed a $375 million federal relief grant to the states, Hoover rallied his supporters to prevent the bill from passing. He also succeeded in heading off a measure to grant relief to drought-stricken Arkansas farmers on the grounds that to

READING 7

One Family
in the Great Depression

Suffering took many forms in the Great Depression. The following excerpt from Studs Terkel's Hard Times, *a volume of interviews with people who lived through the Depression, presents one woman's memory of her childhood during those bad years. The speaker, a middle-aged waitress, was interviewed in the late 1960s.*

I remember all of a sudden we had to move. My father lost his job and we moved into a double-garage. The landlord didn't charge us rent for seven years. We had a coal stove, and we had to each take turns, the three of us kids, to warm our legs. It was awfully cold when you opened those garage doors. We would sleep with rugs and blankets over the top of us. Dress under the sheets.

In the morning, we'd get out and get some snow and put it on the stove and melt it and wash around our faces. Never the neck or anything. Put on our two pairs of socks on each hand and two pairs of socks on our feet, and long underwear and lace it up with Goodwill shoes. Off we'd walk, three, four miles to school.

My father had owned three or four homes. His father left them to him. He lost these one by one. One family couldn't pay the rent. They owned a bakery shop. They used to pay him off half in money, half in cookies. We lived on cracked cookies and those little bread things. So my father was pretty sharp in a way.

He always could get something to feed us kids. We lived about three months on candy cods, they're little chocolate square things. We had these melted in milk. And he had a part-time job in a Chinese restaurant. We lived on those fried noodles. I can't stand 'em today. He went to delivering Corn Flake samples. We lived on Corn Flake balls, Rice Krispies, they used to come out of our ears. Can't eat 'em today either. Can't stand 'em. My mother used to make the bread, put it under a blanket to raise. Oh, that was tasty. I never tasted such good bread since.

Every Sunday we used to go house hunting. That was a recreation during the Depression. You'd get in the Model A with the family and go look at the houses. They were all for sale or rent. You'd go look and see where you could put this and where you could put that, and this is gonna be my room. I knew where I was gonna have my horse in the barn. My mother'd go down in the basement, saying, "Oh, this is well constructed. This is where we're gonna put the potato bin, this is where we're gonna put the onions." We knew just where everyone was gonna be. (Laughs.)

Source: Studs Terkel, *Hard Times: An Oral History of the Great Depression* (New York: Avon, 1971), p. 116. Copyright © 1970 by Studs Terkel. Reprinted by permission of Pantheon Books, a Division of Random House, Inc.

provide such aid would damage "the spiritual responses of the American people." In mid-1932 he relented a bit and approved a measure for a $300 million RFC loan to the states for relief. But the amount was grossly inadequate. The governor of Pennsylvania estimated that under the bill each relief family in his state would receive a few pennies a day.

In later months and years the public would forget that Hoover had been considered the great humanitarian and remember his callous response to the unemployed after 1929. The word "Hoover" soon became a prefix for calamity. "Hoovervilles" were collections of squatters' shacks constructed of scrap metal, tar paper, or wooden crates. Virtually every city and town had one—the largest was in St. Louis and had more than a thousand residents. "Hoover wagons" were dilapidated cars pulled by mules. "Hoover blankets" were newspapers tucked under threadbare clothes for warmth. Most graphic of all, "Hoover flags" were empty pockets turned inside out.

But nothing damaged the president's reputation as a humanitarian more that his handling of the Bonus Army affair. Like other Americans World War I veterans had been hard hit by the Depression. In 1924 Congress, as we saw, had authorized veterans bonus certificates that could be redeemed in cash in 1945, but this scarcely helped now when the need was so great. In 1931 veterans groups induced Congress to authorize granting half the bonus immediately. Hoover vetoed the bill, but Congress overrode his veto. Soon after Senator Wright Patman of Texas proposed paying the remaining half of the bonus with an issue of paper money. In Patman's view the scheme would not only benefit the veterans but also the economy by pumping up drastically deflated prices.

Hoover vehemently opposed the Patman measure, but veterans organizations rallied around it and in early 1932 organized a "Bonus Expeditionary Force" to march on Washington and camp out until Congress passed the bill. By the middle of June over 12,000 bonus marchers had arrived in the capital, some with their families, and were living in abandoned buildings left over from the war period and in a tent-and-shack settlement built at Anacostia Flats. When Congress failed to pass the bill most remained to protest, vowing to "stay till 1945."

The Bonus Army was well disciplined and well behaved, yet at the end of July Hoover ordered the police to clear the veterans from the abandoned buildings. In the process two protesters were killed and the government, fearing trouble, sent the army to Anacostia to clear out the remainder. Under the direction of Army Chief of Staff Douglas MacArthur, infantry, cavalry, and tanks descended on the Flats as if attacking

"Hoovervilles" in New York City's Central Park. (The Bettmann Archive)

a division of enemy troops and burned the camp and drove the veterans off. The administration charged that the Bonus Army had been infiltrated with criminals and Communists. But the public did not accept this conclusion. The journalist Walter Lippmann condemned the president for never taking "the trouble to confer with the bonus marchers." To many Americans it seemed another instance of the government's indifference to human suffering and its determination to do nothing to change the course of events.

The End of the Republican Era

As the months passed, Hoover's reputation followed the economic spiral—down, down, down. Much of this was unfair. He was not responsible for the debacle, and few other public leaders would have done any better in reversing it. No one, in truth, knew what had caused the economic collapse and no one could be sure how to reverse it. Yet whether deserved or not, Hoover's popularity sank steadily as the Depression settled over the nation like some poisonous cloud.

The one break in the gloom as 1932 began was the imminence of a national election and with it the possibility of a new hand at the political helm. Whatever their hopes few Americans could anticipate that they were about to experience the most massive political transformation since the Civil War.

The Depression's Social and Political Effects

The early 1930s was one of the most tumultuous political eras the Western world ever experienced. In France the worldwide depression led to the first victory of a socialist government. In Germany it helped destroy the democratic Weimar Republic and replaced it with the Nazi dictatorship of Adolf Hitler. Elsewhere in Europe it encouraged the growth of radical movements of either left or right that challenged liberal democracy.

In America too the economic crisis produced dissent and upheaval. Much of this was grass-roots and spontaneous. Farmers resisted the attempts of banks and public officials to sell their land, animals, and homes for nonpayment of taxes or mortgages. When the sheriff tried to auction off their property, they collected friends and colleagues and drove the bidders off or forced auctioneers to accept twenty-five cents for a horse or a dime for a cow and then returned the property to the foreclosure victim. In Iowa Milo Reno, a leader of the Iowa Farmer's Union, organized a Farm Holiday Association to limit the shipment of food to Sioux City until farmers got prices they considered fair. Iowa farmers placed logs across the highways, punctured truck tires, and smashed truck windshields to keep produce from getting to city consumers. In Wisconsin other farm activists dumped milk in roadside ditches to raise its price. Workers also at times resorted to illegal and sometimes violent means to express their anger or protect themselves against disaster. In March 1930 a thousand men waiting in line for a Salvation Army food handout in New York attacked two trucks delivering baked goods to a hotel and decamped with their contents. In July 1931, 300 unemployed men descended on the storekeepers of Henryetta, Oklahoma, and threatened to use force if they were not given free food. By the following year looting of food stores by the jobless had become a nationwide phenomenon. Around the country, meanwhile, working men and women, sometimes led by Communists, held protest meetings and rallies that at times turned into riots.

The Depression also encouraged broad ideological attacks on liberal democracy in the United States as it did in Europe. During the prosperous twenties the two Marxist parties, the Socialists and the Communists, had declined to mere squabbling sects. Hard times increased the membership of both groups and, in the case of the Communists, extended their influence far beyond their dues-paying members. Through a wide range of "front" organizations the Communist party appealed to critics of the shaky capitalist order, to men and women dismayed by the rise of Hitler in Germany, and to minority groups who felt victimized by American racism and bigotry. Its influence eventually spread widely among artists and intellectuals whose existing alienation from mainstream American life became far more intense with the accelerating social and economic breakdown. In later years many of the nation's brightest and most creative men and women would regret their entanglement with the Communist party. But their willingness to lend their names to Communist causes during the 1930s amplified the voice of this tiny sect far beyond its actual membership.

The economic collapse also encouraged a more indigenous sort of political dissent. Throughout the country native populistic movements sprang up that were dedicated to redesigning the existing social system. In the South Senator Huey Long of Louisiana, a maverick Democrat with roots in southern populism, advocated a "share our wealth" program that promised to confiscate all personal fortunes above a certain amount and distribute them widely, guaranteeing every family a home, a car, a radio. Elderly people would be assured a pension and every worthy youngster a college education. In Royal Oak, Michigan, a suburb of Detroit, the Reverend Charles Coughlin, a Catholic priest whose broadcast sermons reached millions, demanded inflation of the currency, nationalization of the banking system, and a program of "social justice" to end the supposed abuses of capitalism. In California Francis Townsend, an elderly physician proposed a federal pension of $200 for every man and woman over sixty-years-old "on condition that they spend the money as they get it." This would, he said, not only help the indigent elderly; it would also restore the economy.

But none of this adds up to the convulsive political events that afflicted Europe in the wake of hard times. When we consider the extent of the human misery the Depression produced, we cannot but be amazed at the patience and forbearance of the American people. Yet in America too the Great Depression had a powerful political impact: out of it emerged the movement we call the *New Deal*. While preserving the essentials of democratic capitalism, the New Deal would break with the laissez-faire, "rugged individualism" that had marked much of our history and establish a new, vastly augmented role for the federal government in American life.

The Election of 1932

But as the presidential election year approached, all that was unforeseen and in the future. Most Americans waited patiently through the grim weeks of closing factories and offices and swelling unemployment. The explanation for their forbearance in the face of disaster lies in the hopes ordinary citizens still reposed in the regular political process. In November 1932 the voters would have a chance to change the man and the administration in Washington.

On the Republican side the nominee would clearly be the incumbent. No matter how damaged he was by the economic collapse, the party would not deny President Hoover another chance. But help for the suffering public could not be expected to come from that side. To many voters Hoover and the Republicans meant more of the same policies—and the same failures. The Democrats had a number of eager candidates including Governor Albert Ritchie of Maryland, Speaker of the House of Representatives John Garner of Texas, and former Secretary of War Newton D. Baker. Al Smith too wanted the nomination again and had a strong and loyal following. But the front-runner as the nomination season opened was Governor Franklin D. Roosevelt of New York.

Franklin Delano Roosevelt

To many Franklin Roosevelt seemed a copy of his remote cousin, his wife's uncle, the beloved Teddy. The two men came from the same social class: the old Dutch-English "Knickerbocker" gentry of New York. They had similar careers: state legislators, assistant secretaries of the navy, and governors of New York. Franklin Roosevelt too had been a progressive before 1917, although on the Democratic rather than the Republican side of the political line.

In 1920 the young New Yorker had been the Democratic vice presidential candidate with James Cox and, after that thumping electoral defeat, had returned to private life, setting his sights, like so many other Americans during the twenties, on making money. But he was not suited for private life and the bond business. With unusual good looks, immense personal charm, and the self-confidence that comes perhaps only from being the adored only son of an ambitious mother, he was a natural-born politician in the tradition of the patrician democrat, the champion of the people who himself springs from the elite.

In 1921 Roosevelt had contracted polio while on vacation at his family's summerhouse in Canada. The illness made him unable to walk without braces and a cane for the rest of his life. During the long struggle to regain some muscle control, his wife Eleanor and his aide Louis Howe kept his political fortunes alive. In 1928, at the urging of Al Smith, the Democratic party's presidential nominee, he ran for governor of New York. Smith was swamped by Hoover, but "FDR" won the New York statehouse by a small vote. Smith would never forgive Roosevelt.

As governor Roosevelt began as a moderate progressive in the Al Smith tradition. As the Depression's effects began to settle over the nation, he called for state-financed relief and marshaled New York's resources to provide jobs for the growing army of unemployed and needy, the first governor to do so. In 1930 he won reelection by a record 725,000 votes.

Early in 1932 Roosevelt began to campaign quietly for the Democratic presidential nomination. At the Chicago convention the stop-Roosevelt forces managed to prevent his nomination for three full ballots until the supporters of Garner, promised the vice presidential spot for their candidate, switched their votes, putting the New York governor over the top.

Roosevelt took the unprecedented step of flying to Chicago to accept the nomination in person. He told the cheering delegates that the Democrats "must be the party of liberal thought, planned action, of enlightened international outlook, and the greatest good to the greatest number of our citizens." He endorsed federally financed relief for the unemployed, stock market regulation, public works, tariff reduction, lower interest rates, repeal of the Prohibition amendment, and economy in Washington. At the end of his speech he declared, "I pledge you, I pledge myself, to a new deal for the American people."

A Vote for Change

The election was a walkover for the Roosevelt-Garner ticket. (See Figure 7–2.) Hoover had been renominated in Chicago on a platform of higher tariffs, government

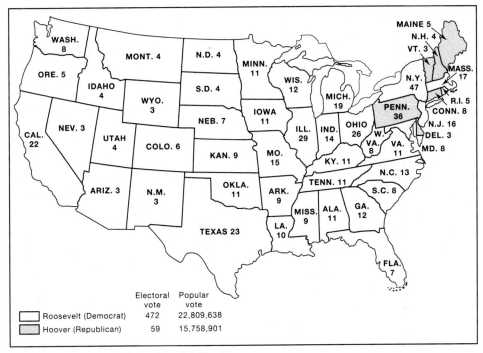

Figure 7–2   The 1932 Presidential Election

spending cuts, no federal relief measures, and a balanced budget. The platform praised the president as a wise leader, "courageous, patient, understanding, and resourceful." The Republicans fudged the Prohibition issue. Their campaign was lackluster, smelling of failure from the outset. In Des Moines farmers paraded in the streets with signs that proclaimed "In Hoover we trusted; now we are busted." In Detroit a crowd at the train station greeted Hoover with catcalls and boos.

The Roosevelt campaign did not evoke wild enthusiasm. The people wanted a messiah, but they did not know for sure what the Democrats were offering. Yet the turnouts for Roosevelt were large and the campaign from the beginning wore the air of victory. And victory it was. Roosevelt got 23.8 million popular and 472 electoral votes to Hoover's 15.7 and 59. Now the public would learn what Franklin Roosevelt meant by a "new deal."

FOR FURTHER READING

For the sources of twenties prosperity see George Soule, *Prosperity Decade: From War to Depression, 1917–1929* (1947). For Ford see Allen Nevins and Frank Ernest Hill, *Ford: Expansion and Challenge, 1915–1933* (1957). The influence of the automobile industry on the economy as well as society is covered in James B. Flink, *The Car Culture* (1975). A fine new *history of advertising during the 1920s is Roland Marchand's Advertising the American Dream: Making Way for Modernity, 1920–1940* (1985).

Several important books on the origins of the economic collapse of 1929–1933 and the reasons for its persistence are Peter Temin, *Did Monetary Forces Cause the Great Depression?* (1976); Lester V. Chandler, *America's Greatest Depression, 1929–1941* (1970); and Charles P. Kindleberger, *The World in Depression, 1929–1939* (1973). On the stock market crash see John K. Galbraith's witty *The Great Crash, 1929* (1955) and Robert Sobel, *The Great Bull Market: Wall Street in the 1920's* (1968). On the foolish and damaging response of the Federal Reserve system to the crisis see Elmus R. Wicker, *Federal Reserve and Monetary Policy, 1917–1933* (1966). On the debt problem of the interwar period see Herbert Feis, *The Diplomacy of the Dollar, 1919–1932* (1950) and Joseph Brandes, *Herbert Hoover and Economic Diplomacy, 1921–1928* (1962).

For the Hoover response to the worsening economy see Albert U. Romasco, *The Poverty of Abundance: Hoover, the Nation, the Depression* (1965) and Jordan Schwartz, *Interregnum of Despair: Hoover, Congress, and the Depression* (1970). On the Reconstruction Finance Corporation see Jesse H. Jones and Edward Angly, *Fifty Billion Dollars* (1951).

For how people fared during the hard years of the Great Depression, see Caroline Bird, *The Invisible Scar: The Great Depression and What It Did to American Life, From Then Until Now* (1966). Also consult David Conrad, *Forgotten Farmers: Sharecroppers and the New Deal* (1965); Irving Bernstein, *Turbulent Years: The American Worker, 1933–1941* (1970); and Raymond Wolters, *Negroes and the Great Depression: The Problem of Economic Recovery* (1970).

For material on Franklin Roosevelt and the 1932 election see the reading suggestions at the end of the next chapter.

8
The New Deal

Franklin Delano Roosevelt, elected president of the United States in 1932, promised the American people "a new deal." (AP/Wide World Photos)

The New Deal Begins

Until 1936, when the Twentieth Amendment went into effect, the waiting period between presidential election and inauguration lasted a full four months. Not until March 4, 1933, did Franklin D. Roosevelt (FDR) take the oath of office and deliver his inaugural address to a waiting, uncertain nation.

The country was in deeper crisis than ever by this point. Successive rounds of business bankruptcies and months of farmers' and homeowners' mortgage delinquency had shaken the banks. Monumentally mismanaged, the Federal Reserve, supposedly "the bankers' bank," had failed to provide the support needed for a financial system in crisis. In late February a great wave of bank failures swept the nation wiping out the deposits and life's savings of thousands. Failure bred further failure. Depositors were soon besieging even sound banks to withdraw their accounts. Since no bank could meet all its obligations at the same time, these too soon faced bankruptcy. By the time of the inauguration, it looked as if the nation's financial structure faced total collapse.

FDR's inaugural address was more important for its tone of confidence, the sense it conveyed that someone was finally in charge, than for its actual policy proposals. "[L]et me assert my firm belief that the only thing we have to fear is fear itself—nameless, unreasoning, unjustified terror," the new president intoned. He would ask Congress for a plan of action but if it did not act he would ask for "broad Executive power to wage a war against the emergency, as great as the power that would be given me if we were in fact invaded by a foreign foe." If short on specifics the address rang with confidence and determination. Millions of citizens heard it over the radio and many thousands wrote in the next few days to tell the president how his words had restored their hope for the future.

The next three months—the so-called First Hundred Days—was one of the most extraordinary periods in American legislative history. Congress passed, and the president signed, more major laws than at any comparable period of our past.

Roosevelt had not reduced his New Deal to a formula that he could rattle off to Congress and the American people. In fact there would never be a simple principle that defined the entire movement launched that bleak early-March day.

The new president was surrounded by advisers pushing him in at least three different directions at the same time. First there was the position favored by the "brain trust," the collection of Columbia University professors including Raymond Moley, Adolf Berle, and Rexford Tugwell, that he relied on for fresh ideas. Like the New Nationalism progressives earlier, these men believed that big economic units were unavoidable. It was time for government to end the chaos of dog-eat-dog competition and introduce planning and rationality into the economy. As for the Depression, it was caused by underconsumption—too little public purchasing power. The incomes of average Americans accordingly had to be raised to enable them to buy all the goods that a productive economy could produce. Many of these advisers had been impressed by the effectiveness of government-business cooperation during the World War and considered this relationship a valid formula for meeting the current crisis.

Another influential group of FDR advisers derived from the Wilson-Brandeis

School of the progressive era. One wing of these progressives was rooted in the South and Midwest and included old insurgents such as Robert La Follette, Jr., and George Norris. Another, surrounding law professor Felix Frankfurter of Harvard, was eastern-urban based. Both circles favored a Wilsonian break up of big monopolies, government regulation, and return to business competition to restore the nation's economic health. The eastern group had no consistent formula for solving the most pressing problems of immediate economic catastrophe. The westerners and south-erners tended to favor the old populist solution—price inflation to improve the well-being of farmers and manufacturers.

A final group seeking to guide Roosevelt were the conservative Democrats surrounding Vice President Garner. Some of these men were conservative southern-ers, others were part of the Democrats' small eastern business wing. The president, they said, should avoid heavy federal spending at all cost. Somehow the economy would right itself, if only the government retrenched and stayed out of the way.

In recent years some scholars have faulted Roosevelt for failing to seize the opportunity to alter fundamentally the distribution of wealth and economic power in the United States. So great was the crisis, they say, that the president might have nationalized the banks and the giant industrial corporations and taxed out of existence some of the major private fortunes. In effect he might have imposed some version of socialism on the country. The argument says much about the agendas of the scholars themselves, but it ignores the realities. No radical wealth-redistribution scheme that might have been imposed in the midst of national crisis would have lasted beyond it. Once the nation had reached an even keel, the reaction would have been equally great in the opposite direction. Socialism was not a possibility in 1930s America, if it was desirable at all.

The criticism also does not take into account Roosevelt's own practical bent. FDR himself was a Wilsonian progressive and rather inclined to the second group of advisers previously mentioned. But he was also a pragmatist who eschewed strict ideological consistency. "Take a method and try it," he would say. "If it fails, admit it frankly, and try another." In the end the New Deal would be a jumble of separate elements, in Moley's phrase much like "the accumulation of stuffed snakes, baseball pictures, school flags, old tennis shoes, . . . and chemistry sets in a boy's bedroom." Some would work; some would fail.

The First Hundred Days

The "First Hundred Days" of FDR's administration began in gloom and acute crisis and ended in exhilaration and hope. On Sunday, the day following the inaugural, Roosevelt issued two edicts, one calling Congress into special session on March 9, and another halting all gold transactions and declaring a national bank "holiday" that closed all the nation's banks. These were stopgap measures, but he had already directed the secretary of treasury to prepare an emergency banking bill to deal with the financial crisis. During the ensuing days the public had to do without cash, but the bold step broke the mood of gloom and restored the public's sense of direction.

When Congress met, the administration submitted a bill giving the president power over international gold movements and providing for an orderly process of reopening those banks that were sound and reorganizing the rest. Some people had expected the president to ask for a government takeover, but Roosevelt wanted toavoid any hint of radical action. Circumstances called for restored confidence in the financial system, not worrisome experiment, he felt.

The next day Roosevelt asked for and got a major cost-cutting bill that slashed veterans' payments and federal employees' salaries. Whatever his later reputation, here Roosevelt was expressing his fiscal conservatism. Many liberal Democrats bridled at the hardship the measure was certain to create for veterans and others. But even they did not proclaim the necessity of maintaining demand for goods and services to shore up farmers and manufacturers. Several days later Congress voted to repeal the Prohibition amendment and, as an interim measure, authorized the production and sale of beer.

This first burst of activity achieved its intended psychological effect. When the banks opened the public accepted their soundness, and the threat of financial breakdown was over. The slide downward had been checked, and public confidence began to grow. "The people trust this admin[istration], as they distrusted the other," Agnes Meyer, wife of Washington *Post* editor Eugene Meyer, wrote in her diary. "This is the secret of the whole situation."

The AAA

But there was nothing in these first few weeks that provided any basis for believing that the government was tackling the fundamental problems. Indeed among the party liberals there was a growing sense that FDR had surrendered to the party's conservative wing. Then on March 16 Roosevelt submitted to Congress his agriculture recovery bill, the Agricultural Adjustment Act (AAA), proposing a series of sweeping changes in the relations between the government and the farm sector of the economy.

The AAA of 1933 proposed to give the federal government unprecedented powers over agriculture so as to raise farm prices and stabilize farm income. Based on the perception that overproduction was the central problem, it authorized a new Agricultural Adjustment Administration to establish tight acreage quotas for farmers of key crops. These restrictions would cut total output. By itself this reduced output promised to raise prices, but in addition, to compensate farmers for smaller crops, the AAA would pay them a certain amount per restricted acre, the money to come from a tax placed on processors of agricultural crops—millers, meat-packers, textile manufacturers, and others.

The plan appealed to many farm groups, and in fact they had been carefully consulted when the bill was being considered. It also expressed many of the views of the brain trust planners. The theory of both was that by saving the farmers from disaster and putting money in *their* pockets, it would stimulate the rest of the economy and reduce unemployment. Unfortunately it was a scheme of contrived scarcity at the very time when millions were having difficulty putting food on their tables and clothing on their backs. The irony was underscored soon after the bill passed, when, to meet the 1933 quotas, farmers plowed up already planted cotton fields, slaughtered millions of young pigs, and let peaches rot on the trees—all while people went hungry and cold in the streets of the cities. These measures, admitted Secretary of Agriculture Henry A. Wallace "were not acts of idealism in any sane society." They could only be justified by the nation's emergency.

The NIRA

The AAA of 1933, was Roosevelt's chief proposal to stimulate agricultural recovery. The National Industrial Recovery Act (NIRA) was his plan to restore industry.

Like the AAA the NIRA reflected the planning impulse of Roosevelt's brain trusters, although labor leaders, business tycoons, and old progressives also influenced its shape. As with so much else in the early New Deal, the NIRA seemed to be a collection of proposals loosely held together by a common name.

Again like the AAA it reflected the view that overproduction was a major source of the economic collapse. One part of the measure was designed to cut output and reduce "wasteful" competition in the name of industrial recovery. Under the supervision of the new National Recovery Administration (NRA) businesspeople in each trade or industry would draft codes of fair competition that, despite the antitrust laws, would permit them to set prices and restrict production. Thus protected against both the excessive output and ruinous cost cutting that the slump had brought, bankruptcies would cease, prices would rise, and industry would stabilize.

The new law ignored the consumer protection principle that had informed the progressive movement of the pre–World War I era. But it did not exclude labor from its benefits. Many of the codes negotiated provided for industry-wide minimum wages, a shorter work week, and the elimination of child labor. Section 7(a) of the act was a major breakthrough for the American trade union movement. Under its terms, for the first time businesspeople as a class pledged to accept "collective bargaining," that is, the right of their employees to negotiate wage, hours, and working conditions through unions without interference or intimidation. The purpose of the labor provisions was the raising of industrial wages and the creation of new jobs. Both effects, the bill's sponsors claimed, would help to pull the nation out of the economic doldrums.

A final section of the bill provided for a Public Works Administration (PWA) with a budget of $3.3 billion. This money was to be spent on a wide variety of projects including roads, public buildings, electric transmission facilities, coastal protection schemes, hospitals, and reservoirs, all to create jobs for idle workers. It was the only part of the bill that sought to tackle the problem of the jobless in a direct way.

More Legislation

Several other measures of the administration's first weeks dealt with pressing social or economic problems. To counter the flight of gold abroad and its disappearance into private hoards, the president removed the nation from the gold standard. Henceforth it would not be possible to exchange paper money for gold coins at the local bank. To find jobs for idle young men in city neighborhoods and put their labor to good use improving roads and other facilities in national forests and parks, Congress established the Civilian Conservation Corps (CCC). Fearing that young women would be neglected, the president's socially conscious wife, Eleanor, and other influential women interceded and managed to get several CCC programs reserved for unemployed young women. In these same weeks Congress also transferred $500 million dollars of federal money to the states for relief for the poor and hungry and established the Home Owners' Loan Corporation to refinance mortgages of people who could not pay their loans to the savings banks or mortgage companies and so faced the loss of their homes.

Most of this early legislative barrage was aimed either at relief of some group facing painful immediate distress—the jobless, homeowners, young people— or to help the recovery of some major economic segment—industry or agriculture. But from the beginning the Roosevelt administration also adopted a program of reform.

In late May, under the influence of the searching Senate hearings into Wall Street practices conducted by Judge Ferdinand Pecora of New York, Congress passed the Securities Act giving the Federal Trade Commission the power to regulate issues of stocks and making company directors liable for misrepresenting such issues. Soon after this Congress passed a more sweeping measure, the Glass-Steagall Act, forcing banks to detach their investment banking from their commercial banking operations to break the dangerous tie between the banking system and the stock market. This bill also established the Federal Deposit Insurance Corporation (FDIC) to guarantee that bank depositors could recover their savings if the bank where they kept their money failed.

One of the boldest innovations of the First Hundred Days was the Tennessee Valley Authority (TVA), the fulfillment of George Norris's dream of the public development of the Tennessee Valley. Roosevelt was a conservationist very much in the progressive tradition. He favored the careful use of the nation's natural resources and, like Norris, saw the Tennessee Valley as a source of cheap public power. But his vision went beyond this. FDR favored a central planning body that would not only restore the Valley's abused and neglected natural endowment, but remake the social and economic life of the entire region. A number of his advisers believed that the experience of a successful Tennessee Valley plan might even inspire other efforts at regional development.

On April 10 Congress passed the TVA bill and placed Arthur Morgan, an eminent engineer, in charge. Morgan shared FDR's larger vision. TVA would not be "a dam building job, a fertilizer job, or power-transmission job," he declared. Its result would be the "improvement of . . . [the Valley's] total well being, in physical, social, and economic condition." The results were impressive. By the mid-1940s the Valley, for half a century an abused, impoverished part of the Deep South, was a bustling hive of factories, prosperous farms, and thriving recreation areas.

Congress adjourned on June 16, exactly a hundred days after it convened in special session in early March. It had enacted a mass of legislation unheralded in American history in its concentration and its boldness. The president had been ably helped by men such as senators Norris, Robert Wagner of New York, Robert La Follette, Jr., of Wisconsin, and Edward Costigan of Colorado. His brain trust and the flock of bright young people—lawyers, journalists, college professors, social workers—who accompanied them to Washington had been vital in the spinning off of new ideas and the drafting of legislative "clauses" and "titles." Many more would come in the ensuing months to help administer the new "alphabet agencies" Congress had established.

But it was Roosevelt who had initiated the legislation, and it was his support that had carried it through. His leadership was not always efficient. The president liked to play one aide off against another and often gave opposing subordinates the impression that he was on their side. This made him seem devious and, at times, two-faced. But apparently it did not seriously damage the administration. FDR's most effective leadership skill was his ability to marshal public opinion in his favor. The president was a political actor with a warm and mellifluous voice that he used with extraordinary effect on the radio. His "fireside chats" to the American public inspired confidence in the administration and helped to rally public support for any initiative he wanted. Many shrewd observers had considered Roosevelt a charming lightweight before March. By June 1933 they knew they had been mistaken. As the old progressive newspaper editor and early FDR critic William Allen White wrote, he had "developed magnitude and poise, [and] more than all, power! I have been a voracious feeder in the course of a long and happy life and have eaten many things, but I have never had to eat my words before."

The Results of the Early New Deal

How effective was this mass of legislation in meeting the dreadful crisis of the day? The answer must be: only moderately. With the enormous advantage of hindsight, we would say today that in addition to some solid hits, the New Deal committed several serious errors and failed to try some important plays.

One clear administration success was lifting the specter of serious physical want from the shoulders of the unemployed. The half-billion-dollar federal appropriation in 1933 to help the states provide relief had been a mere drop in the bucket. It had also been a handout, without related work obligations, and such a "dole," many believed, was bad for morale. But at least the federal relief contributions kept people from starving. This willingness to break with the traditional federal hands-off policy toward victims of the business cycle earned the New Deal the gratitude of millions of ordinary Americans. But it did not bring full employment or end the Depression. Nor did the two major recovery programs, the NIRA and the AAA.

The AAA was the more successful of the two. Between 1933 and 1935 wheat production fell by fifty or sixty million bushels a year, cotton output by ten to thirteen million bales, tobacco by 500 million pounds, and other crops in varying amounts. The government raised over a billion dollars in processing taxes to pay for the crop reductions. The effect on farm income was substantial. Total cash income from agriculture rose almost 24 percent in 1933 and about 15 percent in each of the succeeding years.

But the law obviously cost consumers much money in the form of higher prices for both farm commodities and the products manufactured from them. It also hurt many tenant farmers, especially southern cotton sharecroppers, who found it difficult to collect their share of the cash payments for crop reduction. In some cases to avoid paying tenants or sharecroppers anything at all, landlords simply refused to negotiate annual rental agreements and demoted tenants to the level of hired hands. In other cases the cash they received for acreage reduction enabled landlords to buy tractors, thus replacing human labor entirely. The net effect was to create a surplus of unwanted people in the cotton South, especially Oklahoma and Texas. Meanwhile in the wheat belt years of careless farming capped by unusually hot and dry weather during the summers of 1932 to 1936 turned millions of acres into a near desert of parched soil that became a "dust bowl" where crops died and blowing top soil turned midday into night.

Before long, streams of refugees from the upper South and the Plains were setting off by the thousands for California, the promised land, their meager household goods piled high on broken-down trucks. There these "Okies" hoped they would find an easier life. Many found instead a community itself battling to survive and unwilling to welcome the newcomers with open arms. In 1939 the novelist John Steinbeck depicted the painful Okie experience in *The Grapes of Wrath,* the story of the Joad family and their tribulations on the road and in California. Many African-American tenant farmers set off for the cities of the Northeast and Midwest, continuing the exodus out of the Black Belt that had begun earlier in the twentieth century.

The New Deal's major industrial recovery measure, the NIRA, was even more problematic in its results. Chosen to head the National Recovery Administration was

Sharecroppers on the road after being evicted from their tenant farms. (Library of Congress)

General Hugh S. Johnson, a red-faced, barrel-chested former West Pointer with an aggressive manner and a sharp, profane tongue. Johnson understood the difficulties of his job. "This is just like mounting the guillotine on the infinitesimal gamble that the ax won't work," he remarked. He was an effective propagandist for the NRA and designed a blue eagle symbol with the legend "We Do Our Part" to secure wide public cooperation; these logos were plastered on storefronts, newspaper mastheads and billboards all over America. In New York an NRA parade down Fifth Avenue was the largest parade the city had ever witnessed, with 250,000 people marching to the strains of "Happy Days Are Here Again."

The ballyhoo generated enormous initial enthusiasm for the NRA and helped spark a miniboom in industry. In the first three months Johnson also squeezed out codes of fair competition from all ten of the major targeted industry groups. It looked as if the major New Deal business recovery scheme was on its way.

By 1934 it began to sour. Critics were soon denouncing the NRA for fostering monopoly and thereby hurting small business and the consumer. Johnson himself soon came under attack, his critics claiming he drank too much, was hot tempered, and lacked judgment. In September 1934 Roosevelt replaced him as head of the NRA with Donald Richberg, a man more willing to follow the lead of business itself than his predecessor.

But matters improved little. NRA, whatever its other failings, lacked the mechanism to restore business and industry. What was needed was a major shot of new purchasing power, more public income to increase demand. If goods had begun to move out of the store and warehouse doors, manufacturers would have hired more workers and bought more machines to replenish their stocks. But there was no way that the NRA could achieve this effect. It was not enough just to cut competition and let it go at that.

The RFC

Somewhat closer to the actual needs of the weak economy was the work of the Reconstruction Finance Corporation (RFC), a lending agency founded by Hoover, as we saw, to bail out the banks and major industries. Hoover's appointees at the RFC had pursued conservative lending policies designed at most to preserve the existing industrial structure. Roosevelt's appointee, the freewheeling Texan Jesse Jones, adopted bolder policies. Jones lent large amounts of money to investors in new enterprises to enable them to expand. He served in effect as a modern venture capitalist who finances interesting innovative enterprises. His policies could not fail to stimulate business.

Deficit Spending

Yet despite all these measures recovery remained slow and halting. In 1935 approximately 10.6 million Americans, over 20 percent of the labor force, remained jobless; the following year it was still 9 million, almost 17 percent of those hunting for work.

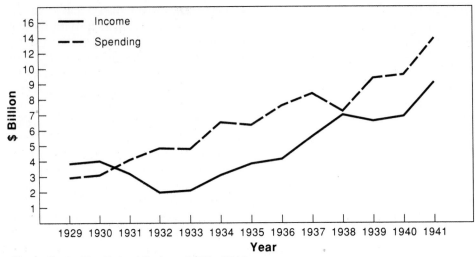

Figure 8–1   The Federal Budget, 1929–1941

Source: *Historical Statistics of the United States* (Washington: U.S. Bureau of Census, 1975), p. 1105.

The stubborn hold of the Depression puzzled and frustrated contemporaries. A few, influenced by the British economist John Maynard Keynes, believed that massive deficit spending by the government would restore demand and restart the economy. Roosevelt and his supporters talked about "pump-priming," a temporary shot of government money to get things moving. Through most of the decade, moreover, the federal government ran annual deficits, an excess of spending over income. (See Figure 8–1.) But this was not intentional deficit spending; it was only the unavoidable consequence of trying to keep people from starving. And whatever deficits the federal government piled up were offset by sharp cuts in local government outlays as states, counties, and cities fought to avoid bankruptcy. Roosevelt and most of his colleagues never understood the Keynesian concept of sustained treasury deficits to make up for weak private consumer and investor demand. Keynes actually came to the White House in May 1934 to talk to Roosevelt but neither man understood the other. "I don't think your President Roosevelt knows anything about economics," Keynes wrote to an American friend after the meeting.

The Second Hundred Days

Roosevelt responded to the slow pace of recovery, and to his critics, by a burst of innovative legislation designed not only to put people to work but to prevent future economic disasters and end long-standing economic and social inadequacies. Historians call this reform push either the "Second Hundred Days" or the "Second New Deal."

The WPA

One of the first measures of the Second Hundred Days was the Emergency Relief Appropriation Act of April 1935 providing $5 billion for relief, the largest sum ever authorized in a single law to that time. This huge amount was to be used for work relief, jobs on public projects for the unemployed. The public-works section of the NIRA had provided something similar. But PWA administrator, Secretary of Interior Harold Ickes, was a man fearful of waste and corruption, and he had insisted on extensive planning and review. As a result PWA projects were slow-starting, long-term undertakings that produced few new jobs to meet the unemployment emergency. The new Works Progress Administration (WPA) emphasized projects that would use more labor than materials and put people to work as quickly as possible.

The WPA was given to Harry Hopkins to administer. Hopkins was a rumpled, chain-smoking, former social worker, whose cynical, tough-talking manner hid a sensitive social conscience. He had been in charge of the earlier federal relief program and had offended Ickes by his free-spending ways and angered Demo-cratic political leaders by his refusal to allow the relief program to become a patronage trough. Now he took command of the enormous new relief fund determined to give jobless people income while at the same time preserving their self-respect.

In the end, pressed by the need to keep people from hunger, many WPA projects were make-work affairs after all, little more than the "leaf raking" the agency's critics charged. Despite every effort to avoid it, moreover, a large amount of money went into the pockets of jobless men and women without any work contribution at all. Yet the WPA managed to build or restore 5,900 school buildings, 13,000 playgrounds, 2,500 hospitals, and 1,000 airports.

WPA was even better in creating "software" than "hardware." Hopkins believed that artists, writers, performers, and students deserved help as much as other unemployed Americans and established WPA projects to preserve their skills and talents and make them available to the public. The WPA's Federal Theater Project employed directors, actors, playwrights, and scenic designers to present comedies, dramas, and puppet shows in cities around the country. To Americans in smaller communities, a touring WPA company was often the first taste of professional live theater. The Federal Writers' project put hundreds of budding writers and a few established ones to work writing state guidebooks, volumes of a *Life in America* series, and a set of ethnic studies. Under the Federal Art Project hundreds of artists painted murals for post offices and other public buildings and gave free art lessons at night in schools, settlement houses, and churches.

One WPA project, the National Youth Administration (NYA), was devoted solely to rescuing young men and women from joblessness and keeping them in school. NYA funds went to 600,000 college students and 1.5 million high-school students for both routine clerical jobs and projects such as compiling catalogs of public documents or indexes of major newspapers. NYA also employed young people not in school on such projects as repairing automobiles, landscaping parks, and building tennis courts.

The NYA outshone most other New Deal agencies in conferring benefits on

This mural (by Howard Heath) in a Walton, Connecticut, school was created for the New Deal's WPA. (Brown Brothers)

African-Americans. Under black educator and activist Mary McLoed Bethune, named head of the NYA Negro Affairs Division in 1936, the agency distributed funds that enabled young African-American men and women remain in school. Bethune later told the president that the money had brought "life and spirit to . . . many thousands who for so long have been in darkness." The NYA also utilized African-American talents in policy-making roles and as administrators. African-Americans "were sought and used in building the NYA program from the bottom up," declared one black newspaper. "The NYA," it noted, was "ahead of all the Federal agencies working toward the full integration of colored people."

The New Deal and Economic Security

Roosevelt and his colleagues never did find a way to restore full employment. Yet they earned the gratitude of millions of Americans and assured their continuing faith in the system of democratic capitalism. The answer to this apparent paradox lies in part in the Second New Deal's successful effort to reduce the deep-running insecurities faced by millions of Americans.

The New Deal and Labor

Organized labor was one of the New Deal's major beneficiaries. Roosevelt himself was not an intrepid champion of urban labor, nor a close friend of trade union leaders. But these deficiencies were offset by people close to him: Eleanor Roosevelt; Secretary of Labor Frances Perkins, the first woman cabinet member; the old Bull Mooser, Harold Ickes; Senator Robert Wagner of New York: Harry Hopkins; and other prominent New Dealers.

The Depression had decimated the existing trade union movement. Not particularly strong even during the prosperous twenties, unions fell apart when hard times and mass unemployment struck after 1929. Yet at the same time the economic debacle stigmatized the probusiness, antilabor attitudes of the 1920s. Roosevelt's election by itself restored hope, and by the summer of 1933 trade union organizers were signing up new members with the slogan, "The president wants you to join the union."

Section 7(a) of the NIRA served to further stimulate union revival. Employers resisted accepting the clause's collective bargaining provisions, and to prevent recovery-damaging strikes, FDR created a series of labor boards to interpret the measure. These agencies established the principle of government-supervised secret elections to decide whether workers favored a union to serve as their bargaining agent. If so, employers would have to bargain with these unions.

Section 7(a) placed a great burden on the nation's union leaders. They now had their hunting license, but it was up to them to bag the game. If a substantial part of American workers were to join unions, they would have to be convinced by dedicated organizers that it was in their best interest to do so. Employers could be expected to fight back with every weapon at their command, including physical and economic intimidation.

For a time it looked as if the game would be lost. In early 1935 the United States Supreme Court declared the National Industrial Recovery Act unconstitutional on the grounds that the law delegated excessive legislative power to the executive branch and, contrary to the commerce clause of the Constitution, allowed the federal government to regulate business within a state as well as business between the states. Fortunately for the unions Senator Wagner and his colleagues were able to rescue NIRA's labor provisions with the Wagner-Connery National Labor Relations Act of July 1935. This measure went beyond Section 7(a) by making the National Labor Relations Board a permanent body and giving it expanded powers. Not only could it conduct and supervise collective bargaining elections; it could also restrain business from "unfair labor practices," including firing workers for union membership and refusing to bargain with unions.

Thus far it was the liberal politicians who were largely responsible for labor's gains. If American wage earners had been forced to rely on the leadership of the American Federation of Labor (AFL), the nation's most important labor body, nothing would have happened.

The CIO

By the 1930s the AFL was suffering from severe hardening of the arteries. Its membership of a little over two million consisted primarily of skilled male craftworkers—printers, carpenters, plumbers, electricians, and the like—many of them native-born Americans. AFL leaders such as William Green and Matthew Woll were content with this situation. Slothful, snobbish, and bigoted, they were uninterested in organizing the semiskilled and unskilled workers in heavy industry, many of whom were women or men of recent immigrant stock.

But not all trade union leaders were indifferent to the opportunity the times offered. Men such as John L. Lewis of the miners and Sidney Hillman of the garment workers favored *industrial unions* organized along industry-wide lines and already headed weak versions of these. At the annual AFL convention in October 1935 Lewis and his colleagues raised the banner of revolt against the old do-nothing leaders and tripped off a major battle. Feelings ran high on both sides. At one point Lewis threw a punch at Big Bill Hutcheson of the carpenters, knocked him down, and jumped on him while he lay sprawled on the floor. Three weeks later Lewis, Hillman, David Dubinsky, and several others formed the Committee for Industrial Organization (CIO) as a division within the AFL. In 1936 the parent body expelled the CIO, which soon changed its name to Congress of Industrial Organizations.

Now began the bitter struggle to turn CIO constituent paper organizations into powerful, effective bodies that could force employers to accept collective bargaining. The United Automobile Workers' (UAW) drive to organize the automobile industry opened in late 1936 when General Motors workers in Flint, Michigan, staged a sit-down strike, refusing to leave the factories until their demands for union recognition and a work contract were met. Management bitterly denounced what was clearly an illegal action, and for a time it looked as if pitched battles would erupt between the determined strikers and the police or National Guardsmen sent to evict them. Governor Frank Murphy of Michigan intervened, however, and prevented violence. In mid-February GM capitulated. It recognized the UAW as the workers' bargaining agent and set up grievance machinery for adjusting labor-management disputes. In April 1937 Chrysler Corporation surrendered and also recognized the UAW. Ford, the most antiunion of the three major car manufacturers, held out for many months longer, using company guards to beat union organizers and prounion workers. Finally in mid-1940, following a major strike, Ford too gave in.

The success of the UAW encouraged workers in the nation's other industries. A popular song, heard at the GM strike, inspired unskilled workers to enroll in CIO locals:

When they tie a can to a union man
Sit down! Sit down!
When they give him the sack, they'll take him back
Sit down! Sit down!

One by one steel, coal, rubber, and textiles fell to the organizing efforts of the CIO. By 1941 the national union had between 2.5 and 5 million members, a large proportion of all unionized industrial workers. There would be further rapid union

Automobile workers entertain themselves during a sitdown strike in January 1937. (AP/Wide World Photos)

growth during the war years to come. By 1945 Big Labor had joined Big Business as a mover and shaker of the nation's economic and political life.

Rugged Individualism versus Security

The CIO brought some security and economic stability to the lives of millions of working men and women. But there remained large areas of American life and large elements of American society still unprotected from the uncertainties of life and a changeable economy. For many years the citizens of other industrialized nations—Britain, Germany, Australia, the Scandinavian countries—had been protected by old-age pensions, unemployment insurance, and even national health insurance systems. Americans, citizens of the richest nation of all, were forced to accept all the hazards and uncertainties without any kind of social insurance.

Social insurance had been talked about in America during the progressive reform era, but nothing had come of it. Now, during 1934 and 1935, a number of factors converged to alter the intellectual and political climate.

First the crisis in the freewheeling 1920s economic system had cleared the ground for all varieties of reform. The Crash and Depression had put on the defensive the rugged individualism of the past and those who maintained that people must be entirely on their own in the race of life. The new mood also reflected Roosevelt's fear of his left critics, especially, Long, Townsend, and Coughlin, and his desire to steal their thunder.

Roosevelt, moreover, had lost faith in the government-business cooperation expressed in the NIRA. Where once they had been willing to try New Deal solutions, businesspeople were now on the attack. Their chief forum was the Liberty League, formed in August 1934 by conservative politicians and industrial leaders. League pamphlets described the government under the New Deal as bankrupt, tyrannical, and socialistic. The Roosevelt administration was miring the nation in a "quicksand of visionary experimentation" and was creating "an ever spreading governmental bureaucracy" that would soon mean "the end of democracy." If such critics opposed him, the president felt, he had no reason to appease them any longer. Finally there was the 1935 Schechter decision of the United States Supreme Court declaring the NIRA unconstitutional. Although the administration deplored the decision at the time, it freed it to reassess its probusiness approach.

The Social Security System

In June 1934 Roosevelt named a cabinet Committee on Economic Security, headed by Labor Secretary Frances Perkins, to consider a comprehensive social insurance scheme. With little debate this group endorsed a system of old-age and survivors' benefits financed by a tax on wages. The committee divided on an unemployment insurance scheme, however, between those reformers who wanted an all-federal system that would establish uniform standards for the whole nation and those who supported a joint state-federal scheme that would allow states to vary the amounts to be paid to the unemployed and permit a certain amount of local experimentation. In the end the committee adopted the state-federal system.

In January 1935 the president sent the social security bill to Congress. In the ensuing debates conservatives argued that the scheme would make every one a dependent of the all-powerful government. African-American workers, conservative southerners charged, would "sit around in idleness . . . supporting their kinfolks on pensions, while cotton and corn crops are crying for workers." A northern Republican insisted it "would take all the romance out of life" by protecting people against the normal uncertainties of existence. Despite such attacks the bill passed and was signed into law in August 1935.

The Social Security Act established a joint state-federal system of unemployment insurance to be paid for by a federal tax on employers' payrolls. It authorized federal grants to the states to help the destitute blind; to support homeless, crippled, dependent, and delinquent children; and to fund several kinds of public-health care. Its most important provision was a system of old-age and survivors' insurance to be paid out of a fund raised by taxes on wages and salaries.

Although a landmark for millions of Americans, it created only a modest social insurance system compared to those of other countries. The American Medical Association had lobbied hard to block "socialized medicine," and the bill contained no health insurance provision. Old-age pensions were to be paid for by future pensioners themselves rather than by federal taxes, which might have had income redistribution effects. But not only did the measure fail to redistribute income, it also withdrew a large amount of purchasing power from the income stream at the very time when every dollar was needed to keep the economy fueled. The measure's unemployment insurance sections, moreover, allowed the states to adopt widely differing standards of support for the unemployed, an arrangement that led to totally inadequate support levels in the poorer states of the South and upper Midwest.

In later years some of the system's initial failings were remedied. Yet it continued to stir passionate debate. The political left would continue to view it as insufficiently redistributive or inadequate to the true needs of the poor. Recently some liberals have called it a boondoggle for prosperous older people at the expense of the poor and the young. The political right has blasted it as too expensive and charged that it created a permanent class of poor people unable to free themselves from public dependency. Yet it was a system whose time had come. The United States had finally joined the other industrial nations. Americans were no longer willing to accept the limitless risks of a laissez-faire economy; if not social security, then socialism. More than any other single measure, for good or ill, it helped create the modern welfare state.

Other Second Hundred Days Legislation

Many other proposals poured from the White House in the last months of Roosevelt's first term. The administration secured passage of the Public Utilities Holding Company Act, forbidding concentrated control by a few firms of the utility industry; a new Banking Act, strengthening the Federal Reserve Board's control over the nation's credit and banking system; the Revenue Act of 1935, increasing the income tax rate on upper income earners and on gifts and estates; and the Frazier-Lemke Farm Mortgage Moratorium Act, protecting farmers against foreclosure for inability to pay their mortgages.

The Soil Conservation and Domestic Allotment Act of early 1936 was designed to save the crop restriction provisions of the AAA after the Supreme Court, in *U.S.* v. *Butler* (1936), had declared unconstitutional its processor tax provision. Now, instead of paying farmers to reduce acreage for unabashed price raising purposes, they would be paid—by the federal treasury—to preserve soil fertility by removing such "soil-exhausting" crops as corn, tobacco, wheat, oats, and cotton, from production.

The Roosevelt Coalition

By this time the administration faced the 1936 presidential election, which promised to be a referendum on the entire New Deal. Roosevelt had reason for confidence. Although the economy was still well below its full-employment level, it had improved substantially, and the public felt that more progress was imminent. More importantly, Roosevelt had rescued millions from the despair that faced them in March 1933. Homeowners had saved their homes from foreclosure, farm prices were up and farmers were better off than during the worst days of 1933, young people had been able to stay in school or had found healthy jobs in the country through the CCC, the elderly could now look forward to retirement pensions for the first time, and industrial workers had unions to support them in the battles with management over wages and hours. All these people inevitably felt grateful to FDR and his party for the gains they had made and the catastrophes they had avoided.

African-Americans and the New Deal

African-American citizens also had come to admire Roosevelt and the New Deal. Among the poorest Americans even during the 1920s, they had suffered the worst when the economy collapsed. Many even in prosperous times had worked at marginal jobs. With the Depression these quickly vanished. When employers cut their work force, blacks, usually with little seniority, had often been the first to get pink slips.

And African-Americans suffered other ills besides unemployment and low income during the 1930s. In the South the Jim Crow system of legal segregation in schools, transportation, and all public accommodations reigned without much change from the early part of the century. African-American southerners also received unequal justice, with lynching all too often meted out to African-American men accused of crimes such as murder or rape of white victims. Finally, blacks in the South were denied the right to vote either by intimidation or various legal tricks such as a poll tax, the Fourteenth and Fifteenth amendments to the Constitution notwithstanding. In the North race discrimination was not buttressed by law, but it prevailed informally in jobs, housing, restaurants, hotels, and college admissions.

The new Deal did little to change the social and political inferiority of African-Americans. Periodic efforts by a few liberal members of Congress and by southern white women led by Jessie Daniel Ames to outlaw lynching by federal law and attempts to eliminate the poll tax in federal elections led nowhere. Although Roosevelt denounced lynching, he refused to fight for an antilynching bill, lest the powerful southern leaders in his own party hold up important New Deal legislation. Eleanor Roosevelt and Interior Secretary Harold Ickes, however, became champions of black Americans. A long-time member of the NAACP, Ickes appointed several African-Americans to important Interior Department offices and included blacks in some of the new public-housing schemes. He and Eleanor Roosevelt came to the defense of Marian Anderson, the famous African-American contralto in 1939 when the conservative Daughters of the American Revolution (DAR) denied her the right to sing in an auditorium at their Washington headquarters. Mrs. Roosevelt, a member of the DAR, attacked the organization for its bigotry and resigned from it in protest. ickes, in charge of Washington's various monuments, granted Anderson a permit to sing at the Lincoln Memorial.

The New Deal provided more substantial benefits through its economic programs. African-Americans did not gain much from the NIRA and, since many black southern farmers were tenants and sharecroppers, the AAA had even hurt them. Far better were New Deal relief programs. These did not discriminate racially and, although their benefits were modest, they were not much worse than the low wages that African-American workers normally earned even in good times. As we have seen, the National Youth Administration proved particularly valuable to young unemployed blacks facing a bleak job market.

Eleanor Roosevelt, shown here speaking to farmers, was as controversial as her husband. She was an especially effective voice within the administration for the downtrodden and neglected segments of American society. (Library of Congress)

Whether symbolic or real, New Deal benefits would revolutionize African-American voting patterns. By 1932 black voters in the North had already begun to desert their traditional Republican allegiance forged in the days of Abraham Lincoln and Reconstruction. During the election campaign that year Robert Vann of the *Pittsburgh Courier* told his African-American readers to "turn Lincoln's picture to the wall." Four years later as the election of 1936 approached, they needed no urging. More and more African-American voters had shifted into the Democratic column, helping to create a powerful new political coalition.

Other Coalition Members

The New Deal coalition was even broader than this, however. For the next thirty years families of union members would remember the New Deal's friendly attitude toward organized labor and the blue-collar worker and vote Democratic. The coalition also included the teeming white ethnic population of the cities—the first- and second-generation Italians, Poles, Jews, Greeks, Hungarians, and other immigrants of the 1890–1925 period. Many of these people were still working-class and were major beneficiaries of New Deal relief and employment programs.

Intellectuals too joined the coalition. The nation's writers, artists, academics, and thinkers generally were liberals; men and women who favored activist government committed to reducing extremes of wealth and power, capable of rational planning for the future, and tolerant of differences in race and creed. Initially skeptical of Roosevelt they became more enthusiastic as he shifted to reform. Among the radicals in the intellectual community the move was abetted by the Communist party's new "united front," alliance-with-liberals line after 1935, when the Soviet Union began to feel threatened by Nazi Germany. The ties were reinforced by the administration's need for skilled minds. Many academics, for example, were drawn from the universities and took jobs in New Deal alphabet agencies where they supplied fresh ideas.

Add to these elements the South, still normally "solid" for any Democrat, and the traditionally Democratic city machines, and the result was an unbeatable political combination for 1936.

But such a sociological balance sheet does not do justice to the breadth of Roosevelt's appeal. He was an enormously magnetic man who inspired confidence in a frightened public seeking reassurance. Of course his charisma and charm did not win everybody. In the prosperous suburbs he was detested as "a traitor to his class." A famous cartoon of the day depicted a distraught child at the door of her large suburban house pointing out to her mother a word scrawled on the sidewalk in front of the house. The child says, "Mother, Wilfred wrote a bad word!" The word was "Roosevelt." But for every disgruntled conservative who despised "that man in the White House," there were a dozen ordinary citizens who adored him.

The 1936 Election

The Democrats nominated FDR by acclamation at Philadelphia in June 1936 on a platform endorsing "protection of the family and the home," "establishment of a democracy of opportunity for all the people," and "aid to those overtaken by disaster." The convention also finally repealed the rule requiring a two-thirds majority of delegates for nomination. Roosevelt's acceptance speech denounced the "economic royalists who had controlled the government under previous administrations and proclaimed that every citizen "must have equal opportunity in the market place." "This generation of Americans," the president concluded, "has a rendezvous with destiny." It was clear that the liberals' push for a juster and more prosperous society was not yet over.

The Republican candidate was Governor Alfred Landon of Kansas, a moderate and decent man with a wretched speaking style and little personal magnetism. There was no real contest. The Republicans appealed to old, traditional American ways, hoping that nostalgia would get them through. The Liberty Leaguers and other conservatives came flocking to Landon, but overall the GOP campaign for the good old days was powerless against FDR's personal popularity and the public's sense that the New Deal had saved them from catastrophe and set the nation on a new, and better, track. Some Republicans had hoped that Roosevelt's opponents on the left—Long, Coughlin, and Townsend—might run a separate ticket and draw away Democratic votes, enabling their candidate to win. But the scheme for an effective third party collapsed when a disgruntled doctor assassinated Long at the Louisiana State capitol in Baton Rouge. Coughlin did back a Union party ticket with William Lemke, a populist North Dakota congressman, as its candidate, but the new organization was a feeble entity from the outset. In the end it was a Roosevelt landslide: FDR won 27.8 million popular votes to Landon's 16.7 million and Lemke's 890,000 and took every electoral vote except the eight of rock-ribbed Republican Maine and Vermont. The Democrats also swept Congress, piling up unprecedented majorities in both houses.

The New Deal in Retreat

After such a resounding mandate most Americans were prepared for a further large installment of liberal reform when FDR's second term began in January 1937. Roosevelt's second inaugural address, with its reference to "one-third of a nation ill-housed, ill-clad, ill-nourished," implied a major push against poverty and inequality and seemed to confirm expectations. (See Reading 8.)

The Court-Packing Scheme

But the administration's first major legislative proposal was not another piece of social reform. Rather it was a federal court reorganization scheme, and it so offended even middle-of-the-road Americans that it knocked most of the wind out of the New Deal push.

Ever since the Supreme Court's striking down of the NIRA, the AAA, and several other pieces of New Deal legislation, Roosevelt had seen the Court as a major roadblock to social progress. Composed of "nine old men" whose social and political views has been formed in more conservative times, it had made itself the watchdog of privilege. If the New Deal was to advance along the reform road, FDR felt, it must first push the judicial roadblock aside.

Roosevelt might have proposed a constitutional amendment to reduce the power of the Court to review acts of Congress. But amending the Constitution seemed too cumbersome. Instead in his judiciary reorganization bill he proposed to increase the number of Supreme Court members from the existing nine to as many as fifteen, an additional one for each judge who reached the age of seventy and refused to resign. This would give him the opportunity to appoint new justices friendly to his policies. The president promoted his scheme as a way to get fresh, young blood on the Court and make it more efficient, but it was instantly spotted as a plan to "pack" the Court with pro-New Deal members, and raised a thunderous political storm.

Objections came from every quarter. Conservatives, of course, were outraged at the attempt to bypass the one government branch willing to stand up to the "radical demagogue" in the White House and his "socialist" plans. Traditionalists, who venerated the Constitution, deplored any attempt to alter the relations of the judiciary to the executive branch. Some liberals feared that in the future a conservative president might pack the court to overturn the civil liberties protections of the Constitution. Many people felt that Roosevelt's approach was devious. If he wanted to change the Court, he should not dress his proposal up with all this talk of "efficiency." A liberal Democratic newspaper pronounced it "too clever—too damned clever."

READING 8

FDR's Second Inaugural Address

On January 20, 1937, Franklin Roosevelt delivered his second inaugural address to the American people. The speech reviewed in general terms the achievements of his first administration but then went on to announce a new agenda for the second. As the excerpt below suggests, this program, even more than the policies of FDR's first term, would be devoted to reducing inequality. Americans, the president declared, must dedicate themselves to building "on the old foundations a more enduring structure for the better use of future generations," using the "new materials of social justice." The speech represents the high-water mark of the New Deal. In light of what actually ensued, there is more than a little irony in FDR's words.

. . . Our progress out of the depression is obvious. But that is not all that you and I mean by the new order of things. Our pledge was not merely to do a patchwork job with second-hand materials. By using the new materials of social justice we have undertaken to erect on the old foundations a more enduring structure for the better use of future generations.

In that purpose we have been helped by achievements of mind and spirit. Old truths have been relearned; untruths have been unlearned. We have always known that heedless self-interest was bad morals; we know now that it is bad economics. Out of the collapse of a prosperity whose builders boasted their practicality has come the conviction that in the long run economic morality pays. We are beginning to wipe out the line that divides the practical from the ideal; and in so doing we are fashioning an instrument of unimagined power for the establishment of a morally better world.

This new understanding undermines the old admiration of worldly success as such. We are beginning to abandon our tolerance of the abuse of power by those who betray for profit the elementary decencies of life.

In this process evil things formerly accepted will not be so easily condoned. Hard-headedness will not so easily excuse hard-heartedness. We are moving toward an era of good feeling. But we realize that there can be no era of good feeling save among men of good will.

For these reasons I am justified in believing that the greatest change we have witnessed has been the change in the moral climate of America.

Among men of good will, science and democracy together offer an ever-richer life and ever-larger satisfaction to the individual. With this change in our moral climate and our rediscovered ability to improve our economic order, we have set our feet upon the road of enduring progress.

Shall we pause now and turn our back upon the road that lies ahead? Shall we call this the promised land? Or, shall we continue on our way? For "each age is a dream that is dying, or one that is coming to birth."

Many voices are heard as we face a great decision. Comfort says, "Tarry a while." Opportunism says, "This is a good spot." Timidity asks, "How difficult is the road ahead?"

True, we have come far from the days of stagnation and despair. Vitality has been preserved. Courage and confidence have been restored. Mental and moral horizons have been extended.

But our present gains were won under the pressure of more than ordinary circumstance. Advance became imperative under the goad of fear and suffering. The times were on the side of progress.

To hold to progress today, however, is more difficult. Dulled conscience, irresponsibility, and ruthless self-interest already reappear. Such symptoms of prosperity may become portents of disaster! Prosperity already tests the persistence of our progressive purpose.

Let us ask again: Have we reached the goal of our vision of that fourth day of March, 1933? Have we found our happy valley?

I see a great nation, upon a great continent, blessed with a great wealth of natural resources. Its hundred and thirty million people are at peace among themselves; they are making their country a good neighbor among the nations. I see a United States which can demonstrate that, under democratic methods of government, national wealth can be translated into a spreading volume of human comforts hitherto unknown, and the lowest standard of living can be raised far above the level of mere subsistence.

But here is the challenge to our democracy: In this nation I see tens of millions of its citizens—a substantial part of its whole population—who at this very moment are denied the greater part of what the very lowest standards of today call the necessities of life.

I see millions of families trying to live on incomes so meager that the pall of family disaster hangs over them day by day.

I see millions whose daily lives in city and on farm continue under conditions labeled indecent by a so-called polite society half a century ago.

I see millions denied education, recreation, and the opportunity to better their lot and the lot of their children.

I see millions lacking the means to buy the products of farm and factory and by their poverty denying work and productiveness to many other millions.

I see one-third of a nation ill-housed, ill-clad, ill-nourished.

It is not in despair that I paint you that picture. I paint it for you in hope—because the Nation, seeing and understanding the injustice in it, proposes to paint it out. We are determined to make every American citizen the subject of his country's interest and concern; and we will never regard any faithful, law-abiding group within our borders as superfluous. The test of our progress is not whether we add more to the abundance of those who have much; it is whether we provide enough for those who have too little.

If I know aught of the spirit and purpose of our nation, we will not listen to Comfort, Opportunism, and Timidity. We will carry on.

Overwhelmingly, we of the Republic are men and women of good will; men and women who have more than warm hearts of dedication; men and women who have cool heads and willing hands of practical purpose as well. They will insist that every agency of popular government use effective instruments to carry out their will.

Government is competent when all who compose it work as trustees for the whole people. It can make constant progress when it keeps abreast of all the facts. It can obtain justified support and legitimate criticism when the people receive true information of all that government does.

If I know aught of the will of our people, they will demand that these conditions of effective government shall be created and maintained. They will demand a nation uncorrupted by cancers of injustice and, therefore, strong among the nations in its example of the will to peace.

Today we reconsecrate our country to long-cherished ideals in a suddenly changed civilization. In every land there are always at work forces that drive men apart and forces that draw men together. In our personal ambitions we are individualists. But in our seeking for economic and political progress as a nation, we all go up, or else we all go down, as one people.

To maintain a democracy of effort requires a vast amount of patience in dealing with differing methods, a vast amount of humility. But out of the confusion of many voices rises an understanding of dominant public need. Then political leadership can voice common ideals, and aid in their realization.

In taking again the oath of office as President of the United States, I assume the solemn obligation of leading the American people forward along the road over which they have chosen to advance.

While this duty rests upon me I shall do my utmost to speak their purpose and to do their will, seeking divine guidance to help us each and every one to give light to them that sit in darkness and to guide our feet into the way of peace.

Source: The Public Papers and Addresses of Franklin D. Roosevelt, vol. 7 (New York: Macmillan, 1941), pp. 1–6.

The court reorganization scheme afforded an excuse for some politicians to desert Roosevelt and the New Deal. During the first few years many conservatives had reluctantly gone along with him, propelled by the public's enthusiasm and their own fear of economic collapse. Now they could hide behind a shield of outrage at FDR's attack on a sacred institution. When over the next few months Congress considered the court reorganization plan, every politician who had a grievance against FDR, against the New Deal, against Mrs. Roosevelt, or against almost anyone connected with the administration, rose to defend the Court. The final blow to the plan came on

April 12 when the Court voted to uphold the constitutionality of the National Labor Relations Act.

This was a key piece of New Deal legislation. Outwardly the President was jubilant. But inwardly his feelings were mixed. The Court, it seemed, had abandoned its obstructionist attitude, but it had also dealt the court reorganization plan a fatal blow by removing any excuse for changing the way the judges were selected. On July 22 the administration forces in Congress, seeing the handwriting on the wall, withdrew the court reorganization bill, abandoning the ill-conceived attempt to change the relations between the executive and judicial branches of the government. Ironically, as a result of deaths and retirements during the next three years, FDR was able to appoint four new Supreme Court justices, completely turning the court around philosophically and ideologically.

The Court fight was a stinging defeat for FDR's leadership, the first major gap in a hitherto unbroken string of legislative successes. It came at the time of the Michigan sit-down strikes, when many middle-class Americans believed social upheaval imminent. In 1937–38 there had also been an abysmal economic tumble as a sharp cutback in government spending overlapped the first payments into the social security pool and a foolish credit-tightening move by the Federal Reserve System. Abruptly the stock market took a nosedive and two million more Americans returned to the unemployment rolls. (See Figures 7–1 in Chapter 7 and 8–1 earlier in this chapter.) Roosevelt primed the pump through new RFC loans and by expanding the WPA rolls. The Federal Reserve did its part by easing credit. The crisis passed, but the unexpected slump further undermined the administration's support.

Additional Legislation

Thus by the opening months of his second term Roosevelt's aura of invulnerability had largely disappeared. During the next four years he was able to get some additional social and economic legislation passed. In February 1938 Congress enacted a new Agricultural Adjustment Act authorizing crop loans for farmers, giving the secretary of agriculture power to establish acreage quotas for staple farmers, creating a permanent soil conservation program, and providing crop insurance. In April 1938 it appropriated almost $4 billion for public works to jog the economy into life again. In June it passed the Food, Drug, and Cosmetic Act, broadening the progressive era protection of consumers against fraudulent and misleading claims, and the Civil Aeronautics Act, allowing the Civil Aeronautics Authority to oversee the burgeoning airline industry. That same month Congress passed the last of the era's major pieces of social legislation, the Fair Labor Standards Act. This law established a minimum wage of forty cents an hour and a maximum workweek of forty hours for millions of American workers.

Compared to the deluge of major reform measures of the first term, however, these achievements were modest. In part the problem was the exhaustion of ideas. No one really knew where to go after this to end the Depression, and for a time those New Dealers from the Wilson-Brandeis tradition of "trust busting" were given a hearing. In early 1938 Congress authorized a major investigation of monopoly in industry under the auspices of the Temporary National Economic Committee (TNEC).

The TNEC's three-year investigation was accompanied by a flood of antitrust prosecutions by Assistant Attorney General Thurman Arnold. The trust-busting campaign achieved little; the economy did not improve.

The Roosevelt "Purge"

During the midterm Congressional elections of 1938 Roosevelt decided to campaign against those members of his own party, mostly southerners, who had deserted him and joined the Republican conservatives to defeat, delay, or weaken New Deal legislation. These men, he felt, must be read out of the party if the Democrats were to stand for liberalism. The attempt to create a national Democratic party with a consistent political philosophy was an appealing goal. But it ignored the local bases of party politics in America and the extent to which even members of Congress spoke for local interests. Many otherwise loyal Democratic voters resented the president's barnstorming around the country making speeches against local conservative Democratic candidates. They called it a "purge" and refused to accept his advice. In the end the president suffered a serious defeat. Most of the conservative Democrats whom he opposed were renominated, and in the November elections the lopsided Democratic congressional majority was sharply cut back. All told, the president had suffered a major political defeat, further damaging his prestige and making it even more difficult for him to extract additional legislation from Congress.

As a person and a leader—although detested by the business classes—FDR continued to be popular among the voters. But by now fewer people believed that the administration had the solutions to the country's major domestic problems. After November 1938 the New Deal was virtually dead.

The New Deal Balance Sheet

But the New Deal would not be forgotten. It had transformed American life in permanent ways and it had done so through democratic processes while keeping fundamental American political institutions intact.

The New Deal had not ended the Depression, but it had changed the way Americans looked at national economic setbacks and how they would deal with them in the future. In 1929 people assumed that major downturns in the business cycle were like untreatable diseases: little could be done about them except, perhaps, to make the patients a little more comfortable. After 1932 Americans would insist that the government in Washington intervene aggressively to stem downturns and reverse them if possible and that it had a responsibility to keep people from physical want, to prevent them from losing their farms, homes, businesses, and self-respect. The New Deal did not solve the riddle of how to end the Depression—although it foreshadowed later Keynesian solutions—but it did set the precedent of activist federal intervention that each later generation would follow when needed.

Even more important than its activist response to the business cycle was the New Deal's inauguration of the welfare state. However prosperous, the economy of the freewheeling 1920s provided little security, a failing soon made especially pointed by the post-1929 economic collapse. Loss of job, accident, old age, widowhood, and orphan-status led to impoverishment and real want. New Deal unemployment insurance, old-age pensions, and aid to dependent mothers and children and to the handicapped—the system referred to loosely as Social Security—put a floor under society's less-affluent and less-powerful citizens. It also added an element of stability to the economy. People's incomes did not suddenly cease when they lost their jobs: they could get unemployment insurance or, if 65 years old or over, take their pensions and leave the job market. Later administrations, even conservative Republican ones, would come to accept the inviolability of the welfare state in some form, and the original components were supplemented and strengthened.

All of this made the federal government an extraordinary force in American life. In the past, except in times of war, the government in Washington, with its small budgets, few thousand employees, and limited sphere of activity, had been a minor presence in people's lives. After 1933 Treasury outlays soared, bureaucracies ballooned, and the federal government took on enormous new responsibilities. Good or bad, Washington became the ultimate resource for solving the major problems that beset Americans and a focus as never before of their hopes and disappointments.

The New Deal also created a new set of power blocs. After 1945 Big Labor joined Big Business as a major player in the political arena. Especially under Democratic administrations it would exert broad influence in the legislative field and help to offset the power of organized capital. If the immediate post–World War II era was more liberal than the 1920s, it was in part owing to the influence of the trade union leaders on the politicians.

Some of these effects would not be felt until years had passed. Meanwhile as Roosevelt's second term drew to a close, the upheavals produced by the world economic crisis in Europe began to demand the attention of the administration as well as of Americans in general. Was the United States once more fated to become enmeshed in the Old World's tangled difficulties and passionate disagreements?

FOR FURTHER READING

The best one-volume treatment of the New Deal is still William Leuchtenberg's *Franklin D. Roosevelt and the New Deal, 1932–1940* (1963). A magisterial evocation of the New Deal era from a distinctly New Deal perspective is Arthur Schlesinger, Jr.'s three volume *The Age of Roosevelt* (1957–1960), interrupted when Schlesinger joined the Kennedy administration. An older, but still useful, treatment of the nation's economy during the 1930s is Broadus Mitchell's *Depression Decade: From New Era through New Deal, 1929–1941* (1947). An interesting brief critique of the New Deal from the left is Paul Conkin's *FDR and the Origins of the Welfare State* (1967).

For a description of the brain trust by one who belonged to it see Rexford Tugwell, *The Brains Trust* (1968). Roosevelt's leadership is favorably evaluated in James McGregor Burns, *Roosevelt: The Lion and the Fox* (1956). A hostile treatment of the Roosevelt leadership from the political right is Edgar E. Robinson's *The Roosevelt Leadership* (1955). FDR's economic ideas are described in David D. Fusfield, *The Economic Thought of Franklin Roosevelt and the Origins of the New Deal* (1956). A fairly recent evaluation of the Roosevelt reforms in general is Gary M. Walton (ed.), *Regulatory Change in an Atmosphere of Crisis: The Current-Day Implications of the Roosevelt Years* (1979).

The literature on specific measures and programs of the New Deal is voluminous. Some of the best works include William F. McDonald, *The Federal Relief Administration and the Arts* (1969); Daniel S. Hirschfield, *Lost Reform: The Campaign for Compulsory Health Insurance from 1932 to 1943* (1970); Betty Lindley and Ernest K. Lindley, *New Deal for Youth* (1938); Roy Lubove, *The Struggle for Social Security, 1900–1935* (1968); John K. Galbraith and Gove Griffith Johnson, Jr., *Economic Effects of the Federal Public Works Expenditures, 1933–1938* (1940); John A. Salmond, *The Civilian Conservation Corps, 1933–1942* (1967); C. L. Harriss, *History and Policies of the Home Owners' Loan Corporation* (1952); Michael Parrish, *Securities Regulation and the New Deal* (1970); John A. Brennan, *Silver and the First New Deal* (1969); Lester V. Chandler, *American Monetary Policy, 1928–1941* (1971); Robert Himmelberg, *The Origins of the National Recovery Administration* (1976); Sidney Fine, *The Automobile under the Blue Eagle* (1963); Ellis Hawley, *The New Deal and the Problem of Monopoly* (1966); Herbert Stein, *The Fiscal Revolution in America* (1969); John L. Shover, *Cornbelt Rebellion: The Farmers' Holiday Association* (1965); Gilbert C. Fite, *George N. Peek and the Fight for Farm Parity* (1954); Sidney Baldwin, *Poverty and Politics: The Farm Security Administration* (1968); Wilmon H. Droze, *High Dams and Slack Waters: TVA* (1965); and Harry A. Millis and E. C. Brown, *From the Wagner Act to the Taft-Hartley Act* (1950).

For some important people surrounding the New Deal see T. Harry Williams, *Huey Long* (1970); Robert E. Sherwood, *Roosevelt and Hopkins: An Intimate History* (1950); Harold L. Ickes, *The Autobiography of a Curmudgeon* (1943); Charles J. Tull, *Father Coughlin and the New Deal* (1965); and Julius Pratt, *Cordell Hull, 1933–44* (1964). Finally, on one key person in the Roosevelt administration see Joseph P. Lash, *Eleanor and Franklin* (1971).

9
World War II

Bombs exploding as Japan attacks Pearl Harbor, Hawaii, on December 7, 1941. (National Archives)

The Isolationist Impulse

Even during the 1920s the United States never withdrew from world affairs. Between 1919 and 1929 Americans enthusiastically sought markets and borrowers abroad. They were also active diplomatically in regions of traditional American concern: the Far East and Latin America. But the United States withdrew from the conflicts of Europe, that small westward projection of Asia that continued to control the economic and political destinies of the world. This removal from Europe's problems proved to be a critical error with immense consequences.

During the twenties old Wilsonian internationalists tried to affiliate the United States with the League of Nations and the World Court. But these efforts were stymied by the overriding public mood of *isolationism*. Dating to the earliest years of the republic when America seemed safe behind its three thousand-mile-wide Atlantic moat, isolationism combined disdain for European contentiousness with suspicion of wily foreigners and a sense of American moral superiority. Why become enmeshed in Europe's tangled affairs? This isolationist perspective was weaker in the Northeast, the Pacific Coast and the South, regions with closer cultural and economic ties to distant nations. It was strongest in the nation's heartland. "To hell with Europe and the rest of those nations," declared Minnesota Senator Thomas Schall.

During the late twenties and early thirties traditional isolationism was reinforced by a powerful reaction against World War I. Increasingly that war came to seem a colossal blunder. Worse still it appeared that America had been drawn into it, not by any legitimate interest, but by phony Allied propaganda and a conspiracy of arms manufacturers and bankers whose only goal was profit. In April 1934 *The Merchants of Death,* a book describing how the nefarious munitions producers had encouraged war, became a selection of the Book-of-the-Month Club. A year later Walter Millis's *Road to War,* blaming a foolish insistence on neutral trading rights and a propaganda deluge for embroiling America in a pointless war, became a best-seller.

Such views were powerfully reinforced by a 1934 congressional investigation, headed by Senator Gerald P. Nye of North Dakota, of how America entered the war. The Nye Committee report, fourteen hundred pages long, concluded that international bankers, armament makers, and their lobbyists had bamboozled the nation into declaring war purely for their own profit. Thereafter Senator Nye became a sought-after lecture-circuit speaker who brought his isolationist message to churches, synagogues, and service clubs, exhorting the public never again to make the mistake it had in 1917.

The revulsion against European entanglement was aggravated by the war debt problem. After the onset of the Depression the former Allied nations cut their loan payments to the United States to tiny token amounts. This resolution of the long-bubbling war debt issue left a bad taste. How could such deadbeats, many Americans asked, ever have deserved our support when they got into trouble?

Pacifism, isolationism, and public revulsion against World War I, combined with a major crisis over Italian aggression against Ethiopia in East Africa, produced a wave of neutrality legislation intended to keep the United States out of future foreign wars. In April 1934 Congress enacted the Johnson Debt Default Act prohibiting loans to any country that had ceased to pay its debts to the United States. In August 1935 Congress forbade arms sales to any belligerent nation, prohibited the transport of weapons in American ships to any belligerent port, and barred American citizens from travel on the ships of any belligerent except at their own risk. Six months later it banned loans to any belligerent nation. In May 1937 nations at war were required to pay cash and carry in their own ships *all* matériel purchased in the United States, not merely arms and munitions. All told, these "neutrality laws" were intended to help the United States avoid the temptations and pitfalls that had, supposedly, embroiled it in the war of 1914–1918.

The Rise of the Dictators

Unfortunately the Neutrality Acts did not reckon with the fast changing reality of the contemporary world. At the very time Congress was seeking to detach the United States from Europe's and Asia's quarrels, forces were being unleashed that would threaten the existing international order and destroy the illusion that the world's richest and most powerful nation could withdraw behind its oceans.

In Europe the end of World War I had brought confusion and disorder. The collapse of the Hapsburg Empire had created a cluster of small squabbling states in central Europe, many made up of antagonistic nationalities. In Russia the Bolsheviks had firmly established their Soviet regime by 1921 and were proclaiming the imminence of Communist revolution throughout Europe and eventually the world.* In Italy the war had weakened both parliamentary democracy and the economy, and in 1922 conservative Italians had turned to a strong man, Benito Mussolini, to restore order and prepare the nation for glory and Mediterranean leadership. *Il Duce* (the leader) abolished the parliamentary system, brutally destroyed his enemies to the left, and established a new authoritarian regime, called *Fascism,* that proclaimed the superiority of discipline over freedom, the state over the individual, and the heroic over the practical.

Nazi Germany

Most threatening of all by the early 1930s were developments in Germany. After a shaky start the regime of the Weimar Republic, which had succeeded the kaiser's empire in Berlin, experienced a few years of prosperity. From 1919 to 1933 Germany functioned as a modern democratic state noted for its cultural creativity.

Despite its accomplishments—in some cases because of them—the Weimar regime had many enemies among its own people. Right-wing Germans despised the republic as a regime imposed by the victors. The nation's defeat in 1918, they insisted, was not legitimate; it came as "a stab in the back" by Jews and radicals. Such people

---

*In 1922 what had been the Russian Empire became officially the Union of Soviet Socialist Republics (USSR), or Soviet Union. Formally Russia is one of the republics in the Soviet Union. But *Russia* and *Soviet Union* are still often used interchangeably, particularly when discussing World War II, and will be so used in this chapter. Later chapters will use *Soviet Union* exclusively.

deeply resented the Versailles Treaty *diktat* that blamed Germany for the war, compelled it to pay billions in reparations, stripped it of its colonies and some of its European territory, and forced it to disarm almost completely. On the other side the far left liked the Weimar regime no better. Opposed to parliamentary multiparty democracy and to capitalism, the Communists strove to replace the republic with a Soviet-type, one-party regime.

Leader (*Führer*) of the farthest right was Adolf Hitler and his National Socialist (*Nazi*) party. Hitler was an Austrian-born fanatical German nationalist who had fought in the kaiser's army during the war. As a youth in Vienna he had absorbed the virulent antisemitism that had marked Austria in its late imperial years and blamed Germany's half-million Jews for the nation's ills. Hitler's antisemitism mined a deep lode of anti-Jewish feelings that had marked much of Christian Europe since the Middle Ages but added to that brew a pseudoscientific theory that regarded north Europeans as a superrace, superior to all other groups, white as well as "colored," and entitled to rule the others. Hitler promised that when he achieved power he would destroy the liberal, democratic republic; eliminate all Jewish influence in German life; suppress the Communists; and free Germany from the humiliating conditions imposed by Versailles.

Although the Nazi ideology and program had supporters in the Weimar Republic, Hitler's quest for leadership made little headway during the late 1920s. The Nazis won seats in the German Reichstag but never came close to a majority. Then the Depression struck Germany, producing mass unemployment and bloody social strife between far left and far right. Promising to restore prosperity and prevent a Communist takeover, the Nazis made rapid gains. In panic the leaders of the republic in January 1933 appointed Hitler chancellor of the German nation. He promptly set about imposing a dictatorship and putting the Nazi program into effect.

Nazi policies destroyed the foundations of liberal, democratic society. The Nazis brutally repressed all political opposition from center to far left; deprived Jews of their German citizenship and severely limited their economic and professional activities; ended free press and free speech; and placed the Nazi party firmly in control of all aspects of German political, social, and cultural life, creating thereby a *totalitarian* state—the "Third Reich"—that obeyed no law except Hitler's will.

Democrats and liberals around the world watched the destruction of Weimar constitutionalism and the turn to totalitarian barbarism with horror. But Germany's neighbors were even more aghast at Hitler's warlike behavior. The Nazi leader quickly tore up the Versailles Treaty and began to rearm Germany. In October 1933 he removed the Reich from the League of Nations. In 1936 he sent troops into the Rhineland, German territory that had been demilitarized after 1918 to protect France against resurgent German power. That same year Hitler and Mussolini, recognizing a kinship of resentment against Britain and France and a shared lust for greater power in Europe, signed a treaty creating an alliance—the *Axis*—against the democracies.

Japan

Meanwhile in the Far East another aggressive and authoritarian regime was disturbing the status quo. Japan in the late 1920s was a half-westernized nation of proud and ambitious people. Having come late to the nineteenth-century great-power scene, the Japanese felt themselves a "have-not" nation entitled to make up for lost time at the expense of China, an immense and politically feeble and divided neighbor. In 1931 they wrested Manchuria from the Chinese Republic, in the process violating the Nine Power Treaty of 1922 guaranteeing China's territorial integrity. Secretary of State Henry Stimson announced that the United States would not officially recognize any arrangement that impaired the independence or sovereignty of China. The Japanese were not impressed by this so-called Stimson Doctrine since it was not backed by force. In late 1934 they renounced the shipbuilding limitation provisions of the Washington Naval Treaty, in effect challenging the United States and Britain to a naval race. In November 1936 Japan and Germany signed an agreement aimed against world communism. Almost immediately Italy too signed the pact. The three authoritarian nations were now linked by a loose alliance.

In 1937, after a supernationalist group came to power in Tokyo, Japan attacked China proper as part of a program of conquest and dominion it disguised under the name of the Greater East Asia Co-Prosperity Sphere.

Preliminaries to War

By this time Europe was in an uproar. In 1935 fascist Italy, propelled by Mussolini's dream of restoring Rome's ancient glory, had attacked the weak African nation of Ethiopia. The League of Nations, led by France and Britain, imposed economic sanctions on Italy that proved ineffective, in part because the United States continued to sell Italy oil. In 1936 the Italians formally incorporated Ethiopia into their empire.

The battle over Spain was another preliminary to World War II. In 1936 Francisco Franco, a right-wing Spanish general, rose in revolt against the left-democratic government of his country. Spain quickly became an international ideological battleground with liberals and radicals defending the Loyalists in Madrid and the political right supporting Franco. Spain soon became a dress rehearsal for World War II as the Soviet Union provided arms, money, and political guidance for the Loyalists while the Germans and Italians supplied planes, tanks, pilots, munitions, and political support to the Rebels. In America many conservative Catholics sided with Franco; liberals and leftists, including many intellectuals, endorsed the Madrid government and several thousand Americans, mostly radicals, went to Spain to fight for the Loyalist cause. Eventually Franco and his forces defeated the Loyalists and established an authoritarian, fascistlike regime in Spain.

Hitler by now had become an immense threat to a stable European order and a terrifying challenger of liberal, democratic values. Once in power Hitler began a forced-draft rearmament program, and with each passing month German military power grew. Meanwhile opposition to the Third Reich was systematically destroyed or driven out. Hundreds of Germany's most talented scholars, scientists, and artists—Jews and anti-Nazis—fled as refugees to Western Europe; an especially large contingent, including physicist Albert Einstein, novelist Thomas Mann, film director Billy Wilder, composer Arnold Schoenberg, and philosopher Herbert Marcuse, came to the United States.

However barbaric the Nazi policies many Germans took pride in the Third Reich's new strength and assertiveness and endorsed "Aryan" racial self-glorification. By 1937 Hitler had few internal opponents.

But he had made many enemies abroad. In 1938, with the help of local Nazis, the Führer annexed German-speaking Austria and began to make territorial demands on his neighbors, Czechoslovakia and Poland, two nations created by the Versailles Treaty and incorporating former German territory or German-speaking people within their boundaries.

Failure of Appeasement

Britain, France, and the Soviet Union were alarmed by the resurgence of German strength and the new German assertiveness but found it difficult to agree on policies to stop the Nazis. People in the west European democracies feared that confronting Hitler would precipitate another international bloodbath like 1914 to 1918, this time with air power sparing no one behind the front lines. Perhaps Hitler could be appeased by making concessions. After all, his shrill demands and assertions were probably nothing more than rhetoric.

Appeasement soon bore bitter fruit. Six months after the annexation of Austria

The Munich Conference of September 1938 at which Great Britain and France erroneously thought they had successfully appeased Germany. From left to right are Neville Chamberlain of Britain, Edouard Daladier of France, Adolf Hitler of Germany, and Benito Mussolini of Italy. To Mussolini's left is Italy's foreign minister Galeazzo Ciano. (UPI/Bettmann Newsphotos)

Hitler created an international crisis by demanding the cession to Germany of the German-speaking Sudeten region of the Czech Republic. The Czechs turned to Britain and France for support; but instead, at a four-power conference in Munich, Britain's Neville Chamberlain and France's Edouard Daladier surrendered to Hitler backed by Mussolini. The Czechs must yield Sudetenland to Germany, they said; they would not support Czech desires to preserve their territorial integrity. Without British-French support the Czechs were forced to bow to Hitler's demands. Europe heaved a sigh of relief, and in Britain and elsewhere Chamberlain was proclaimed a hero when he returned from Munich and proudly announced that he had achieved "peace in our time."

But appeasement did not work. In March 1939 Germany blatantly violated its agreement to stop at the Sudetenland and annexed the remainder of the Czech Republic. Hitler soon made demands on Poland for territory. By now the British and the French were convinced that Hitler's appetite could not be satisfied. Germany had once more become a major threat to the European balance of power and must be stopped. Although not yet militarily ready, they agreed to back Poland if the Germans attacked. They also opened talks with the Soviet Union, Poland's eastern neighbor, to consider cooperation, but mutual suspicions between the capitalist democracies and the Soviet communists along with Poland's refusal to allow Russian troops to enter its territory if the Germans attacked prevented any meaningful united policy of "collective security." Faced with the new British-French resolution, Germany temporarily backed off, but with each passing month war preparations and expectations grew. By the summer of 1939 it looked as if a general European war was just months away.

FDR's Foreign Policy

During these years of mounting international crisis almost all Americans thanked their lucky stars that they were separated from the danger spots by two wide oceans. Most deplored the rise of the militarists and aggressors, but all except a small minority believed the United States could avoid becoming involved.

Roosevelt was one of this minority. He belonged to the influential northeastern elite with close ties to Europe. Although he had retreated from his Wilsonian internationalism during the isolationist era of the late 1920s and early 1930s, he had never entirely abandoned it. FDR's belief in collective security was reinforced by his secretary of state, the crusty former Tennessee congressman Cordell Hull.

Yet FDR was cautious in proposing international cooperation to stop the aggressors. Isolationism and pacifism were far too powerful to be confronted head-on. The American people must be weaned away from their illusions and brought to see the necessity of intervention in slow stages. This cautious policy required a certain amount of deviousness and would lead critics to claim that Roosevelt deliberately deceived the American people. Some even charged—unfairly—that he did so primarily to rescue the faltering political fortunes of his party and the New Deal.

Certain aspects of Roosevelt's internationalism were frankly and openly expressed, however. FDR and Cordell Hull pushed hard to improve relations with America's southern neighbors. The *Good Neighbor Policy* reinforced the revived friendship with Latin America inaugurated by the Republican administrations of the 1920s. In late 1933 Hull supported a declaration of the Latin American Republics at Montevideo, Uruguay, opposing armed intervention by one nation in another's affairs. Thereafter, the interventionist (Theodore) Roosevelt Corollary was largely abandoned by the United States. Friendship with Latin America would prove a valuable asset after America's entrance into World War II.

The new internationalism also took economic forms. Hull and Roosevelt both shared the free trade attitudes then deeply embedded in Democratic party tradition. Under the Trade Agreements Act of 1934 they negotiated a series of "reciprocal trade agreements" with foreign nations to mutually reduce duties on one another's exports. Although this policy did not produce drastic lowering of world trade barriers, it helped stem their rise and became the precedent for still freer international trade in the years after 1945.

When it came to collective security in Europe, however, FDR treaded cautiously at first. Although he deplored the Franco revolt in Spain, he refused to exempt the Loyalist government from provisions of the Neutrality Act's arms embargo clause. He also sympathized with the Ethiopian victims of Italian aggression but felt unable to cooperate with the League of Nations when it imposed sanctions on Italy because he feared that the isolationists would object. Yet even in this early period FDR longed to do something about the expansionism of the Axis powers, and in an address in Chicago in October 1937 he spoke up against "the present reign of terror and international lawlessness." This had reached a "stage where the very foundations of civilization . . . [were] severely threatened." At this point FDR was probably testing the public's attitude more than anything else. He knew he was in no position to do more for collective security than condemn the aggressors and merely offered the suggestion that peaceful nations "quarantine" the Axis powers, treat them in effect as bearers of some foul and infectious disease.

War Begins in Europe

Hoping to avoid a general European war, Roosevelt addressed notes to Italy and Germany in the months following Munich asking them to renounce the use of armed force against a long list of small European nations. Both dictators ridiculed the president, confirming pessimists' worst fears of their intentions. The final crisis in Europe came in summer 1939 when Hitler made new demands on Poland designed to pick a fight even at the risk of war with Britain and France. To neutralize possible Russian support for the Poles, Germany in August 1939 secretly negotiated a nonaggression pact with the Soviet Union, although Hitler had long proclaimed his hatred for communism and his contempt for the Slavic peoples.

On September 1, 1939, German *panzers* (tanks) roared across the German-Polish frontier and cut through a brave, but ineffectual, Polish resistance.

On September 3 Britain and France declared war on Germany. It did not save their Polish ally. The French and the British did little more than fire a few guns at the weak German units left to face them along the French-German border. Any chance that Poland might preserve its independence was destroyed when the Russians, in accordance with secret provisions of the Nazi-Soviet Pact, marched into Poland from the east on September 15. In a few weeks the Nazi juggernaut had destroyed the last pockets of Polish resistance and imposed a harsh regime on the country, one that would soon resort to terror and mass murder.

Americans had no desire to enter the fight, but from the first they overwhelmingly sympathized with the Allies, as Germany's opponents were again called. Pro-Ally sympathy soon made the arms embargo provision of the Neutrality Act, a measure that penalized the French and British, the target of attack. The battle for arms embargo repeal was bitterly fought. Old-line Senate isolationists such as Robert La Follette, Jr., (son of "Fighting Bob"), Hiram Johnson, Gerald Nye, and William Borah vowed to fight "from hell to breakfast" to stop repeal. Borah told the American people in a radio address that arms sales to the French and British would soon be followed by loans, as in World War I. "You will send munitions without pay," he warned, "and you will [then] send your boys back to the slaughter pens." Despite the opposition, in early November, Congress passed the Neutrality Act of 1939, allowing belligerents to purchase American manufactured guns, planes, ammunition, and other war matériel—if they paid cash and carried the weapons away in their own ships. "Cash and carry" was the first step in the process of American intervention in the war on the side of Hitler's enemies.

The Fall of France

For weeks following Poland's surrender, the European war was a series of small skirmishes along the French-German border, in the air, and on the high seas. Neither side suffered many casualties or achieved major gains. Remembering the murderous trench warfare of the western front in 1914–18, many people called the winter of 1939–40 the "phony war." Then in April the Germans mounted a bold attack on Norway and Denmark right under the nose of the British navy. Little Denmark fell without a fight. The Norwegians, helped by the French and British, held out for a few weeks and then surrendered. Worse quickly came. Scarcely stopping for breath, German *panzer* columns sliced into Holland and Belgium on May 10 and destroyed resistance in a matter of days. The main German assault, however, came through the supposedly impassable Ardennes Forest against the French, who had shifted the weight of their forces northward to meet the enemy in the Low Countries. Defeat in Norway and the failure to prepare for the German attack in the west tumbled Neville Chamberlain from office as Britain's prime minister. Parliament replaced him with the vigorous Winston Churchill, a long-time opponent of Chamberlain's appeasement policies.

The change in British leaders was not enough to change the course of events. The masses of German armor and infantry, aided by the terrifying *Stuka* dive-bombers of the *Luftwaffe* (air force), smashed everything in its path. The British and the French appealed desperately for American aid. Paul Reynaud, the French premier, asked Roosevelt for "clouds of planes" and pleaded with the president to reach "across the ocean to help us save civilization." But however sympathetic, Roosevelt could not comply without congressional support. In a few weeks the French army collapsed and the Germans entered Paris. The British forces in northern France, sent during the phony war, retreated to the English Channel coast at Dunkirk and were saved from German capture by a flotilla of naval and civilian ships, hurriedly dispatched from every port in Britain. Meanwhile Mussolini, who had been playing a waiting game, decided that it was time to join his Axis partner or be dealt out of any victorious peace settlement and invaded France from the southeast. On June 23 the French signed an armistice with the Germans that established a broad German occupation zone along the Channel and Atlantic coasts, including Paris, but left control of the south and east to a regime under Marshal Henri Pétain headquartered at Vichy.

America Reacts

The American public watched the awesome power of the German army and air force with horror. In four years of fierce fighting during the previous war the Germans had never taken Paris. Now in a matter of weeks the French had been routed and the British reduced to near impotence. How would it end? And would the United States be next?

Today the possibility of a German attack on the United States may seem preposterous. In 1940 the Atlantic was an insuperable barrier to any aggressor who lacked overwhelming command of the high seas. And as during 1914 to 1918 Germany's chief strength on the oceans consisted of a fleet of submarines, useful against enemy merchant shipping but incapable of carrying troops and supplies for a long-distance invasion. But what if the Germans gained possession of the French and British fleets, a combined naval force that exceeded America's? Such a possibility gave many Americans, high and low, the jitters.

And there were other dangers. America and Nazi Germany were ideological enemies. "Two worlds are in conflict, two philosophies of life," Hitler himself said. Nazi Germany's amazing triumphs had seized the imaginations of many people around the world, and there seemed reason to fear Nazi ideological penetration of the Western Hemisphere and even the United States itself, where a German-American Bund supported the Nazi cause and some American intellectuals were beginning to talk of Nazism as "the wave of the future." There was also the danger of slow encroachment on American economic and strategic interests—in Latin America, especially—by a powerful and expansionist Germany, unchecked by substantial opponents. All told, Axis gains did not bode well for the United States. "Defeat for [the] Allies," declared the interventionist *Nation,* "would seriously undermine American security. It would bring Hitler and Hitlerism to our very door."

By the summer of 1940 millions of Americans were convinced that the United States must prepare for any eventuality. In June Roosevelt established the National Defense Research Committee, later called the Office of Scientific Research and Development, to create new weapons for the armed forces. Soon after this he appointed two new, more energetic, service chiefs, former Secretary of State Stimson as secretary of war, and Frank Knox as secretary of the navy. On June 22 Congress approved a new tax measure to raise almost a billion dollars for national defense and passed the Smith Act, making it unlawful to advocate or teach the overthrow of the state or federal governments by force or violence. In mid-September Congress passed the Selective Service Act establishing the first peacetime military draft in U.S. history.

Over sixteen million young men registered for Selective Service. They were soon streaming off to army camps for basic training and one year of military service.

Meanwhile in the press, from the platforms, and over the airwaves a bitter battle raged between the advocates of isolation and those of increasing intervention. The isolationists' chief organization was the America First Committee, formed in July 1940 to prevent American intervention in the European war. Many America First leaders were moved by the sincere belief that democracy at home could "be preserved only by keeping out of the European war." But others were motivated by hatred of Roosevelt and a few by pro-Nazi sentiments and even antisemitism. Among the latter, it seemed, was Charles Lindbergh, hero of the first solo flight across the Atlantic; he had visited Nazi Germany and been impressed by Hitler and the growing power of the Nazi war machine. At one point "Lindy" identified the "warmongers" in the country as the "Anglophiles," the Roosevelt administration, and the Jews. The latter, he said, had "undue influence in our motion pictures, our press, or radio, and our government," and he warned that they would be blamed if the United States entered the war.

On the other side of the struggle was the Committee to Defend America by Aiding the Allies, headed by the old progressive essayist and editor William Allen White. With three hundred chapters throughout the country the Committee organized petition- and letter-writing campaigns, held rallies, sponsored radio broadcasts, and prepared newspaper advertisements to warn of the Nazi danger and demand aid to Hitler's enemies. By aiding France and Britain, America might avoid war, its message proclaimed. But it is clear that many members and supporters privately believed that the Nazi menace could be stopped only by direct American involvement.

Aid to Britain

The media battle in America paralleled the lethal air battle in Britain. After Dunkirk the British found themselves fighting alone, their ragged, ill-equipped remnant of an army facing Hitler's massive, victorious war machine across the English Channel, just 50 miles away. Churchill, a master of English prose, sustained morale by calls for sacrifice and defiant pledges "to fight on the beaches, . . . fight on the landing grounds, . . . fight in the fields and in the streets, . . . fight in the hills; we shall never surrender." Before attempting a Channel crossing, Hitler sought air supremacy over Britain, and beginning in August 1940 sent fleets of German bombers to blast British military installations and break British civilian morale. The Royal Air Force, although outnumbered, challenged the Germans in fierce dogfights in the skies and exacted a immense toll. Meanwhile Britons huddled in shelters, and thousands died. By the summer of 1940 shortwave radio was able to report events live from Europe, and millions of Americans could hear Edward R. Murrow and other reporters from London describing the bombings with the sounds of actual explosions and sirens in the background. The CBS and NBC broadcasts powerfully reinforced American sympathy for the British people.

But Britain's plight demanded more than sympathy. The United Kingdom was a small island nation dependent on its empire for manpower and on the world for supplies. Its mastery of the seas was essential to survival, and German submarines were more dangerous even than Air Marshal Hermann Goering's *Luftwaffe*. By June of

1940 the Germans were sinking almost 300,000 tons of British shipping a month. If these losses were not stopped Britain would be forced to surrender.

In May Churchill had asked the United States to give Britain fifty of its mothballed stock of World War I destroyers to help escort ship convoys carrying American arms and supplies. But Roosevelt, with the isolationists at his back, hesitated so long that William Allen White believed he "had lost his cud." Then White and his interventionist colleagues had a brainstorm. Why not exchange the destroyers for naval bases on British territory in the Western Hemisphere and a guarantee that Britain would never surrender its fleet to the Germans? Such an arrangement could be pictured as a security measure for the United States, not an act of generosity toward Britain. This scheme got Roosevelt off the hook and by September he was able to conclude the destroyers-for-bases deal with Britain.

The 1940 Election

By this time the United States was in the midst of a presidential election campaign and the issue of war or peace inevitably intruded. Although the country had a no-third-term tradition there was no constitutional bar (as there would be after the passage in 1951 of the Twenty-second Amendment) to Roosevelt seeking another term as president. A wily politician determined to avoid lame-duck status, FDR kept the nation guessing about his intentions and then maneuvered the Democrats into converting his renomination at the Chicago convention into a "draft." The Republicans chose a relative unknown, Wendell Willkie of Indiana, a former utility magnate, but a man who represented the party's more liberal, internationalist wing.

Republican isolationists painted the president as a warmonger, but at first Willkie, himself pro-British, avoided foreign policy attacks. Then as his standings in the polls flagged, he warned that American troops were "already almost on the transports." Roosevelt defended his peaceful intentions. The charge that the American government had "secretly entered into agreements with foreign nations" was a "fantastic mis-statement," he told a Philadelphia audience on October 23. In Boston on October 30 he declared that he had "repeated . . . a hundred times, . . . your boys are not going to be sent into any foreign wars."

Actually the threat of war and the sense that if it came the experienced FDR would make the better leader, worked to the president's advantage. Pollsters before November discovered that a majority of voters favored Willkie if the war was excluded from consideration. But most Americans took the possibility of war very seriously and on election day the voters returned FDR to office for a third term with a twenty-seven to twenty-two million popular majority.

America Goes to War

After the election the president's attention once more turned to preserving Britain's ability to resist. By this time Britain's orders with American firms for arms, ships, planes, and munitions far exceeded its means, even if it sold off all its assets in the United States and abroad. Roosevelt knew how wary Americans remained of lending money to any belligerent, but he soon came up with a clever scheme to get around their resistance. In a press conference on December 17 he used the homey illustration of a householder lending a neighbor his hose to fight a fire, only asking that it be returned when the emergency was over. Why not "lease and lend" war matériel to Britain on the same basis? When the war was over the British would repay the supplies they had borrowed in kind. A week later the president delivered one of his famous fireside chats describing how Britain was fighting America's battle as well as its own and how its defeat would cause serious dangers to the United States. The United States must become "the great arsenal of democracy" to keep Britain going and repel the Axis enemy from its own gates. (See Reading 9.) Soon after this polls showed that fully 80 percent of the American people approved the concept of all aid to Britain short of war. In March 1941 Congress passed the Lend-Lease Act appropriating $7 billion for arms to be "lent" to any nation whose defense the president deemed vital to American safety.

Crisis with Japan

The perceived dangers to America, during the last half of 1940, did not all come from Europe. Across the Pacific American interests also seemed to be in jeopardy. There the Japanese, taking advantage of events in Europe that weakened the western colonial powers, were aggressively pushing their Greater East Asia Co-Prosperity Sphere and threatening American interests. In June 1940 they forced the French to cease sending aid to the Chinese nationalist leader, Chiang Kai-shek, chief opponent of their effort to dominate the country. They also pressured Britain to cut off aid to Chiang. In August the Japanese demanded that the Vichy government in France allow them to build military bases in the French colony of Indochina. It soon looked as if the Dutch East Indies with its vast supply of oil, a commodity resource-poor Japan desperately needed, would become the target of Japanese demands as well.

The American government might have ignored these aggressive moves in the interest of dealing first with Hitler, already perceived as the chief threat. But America had long been the arbiter of stability in the Far East and defender of an independent China, and Roosevelt felt that the Japanese must be deflected from their aggressive course. At first Washington tried moderate countermeasures. In late September 1940 the United States announced that it would embargo all scrap iron shipments to Japan, a move that promised to hobble the Japanese steel and shipbuilding industry. It avoided using the more powerful oil embargo, however, holding this action in reserve if the Japanese continued their aggressive moves.

If anything, America's efforts to restrain the Japanese only egged them on. In September 1940 Japan signed the Tripartite Pact with Germany and Italy, stating that if any of the three signers went to war with any country not then a belligerent in the European war, the others would come to its aid. The pact was clearly aimed at the United States, because in a separate clause it specifically declared that the Soviet Union, whose relations with Japan were poor, was exempt from this provision. Roosevelt and Hull had intended to stall the Japanese expansionists, but they were unintentionally goading them into bolder efforts to take advantage of the Western nations while the latter were weakened or distracted by events in Europe.

READING 9

The Isolationist Viewpoint

*The isolationists fought Roosevelt's efforts to bolster Britain in the months
following the fall of France in every way possible. One of their most ardent
spokespersons was Senator Burton K. Wheeler, a Democrat from Montana.
In mid-January 1941 Wheeler gave the following radio talk in reply to
FDR's proposal for a lend-lease program to supply besieged Britain with
American arms.*

The lend-lease policy, translated into legislative form, stunned a Congress and
a nation wholly sympathetic to the cause of Great Britain. The Kaiser's blank
check to Austria-Hungary in the first World War was a piker compared to the
Roosevelt blank check of World War II. It warranted my worst fears for the
future of America, and it definitely stamps the President as war-minded.

The lend-lease-give program is the New Deal's triple A foreign policy; it
will plow under every fourth American boy.

Never before have the American people been asked or compelled to give
so bounteously and so completely of their tax dollars to any foreign nation.
Never before has the Congress of the United States been asked by any
President to violate international law. Never before has this Nation resorted
to duplicity in the conduct of its foreign affairs. Never before has the United
States given to one man the power to strip this Nation of its defenses. Never
before has a Congress coldly and flatly been asked to abdicate.

If the American people want a dictatorship—if they want a totalitarian
form of government and if they want war—this bill should be steam-rollered
through Congress, as is the wont of President Roosevelt.

Approval of this legislation means war, open and complete warfare. I,
therefore, ask the American people before they supinely accept it, Was the last
World War worth while?

If it were, then we should lend and lease war materials. If it were, then
we should lend and lease American boys. President Roosevelt has said we
would be repaid by England. We will be. We will be repaid, just as England
repaid her war debts of the first World War—repaid those dollars wrung
from the sweat of labor and the toil of farmers with cries of "Uncle Shylock."
Our boys will be returned—returned in caskets, maybe; returned with
bodies maimed; returned with minds warped and twisted by sights of horrors
and the scream and shriek of high-powered shells.

Considered on its merits and stripped of its emotional appeal to our
sympathies, the lend-lease-give bill is both ruinous and ridiculous. Why
should we Americans pay for war materials for Great Britain who still has
$7,000,000,000 in credit or collateral in the United States? Thus far England

has fully maintained rather than depleted her credits in the United States. The cost of the lend-lease-give program is high in terms of American tax dollars, but it is even higher in terms of our national defense. Now it gives to the President the unlimited power to completely strip our air forces of its every bomber, of its every fighting plane.

It gives to one man—responsible to no one—the power to denude our shores of every warship. It gives to one individual the dictatorial power to strip the American Army of our every tank, cannon, rifle, or antiaircraft gun. No one would deny that the lend-lease-give bill contains provisions that would enable one man to render the United States defenseless, but they will tell you, "The President would never do it." To this I say, "Why does he ask the power if he does not intend to use it?" Why not, I say, place some check on American donations to a foreign nation?

Is it possible that the farmers of America are willing to sell their birthright for a mess of pottage?

Is it possible that American labor is to be sold down the river in return for a place upon the Defense Commission, or because your labor leaders are entertained at pink teas?

Is it possible that the American people are so gullible that they will permit their representatives in Congress to sit supinely by while an American President demands totalitarian powers—in the name of saving democracy?

I say in the kind of language used by the President—shame on those who ask the powers—and shame on those who would grant them.

You people who oppose war and dictatorship, do not be dismayed because the war-mongers and interventionists control most of the avenues of propaganda, including the motion-picture industry.

Do not be dismayed because Mr. Willkie, of the Commonwealth & Southern [a wealthy utility company], agrees with Mr. Roosevelt. This merely puts all the economic and foreign "royalists" on the side of war.

Remember, the interventionists control the money bags, but you control the votes.

Source: Burton K. Wheeler, "American Radio Forum of the Air," January 12, 1941.

Events in Europe

By the fall of 1940 the Royal Air Force had won the Battle of Britain, the air war in the skies over the United Kingdom. But Hitler seemed as powerful as ever on the continent where the conquered peoples, still stunned by Germany's blitzkrieg victories, had not yet begun to organize resistance to the brutal Nazi occupation. In April 1941 German forces, moving to rescue the Italians from an ill-starred assault on Greece, invaded the Balkans themselves. British forces from North Africa rushed to help the Greeks, but by June 1 the Germans had added Yugoslavia and Greece to their list of conquests. Helped by the diversion of British strength to defend Greece, the brilliant German General Erwin Rommel attacked the British in Libya and drove them back to Egypt.

Then Hitler made his first big mistake. Flush with an unbroken string of victories on land, Hitler, ignoring the 1939 treaty, sent his mighty army eastward across the Polish border into the Soviet Union in late June 1941. During the months following the September 1939 invasion of Poland, the Russians, however suspicious of Hitler, had servilely supplied him and his military machine with vital supplies of wheat, oil, and steel under the terms of the Nazi-Soviet Pact. Pro-Soviet defenders of the pact claimed Soviet leader Joseph Stalin was playing for time, but the Soviets had not used the interval to prepare for a possible onslaught. The German attack caught them completely by surprise and enabled the invaders to destroy hundreds of planes and tanks and capture or kill thousands of Soviet troops in the first few days. By November 1941 the German *Wehrmacht* (army) had surrounded Leningrad, reached Sevastopol in the Crimea, and were at the gates of Moscow itself.

Hitler's decision to invade Russia was the biggest strategic blunder he ever made. But for a time it looked as if the Soviet Union too would fall before his military might. Churchill, operating on the principle that the enemy of my enemy is my friend, speedily offered Russia aid to fight the Nazis. Roosevelt had to move more slowly. Some Americans regarded the struggle between the Soviet Union and Germany as a fight between "Satan and Lucifer" and hoped the two would destroy one another. Others, however, surmounted their distaste for the Soviet Union and its Communist principles. Roosevelt himself agreed with Churchill, and in late July 1941 he dispatched his close adviser Harry Hopkins to Moscow, to offer munitions and supplies to the beleaguered Soviets. Tell Stalin, the president instructed Hopkins, that "we mean business on a long-term supply job." In the end billions of dollars of American lend-lease equipment would help the Russians stop the German attack.

A Shooting War

By this time the North Atlantic, the chief highway for arms to Britain as well as the Soviet Union, had become a crucial battleground. And all was not well in the Battle of the Atlantic. Each month submarines were sending an ever-larger portion of America's "tools of war" to the bottom. What was the point of American matériel aid if it did not arrive? The solution was American convoys, but that was an act of war.

Roosevelt by now believed American entrance into the war was unavoidable, but he also knew that most Americans were not yet ready, and so he moved cautiously at first on the convoy issue. In the spring of 1941 he transferred a portion of America's Pacific naval forces to the Atlantic to engage in "patrolling." The ships would ply the waters where German submarines operated and warn the British navy of any they detected. On April 9 the president announced an arrangement with the Danish government-in-exile to take over Greenland and there build air and naval bases to be used in patrolling the North Atlantic sea lanes. In July, by agreement with its government, the United States sent troops to Iceland, another country strategically located athwart the sea routes to Britain and the Soviet Union.

Bit by bit the United States was becoming a virtual ally of Great Britain, a relationship underscored by the meeting of Roosevelt and Churchill at Argentia Bay off Newfoundland in August 1941. There the two leaders got to know one another and drew up the "Atlantic Charter." Although America was not an official belligerent, this document in effect was a statement of war aims. Both nations renounced any interest in territorial gains; pledged to oppose territorial changes contrary to the wishes of the inhabitants; and expressed support for political self-determination for all people, freer world trade, freedom from want and fear, freedom of the seas, and disarmament of all aggressors pending some sort of permanent international peace body. The Atlantic Charter was the public part of the British-American discussions. But the two leaders also considered how the United States could be brought into the war. According to Churchill's private report to the British cabinet on his return to London, FDR promised him that "he would wage war but not declare it and that he would become more and more provocative. . . . The President . . . made it clear that he would look for an 'incident' which would justify him in opening hostilities."

Although the United States was acting like a cobelligerent, most Americans still opposed an actual shooting war that would involve sending millions of troops overseas. The public resistance to any greater sacrifice was dramatically highlighted by the vote in Congress just days after the meeting at Argentia Bay. By this time the one-year service term of draftees was running out and by law they would soon all return to civilian life. To prevent the collapse of the army, the administration proposed to extend the service period to eighteen months. In the House the extension passed by a one-vote majority out of 405 cast.

During the fall of 1941 Roosevelt sought his "incident" on the North Atlantic. On September 4 a British plane radioed the American destroyer *Greer,* on patrol off Iceland, that a German submarine had been spotted 10 miles ahead. The destroyer pursued the submarine, which fired a torpedo; the *Greer* answered with depth charges. In the end no one was hurt, but in a radio talk to the American people Roosevelt announced that a submarine had fired on an American naval vessel "without warning" and called the incident "piracy—piracy legally and morally." From now on, he declared, American ships would no longer wait to be attacked; they would fire first. Most Americans accepted FDR's version of the event and endorsed the "shoot on sight" policy, although it amounted to a virtual undeclared war with Germany on the high seas.

On October 9 Roosevelt asked Congress to repeal those sections of the neutrality acts that forbade arming of U.S. merchant ships. While Congress debated the repeal, a German submarine torpedoed the American destroyer *Kearny* off Iceland with the loss of eleven lives. "We . . . wished to avoid shooting," FDR announced after the *Kearny* attack, "but the shooting has started. And history has recorded who fired the first shot." Soon after, a German submarine sank the *Reuben James* on convoy duty in the same area. One hundred sailors went down with their ship. On November 17 Congress authorized the arming of U.S. merchant vessels and removed the ban on their carrying cargo to belligerent ports.

With each passing week the United States was moving rapidly toward full belligerent status. Only Hitler's reluctance to confront America directly prevented all-out war. In time, undoubtedly he would have lost patience and retaliated. But war reached in such a way would have troubled many Americans, and Roosevelt would not have achieved the unity of purpose and the will to win that he wanted. Knowing as we do the full extent of Nazi beastliness and the grave danger that Hitler and Nazism posed to civilized life, we find it hard to condemn FDR. But there are critics who believe that his lack of candor created a bad precedent for later presidents whose causes were far more ambiguous. In 1971 while the United States was mired down in the Vietnam War, Senator William Fulbright claimed that FDR's "deviousness in a good cause made it easier for LBJ [President Lyndon B. Johnson] to practice the same deviousness in a bad cause."

Pearl Harbor

Roosevelt did not need his incident in the Atlantic. In early December 1941, half a world away, Japan committed a heinous act that ended America dissent and created an instant consensus to defeat the Axis powers no matter what the cost in lives and money.

For a time during early 1941 Japan had sought a peaceful settlement of outstanding differences with the United States through direct talks between Secretary Hull and Japanese Ambassador Kichisaburo Nomura as well as through intermediaries. Both sides talked past one another. Hull and Nomura dispensed with a translator, and we now know that neither side fully grasped what the other meant. What was clear, however, was that Japan was not willing to leave China, although in exchange for U.S. resumption of vital raw materials exports it agreed to abandon its expansion into Southeast Asia. This was not enough for the United States, and the talks only led to further mutual exasperation.

Germany's unexpected invasion of the Soviet Union in June 1941 presented Japan with two tempting options. It could attack its traditional enemy Russia when it was vulnerable and eliminate once and for all an impediment to its ambitions in Asia. Or it could move against the British, French, and Dutch colonies to the south, secure in the knowledge that the Soviets would be in no position to obstruct its actions. In a series of momentous cabinet meetings in late June 1941 the Japanese government, goaded by the militarists, decided to turn south despite the "possibility of being involved in a war with England and America."

The American government knew of this secret plan almost immediately. American naval intelligence officers had cracked the Japanese codes and were reading top secret dispatches to and from Japanese officials. The administration debated the appropriate response, with some of FDR's advisers pushing a complete oil embargo and others warning that this would simply provide Japan with a further motive for expansion south. In the end, through a series of oblique and confused moves, the United States embargoed oil.

The skeptics were right. Each day the island empire consumed another 12,000 tons of petroleum. With only an eighteen-month supply on hand, Japan now decided to move against the oil-rich Dutch East Indies come what may. Joseph Grew, U.S. ambassador in Tokyo, wrote in his diary soon after the oil embargo, "The obvious conclusion is eventual war."

As the Japanese oil gauge moved toward empty, the need to act became ever more urgent. At first the Japanese attempted to break the impasse diplomatically through a meeting between Prime Minister Prince Fumimaro Kenoye and Roosevelt. Suspicious of the Japanese since he became secretary of state, Hull demanded that before such a meeting the Japanese agree to abandon their imperial ambitions in Asia. Hull's preconditions ended Kenoye's efforts. By this time the Japanese military leaders had decided that if no settlement with the United States had been reached by October, the army and navy would move against the Dutch East Indies. On October 16 Prince Kenoye resigned as prime minister and Hideki Tōjō, leader of the military expansionists, took his place.

Soon after, the Tōjō cabinet debated once more the issue of peace or war. In ten days of discussion the Japanese leaders decided that they would continue to negotiate with the United States for another month, but if the Americans had not resumed trade by the end of November, Japan would attack. As Tōjō expressed it, "Rather than await extinction, it [would be] better to face death by breaking through the encircling ring." On November 14, in a move to disarm the United States, the Japanese sent veteran diplomat Saburo Kurusu to Washington to present new options. Once more the Americans knew in advance what the Japanese would propose and also that war was close. Playing for time, Hull submitted counterproposals while the American military chiefs sent out warnings of possible attack to all Pacific military commanders. Although it was clear that a major thrust was imminent most of the experts believed it would be to the south against the Dutch, the French, or the British.

The experts had only half the story. Japan would move against the European colonies in Southeast Asia, but it would first try to destroy American naval power in the Pacific by a surprise attack against the main U.S. Pacific naval base at Pearl Harbor, Hawaii. American military leaders should have recognized the possibility of an attack on the Pacific fleet at "Pearl"; since 1931 every graduating class of Japan's naval academy had been required to answer the examination question: "How would you execute a surprise attack on Pearl Harbor?" But the commanders in Hawaii were complacent, perhaps deceived by a racist contempt for the Japanese as little yellow people who wore kimonos and made shoddy gewgaws for export.

On November 25 an immense Japanese armada of destroyers, cruisers, battleships, and aircraft carriers left the Kuril Islands and slipped quietly through the foggy North Pacific heading east, then south. The plan called for Nomura and Kurusu in Washington to present a long document to Hull on December 7, ending with what amounted to a declaration of war. Minutes *after,* according to the blueprint, the Japanese carrier planes would hit the American ships at Pearl Harbor. But something went wrong with the timing and Japanese bombs were already falling on Hawaii before the entire message could be delivered.

December 7 was a peaceful Sunday morning at Pearl Harbor, with sailors sleeping, eating breakfast, or lazing around the deck of their ships. Shortly after 7:30 A.M. a bosun's mate noticed a flock of planes circling at a distance, but assumed it was some sort of Army Air Corps drill. In fact it was the dive-bombers and fighter planes of the Japanese task force that had left their carriers an hour before. Within minutes they were streaking across the sky over Pearl, their machine guns blazing, and their bombs and torpedoes raining down on the unsuspecting Americans below.

At Hickman and Wheeler airfields the Air Corps planes were lined up wing-tip-to-wingtip for better protection against possible saboteurs and were virtually all destroyed. Few rose to challenge the Japanese attackers. The chief blow landed on the fleet of battleships, cruisers, and destroyers lined up at the quay at the naval base. In minutes "Battleship Row," ripped by fierce explosions, turned into a mass of smoke and flame. Hundreds of sailors died in the blasts or were drowned when their ships capsized and went to the harbor bottom. In less than two hours the planes with Japan's rising sun emblem had finished their work and were winging their way back to their carriers. All told 2400 Americans died in the attack and nineteen American ships, including five of the eight battleships, were either destroyed or seriously damaged. Fortunately most of the Pacific fleet's carrier force was on a training mission away from base and was untouched. As it was, the Japanese had succeeded in crippling for many months America's ability to stop their thrust into the South Pacific.

News of the surprise attack reached a nation in the midst of its Sunday leisure. On the East Coast many Americans first learned of the catastrophe when a breathless bulletin interrupted the broadcast of the 3 P.M. New York Philharmonic concert. In Phoenix they heard what had happened when they phoned the *Arizona Republic* for the score of the Chicago Bears–St. Louis Cardinals game. In Denver KFEL broke into a religious program to announce the attack.

The president in Washington had gasped when Navy Secretary Frank Knox phoned to tell him the news. Roosevelt immediately called Hull and then sat quietly for almost twenty minutes composing his thoughts. His feelings were undoubtedly mixed: dismay at the certain losses and also relief that the long wait was over. At Chequers, his country house, Churchill heard a BBC radio bulletin and immediately phoned the White House. "They have attacked us at Pearl Harbor," Roosevelt told the prime minister, "We are all in the same boat now." Churchill's heart leaped for joy. America was in the war! Britain would now survive!

The next day Roosevelt appeared before Congress to deliver his war message. December 7, he announced, was "a date that will live in infamy." While in the midst of negotiations the Japanese had deceitfully attacked an unsuspecting nation. Many lives had been lost and American naval and military forces had been severely damaged. By now news had reached Washington of a general Japanese Pacific offensive, and the president listed the other places where the Japanese had struck: Malaya, Hong Kong, Guam, the Philippines, and Wake Island. "No matter how long it may take us to overcome this premeditated invasion, the American people in their righteous might will win through to absolute victory," he promised, drawing cheers and thunderous applause from the members of the House and Senate. Congress responded with a declaration of war by an almost unanimous vote. "The only thing to do," declared isolationist Senator Burton K. Wheeler, "is to lick hell out of them."

One question remained in suspense for several days: what about Hitler and the Germans? It is not entirely clear that the American people would have been enthusiastic about a two-ocean war at just this time. Fortunately Germany and Italy ended the uncertainty by declaring war themselves on December 11. The United States was now a full-scale partner of Britain and the Soviet Union in the greatest war in history.

The Battlefronts

Everywhere in the opening months of 1942 the anti-Axis powers were on the defensive. (See Figures 9–1 and 9–2.) On the European continent Hitler ruled from France to Poland, either directly or through puppet regimes, although in London, a half-dozen governments-in-exile retained the loyalty of their captive peoples and control of various overseas colonies and small military forces. Most important of these shadow governments was the "Free French" regime organized by General Charles de Gaulle, a proud and stubborn man whose fierce patriotism had not permitted him to accept the Vichy surrender.

Elsewhere the Axis powers were on the march. In Russia winter had stalled the powerful German advance, but it resumed in the spring of 1942, and by August the Wehrmacht had reached the Don River, 600 miles into the heart of the Soviet Union and would soon invest Stalingrad, a major transport hub on the Volga. In North Africa in May Rommel attacked the British, captured Tobruk, and by July was within 60 miles of Alexandria, Egypt. On the Atlantic the German submarine kill soared, with the U-boats sending 1600 Allied ships to the bottom in 1942 alone, often just a few miles off the beaches of the American Atlantic and Gulf of Mexico coasts.

The Japanese gains were spectacular. Japanese forces invaded neutral Thailand and British Malaya on December 8. Two days later their torpedo planes sank the *Prince of Wales* and the *Repulse*, the backbone of British naval power in the Far East. American Guam and Wake Island and British Hong Kong all fell in late December. On January 11 Japanese troops invaded the Dutch East Indies. A combined Allied naval force tried to stop them but was defeated in the Battle of the Java Sea. Java, the chief Dutch East Indies island, succumbed soon after. On February 15 the British, deprived of naval protection, surrendered their sixty-thousand-man garrison at Singapore, the military linchpin of their far eastern empire, to General Tomoyuki Yamashita. In June Japanese forces captured Attu and Kiska, islands in the Aleutian extension of Alaska.

The worst American loss in these early months was the Philippines. Landing on Luzon in mid December, the Japanese quickly took Manila and overwhelmed the weak Filipino-American forces under General Douglas MacArthur. MacArthur and his men retired to Bataan Peninsula and Corregidor, the fortress in Manila Bay, and held out for weeks against great odds. On May 6 the American and Filipino troops surrendered to the enemy and were marched off to prisoner-of-war camps where many would die of beatings, disease, and starvation. Before the American forces capitulated, MacArthur and his family were rescued by daring PT (propeller torpedo) boat captains and brought to Australia where the general was put in charge of Australian-American forces gathering to meet and roll back the Japanese forces.

During these grim months of retreat the British and American leaders made several major strategic decisions. In a series of meetings in Washington Roosevelt and Churchill agreed that Hitler would be the first priority; the war with Japan would be a holding action until the Germans were on the run. They also agreed that the first move in the British-American counteroffensive would be the invasion of Vichy-controlled French North Africa to expel the Axis from the south shore of the vital Mediterranean. On January 1 the two leaders issued the "Declaration of the United

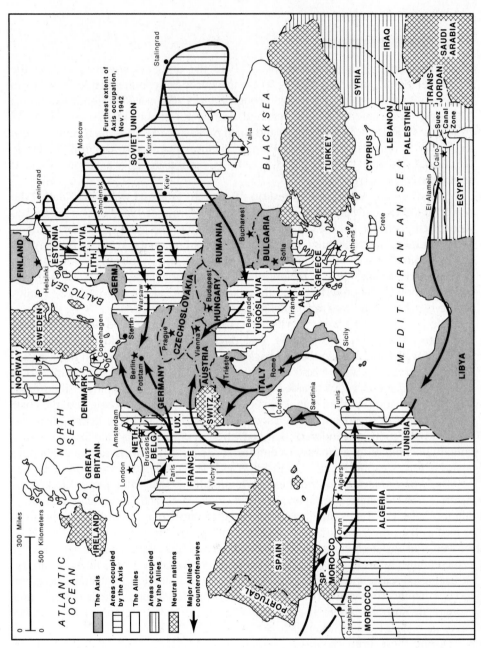

Figure 9–1 *World War II in Europe*

Nations," signed by the United States, Britain, the countries of the British Common-wealth, the European governments-in-exile, several anti-Axis Latin American nations, and the Soviet Union. This document established a loose alliance of anti-Axis countries, named by FDR the *United Nations,* and pledged them to adhere to the principles of the Atlantic Charter.

The Tide Turns

Although Hitler was top priority, the first American military successes came in the Pacific. In the Battle of the Coral Sea on May 7 and 8 neither the Japanese nor the American flagships saw the other; the damage was inflicted solely by airplanes. American losses, including the sinking of the carrier *Lexington,* were serious, but the engagement checked the Japanese threat to Australia. Even more decisive was the Battle of Midway in early June, precipitated by Admiral Isoroku Yamamoto's desire to draw the American navy, still weakened by Pearl Harbor, into a decisive battle that would open Hawaii to invasion and perhaps even permit a devastating attack on the American Pacific Coast.

The Japanese flotilla consisted of over a hundred war vessels including eleven battleships and four carriers. Eighty transports were crowded with troops. Yamamoto tried to disguise his target, but Admiral Chester Nimitz knew, through deciphered code intercepts, where his opponent intended to go and made plans accordingly. When the Japanese arrived off Midway, the Americans were ready and carrier planes from the *Hornet, Enterprise,* and *Yorktown* sank all four of Yamamoto's carriers. Deprived of air cover, the Japanese had no choice but to retreat. The Japanese navy remained intact, but having lost much of its air support, it was badly crippled. We can now see that the American victory at Midway turned the Pacific war around. Thereafter the Japanese tide began to recede.

Encouraged by the naval success in August, the Americans invaded the island of Guadalcanal in the Japanese-occupied Solomons. In bitter fighting in the tangled jungle and in the surrounding air and sea, the American forces slowly extended their control over the island. But not until February 1943 did the Japanese abandon their attempt to retain it.

In early November the Americans and British launched Operation Torch, the long-planned invasion of French North Africa. Under the command of Dwight D. Eisenhower, a young protégé of the American Chief of Staff George Marshall, British and American forces landed in Casablanca, Oran, and Algiers. The Allies hoped that Admiral Jean-François Darlan, the Vichy French official on the scene, would cooperate. But Darlan, a toady of the Nazis, disliked the Americans and British and despised de Gaulle, the man who had come to embody the Free French resistance to Vichy. He refused to order the French troops in North Africa to lay down their arms without the permission of Pétain in France, and the Americans and British soon found themselves fighting the French. At this point Hitler ordered his army to occupy the rest of France over Vichy's protest. This gave Darlan the excuse he needed to yield, and he agreed to surrender on condition that he be recognized as the chief of state in French North Africa. The British-Americans, anxious to consolidate their hold, agreed. De Gaulle's Free French supporters and many American liberals denounced the deal with Darlan

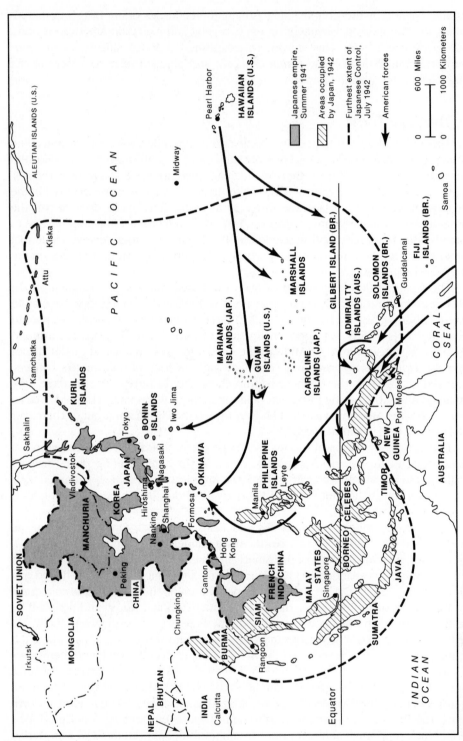

Figure 9–2 World War II in Asia

as an odious surrender to expediency. Fortunately for Allied unity Darlan was assassinated soon after and Henri Giraud, a general untainted by Vichy collaboration, succeeded him.

The British-American invasion of French North Africa foreshadowed the end of Axis power on the south rim of the Mediterranean. Early in 1943 the British Eighth Army advancing from the east attacked the *Afrika Korps* under Rommel, pushing the Germans against the Americans to the west. At Kasserine Pass in Tunisia Rommel's veterans inflicted a serious defeat on the untried Americans. But by early May the outnumbered Afrika Korps had run out of steam. Rommel escaped, later to face the Allies in France, but 250,000 of his men surrendered to the British-Americans.

Eastern Europe and Nazi Racial Policies

By now the tide had turned on the Soviet front as well. Hitler might have demolished the Soviet Union if not for his monstrous racial policies. He considered the Slavic people subhuman and sought simultaneously to destroy their culture and make them slaves of the German *Herrenvolk* (master race). The *Gestapo* (secret police) and the SS (*Schutzstaffel*; elite troops) summarily shot thousands of Polish, Ukranian, and Russian intellectuals and officials. They treated ordinary peasants and workers with calculated brutality, especially when they would not cooperate with the Nazis. To free German manpower for military service, the Nazis forced thousands of Europeans to work as "slave laborers" in German factories under inhuman conditions that finished off many more thousands.

Far worse was the systematic campaign, the *final solution,* to destroy the Jewish communities that had existed in Europe since the time of the Romans. By 1943 approximately eight or nine million Jews lived under Hitler's thumb, the majority in Poland, the Ukraine (a republic of the Soviet Union), the Balkans, and western Russia. These people received no mercy from the Nazis. Killing squads (*Einsatzgruppen*) moved in behind the Wehrmacht as it advanced eastward into the Ukraine and Russia and shot thousands of Jews—men, women, and children—to death. Beginning in 1941, the Nazis began to move Jews from all over occupied Europe to death camps in Poland, where they systematically murdered hundreds of thousands through starvation, overwork, and mass gassing with Zyklon-B, a deadly nerve gas. By 1942 reports of this hideous genocide policy began to reach the Western nations, but much of it was not believed. With some heroic exceptions, the non-Jews among the general populace of occupied Europe, even when they knew of this "Holocaust," as it has come to be called, did not, or could not, do anything to stop it. Six million Jews, millions of Poles and Russians, many thousands of Gypsies, Slavs, French, Dutch, and Greeks, as well as political anti-Nazis and thousands of so-called deviants (mentally ill people, homosexuals, and others) perished at German hands before the Nazi defeat stopped the slaughter.

This bestial behavior made "collaboration" with the Nazis repulsive for most people of the occupied countries. Resistance movements sprang up, which were soon engaged in guerrilla war with the occupying German forces. In the Soviet Union, even though many people had little love for the Communist government, few would cooperate with the invaders after the first few months; thousands eventually joined the "partisans," irregular soldiers who operated behind the Nazi lines harassing the Wehrmacht at every chance.

By July 1942 Hitler's army had reached the city of Stalingrad on the Volga River. There the Soviet troops were ordered to stand. For five months the two armies fought ferociously for a few houses, a few streets, a few yards of ground amid the heat, smoke, and noise of modern weapons, the agony of torn flesh, and the stench of rotting corpses. In November the Russians counterattacked in force and surrounded the 200,000 men of the German Sixth Army. Far gone in illusions of omnipotence, Hitler refused to allow the trapped generals to break out of the Russian ring and retreat. Despite his orders, on February 2 the German commander surrendered his depleted forces of 90,000 men.

The defeat at Stalingrad ended the myth of German military invincibility. In the spring of 1943 the Nazis were able to resume the offensive in the Ukraine. But this time they were stopped in their tracks by a vastly expanded and far better equipped Soviet army, partly supplied by American lend-lease matériel. From this point on the Germans only retreated, fighting brilliant and effective rearguard actions, but moving

The horror of the Nazi death camps was fully revealed to the world only at the end of the war, when they were liberated by advancing Allied armies. This May 1945 photo shows German civilians being forced by U.S. troops to confront what had been done at the Landsberg camp. (AP/World Wide Photos)

steadily back under the remorseless pressure of the Soviets. It was only a matter of time before Soviet troops would cross the border of the *Vaterland* itself.

The Home Front

U.S. and Allied military victories in the field were made possible by successful mobilization at home. America did succeed in becoming the "arsenal of democracy." By 1944, the last full year of war, American factories and fields were producing 30,000 tanks; 100,000 planes; 2,000 ships; and vast quantities of munitions, guns, supplies, and food for American military forces and for its United Nations allies. No soldier, sailor, or airman was as well equipped as the American *GI,* (from "government issue"), the popular name for the ordinary fighting man. Heading the centrally directed industrial mobilization was the War Production Board under the direction of Donald M. Nelson.

Rationing and Price Controls

The industrial achievement was not painless. Resources had to be reallocated from the civilian to the military sectors. After 1942 civilian automobile production ceased and car factories were shifted to tank, aircraft, and military vehicle production. Americans were forced to make do without the cherished annual car model change. The military also laid claim to much of the country's rubber, gasoline, aluminum, and steel supplies.

With the government siphoning off so much of the nation's productive capacity, it was impossible to rely on the processes of the free market. Rationing of rubber tires began just after Pearl Harbor, and the government added sugar, coffee, gasoline, oils, shoes, meat, and other products to the list as the months passed. Yet at no time during the war did Americans face serious deprivations; no other major belligerent nation sacrificed so little of its standard of living. In fact many American families, on short rations through most of the economically depressed 1930s, found the amount allotted to them under the rationing system more than enough. "Big ticket" items—new houses, cars, and electrical appliance—would be hard to get after 1942, but there was an abundance of food and clothing.

Most Americans complied with the rationing laws, feeling that they were "doing something" to help win the war. But some patronized black marketeers, illegal sellers of scarce goods who accepted extra cash in lieu of ration stamps, or purchased counterfeit stamps, or cheated to get more than their share in other ways.

Inflation was a more serious problem. Fortunately there was much slack in the economy left over from the Depression, and at first jobless workers and unused industrial capacity could be reemployed without creating shortages. This advantage did not last long. By 1942 unemployment had disappeared. Employers, eager to meet their war contract deadlines and guaranteed a profit by the government under a "cost plus" arrangement, bid enthusiastically for workers. Thousands of older men who had not worked for years took jobs; thousands of women joined the labor force. "Rosie the Riveter," wearing overalls, with her hair wrapped in a turban and a determined look on her face, became a homefront heroine. At long last the Depression was over;

Americans were soon better off than they had been since 1929. In fact the war had a long-term effect on income distribution in the United States. By eliminating the stagnant pool of the unemployed, it shifted the proportions of income in favor of the lower brackets, a condition that continued well into the postwar period.

Unfortunately the war threatened to overstimulate the economy. By 1945 the federal government's expenditures were running at $100 billion a year, more than ten times the largest yearly budget in peacetime. Government taxes also rose drastically. Millions who had never paid an income tax before found themselves on the federal tax rolls. Federal collection procedures, moreover, were improved by withholding taxes directly from employee's paychecks for the first time. Yet only $130 billion of the war's enormous $320 billion cost was offset by taxes. The rest was met from borrowing or, in effect, creating money. This meant a tremendous excess of cash in the pockets of American wage earners and businesspeople. Some of this surplus went into war bonds or other forms of savings. Abundant dollars, however, were soon chasing scarce goods, the perfect formula for inflation, and it became necessary to control prices.

The Office of Price Administration (OPA) sought to perform this task and did so relatively well. Under Leon Henderson and later Chester Bowles the OPA managed to hold price rises to under 10 percent a year between 1942 and 1945. But its work required an army of clerks, economists, and assorted paper pushers and produced mountains of red tape. The public often resented its actions. When the OPA decided to use homemakers as price checkers, the public denounced the "snoopers." The government also sought to control inflation through the National War Labor Board. When its rules failed to halt wage inflation, Roosevelt issued a "hold-the-line" order freezing prices, wages, and salaries.

Managing Opinion

Restored prosperity was clearly a wartime benefit. Other homefront changes were more ambiguous. The United States went to war a remarkably united nation. Even the most ardent isolationists felt the surge of righteous anger after Pearl Harbor and supported the all-out war effort. But nothing was left to chance. In 1942 Roosevelt established the Office of War Information (OWI) to serve essentially as a propaganda agency. Under the respected journalist Elmer Davis, however, the OWI managed to be relatively objective in its reporting of battlefront and homefront events, although Republicans and conservatives attacked it as pro-New Deal. Private groups, including moviemakers, novelists, journalists, radio broadcasters, and advertisers, also beat the patriotic drum. As in 1917 and 1918 movie stars were prominent at war bond rallies and as purveyors of patriotic attitudes. Dorothy Lamour, dressed in her famous sarong, helped sell over $350 million of war bonds. Ronald Reagan, the handsome Hollywood leading man, made patriotic documentaries.

Wartime Intolerance

The pro-war campaign was not excessively strident. World War I propaganda had created a wave of intolerant superpatriotism, and radicals and German-Americans had been its victims. This time there was relatively little chauvinism. Neither German-nor Italian-Americans suffered discrimination. And because the Soviet Union was a "gallant ally," neither did most leftists.

But tolerance did not extend to the Japanese-Americans on the Pacific Coast. These people, many of them *nisei* (American-born), had long been targets of white prejudice. Already vulnerable, when Japan attacked Pearl Harbor their circumstances worsened. In March 1942 panicky state and federal officials, fearful of sabotage and incited by bigots, ordered the Japanese removed from the Pacific Coast to the interior of the country. None of the Japanese-Americans was shot or starved, but 110,000 were forced to leave their homes on short notice, often selling their property at panic prices, and were relocated in internment camps in remote mountain and desert areas. There they lived behind barbwire in spartan, flimsy barracks until late in the war. The American Civil Liberties Union would call the treatment of the Japanese-Americans the "worst single wholesale violation of civil rights of American citizens in our history."

Despite their treatment most nisei remained loyal to the country that had spurned

During the war the United States forcibly relocated thousands of innocent Japanese-Americans living along the West Coast to crowded internment camps. Not until more than forty years later did the government unqualifiedly admit that the action was wrong. (The Bettmann Archive)

them. When Secretary of War Stimson announced that the U.S. Army would accept nisei volunteers, 1200 immediately enlisted. Many served in Italy, and their record for courage and enterprise far exceeded the average.

African-Americans

African-Americans experienced the war as a mixture of good and ill. Close to a million served in the armed forces, but almost entirely in segregated units. Most of these were confined to noncombat operations, such as truck driving or quartermaster duties, and usually under the command of white officers. When the war began the army had only two black officers, and the navy, none. Only late in the war did the authorities lower the barriers to mixed units and assign African-American troops to combat missions. Black GIs frequently took their training in southern army camps where they encountered the legal segregation of Dixie and the overt racism of the white community. For northern blacks, especially, contact with southern racism was often a bitter experience.

On the home front African-American civilians succeeded in getting some portion of the benefits conferred by a booming economy. But not without a fight. In January 1941, as the American defense effort began to accelerate, A. Philip Randolph, head of the Pullman Porters Union, the nation's largest black labor organization, threatened a march on Washington unless the government forbade race discrimination in defense plants. To avoid disruption of the rearmament drive, in June FDR issued an executive order prohibiting hiring discrimination by plants with defense contracts. He also established a Committee on Fair Employment Practices to monitor compliance with the order. Generally speaking, the arrangements worked. Millions of African-American men and women found jobs in war plants, many earning decent wages for the first time in their lives.

The gains for African-Americans created social tensions, however. The promise of good jobs brought another wave of rural black people from the deep South to the North and West. Like all such migrations, the influx caused crowding and job competition and aroused fears and hostilities. In a few places it led to violence. In mid-1943 a race riot in Detroit resulted in the death of twenty-five blacks and nine whites before federal troops restored order. Yet the gains outweighed the losses. By the end of the war the African-American community was more prosperous, more confident, and better prepared to move aggressively against the legal and the informal discrimination that remained in American life.

Women in Wartime

The war affected women's lives in many ways. Most continued in traditional roles as homemakers and mothers, they experienced the war as consumers or through the anxieties of having sons, brothers, and husbands on the fighting fronts. Many, however, contributed more directly to the war effort.

Single women had long been important members of the labor force, typically as service-job workers. Now many married women responded to the economy's need to fill vacant jobs previously held by men. At defense plants women were employed as

The war created many jobs for women and opened thousands more that previously had been filled by men. (Library of Congress)

assemblers of airframes, engines, parachutes, gas masks, artillery shells, and airplane propellers. They operated hand drills and wired instrument panels. Women also found work in the surging government bureaucracy. Most women were paid less than their male counterparts, but generally speaking this discrimination was taken for granted and there were few protests. On the home front women also served as volunteers for bond drives, ration boards, the Red Cross, and civil defense. Several thousand more adventurous young women joined women's auxiliary groups in the armed services as WACS (army), WAVES (navy), WASPS (air corps), or SPARS (coast guard). By the end of the war women workers had become, according to Eleanor Roosevelt, "an indispensable part of the life of the country."

The War and New Technology

World War II was a powerful stimulus to technological advance. Forced to deal with the health problems of millions in the military, doctors and scientists in the

United States and other allied nations developed new mass-produced antibiotics, drugs against malaria, insecticides, and new ways of preserving and transfusing blood. Other war-induced innovations included radar, perfected by the British, and rocket engines, developed by the Germans, but quickly copied by the Allies. To deal with the complex problems of calculating artillery trajectories, American engineers and mathematicians took the first steps toward developing the modern electronic computer.

The most startling and momentous technical breakthrough of all was the work of the Manhattan Project, a secret program launched by Roosevelt in 1943 on the advice of Albert Einstein and other scientists. Having learned that German physicists had successfully split the atom, causing the release of enormous energy, these scientists immediately saw that here was the basis for a terrifying weapon. In Hitler's hands it would mean the end of civilization. Shortly after the outbreak of the European war in 1939, Einstein wrote Roosevelt about the discovery of atomic fission and warned of its dangers if developed into a weapon by the enemy. The president took the warning seriously and told his subordinates to pursue the matter.

In May 1943, with the war in full cry, the government established the Manhattan Project, with research sites in Tennessee, Washington, and New Mexico, to purify uranium 238 and create an atom bomb. On July 16, 1945, billions of dollars and thousands of workhours later, a handful of scientists waited in the New Mexico desert, fifty miles from Alamogordo, while the switch was thrown and the countdown began for the first atomic explosion. At 5:30 A.M. there was a blinding flash reflected off the distant hill; seconds later came a fierce wind followed by an immense roar. And then the fireball—expanding out and up, and turning into a giant, glowing mushroom-shaped cloud. It was the dawn of a new, more anxious age for all humanity.

The 1944 Election

The war did not put an end to politics and the two- party system of course. In 1944 FDR announced that he had exchanged the role of "Dr. New Deal" for "Dr. Win the War." In fact, the New Deal reform impulse was already played out and the war only confirmed it. There was much talk of suspending political competition for the duration of the war in the interest of national unity. Yet despite the rhetoric about a people united for the sole purpose of defeating the enemy, politics continued. In the congressional elections of 1942 the Republicans made gains and in alliance with southern Democrats achieved informal control of both houses of Congress. In 1944 FDR, although in ill-health, ran for president again, this time against Thomas Dewey, the governor of New York. FDR's running mate was not vice president Henry Wallace, the former secretary of agriculture, who had replaced Garner in 1941. Considered an erratic man and an ultraliberal, Wallace was vetoed by the party's conservatives. Instead, the vice presidential candidate was Harry Truman, the feisty senator from Missouri. Truman, although formerly a Kansas City machine politician, had favorably impressed many Americans through his National Defense Program Investigating Committee, which uncovered waste and corruption in military supply procurement.

In November the FDR-Truman ticket defeated the Thomas Dewey–John Bricker ticket by a popular vote of 25.6 million to 22 million.

Planning for Peace

As the Axis tide receded, the thoughts of United Nations leaders turned to the peace settlement ahead. In October 1943 in Moscow, American, British, and Soviet officials held their first major talks about the postwar future. The British and Americans promised to open a second front in Western Europe as soon as possible. Stalin promised in return that after Germany's defeat, the Soviet Union would join the war against Japan. The three powers also established a European Advisory Commission to formulate postwar policy for Germany and, joined by China, agreed in a general way on a new postwar international body on the League of Nations model.

The following November Roosevelt, Churchill, and Chiang Kai-shek, meeting in Cairo, agreed to prosecute the war in the Far East until Japan unconditionally surrendered; to strip Japan of all her territorial gains since 1914; to return Manchuria and Formosa to China; and to guarantee that Korea, a longtime Japanese dependency, would eventually be free. "Unconditional surrender," originally announced by Roosevelt and Churchill at their Casablanca Conference in January 1943, was a stirring slogan, but by discouraging elements in the enemy nations that favored a negotiated peace, it probably prolonged the fighting and dying.

After the Cairo meeting Churchill and FDR flew on to Tehran, Iran, where they met Stalin face-to-face for the first time and confirmed most of the decisions reached earlier that year in Moscow. The three world leaders got along well personally, but one ominous note appeared. The Russians insisted on keeping the Polish territory that they had seized as part of the Nazi-Soviet Pact of 1939. Poland, they said, could compensate itself to the west at the expense of Germany. The Polish government-in-exile, located in London, bridled at the surrender of territory long part of Poland and rejected the plan despite British pressure. There was also controversy over who should govern Poland after Germany's defeat. The Western powers considered the London exiles the legitimate rulers of Poland; the Russians saw them as anti-Soviet bourgeois politicians whom they did not want exercising power on their western border. Observers could see trouble ahead.

The following year the United Nations (UN) powers held several more important meetings to decide the shape of the postwar world. In early July at Bretton Woods in New Hampshire, forty-four nations planned for postwar international trade by establishing an International Monetary Fund of almost $9 billion to secure stable ratios among international currencies. At Dumbarton Oaks, outside of Washington, the following month the UN powers agreed on basic principles for a new international peacekeeping organization. Between these two meetings one disquieting event took place. On July 27 the Soviet government had recognized as Poland's legitimate government the Polish Committee of National Liberation (later called the Lublin Committee), a pro-Soviet group organized in Moscow.

Victory

The Second Front in Europe

Meanwhile the war went on. U.S. Flying Fortress bombers based in Britain began to bomb military and industrial targets in German-occupied Europe in August 1942. By the following year hundreds of American and British planes were unloading vast tonnages of high-explosive and incendiary bombs on Germany itself. The bombing campaign increasingly became a terror strategy designed to destroy civilian morale and the enemy's will to resist.

In May 1943 the British and Americans met in Washington, and decided to open a second front by a cross-Channel invasion of Hitler's "fortress." For many months the Russians had pleaded for such an attack to relieve the agonizing pressure on them. Churchill, remembering the extraordinary British losses of 1914–18, had resisted, favoring instead an attack across the Mediterranean on Hitler's "soft underbelly." Now, however, with millions of American GIs on British soil and a massive British-American buildup of arms and supplies, he approved the cross-Channel attack for the spring of 1944.

In reality both schemes were tried. After defeating Rommel and the Afrika Korps in North Africa, the Americans and British invaded Sicily in July 1943 and conquered the island in a month. The fall of Sicily undermined Mussolini and led to a coup in Rome. On July 25 the Italian king, Victor Emmanuel III, announced Il Duce's resignation and replacement by Marshal Pietro Badoglio. Badoglio promptly dissolved the Fascist party and opened peace negotiations with the British and Americans. In September after British forces crossed the Straits of Messina to the Italian mainland, Italy officially surrendered. Unfortunately Badoglio could not make good a peaceful takeover of the Italian boot. The Germans quickly moved in to fill the vacuum, rescued Mussolini, and set him up as a puppet ruler in the Italian north. For many months they fought an effective holding operation in Italy, tying up thousands of British-American troops who might have been better used elsewhere. Not until June 4 did American soldiers enter Rome, and it would be months longer before all resistance ceased in northern Italy.

The British-American invasion of France, Operation Overlord, came on June 6, 1944. It was led by Dwight Eisenhower, who had supervised the North African operation. Eisenhower was not a brilliant field commander like his subordinate George Patton. His talent lay in organization and in getting men with clashing interests and personalities to cooperate. Only he, perhaps, could have smoothed the differences between the competing and mutually jealous air, ground, and sea services and yoked the cocky and overbearing Americans together with the defensive and condescending British.

The cross-Channel invasion was the largest amphibious operation in history. On "D-day," 4,000 barges and landing craft, carrying 70,000 British, Americans, Free French, and other Allied troops, crossed the Channel to the beaches of Normandy. The landing craft were protected by a giant naval armada of 1,200 ships and an air cover of 7,500 fighter planes. By now the Germans had completely lost the air war and the once-mighty Luftwaffe could do nothing to stop the invasion. Although the Germans inflicted heavy casualties on the American troops landing at Omaha Beach and elsewhere, they could not prevent the Allied troops from establishing a bridgehead. By the end of the first day the long-delayed second front was a reality.

The initial successes could not be immediately followed up. Thousands more troops were soon ferried across the Channel to reinforce the initial landing force, but for weeks the Allied forces remained bottled up in a small pocket near Caen on the Normandy coast. Then in late July, led by General George Patton's Third Army, they broke out and swept south and east toward Paris and the German border. On August 15 the U.S. Seventh Army landed on the French Mediterranean coast and drove north to take the Germans in the rear. On August 25 Free French and American forces liberated Paris, spared from destruction by the local German commander. During August and September the Netherlands and Belgium were liberated. In the east the Russians had launched their 1944 summer offensive along an eight hundred-mile front, and by the end of August they had pushed the Germans out of most Soviet territory. By early fall the Russians had cut into Poland and the Balkans and were in sight of Germany itself.

Hitler's End

By all reasonable estimates Germany had lost the war. At a comparable stage in 1918 the kaiser had given up. But Hitler, never the most mentally stable man, was by now far gone to paranoia. Buoyed up by visions of fantastic new weapons or fortuitous disasters to his enemies, the Führer insisted that Germany fight on to victory or total doom. Not all Germans were willing to see themselves or their country destroyed, and in July 1944 a group of anti-Nazi officers and civilians, including General Rommel, attempted to assassinate Hitler by detonating a bomb under a table where he sat. The Führer was injured but survived. The plotters were rounded up and brutally executed. Rommel was allowed, for his past services to Germany, to take his own life.

Although reeling, the German war machine was still alive. On June 14 the Germans launched the first pilotless, "buzz-bomb" attacks on London; in retaliation, they said, for the fierce British-American bomber raids that had turned many German cities into oceans of fire and killed thousands of German civilians. In early September they fired V-2 rocket missiles at London. The V-2s, the first ballistic missiles, ushered in a new age of warfare. Fortunately for British civilians the Allied armies were able to capture the launching sites before the new weapons could reduce all of Great Britain to rubble.

The final gasp of the German army in the west came in the Battle of the Bulge in heavily wooded eastern France in December 1944. There the Germans attacked inexperienced American troops, pushed them back 50 miles, and threatened a major breakthrough in the Allied lines. The Germans were finally stopped after a few weeks, but the battle slowed the Allied advance into Germany by more than a month.

In the first weeks of 1945 the Russians launched their final offensive. On January 17 they captured Warsaw and soon after reached Germany's prewar eastern border. One month later American troops crossed into Germany from the west. In April Soviet troops entered the outskirts of Berlin, where Hitler and his small entourage of fight-to-the-death loyalists had holed up in the Chancellory bunker, determined to die with their beloved "Thousand Year Reich." By now Germany was a nation in dissolution, its cities in ruins and thousands of refugees fleeing westward to escape the Russians.

German fear of the Soviet armies was not misplaced. Many of the Soviet troops were bent on revenge, and they often treated German civilians brutally. But whatever atrocities the Germans experienced paled by comparison with the horrors perpetrated by the Nazis at Auschwitz, Treblinka, Belzec, Sobibor, Majdanek, and other "death camps" in Poland and elsewhere that were exposed to the full light of day by the Allies' advance.

On April 25 U.S. and Russian troops coming from opposite directions met at Torgau on the Elbe River. Three days later Italian resistance fighters captured Mussolini as he attempted to flee to Switzerland and beat him to death. His body and that of his mistress were hanged upside down from a pole in a public square. Hitler lived only a few days longer. With Berlin burning around him and Russian troops blocks away, he committed suicide on April 30 in his underground bunker.

On May 7 Admiral Karl Doenitz, Hitler's successor, accepted unconditional surrender terms. Soon after, the fighting in Europe stopped. Hitler's demented dream of world domination had ended.

The Fall of the Rising Sun

By now Japan too was tottering. After Midway and Guadalcanal the Americans, the British, and the Australians began a general advance in India, Burma, and the Central Pacific that slowly rolled back the early Japanese gains. Although Asians themselves, the conquering Japanese had brutally treated Indonesians, Filipinos, Burmese, Malaysians, Pacific islanders, and other Asian peoples, and had hurt their cause.

The far-flung Japanese Empire was mostly water and depended on open sea lanes to function coherently. As American submarine commanders learned their business, more and more Japanese merchant tonnage went to the bottom. Shipping became increasingly scarce, and the empire soon fell into disconnected pieces, a process that deprived the Japan of the very resources it had launched the war to obtain.

The Allied counterattack was not confined to naval action. In mid-1943 MacArthur's men began to advance north from Australia. First the combined American-Australian forces reconquered New Guinea and then attacked the central Solomons. Late in 1943 Admiral Nimitz, in command of both naval and military forces, began to move on the Japanese-held islands from the east. The operations of the American forces were amphibious. First the air force and navy sought to establish air and sea superiority over and around the island target. Next came the mass bombings and naval shelling to soften the entrenched enemy positions. Soldiers and marines then poured onto the beaches in landing barges, followed by the heavy equipment.

The Japanese proved tenacious and difficult foes, often fighting to the last man and ending their resistance only with a suicidal *banzai* charge against the Americans. Even civilians refused to allow themselves to be captured. At Saipan, invaded by the Americans in June 1944, hundreds of women and children leaped off cliffs into the sea rather than be taken prisoners. In late 1944, with most of their trained pilots killed, the Japanese sent barely trained youngsters on *kamikaze* suicide missions to smash their bomb-loaded planes onto the decks of American invasion ships. Off Okinawa in 1945 the *kamikazes* sank twenty-four American ships in a single day. Americans saw this tactic as "fanaticism," and it confirmed racist views that the "Nips" were not fully human.

In mid-1944 American forces reached the Philippines, fulfilling MacArthur's promise, "I shall return." The Japanese tried to intercept the American troop transports with their still-formidable fleet. In two enormous naval engagements, the Battle of the Philippine Sea (June 19–20) and the Battle of Leyte Gulf (October 23–25), the American navy virtually destroyed the Japanese fleet and sealed Japan's fate.

Yet the American attack continued remorselessly. Soon after the Philippine campaign, fleets of B-29s from newly captured Saipan in the Marianas began to pound the Japanese home islands. Almost unopposed, the Superfortresses dumped thousands of tons of high explosive and incendiary bombs on Japanese cities, with Tokyo the favorite target. Many city neighborhoods, constructed of flimsy bamboo and paper, turned into searing furnaces. The B-29 Tokyo raid of March 9, 1945, destroyed over 267,000 buildings and killed or maimed 185,000 Japanese civilians, with the loss of only fourteen American planes. Japanese civilian morale plummeted. For the first time sensible Japanese realized that their country had lost the war. But worse was yet to come for the Japanese people.

FDR's Death and the Atom Bomb

On April 12, 1945, Roosevelt died of a stroke at Warm Springs, Georgia, where he had often vacationed. He had not been well for many months and in retrospect we can see that he probably should not have run for a fourth term. Critics later charged that his weakened condition had led him to concede too much to the Russians at the February conference with Churchill and Stalin at Yalta in the Soviet Crimea. There the Big Three, now confident of victory in Europe, had agreed on three zones (later four, to include France) of military occupation for postwar Germany and a Four Power Commission to govern the country. Control of Berlin, within the Soviet zone, was also to be divided among the powers, with freedom of transit guaranteed through the rest of Germany. In addition the Big Three agreed on the structure of the new international collective security body called the United Nations; accepted Soviet demands that the Lublin Committee, slightly expanded, become the basis for Poland's postwar government; agreed to transfer some Japanese-controlled territory in the Far East to the Soviet Union after a Pacific victory; and awarded the Soviets an occupation zone in postwar Korea. Critics later attacked the surrender of Poland's autonomy and the concessions to the Russians in East Asia, but they ignored the fact that Soviet forces had already overrun Poland by early 1945 and the Russians could impose any government they wanted, while in the Far East the war was far from won and the British and Americans still felt they needed Soviet help.

In any event, Vice President Harry Truman, who took the presidential oath of office that early April afternoon, was ill informed about many aspects of the war and had heard only rumors of the Manhattan Project. Uncertain whether to use the atom bomb or not, he consulted his scientific advisers. In June, convinced that the Japanese would fight to the end if their home islands were invaded, the advisers recommended that the bomb be used against Japan as soon as possible. "We can," they wrote, "promise no technical demonstration likely to bring an end to the war; we can see no alternative to direct military use."

In later years critics charged that the decision to drop the bomb was racist; that it would not have been used against the Germans. They have also charged that it was intended primarily to intimidate the Soviet Union by demonstrating American military power, and as such was the opening gun of the Cold War. Human motives are seldom simple, but the weight of evidence suggests that the decision to use the bomb on Japan was based largely on the conviction, valid or not, that it would shorten the war and save the lives of thousands of Americans and, for that matter, of thousands of Japanese as well.

After the successful New Mexico test of the bomb, Truman gave the signal on July 24 to proceed with the attack. But first he delivered a "last-chance warning" to the Tokyo government. In the Potsdam Declaration (July 26, 1945) he, Churchill, and Chiang Kai-shek warned Japan that if it did not surrender unconditionally it would face "prompt and utter destruction." The reaction in Tokyo was mixed. Some officials urged a favorable response. Others dismissed the warning with contempt. It was this second reaction that impressed Truman, and he ordered the plan to use the A-bomb to go forward.

Early on the morning of August 6 the *Enola Gay,* a B-29 Superfortress captained by Colonel Paul W. Tibbetts, Jr., left Tinian Island near Guam and headed northwest across the Pacific. The plane arrived over Hiroshima, a city of 350,000 people, shortly after 9 A.M. and dropped its deadly load. In seconds 60,000 people died, some disappearing off the face of the earth without a trace, vaporized by the intense heat. Three days later the United States dropped another bomb on the city of Nagasaki killing 35,000 people. (In both cities, thousands more died later.)

Japan Surrenders

Not surprisingly the atom bomb made headlines around the world. Even people of modest education could see that warfare, possibly even the world as a whole, had been transformed. In Japan it took several days for the reality of America's awesome new weapon to sink in, and by then, the Soviet Union, now free of the German menace and anxious to be cut in on the far eastern spoils, had joined the war. In any other nation there would have been little disagreement about the need for quick capitulation. But Allied unconditional surrender terms and Japan's pride made its leaders balk. In the military many of the younger officers favored "one last battle on Japanese soil." Fortunately Truman and his advisers had agreed that unconditional surrender notwithstanding, they would allow the emperor to remain in power. At this point Emperor Hirohito, until then a distant but semidivine figure, intervened and made it clear that he wanted the war ended. "The unendurable must be endured," he declared.

The formal surrender of Japan took place on September 2, on the deck of the American battleship *Missouri* in Tokyo bay with representatives of all the Allied powers present to see Japan bend its knee. The American flag raised over the

On August 6, 1945, the United States dropped one small—by today's standards—atom bomb on Hiroshima, Japan, a city of 350,000 people. A month later, with most major streets cleared and bridges rebuilt, the city looked like this. (AP/Wide World Photos)

battleship was the thirty-one-star banner carried by Commodore Matthew Perry in 1853 when he had anchored in the same bay and negotiated the treaty that opened Japan to foreign trade and influence. But this time American troops had landed as an army of occupation.

Celebration

Back home "V-J Day" set off a wild celebration. In New York two million people gathered in Times Square to cheer, snake-dance, conga, and generally make a giant, joyous racket. There were similar scenes in all the nation's cities. Judging by the news photos, servicemen everywhere used the occasion as an opportunity to kiss pretty girls on the streets.

Few of the celebrants paused to consider the costs: over 320,000 American service personnel died in World War II; 800,000 had been wounded or captured. Compared to the other major belligerents who, in addition to military deaths and injuries, had suffered heavy civilian casualties, these were moderate losses. (More than 7 million Soviet soldiers died in the war, for example, 3.5 million Germans, and 2.2 million Chinese; civilian deaths were many millions more.) Yet they were the worst for the United States since the Civil War. These facts were forgotten in the flush of relief, but it would not take long for Americans to learn that peace, too, had its hazards and its challenges.

FOR FURTHER READING

On the origins of World War II in Europe see Laurence Lafore, *The End of Glory: An Interpretation of the Origins of World War II* (1969) and Keith Eubank, *The Origins of World War II* (1969). For Hitler's career and the nature of Nazi Germany see Allen Bullock, *Hitler: A Study in Tyranny* (1962); Richard Grunberger, *The Twelve-Year Reich: A Social History of Nazi Germany* (1971); and Karl Schleunes, *The Twisted Road to Auschwitz* (1970). Denis Mack Smith's biography, *Mussolini* (1982), tells the story of Italian fascism. The Munich Agreement and the appeasement policy are described in Keith Eubank, *Munich* (1963); World War II's European phases are described in Gordon Wright, *The Ordeal of Total War, 1939–1945* (1968); the Nazi-Soviet war is described in Alan Clark, *Barbarossa: The Russian-German Conflict, 1941–1945* (1965).

Several important general works on FDR's foreign policy and America's road to World War II include Robert Dallek, *Franklin D. Roosevelt and American Foreign Policy, 1932–1945* (1979); Robert Divine, *The Illusion of Neutrality* (1962) and his *Reluctant Belligerent: American Entry into World War II* (1965); James M. Burns, *Roosevelt: The Soldier of Freedom* (1970); and John E. Wiltz, *From Isolation to War, 1931–1941* (1968). A recent work that depicts FDR as both cautious and decisive is Waldo Heinrichs, *Threshold of War: Franklin D. Roosevelt and American Entry into World War II* (1988).

Two scholars have attacked Roosevelt for dishonestly maneuvering the American people into war for politically self-seeking reasons. See Charles A. Beard, *President Roosevelt and the Coming of War, 1941* (1948) and Charles C. Tansill, *Back Door to War* (1952).

On the isolationist impulse see Selig Adler, *The Isolationist Impulse: Its Twentieth Century Reaction* (1958) and Wayne S. Cole, *Senator Gerald P. Nye and American Foreign Relations* (1962). For a later phase of the isolationist drive see Cole's *America First: The Battle against Intervention, 1940–1941* (1953).

Aid to Britain and the Allies is dealt with in Philip Goodhart, *Fifty Ships that Saved the World: The Anglo-American Alliance* (1965) and Warren Kimball, *The Most Unsordid Act: Lend-Lease, 1939–1941* (1969). On the crisis with Japan see Robert Butow, *Tojo and the Coming of War* (1961); Herbert Feis, *The Road to Pearl Harbor* (1950); and Paul W. Schroeder, *The Axis Alliance and Japanese-American Relations, 1941* (1958). A work that sympathizes with Japan's plight before, during, and after Pearl Harbor is John Toland, *The Rising Sun: The Decline and Fall of the Japanese Empire, 1936–1945* (1970). An analysis of the circumstances leading up to Pearl Harbor that blames American unpreparedness on a communications glitch is Roberta Wohlstetter's *Pearl Harbor: Warning and Decision* (1962).

On the fall of the Philippines see Louis Morton, *The Fall of the Philippines* (1953); on Japan's military victories and eventual defeats consult Charles Bateson, *The War with Japan: A Concise History* (1969). For the naval war against Japan and Germany see Samuel Eliot Morison, *Two-Ocean War: The Navy in the Second World War* (1963). Midway deserves a separate look, and Walter Lord's popular *Incredible Victory* (1967) provides it. The war in Europe and North Africa is covered in Dwight D. Eisenhower, *Crusade in Europe* (1948); Charles Brown MacDonald, *Mighty Endeavor: American Forces in the European Theater in World War II*

(1969); Cornelius Ryan, *The Longest Day, June 6, 1944* (1959); Hugh M. Cole, *Ardennes: Battle of the Bulge* (1965); and Martin Blumenson, *Breakout and Pursuit* (1961).

For Nazi behavior in occupied Europe see Alexander Dallin, *German Rule in Russia, 1941–1945* (1957) and Robert Paxton, *Vichy France: Old Guard and New Order, 1940–1944* (1972). The Holocaust is vividly described in Lucy Dawidowicz, *The War against the Jews, 1933–1945,* (1975) and more completely in Martin Gilbert, *The Holocaust: A History of the Jews of Europe During the Second World War* (1985). For the failure of American policies to deal with the refugee crisis see David Wyman, *The Abandonment of the Jews: America and the Holocaust, 1941–1945* (1984) and Henry L. Feingold's *The Politics of Rescue: The Roosevelt Administration and the Holocaust, 1938–1945* (1970).

There are a number of good general books on the American home front in wartime. See the informal Richard R. Lingeman, *Don't You Know There's a War On?: The American Home Front, 1941–1945* (1970). More scholarly and critical is John Blum's *V Was for Victory: Politics and American Culture During World War II* (1976). On the treatment of the Japanese-Americans see Roger Daniels, *Concentration Camp USA: Japanese-Americans in World War II* (1971). For information on the wartime experiences of other groups see Karen Anderson, *Wartime Women: Sex Roles, Family Relations, and the Status of Women During World War II* (1981) and Robert Shogan and Tom Craig, *Detroit Race Riot* (1964). Antiwar feelings are described in Lawrence Wittner, *Rebels Against War: The American Peace Movement, 1941– 1960* (1969).

The economic phase of mobilization is covered in Donald Nelson, *Arsenal of Democracy* (1946); Arthur J. Brown, *The Great Inflation, 1939–1951* (1955); Walter W. Wilcox, *The Farmer in the Second World War* (1947); and Clarence D. Long, *The Labor Force in War and Transition* (1952).

On the development of the Atom bomb see Richard Rhodes's lengthy but fascinating *The Making of the Atom Bomb* (1986). On the bombing of Hiroshima see John Hershey, *Hiroshima* (1946); on the decision to drop the bomb see Herbert Feis, *The Atomic Bomb and the End of World War II* (1966).

Wartime diplomacy and preparations for a new world order are described in Robert Devine, *Second Chance: The Triumph of Internationalism in America During World War II* (1967). A dissenting view from the left of American wartime diplomacy is Gabriel Kolko, *The Politics of War: Foreign Policy, 1943–1945* (1968). A centrist view is Gaddis Smith, *American Diplomacy During the Second World War, 1941–1945* (1965). Works on special diplomatic topics include Diane Clemens, *Yalta* (1970); Herbert Feis, *Between War and Peace: The Potsdam Conference* (1960); E. F. Penrose, *Economic Planning for Peace* (1953); and Ruth B. Russell, *History of the United Nations Charter: The Role of the United States, 1940–1945* (1958).

10
Postwar and Cold War America

Suburbia, U.S.A.—a home in a community like this was the aspiration of many Americans in the immediate post–World War II years. (Library of Congress)

War's Aftermath

In the immediate excitement and joy at victory few Americans could have thought seriously about the postwar world. If they considered the future in those heady days of mid-August they probably focused on resuming normal life, greeting returning family and friends, buying new cars, and going back to school. If they thought about more general matters they probably worried about the economy: would good times continue? Surely few spent much time pondering the future world international order. Fewer still could have envisaged an era where superpower rivalry would profoundly affect many aspects of daily life.

The New Internationalism

The war destroyed isolationism, and long before V-J Day most Americans had concluded that this time, unlike 1918, the United States must remain an active player on the world stage. To some extent the new internationalism reflected a new collective national egotism. Through its might and will it had destroyed the most vicious enemies the world had ever seen and had emerged more powerful than ever. The United States now had a responsibility to lead the world in the ways of peace and prosperity. In 1941 Henry Luce, head of the powerful Time-Life publishing empire, coined the phrase "the American century" to describe his vision of a new international order under benevolent American leadership.

There were also more practical motives for avoiding isolationism this time: world peace. Without American participation in collective security arrangements the United States would find itself forced once more to rescue the world from an oppressor. Shortly before his death FDR summed up this view, "We shall have to take responsibility for world collaboration or we shall have to bear the responsibility for another world conflict."

The new internationalism was embodied in a supernational peacekeeping organization to succeed the old, defunct League of Nations. Called the United Nations (UN) after the wartime anti-Axis alliance and meeting first in San Francisco in April 1945, the new body was given a structure similar to the League: a powerful Security Council composed of the major powers, an Assembly representing all the member nations, a new International Court of Justice, and a cluster of agencies to help publicize and ameliorate world social and medical problems. Despite some effort to give the UN teeth and an independent voice, time would show that, like the League, it could not replace the long-standing system of power politics or settle major international differences when these involved the great powers.

Yet for a time Americans supported the UN enthusiastically as a symbol of the nation's new commitment to collective security and a long-overdue atonement for rejecting the League of Nations. On July 23, 1945, the United States Senate by a historic vote of eighty-nine to two passed the UN Treaty, making this country the first nation to formally sign the charter. American ardor for the new international body was reinforced when the decision was made to locate its permanent headquarters in New York.

The public commitment to activism in world affairs must not be exaggerated. There was a countercurrent, reflecting a desire to get on with ordinary living and resume day-to-day life, that resembled the retreat to privatism of the 1920s. This attitude would brook no delay in getting "the boys" home as soon as possible regardless of America's international responsibilities and the needs of the occupation forces in Japan and Germany. Spouses, parents, and other relatives bombarded members of Congress, administration officials, and military brass with demands that discharges be speeded up. Encouraged by tearful or peevish letters, GIs themselves staged "Wanna-Go-Home" riots in major military centers from the Philippines to France. Under such pressure it proved politically impossible to follow demobilization procedures that met America's military and occupation needs. Within months the armed forces of the United States had virtually melted away.

Readjustment

Once home former GIs faced wrenching problems of readjustment. Unlike Vietnam War veterans in the 1970s returning service men and women in 1945–46 were given heroes' welcomes. Johnnie, or Joe, or Jane came home to celebrating relatives and friends and huge "Welcome Home" banners stretched across the doorway. Most took time off, living on their military discharge pay, while they considered how to resume civilian life. In 1944 Congress had passed the Servicemen's

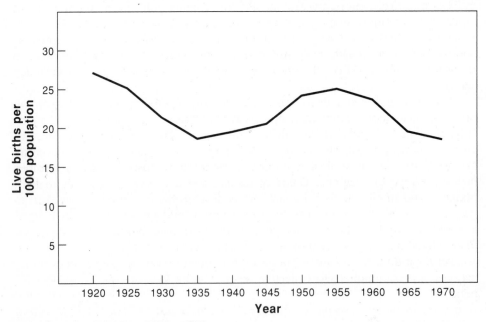

Figure 10–1 Birthrates, 1920–1970

Source: *Historical Statistics of the United States* (Washington: U.S. Bureau of the Census, 1975), p. 49.

Readjustment Act guaranteeing a year's unemployment pay of $20 a week to returned service personnel, providing money for tuition and maintenance for veterans who wanted to resume or begin schooling, and offering loans to buy homes or start businesses. This "GI Bill of Rights" helped enormously to ease the transition to civil life once the veteran had decided what to do.

And yet despite the psychological and material aid many World War II veterans struggled with serious personal difficulties. Some had been physically or emotionally scarred by their experiences and found it difficult to adjust to the humdrum routines of peacetime. Others returned to find that stored up problems were now free to boil over. There had been many hasty wartime marriages of ardent young men and women who scarcely knew one another. Often these could not stand the strain of everyday existence once peace returned. In 1946 the divorce rate rose dramatically.

Yet for every former GI who regretted a wartime marriage, there were a dozen who looked forward to one in the near future. Thousands of young people had postponed matrimony for the duration of the war and now quickly tied the knot. If the divorce rate soared, so did the marriage rate.

And so did the birthrate. For many years population experts had noted the decline in American fertility. During the Depression it fell still further. Long-term population projections of the late 1930s predicted ever-fewer children and ever-smaller families. But then came the war and the peace. Birthrates leaped. (See Figure 10–1.) During the next twenty years there would be a startling "baby boom" that would mold American values and alter American life for a generation.

Togetherness

In part this upward tilt of the fertility curve represented ex-servicemen and their wives making up for lost time. It also represented a remarkable shift in values.

Many women had enjoyed the work experience of the war period and sought to stay in the labor force after 1945. Some did, but others were forced out by employers who either disliked women workers or felt they must make room for returning veterans. But many women also welcomed the opportunity to get back to home and family.

Such attitudes made a deep impression on national values. The later forties and the fifties would be the era of "togetherness," when all the popular media, led by *McCall's*, the *Ladies Home Journal,* and other women's magazines, beat the drums for family cohesion and traditional domestic values. Life, they said, should revolve around the home and children. Women must renounce careers outside the home. Domesticity, the opinion-makers proclaimed, must be women's chief end. As journalist Agnes Meyer wrote in 1950, "woman must boldly announce that no job is more exacting, more necessary, or more rewarding than that of housewife and mother." The advice was intended to apply to both sexes, and to some extent it did. Men too in the postwar years sought satisfactions in family life and activities around the home. Do-it-yourself home repairs and the garage workshop became a prominent feature of the new life-style.

Suburbia

With millions of men returning from Europe and the Far East, getting married, and planning families, no problem after 1945 seemed more urgent than housing. Hard times during the 1930s had hurt the construction industry and left the nation with a severe housing deficit. During the war home construction had been suspended to conserve scarce building materials and labor. Now, after 1945, everyone wanted a place to live—and as quickly as possible.

But providing the millions of new homes and apartments needed was difficult. Resources had to be shifted from military production to civilian construction, land had to be bought, and loans had to be negotiated. The process was glacial, and the housing shortage quickly became a scandal. In the months after V-J Day thousands of veterans either moved in with their families or made do with makeshifts. Some lived in garages, cellars, or even automobiles. In Chicago the city turned over 250 old streetcars to veterans to make into dwellings.

Everyone had a plan for ending the housing shortage quickly. Seemingly plausible were schemes to build houses on assembly lines, like ships, cars, and planes during the war. But the idea simply did not work. Local housing ordinances, labor union rules, and most of all, traditional personal tastes, quickly punctured the "prefab" balloon. By 1949 or 1950 the answer was found in the "Levittown" suburb, named after William Levitt, a Long Island, New York, builder whose approach was soon widely imitated.

Levittown and its equivalents confirmed the triumph of suburbia over the cities. Levitt and Sons avoided the cities where land and labor were expensive. Instead, they bought up potato and cornfields close to major roads and commuter rail lines. Although the houses did not actually roll off assembly lines, Levitt used the latest mass-production, low-cost construction technology. One Levitt crew would descend on the building tract with bulldozers to clear and grade; another would pour hundreds of slab foundations; another crew would erect precut walls. The lumber and hardware for the houses were prepared in Levitt mills. The structures were two-bedroom houses available in only a limited number of models. But by varying the paint color and the placement of each house on its lot the builder avoided excessive sameness. With built-in refrigerator, washing machine, and oven Levittown homes cost as little as $7,000. By 1950 there would be over 10,000 houses in the first Levitt community, inhabited by over 40,000 people.

Levittowns soon sprang up all over the country. (See the photograph opening this chapter.) As their incomes grew, families would move to more expensive suburban development, or add on new rooms to their initially small dwellings. There had, of course, been suburbs before, but these had primarily housed the affluent. After 1950 an ever larger portion of the American population lived in single-family dwellings outside the city centers. The suburban way of life soon became the norm among middle-class, white Americans.

Intellectuals and aesthetes criticized suburbia as boring, materialistic, philistine, and above all, conformist and homogenized. As pop sociologist John Keats wrote, if you lived in the new postwar suburbs, "you can be certain all other houses will be precisely like yours, inhabited by people whose age, income, number of children, problems, habits, conversation, dress, possessions, and perhaps even blood type are also precisely like yours."

The critics were not entirely wrong; suburban life had its drawbacks. Mothers found themselves enslaved to the family car, forced to chauffeur themselves and children everywhere—to school, to lessons, to the supermarket, to the dentist. While their husbands worked in the city with adult colleagues, they sometimes found young children their only company, and often trying company by the end of the day. And undoubtedly there were fewer cultural advantages in the suburbs, although in truth it is not clear how many Americans missed live theater, museums, and concerts.

But there were also compensations. Suburban isolation was offset through various kinds of social networks. Women created informal neighbor groups among themselves. Church membership soared. In 1940 only 50 percent of American families belonged to religious denominations. By 1960 a total of 63 percent claimed formal membership in some church group, with much of the gain coming in suburban communities. Parent-teacher groups, lodges, and civic associations also compensated for the absence of the close physical contact of city life. Yet to many new residents of suburbia these were not really necessary. The trees, grass, good schools, safe streets, and order compensated for all that they had left behind in the city.

Minorities

Not all Americans shared the suburban experience. As urban middle-class and skilled blue-collar families decamped for the suburbs, they left behind the largely African-American and Hispanic poor. Soon after 1945 these people were joined by new waves of immigrants from Puerto Rico, Mexico, and other parts of Latin America, as well as further increments of rural black southerners.

The African-American and Hispanic inner-city ghettos reflected the marked inequalities and prejudices of American life. Few minority people could afford even the bargain-basement Levitt house, but even if they could, they would have been kept out by formal or informal racial and ethnic suburban exclusion practices. Increasingly, the demographic landscape would shift in the direction of white suburban rings enclosing black and brown central urban cores.

The trend had unfortunate social consequences. In 1945 the inner cities were not yet disaster areas. The presence of middle-class people helped anchor the neighborhoods and guarantee decent city services. Families remained intact; crime, although higher than elsewhere, had not yet gotten out of control; and most important of all, drugs had still not undermined the foundation of social life.

The white, middle-class exodus helped concentrate and aggravate social pathologies. More and more the inner cities became the exclusive habitat of the poor, people who needed expensive medical, social, and educational services they could not afford. The departure of the middle-class, however, inevitably eroded the cities' tax bases. At the very time that the need for social services was growing, then, the cities were becoming less able to pay for them. To compensate for a declining number of middle-class taxpayers, those who remained were taxed more heavily. This response, in turn, goaded even more people to leave the city. It was a vicious cycle that would only get worse with each passing year.

The Postwar Economy

Although clearly its benefits were unequally distributed, the postwar era was a time of buoyant prosperity. To many people affluence came as a surprise.

The war, as we saw, brought immense economic improvement, wiping out Depression unemployment and adding to the capital stock of the nation. Between 1939 and 1945 per capita income doubled. But would this all change, Americans wondered, when peace returned? If prosperity had been fueled by immense government expenditures for arms, what would happen when these outlays stopped? In the closing months of the war many of the economic seers predicted that the postwar era would see a return to mass unemployment and harsh social strife.

What the prophets of doom had not reckoned with was pent-up demand. With new automobiles, houses, electrical appliances, and other expensive durables almost impossible to buy during the war, Americans were forced to save. Personal savings totaled about $2.6 billion in 1939. By 1945 it had skyrocketed to $29.6 billion. After V-J Day Americans waited eagerly for that new house with a picket fence, that new Ford or Chevrolet, that new automatic washing machine—and they had money in their bank accounts to pay for it.

It took time to "reconvert" from tanks to cars, from barracks to houses, from guns to appliances, and during the interval consumers complained bitterly—and bid against one another for still-scarce goods. Inflationary pressures quickly built up. The Office of Price Administration (OPA), the wartime price-control agency, tried to hold down prices, but with the psychological restraints of wartime patriotism gone, retailers and wholesalers refused to sell at regulated, legal prices. Scarce goods soon became available only on black markets at any price the seller could get. Inevitably OPA itself became a battleground. Many people blamed the agency for the shortages and black markets. Others, however, including most New Dealers, insisted that without continued regulation prices would shoot through the roof and precipitate another depression.

Fortunately the shortages did not last. By 1947 or 1948 American industry had converted to peacetime demand and was pouring out a flood of goods from rubber bands to limousines. By the end of 1948 the Big Three auto companies—Chrysler, Ford, and General Motors—and the half-dozen car independents then still in business were producing 5 million cars a year. In 1950 American manufacturers turned out 6.2 million refrigerators and 14.6 million radio sets. There was also an entirely new consumer durables industry. That year American electronics firms assembled 7.4 million television sets and were shipping them to consumers as fast as they came off the production line.

Rapid reconversion prevented the worst fears of the economic pessimists. Jobs appeared for over 13 million discharged GIs almost as if by magic. The number of gainfully employed Americans in 1950 was 63.5 million. Unemployment in 1946 was 2.3 million, but by 1953 it was down to 1.8 million. Gross National Product, measuring the total output of goods and services, climbed from $208 billion in 1946 to $504 billion in 1960. This increase translated into a 3.2 percent annual rate of economic growth during the 1950s. It was not spectacular measured against the long-term trend. Nor was it smooth. During the decade and a half following V-J Day there were a

Consumer durables like these washing machines poured off American assembly lines in the postwar years to satisfy pent-up demand. (UPI/Bettmann Newsphotos)

number of minor recessions when unemployment spurted. But to people used to the no-growth or even negative growth of the 1930s, the American economy's performance after 1945 seemed almost miraculous.

Pent-up civilian demand explains the postwar boom only in part. By 1945 the major industrial nations of Europe and Asia, their capital worn-out or destroyed, could no longer supply their own citizens' needs for basic items of food, clothing, and shelter. War devastation also made most of the belligerents incapable of supplying their prewar foreign customers. The United States, its mainland territory untouched by bombs or warring armies, inevitably stepped into the breech. And American industrial products were respected. American technology, after all, had produced the tools, including the atom bomb, that won the war. No country, it seemed, could make things better or cheaper. For several years following 1945 the United States would produce a third of all the world's goods. This enviable situation could not last, but for a time it enormously stimulated American production.

A longer range element in the postwar prosperity was the American investment in education and research. In the postwar era technical and scientific knowledge increasingly drove the economy.

A number of major postwar industries—electronics, pharmaceuticals, atomic energy, aircraft—benefited from the government's massive wartime investments in weapons research. After 1945 the education benefits of the GI Bill of Rights enabled thousands of young men and some young women to become scientists and engineers.

Toward the end of the 1950s Americans' confidence in their educational system faltered. Already under attack as excessively concerned with "life adjustment" rather than hard science and basic skills, it seemed even more inadequate after the Soviet Union's 1957 success in launching *Sputnik,* the first successful artificial space satellite. In response Congress passed the National Defense Education Act (1958), which provided low-cost loans to college students who promised to teach in the public schools and large matching-basis grants to colleges for laboratories and to encourage math and foreign-language teaching. The law increased the number of engineers and scientists and helped place American universities at the cutting edge of new technology and science. By 1960 it was clear that American investment in "human capital" and the "knowledge industries" had become a major source of economic growth.

Truman and the Fair Deal

The New President

Harry Truman, Roosevelt's successor, was not as sophisticated or politically skilled as his predecessor. He was a simpler, earthier man, whose strong suit was common sense and the ability to learn from experience. Despite his early connection with Kansas City machine politics he was personally incorruptible and he shared FDR's broad liberal sympathies. Americans liked the fact that he went in person to his Washington bank and that he called Bess Truman, his plain but sensible wife, "mother." But at times they deplored his profanity and his "undignified" belligerence. When a Washington music critic attacked the vocal abilities of his daughter Margaret, a would-be professional singer, the president wrote him a letter.:

> I have just seen your lousy review of Margaret's concert. . . . It seems to me that you are a frustrated old man. . . . Some day I hope to meet you. When that happens you'll need a new nose, a lot of beefsteak for black eyes, and perhaps a supporter below.

During his first few months as president, Truman seemed a bumbler. Soon after taking office, he and Congress got into a battle over extending price and rent controls. The president seemed to waffle, creating the impression that he was a confused man. His performance in dealing with labor troubles during early 1946 also seemed inconsistent. Concerned with declining overtime pay, temporary unemployment, and rising prices, labor was restless in the immediate postwar period and was determined to increase wages. Management resisted union demands and by January 1946 several million workers were on strike.

The president considered organized labor's demands excessive. Truman denounced the striking unions and brought the struck industries under his executive authority. He also asked Congress for additional authority to regulate labor and the unions. Union workers, a vital element in the Democratic coalition, resented the president's response. "Let Truman dig coal with his bayonets," declared John L. Lewis, the feisty leader of the United Mine Workers, after the president had the army seize the mines. And in the end, despite the president's vigorous intervention, the mine workers got what they wanted.

The Eightieth Congress

In November 1946 the voters elected a Republican Congress, the first since 1928. Convinced that they now had a clear conservative mandate, the Republican majority in the Eightieth Congress sought to lower taxes on upper-income recipients, reduce farm price supports, and generally speaking prevent any further liberal reform. They rejected the president's requests for a public housing bill, national health insurance, federal aid to education, a voting rights act, an antilynching measure, and a permanent Fair Employment Practices Commission. These last three measures were aimed at racial discrimination against African-Americans and offended most of the southern members of Truman's own party even more than they did the Republicans. The racial conservatives were further angered when, by executive order, Truman established a committee to investigate race segregation in the military services, setting in motion measures that soon ended the Jim Crow armed forces.

The one request the Republican Congress granted the president was a stiff labor regulation law. The Taft-Hartley Act of June 1947 expressed the conservatives' view that organized labor had grown far too powerful under the New Deal. It banned the closed shop, a practice that required employers to hire only union members; it permitted employers to sue unions for broken contracts or for damage incurred in strikes; it allowed the federal government to impose an eighty-day cooling-off period for any strike that endangered national health or safety. The act also required unions to make public their financial dealings, forbade unions to make direct contributions to political campaigns, and required union leaders to take an oath that they were not members of the Communist party.

The Taft-Hartley Act was a more stringent law than Truman wanted. "We do not need and we do not want, legislation which will take away fundamental rights from our working people," he declared in a radio message to the American people. He vetoed the measure, restoring some of his credibility with liberals and organized labor. But Congress overrode his veto and Taft-Hartley became law.

Besides Taft-Hartley the only important legislation of this Congress was the National Security Act, a measure that echoed the growing fear of Soviet power. The law unified the armed services under a single cabinet head, the secretary of defense, created the National Security Council to advise the president on national security matters, and established the Central Intelligence Agency (CIA) to gather information abroad pertaining to America's international security.

The Election of 1948

By the eve of the 1948 presidential election it looked as if Truman had alienated almost everyone. To his right were the conservative Republicans and southern

Democrats who disliked either his political or his racial policies or both. In the middle were labor leaders who resented what they considered his union-busting tactics. To his left was a contingent of liberals who compared him unfavorably with FDR as well as people who disliked his strong anti-Soviet policies.

Many of the foreign policy dissenters had begun to rally around Henry Wallace, the former vice president whom Truman had inherited as secretary of commerce from Roosevelt. In September 1946 the president fired Wallace for attacking the administration's foreign policy at a Soviet-American friendship rally in New York. Wallace become an instant hero to those who blamed the United States for the growing Soviet-American hostility.

The president had his supporters. The Democratic party regulars—voters and bosses—liked "Harry," or at least preferred him to the Republicans. He even had some organized support among the true-blue liberals, including the Americans for Democratic Action (ADA), organized in 1947 by academics, politicos, and liberal trade union leaders and dedicated simultaneously to anticommunism abroad and further social reform at home. Although many ADAers were initially skeptical of Truman, they eventually endorsed him for reelection.

In 1948 at their national convention in Philadelphia the confident Republicans turned once again to Governor Thomas E. Dewey of New York as their presidential candidate. Despite his spotty record Truman won the Democratic nomination in the same city three weeks later.

The nomination seemed an empty honor. Given his record thus far, few at the convention thought Truman could win in November. Doubt turned to near certainty when, responding to adoption of strong civil rights platform plank supported by Minneapolis Mayor Hubert Humphrey and other liberals, many southern delegates walked out of the convention and formed a separate ticket. Truman's combative acceptance speech restored some confidence. The president lambasted the Republican Congress and declared his intention to call it back into session to consider a long list of important social legislation. If the Republicans refused to pass his measures, they would prove to the voters that they were obstructionists.

The special session of Congress confirmed Truman's expectations. Presented by the president with a long "shopping list" of "must" legislation, it dithered and squabbled and enacted nothing. Truman would now be able to make the "Do-Nothing" Eightieth Congress his campaign whipping boy.

Yet as the weeks passed it seemed unlikely that Truman could win. Beside Dewey the president faced Governor J. Strom Thurmond of South Carolina on the ultraconservative States' Rights ("Dixiecrat") ticket and Henry Wallace, nominated by the Progressive party of America, an organization controlled by pro-Soviet ultra-liberals and hidden Communists. The first threatened to deprive him of the solid South, the second of left-liberal groups in the big urban-industrial states.

Yet Truman confounded the experts and the polls. (See Figure 10–2.) With little money and virtually no press support he mounted a "whistle-stop" campaign to show himself personally to as many voters as possible. Traveling 32,000 miles by train, the president made hundreds of addresses, many off the rear observation car platform to small clumps of people who appreciated the opportunity to see their president. Truman pulled out all the old populist stops, attacking the do-nothing Congress, "Wall Street reactionaries," "gluttons of privilege," "bloodsuckers with offices in Wall

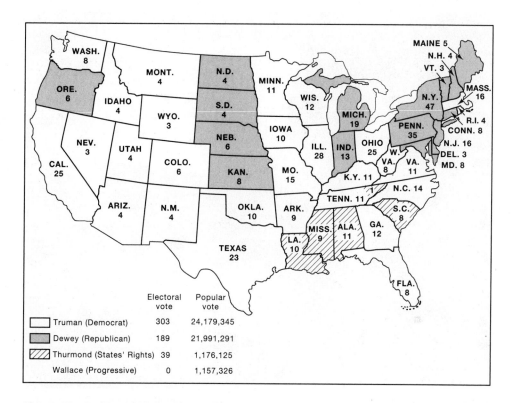

Figure 10–2 The 1948 Presidential Election

Street," and "plunderers." The pollsters continued to predict a Republican triumph, but beneath the surface Truman had awakened fears in millions of farmers, wage earners, and other voters that a Republican victory would jeopardize the gains of the New Deal. He had also projected an attractive image of a scrappy and principled man fighting "the interests."

Truman went to bed election night at 7 P.M. with the pundits still predicting a Dewey sweep. He awoke at 4:30 A.M. to find himself reelected with a plurality of twenty-four million to twenty-two million popular votes and a safe electoral majority of 303 to 189. Thurmond had taken part of the deep South as expected; Wallace had won a million votes largely in New York and California. But organized labor, African-Americans, farmers, unmovable Democrats, and the coattails of popular local Democrats had put Truman over the top.

The Fair Deal

Truman delivered his State of the Union message to the new Congress on January 5, 1949. In it he laid out a program that he called the *Fair Deal,* in obvious echo of FDR's great reform agenda. The president asked for a national health insurance plan, a tax cut for low-income people, a higher minimum wage, new federally financed

On the morning after the 1948 election, President Truman gleefully displays a Chicago newspaper whose early edition had announced his defeat. (UPI/Bettmann Newsphotos)

low-cost housing, a new farm price support system (the Brannan Plan) that would allow consumer prices to fall without penalizing growers, federal aid to schools, new civil rights legislation for African-Americans, and repeal of the Taft-Hartley Act.

The Eighty-first Congress, under nominal Democratic control, was not as obstructionist as its predecessor. It raised the minimum wage from forty cents to seventy-five cents an hour, expanded and improved social security coverage, passed a modest public-housing act, and provided federal funds for medical research and hospital construction. But it rejected all the other suggestions for domestic change the president proposed. Once more, as during Roosevelt's second term, the coalition of southern Democrats and Republicans had managed to frustrate a liberal president with a substantial public mandate.

The Cold War Erupts

Truman's place in history does not depend on his domestic accomplishments but on his handling of the major international crises of the early postwar era. Truman and his foreign policy advisers, George Marshall, and Dean Acheson, fathered the contain-ment policy that defined the nature of Soviet-American relations for a generation.

Americans have debated endlessly the question of blame for the *Cold War*, the postwar superpower rivalry. One group of scholars, the "revisionists," is highly critical of U.S. policy. America, they say, was insensitive to valid Soviet fears of encirclement, was often the aggressor in superpower relations, frequently acted as a conservative neocolonialist world force, and was moved by arrogance, capitalist greed, or powerlust—or all three. The United States in its own way was a missionary nation determined to impose its system and its will on the world. In this view the Cold War was avoidable and it was ultimately American intransigence or drive for dominance that made it possible.

The more common perspective, at least during the 1950s, was that the Cold War confrontation derived either from traditional Russian expansionism or from Soviet zeal for the ultimate triumph of communism over capitalism. Only American might stood between the world and enslavement to Soviet tyranny. This view drew strength from the undeniable paranoia of Soviet leader Joseph Stalin in his last years and the oppressiveness of the Soviet regime under Stalin and his successors both within Soviet borders and in the East European nations that had fallen under Soviet control after 1945. In this approach too, the Cold War was avoidable—if only the Soviet Union had not provoked it time and time again.

In all likelihood neither side is entirely correct. The Soviet-American confronta-tion that we call the Cold War may well have been inevitable. Mutual suspicions marked Soviet-American relations from the outset. From the 1920s on many Americans saw Soviet communism as a serious threat to religion, democracy, and capitalism and the American Communist party as a subversive influence in American life. Such views had encouraged the 1920s Red Scare, delayed diplomatic recognition of the Soviet Union until 1933, and led to the creation of the House Committee on Un-American Activities in 1938 to investigate subversive groups. On the other side, fueled by the capitalist nations' efforts to suppress the Bolshevik Revolution in 1918–1920, the Soviet indictment depicted the United States as the chief exemplar of the exploitive and greedy capitalist system intent on encircling and crushing "socialism" in the Soviet Union and preventing social change in the rest of the world.

Both sides suspended their suspicions during World War II and managed to cooperate to defeat the Axis. For a time, in fact, the Soviet Union was popular with Americans for its impressive performance against Nazi Germany, and pro-Soviet enthusiasm brought new recruits for the American Communist party. But the honeymoon did not last.

The Power Vacuums

The war and Axis defeat transformed the balance of international power. Britain emerged exhausted and depleted, its industrial plant decayed, its overseas invest-ments drained, and its empire torn by internal stresses. France, the other great prewar democracy, had been occupied by the enemy for five years and had lost any serious claim to world leadership. After 1945 it too faced strains within its overseas empire.

Germany, Italy, and Japan were, of course, the most enfeebled of the prewar great powers. Japan, after V-J Day, was a shambles, its industry destroyed, its cities ravaged, and its people frightened and uncertain of what to expect from the American conquerors and occupiers. In Germany near starvation prevailed in the months after Hitler's fall. Cities were smoking ruins, the monetary and banking systems had collapsed, factories were idle. Italy too was a ruin with its industry depleted and its people uncertain of the advantages of liberal parliamentary democracy.

Europe's decline meant that the powers, primarily Britain and France, that had long been the balance wheel of the international order had ceased to play major roles in world politics. This left the Soviet Union and the United States, the two "superpowers," facing one another around the world without intermediaries. Both were inexperienced; neither was used to world leadership. In addition, having lost 20 million citizens during the German invasion, the Soviet Union was especially sensitive to perceived threats to its security.

In 1945–46 millions of displaced persons—survivors from the concentration and death camps, prisoners of war, and people fleeing the vengeful Soviet forces—moved here and there across the European landscape seeking a permanent haven. The United States provided several billions to the United Nations Relief and Rehabilitation Administration to help these refugees. It also modified its strict immigration quotas to admit several hundred thousand displaced persons. But for many months after the Nazi collapse, Europe and its people faced extreme distress. Everything else but survival went by the board.

Misery and frustration left many Europeans susceptible to communist ideology, and in France, Italy, Greece, and other countries pro-Soviet parties attracted mass support. Fearful of Soviet encroachment into western and southern Europe, American policy-makers inevitably sought to prop up regimes that promised to resist the Soviet Union's supporters even when those governments were authoritarian and oppressive.

Closely related to the British-French decline was the emergence of a new arena for competition: the non-European, former-colonial world. Here the old Western empires were rapidly disintegrating, creating immense power vacuums that both the United States and the Soviet Union rushed to fill.

In the Far East Japan's early wartime victories had undermined the myth of the white race's invincibility. With the European nations gravely weakened, this new attitude encouraged nationalist, anticolonial movements throughout the non-European world. In August 1947, after decades of struggle led by Mohandas Gandhi, India became an independent republic. The next year Ceylon (Sri Lanka) and Burma also won their freedom from Britain. Meanwhile anticolonial wars had erupted in Indonesia against the Dutch and in Indochina between the French and the Vietnamese led by Ho Chi Minh.

Almost everywhere in the non-European world nationalism was on the rise. In Africa independence movements in the Gold Coast (Ghana), Kenya, Algeria, Madagascar, and other countries emerged to challenge the colonial powers.

In the Middle East too nationalism challenged the former European masters. In Syria, Iraq, and Lebanon resurgent Arab nationalism soon forced Britain and France to surrender the power they had exercised under old League of Nations mandates. An especially troublesome spot was Palestine, where the Jewish minority launched an uprising against the British regime for its refusal, in response to Arab opposition, to admit Jewish survivors of the Holocaust. In 1948 Britain abandoned the Palestine mandate, and the United Nations partitioned Palestine. Neither Jews nor Arabs accepted the partition and instead went to war. In the end the Jews defeated the Arabs and, with both American and Soviet encouragement, established the new state of Israel. Thousands of Arab refugees fled Palestine to Jordan and other Arab states. Thereafter Israel become an embattled nation whose existence and survival would be a major source of conflict in the region. (See Figure 14–2 in Chapter 14 for a map of the area.)

In many of these emerging "Third World" nations, nationalism was linked with communism. Ho Chi Minh in Vietnam, for example, was a disciple of Lenin. Americans found it difficult to separate the nationalist aspirations of the anticolonial movements from their Marxist component, and the United States frequently placed itself on the side of forces resisting change. The Soviet Union, on the other hand, made it difficult for the United States to avoid this choice through its enthusiastic support of anticolonial "wars of national liberation."

The Chinese Revolution

The most momentous postcolonial upheaval of all took place in China. During World War II the United Nations (Allied) powers, including the Soviet Union, had treated Nationalist China under Chiang Kai-shek as virtually an equal partner in the anti-Axis coalition. In fact China remained bitterly poor and disorganized; its ruling party, the Kuomintang (Nationalists), was corrupt and had limited popular support. Confronting Chiang and his party was Mao Tse-tung (Mao Zedong) and the Chinese Communists with their stronghold in the northern part of the country. Mao and his followers were Leninists whose dogmatism would be fully displayed in the self-destructive 1960s "Cultural Revolution." But in the immediate post-1945 era their promises of land, their dedication to fighting the Japanese invader, and their apparent incorruptibility brought them the respect and support of the vast Chinese peasantry.

Although from 1945 on Mao and Chiang were locked in a fierce combat for supremacy, China was not at first a battleground between the superpowers. At the end of 1945 Truman sent former army Chief of Staff George Marshall to China to seek a compromise between the rival groups. Marshall negotiated a truce in the fighting and then an agreement for a coalition government. But this arrangement soon broke down, and by mid-1946 the two sides were once more at one another's throats.

For the next three years the United States tried to bolster Chiang against the Communists with money, advice, and arms. Nothing helped. The Nationalists were inept and dishonest and the aid sent them was squandered or stuck to the fingers of Nationalist officials. Much of the American arms supplies were sold on the black market or allowed to fall into Communist hands. In 1949 Mao's troops defeated the Nationalists and forced them to flee to the island of Taiwan off the China coast. There Chiang and his followers established themselves as China's legitimate government, hurled defiance at the Communist People's Republic ("Red China"), and promised one day to reconquer the mainland.

China's fall to the Communist camp seemed an ominous victory for the Soviets. Even Americans who saw no way that their country could have saved Chiang from defeat agreed with Secretary of State Dean Acheson that Mao's regime would "lend itself to the aims of Soviet Russian imperialism." This fear became a loaded political issue when right-wingers insisted that China had been "lost," not by Nationalist incompetence and corruption but by the errors of the Truman administration, if not actual treason in high places in Washington.

The Bomb and the Arms Race

Hovering over the emerging superpower rivalry and making it more threatening than any previous international competition was the specter of "the Bomb."

The Soviet Union knew of America's drive to develop the atom bomb even before the war ended. After Nazi defeat the Soviet government brought captured German scientists to the Soviet Union and put them to work with their own scientists to duplicate the American effort. The Soviets would have developed their own atom bomb in any case, but they were able to accelerate the process by effective espionage in America and Britain. In 1949 the Soviet Union exploded its first atomic weapon, ending the brief American nuclear monopoly.

The atom bomb competition was only the beginning of the nuclear arms race. Both sides were soon rushing to develop the far more powerful hydrogen bomb and then competing to perfect delivery systems to ensure that the bombs hit their targets. By the 1960s both sides, using the most sophisticated technology available, had developed intercontinental ballistics missiles, giant rockets that could soar in vast arcs over continents and oceans to deliver nuclear warheads with pinpoint accuracy on enemy cities and military installations. Year after year these new weapons would grow in number and power so that they threatened the very existence of humankind. The testing needed to develop increasingly effective nuclear devices by itself released vast amounts of radiation into the atmosphere, endangering the health of millions of people, present and future.

Nor was the competition confined to nuclear weapons. Both sides poured billions into planes, ships, tanks, and guns. Both maintained enormous standing armies and navies. Some people believed these outlays stimulated economic growth and the development of new technology. Others were convinced that they starved society of the resources it needed to improve the quality of life and ultimately even slowed economic growth rates.

Early efforts to control the arms rivalry foundered on the rock of big-power mutual suspicions. The Soviets at first were behind in the nuclear race and refused to stop until they had caught up. The Americans recognized that in an open society they could not conceal violations of any arms limitation agreement while the closed Soviet society could easily do so unless it permitted on-site inspection of arms manufacturing facilities. In 1946 the United States proposed the Baruch Plan, offering to place atomic energy and weapons under UN control with unrestricted inspection of nuclear facilities. The Soviets, suspicious of the Western-dominated UN and behind in atomic development, rejected the idea. And yet the world survived, if only because neither superpower could be certain it would win a nuclear exchange. In fact, ironically, the existence of nuclear weapons served to prevent a major war between the superpowers. Mutually assured destruction (MAD), however chancy, came to be the ultimate deterrent of World War III.

Containment in Europe

Yet MAD did not prevent a succession of dangerous confrontations between the superpowers or their surrogates.

Difficulties between the Western nations and the Soviet Union go back to the war period itself and can be detected earliest in their disagreements over Poland. They also intruded at the April 1945 founding UN conference in San Francisco, where the Soviet's demand that the big powers have a veto over what issues the Security Council could discuss almost scuttled the meeting. In subsequent months the Soviet Union reneged on promises for free elections in the countries of Eastern Europe that were liberated from Nazi control by Soviet troops. By 1946 most of these—Bulgaria, Rumania, Poland, and Hungary—had become Communist-ruled satellites of the Soviet Union.

Conquered Germany too became an early bone of East-West contention. During the Big Three conference at Potsdam, Germany, in July and early August 1945 the Soviets had agreed to treat Germany as a single economic unit and accept a precise plan for German reparations. It quickly violated these promises. Thereafter the last traces of Big Three cooperation and goodwill quickly faded.

An overall American policy toward the Soviet Union soon began to gel. On February 22, 1946, an eight-thousand-word telegram arrived in Washington from George F. Kennan, an expert in Soviet affairs stationed at the U.S. Embassy in Moscow. Kennan's "long telegram" analyzed Soviet foreign policy in historical perspective and emphasized its continuity over generations. Russian expansionism predated the Bolshevik Revolution, he said. It had originated in the Russians' geographical insecurity and in the need to distract the Russian people from tyranny and poverty at home and would continue under the Soviet regime for the same reasons. The implications were clear: despite any attempt at negotiation, the Soviet Union would remain belligerent and uncooperative; it could be stopped only by strong counter-measures.

Soon after, former British Prime Minister Winston Churchill gave a name to the growing barrier between East and West. Speaking at Fulton, Missouri, on March 5, Churchill declared that "from Stettin in the Baltic to Trieste in the Adriatic, an Iron Curtain has descended across the Continent" of Europe. On the one side was democracy, on the other, "police governments." Unless the West took heed, subversive Communist groups would undermine democracy in the West as well. Britain and the United States, Churchill concluded, must continue to cooperate in the postwar period to ensure Europe's freedom.

Many Americans were not yet ready to take a strong line against the Soviet Union or help bolster the Western European democracies. Most, as we saw, had acquiesced in the rapid decline in U.S. military strength after V-J Day. In September 1945 the U.S. abruptly terminated lend-lease aid to Britain, leaving that depleted country in the economic lurch. When the administration proposed a $3.75 billion low-interest loan to replace it, Congress dragged its feet for many months and insisted on extracting many trade concessions from its former ally before granting the request.

The Truman Doctrine and the "X" Article

American policy began to stiffen when George Marshall became secretary of state in January 1947, replacing James Byrnes. Soon after accepting office, Marshall learned that the British government intended to withdraw all military and economic aid from Greece and Turkey. For a century Britain had imposed peace and order in the Near East, but now it could no longer afford this role. Both Mediterranean countries were in danger, Greece from a leftist uprising against the unpopular monarchy and Turkey from Soviet military pressure on its northeastern frontier. Clearly if the United States did not step into the breach, there was a distinct chance that both these nations would become part of the Soviet orbit.

The crisis in Greece and Turkey produced a revolution in American foreign policy. Should the United States become the guarantor of stability in distant southeastern Europe? To do so would be a major break in American foreign policy. True, the country had entered two world wars to stop a perceived aggressor in Europe, and it had finally agreed to participate in a worldwide peacekeeping organization. But should it also, on its own, seek to substitute for Britain and France around the globe as the regulator of major international change?

Marshall and Truman quickly decided that the United States must fill the vacuum in the eastern Mediterranean or see Soviet power spread over areas where Russia had never before prevailed. On March 12 the president appeared before Congress to request $400 million of economic and military aid to Greece and Turkey. The United States, he said, must "support free peoples who are resisting attempted subjugation by armed minorities or outside pressures." If America faltered in its leadership of the "free peoples of the world," it might "endanger the peace of the world." Both the political left and the right opposed this *Truman Doctrine*. Much of the left still saw the Soviet Union as a benevolent force in the world and regretted the breakup of the wartime Big Three alliance. The right was still isolationist, especially as regards Europe. Senator Robert Taft of Ohio, the leader of the Republican conservatives, condemned the Truman proposal as an "international WPA" that would drain the American economy. Walter Lippmann, the venerable political pundit, warned that it was a dangerous open-ended commitment without foreseeable limits.

Despite the opposition Congress made the appropriation. Pressure on Turkey diminished, while in Greece American aid combined with the refusal of Yugoslavia's independent Communist government under Marshal Tito to allow the leftist guerrilla forces sanctuary enabled the Greek government to survive.

But what about other soft spots in Europe? Should the Truman Doctrine be expanded beyond Greece and Turkey? In July the journal *Foreign Affairs* published an article signed "X" that spoke to this issue. It was by Kennan once again, and it represented the views of an influential circle of foreign policy experts including Kennan, Averell Harriman, Dean Acheson, and Charles Bohlen, most of whom had learned their foreign policy principles at the feet of Henry Stimson, Herbert Hoover's secretary of state. All believed that the United States must "contain" the Soviet Union if it was to avoid being overwhelmed itself. The article endorsed as the main element of U.S. policy toward Europe "a long-term, patient, but firm and vigilant containment of Russian expansive tendencies." Only such an approach could result "in either the break-up or the gradual mellowing of Soviet power." The Kennan article supplied an intellectual rationale for an open-ended *containment policy.*

The Marshall Plan

The European winter of 1946–47, one of the harshest on record, posed an immediate crisis. Subzero temperatures, heavy snowstorms, and transport break-downs added to Western Europe's immediate postwar miseries and played into the hands of the pro-Soviet left. In Italy, Germany, and France the Communists, proclaiming capitalism defunct and incapable of supplying a decent living standard for ordinary men and women, gained thousands of adherents. To the foreign policy experts in the U.S. State Department, rescuing Western Europe's economy seemed essential to preserving democratic government in a vital part of the world.

The result was the *Marshall Plan,* first presented by Secretary Marshall in a speech at Harvard in June 1947 and then, in September, submitted by Truman to Congress as a request for $17 billion in American grants and loans to help Europe recover economically. Under the plan the European countries would themselves work out a recovery program, and the United States would stand behind it. Marshall announced that all European nations, even the Soviet Union, could join the plan, but the Soviets and their satellites, suspecting an American trick, refused to attend the initial planning conference in Paris in July and later rejected the scheme drawn up by the sixteen participating nations to facilitate European recovery. Early in 1948 Congress approved the aid request, and ships were soon speeding across the Atlantic carrying American raw materials and manufactured goods to help Europe get back on its feet.

The Marshall Plan (European Recovery Program) worked magnificently well. In all the United States contributed about $13 billion to financing the scheme. The aid rescued Europe from collapse and was soon making a major contribution to reviving output and employment all over the continent west of the Iron Curtain. It also provided the impetus for further European economic cooperation in the shape of the European Economic Community, or Common Market, which soon generated additional prosperity.

The Marshall Plan evoked European gratitude. The London *Economist* called it "the most . . . generous thing that any country has ever done for others." But the goals were not solely altruistic. The United States was determined to stop the Soviet Union and in this it succeeded as well. Although the Western European Communist parties did not suddenly disappear, they ceased to grow, and Communist regimes failed to gain power through regular electoral means. In American terms Europe was "saved."

The Berlin Blockade

But the Cold War continued. In 1947 the Soviet Union revived the Communist International, the directing body of the Communist parties around the world, after having let it lapse during World War II. The following year the Soviets contrived the overthrow of the democratic government of Czechoslovakia and converted that nation into another satellite. Soon after, Stalin threatened to push the French, British, and Americans out of Berlin, an exposed salient of the West deep within the Soviet's own tightly controlled East German occupation zone. (See Figure 10–3.)

Stalin's Berlin policy was his response to British-French-American efforts to unify their three occupation zones—West Germany—and revive its economy. The Western powers hoped to save themselves from the continuing burden of keeping the Germans alive, although they were not indifferent to the value that a revived Germany could play in offsetting the Soviets. In late 1946 they merged the economies of their three zones, and then in June 1948 they reorganized the German monetary system to end the rampant inflation and restore economic confidence. The effects were dramatic.

Figure 10–3 Divided Germany

The German economy rebounded strongly, kicking off an expansion that would soon be called the "German miracle."

In late July the Soviet Union, violating wartime agreements, cut off rail and highway traffic between West Germany and Berlin. This move threatened to starve the population of the city's Western zones. But what should the Western nations do? Any attempt to break through the blockade by land promised a major military confrontation with the Soviet army and, in all likelihood, the outbreak of World War III. The solution was a massive rescue operation by hundreds of cargo planes flying around the clock to deliver daily the 4000 tons of food, fuel, clothing, and other items needed by the besieged city's 2.5 million people. By the spring of 1949 the planes were bringing in far more than the minimum amount and the Soviets were beaten. On May 12 they removed the rail and road barriers, and the trains, cars, and trucks resumed their movement to Berlin.

Soon after, under the aegis of the Western powers, West Germany became the independent Federal Republic of Germany with its capital at Bonn and a constitution modeled on that of pre-Hitler Weimar. To counter this development, the Soviets organized its own occupation zone into the German Democratic Republic (East Germany) as one of its cluster of satellites.

West Berlin children happily watch an American plane bring food and other supplies to the city during the Berlin Blockade. (The Bettmann Archive)

NATO

The culmination of the American containment policy was the creation of the North Atlantic Treaty Organization (NATO) in 1949. Originally composed of the United States, Canada, and ten European countries including France, West Germany, Britain, Italy, and the Low Countries, it was augmented by the addition of Greece and Turkey in 1952. (France ceased active participation in 1966.)

The NATO treaty was another sharp break with America's traditional foreign policy, which had always avoided "entangling alliances" with other nations. The treaty bound the signers to a mutual defense agreement. "[A]n armed attack against" any one of them in Europe or North America would be "considered an attack against all of them" and they would take collective action, "including the use of armed force," to stop it. Recognizing the special role in the alliance of the American superpower, the participating nations chose Dwight Eisenhower, the commander of the armies victorious against the Nazis, as head of NATO forces. A few years later the Soviet Union formed the Warsaw Pact with its Eastern European satellites to counterbalance NATO. (See Figure 10–4.)

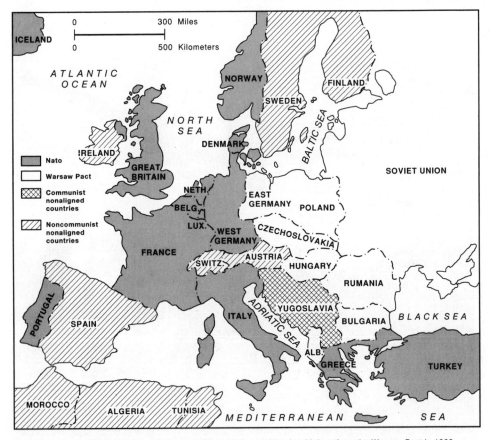

Note: France ceased participating actively in NATO in 1966, and Albania withdrew from the Warsaw Pact in 1968.

Figure 10–4 The Cold War in Europe

The Korean War

Was Red China the same threat to the status quo and American interests in East Asia as the Soviet Union in Europe? Most American policymakers believed the answer was yes. By 1950 Mao and his colleagues had consolidated their hold on the mainland and were demanding control of "all of China," meaning Chiang Kai-shek's domain of Taiwan. Early in 1950 the People's Republic and the Soviet Union concluded a military pact, confirming the equivalence of the two Communist powers in the eyes of many Americans.

Far Eastern Policy

American policymakers were divided over the U.S. role in the Far East. The members of the foreign policy establishment responsible for containment were generally "Europe firsters" who believed the Soviet Union the truly dangerous enemy. As of early 1950 the Europe firsters were still skeptical of Chiang and his self-serving and corrupt officials. Another group, however, composed of assorted isolationist and "old China hands"—missionaries, diplomats, businesspeople, and teachers with personal and family connections with pre-Communist China—saw the Communist advance in the East as even more dangerous. These men and women formed a loosely defined group called the "China Lobby." They blamed the Truman administration for "losing" China to the Communists and sought to oust Mao and his regime from power and return Chiang and the Kuomintang to the mainland. They succeeded in preventing U.S. recognition of Red China and were able to exclude the People's Republic from the UN through repeated U.S. vetoes in the Security Council.

In 1950 the American presence in the Far East was still formidable politically, although not militarily. In Japan General Douglas MacArthur, head of the occupation forces, had swept away the quasifeudal political system and imposed a democratic government on the Japanese people. He had also, to a lesser degree, democratized the social system. Although they had loathed and feared the Americans during the war, the Japanese embraced the occupiers and their reforms enthusiastically. The country remained bitterly poor in 1950, but the foundation had been laid for the enormous economic surge of the 1960s.

In late June 1950 far eastern policy suddenly became a prime American concern when North Korean troops swept across the thirty-eighth parallel and invaded South Korea. The two Koreas were a product of the Allied agreements at Cairo, where the former "Hermit Kingdom" had been promised its freedom from the Japanese occupiers "in due course," and at Yalta, where the country had been divided at thirty-eight degrees north latitude into a Communist, pro-Soviet regime in the north and a pro-Western, although not democratic, administration in the south.

Each government, North and South, wished to reunify the nation under its own auspices, but that of the South, under Syngman Rhee, had been militarily starved by the United States, while that of the North had been provided with powerful arms by the Soviets. The North Korean attack may have been inspired by the Russians. Certainly American officials thought so. The connection between the Soviet Union and the regime in North Korea, according to one U.S. official was similar to the one "between Walt Disney and Donald Duck." The attack probably had been encouraged unwittingly by a January 1950 statement by Dean Acheson, Marshall's successor as secretary of state, that the United States did not consider South Korea a vital part of America's defense perimeter. Whether instigated by the Soviets or not, the attack appeared to be an opportunistic Communist attempt to change the far eastern status quo by military means.

The response in Washington was swift. Despite Acheson's earlier statement the American government perceived that the attack, if unanswered, would encourage further aggression by the Communists. Now the containment policy was to be applied to the Far East as well.

America Intervenes to Save South Korea

Truman moved fast to meet the invasion before the weak South Korean army collapsed. Taking advantage of an unexpected Soviet absence from the UN, the United States was able to secure a Security Council resolution demanding a cease-fire and withdrawal of the attacking forces. Two days later the UN also asked member nations to assist the South Koreans. UN participation sanctioned the United States calling the Korean War a "police action." Congress was never asked to declare war.

Sixteen nations sent troops and supplies to Korea, but the United States bore the brunt of the defense. On June 29 the president authorized MacArthur to use all the forces available to him in Japan to stop the invasion, thus committing the United States to a major land war in the Far East. Senator Taft and other Republicans objected to the haste of the decision; influential Democrats advised Truman to ask for a congressional vote of approval for the intervention. But the president, for all his virtues, was a hot-tempered, impetuous man, and he rejected the advice.

The war at first went badly. By the time the first American troops arrived in Korea, the invaders had easily swept aside the Korean and American defenders and captured Seoul, the South Korean capital. They advanced rapidly south, pushing the South Koreans and the inexperienced and ill-led Americans into a small pocket around the port of Pusan. Here the defenders barely held out while massive supplies and reinforcements arrived from the United States. On September 15 MacArthur, imitating his end runs against the Japanese in World War II, launched an amphibious attack at Inchon close to the thirty-eighth parallel that hit the enemy in the rear. Meanwhile, other American and Republic of Korea (ROK) troops, broke out of Pusan and swept north. The UN forces recaptured Seoul on September 26 and were soon at the thirty-eighth parallel.

With the approval of the UN, the American-ROK forces drove into North Korea and by the end of October were close to the Yalu River, at the Korean-Chinese border. (See Figure 10–5.) Their obvious purpose was to reunite the two sections of the country under Western aegis. Truman and his advisers had considered the possibility of Red Chinese intervention, but despite warnings from Beijing, had accepted MacArthur's conclusion that China was not a serious threat.

MacArthur was wrong. Mao feared a hostile, American-supported Korea on his border, and by mid-October was sending Chinese "volunteers" to bolster the North Koreans. Then in late November the Chinese struck south with thirty-three divisions,

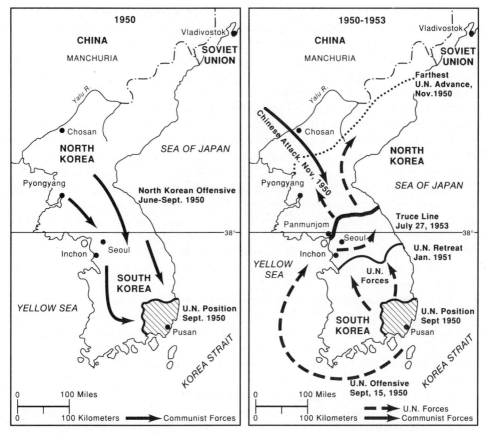

Figure 10–5   The Korean War

many composed of veterans of the long war against Chiang and the Japanese. Despite individual acts of bravery, American troops panicked and fled south the way they had come, abandoning arms, food, tents, supplies, and hundreds of prisoners to the enemy. Thousands of Chinese, facing one of the most bitterly cold winters on record, survived only by using cast-off American blankets, boots, and clothing. It was not a proud page in American military annals. To reduce the pressure, in late December MacArthur proposed that the UN forces blockade the Chinese coast, bomb Chinese war industry, and permit Chiang's military forces to create a "diversionary action" against "vulnerable areas of the Chinese mainland." Truman denied the request, fearing to bring the Soviet Union into the war. He also told the general, a vain and egocentric man who had ruled Japan as his personal fiefdom, that he must issue "no speech, press release, or public statement" on policy without clearance from Washington.

In January the UN forces finally recovered from the initial shock of the Chinese attack and resumed the offensive. They recaptured Seoul again in March and were soon once more at the thirty-eighth parallel.

At this point relations between MacArthur and the administration reached a crisis. In late March Truman told the general that the American government would seek a negotiated peace through diplomacy. MacArthur objected. Soon after this he wrote a letter, read publicly in the House of Representatives, proposing that Chiang be "unleashed" to invade mainland China and urging the United States to shift its overall strategic priority from Europe to Asia.

On April 10 Truman relieved MacArthur of command for insubordination and replaced him with General Matthew Ridgeway. The public split passionately over the MacArthur dismissal. Some approved the president's decision to limit the war and put the general in his place. Others considered the administration weak for refusing to use every means to win the war and for humiliating a great military hero. The MacArthur fans seemed more numerous than the Truman supporters. Thousands of angry and critical letters and telegrams poured into the White House, running twenty to one against the president. One particularly angry voter telegraphed, "Impeach the Judas in the White House who sold us down the river to left wingers and the UN." When the general returned to the United States, his trip across the country became a triumphal procession with ovations, banquets, and rallies in his honor. There was talk of running him for president in 1952.

Public enthusiasm quickly ebbed, however. Congress held extensive hearings on the war that revealed the general's military failings and confirmed the value of the administration's "limited war" position. Despite the shift in attitude the incident revealed a profound American dissatisfaction with any policy that did not produce quick solutions. Critics wondered if Americans were capable after all of pursuing a long-term policy of patient containment.

On July 8 cease-fire negotiations between the UN forces and the Chinese–North Koreans began at Kaesong, close to the thirty-eighth parallel. The fighting continued but was now reduced to furious small-scale firefights and bloody patrol actions, with neither side expecting a breakthrough. The negotiations continued month after month with little visible progress.

Mobilization

By this time the country was on a war footing, with thousands of reserve troops called back into service, and a full-scale draft. In all, over 1.3 million Americans would serve in the Korean theater of war; 54,000 young Americans died. Although there were no serious consumer shortages, prices rose as in World War II, despite official price controls.

Korea was a major step along the Cold War road. In 1949, at the behest of Secretary of State Acheson, the National Security Council had drafted a policy paper (NSC-68) recommending a major rearmament program to meet the growing dangers of Soviet antagonism. The paper had been accepted but it had not been implemented. In 1950 the American defense budget remained a modest $13.5 billion; the nation's total armed forces personnel about 1.4 million. Despite all the tension with the Soviet Union the country remained complacent. Korea changed this drastically. By 1955 America's military budget had soared to almost $40 billion; that year the number of U.S. military personnel reached 2.9 million.

Anticommunism at Home

The Korean War, and especially the frustrating military stalemate, intensified the anti-Communist climate in the United States and set off a campaign against supposed subversives and traitors at home.

The campaign was marked by panic and hysteria. Clearly a small number of American Communists were willing to spy for the Soviet Union. But most members of the Communist party of the United States, however sympathetic to the "Socialist Motherland," were not engaged in espionage. In fact the chief charge against them was that they were subversives. It is true that a few Communists and Soviet sympathizers occupied positions in the media, in Hollywood, in the universities, and in trade unions, and it would be naive to assume that they never used their positions to propagate their political viewpoints. Yet when this is said, it remains true that the handfull of Soviet partisans in the United States never seriously threatened American security or democracy or ever exerted a dangerous influence over American minds. By 1950, however, the United States was suffering from a full-blown anti-Communist frenzy that threatened to undermine the Bill of Rights and damage the very democratic system the crusaders professed to be defending.

It is important to distinguish between the Soviet threat on the one hand and the danger of internal subversion on the other. However valid or invalid the first, the second was clearly unreal. The United States and its capitalist system were never in danger of internal overthrow. Nor was American foreign policy secretly manipulated, as some people felt, by traitors in high places. Yet many Americans were willing to believe that Communist gains in Europe and the Third World were the work of a conspiracy by secret Communists in high Washington office to betray America's interests.

Concern over perceived Soviet expansionism and aggressiveness was the ultimate source of anti-Communism at home. But there were also self-serving gains to be made by playing on, and exaggerating, anti-Communist fears. Obscure politicians could win the limelight and keep it by unmasking hidden Communists in high places; this was the course of Senator Joseph R. McCarthy. One politician could use it against another; Richard Nixon achieved his early political victories in California by charging his opponents with pro-Communist views. It could also serve overall party purposes; some of the less scrupulous Republican leaders of the 1950s accused the Democrats of "twenty years of treason." It was a resource of right against left; conservatives would charge that liberals were "soft on communism," and label their policies "socialistic." Sometimes the gains were purely monetary; more than one former FBI agent or city police detective set himself up as an expert on communism and charged media companies or industrial firms fees to root out Communists among their employees.

Relatively few Americans could resist the anti-Communist wave that swept the country after 1945. Following the discovery in 1945–46 of major Soviet spy operations in the United States, Truman created a commission to look into the question of loyalty among federal employees. Early in 1947 the federal government began the screening of over 3.2 million federal workers, including every clerk-typist, Internal Revenue Service accountant, and postal worker in the country. By 1951 almost 300 had been dismissed and another 3000 had resigned. Meanwhile in December 1947 the attorney general issued a list of ninety organizations, later expanded, that were identified as Communist "front" groups. Membership in any group on the attorney general's list became grounds for suspicion of disloyalty and, in some cases, of dismissal from jobs.

The Hiss and Rosenberg Cases

Public anxiety was fueled by several sensational cases of actual espionage. In the summer of 1948 two witnesses before the House Committee on Un-American Activities (HUAC), Elizabeth Bentley and Whittaker Chambers, both repentant ex-Communists, revealed that a number of American Communists had spied for the Soviets during the 1930s in Washington, D.C. Chambers charged that Alger Hiss, now head of the prestigious Carnegie Foundation for International Peace and once an influential New Deal figure, had been a member of one of these secret rings. Hiss, he claimed, had stolen secret documents from the federal government and turned them over to Chambers to be passed along to Soviet agents.

Hiss appeared before the committee to answer the accusations against him. He denied every charge and made an excellent impression. Urbane, elegant, well-spoken, sincere, he convinced everyone on the committee except the young Republican congressman from California, Richard Nixon, that he was totally innocent. He had never stolen secrets; he had never known Chambers. The committee now recalled Chambers who began to supply circumstantial evidence of his association with Hiss and his family during the 1930s. Armed with this new information, the committee summoned Hiss once again and questioned him closely. Hiss might have confessed to being a Communist during the 1930s; that was not a crime. He might even have admitted that he had taken secret documents; by now the statute of limitations had run out and he could no longer be prosecuted for the offense. He did neither. He denied Chambers's charges again, although admitting he might have known the man under another name. Then he made a fatal mistake. Let Whittaker Chambers make his charges in public, he demanded; if Chambers dared to do so, he would sue him for libel.

Chambers quickly took up the challenge and on a radio program, "Meet the Press," accused Hiss of being a secret Communist and Soviet agent. He then waited for weeks for the promised libel action. When in September 1948 Hiss finally sued for defamation of character, Chambers dramatically revealed a cache of stolen government documents—originals, microfilms, and copies in Hiss's handwriting—that he claimed Hiss had given him years before for safekeeping. Some of these were trivial items, but others contained important secrets.

The Truman administration had been reluctant to prosecute Hiss. Many liberals admired the man and saw him as a symbol of all the New Deal stood for at its best. They also correctly detected in his enemies a partisan zeal to indict the liberalism of FDR and his followers. But confronted with this new, incriminating data, the Justice Department indicted him for perjuring himself before a congressional committee. The first trial resulted in a hung jury. The second trial, ending in January 1950, produced a conviction. The judge sentenced Hiss to five years in prison.

The Hiss case was important as a symbol of Cold War tensions at home. Regardless of Hiss's guilt or innocence, its outcome was a victory for those who believed that Communist gains had been made possible by men in prominent positions who had betrayed their country. If Chambers was right, some New Dealers had committed treason. To those who believed Hiss innocent, his conviction seemed either a case of mass hysteria, like the witch-hunts of the Middle Ages, or a cynical attempt to frame the political left and the New Deal.

The Rosenberg case also reinforced public fears. In 1949 British authorities arrested Klaus Fuchs, an anti-Nazi refugee and naturalized British citizen who as a theoretical physicist had helped the Americans and British develop the atom bomb. A loyal Communist, Fuchs had become a Soviet spy and had passed along secret data to the Soviet Union about atom bomb research. His apprehension in 1950 led, in turn, to David Greenglass, an enlisted man at the U.S. Los Alamos atomic laboratory who had supplied Fuchs with information on the processes for manufacturing the bomb. The trail of contacts finally led to Greenglass's sister and her husband, Ethel and Julius Rosenberg, two Soviet sympathizers. The Rosenbergs denied their guilt and claimed to be victims of Cold War hysteria, but they were both convicted and sentenced to death. Although a portion of the political left rallied to the Rosenbergs, they were executed in June 1953. To this day they remain, in some circles, martyrs of the Cold War.

Joe McCarthy

Korea and its frustrations charged all these Cold War events with special significance and created a demagogue anxious and able to take advantage of the public mood. The man was Joseph R. McCarthy, the Republican junior senator from Wisconsin.

McCarthy, a former state circuit judge, won election to the Senate in the Republican sweep of 1946. McCarthy's victory was due to the weakness of the progressive La Follette state machine and his own supposed (and false) heroic war record. The man had few ideas and little vision. Nicknamed by his colleagues "the Pepsi Cola kid" for his lobbying efforts on behalf of the soft drink manufacturer, he had impressed neither them nor his constituents. By 1950 he was, with reason, worried about reelection two years ahead and desperate for an issue to bring him favorable publicity. Early in the year he had dinner with a friend who advised him that the Communists-in-government issue might be his ticket to reelection. "That's it," McCarthy reputedly declared. "The government is full of Communists. We can hammer away at them."

On February 9, in a speech to the Women's Republican Club of Wheeling, West Virginia, McCarthy charged there were 205 "card-carrying Communists" at work in the State Department, a situation supposedly known to the Truman administration but left uncorrected. On other occasions he cited different numbers. McCarthy was bluffing; he had no idea how many, if any, Communists were in the State Department. Yet in the feverish atmosphere of the day the charge created a sensation. The senator had found his issue and was soon off and running.

McCarthy was a master of obfuscation. When the Democrats investigated the State Department claim, he managed to turn the case into an indictment of the Truman administration for "losing China." Owen Lattimore, a Johns Hopkins University

READING 10

McCarthyism

The right of free expression, even if one is wrong, is a precious part of America's heritage. As a people Americans generally prize their civil liberties, but in moments of fear and panic they sometimes push them aside. One such occasion was the immediate post–World War II era, when many citizens feared the Soviet threat abroad and linked it with subversion at home. These fears were magnified and given focus by Senator Joseph McCarthy of Wisconsin, a demagogue more interested in advancing his own and his Republican party's political interests than in making the country more secure against its enemies. The following is an excerpt from McCarthy's 1950 Lincoln Day speech, the opening shot of his campaign against the forces of "communistic atheism," domestic and foreign. Before he was brought to heel four years later, McCarthy had poisoned the country's political atmosphere and wrecked the careers of hundreds of loyal Americans.

Ladies and gentlemen, tonight as we celebrate the one hundred and forty-first birthday of one of the greatest men in American history, I would like to be able to talk about what a glorious day today is in the history of the world. As we celebrate the birth of this man who with his whole heart and soul hated war, I would like to be able to speak of peace in our time, of war being outlawed, and of worldwide disarmament. These would be truly appropriate things to be able to mention as we celebrate the birthday of Abraham Lincoln.

Five years after a world war has been won, men's hearts should anticipate a long peace, and men's minds should be free from the heavy weight that comes with war. But this is not such a period—for this is not a period of peace. This is a time of the "cold war." This is a time when all the world is split into two vast, increasingly hostile armed camps—a time of a great armaments race.

Today we are engaged in a final, all-out battle between communistic atheism and Christianity. The modern champions of communism have selected this as the time. And, ladies and gentlemen, the chips are down—they are truly down.

Six years ago, at the time of the first conference to map out the peace—Dumbarton Oaks—there was within the Soviet orbit 180 million people. Lined up on the antitotalitarian side there were in the world roughly 1,625 million people. Today, only six years later, there are 800 million people under the absolute domination of soviet Russia—an increase of over 400 percent. On our side, the figure has shrunk to around 500 million. In other words, in less than six years the odds have changed from 9 to 1 in our favor to 8 to 5 against us. This indicates the swiftness of the tempo of Communist victories and American defeats in the cold war. As one of our outstanding historical figures once said, "When a great democracy is destroyed, it will not be because of enemies from without, but rather because of enemies from within."

The truth of this statement is becoming terrifyingly clear as we see this country each day losing on every front. . . .

The reason why we find ourselves in a position of impotency is not because our only powerful potential enemy has sent men to invade our shores, but rather because of the traitorous actions of those who have been treated so well by this Nation. It has not been the less fortunate or members of minority groups who have been selling this Nation out, but rather those who have had all the benefits that the wealthiest nation on earth has had to offer—the finest homes, the finest college education, and the finest jobs in Government we can give.

This is glaringly true in the State Department. There the bright young men who are born with silver spoons in their mouths are the ones who have been worst. . . .

When Chiang Kai-shek was fighting our war, the State Department had in China a young man named John S. Service. His task, obviously, was not to work for the communization of China.* Strangely, however, he sent official reports back to the State Department urging that we torpedo our ally Chiang Kai-shek and stating, in effect, that communism was the best hope for China.

Later, this man—John Service—was picked up by the Federal Bureau of Investigation for turning over to the Communists secret State Department information. Strangely, however, he was never prosecuted. However, Joseph Grew, the Under Secretary of State, who insisted on his prosecution, was forced to resign. Two days after Grew's successor, Dean Acheson, took over as Under Secretary of State, this man—John Service—who had been picked up by the FBI and who had previously urged that communism was the best hope of China, was not only reinstated in the State Department but promoted. And finally, under Acheson, placed in charge of all placements and promotions.

Today, ladies and gentlemen, this man Service is on his way to represent the State Department and Acheson in Calcutta—by far and away the most important listening post in the Far East. . . .

This, ladies and gentlemen, gives you somewhat of a picture of the type of individuals who have been helping to shape our foreign policy. In my opinion the State Department, which is one of the most important government departments, is thoroughly infested with Communists.

I have in my hand 57 cases of individuals who would appear to be either card carrying members or certainly loyal to the Communist Party, but who nevertheless are still helping to shape our foreign policy.

One thing to remember in discussing the Communists in our Government is that we are not dealing with spies who get 30 pieces of silver to steal

*The following statements about Service are grossly inaccurate [Ed. note].

the blueprints of a new weapon. We are dealing with a far more sinister type of activity because it permits the enemy to guide and shape our policy. . . .

As you hear this story of high treason, I know that you are saying to yourself, "Well, why doesn't the Congress do something about it?" Actually, ladies and gentlemen, one of the important reasons for the graft, the corruption, the dishonesty, the disloyalty, the treason in high Government positions—one of the most important reasons why this continues is a lack of moral uprising on the part of the 140 million American people. In the light of history, however, this is not hard to explain.

It is the result of an emotional hangover and a temporary moral lapse which follows every war. It is the apathy to evil which people who have been subjected to the tremendous evils of war feel. As the people of the world see mass murder, the destruction of defenseless and innocent people, and all of the crime and lack of morals which go with war, they become numb and apathetic. It has always been thus after war.

However, the morals of our people have not been destroyed. They still exist. This cloak of numbness and apathy has only needed a spark to rekindle them. Happily, this spark has finally been supplied.

As you know, very recently the Secretary of State [Dean Acheson] proclaimed his loyalty to a man [Alger Hiss] guilty of what has always been considered as the most abominable of all crimes—of being a traitor to the people who gave him a position of great trust. The Secretary of State in attempting to justify his continued devotion to the man who sold out the Christian world to the atheistic world, referred to Christ's Sermon on the Mount as a justification and reason therefor, and the reaction of the American people to this would have made the heart of Abraham Lincoln happy.

When this pompous diplomat in striped pants, with a phony British accent, proclaimed to the American people that Christ on the Mount endorsed communism, high treason, and betrayal of a sacred trust, the blasphemy was so great that it awakened the dormant indignation of the American people.

He has lighted the spark which is resulting in a moral uprising and will end only when the whole sorry mess of twisted, warped thinkers are swept from the national scene so that we may have a new birth of national honesty and decency in Government.

Source: From the *Congressional Record,* 81st Congress, v. 96, part 2 (February 20, 1950).

professor who had served as a State Department adviser on East Asia, was, McCarthy said, a Soviet agent who had deceived his superiors. When Truman and Acheson attacked the senator, he called the president "a son of a bitch" and advised Acheson to seek asylum in the Kremlin.

McCarthy soon went on to attack the widely respected George Marshall, despised by the China Lobby for his refusal to support Chiang during the civil war with Mao and his forces. At Marshall's confirmation hearings as secretary of defense in 1950, the senator announced that he would expose "a conspiracy so immense and an infamy so black as to dwarf any previous venture in the history of man." Despite the attack Marshall was confirmed, but many of his friends would never forgive the senator.

Clearly McCarthy was no respecter of truth, of persons, or even of common decencies. Before long he had developed an approach guaranteed to get him headlines in the nation's papers. He would call a morning press conference and announce that he was calling an afternoon press conference. He made the news both times. He carried around a fat briefcase, supposedly full of written evidence incriminating one person, or whole groups of people, and then refused to show the documents to anyone. He produced nothing, but the performance invariably excited wide speculation.

Despite his incivility and reckless accusatory zeal the senator was a popular man. Supporters flooded his office with mail and contributions. A poll in May 1950 showed that 40 percent of Americans supported him; only 28 percent considered his charges dangerous or untrue. That year he campaigned against some of the congressional Democrats who had opposed him, and their defeat sent shivers down the spines of

Senator Joseph McCarthy, Republican of Wisconsin, and his aide Roy Cohn. (UPI/Bettmann Newsphotos)

would-be opponents. Even at the beginning and within his own party, some people despised the man and loathed his tactics. "I don't want to see the Republican Party ride to victory on . . . fear, ignorance, bigotry, and smear," declared Maine Senator Margaret Chase Smith. But for four years McCarthy managed to terrorize the nation by attacking those who crossed him or whose demise could serve his purposes.

The National Witch-Hunt

McCarthy was not the only Grand Inquisitor during these years. HUAC regularly announced investigations of major American institutions such as Hollywood, the teaching profession, trade unions, and the Protestant churches and then held highly publicized hearings where witnesses were forced to answer questions about their membership in the Communist party. The committee was especially interested in media celebrities—actors, writers, producers, and playwrights—whose presence guaranteed a flood of publicity and justified the committee's continued existence. Some of the nation's most creative people were dragged before the committee including Arthur Miller, Elia Kazan, Lillian Hellman, and Dashiell Hammett. Many of those subpoenaed had indeed flirted with the far left during the 1930s and joined some of the front organizations on the Attorney General's List. Some had been actual Communist party members. But none had spied on their nation. And in any case a democratic society accepts the right of anyone to embrace unorthodox opinions no matter how unpopular. Unfortunately in the heated atmosphere of the day admitting to membership in the Communist party or a front group could ruin a career or a reputation. And if the accused were willing to admit their own political errors, the committee then insisted that they "name names," that is, implicate other people who had shared their views and their former radical activities. Many people who were willing to confess that they had made a mistake themselves were reluctant to squeal on others. Generally the only defense against this process was to plead the Fifth Amendment, the part of the Bill of Rights that allows an accused person to be silent to avoid self-incrimination. "Taking the Fifth" enabled the accused to refuse answers to HUAC questions without prosecution. But it branded one a Communist anyway and produced the same personal stigma as an outright admission of Communist party membership.

The quest for "disloyalty" in these years permeated almost every corner of American life. Colleges, municipalities, and states demanded loyalty oaths of employees as a condition of employment. Private wage earners, especially in the media, were investigated with the help of professional red-hunters who claimed to be skilled in the job of sniffing out subversives. People usually had the right to challenge accusers, but it was often difficult and expensive to clear one's name. Hundreds of completely innocent people fell victim to the excessive zeal or malice of accusers with no effective recourse.

And the federal courts, bowing to the hysteria of the day, failed to protect civil liberties. In 1949 the federal government indicted eleven top leaders of the Communist party for violating the 1940 Smith Act, a measure making it illegal to advocate or teach the overthrow of the government by force and violence. The trial resulted in conviction and prison terms for the defendants. In 1951 in *Dennis* v. *U.S.*, the Supreme Court upheld the right of the government to try people for subversion on the basis of membership in a political party.

The 1952 Election

As the 1952 presidential election approached, the public had become disillusioned with the Truman administration. The little man from Missouri had checked Soviet expansionism in Europe and helped to restore the European economy. But in Asia the United States was hopelessly bogged down in an expensive, no-win war. At home matters seemed to be in a mess as well. Not everybody accepted the McCarthyite view of a nation riddled with disloyalty, but enough Americans believed the "where there's smoke there's fire" thesis that the administration seemed lax in its anti-Communist vigilance.

It also seemed tinged with corruption. No one seriously accused Harry Truman of personal dishonesty, but it was clear that he was surrounded by subordinates who took advantage of inside information or personal contacts to arrange lucrative federal contracts for businesspeople. Such influence peddlers usually charged a 5 percent fee for any contract successfully negotiated. The most blatant offender was General Harry Vaughan, Truman's military aide, who used his influence to get favors for businesspeople, mostly in exchange for contributions to the Democratic party but also, in one case, for a food freezer for his personal use. There was also corruption in the Reconstruction Finance Corporation (RFC), where several of the president's Missouri cronies extended large RFC loans in exchange for favors, including a $9500 mink coat. The Bureau of Internal Revenue, it came out, was also riddled with corrupt officials who took bribes to arrange lower tax bills for private citizens. These scandals produced a wave of prosecutions and convictions and reinforced the impression that Truman and the Democrats had lost their grip.

Gallup polls during 1950–52 showed an approval rating for the president at no more than 25 percent. Three out of four Americans did not believe he was doing a good job. In February 1951 the Twenty-second Amendment to the Constitution, prescribing a maximum of two terms to the president, became the law of the land. The amendment exempted Truman; nonetheless on March 29, months before the 1952 national conventions, he announced that he would not run for another full term.

With the race open on the Democratic side for the first time in twenty years, the competition became intense. Truman's withdrawal made Senator Estes Kefauver of Tennessee, whose investigations of organized crime had attracted national attention, the Democratic front-runner for a time. But the party bosses deplored Kefauver's excessive zeal in connecting racketeers with the big city Democratic machines. The president too disliked Kefauver, who had attacked him for laxity in cleaning up his administration.

Truman favored the governor of Illinois, Adlai Stevenson, the grandson and namesake of Grover Cleveland's second vice president. A thoughtful and eloquent patrician, Stevenson had been elected governor of Illinois on a reform ticket and had established a reputation as a clean-government, moderate liberal. In 1952 he was something of a hero to civil libertarians for his courageous deposition during Alger Hiss's perjury trial endorsing Hiss's reputation for integrity. But Stevenson preferred another term as Illinois governor to the Democratic nomination. His reluctance did not stop his supporters who included, besides the president, the party's ADA liberals and the southern leaders. At the Chicago convention, in something close to an authentic draft, they nominated Stevenson on the third ballot with Senator John Sparkman of Alabama as his running mate.

The Republicans had met two weeks earlier in the Windy City and nominated Dwight Eisenhower and Richard Nixon to head their ticket in November. The choice of "Ike" was a victory for the party's moderates and internationalists who opposed Robert Taft as too conservative and isolationist.

For a time both parties had considered Eisenhower, a man with no clear-cut political affiliations. As late as November 1951 Truman had asked him to consider the Democratic nomination, but Eisenhower had noted that his family affiliation had always been Republican. Yet the general, like Stevenson, was unwilling to actively seek the nomination, wanting it to come to him by acclamation. His Republican supporters took him at his word and had soon organized Citizens for Eisenhower clubs and entered his name in the primaries.

Early in April 1952 Eisenhower asked to be relieved as head of NATO forces in Europe. On June 2 he formally opened his campaign for the Republican nomination with a speech that combined conservative domestic principles with an endorsement of America's international commitments.

Ike came into the Chicago Republican convention with a hard fight on his hands. He had won most of the popular primaries, but the regular delegates from the boss-controlled states had "Taft" written on their hearts. In the end they followed their heads rather than their hearts. The polls showed Eisenhower would win in November; Taft would lose. Ike went over the top on the first ballot. It was, of course, the usual practice for the presidential nominee to chose his running mate with the delegates merely confirming it. Ike did not know this and, in a move borrowed from military staff decision-making practices, called in his supporters and asked them to make the choice. Tom Dewey thereupon named Richard Nixon, the young senator from California, who had made his reputation in the Hiss case.

We Like Ike!

The campaign held few surprises. Stevenson, as expected, proved to be an eloquent, witty, and effective campaigner. But he carried on his back the incubus of Korea, the Truman scandals, and the public's weariness with thirty years of Democratic rule. Eisenhower was a poor speaker with a talent for muddled and nebulous pronouncements. But his middle-American accent, folksy demeanor, and open, cheerful face inspired confidence. He seemed everyone's nice, competent, but undemanding grandfather. After a while, moreover, Stevenson's wit and urbanity began to seem an assertion of his intellectual superiority to his fellow citizens. The Democratic candidate was soon being sneered at as an "egghead."

For a brief period the Democrats thought they had a winning issue when they uncovered a secret "trust fund" financed by rich Californians to help pay Nixon's political expenses. The fund was not illegal, and Nixon was not the only politician who benefited from such largess. Yet it looked suspicious and threatened to cripple the Republican campaign. For a time there was serious talk among Republicans of replacing Nixon as the vice presidential candidate. Then Dewey offered a way out. Nixon should appear on national television and explain himself. If the public response was overwhelmingly favorable he would stay; if not, he would resign.

Nixon gave the speech of his life. He denied that he had received any money personally from the fund and went on to give a family financial statement. He included as his chief assets two heavily mortgaged dwellings, one a small house in California where his parents were living, the other the modest house in Washington. He also listed a two-year old Oldsmobile. His wife Pat, he noted, did not have a mink coat like some of the Democrats' wives. But she looked good in her "respectable Republican cloth coat." In a few sentences the senator had established strong rapport with millions of American wage earners.

The vice presidential candidate now waxed sentimental. It is true that he had taken one gift from a constituent. A benefactor had sent a cocker spaniel to his two little daughters, and Tricia, the six year old, had named it Checkers. "[R]egardless of what they say about it, we're going to keep it." Ever after the talk would be called Nixon's Checkers Speech.

The public loved the speech. Secretaries cried; strong men choked up. Favorable letters poured in to the Republican National Committee. Eisenhower, who had received a special tax exemption for his royalties from *Crusade in Europe*, his best-selling account of World War II, had not liked Nixon's suggestion that all the candidates reveal their personal finances. He never forgave the senator, yet he could count the letters and read the poll results. Nixon stayed on the ticket.

Thereafter the Republican campaign was back on the track. Ike clinched the race on October 24 when he promised that if elected he would go to Korea and settle the stalemate. The Democrats called it a stunt, but many Americans felt it might just do the trick. It made a difference. "For all practical purposes," commented an Associated Press reporter, "the contest ended that night." The results on election day were: Eisenhower-Nixon, 33.9 million; Stevenson-Sparkman, 27.3 million. The Republicans had carried several key southern states and gained control of both houses of Congress by narrow margins. It was a major turnover. (See Figure 10–6.) Describing his feelings, Stevenson used a Lincoln story. After losing an election, Lincoln had said he felt like a small boy who had stubbed his toe in the dark: "he was too old to cry but it hurt too much to laugh."

The Cold War's Distortions

The years immediately following World War II were a time of renewal and new found private satisfactions for many Americans. Times were good and many people felt an expansive sense of new possibilities. And yet hovering over everything was the fear and anxiety that accompanied the Cold War.

However generated, the Cold War had baleful effects on the nation's life in the 1950s. Unused to world political leadership, Americans found the frustrations of international power politics and the ambiguities of Cold War competition difficult to abide. Under unfamiliar pressures they lost their sense of proportion and their respect for dissenting opinions and descended to practices that betrayed the country's best tradition of fair play. America in the fifties was a prosperous nation under a cloud.

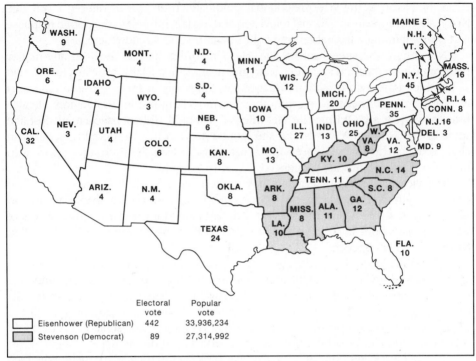

Figure 10–6 The 1952 Presidential Election

Common sense would finally take hold and the worst excesses abate, but McCarthyism had poisoned the political and intellectual atmosphere in unfortunate ways.

FOR FURTHER READING

On the readjustment of veterans the best work is R. J. Havighurst, et al., *The American Veteran Back Home: A Study of Veteran Readjustment* (1951).

The suburbanization of American life and values during the immediate post–World War II years is described critically in John Keats, *The Crack in the Picture Window* (1957) and Richard Gordon et al., *The Split Level Trap* (1960) Two more-recent works on suburbia are Landon Jones, *Great Expectations: America and the Baby Boom Generation* (1980) and Kenneth Jackson's, *Crabgrass Frontier: The Suburbanization of the United States* (1985).

Equally critical of the values of a business society are William H. Whyte, *The Organization Man* (1955) and the novel by Sloan Wilson, *The Man in the Grey Flannel Suit* (1955). A critical and highly influential view of composite American character as it had evolved by the 1950s is the work by David Reisman et al., *The Lonely Crowd* (1958). A sharp indictment of women's status after 1945, as well as a mark of change, is Betty Friedan's *The Feminine Mystique* (1963). More favorable treatments of the suburban experience are Scott Donaldson, *The Suburban Myth* (1969) and Herbert Gans, *The Levittowners: Ways of Life and Politics in a New Suburban Community* (1967). On how blacks have been excluded from the suburban experience see Michael Danielson, *The Politics of Exclusion* (1976).

The economy of the 1950s is covered in Harold Vatter, *The U.S. Economy in the 1950s: An*

Economic History (1963). Two influential contemporary works are John K. Galbraith, *The Affluent Society* (1952) and his *American Capitalism: Countervailing Power* (1956).

Much has been written on the Truman Fair Deal era. For two overall views see Alonzo Hamby, *Beyond the New Deal: Harry S. Truman and American Liberalism* (1973) and Robert Ferrell *Harry Truman and the Modern American Presidency* (1982). Specialized studies of political events during the Truman period include Allen Matusow, *Farm Policies and Politics in the Truman Administration* (1967); Arthur McClure, *The Truman Administration and the Problems of Postwar Labor* (1969); Susan Hartmann, *Truman and the 80th Congress* (1971); and Richard Davies, *Housing Reform During the Truman Administration* (1966).

On the famous election of 1948 see Irwin Ross, *The Loneliest Campaign: The Truman Victory of 1948* (1968); Norman Markowitz, *The Rise and Fall of the People's Century: Henry A. Wallace and American Liberalism, 1941–1948* (1973); and William Barnard, *Dixiecrats and Democrats: Alabama Politics, 1942–1950* (1974).

More has been written about the Cold War than about any other event of the post-1945 era. The issue divided the nation and the division is reflected in the literature. A standard mainstream liberal study of the early phase is Herbert Feis, *From Trust to Terror: The Onset of the Cold War, 1945–1950* (1970). Also see John L. Gaddis, *The United States and the Origins of the Cold War, 1941–1947* (1972) and Adam Ulam, *Containment and Co-existence* (1974). Left revisionist studies that tend to lay the blame for the Soviet-American confrontation at America's door include Joyce and Gabriel Kolko, *The Limits of Power: The World and U.S. Foreign Policy, 1945–1954* (1972) and Richard Barnett, *Intervention and Revolution* (1969). A study of the left revisionists is Robert W. Tucker's *The Radical Left and American Foreign Policy* (1978).

Specific studies of Truman period foreign policy initiatives include William H. McNeill, *Greece: American Aid in Action, 1947–1956* (1957); Hadley Arkes, *Bureaucracy, the Marshall Plan, and the National Interest* (1973); and Bruce Kuklick, *American Policy and the Division of Germany* (1972). American far eastern policy during this period is covered in Herbert Feis, *The China Tangle* (1953).

On the Korean War the best works are Glenn Paige, *The Korean Decision* (1968); David Rees, *Korea: The Limited War* (1964); John Spanier, *The Truman-MacArthur Controversy and the Korean War* (1965); and Clay Blair, Jr.'s behemoth volume, *The Forgotten War: America in Korea, 1950–1953* (1987).

The McCarthy era red scare has also spawned an immense literature. For a sharp general critique of the anti-Communist crusade see David Caute, *The Great Fear: The Anti-Communist Purge under Truman and Eisenhower* (1978). A good anti-McCarthy treatment is Richard Rovere's *Senator Joe McCarthy* (1959). Also see David Oshinsky, *A Conspiracy So Immense: The World of Joe McCarthy* (1983). For defenses of McCarthy and of the anti-Communist purges during the Truman–Eisenhower years see William F. Buckley, Jr., and L. Brent Bozell, *McCarthy and His Enemies* (1954) and Victor Lasky and Ralph de Toledano, *The Seeds of Treason* (1950). The best study of the Hiss affair is Allen Weinstein, *Perjury: The Hiss-Chambers Case* (1978). On HUAC's inquisitorial mode as directed toward Hollywood see Victor Navasky, *Naming Names* (1980). The most effective defense of the era's anti-Communism is Whittiker Chambers's *Witness* (1958). An interesting recent study of the Rosenberg case is Ronald Radosh and Joyce Milton, *The Rosenberg File: A Search for the Truth* (1983).

The 1952 election is dealt with in Heinz Elau, *Class and Party in the Eisenhower Years* (1962). For Adlai Stevenson see Kenneth Davis, *A Prophet in His Own Country* (1957). Nixon writes about his problems during the 1952 campaign in *Six Crises* (1962).

11
Culture and Public Affairs during the Eisenhower Years

Elvis Presley, "the King," elicits a typical reaction from fans during a 1956 performance. (UPI/Bettmann Newsphotos)

Ideas and Values

Compared to the decade that followed, the years of the Eisenhower presidency seem intellectually timid and conformist. In some ways they were; but the period was also a time of needed political consolidation and of creativity in painting, literature, and the popular arts.

The intellectual climate of the 1950s was clearly more conservative than that of the 1930s. During the Depression era the country's most prestigious thinkers had criticized their society from the left of the political spectrum. After 1945 a new mood of affirmation, even self-congratulation, appeared within the American intellectual community.

Some observers have ascribed the new attitude to repression and timidity. And surely fear of McCarthyism was a element in the decline of the left critique. Equally important, however, was the disillusionment of many intellectuals with the Soviet Union and an honest rediscovery of a free society's virtues. The Soviet's paranoia and repressiveness under the cruel dictator Stalin, as confirmed by his successor Nikita Khrushchev in 1956, virtually destroyed any lingering pro-Soviet feelings among all but the most committed Communist party members. Many former supporters of the Soviet Union not only repudiated their political past but came to see the United States as the chief bulwark against Soviet expansionism. And there was also the apparent success of the American economy. Postwar America, after all, was a prosperous land where capitalism, as modified and softened by welfare state safeguards, seemed to have succeeded. What sense did the Marxist critique now make? In 1960 a former Marxist, Daniel Bell, published a collection of essays whose title, *The End of Ideology,* was the requiem for the radical intellectual mood of the immediate past.

The American Celebration

The postwar intellectuals reinforced the celebratory mood of the day in a succession of historical, sociological, and economic essays and books. John K. Galbraith's 1952 work *American Capitalism* admitted to the growth of industrial concentration, but claimed that its political and economic dangers had been offset by the "countervailing" rise of labor unions, the advent of discount retail chains, and the appearance of big government. In American history Daniel Boorstin, Louis Hartz, and Oscar Handlin sought to replace "conflict" views of the American past as formerly expounded by "progressive" historians like Charles Beard and Marxist scholars like Louis Hacker with the "consensus" position that Americans had always agreed on the fundamentals—democracy and private property—and had argued primarily over secondary matters. Political scientists like Robert Dahl meanwhile asserted that decision-making power in American society was not confined to a small elite but resided in a plurality of pressure groups.

Anticonformists

Some social thinkers, inevitably, continued to serve as dissenters and gadflies, but more and more they attacked from the elitist right rather than the proletarian left. John

Keats, in *The Crack in the Picture Window* (1957), depicted suburbia and its inhabitants as intellectually dead and culturally vacuous. William Whyte's *The Organization Man* (1956) disparaged the new, conformist executive class who had come to the top in the postwar years. A similar point was made by Sloan Wilson's novel, *The Man in the Gray Flannel Suit* (1955). The most memorable attack of all came from the sociologists David Riesman, Nathan Glazer, and Reuel Denney in *The Lonely Crowd* (1950). The book, a remarkable best-seller, described with barely disguised disapproval the advent of the new, postwar Americans who lacked any strong inner values and took their cues from the mass society around them. Their predecessors had been "inner directed," guided by internal moral and intellectual "gyroscopes"; the new breed were "other directed," their behavior governed by built-in "radar sets." The new social critics in general disliked mass society and all its tastes including television, big cars with flamboyant tailfins, shopping malls, and ranch-style houses.

Religion and Conservatism

The religious mood of the 1950s was also conservative. From the 1890s onward, although fundamentalism held sway in the hinterland, mainstream American Protestant thought had been liberal, both in theology and in its social orientation. The beliefs in progress, innate human goodness, and perfectability had been incorporated into the Social Gospel preached from the pulpits of a thousand urban Protestant churches.

All versions of religion prospered during the fifties. In 1940 less than half the population of the United States were members of churches; by the late 1950s over 63 percent belonged to some organized religious congregation. There was in this period much talk in the press about the "return to God"; Bible sales soared; politicians turned pious. In 1954 Congress added "under God" to the Pledge of Allegiance and adopted "In God We Trust" as the national motto. One important religious trend was the decline in *sectarianism* and the growth of *ecumenicism,* a unifying impulse among the major faiths. Increasingly during these years there was talk of the "Judeo-Christian tradition," a phrase that sought to embrace Protestants, Catholics, and Jews in a single religious community.

To some degree the greater religiosity of the postwar era was connected with the Cold War. The Communist enemies were atheists; Americans would be believers. It was also associated with the surge to suburbia. Joining a church or a synagogue was one way to reestablish social connections in a new community. It also represented a desire to conform by accepting part of the traditional, vaguely defined, American civic religion. For many people it did not run deep or become solidly incorporated into daily life. But for a time it seemed to confirm the nation's growing conservatism.

There was an irony here. If any serious social philosophy informed the typical churchgoer's religious outlook, it was probably vaguely liberal. People could conquer adversity and perfect themselves and society. The clergy, including Norman Vincent Peale, Monsignor Fulton J. Sheen, and Rabbi Joshua Liebman, told millions from their pulpits, through their best-selling books, and, in the case of Bishop Sheen, from the television rostrum that they could be happy and fulfilled if they used religion as their guide. Even such traditional revivalists as the popular preacher Billy Graham, although rooted in Biblical fundamentals, tended to emphasize religion's value for personal problem solving.

But after 1945 new voices began to be heard as well. The experience of the Holocaust, the threat of the atom bomb, the collapse of European world dominance—all made the optimism of the past seem increasingly fatuous and shallow. How innocent or perfectible were human beings after all, if, after five thousand years of civilization, they could destroy millions of human beings without thinking twice and threaten to do so again?

The man who restored the sense of humanity's imperfections and limitations to mainline, urban Protestantism was the theologian Reinhold Niebuhr, himself a political liberal who believed democracy valid, if only by default. Niebuhr reembraced the venerable Christian doctrine of original sin, long ignored by liberal Protestantism. Without accepting literally the account in Genesis of Adam and Eve's fall and expulsion from the Garden of Eden for defying God, he believed that people were inevitably fallible creatures who could never expect to be entirely free of hate, selfishness, greed, envy, and ambition. The "irreducible irrationality of human nature," he exclaimed, must be acknowledged. Only God was without blemish, and humankind's belief in its own perfectability represented the sin of pride. Under the circumstances there was no reason to believe that any actions of humanity would eliminate evil from the world.

It was during the fifties that, for the first time, a self-conscious conservative intelligentsia took shape. Some of these thinkers, notably Russell Kirk, drew on the conservative tradition of Edmund Burke, the eighteenth-century British political philosopher who had defended traditional society against the excesses of the French Revolution. Others, associated with William F. Buckley, Jr., of the new conservative journal *National Review,* drew from Catholic tradition. Buckley had burst on the intellectual scene in 1951 when, just out of Yale, he had attacked the liberal consensus at elite American universities in his book *God and Man at Yale* (1951). In 1955 the witty, acerbic—and rich—young man founded the *National Review* as a forum for conservative opinion.

The Arts

Painting

During the immediate postwar period the art capital of the Western world moved from Paris to New York. Until the postwar era twentieth-century American painting had been either derivative or provincial. Often trained in France, Italy, or Germany, American painters had followed the lead of the French Impressionists or, later, the Cubists. The naturalistic painters of the pre–World War I Ashcan School had produced some interesting work, but none of it was of world class. During the rebellious 1930s *social realism,* intended to make art an auxiliary of revolution, became popular in the United States. Painters in this mode—Ben Shahn, Jack Levine, William Gropper, Isabel Bishop—depicted weather-beaten farmers or workers, careworn mothers, and down-and-outers, subjects victimized by adversity or oppression. They also painted allegories of political and social injustice including race riots and the Sacco-Vanzetti case. Much of it was unsubtle and mediocre.

Then in the years immediately following the war a new group of American painters—Jackson Pollock, Willem de Kooning, Robert Motherwell, Mark Rothko, Franz Kline, Joan Mitchell, and others—broke out of the conventions of the past and created a dazzling new style that would be called by several names: *Action Painting, Abstract Expressionism,* or the *New York School.*

The action painters, like several previous generations of American artists, lived, worked, and caroused mostly in the lofts and studios of New York's Greenwich Village. But they differed from their predecessors in their conception of what a painting was. They were uninterested in representation. A painting was a visual object that should follow the flat planes of the canvas. Unlike most other artifacts of modern life that were planned and regular, it should be spontaneous. Robert Motherwell in 1950 noted that in the view of his colleagues the "process of painting . . . is conceived of as an adventure, without preconceived ideas." "The need" was for "felt experi-

Seated Woman I, a painting by Abstract Expressionist Willem de Kooning. As in this work, de Kooning did not always eliminate all representational elements. (The Bettmann Archive)

ence—intense, immediate, direct, subtle, unified, warm, vivid, rhythmic." Action painters dripped, threw, smeared, and splattered paint on canvas to create splashes of color, lines, and shapes. Their critics claimed that the whole enterprise was a fraud; their paintings could have been done by monkeys. Their friends saw it as a creative revolution in visual art equal to any of the great aesthetic breakthroughs of the past.

Perhaps carried along by America's postwar power and prestige, the New York abstract expressionists swept the Western art world. They had intended to break out of the limited mold of American provincialism and by the mid-fifties had done so. By that time they were acclaimed throughout Europe, once the sole custodian of the Western art tradition. In 1954 the art critic Clement Greenberg, one of the discoverers of the abstract expressionists, noted that at the recent international Biennale exhibition in Venice, de Kooning's exhibition had "put to shame . . . that of every other painter his age or under."

Literature

American literary achievement during the fifties was not as surprising. For a century individual American writers had enjoyed international recognition. Yet during the 1950s American novels, poetry, and plays won unusual worldwide acclaim.

Two of the literary giants of the fifties were the novelists Ernest Hemingway and William Faulkner. Both received Nobel prizes in the decade, but both were already relics of another era. Hemingway, especially, seemed caught in a rut of monosyllabic supermasculinity. On the other hand the poets Robert Frost and Robert Lowell still had "miles to go." Much of their best work would be done during the two decades following the war.

Of the new crop of writers Norman Mailer, a young man from Brooklyn, was among the most interesting. Mailer's first work, *The Naked and the Dead* (1948), was a war novel in the adversary style of 1930s realist fiction with liberal good guys and semifascist bad guys. Mailer would remain a radical of some sort but increasingly, he become the agent for a new cultural sensibility, one permeated by the quest for sensation through sex, drugs, and violence. In his influential essay, "The White Negro" (1957), Mailer praised the "hipster," the permanent outsider of the ghetto who lived dangerously, in the total present, defying the law and seeking ever more powerful "highs." Mailer was addicted to excess. "The White Negro" praised as a courageous existentialist the ghetto hoodlum who beats in the head of a candy store owner.

Another new novelist who made the military his province was James Jones. *From Here to Eternity,* about army life just before Pearl Harbor as seen through the sensibility of an enlisted man, was the sensation of 1951 and sold four million copies.

During the 1950s the young found their inspiration and recognized their voice in Holden Caulfield, the adolescent hero of J. D. Salinger's *Catcher in the Rye* (1951). The work fits the description by Richard Ohmann of "*the* story" of the fifties novel in which "social contradictions [are] . . . easily displaced into images of personal illness." The sixteen-year-old Holden is a sensitive, rebellious young upper middle-class New Yorker who struggles for authenticity in an adult world full of insincere phonies who lie to themselves and their children. The book became a spectacular hit with the literate young because it spoke to them directly in a way they had never before been addressed and partly, no doubt, because libraries, school boards and even state legislatures, disliking its occasional obscenities and sexual words, tried to ban it. *Catcher's* popularity transformed Salinger into a figure of veneration, a reverence tinged with mystery when he shortly withdrew from the public world and became a quasi-hermit in Vermont.

Serious American theater flourished during the 1950s. Eugene O'Neill, although the twenties were his glory days, had a final burst of creativity during the postwar years with *The Iceman Cometh* (1946) and *Long Day's Journey into Night* (1956). New theatrical figures of great talent included Arthur Miller whose plays *Death of a Salesman* (1948), *The Crucible* (1953), and *A View from the Bridge* (1955) dealt with the personal and social penalties of conformity; and Tennessee Williams, a southerner, whose *The Glass Menagerie* (1945), *A Streetcar Named Desire* (1947), and *Cat on a Hot Tin Roof* (1955) depicted the interplay between illusion and reality that seemed especially vivid in the South.

Southerners and Jews, two social groups hitherto on the edges of American cultural life, came into their literary own during the fifties. Faulkner and Williams were both southern writers, but they were joined by a half-dozen others during the postwar era. Three of the most impressive were Flannery O'Connor, a young Georgia woman, whose "gothic" novels and short stories, including *Wise Blood* (1952) and *A Good Man Is Hard to Find* (1955), depict "grotesque" mountebanks, charlatans, rascals, and characters on the edge of dissolution and decay; William Styron whose *Lie Down in Darkness* (1951) concerns the tragic life and death of a southern girl; and Truman Capote whose *Other Voices, Other Rooms* (1948) dealt with a thirteen-year-old boy who finds, in a spooky, decrepit plantation house with its eccentric inhabitants, his real, although dismaying, self.

Writers who revealed in their work the special irony, skepticism, sense of paradox, and taste for gallows humor that grew out of the American Jewish experience—Bernard Malamud, Philip Roth, and Saul Bellow—also made their mark in this period. Malamud wrote about a generation of Jews still close to their Eastern European roots. *The Assistant* (1957) tells of an Italian clerk employed by a poor Jewish grocer who, when his boss dies, takes on the sorrows and burdens of his employer's life. *A New Life* (1961) is about a Jewish professor from New York in the unfamiliar environment of a far western university. Roth burst on the scene in 1959 with *Goodbye Columbus,* a collection of short works, dealing with the tensions and compromises of Jewish assimilation into prosperous postwar America. The most universalistic of the new Jewish writers was Saul Bellow, a Montreal-born Chicagoan, whose characters in *Seize the Day* (1956) and *Henderson the Rain King* (1959), whatever their ostensible ethnicity, partake of the Jewish experience of survival in the face of adversity.

There were also signs during the decade of a major African-American literary awakening in the work of Ralph Ellison, whose novel *The Invisible Man* (1952) powerfully evokes the social and psychological marginality experienced by black Americans. Another African-American novelist, whose fame would not peak until the following decade, was James Baldwin. Baldwin's *Go Tell it on the Mountain* (1953) dealt with the black migration from the South to the urban ghettos of the North.

The Beats

The *Beat generation* was the fifties' boldest departure from the existing literary tradition. The Beats were social and intellectual rebels strongly influenced, simultaneously, by the underground world of African-American musicians and by the mysticism of Eastern Buddhism. A number were homosexuals who, in the repressive fifties world, found themselves inevitably cast in the role of cultural outsider. Beats despised the "square" suburban, striving, materialist America that had emerged after the war and glorified spontaneity, free instinctual expression, and a relaxed, nonassertive approach to life. Allen Ginsberg, the outstanding Beat bard, would later say that the movement he helped to lead meant "the return to nature and the revolt against the machine."

The first Beats were young men attending Columbia University in New York or living in its environs and included Ginsberg, Jack Kerouac, Neal Cassady, and John Clellon Holmes. They soon linked up with a parallel circle of avant-garde writers in the San Francisco Bay Area. On the West Coast the new literary mood was nurtured by Kenneth Rexroth, a radical critic left over from the thirties, and a young poet, Lawrence Ferlinghetti, whose North Beach bookstore, City Lights, became a sponsor and publisher of the new literary movement.

The Beat literary movement burst onto the reading public's consciousness in 1957 with the publication of Kerouac's *On the Road,* a sprawling picaresque novel of two young men crisscrossing the country by car, experiencing the sounds, tastes, looks, and feels of fifties America like primitives from an alien culture. Although attacked as "typing, not writing," the book sold a half-million copies and put the Beat movement on the map. Ginsberg's long poem "Howl" was a powerful attack on mainstream American society, which he referred to as "Moloch" (after the fearsome god of the ancient Phoencians to whom children were sacrificed), whose "mind is pure machinery! . . . whose blood is running money! . . . whose fingers are ten armies!" Although poetry is seldom as popular as prose, "Howl" struck a resounding chord among the educated restless young and helped shift the country's cultural consciousness.

The Beats soon become role models for a portion of the rebellious young. Defiant young "Beatniks" flocked to low-rent neighborhoods in a few of the country's most cosmopolitan cities, where they lived in sparsely furnished apartments and, like other bohemians before them, challenged the values and sexual taboos of their middle-class parents. Beatniks adopted a distinctive dress style. The men wore sloppy work clothes and sneakers or sandals; the women wore black leotards, drooping peasant skirts, no lipstick, and pony tails. Both sexes smoked marijuana, practiced free love and played at being "creative," with words, or paint, or guitars.

Rock and Roll

The typical beatnik was a young person with artistic yearnings and some higher education, but the mass of adolescents and young adults found other ways to express their rebelliousness. From the beginning of this century the young have often adopted the music of outsiders, of racial minorities, and of the underclass as a way to distance themselves from their parents and their values. Before World War I ragtime played this role. During the twenties it was New Orleans style jazz. In the immediate postwar period folk music, originally cultivated by the political left to express its solidarity with "the people," attracted some of the more-literate young. So did "bebop," the new postwar "cool" or "progressive" jazz style of Dizzie Gillespie, Charlie Parker, Miles Davis, and other sophisticated black musicians. But the real music of post–World War II adolescents was *rock and roll.*

Rock music was woven of many strands. It borrowed from black music—"gospel" and "rhythm and blues." It also incorporated "country," the style of the white, rural South and Southwest. It contained elements of jazz. Rock's original base was the black urban ghettos, but it spread to the larger white community when, in 1951, Alan Freed, a Cleveland disc jockey, began to play rhythm and blues over his station. In 1954 Freed came to WINS in New York where he provided the new music with a greatly expanded showcase.

Rock remained ghetto-rooted until toned-down and prettified. Its first commercially successful practitioner was probably Bill Haley, a white disc jockey from Philadelphia. Haley's hit record of 1954, "Rock Around the Clock," derived from black musician Ike Turner's "Shake, Rattle, and Roll," brought all the strands together and gave a name to the new music. Other musicians—Buddy Holly, the Everly Brothers, "Little" Richard Penniman—quickly came out with their versions of rock and furthered the evolutionary process. Although rock rolled through the cultural world on its own merits, the process was helped immeasurably by record company promotion, the new 45 rpm record, and media showcases like the television program "American Bandstand."

The most famous, or infamous, of the early rock stars was Elvis Presley, a slender young white Mississippian with a smooth black pompadour and sideburns, "bedroom eyes," and pouting lips. Presley had merged the rhythm and blues style of black musicians with white country music and added a large dash of raw sexuality. His suggestive glissandos, heavy rhythmic beat, and swiveling hips excited his audience of young people on the edge of adulthood. (See the photograph opening this chapter.) Older Americans often hated Presley. He seemed a culturally subversive influence. At one point a Jacksonville, Florida, judge threatened to arrest him for impairing the morals of minors. The minors themselves did not seem to mind having their morals impaired; the more their parents objected the better they liked him.

The Commercial Media

Square America had its own popular music and it was not unworthy. The era of "swing" and the big bands—Benny Goodman, Tommy Dorsey, Count Basie, and Glenn Miller—was over, but the musical stage still flourished. In 1943 the musical *Oklahoma,* with scintillating songs by Richard Rogers and Oscar Hammerstein and sophisticated choreography, opened on Broadway to wide acclaim. In 1949 the same musical team created *South Pacific,* with a libretto based on the war stories of James Michener, and appealing melodies such as "Some Enchanted Evening" and "Bali Ha'i."

The nation's chief theatrical showcase was still Broadway in New York, although people elsewhere attended road-company productions of hit Broadway shows, and experimental and repertory companies performed before audiences in other large cities. Most Americans during the fifties, however, satisfied their taste for spectacle and drama through film or television.

The Movies

The years between 1920 and the end of World War II were Hollywood's golden age. This was the era when the major studios—MGM, Twentieth Century Fox, RKO, Warner Brothers, and Paramount—with their vast soundstages and glittering rosters of box-office stars turned out hundreds of movies a year to an immense weekly audience eager for romantic comedies, splashy musicals, cowboy "horse operas," and sentimental dramas. They also produced an occasion "message" film such as the antiwar *All Quiet on the Western Front,* the prison-reform–oriented *I Am a Fugitive from a Chain Gang,* and the sympathetic treatment of the Okie migration to California, *The Grapes of Wrath* .

The large companies made enormous profits not only through movie production, but also because they owned national theater chains that "block-booked" a given studio's whole film output. In 1948 the federal courts declared that the practice violated the antitrust laws and forced the studios to sell off their theater outlets. This quickly ended the studio system. The "majors" soon cut back drastically on their own production and offered their facilities to independent producers who put together "packages" (actors, directors, writers, and camera operators) for a given production.

The change in the industry's structure altered the quality of the product. The independents abandoned the narrow formula movies of the studios and, by and large, produced better, more-original films and fewer "B" efforts. Among the outstanding movies of the fifties were *The African Queen, High Noon, From Here to Eternity, Baby Doll, Shane, Sunset Boulevard, The Wild One, Rebel without a Cause,* and *Some Like It Hot.* But the change in the quality of movies owed even more to the arrival on the scene of a new medium, television, that absorbed the audience for visual potboilers.

The TV Revolution

Television—TV—had been little more than a toy before the war, although by 1939 most of the basic technology had been developed. The war itself preempted electronics production facilities and delayed manufacture of home TV sets. Not until 1946 did the first black-and-white units roll off the assembly lines.

The industry was slow to gain momentum. Television receivers at first were expensive and had small screens; broadcast technique was primitive. It was not possible, for example, to send signals beyond line-of-sight distance, so each station could transmit only to a local audience. In the absence of electronic tape, performances had to be live. And at first there was little to watch.

In May 1947 "Kraft Television Theater" began to broadcast the first live television dramas. Regularly sponsored TV news broadcasting began in the fall of 1947 with the urbane John Cameron Swayze on NBC and Douglas Edwards on CBS as "anchors." But

Television revolutionized American life. These sets, fresh from the assembly line, are being checked. (AP/Wide World Photos)

still the fare was rather thin and the audience limited. New York and Los Angeles were well provided with stations, seven in each, but even some rather large cities—Austin, Texas; Portland, Oregon; and Little Rock, Arkansas—had none as late as 1952.

By the early fifties, however, the networks had launched some of their top shows, including Milton Berle's "Texaco Star Theater" and Ed Sullivan's "Toast of the Town." Also widely popular was the sitcom "I Love Lucy" featuring Lucille Ball and her husband, Desi Arnez, and the ninety-minute-long variety program "Your Show of Shows," with the hilarious Sid Caesar and Imogene Coca.

Even before the first coast-to-coast hookup in 1951, television had begun to alter people's lives. The early owners of sets had been minor celebrities on their block and had to fend off neighbors trying to invite themselves in to see the latest marvel. By 1952 almost twenty million American homes had TV sets, about half the total number of homes. These sets often occupied the place of honor in the family living room, and meals, leisure, bedtimes, and even romance were all modified or postponed to accommodate it. Family closeness and interaction suffered, or at least underwent a major change. No family institution could stand up to the attractions of "the tube." To guarantee that family mealtimes would not interfere with favorite programs, Swanson and other food processors developed the frozen TV dinner that could be heated in the oven and eaten in front of the set.

The other media suffered from television's popularity. During the 1930s publishers had preserved their markets during a time of economic slump by developing new printing and packaging techniques. The Depression years had seen the rise of the photo magazines *Life, Look,* and their imitators. During this period book publishers had discovered how to print book pages on the high-speed presses designed for magazines and how to fasten pages firmly to paper covers with glue. These books, generally reprints of hardcover works, could be marketed from train station and drugstore racks and sold for as little as a quarter. This paperback revolution saved many publishers from bankruptcy.

After World War II the publishing industry faced new challenges. Paperback book sales expanded. But taken together the sales of books, magazines, and newspapers, forced to compete with the riveting moving images on the home screen, failed to keep up with the rising population and improving national educational levels.

The movies, already in disarray over the courts' theater divestment ruling, suffered another blow from television. Film attendance dropped sharply. Why bother to pay the money and expend the effort to get to the local movie house when you could sit in the comfort of your living room and see the "I Love Lucy" show for nothing? The movie producers countered the threat with wide-screen Cinerama and then CinemaScope, visual techniques that television could not imitate. They also reached out to a more sophisticated audience than TV, a "family" medium that had to avoid offending parents of young children. Bit by bit the old production code self-censorship forbidding nudity, sexual acts, blasphemy, and obscenity in films began to be relaxed. In 1961 the Supreme Court ruled that film was entitled to First Amendment protection as free speech and states could not impose movie licensing requirements. Not until 1968 did the present system of ratings, from G (family fare, suited to even young children), to X (frank pornography), come into effect. Yet by the end of the fifties films produced in America had attained a level of maturity and honesty at times not much below the legitimate stage.

TV and Politics

Television also affected the political process. The first national conventions to be televised were those of 1948. Both were held in Philadelphia because that city was now connected by cable to New York, Washington, and other eastern and midwestern cities, and millions would be able to see the proceedings. The campaign itself suggested that TV was not, or not yet, a potent political force. Dewey took to the airwaves; Truman, in part to save money, whistle-stopped from the back of trains. And, as we saw, Truman won.

In 1952, however, television made a difference. This time the networks were able to find sponsors for the proceedings. Westinghouse bought the whole convention coverage package on NBC, and millions of older Americans probably remember Westinghouse announcer Betty Furness opening and closing refrigerator doors better than they do the convention itself.

Whether television was responsible or not, Eisenhower's victory in 1952 made the new medium a vital, even governing element, in the political equation. Thereafter, critics would charge, American politics became a contest of competing spectacles and images rather than of competing ideas. The critics exaggerated the importance of issues in pretelevision elections, but there can be no doubt that at times following 1952 the public seemed to judge candidates more for their telegenic qualities than for their intelligence.

There was another side of the coin, however. At times TV could be a remarkable dissector of character and personality, and a brilliant illuminator of events. In 1954 its power to deflate demagogues was demonstrated by the Army-McCarthy hearings (discussed later in this chapter). In later years, too, it would, more than once, serve the republic's citizens well.

The Eisenhower Administration

The party and the people who came to office in January 1953 were not experienced in the art of government. For twenty years the Republicans had been on the outside looking in, playing the relatively easy role of naysayer and critic. Republicanism had come to mean opposition to an active, interventionist federal government, "fiscal responsibility" (balanced federal budgets), and sympathy for the needs of business and the successful middle class. These positions could be maintained in all their purity when the Democrats occupied the White House. It would not be so easy when they, the Republicans themselves, controlled the executive branch. Making matters all the more difficult from 1954 on, the Democrats would control both houses of Congress, with power to veto any major changes their opponents proposed.

Recent scholars, dismayed by the turmoil of the 1960s and by the costly entanglement in Vietnam, have praised the Eisenhower administration effusively. Ike, they say, was personally warm, reassuring, and effective. He accomplished what had to be done, avoiding war, preserving the essentials of the welfare state, and quietly disposing of McCarthy. His was a "hidden-hand presidency," says Princeton political scientist Fred Greenstein. Even Ike's public inarticulateness now seems a virtue to some. His broken syntax and obscurity when he talked to reporters, they say, avoided unnecessary confrontations and papered over difficulties.

In truth Eisenhower presided over the sort of administration that suited the American people in the 1950s. His cabinet, except for Labor Secretary Martin Durkin, a union leader who soon resigned, was drawn from the ranks of business. Critics said it consisted of "eight millionaires and a plumber." Inexperienced in the pieties of democratic politics, they often seemed to confuse the interests of business with those of the American people at large. Charles E. Wilson, the former president of General Motors, aroused a populist storm, even before he was confirmed as secretary of defense when he declared, "What was good for our country was good for General Motors and vice versa." Yet it is probably true that not since the 1920s were Americans as willing to accept the values of the business community as during the 1950s.

For good or ill, the president relied more on his cabinet and other subordinates than most of his predecessors. Ike as president used the same staff system he had employed in the army. He seldom made decisions without reports on the issues from bureaucrats and high officials. These were coordinated by the president's chief aide, former New Hampshire Governor Sherman Adams. Adams also screened the president's many visitors and was often called "Sherm the Firm" or the "Abominable No-Man." But the overall outcome seemed to be indecision. According to participants, cabinet discussions meandered and wandered from the point to a maddening degree; no conclusions ever seemed to be reached.

Legislative Accomplishments

Still many things were accomplished, although liberals did not always like the results. The administration eliminated several outmoded programs that had lasted since New Deal days, including the Reconstruction Finance Corporation, and reduced the number of federal employees by 200,000 during its first term. Adopting the policies of Secretary of Agriculture Ezra Taft Benson, it tried, although unsuccessfully, to whittle down the government's commitment to farm price supports. It cut the federal government's involvement in electric power production and sought to restore a business presence to the Tennessee Valley Authority through a contract with the Dixon-Yates syndicate. This scheme failed when the Democrats uncovered a conflict of interest violation in the key contract negotiation.

Despite the administration's conservative orientation it sponsored some liberal measures. Eisenhower often got along better with the Democratic leadership in Congress than with the right wing of his own party, perhaps in part because like himself, House Speaker Sam Rayburn and Senate Majority Leader (after 1954) Lyndon Johnson, were Texans. With their help he was able to get enacted laws broadening social security coverage to an additional 7.5 million people and improving its benefits, establishing a new Cabinet-level department—Health, Education and Welfare (HEW)—to administer federal welfare and education programs, creating a modest federal housing program for people displaced by urban renewal or slum clearance, and establishing a federal system of grants to states to improve educational facilities. The year after the Soviet Union's successful launching of *Sputnik* in 1957, Congress established the administration-sponsored National Aeronautics and Space Administration (NASA) to coordinate U.S. space efforts and enacted the National Defense Education Act to encourage science and foreign-language training in the nations' schools and colleges.

The Eisenhower era legislation with the most far-reaching effects was the Highway Act of 1956. This bill, strongly supported by the trucking firms, the automobile companies, and the construction industry, authorized the outlay of $32 billion for a forty-one-thousand-mile system of four-lane, limited-access interstate roads to connect every big city in the nation. The program was to be financed by new gasoline taxes the proceeds of which would be placed in a trust fund and reserved for road construction and repair.

The new interstate highway system undoubtedly benefited the nation. It improved highway safety, lowered transportation costs, and stimulated the automobile, trucking, motel, and tourist industries. But it also had its debit side. Railroad passenger traffic plummeted, making Americans increasingly dependent on the private car. Trucks also hurt rail freight revenues. By the mid-1960s the nation's railroad companies were in serious financial straits and passenger service was being drastically curtailed. The new highway system also helped hollow out the city centers. They encouraged suburban development and middle-class flight. By making enormous new shopping centers accessible, the new roads and superhighways cut into downtown business. Before long the business cores of many American cities were a blight of boarded-up stores and empty offices; the customers and the clients had all departed for the outlying suburban shopping malls.

The End of McCarthy

Eisenhower's 1952 victory brought McCarthyism (see the previous chapter) down. But not immediately.

Everyone expected McCarthy to soften his attacks on subversives and "security risks" in government now that his own party was in power. But the senator thrived on publicity and, unwilling to slip back into the shadows, refused to slow his pace.

During the first Eisenhower Congress McCarthy attacked the administration's list of new appointees as riddled with people of suspect loyalty. He and ultraconservative Senate Republicans tried to prevent the appointment of Charles Bohlen as ambassador to the Soviet Union, accusing that long-term public servant of possible disloyalty. When Secretary of State John Foster Dulles came to Bohlen's defense, McCarthy called him a liar and demanded that he testify before the Senate under oath. In the end Bohlen was confirmed, but the clash so bruised the administration that it was reluctant to challenge the senator again.

McCarthy was soon on the rampage once more. His next target was the Voice of America, a federal agency which broadcast news of American positions on issues and events to listeners around the world. In late November 1953 McCarthy attacked the record of the Republican administration in purging Communists from government. It was "infinitely" better than the Democrats', he stated, but it was far from perfect. He also went out of his way to criticize the administration's support of financial aid to Britain when that country continued to trade with our avowed enemy, the People's Republic of China.

Eisenhower abhorred McCarthy. He had never forgiven the Wisconsin senator for his attacks on the president's old army boss George Marshall, and he was infuriated by his criticism of the administration's foreign policy and its record on security risks. But Ike had little taste for slinging mud with the Senator. He also feared the man. By this time McCarthy had thoroughly intimidated virtually everyone in public life. Rather than taking him on directly, the president bided his time waiting for McCarthy's own excesses to bring him down.

These were not long in coming. In early 1954 the senator tangled with the army over its alleged laxity in ferreting out disloyalty. In response the army claimed that McCarthy and his aide Roy Cohn had sought special favors for G. David Schine, a former McCarthy assistant who had recently been drafted. Congress decided to investigate, and authorized hearings before McCarthy's own subcommittee, with the senator replaced temporarily as chairman by Senator Karl Mundt of South Dakota.

The televised Army-McCarthy hearings began in the Senate Caucus Room on April 22, 1954. Eight weeks later McCarthy's shadow over the nation's life had lifted.

McCarthy's nominal adversary was Army Secretary Robert Stevens and the army brass. But his real opponent—and nemesis—was Joseph Welch, the army's puckish, civilian counsel, a shrewd Boston lawyer with a carefully cultivated low-key style. The proceedings were telecast and millions of American tuned in to see the hearings or saw excerpts on the evening news.

The Wisconsin senator came across as a Hollywood villian. A physically unattractive man, his head was too large for his body, his features were coarse, and under the glaring television lights, he could not disguise his permanent five o'clock shadow. He was incapable of obeying the traditional rules of parliamentary order and ordinary civility. He bullied witnesses, interrupted the proceedings with invalid points of order, and frequently contradicted himself without seeming to care. Welch at first bided his time, getting the measure of the man, a type not familiar to Boston's elite. Then gradually he began to reveal how McCarthy had subverted government officials in his pursuit of dirt and how he had falsified evidence regarding the army's relations with Schine.

The hearings concluded with a 7400-page report that blamed both McCarthy and the army. But it soon became clear that the senator had been mortally wounded. McCarthy's approval rating in the polls had dropped 22 percent by August. Even conservative Republicans now concluded that he had outlived his political usefulness.

Even before the hearings ended, Republican Senator Ralph Flanders of Vermont, had introduced a resolution to censure McCarthy on the grounds that his behavior was "contrary to senatorial traditions and tend[ed] to bring the Senate into disrepute." After the hearings the resolution was debated fully. The vote, taken on December 2, condemned McCarthy. His spell was broken. Eisenhower greeted his Cabinet soon after with the joke: "McCarthyism is now McCarthywasm."

And in fact the senator's reign was over. He continued to have followers and he continued to make charges. But the media ceased to take him seriously and often failed to report his latest claims. Worst of all his Senate colleagues now chose to ignore him, and increasingly he became a lonely, isolated man. He died in May 1957 of liver disease brought on by heavy drinking.

The anti-Communist crusade McCarthy had profited from and fostered was by no means over. The far-right John Birch Society, founded by a Boston candy manufacturer in 1959, continued to beat the Communist conspiracy drums and to accuse people of secret subversion. The Birch Society, with chapters in scores of cities, attacked President Eisenhower for communist leanings and mounted a campaign to impeach Chief Justice Earl Warren. A number of organizations, including Billy James Hargis's Christian Crusade and Fred Schwarz's Christian Anti-Communism Crusade, combined religious fundamentalism with a passionate zeal for detecting and rooting out Communist influence in American life. And yet with McCarthy himself gone, the frenzy receded and Americans were able to bring the internal Communist threat into reasonable perspective.

The 1956 Election

Despite President Eisenhower's personal popularity, the Republicans remained the minority party. In 1954 the Democrats recaptured control of both houses of Congress. Nineteen fifty-six, however, promised to be better for the GOP because Ike would head the ticket again. But then in September 1955 the president suffered a

The Eisenhowers (right) and the Nixons at the 1956 Republican National Convention.
(UPI/Bettmann Newsphotos)

heart attack while on vacation in Denver. He sprang back quickly and by early 1956 had resumed his full duties. In March he announced that he would accept renomination. Then in June he suffered another medical mishap and had to be operated on for an intestinal obstruction. He recovered quickly from this affliction too and was renominated, with Nixon again, at the Republican National Convention in San Francisco.

The Democrats turned a second time to Adlai Stevenson, pairing him with Senator Estes Kefauver of Tennessee. Stevenson had thrown the choice of vice presidential candidate to the convention itself, and in the contest Kefauver narrowly defeated the young senator from Massachusetts, John F. Kennedy.

The campaign was uninspiring. Stevenson seemed less sparkling than the first time. He tried to capitalize on fears of the president's mortality and on Ike's penchant for "golfing and goofing." But no matter how ominous Ike's medical record, he now seemed in radiant good health and most Americans did not believe the country had suffered from his inattention. In the end, it was an Eisenhower-Nixon landslide, with the Republican candidates winning 457 electoral votes to 73 and a popular vote majority of 35.6 million to 26 million. But again it was a personal not a party victory. Stevenson's biographer has written that Ike's triumph "expressed the dominant mood of the country and . . . the warm affection he personally inspired." The Democrats actually increased their majorities in both houses of Congress.

The Civil Rights Movement

No group in America benefited as little from social change in the immediate postwar era as African-Americans. By the Eisenhower years there had been some progress on the racial front. During the Truman administration segregation in the armed forces had ended. In 1947 the brave move of Brooklyn Dodgers' manager Branch Rickey to hire Jackie Robinson as second baseman had finally broken the disgraceful Jim Crow barrier in the all-American pastime. There had been, moreover, a slow evolution of antiracist ideas among liberal and better-educated white people influenced by the sociological and anthropological studies of Gunnar Myrdal (*The American Dilemma*) and Melville Herskovits (*Patterns of Negro Segregation*). Yet through the mid-1950s the racial regime that had taken shape after Reconstruction remained in place almost everywhere.

In the North there was no legal basis for segregation or race discrimination. African-Americans could run for office and exercise their right to vote. Government services were, by and large, fairly apportioned. Yet private schools, hotels, employers, landlords, realtors, and restauranteurs excluded blacks or discriminated against them through unspoken agreement. Inevitably bigotry adversely affected the housing, income, education, and health of black people in the northern cities.

The situation in the South was far worse. There segregation by Jim Crow law was still alive and thriving. In almost every aspect of daily life state or local law prescribed separate facilities for black and white citizens. African-American and white children went to separate schools from kindergarten through university graduate and professional programs. Blacks were kept separate from whites on buses, streetcars, trains, and in terminal waiting rooms. African-Americans were not allowed to eat in most restaurants and were excluded from hotels as well as many parks and swimming pools. Churches were either black or white, almost never both. There had been legal challenges to the local and state segregation laws under the "equal protection of the laws" provision of the Fourteenth Amendment of the Constitution, but most of these had been denied. In the landmark case of *Plessy* v. *Ferguson* (1896) the Supreme Court had declared that equal protection could be satisfied if the governments in question guaranteed that the separate facilities were kept roughly equal in quality. But in fact little was done to enforce even this weak protection until well past World War II. Almost everywhere, as the fifties began, the black schools, swimming pools, waiting rooms, and bus facilities were shockingly inferior to their white equivalents.

There was also the crucial issue of voting rights. No one could deny that the Fifteenth Amendment made exclusion from the ballot because of race illegal. Yet in most places in the South African-Americans were kept from voting by rigged registration rules, intimidation, and a flock of subterfuges. The net result of Jim Crow and the absence of basic civil rights was a de facto caste system in the South that made a mockery of American democracy.

The Jim Crow system in the South, begun in the late nineteenth century, meant discrimination and humiliation for African-Americans. (Library of Congress)

The Attack on Jim Crow

During the Eisenhower years came the major breakthroughs that in a decade, would wipe out the Jim Crow system and elevate African-Americans to full citizenship if not full economic and social equality. The change was launched by the National Association for the Advancement of Colored People (NAACP), the African-American defense organization formed before World War I.

The attack began at the educational summit. During the late 1940s the NAACP instituted a series of suits against southern governments for excluding black students from all-white state university graduate and professional programs. The federal courts agreed that the alternatives offered African-American applicants did not meet even the semblance of equality and thus the students could not be excluded.

But these judicial victories only affected a tiny portion of Jim Crow. Then in 1951 Thurgood Marshall, attorney for the NAACP, commenced suit against the segregated public school system of Topeka, Kansas, a northern community with southern principles. Drawing on the work of sociologists and psychologists, Marshall and the other NAACP lawyers charged that separate facilities imposed a damaging psychological and social stigma on African-American children and hence were inherently unequal. On May 17, 1954, in an unanimous decision that ranks with *Marbury* v. *Madison* and *Dred Scott* v. *Sandford* as historic events, the Court accepted this position in *Brown* v. *Board of Education of Topeka*. In "the field of public education," declared Chief Justice Earl Warren, "the doctrine of 'separate but equal' has no place." (See Reading 11.) Soon after this, the Supreme Court directed lower federal courts to require admission of black students to formerly white schools "with all deliberate speed."

The *Brown* decision began the painful destruction of Jim Crow. But it was one thing for the federal courts to rule; it was another to get the relevant authorities to comply. School desegregation, in part or in whole, came quickly in the upper South and neighboring areas, especially Oklahoma, Kentucky, West Virginia, Maryland, Delaware, and Washington, D.C. But in the deep South many officials, with the powerful support of the Ku Klux Klan and a new group, the White Citizens' Councils, vowed to resist.

The next five years were full of fierce contention between African-Americans and their supporters and the conservative intransigents and outright bigots who cried "never" to desegregation. When a twenty-six-year-old African-American woman, Autherine Lucy, attempted to enroll in the University of Alabama in 1956, the Regents resisted, and she was attacked by shouting, stone-throwing mobs. In Clinton, Tennessee, a thousand whites, egged on by John Kasper, a racist zealot from Washington, D.C., rioted when the courts ordered twelve black students admitted to the local high school. The mob overwhelmed the town's small police force and was stopped only when state troopers and National Guardsmen arrived.

In 1957 the federal government itself had to intervene in Little Rock, Arkansas, to enforce the *Brown* decision. Eisenhower had spent most of his professional life in a segregated army and, like many conservatives, believed that you could not force people to be virtuous. "You cannot change the hearts of people by law," he said. Moreover he was skeptical of the *Brown* decision and later announced in private that his most foolish decision had been to appoint Earl Warren to the Supreme Court. But the president also would not allow federal law to be flouted, and at Little Rock when Governor Orval Faubus of Arkansas called up the state National Guard to prevent the admission of African-American students to all-white Central High, Eisenhower ordered in a portion of the 101st Airborne Division to escort the children through the mob of jeering whites who were screaming "Two, four, six, eight, we ain't gone to integrate." The troops' presence infuriated the white supremacists, but they yielded to fixed bayonets. In a few weeks passions had cooled and the escorts ceased. Central High had been desegregated and the law of the land upheld.

There were few other Little Rocks. Most communities acquiesced in the *Brown* decision at least to the point of admitting a token number of African-American students. Many northern cities were for a time spared the problems of integrating the schools by a housing pattern that was itself segregated. Black children could be excluded from white schools simply because they lived in different school districts. Where this process failed to work, white parents sometimes withdrew their children from the public schools entirely and paid tuition to enroll them in private schools. More and more big city schools became all black. However accomplished, school segregation survived as a practical fact. As of the 1962–63 school year less than one-half of one percent of African-American school children in the deep South were attending integrated schools. Yet an immensely important principle had been established: segregation was unconstitutional.

READING 11

The Supreme Court Rules on Public School Segregation

No decision of the United States Supreme Court has had such momentous social consequences as Brown v. Board of Education of Topeka, *delivered on May 17, 1954. The unanimous decision, written by Chief Justice Warren, reversed the ruling of the Court in* Plessy v. Ferguson *(1896) that separate facilities in public accommodations for whites and blacks did not violate the Fourteenth Amendment's equal protection clause as long as they were equal facilities.* Plessy *had allowed fifty years of Jim Crow in the South and had stigmatized millions of African-Americans with the badge of inferiority. Now that the Supreme Court in* Brown *had finally invalidated the separate-but-equal doctrine in the public school systems, the rest of Jim Crow clearly was threatened. In a single brief ruling the Warren Court had broken the racial logjam and launched a social revolution in the South.*

These cases come to us from the States of Kansas, South Carolina, Virginia, and Delaware. They are premised on different facts and different local conditions, but a common legal question justifies their consideration together in this consolidated opinion.

In each of the cases, minors of the Negro race, through their legal representatives, seek the aid of the courts in obtaining admission to the public schools of their community on a nonsegregated basis. In each instance, they have been denied admission to schools attended by white children under laws requiring or permitting segregation according to race. This segregation was alleged to deprive the plaintiffs of the equal protection of the laws under the Fourteenth Amendment. In each of the cases other than the Delaware case, a three-judge federal district court denied relief to the plaintiffs on the so-called "separate but equal" doctrine announced by this Court in Plessy v. Ferguson, 163 U. S. 537. Under that doctrine, equality of treatment is accorded when the races are provided substantially equal facilities, even though these facilities be separate. In the Delaware case, the Supreme Court of Delaware adhered to that doctrine, but ordered that the plaintiffs be admitted to the white schools because of their superiority to the Negro schools.

The plaintiffs contend that segregated public schools are not "equal" and cannot be made "equal," and that hence they are deprived of the equal protection of the laws. Because of the obvious importance of the question presented, the Court took jurisdiction. Argument was heard in the 1952 Term, and reargument was heard this Term on certain questions propounded by the Court.

Reargument was largely devoted to the circumstances surrounding the adoption of the Fourteenth Amendment in 1868. It covered exhaustively consideration of the Amendment in Congress, ratification by the states, then existing practices in racial segregation, and the views of proponents and opponents of the Amendment. This discussion and our own investigation convince us that, although these sources cast some light, is not enough to resolve the problem with which we are faced. At best, they are inconclusive. The most avid proponents of the post-War Amendments undoubtedly intended them to remove all legal distinctions among "all persons born or naturalized in the United States." Their opponents, just as certainly, were antagonistic to both the letter and the spirit of the Amendments and wished them to have the most limited effect. What others in Congress and the state legislatures had in mind cannot be determined with any degree of certainty.

An additional reason for the inconclusive nature of the Amendment's history, with respect to segregated schools, is the status of public education at that time. In the South, the movement toward free common schools, supported by general taxation, had not yet taken hold. Education of white children was largely in the hands of private groups. Education of Negroes was almost nonexistent, and practically all of the race were illiterate. In fact, any education of Negroes was forbidden by law in some states. Today, in contrast, many Negroes have achieved outstanding success in the arts and sciences as well as in the business and professional world. It is true that public education had already advanced further in the North, but the effect of the Amendment on Northern States was generally ignored in the congressional debates. Even in the North, the conditions of public education did not approximate those existing today. The curriculum was usually rudimentary; ungraded schools were common in rural areas; the school term was but three months a year in many states; and compulsory school attendance was virtually unknown. As a consequence, it is not surprising that there should be so little in the history of the Fourteenth Amendment relating to its intended effect on public education.

In the first cases in this Court construing the Fourteenth Amendment, decided shortly after its adoption, the Court interpreted it as proscribing all state-imposed discriminations against the Negro race. The doctrine of "separate but equal" did not make its appearance in this Court until 1896 in the case of Plessy v. Ferguson, supra, involving not education but transportation. American courts have since labored with the doctrine for over half a century. In this court, there have been six cases involving the "separate but equal" doctrine in the field of public education.

In approaching this problem, we cannot turn the clock back to 1868 when the Amendment was adopted, or even to 1896 when Plessy v. Ferguson was written. We must consider public education in the light of its full development and its present place in American life throughout the Nation.

Only in this way can it be determined if segregation in public schools deprives these plaintiffs of the equal protection of the laws.

Today, education is perhaps the most important function of state and local governments. Compulsory school attendance laws and the great expenditures for education both demonstrate our democratic society. It is required in the performance of our most basic public responsibilities, even service in the armed forces. It is the very foundation of good citizenship. Today it is a principal instrument in awakening the child to cultural values, in preparing him for later professional training, and in helping him to adjust normally to his environment. In these days, it is doubtful that any child may reasonably be expected to succeed in life if he is denied the opportunity of an education. Such an opportunity, where the state has undertaken to provide it, is a right which must be made available to all on equal terms.

We come then to the question presented: Does segregation of children in public schools solely on the basis of race, even though the physical facilities and other "tangible" factors may be equal, deprive the children of the minority group of equal educational opportunities? We believe that it does. . . .

To separate them from others of similar age and qualifications solely because of their race generates a feeling of inferiority as to their status in the community that may affect their hearts and minds in a way unlikely ever to be undone. The effect of this separation on their educational opportunities was well stated by a finding in the Kansas case by a court which nevertheless felt compelled to rule against the Negro plaintiffs:

> Segregation of white and colored children in public schools has a detrimental effect upon the colored children. The impact is greater when it has the sanction of the law; for the policy of separating the races is usually interpreted as denoting the inferiority of the Negro group. A sense of inferiority affects the motivation of a child to learn. Segregation with the sanction of law, therefore, has a tendency to retard the educational and mental development of Negro children and to deprive them of some of the benefits they would receive in a racially integrated school system.

Whatever may have been the extent of psychological knowledge at the time of Plessy v. Ferguson, this finding is amply supported by modern authority. Any language in Plessy v. Ferguson contrary to this finding is rejected.

We conclude that in the field of public education the doctrine of "separate but equal" has no place. Separate educational facilities are inherently unequal. Therefore, we hold that the plaintiffs and others similarly situated for whom the actions have been brought are, by reason of the segregation complained of, deprived of the equal protection of the laws guaranteed by the Fourteenth Amendment. This disposition makes unnecessary any discussion whether such segregation also violates the Due Process Clause of the Fourteenth Amendment. . . .

Source: Brown v. Board of Education of Topeka, 347 U.S. 483 (1954).

Martin Luther King, Jr.

Obviously an enormous battle still remained before the anti–Jim Crow decisions of the courts and federal agencies could meaningfully affect the daily lives of African-American southerners. The courts would have to deal with each instance of Jim Crow legislation and then local people would have to challenge racist diehards who sought to keep the practice even after the law was gone. And there still remained the critical problem of voting rights, and beyond that the fundamental issues of job discrimination and black working-class poverty. The federal government, clearly, could help, but it also could not be counted on to send troops to ferret out every violation of federal law and enforce every court order. Black southerners would have to force the issue themselves. The task required new leadership and new tactics, and both suddenly appeared in Montgomery, Alabama, in late 1955.

Montgomery, the capital of Alabama and "Cradle of the Confederacy," was a thoroughly segregated city. Jim Crow was everywhere, but it was encountered in its most humiliating form on the local bus line where, as in other southern cities, African-American passengers were expected to sit at the back of the vehicle and surrender their seats to white passengers whenever the "whites only" section was fully occupied. On December 1, 1955, Rosa Parks, a middle-aged black seamstress returning from a hard day's work in a downtown Montgomery department store, refused to give up her seat to a white passenger who had just gotten on. Mrs. Parks was arrested and fined ten dollars for violating a Montgomery ordinance.

Montgomery African-American leaders, many of them clergymen, had long brooded over the degrading bus system, and they now seized on the occasion to take action. Meeting at the Mt. Zion African Methodist Episcopal Church, they decided to call a boycott of the bus company to last until it had agreed to seat black passengers on a first-come, first-serve basis and hire black bus drivers for runs in black neighborhoods. The company refused, and the boycott began.

The boycott organizers called on the young pastor of the Dexter Avenue Baptist Church, the Reverend Martin Luther King, Jr., to lead the campaign. Although he was still new to the community, King accepted. It was an event that would ring loudly through the decade and beyond.

King was the son of a successful Baptist minister in Atlanta, Georgia, a southern city where racism seldom showed itself brazenly. He had taken his B.A. at all-black Morehouse College and then escaped Jim Crow for a time by going north to study theology at Crosier Seminary in Pennsylvania and take a Ph.D. in philosophy at Boston University. In 1954 he accepted the call to become minister at the Dexter Avenue Church at $4200 a year, the highest salary paid any Montgomery African-American minister.

King's philosophical studies had exposed him to the egalitarian Social Gospel views of Walter Rauschenbusch; the pacifism of the Reverend A. J. Muste; and the nonviolent protest philosophy of Mohandas Gandhi, the anticolonial political leader of India. He was intrigued by nonviolence as a protest tactic, but he was not yet a full believer in Gandhi's *satyagraha,* civil disobedience against the oppressor as a way to defeat oppression.

The fiery, year-long Montgomery bus strike in 1955–56 tempered and matured King. African-American Montgomeryans organized car pools or walked to work to avoid patronizing the Jim Crow bus line. They accepted the sacrifice with good humor. An elderly black woman en route to her job refused an offer of a ride from a white reporter, "My feet is tired, but my soul is rested," she remarked. Most white Montgomeryans feared change. The Ku Klux Klan bombed King's and other boycott leaders' houses and burned black churches. Hotheads in the African-American community were ready to riot, but King knew that counterviolence would only hurt the civil rights cause and restrained them. "We are not advocating violence," he told his followers. "We must love our white brothers no matter what they do to us." King's leadership and Christian message made him a figure of international reputation.

Although badly hurt by the boycott, the bus company held out stubbornly, and defeat only came through a Supreme Court decision on December 20, 1956, declaring Alabama's Jim Crow transportation laws unconstitutional. Shortly before 6 A.M. the following morning, King and his associates boarded a Montgomery city bus, paid their fares, and sat down in front seats.

King's Montgomery success led to the formation in Atlanta early in 1957 of the Southern Christian Leadership Conference (SCLC). Dedicated at first to ending Jim Crow in public transportation, SCLC soon took on all segregation and the denial of voting rights as well. At SCLC King collected a roster of unusually able aides and allies, including Bayard Rustin, Ralph Abernathy, Fred Shuttlesworth, Wyatt Tee Walker, Andrew Young, and Ella Baker. Some of these people were relatively new to the struggle, others—like Rustin and Baker—were battered veterans of the civil rights wars. In the next few years King and SCLC led the effort to dismantle the century-old edifice of legal segregation and restore African-American voting rights. They would win amazing victories, but the road would be rough and, despite satyagraha, marked with disorder and violence.

The Cold War Continues

The Eisenhower years also saw a modest easing of international tensions. In late November 1952, soon after his election, Ike had kept his promise and gone to Korea to try to end the stalemate in the armistice negotiations. The seventy-two-hour visit, mostly spent looking at situation maps and greeting service personnel, accomplished little. Then in March 1953 Soviet leader Joseph Stalin died, and suddenly new doors opened. On April 16 Eisenhower gave a major foreign policy speech calling for an end to international tensions and a serious effort at world disarmament. At the same time the Americans let it be known that if the stalemate in Korea did not end soon, the United States might resort to dropping an atom bomb on a North Korean target.

These developments were felt in the Far East. On July 26, 1954, despite the efforts of South Korean President Syngman Rhee to sabotage an agreement, the two sides signed the armistice document. Neither the Communists nor the United Nations forces had won. Prisoners were to be exchanged, although many of the captured Chinese and North Koreans did not want to return to their Communist nations. But the two sides would remain in place, almost exactly where they had been in June 1950. Korea would continue to be a nation divided into two hostile parts. But for most Americans the important thing was that the war was over.

Eisenhower continued the containment policy of his predecessor in a general way. But his foreign policy had its own special features.

It was a strange mixture of the pacific and the belligerent. At times the president and his chief foreign policy adviser, Secretary of State John Foster Dulles, sought to avoid entanglements that promised to stretch American commitments too far. Vietnam (discussed in Chapter 13) was an example of judicious limitation, at least at first. In Iran, an oil-rich Islamic country bordering the Soviet Union, however, Eisenhower showed no such restraint. In 1953 the United States, acting through the CIA, arranged a coup to overthrow Mohammad Mussadegh, a left-wing Iranian leader suspected of pro-Soviet goals. Four years before Mussadegh had evicted Shah Mohammed Reza Pahlavi from power and nationalized the Iranian oil industry. The coup returned the shah to power; Iran became an important American friend in the Middle East, although beneath the surface anti-shah, anti-American forces, from both the left and right, continued to seethe.

In Europe American policy was activist. Secretary Dulles, although he had spent his life studying the complexities of foreign policy-making, was given to simplistic saber rattling to frighten the Soviets. In a radio talk in January 1953 he promised the "captive peoples" of the Soviet satellite nations that they could "count on" the United States for support against their Soviet oppressor. In February the administration introduced a resolution in Congress, written by Dulles, denouncing the Soviet occupation of Poland, the Baltic states, Hungary, Czechoslovakia, and the other "captive nations."

Americans generally deplored the Soviet occupation of the small nations on its western border, but many sensible people believed the captive peoples position to be essentially foolish and dangerous propaganda. The United States, they noted, might well encourage hopes among the Eastern Europeans that it could not satisfy. When in 1956 the Hungarians rose against their Soviet occupiers, the United States indeed sat back and did nothing. Soviet troops and tanks soon crushed the brave revolt. The Hungarian "freedom fighters," critics said, were in part victims of unrealistic expectations inspired by Dulles three years before.

Massive Retaliation and a Summit Conference

Dulles's "massive retaliation" policy, announced in early 1954, was another risky foreign policy position. The president deplored the enormous expenditures for armaments but at the same time, of course, had no intention of leaving the West defenseless against Soviet expansionism. What he sought was "a bigger bang for the buck." He recognized that conventional mass armies with their millions of men and thousands of tanks were enormously expensive to maintain and sought to cut the ground forces budget. Between 1953 and 1960, helped by the end of fighting in Korea, Eisenhower reduced the army from 1.5 million to 873,000 men.

But how could deterrence be preserved without large, well-equipped American military forces? The answer seemed simple: by building up our nuclear weapons arsenal to the point where any aggressor would face total annihilation if it persisted. The United States had already detonated its first hydrogen bomb in late 1952. Thereafter the Defense Department concentrated on refining nuclear weapons through prolonged atmospheric testing in Nevada and in Bikini Atoll in the Marshall Islands and on developing improved delivery systems, especially intercontinental ballistics missiles (ICBMs). Not until early 1960 did the ICBMs become truly reliable, but on January 12, 1954, Dulles felt free to declare that in the future the United States would use massive nuclear retaliation against any hostile act "at times and places of our own choosing."

The nuclear arms race was profoundly disturbing to many Americans. Many feared the danger to health and life from the radiation fallout that accompanied the weapons-testing program. An all-out nuclear war itself seemed too horrible to contemplate. In 1957 *On the Beach,* a popular novel (and subsequently a successful movie) set in Australia, depicted what presumably would happen following a nuclear war among the great powers. The war had wiped out all human beings in the Northern Hemisphere, and as the story opens, Australians await the arrival of the deadly radiation cloud, their own deaths, and the end of the human race.

To some people massive retaliation was a seriously flawed strategy. A small number of critics believed that nuclear weapons were inadmissible under all circumstances, even to stop a full-scale Soviet attack on NATO or the United States itself. They often advocated unilateral disarmament, the abandonment by the United States of its nuclear armaments even without an equal response by the Soviet Union. This position was sometimes condensed to the slogan, "better red than dead." At the other extreme were advocates of a nuclear preemptive first strike against the Soviet Union to catch it by surprise and destroy its power before it could retaliate. But most Americans accepted a middle position: while nuclear war must be avoided at all cost, it could not be precluded in the event of a Soviet attack either on the United States itself or on our NATO allies.

What seemed wrong with massive retaliation was that it threatened to start a nuclear war over even marginal concerns. Having reduced its capacity for responding to danger with conventional forces, America would have either to respond to every Communist challenge with a nuclear holocaust or accept certain defeat. Unfortunately as events would soon show, the other alternative—of engaging the enemy at the periphery with conventional military forces—had its dangers too.

During Eisenhower's eight years as president, America's foreign policy fortunes gyrated wildly. Stalin's death led to a notable softening of Soviet policy. In 1955 the Soviets finally agreed to leave their occupied zone in Austria, permitting that country to become a united, independent, neutral nation. After 1953 more and more was heard of "peaceful coexistence" between the superpowers.

But a temporary easing of Cold War tensions did not keep both sides from maneuvering for improved military positions. In 1952 the European members of NATO established the European Defense Community to coordinate their response to a Soviet military threat. But then France, overconscious of its past glories, had second thoughts and, despite Dulles's threat that the United States would engage in an "agonizing reappraisal" of its commitment to European defense if France did not follow through, decided not to join. In 1955 the Soviet Union, fearful of NATO's military revival, arranged the Warsaw Pact, which bound the Eastern European satellites to it in a tight military alliance.

Despite this jockeying for military advantage, efforts at reconciling East-West differences continued. In the summer of 1955 Eisenhower and British and French leaders met at Geneva with Soviet leaders Nikolai Bulganin and Nikita Khrushchev to discuss problems between NATO and the Warsaw Pact nations. This was the first of the postwar summit conferences, and many people had high hopes for its success. But little was accomplished.

A major issue was the fate of Germany, divided since the war into two competing halves. The Americans proposed a unified German nation with the right to join NATO if it wished. The Soviets, not surprisingly, rejected this proposal and countered with a unification plan that required withdrawal of all foreign troops from Germany and a general European security agreement. Eisenhower also proposed a sweeping "open skies" disarmament agreement that would have allowed each nation almost complete access to the other's military installations to verify any arms reduction arrangement. Barely out of the paranoid Stalin era and rulers of a still-repressive, authoritarian state, the Soviets did not take this seriously, and it probably was not taken very seriously by the Americans either.

The Suez Crisis

Despite the absence of significant results the world hailed the "spirit of Geneva," as sign of a new, cordial attitude between the superpowers. The optimistic mood lasted for a scant few months. In 1956 events in the Middle East demonstrated that the superpower rivalry could be played out through surrogates in the Third World as well as directly.

Egypt and Israel were the focus of the new clash. Although Israel had established its independence in 1948, its neighbors were pledged to destroy it, claiming that it was an alien intrusion into the Muslim world and a state occupying what was by right the territory of the predominantly Muslim Palestinians. Israel's most formidable enemy was neighboring Egypt, a country that had recently thrown off British rule, and under its aggressive new ruler, Gamal Abdel Nasser, was intent on establishing its leadership of the Arab world. Nasser launched continuous guerrilla attacks across the Egyptian-Israeli border and promised to destroy the Jewish state.

As part of his ambitious plans Nasser sought control of the Suez Canal, the man-made waterway through Egypt connecting the Mediterranean and Red seas that provided a vital commercial and strategic shortcut to sailing around Africa. Built with British money during the previous century, it had at one time been a critical link between Britain and its Asian empire. In the postwar period it remained a major route of international trade and its tolls continued to be an important revenue earner for Britain and France.

Several nations were willing to underwrite Nasser's ambitions. The Soviet Union supplied him with large quantities of arms. For a time the United States promised to lend him money to build a vital dam at Aswan on the Nile River but then withdrew the offer when Dulles decided that Nasser was getting too close to the Soviets. Meanwhile the Israelis, fearing growing Egyptian power, had asked America for arms. Eisenhower refused, claiming it would only lead to a middle eastern weapons race.

In July 1956 Nasser seized control of the Suez Canal and declared he would use its revenues to build a dam at Aswan. He also closed the international waterway to all

Israeli shipping contrary to long-established international agreement mandating an open canal. After months of fruitless negotiation Israel invaded Egypt and advanced to within 10 miles of the canal. Meanwhile the French and British, in secret collusion with Israel, had dropped paratroopers and seized control of the waterway.

The French-British-Israeli collaboration created an international crisis. The Soviets threatened to send troops to protect its new Egyptian ally. Eisenhower, who had been kept in the dark by the French and British, became angry and sharply reprimanded the invaders. U.S. pressure forced Egypt's opponents to withdraw, leaving Nasser in possession of the canal. Bowing to Israel's concerns over the constant raids across the Egyptian border, the United Nations agreed to establish a peacekeeping military force in the Sinai region that marked the Egyptian-Israeli boundary. Eisenhower had prevented a major war, but he had also humbled America's allies and encouraged Nasser in his aggressive posture. The Middle East remained a tinder box. (See Figure 14–2 in Chapter 14.)

Berlin

Several major international crises marked Eisenhower's second term. One was the old perennial, Berlin, that detached piece of the new West German republic deep within the East German Soviet satellite.

To both the Soviets and the East Germans the Western presence in Berlin was a serious affront. The West German Federal Republic was now a democratic and prosperous country while East Germany remained poor and authoritarian. From the late 1940s on many thousands of East Germans each year fled across the border to the Federal Republic. The migration not only hurt the East German economy; it also highlighted the serious deficiencies of Communist society relative to the West. Gradually the Communists were able to stem the leak along most of the East-West border, but Berlin remained a serious hemorrhage point for refugees from behind the Iron Curtain.

During this period the Western powers refused to deal with the East Germans on Berlin or any other matter. The Soviet Union, they said, was the legal occupying power and it alone had the right to speak for the Soviet zone of Germany. In November 1958 Khrushchev, now sole leader in Moscow, announced that if an agreement on Berlin satisfactory to the Russians was not reached in six months, the Soviet Union would sign a separate peace treaty with East Germany and turn over to it control of the Soviet zone in Berlin. The implication was that unless the Allies dealt with East Germany, they would face a blockade of Berlin similar to the one of 1948–49.

Khrushchev's ultimatum created an instant crisis. But then it eased. In September 1959 Khrushchev visited the United States and conferred with Eisenhower at Camp David, the presidential retreat in the Maryland mountains. Once again the American and Soviet leaders got along personally, leading a worried world now to hail the "Spirit of Camp David." The two men agreed to hold a four-power summit meeting in May 1960 to discuss Germany and Berlin. Soon after, Khrushchev canceled the ultimatum.

The Soviet leader, however, had second thoughts about relaxing the Berlin pressure. But how could he explain changing his mind? Then just before the scheduled Paris summit, Khrushchev found the out he needed.

On May 1 a high-flying American U-2 spy plane, equipped with radiation detectors and high-tech cameras, was shot down over Soviet territory and its pilot, Francis Gary Powers, taken prisoner. Both nations, of course, regularly spied on one another through conventional human agents and through advanced technology, and each knew of the others' activities. But never before did the Soviets have such dramatic proof of American spying, and on May 5 Khrushchev announced that the United States had been caught engaging in "aggressive acts" against the Soviet Union.

The purpose, he said, was to wreck the summit conference, but he blamed American underlings, not the president. In fact Eisenhower did know about the spy plane operations and had approved them. At first the American government tried to pass the U-2 off as a weather plane, but when it became clear that the Soviets had the evidence, Eisenhower admitted the purpose of the flights and his own knowledge of them.

The leaders of France, Britain, the United States, and the Soviet Union met in Paris despite the U-2 incident. But the Soviets quickly made it clear that they had changed their mind. At the preliminary meeting on May 16 Khrushchev was blunt, accusing the president of "treachery" and of "bandit" acts against the Soviet Union. He then stalked out of the Elysée Palace. The summit collapsed and with it all immediate chance to reduce Cold War tensions.

Cuba and Castro

By the last months of Eisenhower's administration the United States confronted a problem nearer to home as well—in Cuba, just ninety miles off the Florida coast.

For years Cuba had been an informal American dependency, functioning under the shadow of the American (see Figure 5–1 in Chapter 5) colossus. Many Cubans despised Uncle Sam as a colonial power that impeded their country's full independence and upheld Cuban regimes that preserved political and social inequality. And at times the United States *had* clearly used its power to frustrate social change in Latin America. In 1953, for example, the CIA sponsored a coup against Jacob Arbenz Guzmán, the leftist Guatemalan president suspected of pro-Soviet sympathies. The Arbenz government was replaced by a conservative one favorable to the United States.

During the early fifties Cuba was ruled by Fulgencio Batista, a notorious despot who used brutal methods to repress opposition and lined his pockets from the proceeds of gambling and prostituion. Almost everyone in Cuba, including the prosperous, pro-American middle class, opposed the Batista regime. American public opinion too was hostile to the tyrant.

From 1956 on the anti-Batista opposition was led by a bearded young lawyer, Fidel Castro, a former University of Havana student. Castro and his small rebel band established headquarters in the rugged Cuban mountains and from there launched guerrilla attacks against the Batista forces. With the support of the majority of the Cuban people they soon made spectacular gains. On New Year's Day 1959 Batista saw the inevitable and fled into exile.

For a time Americans hailed Castro's victory. He initially denied Communist sympathies, promised democracy, and stated that American property was safe under his regime. The American left would later say that Castro need not have been an enemy of the United States; that the United States itself was responsible for turning the Cuban Revolution in a pro-Soviet direction. Perhaps so but it is clear that Castro was also never the democrat that he claimed. Once in power he established revolutionary tribunals that condemned to death or prison hundreds of accused Batista supporters without benefit of elementary legal protection and imposed censorship on Cuban writers, academics, and journalists. He was soon praising Red China and the Soviet Union and calling the United States "a vulture . . . feeding on humanity." In a matter of months he had lost the support of much of the Cuban middle class, many of whom fled their homeland for Florida.

If American liberals and conservatives deplored Castro's behavior on moral or ethical grounds, the American government saw Castro as a beachhead for Soviet influence in the Americas and resolved to bring him down as it had Guzmán in Guatemala. By the last months of the Eisenhower administration, the CIA was training cadres of Cuban exiles in Florida and Guatemala for an invasion to topple Castro's government and establish in its place one more friendly to the United States.

Ike's Farewell and the 1960 Election

Three days before Eisenhower's second term ended, the president made a farewell speech to the American people containing one of his more interesting statements. Disarmament, he declared, must be one of the nation's highest priorities. Unfortunately over the years there had developed an alliance between American military men and arms manufacturers to build up the nation's arsenal beyond legitimate need. This "military-industrial complex" posed a threat to American democracy. "The potential for the disastrous rise of misplaced power exists and will persist," he pronounced. The statement was surprising from a man who had himself been a career officer in the army, and many Americans took it to heart.

The Candidates

Ike's successor would be the handsome young Democratic senator from Massachusetts, John F. Kennedy, the man who had almost won the Democratic vice presidential nomination four years before.

Kennedy was the second son of Joseph P. Kennedy, a conservative and abrasive millionaire banker, moviemaker, industrialist, and Wall Street speculator from Boston. The Kennedys were an Irish-Catholic family that exhibited in its own history the journey of nineteenth-century Irish immigrants from poverty to affluence. Joseph's father was a successful, self-made man; he himself was a Harvard graduate who made millions in business. Yet he never felt that he had been fully accepted by the Yankee Protestant elite who ruled in Boston and his fierce desire to show the world that the Kennedys took second place to no one was a controlling motive in his behavior. Joseph Kennedy was determined to make one of his sons president and was willing to put his wide connections, his large fortune, and his enormous energy behind this goal. His first choice for high office was his oldest son, Joseph, Jr., but when Joe Jr. was tragically killed in World War II, he turned to John.

In 1946 John Fitzgerald Kennedy was a skinny Harvard graduate who had just returned to civilian life after serving as a naval officer in the Pacific. A war hero who had barely escaped death when a Japanese destroyer sank his PT boat, he ran for Congress in a Boston district and won. In 1952 he unseated Boston Brahmin Senator Henry Cabot Lodge.

As a senator, Kennedy had chalked up a mediocre record. Out of deference to his anti-Communist Catholic constituents, he had tolerated Joe McCarthy, who was a friend of his father. He also had, at times, accepted the positions of southern colleagues on racial issues. Kennedy was a pragmatist rather than an idealist, and it was not clear that he held any clear, uplifting vision beyond "success" for its own sake. In 1960 some members of the liberal intelligentsia supported him but many considered him just another rich young man driven by intense ambition and backed by immense wealth. One liberal would call him the "Democratic Nixon."

With the electorate at large Kennedy's chief handicap was his religion. He was not an especially pious Catholic, but many Protestant Americans, as in the days of Al Smith, considered the Catholic Church an alien and dangerous institution, and felt that a Catholic president might put his religion ahead of his country. Even Democratic leaders who personally dismissed such fears wondered if a Catholic could overcome the bigotry that had helped defeat Smith in 1928.

Kennedy's chief rival for the nomination was Hubert Humphrey, the exuberant senator from Minnesota. Humphrey was a certified liberal, a founder of Americans for Democratic Action, a loyal champion of labor, and a determined advocate of civil rights. But he not only lacked the personal magnetism of Kennedy but also his money and skilled staff. Another Kennedy rival was the Senate majority leader, Lyndon B. Johnson of Texas. The most effective parliamentarian since Henry Clay, Johnson suffered from his identification with the South and his reputation as a wheeler-dealer.

The key primary contest was in West Virginia, an overwhelmingly Protestant state. There Kennedy money and organization helped to overcome Humphrey's pro-labor reputation and anti-Catholic feeling to give the Massachusetts senator a whopping 61 percent majority.

The Kennedy forces came to the Los Angeles Democratic convention in early July with victory in the bag and won on the first ballot. In a move to attract the southern and southwestern vote in November, Kennedy asked Johnson to join the ticket.

The Republicans turned to Richard Nixon, the vice president, as their candidate. Although few Americans loved Nixon and some believed him unscrupulous, he had acquired a new stature since 1952, especially in the foreign affairs realm. Some of this was pure hype. In 1958 he had taken a tour through South America to express U.S. interest in, and goodwill toward, its Latin neighbors. In Peru and Venezuela he had been attacked by screaming mobs and had narrowly escaped personal injury. The press depicted him as a hero. The following year, while attending the Soviet Exhibition of Science, Technology, and Culture in Moscow, the vice president had had an encounter with Premier Khrushchev in the kitchen of a model six-room American ranch house. The two engaged in a debate on the relative consumer merits of their two societies and Americans felt that Nixon had "won." Somehow these two events had been transformed by the media into profound learning experiences for the vice president.

Nixon's only serious potential competitor was Nelson Rockefeller, New York's Republican Governor. Rockefeller represented the party's Eastern liberal wing dominated by "old" families and "old" money, and was an attractive, effective man with a famous name. Fortunately for Nixon, he seemed more interested in influencing the party's ideology than getting its nomination. Rather than challenging Nixon for the nomination, in June 1960, while the Republican Platform Committee was deliberating, he threatened a major platform fight if the vice president did not endorse his liberal domestic policies and acknowledge the need for a larger defense budget. The governor's ultimatum forced Nixon to come to his New York apartment and agree to changes in the platform. Republican conservatives like Senator Barry Goldwater of Arizona attacked the "Compact of Fifth Avenue" as the "Munich of the Republican Party."

With Rockefeller out of the way Nixon's nomination was without serious opposition. As a further sop to the Republican liberals, Nixon chose Henry Cabot Lodge, now ambassador to the UN, as his running mate.

The Campaign

The election contest that followed was one of the most exciting in thirty years. Neither man seemed to have a clear-cut advantage. Kennedy had looks, money, and a beautiful, style-setting wife. He was not above using his sex appeal as a campaign weapon. As reporter Murray Kempton wrote at one point, Kennedy had "treated southern Ohio yesterday as Don Giovanni used to treat Seville." Charisma notwithstanding Kennedy had his liabilities: inexperience, the reputation of a rich playboy, and Catholicism. By contrast Nixon was a veteran politician, came from a solid middle-class background, and had the support of most of the nation's big-business leaders. He was also the heir, or so it seemed, of the beloved Ike. In fact Eisenhower was surprisingly cool to his vice president. At one point when asked what ideas Nixon had contributed to his administration, he replied, "If you give me a week, I might think of one. I can't remember." Still Ike was willing to "do anything to avoid turning [his] chair and the country over to Kennedy" and actively supported the Republican candidate.

The Democrats campaigned on a "missile gap" that some experts thought the Eisenhower administration had allowed to open between the United States and the Soviet Union. (Subsequent intelligence revealed that in fact there was none.) Kennedy promised to close the gap and in general win the competition with the Soviets for the world's favor. He also promised to get a sluggish economy moving again and devote more of the nation's wealth to improving education, helping the poor, and upgrading the country's public facilities. Nixon, predictably, emphasized his experience, especially in foreign affairs, and the accomplishments of the Eisenhower years.

Kennedy's religion could not be avoided as an issue, although the Republican candidate to his credit did not mention it. The Democratic nominee met the Catholic issue head on by an appearance before the Greater Houston Ministerial Association in September. "I believe in an America," he told the Protestant leaders, "where the separation of church and state is absolute—where no Catholic prelate would tell the President (should he be Catholic) how to act, and no Protestant minister would tell his parishioners for whom to vote." The speech undoubtedly helped, although it did not convince the most anti-Catholic voters.

Kennedy also succeeded in overcoming much of the public's concern about his inexperience as an executive. A series of television debates with Nixon from September 25 through October 21 was crucial. The first was in Chicago and was a clear-cut Kennedy victory. The Democratic candidate seemed poised and articulate and he looked good on camera. Suffering from an infected knee, Nixon seemed nervous and tired. He perspired and appeared unshaven. After this first debate many who had doubted Kennedy's maturity concluded that he had handled himself better than the older, more experienced vice president.

Civil rights inevitably became a major campaign issue. A large majority of African-American voters by now were Democrats. But many were disturbed by the power within the party of the southern segregationists; many were also suspicious of the Catholic Church. Kennedy was in a delicate position. He feared the complete defection of the white South, Lyndon Johnson notwithstanding. But he also knew he could not afford to lose the big industrial states with millions of black voters. To his credit he chose to champion the civil rights cause even to the point of obliquely endorsing the use of civil disobedience.

John F. Kennedy and Richard Nixon hold their first 1960 campaign debate. In the center is the moderator, Howard K. Smith of ABC. (UPI/Bettmann Newsphotos)

The real breakthrough in winning black support, however, came late in the campaign when a Georgia judge sentenced Martin Luther King, Jr., to four months at hard labor for attempting to desegregate an Atlanta department store lunch counter. Given the nature of southern jails, there was an excellent chance that King would never leave prison alive. Nixon privately tried to get Attorney General William Rogers to intervene, but Eisenhower vetoed the move. Kennedy called Coretta King, expressing his sympathy and desire to help her husband; Kennedy's brother Robert, his campaign manager, contacted the Georgia judge. The next day King was out on bail. Mrs. King spread the news of Kennedy's intervention, guaranteeing a massive African-American turnout in November for the Democrats.

Kennedy won, but the victory was one of the closest in history. (See Figure 11–1.) The Massachusetts senator received only about 100,000 more popular votes than Nixon out of the 68.8 million cast and carried fewer, although larger, states for an electoral majority of 303 to 219. Even these figures may not be a true measure of Kennedy's electoral weakness. Some scholars believe, as did Nixon himself, that in both Texas and Illinois the Democratic tally had been falsified by the local Democratic machines. Many Republican leaders urged the vice president to challenge the results, but Nixon, recognizing the legal difficulties and not wishing to taint the presidential election process, refused.

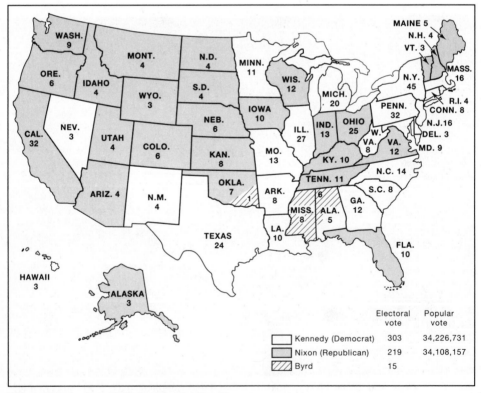

Figure 11–1 The 1960 Presidential Election

An analysis of the returns suggests that, in the end, the religious issue hurt the Democratic candidate after all. Some Republican Catholics no doubt switched to vote for him. Kennedy also got some normally nonvoting Catholics to come to the polls. But on the whole the religious issue had the effect of shifting thousands of Democratic Protestant voters, especially in the South and rural Midwest, into the Republic column. It was Kennedy's good fortune that his gains came in the large industrial states, his losses in places where he either had no chance of winning anyway (the rural Midwest) or where Democratic loyalty was still so ingrained or Johnson's appeal so strong (the South) that the defections were not enough to transfer many whole states to Nixon.

Transition and Balance Sheet

Despite the shadow over the election results, as the country awaited the new administration, many people looked forward to a new political era, one marked by youth, by style, and by bold new initiatives. In more ways than just by the calendar, the fifties were over.

A majority of the nation's most alert and active citizens were probably glad to see the era end. Yet a decade later some would look back to the 1950s with nostalgia. In part their response would reflect the excesses of the 1960s. But it would also derive from the realization that, despite their outward timidity and caution, the fifties had been a creative era when the nation made significant cultural breakthroughs in painting, popular music, literature, and philosophy. Nor was that all. The 1950s had been prosperous years for many Americans and, after the harsh years of depression and war, they had confirmed the promise of American life. Furthermore they had witnessed the start of a social revolution in the South that would not end until the promise of civic equality for all races, first made during Reconstruction, had been realized. All in all, it was not too bad a record.

FOR FURTHER READING

On the intellectual climate of the 1950s see Richard Pells, *The Liberal Mind in a Conservative Age: American Intellectuals in the 1940s and 1950s* (1984). On the new conservatism see Russell Kirk, *The Conservative Mind* (1953); William F. Buckley, Jr., *God and Man at Yale* (1951); Daniel Bell, *The End of Ideology: On the Exhaustion of Political Ideas in the Fifties* (1960); and Hans Hoffmann, *The Theology of Reinhold Niebuhr* (1956).

American painting is covered in Andrew C. Ritchie, *Abstract Painting and Sculpture in America* (1951). Serge Guibaut's *How New York Stole the Idea of Modern Art* (1983) claims that the rise of the abstract expressionists to prominence was related to American political hegemony in the postwar era. On rock and roll see Nik Cohn, *Rock: From the Beginning* (1969) and Charlie Gillett, *The Sound of the City: The Rise of Rock and Roll* (1970). Albert Goldman's *Elvis* (1981) retells the scandal of Elvis Presley's life as well as his contribution to popular music.

Bruce Cook's *The Beat Generation* (1971) and Lawrence Lipton's *The Holy Barbarians* (1959) discuss the Beat dissenters. The movies are discussed in Michael Wood, *America in Movies* (1975). The best discussion of television is Erik Barnouw's *A History of Broadcasting in the United States, Vol. III, The Image Empire* (1970).

Eisenhower and his presidency come under attack in Marquis Childs, *Eisenhower: Captive Hero* (1958) and Emmet John Hughes, *The Ordeal of Power* (1963). More positive are Merlo J. Pusey, *Eisenhower, the President* (1956) and Arthur Larson, *Eisenhower: The President Nobody*

Knew (1968). A recent work that emphasizes how effective Ike was behind the scenes while often seeming to bumble in public is Fred Greenstein, *The Hidden-Hand Presidency: Eisenhower as Leader* (1982). On the Dixon-Yates fiasco see Aaron Wildavsky, *Dixon-Yates* (1962).

The civil rights movement of the 1950s begins essentially with the 1954 *Brown* decision. For the *Brown* case see Richard Kluger, *Simple Justice* (1976). For the conservative response to it see Numan Bartley, *The Rise of Massive Resistance: Race and Politics in the South during the 1950s* (1959). For the early years of Martin Luther King, Jr.'s leadership see the recent book by Taylor Branch, *Parting the Waters: America in the King Years, 1954–63* (1988). Another, much briefer, work that covers the later years of the civil rights movement as well is Harvard Sitkoff, *The Struggle for Black Equality, 1954–1980* (1983). Also see Stephen Oates's eloquent *Let the Trumpet Sound: The Life of Martin Luther King, Jr.* (1982). David Garrow's *Bearing the Cross: Martin Luther King, Jr. and the Southern Christian Leadership Conference* (1986) is more scholarly that Oates's work, but less readable.

The Eisenhower phase of the Cold War is covered in Robert Divine, *Eisenhower and the Cold War* (1981); Townsend Hoopes, *The Devil and John Foster Dulles* (1973); and Roscoe Drummond and Gaston Coblentz, *Duel at the Brink: John Foster Dulles' Command of American Power* (1960). Also see David Wise and Thomas B. Ross, *The U-2 Affair* (1962).

The election of 1960 is skillfully evoked in Theodore White's *The Making of the President, 1960* (1961).

12
The Sixties

Members of the 1960s radical counterculture. (Gene Anthony/Black Star)

Kennedy's New Frontier

Every Democratic administration since 1932 has adopted, or been assigned, a label to describe its program for change. Republican administrations have scorned the practice and for good reason: generally, they have come to office dedicated not so much to new programs as to undoing those of their Democratic predecessors. Franklin Roosevelt's program, of course, was the New Deal, Truman's, the Fair Deal. John F. Kennedy (JFK) called his the *New Frontier*.

Kennedy first used the term in his acceptance speech at the 1960 Democratic convention. His nomination had ushered in a "New Frontier," he declared, "the frontier of the 1960s." It is hard to tell what Kennedy meant, but a certain amount of mystery is appropriate for an acceptance speech; the candidate must not give his opponent in the grueling battle ahead too many targets to shoot at. Yet the New Frontier was not explained much better in Kennedy's Inaugural Address from the Capitol the following January 20. Here was the opportunity to define the New Frontier, but instead once again Kennedy took refuge in eloquent generalities. "Let the word go forth from this time and place, to friend and foe alike, that the torch has been passed to a new generation of Americans . . . tempered by war, disciplined by a hard and bitter peace, proud of our ancient heritage." The speech echoed with uplifting phrases: "the trumpet summon us again," "ask not what your country can do for you; ask what you can do for your country," "we shall pay any price, bear any burden, meet any hardship," and "the common enemies of man: tyranny, poverty, disease and war itself." The public heard the beautiful music and ignored the empty libretto. But one thing was clear: the message was "March." After eight years of consolidation, the nation would be moving again.

The next weeks were a blur of motion. Within two months Kennedy had dashed off thirty-two official messages and recommendations for new legislation, delivered twelve speeches, announced twenty-two executive orders, and held seven press conferences. "He did everything . . . except shinny up the Washington Monument," the journalist James Reston wrote of one of JFK's early days. The public liked the vigor.

They also liked the images. Eisenhower had been the oldest president the nation ever had. Kennedy was the youngest and possibly the handsomest. He was also a cultivated man who seemed to read widely and appreciate the arts. Many intellectuals would be flattered by his interests. But it was more than just the president himself. His wife, the former Jacqueline Bouvier, was beautiful and elegant; his young daughter, Caroline, radiated delicate charm. His cabinet and close circle of advisers were sharp, articulate, and bumptious young men, many from Harvard, who worked hard and played hard and seemed to relish running the greatest nation on earth. Arthur Schlesinger, Jr., the Harvard historian who served Kennedy as a White House aide, would exult, "Never had girls seemed so pretty, tunes so melodious, and evenings so blithe and unconstrained." In later years people compared the "thousand days" of the Kennedy presidency to Camelot, the mythical court of brave knights and beautiful ladies presided over by King Arthur.

Inevitably, the image was not entirely true; this administration like all others had

President Kennedy, his wife,
Jacqueline, and his children,
Caroline and John, Jr.
(UPI/Bettmann Newsphotos)

its share of imperfect people. Many of Kennedy's advisers had more drive than discernment. Some have been described as juiceless technocrats, enamored of the quick-fix solution. The president himself was a flawed man who, as later became widely known, let others write his books and jeopardized his public reputation and the integrity of his office by his womanizing activities. Yet there can be no doubt that the public found the energy and the exuberance of the new administration a tonic for its tired blood. The young, especially, felt the thrill of new possibilities and new directions.

New Proposals

Some of the president's earliest initiatives confirmed the image of the new beginnings. On March 1 he announced the formation of a Peace Corps of young American volunteers who would go abroad to help less-developed nations improve their economies, their people's health, and their educational facilities. The new scheme to help the Third World instantly appealed to the idealism of the young, and even before Congress had passed the necessary legislation, thousands had offered to join. Another early proposal that engaged the public's imagination was the Alliance for Progress, a scheme to help Latin America achieve democracy, economic growth, and social equity through joint U.S. and Latin American cooperation.

At the end of May Kennedy asked Congress for a massive appropriation for an American space program. "I believe," he told the audience, "that this nation should commit itself to achieving the goal, before this decade is out, of landing a man on the moon and returning him safely to earth." The administration was goaded, in part, by the space successes of the Soviet Union since Sputnik in 1957. After several embarrassing failures the United States finally launched its own satellite in late January 1958. But then in April 1961 the Soviet Union announced that it had sent a man into space and recovered him successfully. Kennedy was undoubtedly playing catch-up with America's chief international rival and his space program was part of the continuing Cold War. But it was more. It was also a commitment to a bold human adventure resembling those momentous explorations of early modern times that had brought the European and non-European worlds into contact.

These early, flashy proposals were more successful in winning congressional support than Kennedy's other domestic programs. The new president was not a flaming liberal; at most he belonged among the moderates of his party. To reassure the business community, suspicious of Democrats since the New Deal, he appointed as defense secretary Robert McNamara, former Ford Motor Company executive, and as treasury secretary Douglas Dillon, a conservative Republican with Wall Street connections, although Kennedy offset the latter choice by appointing Walter Heller, a liberal economics professor, as head of the Council of Economic Advisers. But even if JFK had been a radical, the continuing informal coalition of northern Republicans and southern Democrats would have kept bold reform legislation from passing. Time and again liberal measures sent to "the Hill" encountered an impenetrable wall of resistance.

Despite this formidable opposition the president did secure an increase in the minimum wage, a modest federal housing act, and an area redevelopment measure to aid urban and rural depressed areas. In late 1961 under pressure from influential Democratic women he established the President's Commission on the Status of Women with Eleanor Roosevelt as chairperson. The commission's report in 1963 urged an end to job discrimination against women and endorsed day care centers and paid maternity leaves for married working women, but it also pronounced that "the fundamental responsibility" of women was to be "mothers and housewives." This was scarcely revolutionary, yet the commission did bring together a network of women—and some men—alert to feminist issues and helped launch the modern feminist movement.

More than this proved impossible, however. Congress defeated bills establishing a Department of Urban Affairs, a system of medical insurance for the elderly, and federal grants for school construction and teachers' salaries. The administration also found it difficult to get through a substantial federal tax cut that Heller and other Keynesians in and out of the administration believed essential to get the sluggish economy moving briskly again.

Moderate though he was, the president found it difficult to avoid offending business anyway. In April 1962 U.S. Steel, the country's steel-producing giant, announced a sharp price increase. Because steel entered into the manufacture of so many other things, this move promised to accelerate inflation, still modest in the early sixties. At a press conference soon after the company's price hike announcement, Kennedy denounced the company's president Roger Blough for his "public-be-damned" attitude. At the same time Secretary McNamara threatened not to buy steel for defense needs from any company that raised its prices. Blough retreated and rescinded the increases, but neither he nor many of his big-business colleagues ever forgave the president.

Civil Rights Crises

Kennedy came to power at a time when the civil rights movement was entering a more militant, turbulent phase. The change began in February 1960 when four young African-American students at North Carolina Agricultural and Technical College in Greensboro decided to sit down at the whites-only lunch counter of Woolworth and ask to be served. They were refused. The students came back with reinforcements the next day and for many days after, demanding that they be allowed to buy a cup of coffee. Bystanders cursed, spat at, and pummeled the students, but inspired by Martin Luther King's nonviolent philosophy, they refused to retreat or be provoked into counterviolence. The sit-in tactic soon spread to other segregated southern communities where African-American people had long accepted humiliating second-class treatment at local stores.

The brave example of the black students in Dixie acted like a massive electrical shock. Northern white students quickly formed support groups to raise money for their African-American comrades and organized boycotts of northern branches of Woolworth and other five-and-ten chains that had refused service to southern black students. Adult civil rights groups including Martin Luther King's Southern Christian Leadership Conference (SCLC) and the Congress of Racial Equality (CORE) also rushed to help. In April 1960 at a meeting in Raleigh called by Ella Baker of SCLC, the student sit-in leaders organized the Student Nonviolent Coordinating Committee (SNCC), dedicated to achieving an end to racial discrimination through black and white cooperation and the use of nonviolent means. Soon after this SNCC opened its national office in Atlanta in a corner of SCLC's national headquarters.

Early the next year CORE began the first of the "Freedom Rides" to force the desegregation of bus station facilities in southern cities. The riders refused to use segregated terminal rest rooms and coffee shops; they insisted that the recent Supreme Court decision prohibiting segregation in terminals (*Boynton* v. *Virginia*) be obeyed. Like SNCC, CORE was interracial. In these years all the major civil rights groups had a vision of "black and white together" both in the civil rights movement and in the future "color-blind" society it would help forge. When the first two CORE buses left Washington on May 4, half the riders were whites, many of them older members of pacifist groups.

At Rock Hill, South Carolina, a mob of angry whites blocked the entrance to the white waiting room and beat John Lewis, a member of the Nashville SCLC, and Albert Bigelow, a white pacifist, when they tried to enter. As the buses moved south the mobs of white racists, alerted by the media, grew larger and more savage. Attorney General Robert Kennedy, the president's brother, tried to intervene to protect the riders, calling on the governors of Alabama and Mississippi to guarantee order and the safety of the civil rights workers. They were uncooperative.

The administration was in a bind. On the one hand it sympathized with African-American aspirations and in any event needed black votes. On the other hand it also counted on the support of white southern Democrats. Hoping to prevent a showdown, the president called for a cooling off period by both sides, a move that offended many civil rights activists who noted that African-Americans had "cooled it" for several centuries with little to show for it.

Eventually the attorney general dispatched several hundred federal marshals to stop the mayhem and secured a federal injunction forbidding the Ku Klux Klan from interfering with interstate bus travel. On September 22 the Interstate Commerce Commission officially ordered the end to segregation at all bus and train stations.

If the Kennedys hoped that this would end the racial turmoil in the South, they were mistaken. In the fall of 1962 the attorney general was forced to use federal troops and marshals to force Governor Ross Barnett of Mississippi to desist from blocking James Meredith, an African-American applicant, from registering at the University of Mississippi. Many of the soldiers and marshals were injured by taunting, stone-throwing crowds of segregationists; several people were killed in the melees. Meredith was finally registered, but there was a similar confrontation at the University of Alabama during the late spring of 1963 with Governor George Wallace cast in the role of Ross Barnett. Wallace promised to "bar the entrance" of two African-American students to the state university and only backed down when the president ordered the federalized Alabama National Guard to guarantee their admission.

Meanwhile civil rights leaders had launched several major new drives. In 1961–62 they tried to desegregate public facilities in Albany, Georgia, and by early 1962 the small Georgia city had become the arena for a major battle with the segregationists. Faced with a wily police chief who avoided blatant brutality, King and SCLC suffered a defeat. The drive in 1963 to desegregate Birmingham, Alabama's largest city, was more successful. King believed Birmingham a test case. If the city's wall of public and private segregation could be cracked it would "break the back of segregation all over the nation." SCLC's weapons were nonviolent sit-ins and marches designed to advertise the city's racial failings. King understood that the authorities, led by the coarse and brutal police commissioner, Eugene ("Bull") Connor, might well be tempted to use violence against the protestors. Although he did not specifically connive at such a result, he recognized that such behavior would shock the conscience of the nation and help defeat the racists.

The outcome was as expected. Connor used attack dogs and fire hoses against peaceful marchers including women and children. He arrested hundreds. The newspapers and television networks carried pictures and film clips showing the savage confrontations; they profoundly shook the public. President Kennedy said that one picture of a ferocious dog attacking a terrified African-American woman had made him "sick," and he could "well understand why the Negroes of Birmingham are tired of being asked to be patient."

Birmingham was the regional headquarters of many important national business firms. Executives of these companies were disturbed by the turmoil and outrages as were many of the city's local merchants. They were bad for business. Under pressure from the administration and from business leaders elsewhere, on May 10 the city's business and political leaders accepted a settlement that guaranteed desegregation of the city's parks, libraries, and transport action facilities and promised the hiring of African-American workers in the city's downtown department stores. King left Birmingham satisfied that nonviolent civil disobedience could work.

New Civil Rights Legislation

The reverberations from Birmingham went beyond the city. During the Eisenhower years Congress had passed several civil rights bills. The Civil Rights Act of

1957 had established a six-person Civil Rights Commission and a Civil Rights Division in the Department of Justice to protect the voting rights of African-Americans and other minorities. The Civil Rights Act of 1960 had strengthened the voting rights provisions of the earlier measure.

These were weak laws and accomplished little. Now, in the wake of the Birmingham upheaval, Kennedy decided to push for a stronger federal civil rights bill. On June 19, 1963, he sent Congress a proposal giving the attorney general power to initiate school desegregation suits and outlawing discrimination in theaters, hotels and motels, stores, gas stations, restaurants, and ballparks and stadiums. Civil rights militants wanted strong provisions for ending job discrimination included in the bill, but the president knew that he would have a hard time getting the measure through Congress as it was and refused.

Although disappointed, the heads of the major civil rights groups decided to organize a massive summer demonstration in Washington to kindle support for the bill. This gathering would bring together thousands of black and white Americans in a vast outpouring of sympathy for the goal of an integrated society. The administration feared that the demonstration might offend some of the middle-of-the-roaders in Congress whose votes it needed, and only when the civil rights leaders refused to yield did the president give his blessing.

The Reverend Martin Luther King, Jr., (just left of center foreground) leads the 1963 March on Washington for civil rights. (UPI/Bettmann Newsphotos)

The August 28, 1963, March on Washington was the high point of the 1960s civil rights movement. As many as 200,000 demonstrators, including thousands of white people, came to the Mall in Washington to sing "We Shall Overcome" and other civil rights hymns, listen to folksingers including Bob Dylan and Joan Baez, and carry placards announcing "Decent Housing—Now!," "Integrated Schools—Now!," "Effective Civil Rights Laws—Now!" There were a dozen speeches climaxed by King's "I Have a Dream," in which the African-American leader displayed the power of his eloquence and the soaring moral authority of his cause. In sonorous periods that repeated the theme "I have a dream," King told of his vision of the future when "sons of former slaves and sons of former slaveowners" would "sit down together at the table of brotherhood," and when his four children would "not be judged by the color of their skin but by the content of their character." His listeners knew that they had witnessed a historic event and heard a legendary speech. The speech and march transformed King into a world historical figure. In October 1964 he received the Nobel Peace Prize.

Foreign Policy Crises

The Kennedy team brought to the White House a determination to avoid the foreign policy mistakes, as they saw it, of the previous administration. The nation must be prepared to stop the spread of communism around the world even if that entailed risks. The United States must rearm with conventional weapons to provide the "flexible response" required by "wars of national liberation" sponsored by the Soviet Union and China. To ensure the capacity to deal with such events it must further develop its "counterinsurgency" capacity. The troops trained to suppress guerrilla warfare were officially called the "Special Forces Group," and they were fitted with jaunty green berets.

The Bay of Pigs   Kennedy inherited his first foreign policy crisis from his predecessor. For months the Cuban-exile force Eisenhower had authorized had been training in Florida and Guatemala to invade the Cuban mainland. (See Chapter 11.) The CIA and the Joint Chiefs of Staff assured the new president that even a small force of emigrés, landed at the Bay of Pigs on Cuba's south coast, could ignite the anti-Castro opposition and quickly bring the Cuban tyrant down. Although he had his doubts, the president gave the operation the green light in April 1961.

Everything went wrong. To knock out Castro's small air force, old World War II bombers manned by anti-Castro Cubans attacked the Cuban airfields. They did little damage, although the CIA told the president that the Cuban planes had been destroyed. Soon after, five old cargo vessels carrying the invasion force arrived along the Cuban coast with several supply ships. The still-intact Cuban air force quickly sank the vessel carrying most of the invaders' munitions and communications equipment. Nevertheless 1500 Cuban exiles landed on the swampy beach and proclaimed the end of the Castro regime.

The Cuban people did not rise at the announcement, and the invaders were quickly pinned down by thousands of Castro's militia, supported by tanks. The exiles called pitifully for American help; so did the CIA. But Kennedy had already disclaimed any intention of invading Cuba and refused to send reinforcements. After three days the invaders had all surrendered to Castro's forces; they were ransomed by the United States eighteen months later. Cuban-Americans would never forgive the Democrats for the fiasco.

The Bay of Pigs defeat was a humiliation for the president. As one journalist said, the event made Americans look "like fools to our friends, rascals to our enemies, and incompetents to the rest." Kennedy winced as America's enemies chortled at his discomfiture. He would never trust the CIA again, although that did not keep him from condoning its efforts to destroy the Cuban economy by clandestine operations and, possibly, its often fantastic schemes to topple or assassinate Castro.

Encounters with the Soviets   Kennedy was to pay a high price for the Bay of Pigs disaster in his dealings with Nikita Khrushchev. In January 1961 the Soviet premier had declared his country's "unlimited support" to "peoples fighting for their liberation." In this same speech he once more threatened to force the Western powers to abandon Berlin. After the Bay of Pigs Khrushchev apparently concluded that the American president was an inexperienced, insecure, and weak young man who could be easily intimidated.

When the rulers of both superpowers met at Vienna in June, Khrushchev tried to bully the president. The Soviet premier was rude, coarse, contemptuous, and angry. Blaming UN General Secretary Dag Hammarskjöld for the death of Patrice Lumumba, the Soviet's friend in the African nation of the Congo, he demanded that the single UN head be replaced by a "troika" representing the West, the Soviet bloc, and the neutral countries. More important something must be done about Berlin. It was, he said, a bone in the Soviet Union's throat. With or without American consent, the Soviet Union would sign a treaty with East Germany that would end the right of free communication with Berlin. If the United States wanted to go to war over this, so be it.

The president returned to Washington shaken but resolute. On June 26 he told the American public that "if war breaks out it will have been started in Moscow." Kennedy asked for an additional $3.5 billion for defense, issued a call-up of army reserves, and ordered mothballed military planes and ships to be readied for combat. He also urged people to build bomb shelters, a move that set off a wave of half-funny, half-hysterical discussion of the best kind of personal shelters to build, how they should be stocked, and whether they should contain arms to fight off panicky, but improvident, neighbors when apocalypse arrived.

Meanwhile the Soviets had their own plans. For years the exodus of refugees from East to West Germany had been a humiliation for the Communists, underscoring the failings of society behind the Iron Curtain. By 1961 the flood had been lessened by guards and barbed wire along most of the East-West border, but Berlin remained a serious leak. Just after midnight on August 13 the East German army and police descended on the East-West city border; unloaded trucks carrying sawhorses, concrete blocks, and barbed wire; and began to erect a twenty-five-mile wall to separate the city's sections. Four days later the Berlin Wall was completed. All of Germany was now divided by a physical barrier guarded by searchlights and soldiers with rifles and guard dogs.

The Berlin Wall was followed by Soviet resumption of nuclear bomb testing in the atmosphere. For years scientists and medical people had warned of the health dangers of radioactive fallout from nuclear bomb tests. The United States had proposed a scheme to ban atmospheric tests, and although no formal agreement had been reached, both superpowers had suspended them. Now the Soviets set off over thirty new, more powerful bombs that, all told, released more radioactive poisons into the air than all the previous Western tests combined. Kennedy responded by authorizing resumption of U.S. testing.

For a few months in mid-1961 it looked as if the world was on the verge of war. Then in late September Khrushchev began to back off, telling a visiting Western diplomat in Moscow that "Berlin is not such a big problem for me. What are two million people among a billion communists?" In mid October he told a Communist party congress that the Western powers were acting reasonably and there was no need to press the Berlin issue to a showdown. The crisis in Europe was over.

The Cuban Missile Crisis

But not in the Americas. After the Bay of Pigs incident the Cubans, fearful of further United States–inspired attacks, had tightened their ties to the Soviet Union. By 1962 they were importing vast amounts of Soviet arms, sending Cuban technicians and pilots for training in either the Soviet Union or Czechoslovakia, and trading predominantly with the Soviet bloc countries behind the Iron Curtain.

Then in the summer of 1962 Khrushchev recklessly decided to challenge the United States on its home ground by placing in Cuba intermediate-range missiles that were aimed at the United States, ninety miles away. This was the first time the Soviet Union had ever placed nuclear weapons on foreign soil, and they were clearly intended to weaken America's position in the world.

From the beginning the Americans had observed the flow of ships, men, and supplies into Cuba, but not until mid October did U-2 overflights reveal that the Soviets were building missile launch sites in the island and had already delivered thirty or more missiles with nuclear warheads. Something would have to be done quickly if the United States was not to be faced with a nuclear-armed enemy on its doorstep. Suspicious by now of the regular national security apparatus, Kennedy quickly formed an Executive Committee (Ex Comm) of top aides and military officials to advise him on how to meet the challenge.

The Ex Comm group proffered conflicting options. The military men favored an air strike to destroy the launch sites before they could be made operational. A few even advocated an invasion of Cuba. Secretary of Defense McNamara and others urged a blockade that would prevent the installation of more missiles then approaching on Soviet ships. Robert Kennedy, who had taken charge of the group, supported the blockade option.

The president decided that it was important to make the confrontation public. On October 22 he briefed NATO representatives and the Latin American ambassadors on the crisis and that evening he addressed the American people on television. The United States, he said, was declaring a "quarantine" against any additional Soviet deliveries to Cuba and would follow this move by stronger measures if necessary. Any missile launched from Cuba would be treated as a Soviet attack on the United States and lead to full retaliation against Russia itself. It would set off World War III.

Americans, and in fact people all around the world, waited nervously to see how the Soviets would respond. Most Americans apparently believed the president was doing the right thing, but in other parts of the Western world many felt that the United States was playing "chicken" with human survival at stake. The British philosopher Bertrand Russell, an advocate of unilateral disarmament, telegraphed Kennedy, "Your action desperate. . . . No conceivable justification. . . . End this madness."

The next day the Soviets accused the United States of piracy and denied that the missiles were intended for offensive purposes. On October 24 American naval vessels arrived at their positions off Cuba and prepared to intercept twenty-five Soviet merchant vessels steaming for the Caribbean island.

The first signs of Soviet retreat came that same day when, obviously by order from Moscow, the Soviet vessels approaching Cuba stopped. Twelve then turned and headed back toward their home ports. Hearing of the withdrawal, Secretary of State Dean Rusk whispered to National Security Adviser McGeorge Bundy, "We're eyeball to eyeball and I think the other fellow just blinked."

But the crisis was not over yet. In Cuba the hasty preparations to make the missiles operative continued while the UN debated whether the American claims concerning the missiles were accurate. At 6 P.M. on October 26 a long letter from Khrushchev began to arrive by teletype in Washington. The Soviet leader admitted for the first time that Soviet missiles had been placed in Cuba. He also promised to withdraw or destroy these if the United States promised not to attack Cuba.

As Ex Comm was debating whether to accept these terms, another message arrived from Moscow. The Soviet Union would withdraw its missiles if the United States agreed to dismantle NATO missile bases in Turkey, close to the Soviet Union. The American government did not believe the bases valuable and wanted to abandon them anyway, but Washington did not want to do so under the Soviet gun. At this point Ex Comm, backed by the Joint Chiefs of Staff, came perilously close to recommending a combined airstrike and invasion of Cuba. Soviet lives would undoubtedly have been lost; war with the Soviet Union might well have followed.

The president now stepped in and reminded his advisers that the proposed attack threatened the survival of humanity. Fortunately Robert Kennedy had a bright idea. Why not reply positively to the first message and ignore the second? The attorney general and Ted Sorensen, JFK's chief domestic adviser, composed just such a response, and the president dispatched it to Khrushchev that evening, accompanying it with the public statement that he had accepted Khrushchev's proposal. How would the Soviet Union respond?

On Sunday, October 28 at 9 A.M. Washington time, Radio Moscow broadcast a reply to the American note. "In order to eliminate as rapidly as possible the conflict which endangers the cause of peace . . . the Soviet government . . . has given a new order to dismantle the arms . . . described as offensive and to crate and return them to the Soviet Union." Castro was furious; the Soviets had acted without his knowledge. But he had no choice. As for almost everyone else in the world, the sense of relief was overwhelming.

The peaceful end of the missile crisis set the stage for an improvement in Soviet-American relations. Kennedy developed a new confidence in himself and was able to deal with the Soviets less stridently and defensively. The Soviet Union, in turn, proved more conciliatory too, although the missile retreat had hurt Khrushchev and would contribute to his overthrow in October 1964. In June 1963 the United States and the Soviet Union established a "hot line" directly connecting the leaders of both nations, to be used for personal communication in case of another crisis. A month later Britain, the United States, and the Soviet Union agreed on a Limited Nuclear Test Ban pledging the three nations to cease testing nuclear weapons in the atmosphere, under water, and in space. Underground testing could continue, but the increase in atmospheric nuclear pollution would now end.

These post-missile crisis moves reduced international tensions. In Vietnam, however, Kennedy's policies were less successful. These will be considered in Chapter 13.

Destiny in Dallas

In late November 1963 Kennedy, accompanied by his wife, went to Texas to help heal a serious rift in the state's Democratic party. Despite warnings that he would encounter venomous hatred from the far right for his civil rights stand, the president and the first lady had been greeted like visiting royalty in Houston, San Antonio, and Fort Worth.

The presidential party arrived in Dallas on Friday, November 22, and Kennedy, his wife, Texas Governor John Connally, and assorted dignitaries set out by motorcade from Love Field airport to the Dallas Trade Mart where the president was scheduled to deliver a speech at noon.

The day was sunny and pleasant and the crowds lining the route through downtown Dallas were surprisingly large and enthusiastic. The president rode in the backseat of an open Lincoln convertible with Jacqueline by his side and Connally and his wife in the jump seats in front of them. At 12:30 P.M. shots rang out from the sixth floor window of the Texas School Book Depository, a textbook warehouse at the corner of Houston and Elm streets. The president fell over on his wife, hit in the head and neck; Governor Connally, sitting in front, was hit in the back, chest, right wrist, and left thigh. The presidential car sped to Parkland Memorial Hospital, but it was too late. John Kennedy was pronounced dead at 1 P.M. Vice President Lyndon Johnson had been further back in the motorcade, and later that day, while waiting to leave for Washington, he took the presidential oath of office with the stunned and still bloodstained Jacqueline Kennedy by his side.

The killer apparently was Lee Harvey Oswald, an eccentric loner who had defected to the Soviet Union and then, after returning with a Russian wife, became active in a left-wing group called Fair Play for Cuba. The killing excited the wildest speculations that were powerfully reinforced when, two days after his capture, as he was being moved from one local jail to another, Oswald himself was shot and killed by Jack Ruby, a shady Dallas nightclub owner. Oswald had never admitted anything. The left would seek to pin the assassination on the right: Oswald was paid by

Within hours of the assassination of President Kennedy on November 22,1963, Lyndon B. Johnson took the presidential oath as his successor. At Johnson's right is his wife, Lady Bird; to his left is Kennedy's widow, Jacqueline, her clothes stained by her husband's wounds. (UPI/Bettmann Newsphotos)

right-wing southern fanatics who hated Kennedy's civil rights stand or by the FBI or CIA with their own bizarre agendas. The right would blame the left: Oswald was an agent of either Castro or Khrushchev. President Johnson appointed a commission headed by Chief Justice Earl Warren to investigate the horrible and strange events. Despite the twenty-six-volume Warren Commission Report that found both Oswald and Ruby had acted alone, Americans' imaginations soared. Conditioned by years of conspiracy theories, CIA escapades, and spy thrillers, many people refused to accept the Warren Commission's conclusions. Some popular theories speculated that there was more than one killer, that Oswald could not have fired the gun, that he was a "Manchurian Candidate" (the name of a movie of the period), a man programmed to kill by some sinister group.

The president's assassination lacerated the nation. Although Kennedy had won by the narrowest of margins in 1960 and had made additional enemies, especially on the right, he had gained many more friends. Few people any longer feared his religion, and millions had come to admire his grace, eloquence, wit, and growing maturity in office. He seemed to millions a radiant young hero. Today it is known that there was base metal alloyed with the gold, but few people in 1963 knew of the president's personal moral lapses or the shabby plots against Castro. There was every indication that he would win big in 1964, especially if, as seemed likely, the Republicans turned to Barry Goldwater, the leader of the party's right wing.

Millions of stunned Americans watched on television the solemn funeral ceremony in Washington on November 25: the coffin resting on a gun carriage pulled by matched gray horses; the muffled drum rolls; the moving mass by Cardinal Richard Cushing of Boston, the Kennedys' old family friend; little John Jr. saluting his father outside the Washington church; and the internment at Arlington cemetary. It produced an outpouring of national grief unequaled since Lincoln's death a century before. In later months many people would say that what had kept them from panic was the firm and steady hand of the new president, Lyndon Johnson.

Johnson Takes Over

The new president was a very different man from his predecessor. Kennedy loyalists, drawing on Shakespeare, would use the phrase "Hyperion to a satyr" to compare the two. It was grossly unfair. Lyndon B. Johnson (LBJ) was not handsome; he was not young; he was not witty; he was not polished; he was not elegant. Johnson had a coarse and bullying streak. He sometimes forced subordinates to accompany him into the toilet while he dictated memos or lectured them. When he wanted political favors, he seized people by the lapels, thrust his face into theirs, and delivered long monologues on why they must do what he wanted. This was called "the treatment" and it was often effective. The new president was a virtuoso of revenge. People who crossed him risked having their political legs, if not worse, cut off. Furthermore he was "new money" rich, unlike the Kennedys whose fortune had been won a generation previously, and his methods of acquiring wealth—using political influence to gain ownership of Texas television stations, for example—were not always savory.

But great failings were accompanied by great virtues. Although now a rich man, Johnson had never forgotten his youthful poverty and the poverty of Mexican-Americans and Texas hill country farmers during the Depression. His hero was Franklin Roosevelt, for whose National Youth Administration he had worked, and he sincerely hoped to complete the New Deal program of weaving a security net for ordinary Americans and creating new opportunities for the nation's outsiders. He also commanded uncommon legislative skills. His years as Senate minority and majority leader had trained him to manipulate Congress as no other previous president. In many ways he had the parliamentary dexterity of a British prime minister. Unlike his predecessor who did not command great respect on Capitol Hill, Johnson, at least at first, had Congress securely in hand.

The Great Society Emerges

The new president, taking advantage of public grief and shame over the assassination, moved quickly to propel deadlocked Kennedy legislation through Congress. In the first months he secured passage of an important foreign aid bill, a Higher Education Facilities Act, and the long-blocked tax reduction measure to fire up the economy. Most importantly he got Congress to pass the pending civil rights legislation. The Civil Rights Act of 1964 forbade discrimination in public places; authorized federal suits to desegregate schools; outlawed job discrimination for race, religion, and sex; and swept away barriers to voter registration based on technicalities and on supposed education deficiencies.

A year before his death Kennedy had asked his aides to look into the "poverty problem." Like many other Americans he had read Michael Harrington's recently published *The Other America* showing that millions of citizens, despite overall national affluence, were still poor. Kennedy felt something should be done about it and had asked Walter Heller to come up with the facts and figures for antipoverty legislation. He died before the experts' report came in, but Johnson picked up the idea and expanded it. In January 1964 he called on Congress to declare "an unconditional war on poverty," and soon after introduced the Economic Opportunity Act.

Passed in late August, this measure established the Office of Economic Opportunity (OEO) with an initial budget of $800 million. OEO ultimately planned and administered a wide range of programs: Head Start to give young ghetto children an educational leg up; job training for the poor; a domestic peace corps (VISTA); a neighborhood youth corps to occupy inner city adolescents usefully; and a series of "community action" programs to nurture initiative and competence among the poor. Johnson chose former Peace Corps Director Sargent Shriver, a Kennedy by marriage, as its head.

Johnson also launched several legislative initiatives of his own. During these months Congress enacted the Wilderness Preservation Act to sequester nine million acres of public land for a permanent unexploitable reserve and the Urban Mass Transportation Act to help build or improve city public transportation systems.

In May 1964, speaking to the graduates of the University of Michigan in Ann Arbor, Johnson gave a name to his program. It was now time, he said, to build the *Great Society* where material abundance would provide the basis for "a richer life in mind and spirit." Such a society demanded "an end to poverty and racial injustice." It also demanded not just more, but better. "[T]he city of man [must serve] not only the needs of the body and the demands of commerce but the desire for beauty and hunger for community."

The 1964 Election

During these early months the president had been helped by the desire to memorialize the martyred Kennedy. This impulse could not be expected to last indefinitely. Fortunately for the Great Society the Republican right handed the president an enormous extension of time that he would put to good use.

Although powerful at the grass roots, especially in the Midwest and Southwest, for years the conservative wing of the Republican party had been frustrated in its quest for the presidency. Far too often the party had turned to its moderate wing at the quadrennial presidential nominating conventions. As the 1964 presidential election approached, the Republican right was determined it would not happen again. This time one of their own would carry the GOP banner.

The right had an attractive candidate in Senator Barry Goldwater of Arizona, a handsome former Phoenix department store owner and reserve air force general. Goldwater had published a book, *The Conscience of a Conservative,* urging slashes in federal spending, tough restrictions on organized labor, the end of federal involvement in racial issues, and "total victory" over the Communist effort "to capture the world and destroy the United States." He quickly became the party conservatives' standard-bearer.

The moderate and liberal Republicans led by Nelson Rockefeller and Governor William Scranton of Pennsylvania fought Goldwater and his band of "extremists" at the July national convention in San Francisco. But the Goldwater forces were too aggressive and determined. The Arizona Senator secured the nomination on the first ballot and in a defiant acceptance speech, proclaimed that "extremism in defense of liberty is no vice and . . . moderation in the pursuit of justice is no virtue." Goldwater's campaign, with vice presidential nominee William Miller, an obscure New York Congressman, used as its slogan "A Choice, Not An Echo."

Johnson won the Democratic nomination at Atlantic City by acclamation with Senator Hubert Humphrey of Minnesota as his running mate. The one flaw in what was otherwise a love feast was the challenge by the Mississippi Freedom Democratic party (MFDP) of the regular all-white state delegation, chosen in all-white primaries. Elected by an unofficial "freedom" primary during the Mississippi "Freedom Summer" civil rights drive of 1964, the MFDP delegates, mostly African-American, defended their claim before the credentials committee through the eloquent middle-aged black woman Fannie Lou Hamer, who described the systematic exclusion of black Mississippians from the ballot and argued that MFDP alone supported the president's doctrines and values in Mississippi. But the Johnson forces, fearing loss of the whole South, imposed a compromise that allowed the MFDP only a token representation, although promising to do better in 1968. In later months many young civil rights workers would remember this rebuff with anger.

The presidential campaign was a Republican disaster. Many moderate and liberal Republican leaders refused to work for Goldwater. Thousands of voters, normally Republican, deserted the party. Goldwater had left many hostages to political fortune in past ill-considered proposals and political suggestions. He had offered to sell the respected Tennessee Valley Authority to private interests for a dollar; he had speculated that it might be a good thing if the eastern seaboard were sawed off the continent and allowed to float out to sea; he had suggested the elimination of federal rural electrification programs; he had proposed making social security a voluntary system. As recently as 1963 he had made the frightening proposal that local NATO commanders be given the power to use nuclear weapons in a crisis without presidential authorization. Each of these ideas would return to haunt the candidate.

The Democrats took advantage of every opportunity their opponents gave them. They depicted Johnson as a fatherly, benevolent figure, a reasonable and moderate man compared with the "radical right" fanatic from Arizona who intended to dismantle the welfare state and blow up the world. In fact the president was not exactly a pacifist either. During these months the Johnson administration was committing the United States to an ever-expanding role in Vietnam. In August, citing an attack by North Vietnamese naval vessels on the American destroyer *Maddox,* the president secured the Gulf of Tonkin Resolution from Congress, authorizing the administration to "take all necessary measures to repel any armed attack against the forces of the United States." He would soon use the resolution as a license to expand the American commitment in Vietnam. (See Chapter 13.) Yet during the campaign Johnson pledged "no wider war" and the Democrats felt free to accuse their opponents of being trigger-happy.

The results were no surprise. The Johnson-Humphrey ticket roared to victory with 61 percent of the popular vote, an even larger proportion than FDR had won in 1936. It also took every electoral vote except fifty-two, all of these from the deep South, except Arizona, Goldwater's home state. The new eighty-ninth Congress would have overwhelming Democratic majorities: 68 to 32 in the Senate, 295 to 140 in the House.

The Great Society at High Noon

The next two years were among the most legislatively productive in American history. The president claimed an enormous public mandate, a "consensus" for change that he quickly converted into a reform tidal wave.

The first administration successes came with passage of a federal aid to education bill (the Elementary and Secondary School Act) and the Medicare Act, establishing a system of free medical care for persons over 65 under the Social Security system. Medicare did not provide the full health insurance coverage for all Americans that liberals had urged since the New Deal, but it was an important installment.

In August 1965 Congress enacted an Omnibus Housing Act providing rent supplements for low-income families; in September it established a new cabinet-level Department of Housing and Urban Development and a National Foundation of Arts and the Humanities to encourage music, dance, painting, theater, and research in the humanistic disciplines. In October it passed a Water Quality Act and an Air Quality Act mandating higher standards for the nation's waters and imposing automobile exhaust controls. That same month came a Higher Education Act providing the first federal scholarships for college students. Other measures of that remarkable eighty-ninth Congress included a teacher corps, subsidies for new mental health facilities, aid to urban mass transit, and new consumer protection legislation.

The president was even able to get another installment of civil rights legislation. The Voting Rights Act of 1965 forbade literacy tests as a requirement of voter registration and allowed the federal government to supervise voter registration where there was clear evidence that the local authorities were preventing minorities from registering.

The Tax Cut and Prosperity

Johnson owed his success in part to his legislative skill, in part to the accident of lopsided majorities in Congress. But there was another crucial factor: the nation was prosperous as never before. The tax cut of his first months as president, a measure that benefited the middle class disproportionately, had done the trick. In 1964 the GNP rose an impressive 6.3 percent; in the next year the growth rate rose even faster.

Growth rates per capita during the 1960s would exceed those for any period during this century. At the same time, in the peak years of the Great Society inflation was low, under two percent in 1965 for all consumer prices. Millions of Americans felt flush, expansive, generous. The country surely could afford to allocate some slices of its ever-expanding pie to people who were less fortunate.

An Evaluation of Great Society Programs

It is not clear how effective the Great Society was. Middle-class programs, such as the National Endowments, clearly enriched scholarship and the arts. Many professors have reason to praise Johnson. Programs to improve the environment, although obviously insufficient, were necessary early steps in the long-term campaign to avoid world ecological disaster. Education programs helped thousands of students through undergraduate, graduate, and professional programs. But what about the antipoverty measures, the crux of the Great Society?

Here the experts disagree. Conservative scholars, as we shall see, believe that many of the antipoverty programs did not work. In fact some claim that by creating a high level of dependency, they only created even more poor, people incapable of working and earning their own income. The left criticized the Great Society as too little, too late. It did not redistribute income from rich to poor. Michael Harrington, the man whose exposé of American poverty, *The Other America,* had inspired the War on Poverty, concluded, "What was supposed to be a social war turned out to be a skirmish and, in any case, poverty won."

The truth seems to be rather complex. Clearly the Great Society programs provided jobs for educated men and women, African-American and white—as administrators, office workers, social workers, and teachers of skills. Poverty programs undeniably were pork barrels, and this time new people, some of them ghetto activists with militant goals and advisers with left-liberal social agendas, were being cut in. City mayors, many good Democrats, often objected to local people, especially militants, having direct access to federal money and thereby bypassing them, and these mayors carried their objections to the president and the vice president. The media, meanwhile, gave every excess of the Community Action Programs generous attention, in the process arousing serious public doubts.

But did the programs reduce poverty and even out some of the inequalities of American life? To some extent, apparently, they did. Head Start, a program to teach poor children language and other skills at an early age, seemed to make a difference in the later performance of ghetto children in school and the job market. Job-training programs provided marketable skills for some poor people. Various "entitlements" programs—providing health, education, food, rent supplements, and other services and commodities—raised the income of those at the economic bottom. On the other hand, as Harrington says, poverty won. Its sources lay too deep to be eliminated through programs such as those supplied by the Great Society.

The Breakdown of the Civil Rights Movement

African-Americans, of course, had been major beneficiaries of the upwelling of social generosity. Americans recognized the special afflictions of the country's black people, and Great Society programs had conferred disproportionate boons on the inner-city ghettos. From 1965 on this reservoir of goodwill rapidly drained away. An important piece of the Great Society consensus would break off.

One cause was the changing mood within the civil rights community itself. As early as the Marcus Garvey movement of the 1920s a small minority of African-American leaders had attacked the idea of a nonsegregated, biracial society. Garvey had supported black separatism and urged the return of blacks to Africa. In 1931 Elijah Muhammad, born Elijah Poole, had founded the Black Muslims, a religious group that rejected Christianity as a white people's religion and turned the negative white stereotypes of African-Americans upside down. Muhammad and his disciples called whites "blue-eyed devils," the "human beast," and "liars and murderers," and advocated total separation of black people from white society.

Muhammad's most effective disciple, although later an opponent, was Malcolm X, a young street hustler converted to the Muslim faith while in prison. Malcolm advocated the use of force, although only to protect African-Americans against physical violence, and eventually abandoned antiwhite views. He broke with the main Muslim group under Elijah Muhammad in 1964 and in 1965 was assassinated, allegedly by some of his factional enemies.

The Muslims' chief following was in the northern urban ghettos. In 1966 they were joined by the Black Panthers, organized in Oakland, California by two young African-American junior-college students, Bobby Seale and Huey Newton. The Panthers favored black self-defense against police brutality. Their members wore paramilitary garb and, for a time, carried rifles openly in public. Their macho style and bravado attracted African-American inner-city youths. It provoked the police, and almost from their birth the Panthers and the cops engaged in bloody clashes for which both sides were often to blame.

The Muslims and the Panthers were the fringe. But by 1965 militancy and separatist black nationalism had begun to invade the civil rights mainstream, where a biracial, color-blind society had been the fond goal and nonviolent civil disobedience, the preferred means.

In part the change derived from the struggles of Third World peoples in Africa, Asia, and Latin America to throw off their colonial chains. In Africa by the mid-sixties there were already several independent black nations, and more were soon to follow. Their struggles and successes created a new sense of pride in young African-American men and women. They also provided a model for the African-American experience at home. Black students read *The Wretched of the Earth,* Frantz Fanon's account of the Algerian battle for freedom against the French, and identified with the revolutionists. Weren't African-Americans just a colonialized people like the Nigerians, Congolese, or Algerians who were fighting against European oppressors? This black nationalist mood emotionally bound the new militants to powerful currents sweeping the Third World.

But events at home were even more important than those abroad as a spur to militancy and separatism. In 1964 SNCC launched its "Freedom Summer" project in Mississippi, the South's poorest and most segregated state. Hundreds of northern volunteers, mostly white college students, came to Mississippi to join the SNCC workers and local African-American leaders already on the scene in a program of voter

Black Panthers on the steps of the California Capitol. (AP/Wide World Photos)

registration, "freedom schools" for black children, and the creation of a biracial Democratic party.

The summer started with tragedy. While white student volunteers were training in Oxford, Ohio, to meet the summer's trials and dangers, news arrived that three young civil rights workers in Mississippi, including two northern whites, had disappeared. The volunteers came anyway. They encountered ferocious hostility from white Mississippians who saw them as an invading horde determined to upset the South's delicate racial balance. They received little help from the federal authorities. Over eighty SNCC volunteers were beaten, scores were shot at, and a thousand thrown into fetid jails. One participant later wrote that Freedom Summer had been "the longest nightmare I ever had." On August 13 the bodies of the three missing civil rights workers were found buried in an earthen dam. Later twenty-one white men, including several police, were arrested for the crime. The authorities judged the evidence for a murder charge insufficient, but sixteen of the suspects were later tried for violating the victims' civil rights.

The Mississippi Freedom Summer experience, as hoped, attracted media attention and reinforced northern liberal sympathies for the civil rights cause. Among the participants themselves it produced mixed results. Many white students returned to their northern college campuses convinced that America was an irretrievably racist society. Some of these young men and women would become leaders in the new left student movement just beginning to emerge on college campuses. African-American participants generally felt let down. Many resented the white students who had at times acted arrogantly and when the summer ended, had been able to pull up stakes and return to their safe ivy-walled campuses, leaving them to face the racists' hostility alone. These feelings further encouraged separatism. The experience also weakened SNCC's faith in nonviolence. Turning the other cheek had not protected the volunteers against attack; it had not saved the three murdered civil rights workers. Why not meet violence with violence? Before long the SNCC leaders and other young black militants would proclaim "Black Power" and challenge the nonviolence and biracialism of Martin Luther King and SCLC.

By this time SCLC had passed its peak. In early 1965 King had been able to mobilize the support of white clergy and northern white liberals to further African-American voter registration in Selma, Alabama, over the opposition of Sheriff Jim Clark and Governor George Wallace. The confrontations had been bloody; several white participants, including a Detroit homemaker and a Unitarian minister, had been shot and killed by white racists. Their martyrdom had revolted liberals and provided Johnson with the moral ammunition he needed to induce Congress to pass the 1965 Voting Rights Act.

A year later, during a march for freedom to protest the shooting of civil rights leader James Meredith, the phrase "Black Power" first surfaced. At rallies along the highway to Jackson, Mississippi, the state capital, SNCC leader Stokely Carmichael, a young black firebrand from New York, began to shout "We want black power! Black power!" The older leaders objected. Roy Wilkins of the NAACP denounced the term and the idea as "the father of hatred and the mother of violence." It meant separatism; it meant "going it alone." King, however, feared driving the young militants away and hedged. His hesitation did not help his reputation with the firebrands. By this time SNCC was ridiculing King as "de lawd" and denouncing his faith in nonviolence and "black and white together." Soon after SNCC and CORE expelled their white members to "go it alone."

Black Power frightened and offended many whites who had hitherto supported the civil rights movement. King and others tried to reassure white liberals, but increasingly white people felt hurt and excluded. Many would now stand by the sidelines; some would reconsider earlier attitudes.

King Turns North

By this time Reverend King had turned his attention to the northern inner cities, where African-American ghetto dwellers were beginning to express the new insurgent mood violently. Beginning in August 1965 with Watts in Los Angeles and then for the following three "long hot summers" in Chicago, Cleveland, Detroit, Newark, Washington, and over 100 other cities stupendous riots turned black neighborhoods into smoking ruins that resembled Berlin or Tokyo at the end of World War II. These explosions of rage were often ignited by reports of police brutality; they then fed on the enormous bottled-up resentment of black ghetto dwellers toward white storekeepers, landlords, the welfare bureaucracy, and "the man" generally.

Critics pointed to the self-serving motives of many rioters. Some African-American leaders believed they were only hurting their own cause. Yet they had their defenders. However unfocused, said black militants and white radicals, the rioters were primitive revolutionaries who were acting the only way possible against a system that would no longer yield to persuasion.

King had gone to Watts while the pall of smoke still rose over the city and had resolved to turn his attention to the problems of the northern ghettos. In a sense with Selma and the Voting Rights Act the civil rights movement of the fifties and early sixties had achieved as much as it could. Segregation was gone or going; African-Americans were beginning to vote in the South in large numbers. Yet almost everywhere African-American poverty remained, a reproach to America's promise of opportunity and economic success.

There were many causes of this continuing inferiority. Black education was substandard; blacks were excluded from trade union membership and apprenticeship programs; blacks remained segregated in urban slums where housing was expensive and dilapidated and where jobs and good shopping were limited. Soon after Watts King resolved to turn SCLC's attention to the urban ghettos, concentrating on Chicago and its harsh housing discrimination practices.

In early 1966 King set up headquarters in Chicago and launched a campaign against the North's informal discrimination. African-American ghetto housing must be improved, King announced, and African-American people must be allowed to move to any neighborhood they wished.

It was far harder to desegregate housing then King and his colleagues had anticipated. Landlords and real estate companies resisted changes in their practices. White homeowners feared that blacks would destroy the value of their property and the peace of their communities. In Chicago Mayor Richard Daley claimed that King and his associates were outsiders who were stirring up trouble for no good reason.

King and his followers were not deterred. SCLC and other local African-American organizations mounted protest marches into white neighborhoods; they held rallies downtown to demand an end to segregated housing. The protestors encountered even worse hostility in the tight-knit Chicago ethnic communities than in the South. By now a new force had appeared on the political scene in the shape of "white backlash," a formidable resistance to any further concessions to black protesters. In Chicago backlash citizens—many the white-collar and blue-collar children and grandchildren of European immigrants—felt threatened by African-American political and economic aspirations and asked why they, whose forebears had not received help from the government as had African-Americans, should be made to pay the price of black advancement. When King and his followers marched through backlash neighbor-hoods, they encountered jeers and violence. Many protesters, including King himself, were injured in stone-throwing incidents.

In the end King got the mayor and the city's business, real estate, and financial lead-ers to accept the principle of fair housing. But the pact with the city was an empty ges-

ture, and almost everyone knew it. Chicago, like almost every place else, remained a ghet-
toized city. To save face, however, King pronounced the Chicago campaign a success.

The Poor People's Campaign and Death of King

By late 1967 King had been forced to recognize that the really hard part of the
struggle for racial equality remained. In December King announced that in the spring
SCLC would mount a "Poor People's Campaign" to force the federal government to
provide jobs, education, and housing for the poor—all the poor.

By now the full-scale war in Vietnam was causing serious problems for King and
his civil rights colleagues. The antiwar movement drained off further white liberal
support from the civil rights drive. The war also divided the black civil rights
leadership. The conservative civil rights groups, the Urban League and the NAACP,
were grateful to Johnson and the Great Society for what they had done for
African-Americans and poor people and feared offending the president. The militant
leaders of SNCC and CORE, on the other hand, had little use for Johnson-style
liberalism in any case and saw Vietnam as a white man's neocolonial war against
people of color.

By 1967 King, a man in the political middle, had become a prominent antiwar
leader. He opposed the war in part because he believed in nonviolence. He also
believed that ghetto youths were disproportionately sacrificing their lives while at the
same time the war was starving the Great Society programs that benefited ghetto
dwellers and the poor generally. Although he was reluctant to place himself in
opposition to the Johnson administration, he could not keep silent. In August 1965
King began to denounce the war and demand a negotiated settlement.

The administration struck back. From 1962 on the FBI had been wiretapping King
and his associates on the suspicion that SCLC was being influenced by one or more
secret Communist agents. Even after these charges were laid to rest, J. Edgar Hoover
and his agents continued the surveillance. Eventually they uncovered the fact that King
occasionally drank too much and had committed adultery. Hoping to destroy King's
reputation, Hoover leaked the information to federal officials, prominent journalists,
and religious leaders and had his agents anonymously send King himself a tape of his
sexual indiscretions accompanied with the advice that he commit suicide. After King's
defection to the antiwar movement, President Johnson endorsed Hoover's scheme to
undermine the civil rights leader's moral authority.

On April 4, 1968, Martin Luther King, Jr., was assassinated by James Earl Ray, a
white man probably in the pay of southern racists, as he stood on a motel balcony in
Memphis, Tennessee. King had gone to the city to help striking black sanitation
workers. News of King's murder set off a wave of ghetto riots that put the long hot
summers of the past to shame. Chicago, Baltimore, Detroit, and other cities previously
damaged by riots exploded. Now the nation's capital joined the list of cities looted,
burned, and trashed. It took 55,000 troops around the country to restore order to the
nation's cities.

The Reverend Ralph Abernathy, one of King's lieutenants, now became head of
SCLC. He immediately declared that the Poor People's Campaign would commence
that summer on schedule.

Despite Abernathy's brave efforts, however, he could never take King's place. The campaign's centerpiece was an encampment of African-Americans, white students, and Mexican-Americans near the Mall in Washington, D.C. Called "Resurrection City," it quickly fell into disarray. Rain turned the area into a swamp; vicious elements among the poor themselves preyed on the others. When the campaign disbanded in June, little if anything had been accomplished to extract new legislation from Congress to benefit the poor.

The demise of Resurrection City ended the "Second Reconstruction." It had dismantled the edifice of legal discrimination in America, but it had failed to end the economic and social inequality of white and black in America. Time would show that these were far more perplexing and far more difficult to eradicate within the framework of liberal society than Jim Crow.

The Rise and Fall of the New Left

The militancy boiling up in the civil rights and peace movements was part of a new, radical mood sweeping the nation at large. The new attitude affected adults, but it was especially potent among the educated young.

By the mid-1960s American colleges and universities were overflowing with students. In 1966 there were over five and a half million college students in the United States, a larger number by far than ever before in its history. The educational explosion was fueled in part by the post-1945 "baby boom," a social change that had reversed the century-long trend to lower birthrates. It was also powered by the growing prestige and value of a college degree. Overall prosperity, newly available federal aid, and a strong sense that the technical and professional skills that colleges dispensed were essential to success in the new economy all combined to make B.A.s, J.D.s, and Ph.D.s the goal of an expanding percentage of young men and women. When economists were saying that the universities were the engines of national wealth and power, it was natural for the young to flock to the campuses.

But in addition to those seeking vocations, there were those seeking enlightenment. Especially in the "soft disciplines"—the humanities and the social sciences—students often displayed a less materialistic attitude than those in the career-oriented fields. By the early 1960s many young, middle-class adults were beginning to feel that material success was not enough. American society appeared to have solved most of its economic difficulties, and there was no need for college-educated people to fear joblessness and hunger. Yet having grown up in the properous postwar era when success came easy, the affluent college young took little pleasure from material abundance, a condition that had brought great satisfaction to their parents. American society was still imperfect. Racism remained; the threat of nuclear war remained. Moreover alienation, powerlessness, environmental ugliness, conformity, intellectual barrenness, and intolerance all survived to diminish life in America. The "quantity" problems had been solved; now it was time to tackle the "quality" problems.

The new mood flourished in part as a reaction to the immediate past. During the 1950s dissent and social speculation had been constrained by McCarthyism and the self-congratulatory mood that followed success in World War II and the unexpected burst of postwar prosperity. McCarthy was now gone, and young Americans had come to take prosperity for granted. It was now time for a *New Left*, detached from the old, dogmatic Communist left, to destroy complacency, end the vestiges of inequality, and create a more humane, fulfilling, and democratic society.

Campus Radicalism

Such at least were the professed attitudes and goals of the first wave of student activists. As the fifties ended, here and there on some of the more cosmopolitan campuses small groups of young men and women were beginning to place social and political change on the undergraduate agenda. Some focused on peace; many were for a time drawn into the civil rights movement, especially as support troops for SNCC. Others made civil liberties their chief concern. A sizable proportion of this early group were the children of radicals, including Communists, although most of these "red diaper babies" were not strict Marxists. They no longer glorified the industrial working-class (the proletariat). They believed they themselves were the most potent

Students occupying Columbia University, 1968. (UPI/Bettmann Newphotos)

"agents" of social change. They had abandoned their parents' one-time pro-Soviet viewpoint. If any nation won their admiration it was Cuba, whose young charismatic leader, Fidel Castro, seemed to embody the best of the radical tradition without the dogmatism. Although undogmatic they were not, even at the outset, decorous. Young people are almost invariably swept away by enthusiasms, by passions, by infatuations. From the beginning their seniors often deplored their excesses of deed and word.

The existence of a new campus left burst on the public consciousness in the fall of 1964 when student insurgents at the University of California at Berkeley challenged the university administration's decision, under conservative pressure, to restrict political advocacy on the Berkeley campus. Organized as the Free Speech Movement (FSM), the students occupied the administration building and called a strike when the police ousted them bodily. Sympathetic to free speech and appalled by the police intrusion into academe, the faculty and liberal segments of the California community supported FSM, forcing the administration to relent.

Berkeley was the precedent for a thousand student rallies, strikes, and building takeovers during the next few years. These were directed against university "complicity" in the Vietnam War, against university "racism," against campus recruitment by the military and by companies such as Dow Chemical that made war matériel; and against the impersonality and repressiveness of the campus experience, the "irrelevance" of undergraduate curricula, or some other supposed failing of college life. They would at times force administrators to adopt more "relevant" courses and curricula, abandon paternalistic rules, and exclude unpopular speakers and recruiters from campus. Many of the campus confrontations were led by Students for a Democratic Society (SDS), formed in the early 1960s as the student affiliate of the League for Industrial Democracy (LID), an anticommunist moderate socialist group dating from before World War I.

SDS

SDS's early leaders were a group of young men and women at Ann Arbor, Michigan, including Al Haber, Tom Hayden, Richard Flacks, and Sharon Jeffrey, in tune with the new post-McCarthy student mood. In 1962 the Ann Arbor activists sponsored the Port Huron Statement, which endorsed "participatory democracy" to end powerlessness in America and declared that with blue-collar labor in the rich industrial nations fat and complacent, students were the most promising agents of social change. SDS soon established chapters at other colleges, usually prestigious campuses with a large proportion of cosmopolitan, affluent students.

After 1965 SDS became a major force in the campus anti-Vietnam movement, although the SDS leadership was always curiously reluctant to make the war the organization's chief concern. By 1966 SDS had broken with its parent group, LID, over excluding Communists and opened its membership rolls to hard-line Marxists oriented either to the Soviet Union or Communist China.

SDS fell apart at its national convention in Chicago in June 1969. There the old leaders of 1962 were present, if at all, only as observers. One faction, the "national office," convinced that social change could be midwived only by "wild in the streets" rebellious youth and by Third World revolutionaries like the Black Panthers, fought the hard-line Marxists led by the Progressive Labor party. Afraid to be outvoted, the national office group marched out of the hall leaving Progressive Labor in control. Within months the national office faction was planning to go underground to fight a guerrilla war against American "imperialism." The shell of SDS, under Progressive Labor leadership, ceased to attract members and soon expired.

Before its demise SDS had helped scatter New Left seeds in all directions. College faculties, portions of the literary, artistic, and intellectual communities, journalists, and some professional groups either borrowed its views and rhetoric or actually drew part of their membership from young SDS alumni radicalized in college. By the early 1970s, moreover, several major organs of opinion—the *New York Review of Books* and *The Nation,* for example—were disseminating New Left positions widely among their readers. The journalist Tom Wolfe called the views of the adult intellectual-literary leftists "radical chic." Yet with the demise of SDS the framework of the New Left collapsed. By mid-decade it was gone.

Repression

The New Left had largely destroyed itself by its immaturity, irresponsibility, and inability to understand American realities. But its demise was helped along by its enemies. Not only had the FBI sought to undermine Martin Luther King; it had also tried to confuse and distract the student left and the Black Panthers. Under the label "COINTELPRO," the FBI had infiltrated SDS, the peace movement, and the Panthers. Its purpose was not only to gather information on possible illegal doings but also to sow confusion by dirty tricks. FBI agents, for example, tried to prevent an alliance between SDS and the Panthers by sending anonymous letters purporting to come from one group personally attacking leaders of the other organization. Hoover's agents planted stories about the sexual misconduct of radicals and peace leaders. They induced the Internal Revenue Service to examine the tax returns of left peace movement leaders to tie them up in complex audits. The FBI even established a hit list of dangerous radicals to be rounded up in event of war. All told, whatever the provocation it was not a pretty picture for a democratic society still a long way from the edge of chaos.

The Counterculture

Paralleling and often interlocking with the New Left was the counterculture. This was a movement of revolt against the moral values, the aesthetic standards, the personal behavior, and the social relations of conventional society. (See the photograph opening this chapter.) It differed from earlier bohemias and even from the fifties beatnik phenomenon by its intimate association with consciousness-altering drugs. Although the Beats smoked marijuana ("grass") and even imbibed peyote and psilocybin, they did not make these drugs central to their lives. And they did not have lysergic acid diethylamide (LSD) the most potent hallucinogen of all. So fundamental was this substance to the new bohemia that the novelist Alan Harrington has said that the counterculture was "no more than Beats plus drugs."

Psychedelia

LSD (acid) is an artificial derivative of a natural fungus, first produced by a Swiss chemist in 1943. It stimulates fantastic images and states of mind where circles whirl, solid objects liquify, and colors produce sounds or tastes. LSD "trips," when they do not turn into terrifying nightmares, create the sense in the participant that ordinary perceptions are impoverished and that the world is infinitely richer than it seems. It later became clear that the drug is also harmful genetically, can precipitate psychosis, and might destroy the mental balance of chronic users.

For a time, however, LSD promised a new world liberated from the tedium of ordinary life. In the hands of Timothy Leary, a one-time psychology professor at Harvard, and Ken Kesey, a successful West Coast novelist, along with their friends and disciples, it seemed an instrument for undermining the "square," humdrum world of competitive striving, conventional sexual relations, and "linear" thinking. Leary sought to spread his message of "turn on, tune in, drop out" through a new ecstatic religion with its headquarters in Millbrook, New York. The authorities eventually closed it down and Leary himself ran afoul of the law. Kesey, author of the best-selling *One Flew Over the Cuckoo's Nest,* a novel describing the absurd workings of a mental hospital, proselytized for the new drug-induced utopia through music. The "acid tests," a series of San Francisco area rock and roll concerts charged up with LSD and flashing strobe lights, helped popularize the use of hallucinogen.

"Psychedelic" drugs quickly merged with the rock music scene. The practitioners of "acid rock," including such groups as the Grateful Dead, the Jefferson Airplane, the Fugs, Country Joe and the Fish, and the Quicksilver Messenger Service, incorporated the blasting sounds and sights of the acid experience into their music. Their concerts were celebrations of the new psychedelia. The new hallucinogens also eventually influenced the British groups the Rolling Stones and the Beatles, the latter being four English youths from Liverpool, whose first American visit in 1964 had produced an hysterical outpouring of adulation called Beatlemania. Their song "Lucy in the Sky with Diamonds" of 1967 was a thinly disguised hymn to LSD.

Rock music was a major transmission agent for the drug culture. The concerts at San Francisco's Fillmore auditorium and its imitators in other cities enveloped young people in the words, music, and sights of the acid culture and, often, in clouds of marijuana smoke as well. Rock festivals, beginning with the 1967 outdoor concerts in Monterey, California, were two- or three-day saturnalias of music, acid, and "grass." The festivals culminated with the immense gathering at Max Yasgur's farm in Woodstock, New York, in August 1969. Woodstock brought together all the elements of the counterculture community, including a political branch led by Abbie Hoffman and Jerry Rubin, two radicals who in early 1968 had organized the Yippies, an amalgam of political and cultural dissent. Woodstock seemed to be the beginning of a new counterculture "nation." In reality it marked the beginning of the end of the counterculture as an organized (or semiorganized) movement.

Hippies

Clearly, the most committed inhabitants of psychedelia were the hippies, denizens of a new subculture that abruptly appeared in San Francisco, New York, Los Angeles, and a few other major cities and college towns in 1966–67. Mostly young dropouts from middle-class suburbia, hippies, unlike many New Left activists, totally repudiated their origins. Their parents cherished material possessions; they would cultivate holy poverty. Their parents valued emotional control and self-denial; they would cultivate free expression and hedonism. Their parents were enslaved to competitive, aggressive responses; they would be guided by "love" and "flower power."

The hippie phenomenon first came to the attention of the general public with the "Human Be-In" held in San Francisco's Golden Gate Park in January 1967. Billed as a gathering of the "tribes"—of the "new people" of the new, liberated age—the Be-In announced the appearance of a new self-conscious counterculture community in the adjacent Haight-Ashbury neighborhood.

"The Haight" had its distinctive fauna—natives wearing beards, sandals, leotards, jeans, and miniskirts. It had its distinctive economy—poster shops, coffee houses, "headshops," arts and crafts emporia, and, barely out of sight, a legion of drug pushers. It had its own media and art—underground press, "comix," and psychedelic posters. So distinctive and colorful was this latest version of bohemia that by April 1967 the Grey Line Bus Company was running tours to the Haight for curious squares. By the late spring every rebellious sixteen-year-old was talking about "making the scene" in the Haight during the summer. It would be, everyone said, a glorious "Summer of Love."

The Haight-Ashbury Summer of Love, and its equivalent in New York's East Village, was an extraordinary experience. Thousands of young people crowded the streets and the "pads," "grooving" on grass and acid and the free concerts on Hippie Hill or in Central Park. They lived on money from home, by selling dope, panhandling tourists, or by taking handouts from the Diggers, a group of political-cultural anarchists who opposed private property and made "free" their motto. Many Haight-Asbury and East Village refugees found the experience liberating. But there was another side too. Disease, bad trips, ripoffs, thefts, and rape spread among the "flower children." Several drug dealers and a number of hippies were murdered. When September came many of the visitors were glad to return home.

There would be no more summers of love, but the hippie ethic did not suddenly die. Returnees from Haight-Ashbury and the East Village brought to their college communities and home towns much of the hippie culture. Some hippies sought to make the new ethic a permanent way of life by establishing communes, utopian communities where the new values could replace the old. The public's fascination with the hippie ethic continued and helped make *Easy Rider,* a counterculture movie epic starring Peter Fonda and Dennis Hopper, a big success in 1969. The hippie viewpoint also informed *Hair,* a commercially successful "tribal rock" musical about a young, long-haired man who ends up in Vietnam. *Hair* celebrated the "Age of

Aquarius" where peace, pot, perversion, and "crystal revelation" would all prevail. "Guerrilla theater," a form of street spectacle, also drew on the counterculture style and sought to bend it to political, antiwar, and social liberation ends.

The Sexual Revolution

The counterculture proclaimed the merits of sexual freedom and placed instinctual liberation at the center of its vision. It was responding to major changes in morals and attitudes that affected American society at large.

The sixties decade marked the culmination of a sexual revolution that had been building at least since the forties. In 1948 Alfred Kinsey, a zoology professor at Indiana University, published the epoch-making *Sexual Behavior in the Human Male*. The work made sex seem a less forbidden subject by making it "scientific" and by revealing how common sex outside of marriage actually was. During the next decade Hugh Hefner's *Playboy* magazine, purveying a hedonist message and featuring young women bare above the waist, became the publishing sensation of the era. Soon the courts began to strike down local laws banning obscene books. The process of extending free speech guarantees to sexual expression culminated in the early 1960s with a series of federal court decisions allowing publication of any work so long as it contained a trace of "redeeming social value."

The courts' rulings allowed the open publication for the first time of a number of literary classics, but it also opened the floodgates for much outright pornography. A major beneficiary of this breakthrough was the underground press that appeared soon after. These publications included sexual news and "personals" offering sexual services as a staple of each issue. In 1968 the movie industry finally abandoned its dated "production code" and replaced it with a rating system—"G" (general), "M" (mature), "R" (restricted), and "X" (no one under sixteen admitted)—that allowed the showing of sexually explicit films. Soon scores of city downtowns sprouted X-rated movie houses to cater to the curious. Theater too was soon "liberated." Serious plays displayed nudity and featured dialogue formerly only heard in military barracks or locker rooms. Tom O'Horgan's *Futz* was about a man who loved his pig—physically.

By now sexual permissiveness had developed an intellectual rationale. The neo-Freudian writings of Norman O. Brown and Wilhelm Reich blamed many of society's ills on instinctual repression. Herbert Marcuse, a transplanted Middle European, labeled sexual repression a tool of capitalist domination. Marcuse, especially, became a guru to the counterculture and the spacier segment of the New Left.

The growing sexual permissiveness undoubtedly escalated sexual indulgence. Although the information is inconclusive, it seems clear that young people in the sixties had sex sooner, more often, and in more exotic ways than their parents ever dreamed possible.

The *sexual revolution* of the sixties cannot be ascribed solely to changes in cultural and moral attitudes. Even more important, probably, were two medical breakthroughs of the postwar period: mass produced antibiotics and the birth control pill. These supposedly eliminated the chief inconveniences of casual sex, disease and pregnancy. Together they created for a time a sense of security that promised to make "free love" really free. It was a brief interlude that would not last.

The New Feminism

The social restlessness and discontent and the desire for liberation that stirred African-Americans and youth during the sixties also influenced women. In 1961, as we saw, the President's Commission on the Status of Women had begun to stimulate a new response to women's concerns after the slow years of the fifties. Women, black and white, had also participated in the civil rights movement. They had become activists in the early New Left. These activities conferred new activist skills and aroused new impatience with deference and hierarchies of power. Then in 1963 Betty Friedan, a middle-aged Smith College graduate, helped crystalize a new feminist consciousness with her book *The Feminine Mystique.*

Friedan noted and deplored the decline of women's aspirations during the forties and fifties. She identified the subtle negative effects of sexism and called for a return to feminist activism to wipe out the large remaining areas of social and economic discrimination against women. In an era when all disadvantaged groups were raising the banner of equality against the white male "establishment," the book struck a resounding chord.

In 1966 Friedan and like-minded women formed the National Organization for Women (NOW). (See Reading 12.) NOW, like the NAACP, sought to work through the existing political system, using lobbying techniques and legal challenges against discrimination. In 1967 it endorsed the Equal Rights Amendment, supported by feminists since the 1920s, to insert into the Constitution a prohibition against all discrimination based on sex.

More radical than NOW were *women's liberation* groups, offshoots of the New Left. The pioneer "liberationists" were women who were former members of SNCC, SDS, and similar radical organizations. Although politically radical, these groups had often limited women to routine, unglamourous organization work while the men held the executive positions and became media celebrities. When women members of SNCC and SDS objected to their subordination, the male leaders had often resorted to ridicule and derision.

Rebuffed, the women responded by reevaluating their position in the organizations and reconsidering the place of women in society. They concluded that "sexism" pervaded even the radical movement and that women could not expect it to disappear even if the radicals triumphed and established their "classless society." There must be a separate radical women's movement that would push for women's liberation from male oppression whatever the ideology. They also concluded that the chief oppressor was not capitalism as such. Rather it was "patriarchy," the rule of men, a system that had prevailed since remote times. Patriarchy was the ultimate source of domination and oppression in the world; capitalism was only one form of this system.

The women's liberationists were more radical in their attitudes toward gender and men than other feminists. They generally held that there were no essential differences in personality or abilities between men and women. The observed disparities were the result only of early training and education designed to keep women in inferior positions. These differences were then reinforced by fashion and feminine stereotypes in later life. Some believed that marriage and the traditional

READING 12

The NOW Statement of Purpose

The chief vehicle of the 1960s feminist movement was NOW—the National Organization for Women. Founded in October 1966 as an expression of the feminist surge that followed publication of Betty Friedan's The Feminine Mystique, *NOW represented the views primarily of middle-class, well-educated white women. But despite this limited base, it quickly became the most effective voice of the new women's movement of the sixties.*

We men and women who hereby constitute ourselves as the National Organization for Women, believe that the time has come for a new movement toward true equality for all women in America, and toward a fully equal partner-ship of the sexes, as part of the world-wide revolution of human rights now taking place within and beyond our national borders.

The purpose of NOW is to take action to bring women into full participation in the mainstream of American society now, exercising all the privileges and responsibilities thereof in truly equal partnership with men. . . .

We organize to initiate or support action, nationally, or in any part of this nation, by individuals or organizations, to break through the silken curtain of prejudice and discrimination against women in government, industry, the professions, the churches, the politcal parties, the judiciary, the labor unions, in education, science, medicine, law, religion and every other field of importance in American society.

Enormous changes taking place in our society make it both possible and urgently necessary to advance the unfinished revolution of women toward true equality, now. With a life span lengthened to nearly 75 years it is no longer either necessary or possible for women to devote the greater part of their lives to child-rearing; yet childbearing and rearing which continues to be a most important part of most women's lives—still is used to justify barring women from equal professional and economic participation and advance.

Today's technology has reduced most of the productive chores which women once performed in the home and in mass-production industries based upon routine unskilled labor. This same technology has virtually eliminated the quality of muscular strength as a criterion for filling most jobs, while intensifying American industry's need for creative intelligence. In view of this new industrial revolution created by automation in the mid-twentieth century, women can and must participate in old and new fields of society in full equality—or become permanent outsiders.

Despite all the talk about the status of American women in recent years, the actual position of women in the United States has declined, and is declining, to an alarming degree throughout the 1950's and 60's. . . . Working women are becoming increasingly—not less—concentrated on the bottom of the job ladder. . . . Further, with higher education increasingly essential in today's society, too few women are entering and finishing college or going on to graduate or professional school. . . . In all the professions considered of importance to society, and in the executive ranks of industry and government, women are losing ground. Where they are present it is only a token handful. . . .

Until now, too few women's organizations and official spokesmen have been willing to speak out against these dangers facing women. Too many women have been restrained by the fear of being called "feminist." There is no civil rights movement to speak for women, as there has been for Negroes and other victims of discrimination. The National Organization for Women must therefore begin to speak.

WE BELIEVE that the power of American law, and the protection guaranteed by the U.S. Constitution to the civil rights of all individuals, must be effectively applied and enforced to isolate and remove patterns of sex discrimination, to ensure equality of opportunity in employment and education, and equality of civil and political rights and responsibilities on behalf of women as well as for Negroes and other deprived groups. . . .

WE BELIEVE that this nation has a capacity at least as great as other nations, to innovate new social institutions which will enable women to enjoy true equality of opportunity and responsibility in society, without conflict with their responsibilities as mothers and homemakers. In such innovations, America does not lead the Western world, but lags by decades behind many European countries. We do not accept the traditional assumption that a woman has to choose between marriage and motherhood, on the one hand, and serious participation in industry or the professions on the other. We question the present expectation that all normal women will retire from job or profession for 10 or 15 years, to devote their full time to raising children, only to reenter the job market at a relatively minor level. This, in itself, is a deterrent to the aspirations of women, to their acceptance into management or professional training courses, and to the very possibility of equality of opportunity or real choice, for all but a few women. Above all, we reject the assumption that these problems are the unique responsibility of each individual woman, rather than a basic social dilemma which society must solve. True equality of opportunity and freedom of choice for women requires such practical, and possible innovations as a nationwide network of child-care centers, which will make it unnecessary for women to retire completely from society until their children are grown, and national programs to provide retraining for women who have chosen to care for their own children full-time. . . .

WE REJECT the current assumptions that a man must carry the sole burden of supporting himself, his wife, and family, and that a woman is automatically entitled to lifelong support by a man upon her marriage, or that marriage, home and family are primarily women's world and responsibility—hers to dominate—his to support. We believe that a true partnership between the sexes demands a different concept of marriage, an equitable sharing of the responsibilities of home and children and of the economic burdens of their support. We believe that proper recognition should be given to the economic and social value of homemaking and child-care. To these ends, we will seek to open a reexamination of laws and mores governing marriage and divorce, for we believe that the current state of "half-equality" between the sexes discriminated against both men and women, and is the cause of much unnecessary hostility between the sexes. . . .

IN THE INTERESTS OF THE HUMAN DIGNITY OF WOMEN, we will protest, and endeavor to change, the false image of women now prevalent in the mass media, and in the texts, ceremonies, laws, and practices of our major social institutions. Such images perpetuate contempt for women by society and by women for themselves.We are similarly opposed to all policies and practices—in church, state, college, factory, or office—which, in the guise of protectiveness, not only deny opportunities but also foster in women self-denigration, dependence, and evasion of responsibility, undermine their confidence in their own abilities and foster contempt for women. . . .

We will strive to ensure that no party, candidate, president, senator, governor, congressman, or any public official who betrays or ignores the principle to full equality between the sexes is elected for appointed to office. If it is necessary to mobilize the votes of men and women who believe in our cause, in order to win for women the final right to be fully free and equal human beings, we so commit ourselves.

WE BELIEVE THAT women will do most to create a new image of women by acting now, and by speaking out in behalf of their own equality, freedom, and human dignity—not in pleas for special privilege, nor in enmity toward men, who are also victims of the current, half-equality between the sexes—but in an active, self-respecting partnership with men. By so doing, women will develop confidence in their own ability to determine actively, in partnership with men, the conditions of their life, their choices, their future and their society.

Source: National Organization for Women, Washington, D.C. October 29, 1966.

family were agencies of oppression and wished to change them drastically or even abolish them entirely.

Often in movements for social change the key precipitating element is the sudden awareness of oppression by individuals or some group. In the case of women, said the liberationists, the oppression was often deeply hidden under layers of guilt, stoicism, even love for the male oppressor. The technique for getting to these underlying feelings was "consciousness-raising" (CR), a sort of group therapy, where women gathered by themselves and discussed their problems, often their difficulties with husbands, lovers, and fathers, although with mothers and other women as well. The effect, not surprisingly, was to bring their anger against men to the surface.

Consciousness-raising spread like wildfire in the years just after 1968. For many women CR was primarily a therapeutic technique. But it also served as a recruiting device for the radical wing of the new feminism. Over the next few years a flock of radical feminist groups such as the Redstocking, Radical Feminists, and WITCH appeared to question the fundamental relations of the sexes and indict male-dominated, sexist society. Several of these small organizations produced headlines and aroused both support and antagonism by disruptive tactics. One of their biggest publicity coups came in September 1968 when a group of radical feminists from the New York area picketed the Miss America contest in Atlantic City, charging that contemporary beauty standards were designed to keep women in silken bondage.

The Great Society Ends

As Johnson's full term drew to a close it became clear that he and his programs were in serious trouble.

The president's consensus was unraveling at both ends. To his extreme left were the student rebels and their supporters among the intellectuals. But these were not numerous, and besides their hostility probably helped politically more than it hurt.

Far more serious opponents on his left flank were the anti–Vietnam War group collecting around Senator Eugene McCarthy of Minnesota. These people despised the war and opposed the administration's continued escalation. In late 1967 the antiwar liberals had convinced McCarthy to challenge the president for the Democratic nomination in 1968. Although he considered the attempt quixotic, the senator had agreed and early in the election year had entered the New Hampshire Democratic primary.

The McCarthy drive captured the imagination of thousands of college students who poured into the Granite State to ring door bells, make calls, organize rallies, and stuff envelopes. To everyone's amazement, the challenger almost beat the incumbent president in the primary. Soon after, Robert Kennedy, then U.S. Senator from New York and another antiwar "dove," also threw his hat into the ring.

By this time LBJ realized that the Vietnam War could probably not be won. In January 1968 the Vietcong–North Vietnamese Tet offensive shook the president and undermined the public's confidence that a victory was possible. After Tet Secretary of Defense Clark Clifford and Johnson's closest foreign policy advisers recommended that the United States reduce its Vietnam commitment. (See the next chapter.) Meanwhile the president was also under attack on the right where the Great Society, and indeed the whole thrust of the sixties, had raised up a host of enemies.

Backlash

Much of the problem was beyond Johnson's reach. The American middle-class public had become skeptical of the civil rights movement now that it had shifted its attention north and had entered its black power phase. Among blue-collar white citizens, especially, the mood since the ghetto riots had become frankly hostile to African-Americans. Why were they rioting and destroying property when the country had tried so hard to help them? "We build the city, not burn it down," declared one blue-collar group.

Many of these same "middle Americans"—white, middle- and working-class people of conservative, family-oriented value—deplored other social trends as well. As the central cities decayed, urban crime rates rose. Many middle Americans believed that blacks were primarily responsible for both the decay and the crime. They also deplored the disruptive tactics of the radical students; they saw the counterculture as immoral and disrespectful; they regarded the sexual revolution as dangerous; they considered the radical feminists a disgrace to women. By the late sixties many of these backlash dissenters were enlisting under the banner of Governor George Wallace of Alabama and were spoiling to challenge the reign of the "pointy-headed liberals" who had encouraged the forces of immorality and chaos.

Inflation and a Tax Rise

In the 1966 midterm elections, the Republicans had recovered from the Goldwater debacle and cut sharply into Johnson's lopsided liberal majority in Congress. Further reform might have been possible, nevertheless, if the economy, so successful through most of the Johnson administration, had not begun to falter. By late 1967 the remarkable price stability of the preceding decade came to an end. The following year the consumer price index rose almost 5 percent. At the same time foreigners began to cash in their dollars for gold, pulling the yellow metal out of Fort Knox and the vaults of the New York Federal Reserve Bank. On New Years' Day 1968 the president announced restrictions on American private investment abroad and on the amount of money American tourists could spend overseas. But these were stopgaps, and in early March there was a near panic in the world's gold exchanges.

The basic problems were the federal deficit and Johnson's reluctance to tax the American people to pay for the Vietnam War because he feared that taxes would make the war even more unpopular. Finally in late 1967 he was forced to acknowledge the gap between federal income and outgo and ask for a 10 percent surcharge on federal income taxes.

This was a major defeat for the Great Society. Wilbur Mills, a southern fiscal and social conservative who headed the all-powerful House Ways and Means Committee, refused to sanction a tax increase unless the president promised to cut back on domestic social programs. To stop inflation the president must abandon his remaining reform agenda.

In mid-1968 Johnson finally got his tax increase. But he paid the price. The administration promised Mills that it would trim the federal budget. The president would continue to urge new social legislation to help the country's poor, but he recognized that he could no longer get more money to end poverty. In later years the outlays for the poor would actually grow as cost of living increases and other escalators pushed up dollar appropriations. But after mid-1968 there would be few new initiatives; the spirit of the Great Society experiment had departed.

The 1968 Election

The Candidates

By this time too Johnson had decided to withdraw from the presidential race. Fearing further humiliation in the primaries at the hands of the McCarthy and Kennedy forces and hoping that his withdrawal might encourage a peace settlement in Vietnam, he decided to renounce a second full term. On the evening of March 31 he appeared on national television to speak on Vietnam. Just before signing off the president read an addendum to the speech. He had concluded, he said, that he should not permit the presidency to become involved in the noisy contentions of the coming presidential year. "Accordingly, I shall not seek and I will not accept the nomination of my party for another term as your President."

The 1968 presidential campaign then moved into high gear. With Johnson out of the race, the two antiwar Democratic candidates battled it out in a series of bruising primary fights in Indiana, Oregon, and California. Kennedy's followers included most of the African-American, Hispanic, and blue-collar Democratic voters; McCarthy proved strongest among students, professionals, and suburbanites. The big prize was California, the nation's largest state. In June Kennedy won a close victory there, but in Los Angeles, minutes after his victory statement, the New York senator was gunned down by Sirhan Sirhan, an Arab nationalist who disliked his support for Israel. Within three months the nation had suffered a double trauma of politics by assassination. Many Americans wondered how things had come to such a sorry pass.

Kennedy's assassination made Vice President Hubert Humphrey the front-runner. As vice president, Humphrey, of course, had waited until Johnson's withdrawal to announce his candidacy. By that time it was too late to enter the primaries, but with the support of most of the Democratic mayors and public officials, the trade union leaders, and the party's power brokers, the vice president did not need the primary delegates. He won the nomination over McCarthy easily at the Chicago convention in late August. His running mate was Senator Edmund Muskie of Maine.

Yet Chicago was scarcely a Humphrey triumph. Well before the Kennedy assassination the antiwar left, represented by the National Mobilization Committee to End the War in Vietnam (the "Mobe"), had announced plans to demonstrate for peace in Chicago during the convention. The Yippies, the Rubin-Hoffman attempt to merge radical politics with radical culture, proclaimed their intention to hold a disruptive "Festival of Life" in Chicago to offset the Democrats' "Festival of Death" and provoke the authorities to show the "naked face of power." Fearing that chaos would disgrace his city, Mayor Daley, refused permits to the Yippies or the Mobe for marches or the right to use the parks for sleeping.

McCarthy advised his followers to stay away. And in the end only a few thousand Yippies and Mobe people came. Yet for most of a week the Chicago streets near the convention hotels and convention hall witnessed club-swinging, stone-throwing violence between the police and demonstrators in which scores of innocent reporters and other bystanders were also roughed up and hurt.

An investigating committee later called what had transpired a "police riot." There is strong evidence, however, that Rubin, Hoffman, and their colleagues were intent on a confrontation. Whoever was responsible, the violence in downtown Chicago, transmitted to television viewers all over the nation, created the impression that the Democrats were incapable of keeping order. As a result Humphrey, although despised himself by the militants, suffered in the public estimate.

The Republican convention at Miami Beach was a more sedate affair. After Governor George Romney of Michigan, a naive, well-intentioned man, had destroyed his credibility by confessing to having been brainwashed on Vietnam by U.S. officials in Saigon, Richard Nixon became the clear front-runner. Most of the Republican professionals appreciated his loyal support for Goldwater and his help in restoring the party's fortunes after the 1964 debacle. Nixon's only possible challenger was Governor Ronald Reagan of California, a man who represented the party's most conservative wing. Nixon fended off the Reagan threat by promising the conservative southern Republicans that if nominated he would choose as his running mate a man the South could accept, and if elected he would do nothing to accelerate school desegregation. After nomination Nixon selected as the ticket's vice presidential candidate Spiro Agnew, the governor of Maryland, a man from a border state with a reputation for disliking African-American militants.

George Wallace was also a candidate, having been nominated in September by his own tailor-made organization, the American Independent party. His running mate was air force General Curtis LeMay, a military hard-liner who had once suggested bombing Vietnam "back to the stone age." Wallace attracted a large following in the white South. He also was popular among blue-collar middle Americans and backlash voters generally. Here was a man who would put the kooks and crazies in their place, impose "law and order," stop the campus disrupters, and conclude the war in Vietnam by tough, all-out action instead of the pussyfooting of the Johnson administration.

The Campaign

For a time the Wallace candidacy cut deeply into Democratic ranks. Thousands of blue-collar union members seriously considered deserting their traditional party for the Wallace-LeMay ticket. Nixon too appeared to draw defectors from Democratic ranks. The Republicans followed a shrewd strategy of appealing to the "silent majority." Nixon avoided the bigoted rhetoric of Wallace, although he did not disdain using "code" terms such as "law and order" that touched the same chords. Agnew, however, sounded like a country-club Wallace and had to be toned down lest he offend too many moderates.

For weeks following the Democratic convention the Humphrey-Muskie ticket limped badly. Many of the big money Democratic contributors, seeing the vice president as a loser, refused to help. Johnson had control of a large pool of funds but did not want to release it to the vice president. By the fall American–North Vietnamese preliminary peace talks were under way in Paris and LBJ hoped to prevent the vice president from promising his own independent, soft line that would encourage the enemy to stand tough.

Yet to win, Humphrey had to detach himself from the dead-end Vietnam escalation policies of LBJ. Eventually he found the moral courage to strike out on his own with a statement in Salt Lake City on September 30 that as president he would unilaterally cease all bombing of North Vietnam if the enemy promised to end infiltration of additional troops into the South. It wasn't a dramatic change from the Johnson position, but it did show some independence and brought liberal voters and their contributions back in a wave. Meanwhile the labor unions mounted a major campaign against Wallace among their members, pointing out how, during his gubernatorial administration, Alabama workers had been poorly paid and the state had lacked minimum-wage and child labor laws. As the campaign wound down, union members too began to return to the Democratic fold.

As election day approached the Democrats pulled almost even with the Republicans, while Wallace fell far behind. The results were exceptionally close. (See Figure 12–1.) Nixon got 31.8 million popular votes; Humphrey 31.3 million; Wallace 9.9 million. Less than a one percent margin separated the two major candidates. Nixon received 301 electoral votes, however, with 270 needed to win, and was elected president of the United States. He had succeeded, as his election strategy required, in carrying the traditional Republican states, several of the major industrial states, and the states of the upper South, surrendering only the deep South to Wallace. The Democrats retained control of both houses of Congress, but again the liberals could count on a conservative majority against them.

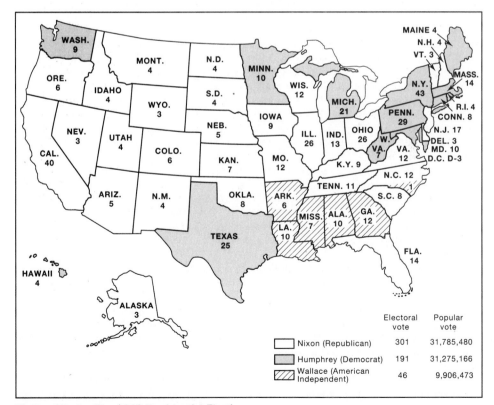

Figure 12–1 The 1968 Presidential Election

The Sixties End

And so the noisy, vivid, militant, confrontationist, chaotic, innovative, outrageous, and prosperous sixties ended, not chronologically, perhaps, but in most other ways. Its critics would call it "a slum of a decade," and clearly its legacy was mixed. An era that began when, briefly, influential Americans concluded that they had solved the problem of abundance and now could confront the issues of quality and equality, it allotted immense energies to flagrant excess—of rhetoric, expression, behavior, and theory. More positively it also witnessed a diminution of power inequality and status rigidities and the legitimation of views and groups once beyond the pale of respectability. Segregation ended, feminism regained its voice, and new sounds, sights, and freedoms found outlet. But it also left behind a legacy of self-indulgence, irresponsibility, and diminished personal and intellectual standards that some believe are with us yet.

FOR FURTHER READING

There are a number of works that attempt to deal with the entire sixties decade. William O'Neill's, *Coming Apart: An Informal History of America in the 1960s* (1970) is amusing as well as instructive. A work covering the same ground by a former SDS leader is Todd Gitlin's *The Sixties: Years of Hope, Days of Rage* (1987). Also see Irwin Unger and Debi Unger, *Turning Point: 1968* (1988), which, despite its title, covers much of the decade.

Two sympathetic works on the Kennedy administration that the student should consult are Arthur Schlesinger, Jr., *A Thousand Days* (1965) and Herbert Parmet's two-volume biography *Jack: The Struggles of John F. Kennedy* (1980) and *JFK: The Presidency of John F. Kennedy* (1983). Two more critical books are Garry Wills, *The Kennedy Imprisonment* (1983) and Henry Fairlie, *The Kennedy Promise* (1976). An interesting assessment of the Kennedy clan is David Burner and Thomas West, *The Torch Is Passed: The Kennedy Brothers and American Liberalism* (1984).

For an overall assessment of JFK's domestic policies see Aidi Donald (ed.), *John F. Kennedy and the New Frontier* (1966). The Peace Corps is discussed in Robert Carey, *The Peace Corps* (1970) and the Alliance for Progress in Herbert K. May, *Problems and Prospects of the Alliance for Progress* (1968). For JFK's early moves against poverty see Daniel Knapp and Kenneth Polk, *Scouting the War on Poverty: Social Reform Politics in the Kennedy Administration* (1971). The space program for the Kennedy years as well as before and after is covered in Walter A. McDougall, *The Heavens and the Earth: A Political History of the Space Age* (1985) The way the economy fared during JFK's administration is described in Seymour Harris, *The Economics of the Kennedy Years* (1964).

There are a number of books on the Kennedys and the civil rights movement. See Carl N. Brauer *John F. Kennedy and the Second Reconstruction* (1977) and Victor Navasky's critical study *Kennedy Justice* (1971).

For the civil rights movement during the sixties see, once again Harvard Sitkoff, *The Struggle for Black Equality* (1983). Also see Clayborne Carson, *In Struggle: SNCC and the Black Awakening of the 1960s* (1980); Mary King, *Freedom Song: A Personal History of the 1960s Civil Rights Movement* (1987); Cleveland Sellers, *River of No Return* (1976); and James Peck, *Freedom Ride* (1962).

Kennedy era foreign policy is discussed in Richard Walton, *Cold War and Counter-revolution* (1972). The Bay of Pigs crisis is covered by Peter Wyden, *Bay of Pigs* (1980). The Cuban Missile crisis is considered in Graham Allison, *Essence of Decision: Explaining the*

Cuban Missile Crisis (1971) and Robert Kennedy, *Thirteen Days* (1969). For the Berlin crisis see Jack M. Schick, *The Berlin Crisis, 1958–62* (1971).

The Kennedy assassination has generated a veritable deluge of studies, most advancing some pet conspiracy idea. The best narrative treatment, however, is still William Manchester, *Death of a President* (1966).

Lyndon Johnson's own defense can be found in his memoirs *The Vantage Point: Perspectives of the Presidency, 1963–1969* (1971). A scathing analysis of Johnson's character before he became president is Robert Caro's *The Path to Power* (1982). More sympathetic is Doris Kearn, *Lyndon Johnson and the American Dream* (1977). An analysis of the Johnson administration from a scholar who was the resident White House intellectual for a time is Eric Goldman, *The Tragedy of Lyndon Johnson* (1969).

The Great Society has been attacked from both the left and the right. Critics on the left include Allen Matusow, *The Unravelling of America* (1984) and Stephen Rose, *Betrayal of the Poor: Transformation of Community Action* (1972). A critic on the right is Daniel Moynihan, *Maximum Feasible Misunderstanding* (1970). For a good overview of the war on poverty see James Sundquist (ed.), *On Fighting Poverty* (1969).

The 1964 election is covered in Theodore White, *The Making of the President, 1964* (1965).

Black power and black nationalism are described in Archie Epps, *Malcom X and the American Negro Revolution* (1969) and Charles Hamilton and Stokeley Carmichael, *Black Power* (1967). Eldridge Cleaver's *Soul on Ice* is a personal memoir of a black power advocate. On the ghetto riots see Joe E. Feagin and Harlan Hahn, *Ghetto Revolts: The Politics of Violence in American Cities* (1973). A brief book on northern students and Freedom Summer is Mary Aickin Rothschild, *A Case of Black and White: Northern Volunteers and the Southern Freedom Summers, 1964–1965* (1982). On another aspect of the Freedom Summer of 1964 see William Bradford Huie, *Three Lives for Mississippi* (1965).

No one has written a history of the emerging sixties backlash, but see Marshall Frady, *Wallace* (1970). Also see Kevin Phillips, *The Emerging Republican Majority* (1969); Patricia Cayo Sexton and Brendon Sexton, *Blue Collars and Hard Hats* (1971); and Andrew Levison, *The Working Class Majority* (1974).

There are many books on the sixties student left and their activities. Among the better ones are James Miller, *Democracy Is in the Streets: From Port Huron to the Siege of Chicago* (1987); Kirkpatrick Sale, *SDS* (1974); and Irwin Unger, *The Movement: A History of the American New Left, 1959–1972* (1974). On the Berkeley Free Speech Movement see Max Heirich, *The Spiral of Conflict: Berkeley, 1964* (1971).

The counterculture is described in Theodore Roszak, *The Making of a Counter Culture: Reflections on the Technocratic Society and its Youthful Opposition* (1969); Martin Lee and Bruce Shlain, *Acid Dreams: The C.I.A. and the Sixties Rebellon* (1985); Charles Perry, *The Haight-Ashbury: A History* (1984); Morris Dickstein, *Gates of Eden: American Culture in the 60s* (1977); and Tom Wolfe's amusing *The Electric Kool-Aid Acid Test* (1969). For the acid rock scene see Ralph Gleason, *The Jefferson Airplane* (1972). There is no adequate history of the sexual revolution, but see Gay Talese, *Thy Neighbor's Wife* (1980).

The student interested in the woman's movement of the 1960s should first consult Betty Friedan, *The Feminine Mystique* (1963). Also see Judith Hole and Ellen Levine, *The Rebirth of Feminism* (1971); Sara Evans, *Personal Politics: The Roots of Woman's Liberation in the Civil Rights Movement and the New Left* (1979); and Robin Morgan (ed.), *Sisterhood Is Powerful: An Anthology of Writings from the Woman's Liberation Movement* (1970).

For the momentous 1968 election see Theodore White, *The Making of the President, 1968* (1969); Lewis Chester, Godfrey Hodgson, and Bruce Page, *An American Melodrama; The Presidential Campaign of 1968* (1969); Arthur Herzog, *McCarthy for President* (1969); and Jules Witcover, *85 Days: The Last Campaign of Robert Kennedy* (1969). Robert Kennedy's whole career is covered eulogistically in Arthur Schlesinger, Jr., *Robert F. Kennedy and His Times* (1974).

13
The Vietnam War

A 1967 anti–Vietnam War protest in Los Angeles. (AP/Wide World Photos)

The Vietnam Morass

Although the growing disunity of the civil rights movement, the radicalization of the left, and the rise of the backlash impulse all weakened the Johnson consensus, it was the Vietnam War, ultimately, that destroyed Lyndon Johnson's administration. This conflict, the longest foreign war in our history, checked the forward momentum of the Great Society and ultimately lead to the president's renunciation of a try for a second full term of office. The war ended, years later, with American goals frustrated and American morale and self-confidence depleted. The meaning of the Vietnam experience is still debated by Americans today.

The Historical Background

Vietnam is an ancient land that Europeans called Cochin China when they first encountered it in the sixteenth century. It was part of a larger cultural entity that included adjacent Laos and Cambodia and, like these other lands, had derived many of its institutions from the neighboring civilizations of India and China. (See Figure 13–1.)

Vietnam, the "lesser dragon," lived in the political shadow of China, the "greater dragon," and had long struggled to remain independent of it. Yet the Vietnamese had borrowed much from the Chinese: government by an educated class of civil servants (mandarins), rule by an emperor, rice culture, and the system of Confucian ethics that emphasized respect for authority and for ancestors.

Europeans—Portuguese, Dutch, French, and British—intent on trade, began to penetrate the region in the sixteenth century. But profits were elusive. The Vietnamese disliked foreigners and, tough and warlike, they could not be strong-armed into yielding trade concessions or other advantages. The Europeans soon lost interest. Yet one aspect of European civilization, Christianity, took deep root. By 1800, thousands of Vietnamese, especially in the northern part of the country, had become Roman Catholics.

Serious French political intrusion into the region began in the 1840s, justified by the Vietnamese emperor's persecution of French Catholic missionaries. In 1861 French forces captured the south Vietnamese city of Saigon (now Ho Chi Minh City) and soon after annexed several south Vietnamese provinces as colonies. Thereafter, bit by bit, France incorporated Vietnam, Laos, and Cambodia into its growing empire as French Indochina, although it retained local officials and even the Vietnamese emperor as intermediaries to transmit its orders and policies to the people.

The French brought their law, schools, language, and economy. Some Vietnamese eagerly assimilated French culture; some went to Paris to further their educations. Many, however, resented French cultural as well as political rule, and resisted. As early as 1859 Vietnamese irregular troops had begun to attack the French authorities and sporadic military resistance continued through the remainder of the nineteenth century.

During the opening years of the twentieth century Vietnamese resentment of French rule was amplified by increasingly exploitive economic policies. These

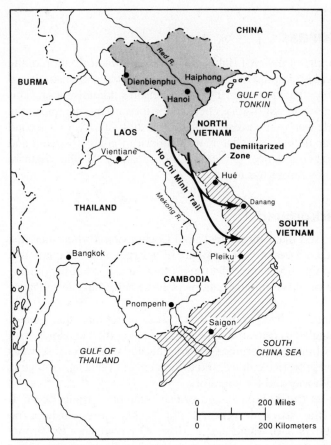

Figure 13–1   The Vietnam War

included turning over vast stretches of rice lands to French and favored Vietnamese landlords and displacing thousands of formerly landowning peasants, establishing large French-owned rubber plantations worked by disease-ridden indentured servants, and creating official monopolies of alcohol, salt, and opium production.

World War II

France's hold on its Indochinese colony weakened after its defeat by Germany in mid-1940. The expansionist Japanese soon began to demand that the French Vichy regime grant them the right to station troops on Indochinese soil. After Pearl Harbor Japanese troops occupied the whole colony, ruling through French Vichy officials. In several East Asian countries, where Japanese conquest displaced the former European rulers, the local people rallied to the new conquerors—at least they were Asian. But not in Vietnam. There the anticolonial movement was led by Ho Chi Minh, a Marxist revolutionary, and he firmly believed that the Allies would eventually defeat Japan and then grant Vietnam its independence.

Ho Chi Minh was a Communist and a nationalist simultaneously. He had left his native country in 1911 and traveled about the West, staying for a year in New York and passing some time in London before settling in Paris during World War I. There his Vietnamese nationalism was reinforced by Wilsonian self-determination doctrines and there, in 1920, Ho became a charter member of the new French Communist party.

In 1924 Ho went to Moscow where he met Soviet leaders Joseph Stalin and Leon Trotsky and studied techniques of revolution. He then returned to East Asia and, from the refugees of China, Hong Kong, and Thailand helped organize movements to overthrow the French and create a united, independent, and Communist Vietnam. In early 1941 Ho slipped across the border into Vietnam disguised as a Chinese journalist and established the Vietminh (the Vietnam Independence League) to fight the Japanese. Believing the time "not yet ripe" for open Communist leadership, the Vietminh proclaimed themselves a front of "patriots of all ages and all types, peasants, workers, merchants, and soldiers."

War against the French

After Japan's defeat the French sought to regain control in Indochina. The Americans were at first skeptical of French goals. In 1943 Roosevelt, who believed the French had "milked" their colony "for a hundred years," proposed an international trusteeship for the country. After FDR's death, however, the pro-French circles in the State Department prevailed, and in May 1945 Secretary of State Edward Stettinius assured the French foreign minister that the United States would support France's claims in the region.

But Ho Chi Minh and his Vietminh colleagues had no intention of letting the French return to power. In September 1945 in the northern city of Hanoi, before the French were able to reassert their authority, Ho and his associates announced the independence of Vietnam. Although a Communist Ho was also a pragmatist and still hoped that the United States might help him rebuff the French when they tried to return. His words from the platform at Hanoi's Ba Dinh Square included lines directly from the American Declaration of Independence.

During the next months confusion reigned in Vietnam with Ho's forces holding in the north and the French easily regaining control in the south. In 1946 Ho agreed to accept Vietnamese inclusion within the "French Union" in exchange for recognition of the "free state" status of the Democratic Republic of Vietnam. This arrangement quickly broke down and the two sides were soon engaged in a bitter war.

American Interest

Despite the early American tilt to the French, it took the Cold War to focus American attention on Vietnam. In 1949 came the North Atlantic Treaty Organization

(NATO), of which France was a key member. Soon after, the Chinese Communists defeated Chiang Kai-shek and took control in Beijing. In 1950 the North Koreans crossed the thirty-eighth parallel launching the frustrating Korean War. (See Chapter 10.) These events forced a reconsideration of the United States' Vietnam policy. France, American policymakers now concluded, must be supported—to keep the French loyal to NATO and encourage them to hold the line against Communist expansionism in Asia. This second goal would be given vivid expression by President Eisenhower at a 1954 press conference when he noted that the Southeast Asian nations were like "dominos." If "you knock over the first one . . . the last one . . . will go over very quickly."

Under President Truman the United States, after extracting promises from the French to accord some degree of autonomy to the Vietnamese under Emperor Bao Dai, had began to subsidize the French effort to defeat Ho Chi Minh and the Vietminh. By 1954 the United States was paying almost 80 percent of the cost of the bitter French-Vietminh struggle.

Dienbienphu and the Geneva Agreements

Despite American financial aid the war did not go well for the French. By the end of 1952 the Vietminh had won control of almost all of northern Vietnam and were intruding into neighboring Laos. Then in July 1953 the United States and the North Korean–Red Chinese allies signed the armistice ending the Korean War. This freed the Chinese to send supplies and heavy weapons to the Vietminh. By 1954 the desperate French were asking for American troops to stop Ho. The United States, having just extricated itself from one land war in Asia (Korea), did not relish entering another. After the British rejected a joint British-American intervention to aid their NATO ally, the Eisenhower administration turned down the French request. French defeat quickly followed. On May 7, 1954, after a fifty-five-day siege, the French surrendered their garrison at Dienbienphu to General Vo Nguyen Giap, Ho's talented military associate, a blow that virtually ended the fighting.

Fortuitously the next day nine nations met at Geneva to consider a Vietnamese settlement. What emerged was an agreement that proclaimed Vietnam free, but divided the country along the seventeenth parallel with a 5-kilometer-wide demilitarized zone (DMZ) to separate the two portions. The Vietminh would withdraw to the north, and the remaining French troops remove to the south pending their departure from the country. Vietnamese civilians would be allowed to choose freely which half of the country they wished to live in. This separation into a north and a south would not be permanent, however. In July 1956 an International Control Commission would call an election to decide what action should be taken to create a united Vietnam.

The United States was present at the conference but did not sign the Geneva Agreement, although it consented to abide by its general terms. Soon after, in an effort to prevent further Communist gains in Southeast Asia, Secretary of State John Foster Dulles induced seven nations with western Pacific interests—Great Britain, France, New Zealand, Australia, Pakistan, Thailand, and the Philippines—to join the United States in creating the Southeast Asia Treaty Organization (SEATO). SEATO, like NATO in Europe, would "act to meet the common danger" of "Communist aggression" in its region. Unlike NATO, however, it would not have a unified military command.

South versus North

Fighting would soon break out again in Vietnam, this time between Ho Chi Minh's Communist government (the Democratic Republic of Vietnam) in North Vietnam with its capital in Hanoi and a new pro-Western regime (Republic of Vietnam) in South Vietnam with its capital in Saigon. The premier of the new South Vietnamese government, under the nominal rule of Emperor Bao Dai, was Ngo Dinh Diem, a Vietnamese Catholic and a sincere Vietnamese patriot but an aloof and austere man of limited vision who easily confused the welfare of Vietnam with the well-being of his own extended family.

During the early months following Geneva several hundred thousand Catholics left North Vietnam for the more congenial south, while many Communists in the south went north to find a similar friendly environment. Diem, who hoped to establish a centralized regime based on traditional Vietnamese concepts of obedience and deference, was soon engaged in bitter struggles with competing religious sects anxious to dominate the country and with remaining Vietminh who had not followed the majority north. With massive injections of American economic aid Diem soon consolidated his power, and in October 1955, in a election managed by his brother Ngo Dinh Nhu, he eliminated Bao Dai politically and had himself elected president of South Vietnam. Fearing a Communist victory, Diem, with United States approval, ignored the Geneva Agreement call for national elections. The partition along the seventeenth parallel, which had started as a temporary expedient, became a permanent reality of Vietnamese life.

From the outset the Eisenhower administration supported Diem as a bulwark against a Communist takeover of the whole country, and the United States quickly superseded the French. Between 1954 and 1959 approximately 2.3 billion American dollars poured into South Vietnam. One-fifth of this was earmarked for Diem's military forces; the rest took the form of economic aid. American officials saw themselves as "nation-building" in Vietnam. They hoped to bring peace and prosperity to the country as an offset to Communist blandishments, but much of the aid was wasted and American demands for land reform were ignored. To make matters worse, Diem and his associates threw suspected political opponents into reeducation camps, arbitrarily abolished elected village governments, and "re-grouped' peasant villagers to prevent opposition by removing them from their accustomed homes near the graves of their ancestors. Before long Diem had stirred up a guerrilla war in the countryside against his regime.

At first the peasant opposition was spontaneous. The North Vietnamese government, although it despised the Diem regime and hoped eventually to impose its own rule over a unified nation, initially gave the anti-Diem guerrillas (soon to be called Vietcong by their opponents and the National Liberation Front by their friends) little help. By 1959, however, the North had changed its mind and was supplying the Vietcong with arms, military advisers, and strategic aid. By 1960 the North Vietnamese were calling for the "liberation" of South Vietnam.

The Kennedy Administration and Vietnam

President Kennedy feared giving his domestic opponents the opportunity to attack his foreign policy as weak. He also believed, as we have seen, that East-West confrontation in the future would take the form of small wars by Soviet and American surrogates and guerrilla disturbances, not head-on superpower collisions. Vietnam seemed an obvious example of this new form of confrontation. Kennedy felt it must be met by counterinsurgency methods and by measures to reduce grievances, including land reform and political reform. Diem must be induced to win the confidence of the Vietnamese peasants to wean them away from the Communists.

Should the Diem regime also be given further military aid? In May 1961 Vice President Lyndon Johnson went to Saigon to report on the Vietnamese situation for the president. Johnson recommended continued massive American aid to avoid a "domino effect," but advised against sending any American combat troops. Such involvement was "not only not required, it is not desirable." Johnson lavishly praised Diem, comparing him to Winston Churchill, although in fact he was privately skeptical of the South Vietnamese leader.

In October 1961, after a summer of turmoil in the Vietnamese countryside, Kennedy dispatched General Maxwell Taylor and White House aide Walter W. Rostow to Saigon to examine the ground once again. The two men recommended sending American military advisers to be attached to Army of Vietnam (ARVN) units and a force of 10,000 combat troops to backstop the South Vietnamese military. The United States should also consider military actions against North Vietnam if it continued to aid the Vietcong.

Kennedy rejected this advice. It would only lead to ever deeper involvement. "It's like taking a drink," he remarked. "The effect wears off, and you have to take another." But he could not resist. He soon increased the number of military advisers in South Vietnam. By the time of his death in late 1963 there were about 15,500 Americans attached to ARVN or the Saigon government to provide expert military and administrative help.

The Elimination of Diem

For a time the policy of help for Diem seemed to work. Under a new counterinsurgency policy, personally administered by Nhu, peasants were herded into fortified, barbed wire-surrounded "strategic hamlets." There they could, presumably, be protected against intimidation by the Vietcong, and the Communist guerrillas in turn could be deprived of supplies and recruits. In fact the program deeply offended many peasants and only helped the Vietcong, but American officials, the first of a long line of naive or self-deluded bureaucrats, reported to Washington that the Communist tide was receding. American journalists stationed in South Vietnam related a much bleaker picture, but Kennedy too was taken in. In his 1963 State of the Union message he informed the American public that the "spearpoint of aggression has been blunted in South Vietnam."

Then Diem made a major mistake. A devout Catholic, in May 1963 he forbade the

A Buddhist immolates himself on the streets of Saigon, June 1963. (UPI/Bettmann Newsphotos)

large Buddhist community in Vietnam from displaying their flags. When a Buddhist crowd at Hue refused to comply, Diem's troops fired into the crowd. A stampede ensued; nine people died. Diem now found himself with a major religious revolt on his hands.

The Buddhists proved to be skilled manipulators of the media. On June 11 a Buddhist monk sat down on the pavement in Saigon, drenched himself with gasoline, and then set himself on fire. Other Buddhist self-immolations followed soon after. In each case the media had been informed in advance and were waiting to take and send the appalling pictures to the international press, which treated the events as examples of the Diem regime's brutality. Kennedy tried to induce Diem to meet the Buddhists' legitimate demands, but Diem resisted all the way.

By the early fall the Diem regime seemed to have lost its grip entirely. The Saigon government began to jail students and to persecute Catholics as well. By now the American president had lost faith in Diem, and in late August the State Department hinted to the American ambassador in Saigon, Henry Cabot Lodge, that the United States would not be opposed to Diem's replacement. On receipt of this message, Lodge informed Diem's enemies in the South Vietnamese army that the United States would not intervene to save him. This was the signal they needed. On November 1 the insurgent generals besieged the government palace. Diem and his brother had escaped, but they were quickly caught and mowed down by a rain of bullets.

Americans hoped that now the needed reforms would be imposed and South Vietnam would be transformed into a stable country, able to defend itself against the

Vietcong guerrillas and serve as a bulwark in Southeast Asia against the spread of the Communist virus. In Saigon too there was new optimism. At news of the anti-Diem coup people danced in the streets and showered the victorious generals with confetti. They even cheered Ambassador Lodge in public. Then, three weeks later, President Kennedy was assassinated in Dallas.

Johnson and Vietnam

Johnson was not as astute an international player as his predecessor. An incomparably skilled legislator, LBJ knew the crochets and crannies of Capitol Hill as no other American. But his foreign policy comprehension did not go much beyond the conventional wisdom of Americans who had learned their lessons in World War II. The president saw Hitler's aggressive expansionism of the 1930s as the relevant precedent for Vietnam. Appeasing the Führer at Munich had only whetted his appetite and led ultimately to a larger war. He sometimes put the matter in earthy language. "If you let a bully come into your front yard one day," he said, "the next day he will be up on your porch and the day after that he will rape your wife in your own bed." Besides America was leader of the "Free World" and if it did not draw the line now, it would lose credibility everywhere, even among its European allies.

Another force that drew Johnson ever further into the Vietnam morass was the masculine need to prevail. Many Americans, certainly many American men, shared this competitiveness, but the president's personal roots in the country's southwest—a "man's country"—amplified this quality in him. To Johnson, and other Americans, losing seemed intolerable. America, he believed, had never lost a war, and he did not intend to be the first president to be at the helm when it happened.

We can now see that all this reasoning was flawed. In part American east Asian policy was based on the fallacy that China was behind the North Vietnamese. Actually the Chinese were wary of the Hanoi regime, which they saw as a potential rival in Southeast Asia. China provided far less of the North Vietnam's military support than did the Soviet Union. It is also clear that the domino effect was an illusion. South Vietnam's final fall in 1975 did not trigger a major wave of Communist takeovers. Nor did the United States' failure to fight to the bitter end convince our NATO allies that we were untrustworthy. On the other hand the administration was not wrong to see the Hanoi regime as authoritarian and repressive. The Communists would prove to be harsh conquerors and rigid ideologues whose rule over a united Vietnam, after peace, would make a shambles of the national economy. As for the "macho" factor, it seems an unconvincing basis for conducting a world power's foreign policy. Besides, even though the United States had never lost a war, it had not actually "won" in Korea, and still the heavens did not fall.

The Johnson Administration's Early Response

However certain that the Communists must be stopped, the new president, anxious to consolidate his home political base, at first soft-peddled Vietnam. In his first State of the Union message in January 1964 he virtually ignored Southeast Asia.

He had not forgotten the war, however, especially since General Nguyen Khanh, the new South Vietnamese leader, seemed no better able to consolidate the country behind him and suppress the Vietcong than Diem. Faced with the continuing danger of Communist takeover, the administration considered a major bombing campaign against North Vietnam but then thought better of it to avoid allowing Vietnam to become a partisan issue in the approaching 1964 presidential election campaign. Seeking some way to defuse the war's political danger, in August, with a dubious attack by North Vietnamese patrol boats on American destroyers as its excuse, the administration requested a congressional resolution of support for a retaliatory policy "to prevent further aggression." All indications were that the American public overwhelmingly supported the administration, and on August 7, by an almost unanimous vote, Congress passed the Tonkin Gulf resolution, granting the president power to "take all necessary measures to repel any armed attack against forces of the United States." In later months the attorney general would claim that the resolution was the "functional equivalent" of a "declaration of war."

Johnson was able to keep Vietnam from becoming a major campaign issue by denying any plan to escalate American involvement. He would "seek no wider war," he told the American people from a dozen rostrums across the country. "We do not want to get tied down in a land war in Asia," he proclaimed in late September. "We are not going to send American boys nine or ten thousand miles away from home to do what Asian boys ought to be doing for themselves," he announced a month later. His enemies later charged that LBJ was following the uncandid precedent of his hero Franklin Roosevelt during the months preceding Pearl Harbor but in a far worse cause. In reality Johnson was in a quandary. He feared he was damned if he did and damned if he didn't. He did not want to be charged with "losing" Vietnam, as Truman had "lost" China; he also did not want a land war in Asia to destroy his consensus and drain all life from the Great Society. His deceptions reflected his own confusion as well as a natural devious streak in his personality.

Rolling Thunder

After November 1964 with the victory over Goldwater behind him, Johnson faced major decisions in Vietnam. In late December Vietcong agents exploded a car bomb beneath the Brinks Hotel in Saigon, housing American military advisers, killing two and injuring fifty-eight. The new American ambassador, General Taylor, along with every other senior officer in Saigon, urged the president to retaliate against North Vietnam. When Johnson demurred, Taylor responded that the United States was "presently on a losing tack" and that to "take no positive action now is to accept defeat." He recommended a major air offensive against the source of Vietcong power, North Vietnam.

In February the president sent National Security Adviser McGeorge Bundy to Saigon to appraise the situation. Bundy had been in Saigon for just a few days when the Vietcong attacked the American base at Pleiku, killing eight American military advisers, wounding a hundred, and destroying ten U.S. planes. After consulting Taylor and General William Westmoreland, the American military commander in South Vietnam, Bundy telephoned the White House advising that the United States commence bombing attacks on North Vietnam promptly. Unless it did so American determination to "stay the course" would be in doubt.

Within hours American planes were bombing a North Vietnamese army post north of the seventeenth parallel. In early March Johnson launched a sustained bombing campaign (*Rolling Thunder*) against targets in North Vietnam to compel the North Vietnamese to desist from further attacks and force them to come to the bargaining table. On March 8 the first U.S. combat troops, sent to protect the Rolling Thunder air base at Da-nang, waded ashore at Nam O Beach. Ten pretty Vietnamese girls carrying flowers greeted them. In early April, with the air war clearly a failure, the president sent additional marines to Vietnam and authorized their use in offensive actions. Soon after this American troops participated in their first "search and destroy" mission against the Vietcong.

The War Goes On

Thus began the full participation of the United States in the longest, and least defensible, war in its history. To Johnson and his advisers the war seemed a valid effort to hold the line against communism. Let Ho Chi Minh and his North Vietnamese Communists succeed in destroying the South Vietnamese government and unifying Vietnam under their rule and what would prevent them from subverting and conquering the rest of Southeast Asia? Only the Red Chinese or the Soviets could benefit from such an outcome.

Had the war been quick and cheap, the American public might have accepted the Johnson diagnosis and prescription. Unfortunately for the administration it could not fight the way Americans preferred—with overwhelming firepower and technology that could pulverize the enemy and bring a quick decision. In Vietnam the enemy seldom appeared in force to fight a battle. Instead they used stealth, ambush, and infiltration to hit the ARVN and the Americans and then escape. Vietnam became a dirty guerrilla war where American soldiers and marines struggled against an elusive foe in an unfamiliar and atrocious environment of jagged mountains, leech-infested tropical swamps, and steaming jungles. Bombing North Vietnam, although it spared American lives, did not work. The air force dropped enormous tonnages of bombs on the Vietcong and North Vietnamese troops south of the seventeenth parallel and on North Vietnam above the line to flatten the enemy and break Communist morale. The attacks failed. The Vietcong lived on a few handfuls of rice a day and were armed primarily with knives, rifles, and light mortars. They had little heavy equipment to destroy. The North Vietnamese economy was primitive by modern standards and, although many North Vietnamese died in the bombing raids, Hanoi's ability to fight was scarcely affected and its resolve to hold out undiminished.

In the end thousands of American ground troops, many of them draftees, had to be sent to the battlefields eight thousand miles away. By early 1968 a half-million Americans were fighting and dying in Vietnam.

The Antiwar Movement

Through the first few years following Rolling Thunder a majority of Americans supported the president. Many agreed that the war was a test of American determination to stop communism around the world. At first antiwar sentiment was confined to the academic community, students, the left, pacifists, and certain portions of the country's intellectual class. Then, as the dreary months passed with mounting costs and casualties, more and more citizens began to perceive the war as a mistake. (See Figure 13–2.) Could defense of a place so remote and alien as Vietnam really be vital to the nation's safety? Democracies are formidable opponents in war when citizens feel their own safety endangered; they seldom will go the distance in a prolonged struggle when the goals are unclear and ambiguous.

The first serious organized opposition to the Vietnam War erupted in March 1965 in response to Rolling Thunder when students and faculty at the University of Michigan at Ann Arbor held the first "teach-in." This was a full day of critical lectures and seminars on Vietnam and American involvement that was quickly copied at other universities and colleges around the country.

The sudden escalation of the war also reactivated established pacifist groups such as the Fellowship of Reconciliation and the War Resisters' League and antinuclear groups like the Committee for a Sane Nuclear Policy. Before many months various "umbrella" peace groups with a wide variety of names and differing positions on how to end the war were marching and rallying to demand a major change in American policy in Southeast Asia.

Some peace advocates were moderate; they wanted the United States to begin serious negotiations with the North Vietnamese and the Vietcong to achieve an honorable settlement, and they usually endorsed petitions and peaceful demonstra-

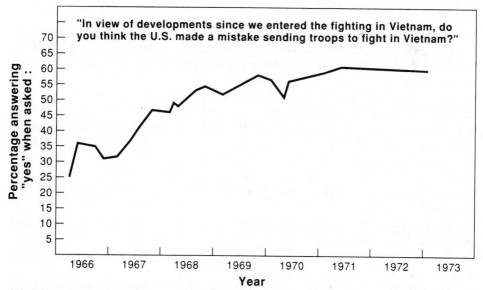

Figure 13–2 Public Opinion on the Vietnam War

Source: Gallup Poll data.

Vietnamese children fleeing a napalm attack. In the background are South Vietnamese soldiers. Scenes like these, shown on evening television, contributed to the American public's disillusion with the Vietnam War.
(UPI/Bettmann Newsphotos)

tions and rallies. Other groups were militant; they insisted that the United States leave Vietnam immediately and unconditionally, and they often supported civil disobedience and at times flaunted anti-American slogans and Vietcong and North Vietnamese flags. Beginning in mid-1965 a few determined antiwar activists began to burn their draft cards.

The most militant "peaceniks" were apt to be college students. Until late in the war college students in good standing were deferred from the draft. Even when white middle-class men could not claim an academic deferment they could often evade service through false medical exemptions or some other manipulation of the draft system. Many sought conscientious objector status. Hundreds fled to Canada where the arm of Uncle Sam could not reach them. Others simply defied the government by refusing to be inducted and accepted jail. In their place the Selective Service system inducted those too poor or too unmotivated academically to attend school. A large proportion of such young men were either black or Hispanic. A line from *Hair*, a popular rock musical of 1968, wittily described the Vietnam War as "white people sending black people to make war on yellow people to defend the land they stole from red people."

Yet white college students were under enormous pressure from the draft, and even when they themselves successfully evaded induction they often felt a heavy burden of guilt over the disproportionate sacrifice of minority young men. Fear and guilt are two potent sources of militancy.

The typical antiwar action was the march to some designated spot—often one symbolically connected with the war—such as the Pentagon outside of Washington, D.C., or the UN complex in New York. Protesters carried banners and signs with

READING 13
A Marine Reminisces about Vietnam

A large proportion of the young men who served in Vietnam came from lower- and working-class backgrounds. Jim Noonan, whose reminiscences are given below, was raised in Brooklyn, New York. A high school graduate, in early 1966 Noonan decided to join the Marine Corps, partly from patriotic considerations. In this reading he recounts his experience in Vietnam, briefly contrasting it with his work among extremely poor people in New York.

I was born in Brooklyn Hospital and educated at Brooklyn College. Still live in Brooklyn. I only left Brooklyn once in my life—that was to Vietnam. And they were shooting at me, so I decided to never leave Brooklyn again.

I got out of high school a year before I joined the Marine Corps. I was not a very promising student and didn't have any college prospects. I was working. And the normal thing for a kid in my neighborhood to do if you weren't in college, you went into the service.

I was deferred because I was the sole support of my mother. My father died when I was fourteen years old and she raised me alone. But it really seemed like it was my duty to go. So on March 2, 1966, I joined the Marine Corps. I enlisted on a buddy plan with George Hankin, who is now a cop in New York City, and Richie Radcliffe. We all went down to Parris Island together.

Richie and I wound up going to Vietnam. But George hurt his arm—he had already broken it playing football—and he didn't go. He was pretty bitter about that because his cousin had been killed in Vietnam. And it was a holy mission for George.

I went to communications school as a message center man, learning to operate teletypes and things like that. From there, I was sent to Vietnam in late September 1966. I was assigned to the 1st Shore Party Battalion in Chù Lai. I remember it was the rainy season. The truck that took us to our outfit couldn't make it in the mud. So they left me out with my seabag over my shoulder. And I hiked the last mile through mud that at times was up to my waist.

I reported to the company office in our base-camp area and they assigned me a bunk. Several months later, when the sun came out, was the next time anything was dry. Mud was just everywhere. We had no electricity. The only reason we had showers was because we found a fuel tank that had fallen off a jet.

I had contact with Vietnamese people in the villages nearby. I have this crazy theory that sanity stops at about the age of eight and begins again at sixty-five. So the children, no matter where you were in Vietnam, provided a certain buffer against insanity.

My mother, my two sisters, and my sister-in-law were always sending me "care packages." I would then hitchhike to this orphanage and give them the canned food from home and play with the kids. In Chu Lai we had Vietnamese working in our base camp. That was something not all of us were comfortable with, but we grew accustomed to it.

One thing that made a dynamic impression on me was the place where these Vietnamese lived. They would come in from the hills to work at the base. Trucks would pick them up and bring them back. They lived in places surrounded by Cyclone fences, with barbed wire on the top. Their huts were fashioned out of flattened beer cans and cardboard boxes. Each night these people would take our garbage. And they didn't take it to make compost— they took it for their dinner. They were transients, refugees. And in a difficult time, they were the ones who had the fewest rights. That made a pretty big impression on me.

Right now, I don't have to close my eyes to get a vision of the children's hospital . . . and a particular kid I probably spent twenty minutes staring at with my mouth open. The wounds on his back and the backs of his legs and buttocks were opened, festering, with flies. No mosquito netting, no bandages, he lay on a dirt floor. It was nothing more than a tent.

My last year in college I worked as a medical technician for New York City's lead poisoning program. I would take kids' blood in tenement buildings. And I had difficulties. The kids in Bedford-Stuyvesant called me "Dracula." I saw serious poverty. I remember walking up to the top floor of a four-story tenement. I wore a white clinical coat because I looked so young that nobody would believe I was able to stick a needle in a kid's arm.

When I reached the top of the stairs, my coat was drenched with sweat. I sat down in front of the kid and I thought I was going to faint. The wall across the room appeared to be moving. It was covered with cockroaches. Thousands of them! It was an ill-lit apartment and the wall was coming in and out, like breathing. But it was the cockroaches crawling all over each other, just festering on there. I saw that kind of poverty. But even still, I've never seen anything like the Vietnamese people gathering our garbage, protecting it like it was precious stones.

In the Chu Lai base camp I lived a relatively secure life. But the worst three days I had in Vietnam was when we were hit with 122-mm Russian rockets and just about everything else the North Vietnamese could throw at us. It was absolutely extraordinary. Everywhere you looked, it was tracer bullets. Every light bulb in our hootches [huts] was shot out. The air mattresses were flattened . . . bullets went through just about everything. And then the 122-mm rockets came in. There's a slight second between the banshee whistling and the explosion. During one of those slight seconds, I just about bit through my lip. It was terrifying.

I came home on Halloween 1967. I arrived at Kennedy Airport with all my nieces and nephews waiting in their Halloween costumes. It was wonderful seeing my mother, my brother, my sisters, and all the kids. My nephew Chip was standing there in a skeleton costume.

My Uncle Jim, my mother's brother, died the day before I came home. He had been sick for a long time, so my nieces and nephews didn't know that he existed. And my nephew Chip heard his mother say, "Uncle Jim died." Now the only Uncle Jim he knew was me. He was very upset. My sister asked him what was wrong. And he said I was dead. She said, "No, No."

When I came home that night, Chip handed me a note that said, "Dear Uncle Jim, I'm glad you're not dead. Love, Chip." It had little American flags, soldiers, a stickmen kind of drawing. You know, the art of a child that age. It was a wonderful note. I couldn't have agreed with him more. So I kept it, and to this day, keep it in my little area for precious things that can't ever be replaced.

Source: From *To Bear Any Burden* by Al Santoli. Copyright © 1985 by Al Santoli. Reprinted by permission of the publisher and E. P. Dutton, a division of Penguin Books USA, Inc.

slogans: "Stop the War," "Out Now!," "America out of Vietnam." (See the photograph opening this chapter.) They often chanted and sang peace songs. At their destinations the protesters listened to antiwar speeches by prominent peace activists, such as A. J. Muste, David Dellinger, and Martin Luther King. The largest and best publicized of these demonstrations took place in New York, San Francisco, and Washington and were usually conducted by antiwar coalitions that often disagreed bitterly over tactics, ideology, and leadership. Most of the demonstrations were orderly, although occasionally some radical splinter insisted on causing trouble.

Campus antiwar demonstrations were often more violent than the city marches. The campus actions frequently had a specific target, usually a campus recruiter such as the navy or a military contractor associated with the war effort. At the universities of California, Wisconsin, and Michigan campus riots broke out when demonstrators sought to stop job interviews with Dow Chemical Company, which manufactured napalm, the incendiary jelly used against guerrillas in Vietnam that produced horrible burns. At Columbia and Pennsylvania universities the targets were university-affiliated institutes that did contract work for the Defense Department.

The President's Deceptions

Anger at the president's Vietnam policies was reinforced by his failure to confide in the American public. Johnson was not a trusting man. His years in the labyrinthine politics of Texas and Washington had convinced him that deception was often wiser than truth. Besides he wanted both "guns *and* butter" and feared that revealing the full costs of the war would jeopardize his cherished Great Society programs. The administration talked constantly of "the light at the end of the tunnel," but the months dragged on without the tunnel's end. Before long critics were referring to the president's "credibility gap."

The president's most serious deception was financial. Johnson avoided asking for new taxes from Congress to pay for Vietnam's costs and instead hid the bill in the Pentagon's huge annual budget. In effect he borrowed the money, creating a federal deficit of almost $10 billion in 1966. By 1968 this figure was over $25 billion. The process only created inflationary pressures. By 1968 consumer prices were rising at almost 5 percent annually, a figure that appeared deeply disturbing after the stable prices of the previous decade.

Pro-War Attitudes

Militancy against the war was met by militancy in its favor. At times antiwar demonstrators were set on by pro-war groups who threw rocks or tomatoes or spray painted the marchers. Conservative and far-right organizations countermarched and counterrallied carrying signs reading "My Country—Right or Wrong," "No Glory Like Old Glory," and "I Wish I Had a Draft Card." Increasingly, the all-out pro-war position became the property of the political right and, along with anger against the civil rights movement, a part of the backlash position that had begun to emerge.

The administration also struck back. Soon after the first draft card burnings Congress made "willful destruction" of a draft card a crime punishable by five years in jail and a $10,000 fine. Federal agents soon arrested several violators.

Johnson believed that the antiwar movement was a powerful weapon of Hanoi and its allies which, unable to match American military might, intended to undermine the American will to fight. He was not wrong about Hanoi's plan for winning. The Communists knew they could not defeat the Americans on the battlefield and that to win they had to shake their enemy's determination. But LBJ also believed that elements in the antiwar movement were in Hanoi's pay and authorized the CIA to investigate links between the North Vietnamese government and the antiwar protesters. It is true that after 1966 a number of American antiwar leaders conferred with representatives of Hanoi behind the Iron Curtain, but no one accepted "Hanoi gold," and the agency did not discover any complicity. The FBI too got into the act as well. One purpose of the agency's clandestine COINTELPRO dirty tricks operation was the harassing of antiwar leaders and the derailing of antiwar demonstrations.

In addition to these covert measures the government took tough legal action against a flock of peace activists, culminating in the January 1968 indictment of Dr. Benjamin Spock, the famous baby doctor, and four other peace activists for conspiring to subvert the draft. None of the defendants in this case, or the others, served time in jail, but this legal offensive drained the energies and depleted the funds of the insurgents.

Tet

However prolonged the fighting and delayed the outcome, not until early 1968 did the administration and large portions of the American public cease to believe that victory was possible. Then during Tet, the Vietnamese lunar New Year, the Vietcong launched an offensive that destroyed all hope and led to a reversal of Johnson's policy.

On January 31 more than 70,000 Vietcong guerrillas and North Vietnamese regulars suddenly struck at a hundred or more South Vietnam cities and towns, including half the provincial capitals, and at a dozen American military bases. At Hue, the beautiful old capital, they took the Citadel, the ancient fortress in the city's center, and then proceeded systematically to murder people identified as "cruel tyrants and reactionary elements." Communist political agents shot, clubbed to death, or buried alive more than 3000 people. Not until late February were they rooted out in house-to-house fighting by marines. Three Vietcong battalions captured Ben Tre in the Mekong Delta and had to be blasted out by artillery and bombs at the cost of half the town's structures. In one of the more deplorable remarks of the war, an American officer explained afterward, "It became necessary to destroy the town to save it." At Khesanh, where the attack began before Tet, the Communist forces besieged a marine garrison, and until it was relieved, worried Americans feared the battle would repeat the French defeat at Dienbienphu.

Psychologically the Vietcong attack on the U.S. Embassy in Saigon was the most telling blow. There nineteen Vietcong commandos, smuggled into the South Vietnamese capital months before, broke into the embassy compound and tried to blast their way into the embassy building itself. They did not succeed. Fleet-footed guards slammed the doors and held them off until troops arrived and killed the intruders. Although the Vietcong had failed, Americans were shocked at the enemy's ability to penetrate to the very core of American power in Vietnam.

The primary purpose of the Vietcong attackers was to demonstrate their prowess and inflict a moral defeat on the Americans and South Vietnamese. They succeeded. The enemy suffered very heavy casualties, yet to a public fed a steady diet of official optimism, the Tet offensive was profoundly disillusioning. Walter Cronkite, the respected CBS anchorman, went to South Vietnam soon after Tet to see what had happened. Hitherto a "hawk" on the war, he reported to the American people that it now seemed "more certain than ever that the bloody experience of Vietnam is to end in a stalemate."

The president himself put on a brave front, but he too was shaken. Soon after Tet, General Westmoreland asked for an additional 206,000 troops. This request precipitated a crisis within the administration. To grant it would be to continue the escalation process, committing even more American resources to the prolonged struggle. To refuse it would require a major reconsideration of American goals. Johnson asked his close military and foreign policy advisers to review the whole Vietnam involvement. The advice of almost all these experienced men was stop the escalation in Vietnam and by slow stages turn the fighting over to the South Vietnamese. The United States must try to get out.

One incident connected with the Tet offensive did not come to the American public's attention until later. Guerrilla wars are dirty wars. There are no front lines or enemy troops wearing identifiable uniforms. Death comes not only from gunfire but from booby traps, ambushes, and poisoned stakes. Both sides use brutal methods and take few prisoners. In Vietnam the inhumanity was compounded by the racial and cultural differences between the antagonists. Many Americans regarded the Vietnamese, even their South Vietnamese allies, as only half-human "gooks."

At Mylai, a small community in coastal Quangngai province, a detachment of American soldiers under lieutenant William Calley was sent to oust suspected Vietcong guerrillas. When they were through they had massacred 300 civilians, many women and children. The army tried at first to cover up the atrocity but could not, and

Calley and another American soldier were eventually court-martialed. Calley was convicted, but many pro-war Americans believed him innocent of serious wrongdoing. For the other side Mylai would become the symbol of all that was evil about the Vietnam War.

The War and the 1968 Election

As we have seen (see Chapter 12), the growing public opposition to the war brought two peace candidates—senators Eugene McCarthy of Wisconsin and Robert Kennedy of New York—into the lists against Lyndon Johnson for the 1968 Democratic nomination. Johnson's moral defeat in the New Hampshire primary and the likelihood that he would also lose in Wisconsin led to his decision at the end of March not to run for another full term.

But the same speech that announced his political decision also offered to stop the bombing of North Vietnam north of the twentieth parallel, most of the country's area, in exchange for peace negotiations. At the same time the president authorized veteran American diplomat Averell Harriman to open peace talks with the Communists whenever they wished. Soon after, the North Vietnamese announced they were ready to parlay, and on May 10, 1968, in a mood of optimism peace talks began in Paris. They would drag on for five years.

The 1968 Humphrey-Nixon presidential campaign did little to advance a peace settlement in Vietnam. By the time the campaign got underway the Paris peace talks had stalled over the issue of making the bombing halt unconditional and whether the Vietcong and the Saigon government should be included in the discussions. If Johnson had agreed to the North Vietnamese conditions it would have helped Humphrey and the Democratic candidate's advisers strongly endorsed it. But the president, seeing acceptance as repudiation of his policies, at first refused. When he decided for the sake of the Democratic ticket to yield, South Vietnamese President Nguyen Van Thieu, believing Nixon a stronger Saigon partisan than Humphrey, refused to go along, and the agreement bogged down. Humphrey came so close to winning that some observers have argued that the last-minute boost of an agreement would have changed the results.

Nixon and Vietnam

By the time Richard Nixon became president in January 1969, approximately 30,000 Americans had died in Vietnam. Nearly 20,000 more would go to their deaths before the fighting stopped. In Vietnam itself American troop morale plummeted when it became clear that winning a military victory was no longer a serious option. Among the fighting troops there were increasingly frequent racial incidents between African-Americans and whites, enlisted men turned to marijuana and hard drugs as a way to face danger and fight off boredom, and discipline all but collapsed in some units where enlisted men "fragged" unpopular officers by rolling live grenades into their tents. And it would get worse. The morale of the American armed forces became one of the most serious casualties of Vietnam.

As president, Nixon pressed efforts to extricate the country from the war. Unlike

Johnson, who had led the country into the Vietnam quagmire, he had no political stake in continuing. But no more than Johnson did he wish to be tarred with defeat. As he would later say, he did not intend to be "the first president of the United States to lose a war." His plan, an elaboration of Johnson's post-Tet policy, called for the progressive withdrawal of all American combat forces from Vietnam and the gradual shift of all military responsibility to the South Vietnam government, whose forces would be built up through massive American aid. This *Vietnamization,* he apparently believed, could lead to peace between the two halves of permanently divided Vietnam, without an American presence.

His optimism was not shared by National Security Adviser (later secretary of state) Henry Kissinger, Nixon's chief agent in the negotiations with Hanoi. Kissinger was a realist who recognized that without American troops the Saigon regime would probably fall. All that could be achieved, as he later phrased it, was "a decent interval."

Whatever the administration's doubts Vietnamization proceeded apace under the new administration. In June 1969 Nixon announced a withdrawal of 25,000 American troops. In September he promised to withdraw an additional 35,000. Meanwhile a flood of American guns, planes, and munitions poured into South Vietnam to build up its forces so that they could do the job themselves.

These moves did not satisfy the antiwar activists, however. In October and again in mid-November student-organized Moratorium Days brought thousands of protesters into the nation's streets and to the nation's capital. Vice President Agnew, the administration's conservative spokesman, denounced the demonstrators and other critics as "an effete corps of impudent snobs who characterize themselves as intellectuals." The president ostentatiously ignored the Washington march by spending the day watching a Redskins football game.

The Cambodia Incursion

Meanwhile the Paris negotiations dragged on inconclusively. The North Vietnamese believed that talking did not preclude fighting and sought every advantage in positioning their forces logistically and winning ground on the battlefield while the talks proceeded. The United States responded by blows intended to raise the costs of continued delay. These began in early 1969 with a secret bombing campaign against North Vietnamese supply lines and depots in Cambodia, Vietnam's supposedly neutral neighbor, that would last for fourteen months. In April 1970 Nixon authorized a limited invasion of Cambodia to deny the North Vietnamese a sanctuary and clean out suspected pockets of Vietcong troops and supplies. Thousands of American and ARVN ground troops swept across the Cambodian border, achieving little in the end.

The incursion created a powerful shock wave at home. By now Nixon had reduced the number of American troops to about half the maximum number in 1968. But despite all the talk of Vietnamization he had now apparently expanded the war. In a matter of days half the campuses in the United States had detonated in strikes and disruptions. Thousands of students ceased attending classes to organize rallies; on many campuses that spring the activists forced cancellation of final examinations.

The Cambodia incursion produced the closest thing to a political massacre that America experienced during the turbulent era following Johnson's Vietnam escalation. Kent State University in Ohio had been only one of the hundreds of campuses that had exploded after Cambodia. But the authorities there were more clumsy and short-tempered than most. On Monday, May 4, 1970, while students were changing classes, the National Guard, untrained in crowd control but called in by Ohio Governor James Rhodes to stop disorder, responsed to taunting and stone-throwing by firing a volley of live ammunition at the students. Four were killed and thirteen wounded. None of the injured or dead was a militant; one was an ROTC member.

Many Americans, perhaps a majority, thought the students deserved what they got. But a substantial—and influential—portion of the public was horrified by the shooting. Thousands of students took to the streets in protest. It seemed the appalling culmination of all the anger, division, and ferocity of a decade.

Peace at Last

Still the war continued with no end in sight. In February 1970 serious peace negotiations had shifted from the formal talks to secret discussions in a dingy Paris suburb between Kissinger and Le Duc Tho, a senior member of the North Vietnamese politburo. Such sub-rosa parleys had the advantage in Kissinger's view of bypassing the press and also the State and Defense departments. For a time these talks made progress and then they too stalled. To force the Communists's hand, in early 1972 Nixon ordered resumption of the long-suspended bombing raids on Hanoi and other North Vietnamese cities. Soon after, he announced the mining of the harbor of North Vietnam's major port, Haiphong, and further heavy bombing raids on the North. These would stop if the enemy accepted a cease-fire. Yet at the same time American troop withdrawals continued with the last American combat units gone by August 13, 1972.

Peace talk progress resumed during the 1972 American election campaign, and on October 26 Kissinger announced a settlement agreement. It proved premature; South Vietnamese President Thieu objected to its provisions and his response scuttled the agreement. Bombing attacks on North Vietnamese targets, suspended to encourage an accord, now were resumed with special ferocity to force the Communists to make further concessions. This reaction may have been decisive. On January 27, 1973, the Americans, North Vietnamese, South Vietnamese, and Vietcong signed a final agreement in Paris ending the Vietnam War.

Peace Provisions

The terms were simple, but at many points ambiguous. The United States would remove its remaining military advisers, and within sixty days North Vietnam would return the 500 or so American prisoners of war in its custody. The fighting in Vietnam would stop, with all forces remaining in place, and the cease-fire would be supervised by an international commission. All military activities in Laos and Cambodia would also cease. To foster the prosperity and guarantee the survival of South Vietnam, the object of American concern for almost ten years, the United States would send modest replacement military aid and a large but unspecified amount of economic aid. The all-important political arrangements were left vague: there would be a National Council of National Reconciliation and Concord composed equally of Saigon government and Vietcong partisans to being together the two sides and eventually arrange free national elections. How this would be accomplished was not clear.

It is hard to believe that Nixon and Kissinger truly believed they had achieved "peace with honor"; it seems unlikely that they did not recognize they had merely constructed a rickety face-saving device. Yet the weary American public cheered the results. America's longest war was over.

The Legacy

The peace in Vietnam lasted little more than two years. It proved impossible to implement the reconciliation terms. Neither South Vietnam nor North Vietnam took them seriously and fighting shortly resumed. This time, without American troops and bombers, the South Vietnamese could not hold, and in early 1975 the North Vietnamese army finally overran the South. Thousands of refugees, many identified with the American regime, fled the country and were admitted to the United States. In late April as the Communist Army entered Saigon, American helicopters transported 1000 panicky Americans and 5000 South Vietnamese from the American Embassy compound in Saigon to U.S. navy ships offshore. It was an inglorious end to the struggle that had cost so much in lives, money, and national morale.

The Communist regime established in South Vietnam proved as repressive and rigid as its enemies anticipated. It clamped down on dissenters with an iron hand, dealt harshly with former opponents and thousands of long-term Chinese residents of Vietnam, and imposed a centralized economic order that soon destroyed the South's economy. Thousands of "boat people" were soon fleeing Vietnam and taking their chances with pirates and storms on the high seas rather than face the harsh regime.

The war left a legacy for Americans. Many, especially those who opposed it, would thereafter be extra wary of American entanglement in anticolonial uprisings. In 1973

One of the last U.S. helicopters to leave Saigon in April 1975, as North Vietnamese troops were closing in. (UPI/Bettmann Newsphotos)

such feelings induced Congress to pass the War Powers Resolution requiring the president to get congressional approval before sending American troops to a combat zone for more than ninety days. In the 1980s, as we will see, resistance to U.S. involvement in Nicaragua drew fuel from the "lesson" of Vietnam. Many of these same people opposed increased arms expenditures and favored nuclear disarmament schemes.

Yet the war's outcome also encouraged the opposite reaction. To other Americans the result seemed a humiliation. The United States had not really been defeated; it had been betrayed by its own people. This must never be allowed to happen again. American must rearm and stand tall. It was this response, this current of opinion, that the political right would tap so successfully in 1980.

FOR FURTHER READING

Students interested in the background of the Vietnam War, as well as the war itself, should consult Stanley Karnow, *Vietnam: A History* (1983). A briefer history of the whole Vietnam involvement is George Herring, *America's Longest War: The United States and Vietnam, 1950–1975* (1986). For treatments that support the Johnson administration positions see Norman Podhoretz, *Why We Were in Vietnam* (1983) and Gunther Lewy, *America in Vietnam* (1978).

The antiwar movement is covered exhaustively in Nancy Zaroulis and Gerald Sullivan, *Who Spoke Up!: American Protest against the War in Vietnam, 1963–1975* (1984) and in Fred Halstead's Trotskyist study, *Our Now!: A Participant's Account of the American Movement against the Vietnam War* (1978). Two books that deal with the country as a whole during the Vietnam era are Alexander Kendrick, *The Wound Within: America in the Vietnam Years, 1945–1974* (1974) and Thomas Powers, *The War at Home: Vietnam and the American People, 1964–1968* (1973). Specialized descriptions of the antiwar movement include Louis Menashe and Ronald Radosh (eds.), *Teach-Ins USA* (1967); Norman Mailer, *The Armies of the Night* (1968); Alice Lynd (ed.), *We Won't Go: Personal Accounts of War Objectors* (1968); and Michael Ferber and Staughton Lynd, *The Resistance* (1971).

The American government's response to the antiwar movement is dealt with in Jessica Mitford, *The Trial of Dr. Spock* (1969); Tom Hayden, *Trial* (1970); and Jason Epstein, *The Great Conspiracy Trial* (1970). A scathing denunciation of government surveillance practices is Frank Donner's *The Age of Surveillance* (1980).

For the Tet offensive and some of its accompaniments see Don Oberdorfer, *TET! The Turning Point in the Vietnam War* (1983) and Peter Braestrup, *Big Story: How the American Press and Television Reported and Interpreted the Crisis of Tet 1968 in Vietnam and Washington* (1983). For the Johnson decision to end escalation see Herbert Schandler, *The Unmaking of a President: Lyndon Johnson and Vietnam* (1977) and Townsend Hoopes, *The Limits of Intervention: An Inside Account of How the Johnson Policy of Escalation in Vietnam was Reversed* (1973). On Mylai, see Seymour Hersh, *Mylai: A Report on the Massacre and Its Aftermath* (1971).

Nixon, Kissinger, and Vietnam are covered critically in Seymour Hersh, *The Price of Power: Kissinger in the Nixon White House* (1983); David Landau, *Kissinger: The Uses of Power* (1972); and William Shawcross, *Side-Show* (1979). Kissinger has ably defended his Vietnam policy in his own *The White House Years* (1979).

Kent State is described in James Michener, *Kent State: What Happened and Why* (1971) and Peter Davies, *The Truth about Kent State* (1973).

14
The Great Malaise

Signs like this one were common in America during the OPEC oil embargo of 1973. (Alain DeJean/Sygma)

The Nixon Administration

From today's perspective the 1970s seem a time of *malaise*. The word, of French origin, was used by journalists and other observers to describe the poorly defined collective illness that seemed to beset the nation during much of the seventies. Those who used the term often meant the state of the economy in the wake of the oil price surge and the energy crisis, but they also applied it to the insecure and dissatisfied political and psychological mood of the American people after 1968.

Richard Nixon helped to create the negative public mood. Nixon was a complex and deeply flawed man. His personality was protean, taking on a bewildering range of shapes to suit the circumstances. This is true of many politicians, but few seemed so lacking in an inner core of authentic self. It was this malleability that led to the frequent assertion of his political allies that there was currently "a new Nixon" in operation who was somehow better than the old one.

As president, Nixon was not especially interested in domestic affairs. From the outset of his political career he had felt most comfortable dealing with foreign policy issues, and even his early identification with anticommunism had been a domestic echo of America's new postwar role in world affairs. Yet he claimed to have a domestic agenda. His fondest desire, he said, was to heal the nation's wounds. In his victory statement soon after the election he recalled a sign carried by a young girl in Ohio during the presidential campaign that read "Bring Us Together." That would be his purpose: bridging the gap between the generations, between the races, and between the parties.

Wooing Middle America

Perhaps the new president really believed these words, but other goals came first. He had promises to keep to the white South for helping him get elected. He also hoped to please "middle Americans," a gentler term than "backlash," for white working- and middle-class people of conservative, family-oriented values. Both constituencies abhorred the perceived cultural excesses of the 1960s and wished to slow the pace of social change that, in their view, was tearing the nation apart. Somehow the federal government must shift its weight to the other side of the scale, toward the forces of consolidation and stability and away from change. In effect the new administration must change sides in the mighty social and cultural war that had erupted during the previous decade.

The shift reflected the administration's own sincere beliefs. But it was also a move to make the Republicans the majority party. During the presidential campaign one of Nixon's advisers had been an astute young political analyst from New York, Kevin Phillips. In 1969 Phillips's book *The Emergence of a Republican Majority,* recommended a new strategy for the GOP. A major shift was underway in American politics, Phillips announced. In the sweep of territory from Virginia to California—"the Sunbelt"—white, old-stock Americans were disgusted by the social and political activism of the day and offended by radical students and intellectuals and by militant blacks. So were many urban, predominantly Catholic, ethnics. Many of those exasperated people were traditional Democrats, but they could be wooed away from their party and converted into Republicans if the GOP made clear its opposition to all forms of militancy. A consistent conservative strategy could transform the Republican party into the normal majority party, a position it had not enjoyed since the rise of the New Deal in the early 1930s.

Judging by their actions, Nixon and his advisers took the Phillips thesis seriously. Nixon had promised to slow the pace of school desegregation in the South, and after taking office, he directed the Department of Health, Education, and Welfare and the Justice Department to ease the pressure on southern school districts to end segregated practices. He later publicly attacked the policy of court-ordered busing of pupils from one school district to another for the sake of promoting racial balance. Under orders from Attorney General John Mitchell, Nixon's former law associate, the Justice Department cooperated with local police departments in cracking down on the Black Panthers and instituted indictments against a variety of antiwar and radical groups.

The president also sought to shift the ideological center of gravity of the Supreme Court. Under Chief Justice Earl Warren the nation's highest court had been a dynamic force in the drive for a more egalitarian and libertarian society. From *Brown* v. *Board of Education* onward, federal judges had pushed the pace of desegregation, had insisted on the right of accused criminals to legal counsel and to keep silent (*Gideon* v. *Wainright* and *Miranda* v. *Arizona*), had required the reapportionment of state legislatures to reflect racial and demographic shifts (*Baker* v. *Carr*), had struck down book censorship statues (*A Book Named 'Memoirs of a Woman of Pleasure'* v. *Attorney General of Massachusetts*), and had denied the right to any local government to mandate prayer or Bible reading in the public schools (*School District of Abingdon Township* v. *Schlempp*). In all these matters the Court had seemingly taken the side of people outside the mainstream or critics of American values, and it had offended the conservative middle American voter.

When Earl Warren retired as chief justice in 1969, Nixon selected Warren Burger, a man less committed to "judicial activism,"—using the federal courts to compel social or political change—to succeed him. Although Burger was a conservative, he was also a believer in the doctrine that the courts should not abruptly overthrow the decisions of their predecessors. His appointment, accordingly, was less helpful than conservatives had hoped in shifting the Court's ideological emphasis. When another vacancy occurred, Nixon determined to select a judge who could be counted on without fail to resist the judicial trends of the recent past. With his debts to Strom Thurmond and other southern Republicans in mind, such a jurist should, he believed, also be a southerner.

Unfortunately for his strategy his first nominee, Judge Clement Haynsworth of South Carolina, had a too blatantly segregationist, antilabor record and was tainted by conflict of interest charges besides. Nevertheless, the Senate's refusal to confirm him angered the president, who promptly submitted the name of G. Harrold Carswell, a Florida federal judge with a record that suggested not only flagrant racism but also legal mediocrity. When the Senate rejected this nomination too, Nixon attacked the Senate's liberal majority as unalterably opposed to giving the South a voice in the governing of the nation. It was clear, he said, that he could not "successfully nominate to the Supreme Court any . . . judge from the South who believes as I do in strict construction of the Constitution." Ultimately the Senate did confirm a conservative, Harry Blackmun, but he was from Minnesota. Although defeated in his attempt to accommodate the traditional South, Nixon had scored points with southern conservatives.

Yet Nixon was not the consistent conservative hard-liner in domestic matters that liberals had feared. Following the advice of his domestic affairs adviser, Daniel Moynihan, a Harvard professor of government who had served under Kennedy and Johnson, he did not dismantle the Johnson poverty programs. To do so, Moynihan said, would create chaos in the inner cities. For a time the president even endorsed Moynihan's plan for a federal takeover of state welfare programs and a federally "guaranteed annual income" for the poor of $1600 per family of four. Attacked by the right as too liberal and by the left as too limited, the scheme died, leaving the country with a welfare patchwork that satisfied no one.

Environmental Issues

The president also responded to the growing clamor over pollution and the general deterioration of the nation's physical environment. The public concern was a delayed response to the downside of the technological revolution of the postwar era that had provided new sources of energy, new industrial processes, new building and packaging materials, and new ways to combat insect pests and weeds that destroyed crops and reduced agricultural output. Many of these advances had unfortunate side effects: they polluted the air, food, and water supplies and in the process increased the incidence of cardiovascular disease and cancer and degraded the beauty and recreational value of the environment.

Fears of the negative effects of technology were not new, of course; they go back to medieval times. The modern *ecology,* or environmental, movement dates, however, from the 1962 publication of Rachel Carson's *Silent Spring,* a description of how DDT and other synthetic insecticides were damaging the nation's natural environment and destroying its animal and plant life. The drive to protect the environment soon merged with a broad-gauged consumer protection movement inspired by Ralph Nader, a Harvard-educated lawyer whose book *Unsafe at Any Speed* (1965) indicted the automobile industry for its excessive focus on styling, speed, and engine power to the neglect of safety. When General Motors (GM) was caught trying to discredit Nader by hiring private detectives to poke into his personal life, Nader sued and won a large financial judgment against the firm. The publicity goaded Congress into passing the first significant auto safety law (the National Traffic and Motor Vehicle Safety Act of 1966) and began the long process of improving highway safety.

Nader soon become father of a powerful new environmental and consumer protection movement. The GM money settlement enabled him to establish his Center for the Study of Responsive Law, staffed by young men and women called "Nader's Raiders" who devoted their skills to ferreting out consumer fraud and environmental wrongdoing. Other environmental groups, including the Sierra Club, the National Wildlife Federation, Friends of the Earth, and the Environmental Defense Fund, also flourished during these years.

There was a strong antibusiness bias to the consumer protection and environmental movements. The consumer advocate-environmentalists often found themselves pitted against oil-drilling companies, the nuclear power and chemical industries, timber and mining firms, drug companies, and steel makers in their battle to limit or regulate extractive or manufacturing processes. In addition some of the newer groups, including Nader and his associates, were products of the insurgent mood of the 1960s. Their survival into the 1970s and 1980s represented a long epilogue for 1960s radicalism and the counterculture. Their critics often accused them of opposing all economic growth through some romantic attachment to an imagined utopian, preindustrial past.

If their ideology had been their sole appeal, the consumer advocate-environmentalists would probably not have made much headway. But they also touched the public's instinct for self-preservation. Many Americans, not just those disposed to dislike business or yearn for the Garden of Eden, were made nervous by the dangerous by-products of modern industrial processes and wished to protect themselves and their piece of America.

It was this mood that led even the probusiness Nixon administration to support environmental legislation. On January 1, 1970 Nixon signed into law the National Environmental Policy Act, requiring federal agencies to issue an "impact statement" for each major project they proposed. In April, following a damaging oil spill in the Santa Barbara Channel off the California coast, Congress passed the Water Quality Improvement Act authorizing the government to clean up oil spills and levy charges on those responsible. In 1970 Nixon also recommended and got an Environmental Protection Agency (EPA) to administer all federal programs to combat pollution. At the same time he proposed a National Atmospheric Administration to deal with the problems of the oceans and the atmosphere. In 1972 Congress passed the Federal Environmental Pesticide Control Act, giving the EPA power to control the manufacture, use, and distribution of pesticides. Soon after, EPA administrator William Ruckelshaus banned DDT from all further use.

Space

One striking triumph of Nixon's first year in office was the moon landing in July 1969. This was the culmination of President Kennedy's 1961 promise to land a man on the moon "before this decade is out" and Lyndon Johnson's continued commitment to that goal. Yet it was in Nixon's administration that, after many billions of dollars and countless man-hours, the manned space program finally achieved Kennedy's end. On July 16 the Apollo 11 mission, with Michael Collins, Edwin Aldrin, Jr., and Neil Armstrong aboard, blasted off from the Kennedy Space Center (Cape Canaveral) in Florida and headed for earth's only natural satellite. Three days later the astronauts placed their command vessel into orbit around the moon, and on Sunday, July 20 Armstrong and Aldrin descended in the *Eagle* landing module to the broken lunar surface. At 10:56 P.M. Eastern Daylight Time, as over half a billion people worldwide watched and listened, Armstrong left *Eagle* and took humankind's first step onto the surface of any celestial body other than earth. Joined by Aldrin, he planted a television camera on a pole, and delighted viewers could see the two men bounding like

July 1969: earthlings walk on the moon for the first time. (UPI/Bettmann Newsphotos)

kangaroos over the stark lunar terrain (the moon's gravitational pull is only one-sixth of the earth's).

Two hours later, after collecting fifty pounds of moon rocks and soil for testing, and planting an American flag and various scientific devices on the surface, the astronauts returned to their mother ship *Columbia* and blasted off for earth. On July 24 the *Columbia* splashed down in the Pacific. President Nixon was on the bridge of the aircraft carrier *Hornet,* waving his binoculars, when the *Columbia* descended on its orange and white parachutes.

Apollo 11 was followed by five other American-sponsored moon landings, each of which gathered additional information about the moon's composition and geology and revealed fascinating data about the nature of the solar system. But then the landings ceased. The Apollo 17 expedition, which returned to earth in December 1972, was the last of the series and, so far, the last time humans touched down on the moon.

By this time the novelty of the moon landings had worn off and enthusiasm had waned. The Apollo series had cost $25 billion, a sum that appalled citizens who worried about the plight of America's needy and underprivileged. Critics claimed, moreover, that the costs had been unnecessary from a strictly scientific point of view: as much or more information could have been garnered by sending unmanned probes at far lower cost. America had been moved more by rivalry with the Soviet Union than by thirst for knowledge, many claimed.

But another explanation of the space program's winding down also fits the facts. Launched in the full enthusiasm of the buoyant early sixties, it expressed the American people's confidence in limitless possibility. By 1970 times had changed. Americans were no longer confident; they also no longer felt flush. Apollo fell victim to the spiritual and material malaise that was creeping across the country by the early 1970s. Its termination, in turn, reinforced the erosion of national morale.

Nixonomics

Declining morale was also linked to economic decline. The decade following 1968 was a period of slowdown, a time when growth rates diminished and America's place in the world economy deteriorated. The effects would reverberate through many areas of national life.

During the twenty year period 1947–1967 the nation had ridden an extraordinary economic wave. Total gross national product (GNP) growth rates had averaged 3.9 percent per year. Productivity per man-hour, an important measure of economic vigor, had grown at a 3.2 percent average annually. Unemployment during this period had run a small 4.7 percent of the labor force. Then about the time Nixon took office, the boom ran out of steam. Between 1967 and 1979 GNP growth slowed to 2.9 annually, productivity increases declined to 1.5 percent each year, and unemployment rose to an average of 5.8 percent. Worst of all, inflation returned with a roar. In the 1947–1967 period consumer price increases had held to about 2 percent yearly; by 1973 they had soared to over 9 percent. In 1979 consumer prices would rise by 13 percent, one of the highest inflation rates in American history. (See Figure 14–1.)

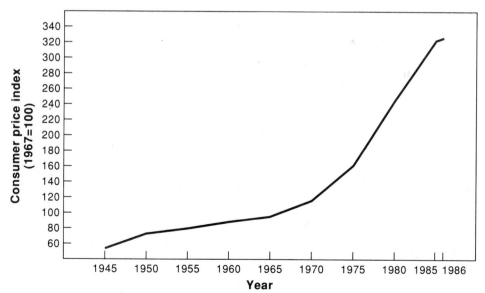

Figure 14–1   The Consumer Price Index, 1945–1986 (1967 = 100)

Sources: *Historical Statistics of the United States* (Washington: U.S. Bureau of the Census, 1975), p. 210, and *Statistical Abstract of the United States, 1988* (Washington: U.S. Bureau of the Census, 1987), p. 450.

The Causes of the Economic Problems

Nixon was not responsible for the national economic slowdown. The start of the inflation surge, for example, was largely the result of Johnson's reluctance to follow pay-as-you-go policies for the Vietnam War and his reliance on federal deficits to pay the nation's bills.

The growth rate decline had even more distant roots. In part America's economic achievements had been due to its easy domination of postwar international markets. This success was as much a product of other nations' limitations following World War II as its own prowess. But by the late sixties the war-torn regions abroad had recovered, and Germany and Japan, especially, had fully modernized their industrial plant. It did not take long before they had become formidable competitors to the United States, not only cutting into America's overseas markets, but winning millions of customers for their products in the United States itself.

This development caught the United States unprepared. As the engine of the free world economy after 1945, America had been a major exporter of capital and under the 1947 General Agreement on Tariffs and Trade had kept its markets open to foreign producers. Along with generous Marshall Plan aid and American willingness to shoulder the immense burden of anti-Communist military defense, this policy had helped revive the free world economy. But as the 1960s drew to a close, American producers found themselves unable to match the costs and the quality of German and Japanese wares, especially in electronics, optical goods, and automobiles. By 1970 German Volkswagens and Mercedes and Japanese Toyotas and Datsuns had begun to flood American streets and highways, cutting deeply into the sales of GM, Ford, and Chrysler. By that time too the thirty-five millimeter camera had become an exclusive Japanese-German preserve and more and more American companies had abandoned television production to Sony, Panasonic, and other Japanese electronics firms. As the new decade began, even the steel industry, the very symbol of America's earlier industrial preeminence, was in serious financial trouble, unable to compete with foreign producers.

The picture was not all dark. American agriculture remained the most advanced and productive in the world, and the United States was able to meet not only its own food needs but the shortfalls of other nations, including the Soviet Union. Furthermore American firms such as Boeing and Douglas supplied the world with most of its civilian airliners. The most advanced sector of American industry was semiconductors and the dazzling computers they made possible. The major breakthroughs in computer science, as in electronics generally, were achieved in American laboratories. In electronics the Japanese had been more skillful in converting basic technology into successful consumer products. Not so with computers, where firms such as IBM, Wang, Cray, and other companies were soon far ahead of everyone else in building large "number crunchers" that enabled industry, financial firms, and government agencies to make their operations more efficient. Still, although there were islands of excellence and competitiveness in the economy, as the sixties gave way to the seventies it was clear that the United States was facing an economic challenge from abroad without precedent since the previous century.

Sagging American exports and soaring American imports in turn created severe financial problems. By 1970 American exports dipped below American imports for the first time in many decades. Americans paid for the excess of imports with dollars and our major trading partners were soon awash with them. By 1971 the West German government alone held more dollars then there was gold in Fort Knox. Because foreigners now had more dollars than they wanted, they sought to exchange them for American gold, a procedure allowed by both American law and the Bretton Woods Agreement negotiated in 1944 as World War II wound down. The drain soon threatened to exhaust the American gold stock.

Nixon's Economic Policies

Nixon dealt with these dangers ineptly. His answer to America's deteriorating trade position was to end the convertibility of American dollars into gold on demand in August 1971. Soon after, in hopes of lowering American prices to foreign customers, the United States devalued the dollar in terms of other national currencies. These moves stopped the gold drain but did little to check the long-term decline of America's productivity and competitiveness relative to other nations.

Nixon's move against inflation was little better. The president, as we saw, inherited the problem from his predecessor. He had long professed to despise tight economic controls by government, but faced with a possible runaway inflation, and fearing its effects on his reelection chances, in 1971 he abruptly changed course. On the same day that he ended the dollar's gold redeemability, Nixon announced that all prices, wages, dividends, and rents would be frozen at existing levels for three months. Compliance by employers, firms, and landlords would be imposed by a Cost of Living Council headed by Treasury Secretary John Connally. Over the next few months the inflation rate slowed, and Nixon announced "Phase Two," which replaced compulsion with voluntary compliance. Phase Two proved largely ineffective; price increases once more accelerated.

Nixon and Foreign Policy

But at best Nixon dealt with domestic problems almost as an afterthought. It was in the shaping of America's relations with other nations that he would, he believed, make his mark in history. Nixon's first secretary of state was William Rogers, a smooth New York lawyer who had served as Eisenhower's attorney general. But Rogers had little to do with the management of foreign policy. Nixon reserved much of the field for himself and in any case preferred to consult his more congenial National Security Adviser Henry Kissinger, a former Harvard professor of government who was a proponent of unsentimental *realpolitik* in the conduct of foreign affairs. Nixon and Kissinger seemed to enjoy intrigue, preferring to deal with foreign leaders by hidden "back channel" routes rather than through the State Department and the usual ambassadorial officials.

Nixon and China

Although progress toward disengagement in Vietnam at first proved slow and discouraging (see Chapter 13), the Nixon-Kissinger team could claim major foreign policy advances on other fronts.

Nixon was no friend of the China Lobby, that group of conservative Americans who abhorred the Chinese Communist regime and had successfully fought every attempt to get the United States to recognize the Beijing (Peking) government and allow admission of the People's Republic to the UN. The president, although a dyed-in-the-wool anti-Communist, understood that Red China would not simply go away if the United States refused to establish diplomatic relations. He also perceived that a major breach was opening between the two largest Communist nations, China and the Soviet Union. Establishing relations with Beijing might enable the United States to use one Communist nation against the other to advance its own interests. In this case Nixon's long-established conservative and anti-Communist reputation stood him in good stead. The political right could not accuse him, as they would a liberal Democrat who sought to deal with China, of betraying his country.

The initial move came from the Americans when in March 1971 the State Department lifted a long-imposed ban on American travel in the People's Republic. By now China had abandoned its bizarre and tumultuous Cultural Revolution and was prepared to deal rationally with its problems. In April the Beijing government responded by inviting the American table tennis team, then playing in Japan, to tour mainland China, all expenses paid. The Soviets recognized the meaning of the event and called the invitation "unprincipled."

The American team was given the red-carpet treatment, and to flatter their guests the Chinese discretely avoided sending their best players to the meets. The positive response of the American people in turn encouraged Kissinger and Nixon to proceed. During the next few months Kissinger made a secret visit to the Chinese capital where he talked at length with foreign minister, Chou En-lai. On July 14, 1971, Nixon informed the American people of Kissinger's visit on national television and declared that he expected to go soon to Beijing himself. Although seeking a new relationship with Beijing, the United States sought to avoid sacrificing its old Kuomintang friends on Taiwan. Nixon tried to pursue a "two Chinas" policy that included keeping Taiwan in the UN. But fired up by the breakthrough, the members of the UN General Assembly voted to exclude Taiwan and admit Red China regardless of the American president's wishes.

In late February 1972 Nixon, his wife, Pat, and an entourage of journalists and advisers flew to Beijing to meet with the Chinese leaders. Relatively little was accomplished in the formal talks beyond an American agreement to withdraw U.S. troops from Taiwan, but the visit prepared the ground psychologically for full diplomatic relations. Americans watched on television in amazement as their president, once the arch anti-Communist, walked along the Great Wall and shook hands with Mao Tse-tung (Mao Žedong). After more than twenty years the two great nations, once close friends, had resumed relations.

Improved Soviet Relations

Kissinger and Nixon also succeeded in improving relations with the Soviet Union, a policy labeled *détente*. For months the national security adviser had been holding secret talks with Soviet Ambassador Anatoly Dobrynin without consulting Secretary Rogers. These had led to closer economic ties with the Soviets, including major grain sales to compensate for the Soviet Union's chronic shortfall in wheat production. But the president and his chief adviser were out for bigger game than improved trade relations. They wanted the Soviet Union to pressure the North Vietnamese into a more reasonable negotiating position at the Paris peace talks and hoped to slow the nuclear arms race and reduce Cold War tensions.

For a time in the spring of 1972 improved Soviet-American relations were endangered when the United States resumed bombing attacks on Hanoi and mined Haiphong harbor, the major North Vietnamese entry port for Soviet supplies. The bombers sank a Soviet ship in the harbor, killing several on board. Fortunately the Soviets chose to ignore the attack. On May 22 Nixon visited Moscow and was greeted cordially by Soviet Premier Leonid Brezhnev. Amid the festivities some actual business was concluded. The United States and the Soviet Union agreed to a series of joint research projects in medicine, to cooperation in space and on environmental matters, and to an end to hostile encounters on the high seas. Most important were a series of agreements on nuclear arms limitations that capped years of negotiations. When incorporated into the Strategic Arms Limitation Treaty (SALT I) of August 3, 1972, these agreements limited the defensive antiballistic missiles that both sides could position and froze offensive nuclear weapons to those already in existence or still under construction.

The Middle East

The Middle East had long been a major trouble spot for the United States. There Israel and its Arab neighbors remained implacable enemies, with the Arabs determined to destroy what they perceived as a Western intruder in their region. Israel's stunning victory in the 1967 Six Day War had expanded its boundaries to include all of Jerusalem, part of Syria, Egypt's Sinai Peninsula, the Gaza Strip, and the West Bank of Jordan. (See Figure 14–2.) The victory had created a new sense of security, even complacency, among Israel's beleaguered people, but it had also increased the hostility of its Arab neighbors and added immeasurably to its dilemma over the Palestinians, the predominantly Muslim inhabitants of what had been the British Palestine mandate, who were now, in much larger numbers, under Israeli rule.

On October 6, 1973, during the Jewish holiday of Yom Kippur, Egypt, now led by Anwar Sadat, and Syria attacked Israel. Caught unaware, the Israelis for several critical days retreated, suffering heavy losses in men and equipment, particularly on the Egyptian front. The war soon looked as if it might become a superpower confrontation, for although the Egyptians had recently thrown out their Soviet advisers, the Soviet Union quickly supplied them with new weapons and when it looked as if the Israelis might be defeated, the United States airlifted enormous amounts of replacement supplies to Israel.

In a few days the tide of battle turned. Israel halted the Arab advance and then launched a counterattack that threatened to destroy the entire Egyptian invasion army. At this point the Soviets intervened politically on behalf of Egypt. They warned that if the Israelis did not desist, they would send troops to stop them. The United States

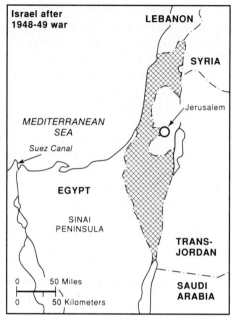

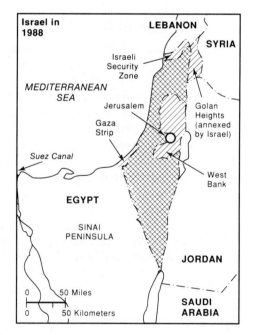

Figure 14–2   Israel and the Middle East

responded by placing its military forces on worldwide alert. Fortunately the Israelis agreed not to proceed any further and to accept a truce with UN forces to supervise the cease-fire.

The Yom Kippur War had repercussions far beyond the eastern Mediterranean. By now many of the industrialized nations, including the United States, had become dependent on middle eastern oil for automobile gasoline, heating fuel, and electric power production. This reliance placed them at the mercy of the Arab oil producers who dominated the Organization of Petroleum Exporting Countries (OPEC). In response to the support of Israel by the United States and several European countries, the Arab producers cut their crude oil production by 5 percent and imposed a complete oil embargo on nations considered friendly to Israel. The embargo itself was soon lifted, but the experience left the Arab nations with a new sense that oil was a powerful international weapon and a new willingness to cooperate for the purpose of raising oil prices. In the next few years, as world petroleum prices quadrupled, Americans and Europeans would hear much of OPEC's economic power, invariably to their dismay.

The Yom Kippur War had another significant and more welcome effect. Although in the end Israel gained the upper hand, the Egyptians' near-victory instilled in them a new confidence. No longer obsessed by a sense of inferiority, they were able to act more generously toward their enemies. When Kissinger, then secretary of state, began a series of whirlwind trips among the various Middle Eastern capitals during the fall and winter of 1973–74 ("shuttle diplomacy"), he managed to negotiate several agreements between Israel and Egypt regarding troop disengagement and other matters. He also won the confidence of Anwar Sadat and was able to draw Egypt into the American orbit.

The 1972 Election and Watergate

Nixon had campaigned hard for Republican candidates during the 1970 congressional elections and sought to use incidents of student heckling and rock-throwing to malign the Democrats. The tactic did not work well. The Democrats gained twelve House seats and eleven governorships.

By the time Nixon returned from his Moscow trip, the country was gearing up for the 1972 presidential campaign. On the Democratic side the obvious front-runner would have been Senator Edward Kennedy of Massachusetts, the only surviving senior Kennedy male and heir to the family mystique. But Kennedy had destroyed his chances in July 1969 when, at Chappaquiddick near Martha's Vineyard, a fatal accident occurred. Leaving a hard-drinking party with a young woman who had been a political worker for his brother Robert, the senator drove his car off a bridge and the young woman drowned. Kennedy himself escaped serious injury. Despite his denials the public believed that he and the girl had left the party for romantic reasons and in his drunken state he had taken a wrong turn. They were also skeptical of his story of how he had tried many times, at risk to himself, to save her. A married man, the senator already had a reputation for infidelity, and the awful incident further damaged his public image.

With Kennedy out, Senator Edmund Muskie of Maine, the Lincolnesque Humphrey running mate of 1968, was the front-runner as the Democratic convention in Miami approached. But Muskie ruined his chances when, viciously attacked by the far-right *Manchester Union Leader* during the New Hampshire primary campaign, he apparently broke down and wept while defending his wife. The public took this as a sign of weakness and Muskie's campaign thereafter collapsed. The backlash-voter hero George Wallace, now back in his home Democratic party, also seemed a serious contender until he was shot and paralyzed while campaigning in Maryland by a publicity-seeking would-be assassin.

Senator George McGovern of South Dakota, a former history professor who belonged to the party's most liberal and dovish wing, soon moved to front place. McGovern benefited from major rule changes adopted at Chicago in 1968 that were designed to open up the party to outsiders. These mandated a better "balance" at national conventions by requiring that in the future there be more African-Americans and other racial minorities, more women, and more young people among convention delegates. No longer would the professionals, the trade union leaders, and the white male politicos determine the results.

At Miami the new groups were present in force; the California delegation even boasted a contingent of people on welfare. The convention seemed a holdover from the sixties with elements of the political left, the counterculture, and various "liberationist" groups highly visible and vocal. These "New Politics" groups controlled the convention, excluding many traditional Democrats from the proceedings and repudiating more conservative views. The convention adopted a left-liberal, strongly antiwar platform and nominated McGovern on the first ballot. It seemed to shrewd observers a pyrrhic victory for the McGovern forces, however. Many conservative and middle-of-the-road Democratic voters watching the proceedings on television felt alienated by the spectacle of the party's conquest by the left. They would not be enthusiastic supporters of the ticket in November.

Nixon and Agnew won renomination without serious opposition at the Republican convention in August on a conservative platform. After the president's opening to China and détente with the Soviet Union, his reputation had soared. Against the unorthodox Democrats his victory seemed a sure thing.

Watergate: Opening Phase

But Nixon and his advisers decided to leave nothing to chance. Running the campaign, under the direction of former Attorney General John Mitchell, was the Committee for the Re-Election of the President (CRP). This committee, soon called "CREEP" by the Democrats, was determined to win and win big in November for the president—and at any cost.

The collection of crimes called *Watergate* grew out of this win-at-all-cost attitude. It also was sustained by Nixon's special failings as a political leader. However skilled in diplomacy, he was politically insecure, suspicious of his opponents, and uncomprehending of the rules of the American political game. His chief advisers—men such as John Mitchell; John D. Ehrlichman, Nixon's domestic affairs adviser; White House Chief of Staff H. R. Haldeman; and John Dean, White House counsel—were even worse. Drawn mostly from the business community where sharp dealing was often the norm, unused to the compromises and restraints of the nation's mainstream political culture, and deeply imbued with the security obsessions that marked the era, they accepted the principle that anything goes in the pursuit of victory. To win in 1972, the public later learned, they were willing to subvert the laws and the spirit of the constitutional processes by which the nation lived.

By the summer of 1972 CRP was rolling in money, much of it extracted from large corporations induced to contribute by promises of favors. After "laundering" in Mexico to disguise their origins, these funds were deposited in secret party accounts or crammed into CRP safes. The flood of green would be used to bury the Democrats in a wave of media ads and massive rallies in the fall.

Another phase of the projected Nixon campaign was "dirty tricks," a "disinformation" and espionage campaign to confuse and obstruct the Democrats. Run by a White House Special Investigations Unit, nicknamed the "plumbers," it had begun as an attempt to plug leaks of confidential administration discussions and activities. The most bothersome of these leaks had been the theft by former Kissinger aide Daniel Ellsberg of the *Pentagon Papers*—hundreds of documents on Vietnam collected as an internal Defense Department report—and their publication in the *New York Times* in June 1971. That September a unit of the plumbers broke into the office of Ellsberg's Los Angeles psychiatrist in search of information that might tarnish Ellsberg's reputation.

CRP borrowed the plumbers' approach and some of their personnel. It funded Republican zealot Donald Segretti's spying and infiltration operations against the Democrats and his scheme to sow dissension in their ranks by mailing letters on bogus Muskie campaign stationary charging other Democratic candidates with sexual indiscretions. Other CRP-financed dirty tricks included an attempt to sabotage Ted Kennedy by concocting phony cables implicating his dead brother John in the assassination of the South Vietnamese leader Ngo Dinh Diem and encouraging Internal Revenue Service audits of prominent Democrats' tax returns to distract them from political activities.

The dirty trick that would backfire and eventually destroy Nixon was the June 1972 break-in at Democratic National Committee headquarters in the Watergate Hotel and office complex in downtown Washington to steal confidential Democratic documents. The operation was conceived by G. Gordon Liddy, counsel to CRP, a man with a James Bond imagination. At one point CRP had considered a million-dollar sequence of kidnappings, phone-tappings, and sexual blackmail operations against Democrats that made even Mitchell blanch. In the end Liddy settled for a much cheaper break-in at the Watergate to rifle the Democrats' files and bug their telephones for useful or incriminating information.

On the evening of June 17, after the failure of an earlier attempt, James W. McCord, Jr., security coordinator of CRP, and four anti-Castro Cuban accomplices succeeded in entering the empty Democratic offices. But the break-in was detected by a security guard and McCord and his four colleagues were caught. When booked at the police station, they all gave aliases and refused to say what they had been doing. Observing the arrest from the balcony of a nearby motel were several other members of CRP, including E. Howard Hunt, a White House consultant.

News of the arrests reached CRP leaders in Los Angeles the next morning when Liddy called long distance. Their immediate reaction was to try to conceal the connection between the break-in and the president's reelection campaign. Unfortunately for CRP it did not take long before the link between the burglars and the Republicans leaked out. On June 19 the police discovered Hunt's name in an address book in possession of one of the arrested Cubans.

At this point, hindsight shows, it would have been politically smart for the president to have admitted that Republican zealots had violated the law and then condemned their acts. Instead Nixon and his staff, under pressure from the indicted men to supply money for legal defense and for their families, agreed to protect the burglars by making the break-in appear to be an anti-Castro Cuban caper. On June 20 the president told White House aide Charles Colson, "We are just going to leave this where it is, with the Cubans." In short order documentary evidence of the operation went into the paper shredders. Other incriminating documents were sent to FBI Director L. Patrick Gray, who, on instructions, burned them. At the same time CRP drew on its vast pool of funds and sent $500,000 in hush money to the indicted men.

The *Washington Post* carried news of the break-in the day after it happened. But at first almost no one paid much attention. At a briefing for reporters on June 19 Press Secretary Ronald Ziegler dismissed the break-in as "a third-rate burglary attempt" too insignificant to comment on. As pressure grew, however, Nixon could not ignore the issue. Finally on August 29 he told reporters that he had already ordered an investigation of the affair by Chief White House Counsel John Dean, and the results had shown that "no one in the White House Staff, no one in this Administration presently employed, was involved in this very bizarre incident" Dean later said this was the first he had ever heard of this "investigation."

Nixon Reelected

By now the presidential election was entering the home stretch. McGovern proved to be an inept campaigner. He had chosen as his running mate the young senator from Missouri, Thomas Eagleton. When shortly after the convention Eagleton confessed that he had twice been hospitalized for emotional problems, McGovern at first defended him and then forced him off the ticket, choosing in his place Sargent Shriver, the former Office of Economic Opportunity head. The incident made McGovern seem both indecisive and self-righteous.

The Democratic candidate tried to recoup by attacking the administration for being too close to business, for its opportunistic economic controls policy, for favoring the rich over the poor, and for spending too much on defense and not enough on domestic welfare programs. He mentioned the Watergate break-in as an example of the administration's disregard of law, but in the absence of any hard evidence of White House involvement, the charge did not stick. McGovern took particular aim at the administration's continued involvement in Vietnam. This too missed its mark. By now Vietnamization had reduced American casualties to the vanishing point.

The election results were not surprising. In the end McGovern got only 37.5 percent of the popular vote to Nixon's 60.7 and won only the liberal state of Massachusetts and the District of Columbia, a predominantly African-American community. There was a massive defection of traditional white Democratic voters. McGovern had not succeeded in surmounting the perception that the party had fallen into the hands of minorities, radicals, and eccentrics, and many Democrats—ethnics, the white South, trade union families—deserted their party. Some obviously voted Republican, yet many Americans still did not like the man in the White House and refused to vote at all. The voter turnout was the smallest in twenty-four years.

Watergate Unravels

By the time of Nixon's second inauguration in January 1973 the Watergate burglars along with Hunt and Liddy were under indictment. As yet no one could pin anything on the president's staff, certainly not on the president himself, although two *Washington Post* reporters, Carl Bernstein and Robert Woodward, had begun to dig deeply into the scandal.

But then, soon after the beginning of Nixon's second term, the White House cover-up plan began to fall apart. The trial in Washington of the Watergate burglars, presided over by "Maximum John" Sirica, a tough federal judge, concluded on January 30, 1973, with their conviction on a variety of charges. At the sentencing in March Sirica read aloud a letter from McCord declaring that "perjury had occurred during the trial" and that "there was political pressure applied to the defendants to plead guilty and remain silent." Clearly, the judge stated, the full Watergate story had not been told.

The McCord statement blew the Watergate affair wide open. In early February the Senate appointed a Select Committee on Presidential Campaign Activities to investigate. The committee was headed by the white-haired, folksy, but Harvard-educated Democrat, Sam Ervin of North Carolina. Over the next few months a parade of witnesses came before the Ervin Committee to testify under oath about their knowledge of the break-in. Meanwhile the Watergate defendants, as yet unsentenced and worried about their futures, remained a serious danger to the administration. On March 22 John Dean told Nixon that Watergate was "a cancer growing on the presidency" and that something must be done to stop its growth. Soon after, he, Haldeman, and the president considered further demands by the Watergate burglars for money and for possible clemency. Nixon told the others that money would be no problem: "You've got to keep the cap on the bottle . . . in order to have any options." He advised that all those who were forced to testify should avoid the risk of perjury charges by claiming faulty memories. Their defense should be that the break-in was connected to national security. The following day in a private discussion with John Mitchell he further declared: "I don't give a shit what happens. I want you all to stonewall it, let them plead the Fifth Amendment, coverup or anything else, if it'll save it—save the plan . . . . Up to this point, the whole theory has been containment, as you know John."

For the next year the intertwined set of scandals called Watergate was never far from headline news. The public absorbed the revelations of reckless disregard for truth, contempt for constitutional processes, and the plain violations of criminal law with fascinated horror as they poured from the televised Ervin Committee hearings, continued grand jury investigations, and the reports of Woodward and Bernstein in the *Washington Post*. Each day, it seemed, brought its appalling disclosures of gross breaches of trust by the administration. Americans learned about the break-in at Elleberg's psychiatrist's office and then the attempt by Ehrlichman at Ellsberg's trial for espionage and theft of the Pentagon documents to suborn the judge by offering him the vacant FBI directorship. They heard about a White House "Enemies List" of antiadministration politicians, professors, and journalists who were tagged for harassment by the Internal Revenue Service and other federal agencies. Ultimately a raft of secondary scandals also came to light: how the administration had settled an antitrust suit in favor of the International Telephone and Telegraph Company in exchange for political contributions, how Nixon had been allowed improper tax deductions for donating his vice presidential papers to the National Archives, how he had used federal funds to improve the grounds of his personal homes at Key Biscayne, Florida, and San Clemente, California.

As the investigators closed in, Nixon was forced to throw some of his staff to the wolves. On April 30, 1973, two weeks after declaring that he was launching searching new inquiries, he announced the resignations of Haldeman, Ehrlichman, and of Attorney General Richard Kleindienst, Mitchell's successor, and the firing of John Dean.

In early May the new attorney general, Elliot Richardson, agreed to appoint a special prosecutor to investigate all aspects of the Watergate affair. On Richardson's advice Nixon chose Harvard Law Professor Archibald Cox for the post on May 18.

The Watergate hearings proved to be as riveting as the Army-McCarthy hearings twenty years earlier. Despite the administration's attempt to prevent the testimony of high officials by invoking the doctrine of executive privilege, Mitchell, Haldeman, Ehrlichman, Dean, and others appeared before the Ervin Committee and revealed much of what had taken place in secret conclaves in the White House and elsewhere. But no one except Dean was willing to accuse the president himself of guilty knowledge or of trying to prevent disclosure of the full facts.

Then on July 16 former White House aide Alexander Butterfield remarked almost casually that for the previous two years all White House conversations had been taped. If the tapes could be procured, it would become possible to know without fail—in the words of Senator Howard Baker of Tennessee—"what the president knew and when he knew it."

Both Cox and the Ervin Committee subpoenaed tapes for key periods. Nixon, claiming executive privilege once more, refused to release them. Cox asked the courts to compel the president's compliance, and Nixon, fearing the prosecutor's zeal and independence, asked Richardson to fire him. When the attorney general refused, the president dismissed him. Nixon then asked the deputy attorney general to do the deed. He too refused and was fired. Finally, concluding this "Saturday night massacre," Solicitor General Robert Bork became acting attorney general and dismissed Cox.

Impeachment and Resignation

Cox's departure did little to help Nixon. Public outrage compelled the president to appoint another special prosecutor. His choice fell on Leon Jaworski, a conservative Houston lawyer who could be expected to be more favorable to the Republican administraton than his predecessor. Meanwhile in October the House Judiciary Committee, under Peter Rodino of New Jersey, began to hold preliminary hearings on the possible impeachment of the president.

While these events were unfolding a scandal erupted around Vice President Spiro Agnew, a man who had become the administration's hard-line voice against the militant students, the peace activists, and the "eastern liberal establishment." Accused of taking kickbacks from contractors while governor of Maryland and of evading income taxes, Agnew resigned on October 10. Following the terms of the twenty-fifth Amendment, Nixon nominated Gerald Ford of Michigan, the House minority leader, to succeed Agnew.

In April 1974 the White House's last-ditch effort to conceal the cover-up began to come apart. On April 11 the Rodino Judiciary Committee subpoenaed forty-two White House tapes; soon after this Special Prosecutor Jaworski, less compliant than had been expected, also demanded to see White House tapes. Nixon resisted bitterly, but on April 30 he released over a thousand pages of edited transcripts, although not the tapes themselves or even transcripts of all the tapes requested. Yet even these revealed the president and his colleagues as unfocused, inarticulate, often truculent, and bigoted men. They also pointed at efforts to prevent the full revelation of Watergate misdeeds. But they failed to reveal any "smoking gun."

In July the House Judiciary Committee began televised discussions of impeachment and at the end of the month voted three articles of impeachment against Nixon: for engaging "personally and through his subordinates and agents in a course of action designed to delay, impede, and obstruct the investigation" of the Watergate break-in and to "cover up, conceal, and protect those responsible" for the break-in; for "violating the constitutional rights of citizens [and] impairing the due and proper administration of justice"; and for defying committee subpoenas, thereby hobbling the impeachment process. But it turned out that the articles, the first voted against a president since 1868, never had to be weighed by the Senate in an impeachment trial.

On August 5 after the Supreme Court had denied Nixon the right to withhold any of the tapes, he surrendered the tapes to Jaworski. One of these, for June 23, 1972, contained the smoking gun. On that day, less than a week after the burglary, the President had discussed the break-in with Haldeman and had told his assistant to stop the CIA and the FBI from proceeding any further on the case. They should be told, he said, that if the purposes of the break-in were revealed it would jeopardize national security. (See Reading 14.)

The publication of the June 23 conversation made it certain that the president would have to leave office. On August 7 senators Barry Goldwater and Hugh Scott, representing respectively the conservative and liberal wings of the Republican party, visited the White House to tell Nixon he must resign to spare the country the long agony of an impeachment trial. That evening Goldwater told reporters he could not count more than fifteen senators who would vote against conviction.

At 9 P.M. Eastern time on August 8, Nixon spoke to the nation on television. He would resign the presidency at noon the next day, he said. The next morning, after a brief farewell to his staff in the East Room of the White House, he and his family flew off for California and retirement from public life. At a little after noon that day Gerald Ford took the oath of office as president of the United States. (Text continues on page 450.)

READING 14

The Watergate Cover-up

Nixon was by no means the most incompetent man who sat in the White House, but he may have been the most devious. Insecure, suspicious, often mean-spirited, he encouraged the deceit and chicanery that led to the Watergate break-in and then fostered the cover-up that turned it into a constitutional crisis. This reading comes from the famous taped private conversations between the president and key White House aides in the weeks after the Watergate burglers were caught. H. R. Haldeman was Nixon's chief of staff; John Dean a White House counsel. These conversations and others like them constituted the smoking gun of presidential complicity in the cover-up attempt that ultimately forced Nixon out of office.

June 23, 1972

Haldeman: Now, on the investigation, you know the Democratic break-in thing, we're back in the problem area because the FBI is not under control, because [Director Patrick] Gray doesn't exactly know how to control it and they have—their investigation is now leading into some productive area. . . . They've been able to trace the money—not through the money itself—but through the bank sources—the banker. And it goes in some directions we don't want it to go. Ah, also there have been some [other] things—like an informant came in off the street to the FBI in Miami who was a photographer or has a friend who is a photographer who developed some films through this guy [Bernard] Barker and the films had pictures of Democratic National Committee letterhead documents and things. So it's things like that that are filtering in. . . . [John] Mitchell came up with yesterday, and John Dean analyzed very carefully last night and concludes, concurs now with Mitchell's recommendation that the only way to solve this . . . is for us to have [CIA Assistant Director Vernon] Walters call Pat Gray and just say, "Stay to hell out of this—this is ah, [our] business here. We don't want you to go any further on it." That's not an unusual development, and ah, that would take care of it.

President: What about Pat Gray—you mean Pat Gray doesn't want to?

Haldeman: Pat does want to. He doesn't know how to, and he doesn't have any basis for doing it. Given this, he will then have the basis. He'll call [FBI Assistant Director] Mark Felt in, and the two of them—and Mark Felt wants to cooperate because he's ambitious—

President: Yeah.

Haldeman: He'll call him in and say, "We've got the signal from across the river to put the hold on this." And that will fit rather well because the FBI agents who are working the case, at this point, feel that's what it is.

President: This is CIA? They've traced the money? Who'd they trace it to?

Haldeman: Well, they've traced it to a name, but they haven't gotten to the guy yet.

President: Would it be somebody here?

Haldeman: Ken Dahlberg.

President: Who the hell is Ken Dahlberg?

Haldeman: He gave $25,000 in Minnesota and, ah, the check went directly to this guy Barker.

President: It isn't from the Committee though, from [Maurice] Stans?

Haldeman: Yeah. It is. It's directly traceable and there's some more through some Texas people that went to the Mexican bank which can also be traced to the Mexican bank—they'll get their names today.

President: Well, I mean, there's no way—I'm just thinking if they don't cooperate, what do they say? That they were approached by the Cubans? That's what Dahlberg has to say, the Texans too.

Haldeman: Well, if they will. But then we're relying on more and more people all the time. That's the problem and they'll [the FBI] . . . stop if we could take this other route.

President: All right.

Haldeman: [Mitchell and Dean] say the only way to do that is from White House instructions. And it's got to be to [CIA Director Richard] Helms and to—ah, what's his name? . . . Walters.

President: Walters.

Haldeman: And the proposal would be that . . . [John] Ehrlichman and I call them in, and say, ah—

President: All right, fine. How do you call him in—I mean you just—well, we protected Helms from one hell of a lot of things.

Haldeman: That's what Ehrlichman says.

President: Of course; this [Howard] Hunt [business.] That will uncover a lot of things. You open that scab there's a hell of a lot of things and we just feel that it would be very detrimental to have this thing go any further. This involves these Cubans, Hunt, and a lot of hanky-panky that we have nothing to do with ourselves. Well, what the hell, did Mitchell know about this?

Haldeman: I think so. I don't think he knew the details, but I think he knew.

President: He didn't know how it was going to be handled though—with Dahlberg and the Texans and so forth? Well who was the asshole that did? Is it [G. Gordon] Liddy? Is that the fellow? He must be a little nuts!

Haldeman: He is.

President: I mean he just isn't well screwed on, is he? Is that the problem?

Haldeman: No, but he was under pressure, apparently, to get more information, and as he got more pressure, he pushed the people harder.

President: Pressure from Mitchell?

Haldeman: Apparently. . . .

President: All right, fine, I understand it all. We won't second-guess

Mitchell and the rest. Thank God it wasn't [special White House counsel Charles] Colson.

Haldeman: The FBI interviewed Colson yesterday. They determined that would be a good thing to do. To have him take an interrogation, which he did, and the FBI guys working the case concluded that there were one or two possibilities—one, that this was a White House (they don't think that there is anything at the Election Committee) they think it was either a White House operation and they have some obscure reasons for it—non-political, or it was a—Cuban [operation] and [involved] the CIA. And after their interrogation of Colson yesterday, they concluded it was not the White House, but are now convinced it is a CIA thing, so the CIA turnoff would—

President: Well, not sure of their analysis, I'm not going to get that involved. I'm (unintelligible).

Haldeman: No, sir, we don't want you to.

President: You call them in.

Haldeman: Good deal.

President: Play it tough. That's the way they play it and that's the way we are going to play it. . . .

* * *

President: O.K. . . . Just say (unintelligible) very bad to have this fellow Hunt, ah, he knows too damned much. . . . If it gets out that this is all involved, the Cuba thing, it would be a fiasco. It would make the CIA look bad, it's going to make Hunt look bad, and it is likely to blow the whole Bay of Pigs thing which we think would be very unfortunate—both for CIA, and for the country, at this time, and for American foreign policy. Just tell him to lay off. Don't you [think] so?

Haldeman: Yep. That's the basis to do it on. Just leave it at that. . . .

September 15, 1972

President: We are all in it together. This is a war. We take a few shots and it will be over. We will give them a few shots and it will be over. Don't worry. I wouldn't want to be on the other side right now. Would you?

Dean: Along that line, one of the things I've tried to do, I have begun to keep notes on a lot of people who are emerging as less than our friends because this will be over some day and we shouldn't forget the way some of them have treated us.

President: I want the most comprehensive notes on all those who tried to do us in. They didn't have to do it. If we had had a very close election and they were playing the other side I would understand this. No—they were doing this quite deliberately and they are asking for it and they are going to get it. We have not used the power in this first four years, as you know. We have never used it. We have never used it. We have not used the Bureau, and we have not used the Justice Department, but things are going to change now. And they are either going to do it right or go.

Dean: What an exciting prospect.

President: Thanks. It has to be done. We have been (adjective deleted) fools for us to come into this election campaign and not do anything with regard to the Democratic Senators who are running, et cetera. And who the hell are they after? They are after us. It is absolutely ridiculous. It is not going to be that way any more.

March 13, 1973

President: How much of a crisis? It will be—I am thinking in terms of—the point is, everything is a crisis. (expletive deleted) it is a terrible lousy thing—it will remain a crisis among the upper intellectual types, the soft heads, our own, too—Republicans—and the Democrats and the rest. Average people won't think it is much of a crisis unless it affects them. (unintelligible)

Dean: I think it will pass. I think after the [Senator Sam] Ervin hearings, they are going to find so much—there will be some new revelations. I don't think that the thing will get out of hand. I have no reason to believe it will.

President: As a matter of fact, it is just a bunch of (characterization deleted). We don't object to such damn things anyway. On, and on and on. No, I tell you this it is the last gasp of our hardest opponents. They've just got to have something to squeal about it.

Dean: It is the only thing they have to squeal—

President: (Unintelligible) They are going to lie around and squeal. They are having a hard time now. They got the hell kicked out of them in the election. There is not a Watergate around in this town, not so much our opponents, even the media, but the basic thing is the establishment. The establishment is dying, and so they've got to show that despite the successes we have had in foreign policy and in the election, they've got to show that it is just wrong, just because of this. They are trying to use this as the whole thing.

March 21, 1973

Dean: So that is it. That is the extent of the knowledge. So where are the soft spots on this? Well, first of all, there is the problem of the continued blackmail which will not only go on now, but it will go on while these people are in prison, and it will compound the obstruction of justice situation. It will cost money. It is dangerous. People around here are not pros at this sort of thing. This is the sort of thing Mafia people can do: washing money, getting clean money, and things like that. We just don't know about those things, because we are not criminals and not used to dealing in that business.

President: That's right.

Dean: It is a tough thing to know how to do.

President: Maybe it takes a gang to do that.

Dean: That's right. There is a real problem as to whether we could even do it. Plus there is a real problem in raising money. Mitchell has been working on raising some money. He is one of the ones with the most to lose. But there is no denying the fact that the White House, in Ehrlichman, Haldeman and Dean, are involved in some of the early money decisions.

> *President:* How much money do you need?
> *Dean:* I would say these people are going to cost over a million dollars over the next two years.
> *President:* We could get that. On the money, if you need the money you could get that. You could get a million dollars. You could get it in cash. I know where it could be gotten. It is not easy, but it could be done. But the question is who the hell would handle it? Any ideas on that?
> *Dean:* That's right. Well, I think that is something that Mitchell ought to be charged with.
> *President:* I would think so too.
>
> Source: From *Hearings Before the Committee on the Judiciary, House of Representatives, 93rd Congress, 2nd Session* (Washington: Government Printing Office, 1974).

The Ford Presidency

Ford's first words to the American people, uttered moments after the swearing-in ceremony, were reassuring. The country's "long national nightmare" was over, he declared. "Our Constitution works. Our great republic is a government of laws and not of men." But many people were not certain that "the system" had "worked" all that well. Without the lucky break of the tapes, after all, Nixon and company might well have succeeded in concealing their illegal cover-up. Doubts were reinforced when the new president pardoned the ex-president, thereby preventing his prosecution for criminal activity. The act seemed all the more misguided in light of the ultimate trial and conviction of most of Nixon's close advisers.

Yet the public wanted very much to like this first unelected president. Ford seemed a solid and personally agreeable, if dull and unimaginative, man. To make up for his lack of foreign policy experience, he retained Henry Kissinger as secretary of state. Since Ford's elevation to the presidency had vacated the vice presidential office, he was charged with selecting his successor. For this post he chose the Republican party's liberal gadfly, Nelson Rockefeller of New York. Both appointments seemed wise choices for a man without a popular mandate.

Economic Policy under Ford

Ford's chief domestic problem was the accelerating inflation. By 1974 prices were rising at the double-digit rate of 11 percent. The next year they slowed somewhat but then in 1979 and 1980 they soared to 12 and then to 13 percent. Inflation would be the most severe economic problem of the late seventies.

Some of this surge could be traced to petroleum price rises by the OPEC oil cartel, newly confident of its strength following the Yom Kippur War. For decades the United States had been a major oil producer and exporter. Gasoline and other petroleum derivatives had been cheap, and Americans had been extravagant in their use of energy. American automobiles, for example, had been notorious gas-guzzlers, getting often no more than 8 or 10 miles per gallon. By the mid-seventies, however, the United States no longer produced enough oil for its needs and was importing millions of barrels annually.

Dependence on imported oil made the OPEC price rises reverberate through the economy. Every item that used large amounts of energy to manufacture immediately leaped in cost. In addition, the soaring price of energy required major redesign of automobile engines, electric generator stations, and housing insulation systems to increase energy efficiency. All of these efforts were expensive and all added further impetus to inflation.

But soaring oil prices were not the only economic problem. By the mid-seventies the United States was suffering from a condition that the wordsmiths called "stagflation." This was the worst of two worlds: stagnation and inflation simultaneously. Not only were prices rising, economic growth was slowing. Annual increases in GNP, which had averaged almost 4 percent a year the previous decade, slowed to about 3 percent during the 1970s. This leveling off was felt in the paycheck of American working people. From 1948 to 1966 average yearly growth in real spendable earnings had run 2.1 percent. Between 1966 and 1973 it dropped to half that rate. During the last two or three years of the 1970s real spendable income actually declined, on average, for American wage and salary earners. Family incomes would continue to rise slowly, but only because more family members, especially wives and mothers, joined the work force.

Accompanying the slower growth was rising unemployment. In the late sixties the jobless rate had averaged under 4 percent; in 1975 it reached 8.5 percent. (See Figure 14–3.) In the past inflation and unemployment had been trade-offs; now the country was afflicted with both of them at the same time.

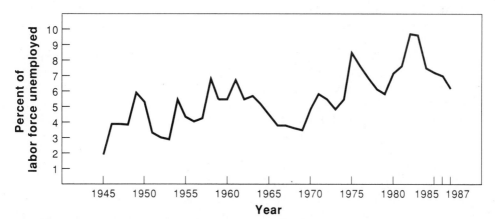

Figure 14–3 Unemployment, 1945–1987

Sources: *Historical Statistics of the United States* (Washington: U.S. Bureau of the Census, 1975), p. 135; *Statistical Abstract of the United States, 1985* (Washington: U.S. Bureau of the Census, 1984), p. 390; *Statistical Abstract of the United States, 1988* (Washington: U.S. Bureau of the Census, 1987), p. 365; and *Monthly Labor Review* (September 1988), p. 65.

The reasons for the stagflation were not clear. Conservative economists blamed government policies. High social security and personal income taxes, overgenerous unemployment insurance benefits, excessive regulation, and heavy taxation of capital gains had either discouraged investment or drained the economy of needed capital funds, they said. Yet at the same time an exaggerated concern with social misfortune and the desire to maintain full employment impelled the government to spend more than it took in, thus pumping up consumer demand and fueling inflation. The conservative experts also tended to believe that American workers were overpaid. Powerful unions, especially in steel, mining, and automobiles, had worked out deals with management that provided ever larger wage hikes without corresponding increases in worker output. The net effect of all of this was inflationary price rises.

Liberal economists tended to blame stagflation on distorting "structural" factors. Inflation, of course, owed much to OPEC's price rigging. But in addition American businessses and industries were themselves responsible for artificially high prices, a result achieved by price collusion and inefficient forms of production, such as annual automobile model changes, that added nothing but costs to the price of a car. Furthermore the vast government outlays on defense were wasteful; not only did they pump money into the economy, they starved it of needed skills and resources. Racism and sexism also exacted high economic costs by wasting the skills of major segments of the American population. Finally there were the shifts from blue-collar heavy industry jobs to white-collar knowledge industry jobs that marked the maturing of the economy. This process had left millions without the skills needed for the job market. No matter how much purchasing power the government created by deficits, these workers would remain unemployed unless and until they were retrained.

Different views led to different prescriptions. Conservatives wanted to lower taxes, especially on capital gains and on people with higher incomes, to encourage investment and creative enterprise. They wanted to offset the government's smaller revenues by cuts in government spending, especially on welfare programs. They also wanted to encourage stiffer domestic competition by ending government regulation, even if this entailed some risk to the environment or to the survival of weaker firms. By the end of the decade conservative economists with views such as these would be called *supply-siders.*

Liberals instead favored sharp cuts in defense spending; a marked increase in government outlays for retraining programs, education, and research and development; and various federal incentive policies focused on specific industries. One unusual development among liberal thinkers was the appearance of high tariff, protectionist views. These were not based on theory, but were a response to foreign competition that threatened the jobs of American industrial workers.

President Ford dealt ineffectively with the economy's problems. A conservative Republican, he was far more concerned with rising prices than with rising unemployment. The president sought to slash government spending for housing, education, and public works and at the same time urged a tax increase to cut down on consumer purchasing power. He also launched a psychological attack on inflation expectations that featured buttons inscribed with the motto WIN (Whip Inflation Now). The campaign accomplished little and critics laughed at its triviality. In truth there were no easy solutions to the stagflation problem, and the president was not wrong in believing that persistent federal deficits were an important part of the problem. The public wanted expensive programs—aid to education, better roads, superior health care, and national security—but preferred borrowing to pay for them rather than taxing themselves.

Legislation and Foreign Policy

Several pieces of legislation during the Ford years reflected the lessons learned during Watergate. In October 1974 Congress strengthened an earlier Freedom of Information Act to allow the public access to data accumulated by the federal government concerning individuals. Ford vetoed the measure on the grounds that it might jeopardize national security. Congress passed it over his veto.

The president approved, however, a new law to reduce the influence of money in politics. The Campaign Finance Law of 1974 established spending limits for primary campaigns, required disclosure of sources and uses of campaign money, and allowed taxpayers to contribute money to presidential campaigns through a tax deduction from their income tax returns. The new law was intended to help make candidates less dependent on fat-cat campaign contributors and lobbyists, but it did not. With each campaign the costs of embarking on the long ordeal of caucuses, primaries, and conventions that preceded nomination continued to grow. Despite the law's intent, money continued to count. In fact with each successive national election there were more numerous and more powerful political action committees (PACs) representing special ideologies or special social and economic interests. Critics claimed that if existing trends persisted the United States would become a plutocracy, a nation ruled by the wealthy.

Ford's foreign policy was an extension of Nixon's. Since most Americans considered the disgraced president more successful at foreign than domestic affairs, this was not surprising. Ford and Kissinger continued to seek some sort of peace between Israel and its Arab neighbors. Like his predecessor the new president visited China and reaffirmed Sino-American friendship. In November 1974 Ford met with Soviet Premier Leonid Brezhnev in Vladivostok and the two continued the nuclear arms limitation process launched with the SALT I agreements by signing a document limiting the number of each country's missile launchers, warheads, and other strategic weapons. Proponents of nuclear disarmament hoped that the agreement would soon be incorporated into formal treaties as SALT II.

The Bicentennial

The highpoint of the Ford years was the 1976 bicentennial celebration of American independence. One hundred years earlier, the country had mounted an international exposition in Philadelphia to commemorate the centennial of American independence. The great 1876 Philadelphia World's Fair had displayed the confident nation's new industrial might and technological prowess. It was here that Alexander Bell's great invention, the telephone, was unveiled.

But in 1976 a vastly richer nation could not find an equivalent focus for the celebration. World's fairs were now enormously expensive events that often produced

The "tall ships" sail through New York Harbor on July 4, 1976. (Black Star/Ted Hardin)

large deficits. The nation was also too divided. Attempts by Philadelphia promoters to organize an international exposition fell afoul of racial squabbling over employment, land use, and other matters. Moreover newer parts of the country wanted their own local celebrations.

In the end, the bicentennial became a decentralized, scattershot affair. Washington, D.C., held a major parade down Pennsylvania Avenue with 500,000 spectators, 60 floats, and 90 marching bands. In San Francisco 6000 people gathered at Golden Gate Park to celebrate both the U.S. bicentennial and the two hundredth anniversary of the arrival of the first Spanish settlers at the site of the future city. The closest thing to a national event took place in New York harbor as sailing ships from many lands cruised through the harbor while millions of spectators watched the tall ships' stately procession. Most Americans did feel a surge of pride on the nation's two hundredth birthday; yet those with a sense of history felt the occasion also reflected a nation afflicted with a new sense of limits.

The 1976 Election

In 1974 the voters expressed their dismay over Watergate by giving the Democrats a smashing victory in the midterm congressional elections. Even Ford's own congressional district, which had been safely Republican since 1912, went Democratic. As the 1976 presidential election approached, it looked as if the national mood had made nonsense of Kevin Phillips' predictions that the Republicans were becoming the normal majority party.

The chief beneficiary of the Democratic surge was the one-term governor of Georgia Jimmy Carter, a Naval Academy graduate, a southerner, and a born-again Christian. Carter's chances for the Democratic presidential nomination would have been virtually nil if not for Watergate. That chamber of political horrors had made millions of voters skeptical of old politicos like Nixon and anxious for a fresh face. The former governor, who prayed daily, also seemed a deeply moral man who would never permit the sort of shabby behavior that had pervaded the White House during the Nixon years. True, Gerald Ford was an honest man, but he was closely identified with the Washington establishment and he had squandered much of his moral capital by pardoning Nixon.

Starting with a name-recognition factor of only 2 percent, Carter campaigned ceaselessly for delegates during the primary period. By the time of the 1976 Democratic convention in New York he had the nomination sewed up and won on the first ballot. He chose for his running mate Senator Walter Mondale of Minnesota.

An incumbent president seldom encounters serious competition for his party's renomination, but Ford, who had not been elected to the office and was a man without much personal magnetism, had to beat off the serious challenge of Ronald Reagan, the conservative former governor of California. Ford narrowly won on the first ballot. He chose Senator Robert Dole of Kansas as his vice presidential running mate.

The Democrats campaigned as friends of the "little man" and enemies of the big corporations. They appealed to African-American voters and women but avoided too close an identification with the "outsiders" who had been such a prominent part of McGovern's campaign four years earlier. Ford campaigned as the more experienced leader and attacked Carter as a man with only the vaguest idea of what he would do as president. As the weeks passed the voters, initially enthusiastic about Carter, began to waver and on election day gave the Democratic candidates a shaky victory of 40.2 million popular votes to their opponents' 38.6 million, and 297 electoral votes to the Republicans' 241. When the analysts examined the returns they concluded that Carter had fashioned his victory from a combination of the South, including states that had been recently drifting into the Republican column, and the traditional Democratic constituency of northern African-American, ethnics, Catholics, Jews, and trade unionists. It seemed doubtful, however, that anyone but a southerner could have carried it off. (See Figure 14–4.)

Jimmy Carter: The Early Months

Despite the narrow victory Carter began his administration on a wave of hope and popular approval. The public liked his common touch. For the swearing-in ceremony he wore a $175 dollar three-piece business suit and took his oath of office with his hand on an old family Bible. After the ceremony he and his wife, Rosalynn, and their daughter Amy walked, rather than rode, at the head of the procession to the White

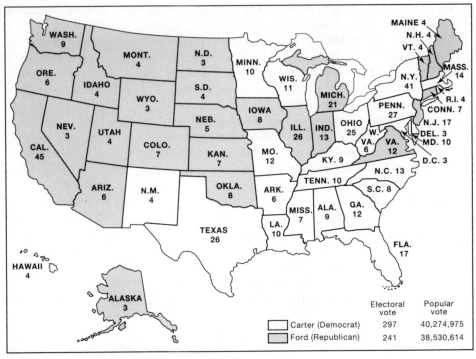

Figure 14–4 The 1976 Presidential Election

President and Mrs. Carter walking up Pennsylvania Avenue after the president's inauguration, January 20, 1977.

House. To further demonstrate their democratic values the Carters enrolled Amy at the local, predominantly African-American, Washington public school.

Energy

The new administration's domestic policies were dominated by the energy crisis. After the OPEC nations lifted the oil embargo in March 1974, petroleum and gasoline once more became abundant, although at much higher prices than ever before. Meanwhile Americans continued to consume energy supplies wastefully, daily increasing American dependence on the Middle East and other foreign regions for their oil supply.

Carter, a former nuclear submarine officer, understood the dangers of American oil dependence. The world's most powerful nation could not permit itself to become hostage to the goodwill of Middle East oil sheiks; Saudi Arabia could not be allowed to make American foreign policy. There was also the matter of international economic relations. If America continued to be dependent on foreign oil, it would have to pay out billions of dollars to the Middle East. This would worsen an already large balance of payments deficit.

The energy dearth also created problems by shifting the nation's regional power balance. The South and West, with their lower cost of living and their warm climate, had long attracted retirees from the North. By midcentury, with so many Americans living into their seventies and even eighties and with federal and private pension plans giving people the freedom to live anywhere in the country, the populations of Florida, Arizona, California, Texas, and other Sunbelt states soared.

Now rising oil prices engineered by OPEC brought further prosperity to Texas, Oklahoma, Louisiana, and other states in the southwestern "oil patch" while simultaneously hurting the northern industrial and farm regions that consumed energy but produced relatively little of their own. Oil patch residents were not always generous in their response to the plight of other Americans. Observers during these years reported bumper stickers on cars in Texas and other oil-producing states saying "Freeze a Yankee" and "Let the SOB's Freeze in the Dark."

Carter first addressed the energy crisis soon after the inauguration in the midst of one of the most severe eastern cold snaps in years. Before the cameras the president wore a heavy wool sweater to show the need to keep home thermostats low. On this occasion he said that his program would "emphasize conservation" and he asked the public to lower its thermostats to 65 degrees during the day and 55 at night. In late April he appeared before Congress and outlined a major energy program. The prices of petroleum, natural gas, and other fuel sources, until now held down artificially by government regulation, should be deregulated to find their own level. This would stimulate exploration for oil and natural gas and help increase domestic sources of supply. At the same time the government should encourage conservation by placing a high tax on imported oil and providing tax credits for people who insulated their houses. But the president's energy program, incorporated into over a hundred separate measures, quickly stalled in Congress.

Part of the problem was regional rivalries. The program promised to shift wealth still further from the North and East to the Sunbelt, where most of the nation's energy derived. There were also ideological difficulties. Liberal critics claimed that making higher prices the chief incentive to conservation hurt the poor far more than the rich. Conservatives responded that the only alternative was some unacceptable bureaucratic system of rationing.

Nuclear Energy and the Environment

The public was also divided over the role of atomic power in any scheme to ease the energy shortage. Since the 1950s the number of power-generating stations based on radioactive fuel had been increasing across the nation. It soon became clear that atomic energy was not the revolutionary breakthrough to cost-free energy that had been predicted just after World War II, but by the late 1970s about 3.5 percent of all U.S. electricity was generated by nuclear power plants.

This was a smaller proportion than in many major industrial nations, yet it raised a storm of controversy. As we have seen, ever since Rachel Carson's *Silent Spring* (1962) the public had worried about human-made environmental disaster and Congress had acted to limit sources of air and water pollution. The passionate environmentalists felt that these controls were too feeble and pointed to recent disasters as warnings: major oil spills along the California coast that threatened to damage Pacific coast ecology; forest damage inflicted by acid rain, the by-product of northeastern and midwestern fossil-fuel consumption; the disastrous erosion of the quality of life by unrestricted suburban growth. The country, they said, must clamp down hard on dangerous environmental practices, even if this meant limits on economic growth.

The proper response to the energy shortage, they insisted, was conservation —lowering energy use. Cars must be made smaller and more fuel efficient; houses must be better insulated; people must lower their thermostats, walk more, and turn off their lights. If energy output had to be increased it should be done by harnessing wind power and natural thermal power. For a time solar panels that could convert the sun's rays into hot water became the rage in some parts of the country. Often connected with such views was a concern for population limitation. People polluted the environment and used up scarce resources, and the sooner the country brought its rate of natural increase down to bare "replacement level," the better.

The environmentalists particularly deplored nuclear energy. Atomic energy plants produced thermal pollution of the water used to cool them, thereby endangering fish and local flora. Their spent nuclear fuel created severe problems of radioactive waste disposal. Most serious of all was the possibility of nuclear accident where failure of equiment or human error might cause a radioactive leak, or worse, a meltdown that would release vast quantities of radioactive gas and soot into the atmosphere. If such an accident occurred thousands might die or contract cancer.

In the last half of the seventies environmental groups used the protest tactics of the sixties to block construction or completion of nuclear power plants. In April 1977 for example, 2000 Clamshell Alliance demonstrators occupied the construction site of a new atomic energy plant going up at Seabrook, New Hampshire. The police arrested 1400 demonstrators. The antiatomic energy groups also pressed legal challenges to nuclear power plant construction. The antinuclear cause received a big lift when a leak developed at the nuclear power plant at Three Mile Island, near Harrisburg, Pennsylvania, in March 1979. Although the leak was contained and no one died, the American public quaked at the apparent narrow escape from a meltdown. Conservatives and power industry spokespeople continued to insist that atomic energy was safe and potentially cheap, but by the early 1980s it had become too difficult and expensive to overcome the public's fears and the environmentalists' challenges. The atomic energy industry soon stopped dead in its tracks. Half-completed plants were abandoned; planning for new ones ceased.

Carter's Political Failings

But the slow progress of Carter's energy program was not just a product of ideological and regional differences. There were serious flaws in the president's way of presenting the energy problem to the American people. Carter often sounded like a preacher calling his flock to repentance. He scolded the public for its energy extravagance. It was their disregard of the future, he said, that had gotten the United States into its current energy bind in the first place. He referred to "limits" and the need to accept a future less prosperous than the past. In July 1979, in a talk from his Camp David retreat often referred to as the "malaise" address, he described the country's "crisis of confidence" brought on by the energy crisis. Soon after, to signal a new beginning for his administration, he fired three of his cabinet members.

Much of what the president said was valid, but the American public did not enjoy being told that it could not have its cake and eat it too. Carter's political sermonizing, moreover, seemed self-righteous and depressing.

The president and his staff also proved inept in the infighting and horse-trading that marks legislative success in Washington. Carter had no experience of the federal government. Indeed that had been one of his political assets in the eyes of the post-Watergate public. But his ignorance and the arrogance of his young staff hurt him seriously in his relations with Congress. The administration offended Democratic leaders by not informing them of impending nominations for major executive positions or by failing to consult powerful members of Congress on matters that came under their legislative purview. Early in his administration Carter vetoed nineteen pet water projects for the West without telling their congressional sponsors in advance; many learned about the action only from their local newspapers. Even in small things the Carter staff lacked tact and courtesy. Hamilton Jordan, a close Carter aide, refused to grant House Speaker Thomas ("Tip") O'Neill's request for extra seats to the inaugural festivities. Thereafter O'Neill always referred to Jordan as "Hannibal Jerkin."

Some of the administration's severest setbacks came on the economic front. As we have seen, ever since the lifting of the Nixon price ceilings, inflation had soared out of control. As prices rose, so did interest rates, in part to discount higher prices and ensure lenders a reasonable return on their money in the future. High interest rates in turn depressed the housing industry because home buying depended on borrowed mortgage money. After 1979 the new head of the Federal Reserve Board, Paul Volcker, deliberately raised the Fed's rediscount rate, its interest charge to private banks, to reduce consumption and hold down prices. The move was unavoidable, but positive results were slow in coming.

For a time in the late 1970s it looked as if inflation had become a way of life and people sought to accommodate to its effects. The results were deplorable. Investors shifted their money from income-generating factories and enterprise into real estate and "collectibles," anything that promised to appreciate in price. The inflation surge also discouraged efficiency. If each month prices were higher, businesspeople, no matter how wasteful their practices, could count on profits. The incentive to increase productivity fell sharply. The inflation also shifted income from some groups to others. People who could pass along their costs to others gained; those on fixed incomes lost.

Carter seemed to have no answers. He favored reduced federal spending and continued high taxes to cool the economy but was unable to inspire the public or Congress with any clear policy. During much of his administration the economy just drifted with inflation seemingly built into the system.

Carter's Foreign Policy

The president's foreign policy balance sheet showed both debits and credits. Carter was determined to put the Vietnam era behind him and to ease Cold War tensions further. In his view this meant avoiding the hard-nosed Kissinger era response of putting America's short-term advantage first. The United States would no longer support authoritarian regimes abroad but use its good offices to induce undemocratic foreign governments to respect human rights. Washington would criticize harsh Soviet policy toward its dissidents who opposed Moscow's repressive domestic policies or who, as Jews, suffered religious persecution. Few Americans quarreled with this response. But the human rights principle was applied inconsistently. At times Washington attacked anti-Communist, pro-American authoritarian governments in the Americas and elsewhere. Conservatives, placing success in the Cold War first, deplored such attacks. At other times the administration overlooked the human rights violations of the United States' authoritarian friends. On these occasions liberals, less concerned with gaining Cold War advantages than with perceived international injustice, complained.

The president offended anti-Communist hard-liners by going beyond Nixon and opening formal diplomatic relations with the People's Republic of China in January 1979. The previous year he had succeeded in inducing the Senate to approve a new treaty with Panama that provided for the eventual transfer of control over the Panama Canal and the Canal Zone from the United States to Panama. Various superpatriot groups considered the treaty a shameful surrender of American rights.

Carter and the Soviet Union

Carter's policy toward the Soviet Union seemed naive to conservatives. Although he condemned Soviet human rights violations, he acted as if the Soviet Union were otherwise trustworthy. In June 1979 he completed negotiations for another Strategic Arms Limitation Agreement (SALT II). This treaty was pending in the Senate when, abruptly in late 1979, the Soviets sent troops into Afghanistan to support a puppet government threatened with overthrow by its domestic opponents.

Afghanistan was close to the Persian Gulf, the vital sea outlet for much of the Middle East's oil supply, and the move shocked the president and the American public. In response Carter withdrew the SALT II treaty from the Senate, canceled large Soviet grain purchase contracts with the United States, embargoed shipments of high technology wares to the Soviet Union, forbade Americans to particpate in the 1980 summer Olympic games in Moscow, and asked Congress for legislation to require draft registration of all nineteen- and twenty-year olds. In his January 1980 State of the Union Address he warned the Soviet Union that the United States considered the Persian Gulf region essential to U.S. national security.

Carter and the Middle East

More than even his predecessors Carter found his administration caught up in the intricacies of Middle Eastern affairs. The president won applause at home for his success in getting long-time enemies Israel and Egypt to agree to a peace treaty.

The possibility of such a pact had appeared unexpectedly in November 1977, when Egyptian leader Sadat visited Israel to discuss differences between the two countries. This was the first break in the Arab line against recognition of Israel, and it made Sadat a marked man to the anti-Israeli Palestine Liberation Organization (PLO) and its supporters in the Arab world. In August 1978 after it appeared that the peace process between Egypt and Israel had stalled, Carter invited Sadat and Israel's Prime Minister Menachem Begin to the presidential retreat at Camp David in Maryland to resume negotiations.

After weeks of hard bargaining that tested Carter's powers of persuasion severely, the two sides reached an agreement. Israel would evacuate the oil-rich Sinai region, occupied after the 1967 war, and return it to Egypt. In return Egypt would recognize Israeli independence and exchange diplomatic representatives with its former enemy. Unfortunately, on the all-important issue of the displaced Palestinians, the agreement settled for vague promises of a future accommodation, terms that the PLO and its Arab supporters rejected. During the next few years Arab resentment of Israel continued and new hatred was spawned against Egypt and the United States. At times it would take the form of terroristic hijacking of American airplanes, kidnappings, and bombings at airports abroad used by American tourists. Yet despite these responses the American public and much of the free world hailed the Camp David results as a major Carter success.

The Iran Hostage Crisis

Almost wholly negative in its consequences and ultimately disastrous for the Carter administration was the triumph of Islamic fundamentalism in Iran. Early in 1979 Shah Mohammad Reza Pahlevi of Iran, the authoritarian ruler who America had helped regain his throne in 1953 (see Chapter 11), was overthrown by a coalition of opponents from his left and right. The shah eventually came to the United States, where he entered a hospital for treatment of cancer. Soon after, Shiite Muslim fundamentalists led by the Ayatollah Ruholla Khomeini gained the upper hand in Iran and brutally suppressed their enemies—both the shah's supporters and the leftists—and imposed a strict religious regime on the Iranian people.

The ayatollah and his followers represented a powerful new force in the Middle East. Violently anti-Western, a throwback to the days of Islamic ultraorthodoxy and religious rule, they appealed to a strong Shiite minority in the Muslim world that resented both the Sunni majority and the modernizing tendencies represented by the West. Their sworn enemies were Israel and the United States, the latter seen as a "great Satan."

In November 1979 a group of fanatical young militants, probably with the approval of the ayatollah, seized the U.S. Embassy in Tehran and refused to release seventy American employees and diplomats. They would hold the hostages, they said, until the United States agreed to surrender the shah and his ill-gotten wealth to the Iranian authorities and apologized for America's past actions toward Iran.

This violation of diplomatic protocol and the law of nations shocked the American people and riveted their attention on events in Tehran for over a year. In retrospect it is clear that Americans allowed their concern for the hostages to eclipse too many other interests and absorb too many energies. The seizure was outrageous, but extricating the hostages and punishing the culprits should not have become an obsession.

Yet it did. Month after month while the United States maneuvered and argued—in the World Court, at the UN, among the other Muslim states—the hostage

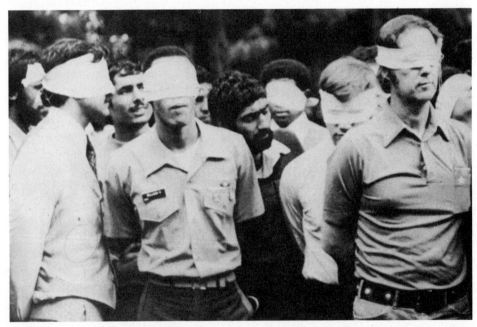

American hostages being paraded in Tehran, Iran, in November 1979. (UPI/Bettmann Newsphotos)

crisis smothered all other news. The American government froze several billion dollars of Iranian funds in the United States and cut off all trade in weapons and other goods to Iran. Individual Americans sometimes vented their frustration by acts of revenge against innocent Iranian students in the United States. On November 17 the Iranians, courting world opinion, released thirteen women and African-American hostages not suspected of espionage but refused to free the remaining fifty-three.

By early 1980 with the presidential election approaching, Carter became desperate. The American hostages were certain to become an important issue in the campaign. In late April, over the opposition of Secretary of State Cyrus Vance, the administration launched a rescue operation by heavily armed helicopters from American naval vessels in the Persian Gulf. This failed dismally. Eight men died in the attempt and the operation had to be aborted. Millions of citizens now felt even more impotent and angry and much of their rage was directed at their own president.

The 1980 Election

Despite the increasing public disenchantment with Carter and a serious challenge from Senator Edward Kennedy, the president could not be denied renomination by the Democrats in 1980. The Republicans turned to Ronald Reagan, the former two-term governor of California and heir of the Goldwater right within the party. They gave the vice presidential nomination to George Bush, a man closer to the Republican center. Some voters who did not like either Carter or Reagan supported Congressman John B. Anderson, a liberal Republican from Illinois, who ran on the Independent ticket.

A former movie actor and erstwhile New Deal liberal, Reagan had drifted to the political right in the 1950s and for a time, after his movie career declined, become a paid spokesman for General Electric. He had been carried into the California governor's mansion in 1966 on a wave of resentment against high taxes and student militancy. In Sacramento Reagan painfully learned the art of compromise and, despite predictions, had moved to the political center.

Yet in 1980 liberals saw his nomination for the presidency as a dangerous challenge to the entire post-twenties political era, and some indulged in loose talk of the coming "fascism" if he won.

In fact, like George Wallace and Richard Nixon before him, Reagan *did* appeal to the backlash against the perceived excesses of the sixties and early seventies. By 1980 African-American militancy, student unrest, and peace marches were things of the past, yet the old resentments—on both sides—lingered.

Reagan profited especially from the seventies' surge of Protestant fundamentalism. He was a product of fundamentalist education—although a divorced man and a lax churchgoer—and he appealed to the fundamentalists' ardent anticommunism, their concern for traditional "family values," their opposition to abortion (which had been legalized by the Supreme Court in 1973) and militant feminism, and their desire to encourage traditional Christianity over a "secular humanism" they claimed had become the nation's predominant faith.

The struggle between fundamentalism and religious liberalism had been part of American cultural life since early in the century. But never before had the fundamentalists been so militant and so well organized politically. During the campaign fundamentalist leaders such as the Reverend Jerry Falwell and Pat Robertson, mobilized as the "Moral Majority," helped rally the devout and raise funds for Reagan. They had the support of Richard Viguerie, a right-wing former Texas lawyer, who organized effective direct-mail fund-raising campaigns for right-wing causes.

Reagan also appealed to voters who felt the Carter administration had ignored growing Soviet strength and had let the United States be pushed around by Iran and other minor powers who no longer feared American might. "Is America as respected throughout the world as it was?" he asked. "Do you feel our security is safe?" Under his administration the country would once more "stand tall."

The highpoint of the campaign was the Carter-Reagan debate on national television. The president proved himself the better informed man, yet Reagan probably "won." The challenger was relaxed and charming, obviously no fascist threat to anyone. How could a man so pleasant, so full of apparent goodwill, harm anyone? The debates helped calm voter fears about a man who had seemed to many at the far-right fringe of American politics.

Yet for a time it seemed that Carter, by getting the embassy hostages released before election day, might pull off a victory. But the Iranians toyed with the United States, and on November 4 they were still captives. Not until January 20, Inauguration Day, did they leave Iran for home. The voting result was a near-Reagan landslide, with the Republican candidate nearly 44 million votes to Carter's 34.7 million. Reagan carried all but four states, winning 489 electoral votes to Carter's 49. (See Figure 14–5.) He would also have a Republican Senate to work with and an ideological, although not a party, majority in the House.

From Nixon to Reagan

The decade that followed the 1960s were depressing years for most Americans. Although Richard Nixon had ended the Vietnam War and lowered tensions between America and the People's Republic of China and the Soviet Union, by the last year of Jimmy Carter's administration Soviet-American relations were worse than during the 1960s. Still more disturbing was the 1980 taking of American hostages by revolutionary Iran Revolution. The hostage crisis tremendously frustrated Americans and reinforced their sense that their country had lost standing in the world.

Conditions at home also gave Americans reasons for gloom. The giant leap of energy prices that followed the OPEC oil embargo of 1973, precipitated a burst of runaway inflation unequalled since the mid 1940s. Many citizens were convinced that the good years of buoyant growth were gone forever.

And political events reinforced the crisis of confidence. Nixon confirmed his enemies' suspicions by plunging the nation into the worst political scandal in its history. Although the country survived Watergate, it emerged with its morale damaged. Carter, the man who might have repaired the nation's collective self-

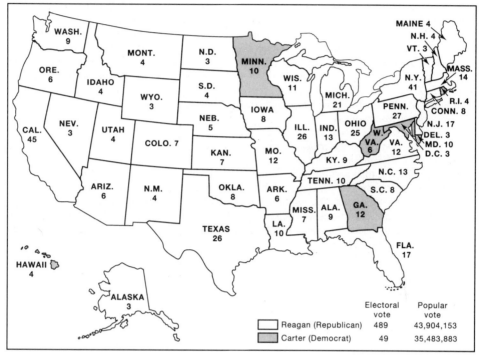

Figure 14–5   The 1980 Presidential Election

esteem, proved ineffectual. He only succeeded in making Americans feel peevish and ill-tempered.

Ronald Reagan was the beneficiary of the public's testy mood as the 1970s ended. The next few years would tell whether he could restore public confidence, revive a faltering economy, and reestablish America's international preeminence.

FOR FURTHER READING

On the Nixon personality see Garry Wills, *Nixon Agonistes: The Crisis of the Self-Made Man* (1971); also Bruce Mazlich, *In Search of Nixon* (1972), a psychoanalytical study.

On the rise of the South to political power see Kirkpatrick Sale, *Power Shift: The Rise of the Southern Rim and its Challenge to the Eastern Establishment* (1975). Peter Carroll, *It Seemed Like Nothing Happened: The Tragedy and Promise of America in the 1970s* (1982) deals with that apparently culturally uninteresting decade in an interesting way.

The beginnings of the post–World War II environment issue is dated from Rachel Carson's *Silent Spring* (1962). For environmentalism thereafter see Frank Graham, Jr., *Since Silent Spring* (1970) and Emma Rothschild, *Paradise Lost* (1973).

Nixon and the Arab-Israeli conflict is described in William Quandt, *Decade of Decision: American Policy toward the Arab-Israeli Conflict* (1977). On the energy crisis the reader should consult Daniel Yergin and Robert Stobaugh, *Energy Future: Report of the Energy Project at the Harvard Business School* (1979). Nixon's economic policies are skewered in Leonard Silk, *Nixonomics* (1972). The welfare reform proposals of the Nixon administration are described in Daniel Moynihan, *The Politics of a Guaranteed Income* (1973).

Nixon and China are covered in Lloyd Gardner, *The Great Nixon Turn-Around: America's New Foreign Policy in the Post-Liberal Era* (1973). On the election of 1972 see Robert Sam Anson, *McGovern* (1972). The most recent installment of America's immigration history is described in David Reimers, *Still the Golden Door: The Third World Comes to America* (1985).

The Watergate literature is more than abundant. Some of the best works are Carl Bernstein and Robert Woodward, *All the President's Men* (1974); Theodore White, *Breach of Faith: The Fall of Richard Nixon* (1975); Jonathan Schell, *The Time of Illusion* (1975); John Dean, *Blind Ambition: The White House Years* (1976): and Leon Jaworski, *The Right and the Power: The Prosecution of Watergate* (1976).

Two works on the Ford presidency are Richard Reeves, *A Ford, Not a Lincoln* (1975) and J. F. ter Horst, *Gerald Ford and the Future of the Presidency* (1974). For the 1976 election see Jules Witcover, *Marathon* (1977).

On Carter, the man and his administration, see James Wooten, *Dasher: The Roots and the Rising of Jimmy Carter* (1978); Haynes Johnson, *In the Absence of Power: Governing America* (1980); and Clark Mollenoff, *The President Who Failed: Carter Out of Control* (1980).

Carter's most conspicuous foreign policy failure was the hostage crisis in Iran. See Barry Rubin, *Paved with Good Intentions* (1980) and Hamilton Jordan, *Crisis: The Last Year of the Carter Presidency* (1982).

15
The Reagan Revolution

Ronald Reagan (left) and George Bush at the 1980 Republican National Convention. (UPI/Bettmann)

The "New Right"

Ronald Reagan's victory was hailed by conservatives as a mandate for a rightward political shift. And they were correct. For years Americans who deplored the social "excesses" of the permissive sixties and the political and economic excesses of liberal government had been preparing for the day. These members of the *New Right* were the spiritual descendants of the traditional Americans who had resisted the new social and intellectual forces of the 1920s and of the Harding and Coolidge Republicans who had turned the nation away from the progressive movement's concern over concentrated private economic power. Like their twenties forebears, they came disproportionately from the country's heartland, now located in the Sunbelt rather than the upper Midwest.

The agenda of these eighties conservatives was, in part, an update of their predecessors'. A lot of it dealt with social issues. Much of the New Right was fundamentalist Protestant in its religious affiliations, although it also included, among others, orthodox Jews who deplored irreligious secular trends, and traditional Catholics who rejected Marxist-influenced *liberation theology* and the liberal theological trends since Pope John XXIII. Many of its supporters, especially fundamentalists, deplored the sway of evolutionary teachings in the schools and demanded equal time for *creationist science,* a doctrine based on the biblical version of life's origins. They lamented the growing secularization of American education. The schools should find time for children's prayers; textbooks should not preach godless *secular humanism;* schools should not be allowed to teach immorality under the guise of sex education.

But to the New Right the imperfections of the schools merely reflected the general deterioration of public morality. Since the sixties, civil libertarians and liberal federal courts had made pornography—in books, magazines, film, and recordings—a pervasive influence in American life, corrupting the nation's youth and undermining the moral code.

Feminism too, the New Right said, was corroding conventional moral values as well as the family. In 1973 the Supreme Court in *Roe* v. *Wade,* responding to the new feminist sensibility, had struck down a Texas law forbidding abortion and opened the door to "abortion on demand" during the first three months of pregnancy. The polls showed that a majority of Americans endorsed freer access to abortion, but to many people of traditional religious background abortion seemed indistinguishable from murder. The social conservatives fought for an anti-abortion constitutional amendment and demanded that the federal government limit abortions at veterans' hospitals. A few extremist "pro-life" groups even resorted to bombing abortion clinics to stop the "murder of the innocents."

Still another feminist issue angered the New Right. Disturbed by the slow penetration of African-Americans and women into the professions, government service, and high-paid blue-collar trades, Congress and the courts had pushed the concept of "affirmative action"—preferential, not merely equal, treatment for minorities and women. This policy, said opponents, penalized white males and violated the principle of merit as a measure of preference. Still worse, they insisted,

Anti-abortion protesters in front of the White House, 1986. (UPI/Tim Clary)

was the newer principle of "comparable worth" that sought to equate the salaries of predominantly female occupations with supposedly similar, but higher paying, male job categories. Feminists and minority-group leaders responded that affirmative action was justified compensation for past race and sex discrimination; comparable worth merely eliminated gender-based job bias. Yet the two demands remained a source of irritation to conservative Americans.

The new assertiveness of homosexuals also vexed the New Right. During the late sixties homosexuals, responding to the decade's "liberationist" impulse, had begun to "come out of the closet" and demand changes to end what they perceived as legal, economic, and social discrimination. Social conservatives considered many of these demands—including the right of homosexual couples to adopt children, the legalizing of homosexual "marriages," and the end of discrimination against homosexual schoolteachers—threats to heterosexual mores and dangers to the traditional family. Conservatives fought back. In 1973 Phyllis Schlafly, a lawyer and mother of six, organized the Eagle Forum to oppose homosexual rights activism and free abortion. When in the early 1980s the horrible scourge of acquired immune deficiency syndrome (AIDS) burst on the scene, some of the more militant social conservatives declared that the disease was God's judgment on homosexuals for their wicked sexual practices.

By the end of the seventies the social and religious right had become a formidable organized force. More than 50 million Americans identified themselves as "evangel-ical" Christians. Not all were militant; not all were political. But many who watched the Reverend Jerry Falwell's "Old Time Gospel Hour" or Jim Bakker's PTL (Praise the Lord) TV ministry also sent money to Falwell's Moral Majority or responded to Richard Viguerie's massive fund-raising letter campaigns for conservative causes and politi-cians. The support of the religious and social right had been an important component of the Reagan victory in 1980.

The Neoconservative Intellectuals

Many New Right attitudes were visceral responses of people who felt bypassed in American life. They were reacting to the policy of inclusion that had marked the years since the 1960s and that seemed to submerge their values, interests, and visions in favor of those groups who at one time were at the periphery of American society. They were generally ordinary people who came to their views through their churches, the popular magazines and newspapers, and word of mouth.

But the New Right was also informed by a growing conservative intelligentsia. The nation had never lacked an intellectual right, but by the late 1970s it was both larger and more confident than ever before. Some of the conservative thinkers, the so-called *neoconservatives,* were associated with the journals *Commentary* and *The Public Interest.* Some were older men and women, many refugees from the left, driven away, they said, by the radical excesses of the tumultuous sixties. Although they had moved right, they usually retained a strong residual attachment to civil rights and civil liberties.

There were, however, several other clusters of conservative thinkers. There was the group of younger intellectuals attached to new conservative "think tanks" such as the American Enterprise Institute and the Heritage Foundation, organizations funded by conservative businesspeople. The magazine *National Review,* founded by William Buckley in 1955, provided a forum for conservative Catholic activists. Among university economists there were disciples of the free-market thinker Milton Friedman and the supply-siders led by Arthur Laffer. A number of conservative academic political scientists were followers of Leo Strauss, a German-born political philosopher. There was also the curious following of Ayn Rand, a Russian-born novelist and philosophical materialist, who despised democracy and touted an exaggerated elitism. The hero of one of her novels, *The Fountainhead,* was a Frank Lloyd Wright–type genius architect whose housing development design is cheapened by the project's financial backers intent on profit. Rather than accept this compromise with standards, he dynamites the whole thing.

Political Positions of the New Right

The New Right intellectuals, by and large, were more concerned with political and foreign policy issues than the social agenda that attracted the religious right. They deplored "big government" as oppressive. It had taken on too much that should be left to the individual. Government could not make up for the deficiencies in private

READING 15

Ronald Reagan Lays Out His Agenda

No one can say that Ronald Reagan did not give fair warning of his intentions both during the presidential campaign of 1980 and in his 1981 inaugural address. Excerpts from that address follow. Reagan said many times before he actually commenced his duties as president that he would cut taxes, cut government programs, and make the United States more powerful militarily. He did indeed accomplish each of these goals but the process would cost the nation dearly. It would be hard to find a better description of this cost than his own inaugural words for his spendthrift predecessors: they had "piled deficit upon deficit, mortgaging our future and our children's future for the temporary convenience of the present." By the time George Bush succeeded Reagan in 1989, the national debt had climbed to well over $2 trillion, almost three times the figure of eight years earlier.

. . . The business of our nation goes forward.

These United States are confronted with an economic affliction of great proportions.

We suffer from the longest and one of the worst sustained inflations in our national history. It distorts our economic decisions, penalizes thrift and crushes the struggling young and the fixed-income elderly alike. It threatens to shatter the lives of millions of our people.

Idle industries have cast workers into unemployment, human misery and personal indignity.

Those who do work are denied a fair return for their labor by a tax system which penalizes successful achievement and keeps us from maintaining full productivity.

But great as our tax burden is, it has not kept pace with public spending. For decades we have piled deficit upon deficit, mortgaging our future and our children's future for the temporary convenience of the present.

To continue this long trend is to guarantee tremendous social, cultural, political and economic upheavals.

You and I, as individuals, can, by borrowing, live beyond our means, but for only a limited period of time. Why then should we think that collectively, as a nation, we are not bound by that same limitation?

We must act today in order to preserve tomorrow. And let there be no misunderstanding—we're going to begin to act beginning today.

The economic ills we suffer have come upon us over several decades. They will not go away in days, weeks or months, but they will go away.

They will go away because we as Americans have the capacity now, as we have had in the past, to do whatever needs to be done to preserve this last and greatest bastion of freedom.

In this present crisis, government is not the solution to our problem; government is the problem.

From time to time we've been tempted to believe that society has become too complex to be managed by self-rule, that government by an elite group is superior to government for, by and of the people.

But if no one among us is capable of governing himself, then who among us has the capacity to govern someone else? . . .

Well, this administration's objective will be a healthy, vigorous, growing economy that provides equal opportunities for all Americans with no barriers born of bigotry or discrimination.

Putting America back to work means putting all Americans back to work. Ending inflation means freeing all Americans from the terror of runaway living costs.

All must share in the productive work of this "new beginning," and all must share in the bounty of a revived economy. . . .

Our government has no power except that granted it by the people. It is time to check and reverse the growth of government which shows signs of having grown beyond the consent of the governed.

It is my intention to curb the size and influence of the federal establishment and to demand recognition of the distinction between the powers granted to the federal government and those reserved to the states or to the people.

All of us—all of us need to be reminded that the federal government did not create the states; the states created the federal government.

Now, so there will be no misunderstanding, it's not my intention to do away with government.

It is rather to make it work—work with us, not over us; to stand by our side, not ride on our back. Government can and must provide opportunity, not smother it; foster productivity, not stifle it.

If we look to the answer as to why for so many years we achieved so much, prospered as no other people on earth, it was because here in this land we unleashed the energy and individual genius of man to a greater extent than has ever been done before.

Freedom and the dignity of the individual have been more available and assured here than in any other place on earth. The price for this freedom at times has been high, but we have never been unwilling to pay that price.

It is no coincidence that our present troubles parallel and are proportionate to the intervention and intrusion in our lives that result from unnecessary and excessive growth of government.

It is time for us to realize that we are too great a nation to limit ourselves to small dreams. We're not, as some would have us believe, doomed to an inevitable decline. I do not believe in a fate that will fall on us no matter what we do. I do believe in a fate that will fall on us if we do nothing.

So, with all the creative energy at our command let us begin an era of national renewal. Let us renew our determination, our courage and our strength. And let us renew our faith and our hope. We have every right to dream heroic dreams. . . .

In the days ahead I will propose removing the roadblocks that have slowed our economy and reduced productivity.

Steps will be taken aimed at restoring the balance between the various levels of government. Progress may be slow—measured in inches and feet, not miles—but we will progress.

It is time to reawaken this industrial giant, to get government back within its means and to lighten our punitive tax burden. . . .

And as we renew ourselves here in our own land we will be seen as having greater strength throughout the world. We will again be the exemplar of freedom and a beacon of hope for those who do not now have freedom.

To those neighbors and allies who share our freedom, we will strengthen our historic ties and assure them of our support and firm commitment.

We will match loyalty with loyalty. We will strive for mutually beneficial relations. We will not use our friendship to impose on their sovereignty, for our own sovereignty is not for sale.

As for the enemies of freedom, those who are potential adversaries, they will be reminded that peace is the highest aspiration of the American people. We will negotiate for it, sacrifice for it; we will not surrender for it—now or ever.

Our forbearance should never be misunderstood. Our reluctance for conflict should not be misjudged as a failure of will.

When action is required to preserve our national security, we will act. We will maintain sufficient strength to prevail if need be, knowing that if we do so we have the best chance of never having to use that strength.

Above all we must realize that no arsenal or no weapon in the arsenals of the world is so formidable as the will and moral courage of free men and women.

It is a weapon our adversaries in today's world do not have.

It is a weapon that we as Americans do have.

Let that be understood by those who practice terrorism and prey upon their neighbors.

I am told that tens of thousands of prayer meetings are being held on this day, for that I am deeply grateful. We are a nation under God, and I believe God intended for us to be free. It would be fitting and good, I think, if on each inaugural day in future years it should be declared a day of prayer.

Source: Facts on File, January 23, 1981.

character and its attempts to do so only led to permanent dependency. As Reagan, their most effective spokesman, would say, "government is not the solution; government is the problem."

Among government's most troublesome exactions, said the New Right, were the taxes it imposed. These were a brake on enterprise. Creative people were discouraged from innovation when they knew that profits would be taxed away by the government. The existing tax system was especially onerous because of "bracket-creep," the automatic increase in tax rates imposed by inflation-fueled wage and salary increases. Cut taxes drastically, especially in the upper-income brackets, and you would stimulate economic growth by offering new incentives to enterprising people. According to the supply-side economists Arthur Laffer, Jude Wanniski, and Martin Anderson, such an approach need not cause serious budget deficits: the surge in economic output would raise the government's overall tax take, largely offsetting the lower tax rates.

Neoconservatives also found taxes deplorable for the uses to which they were put. The 1960s Great Society antipoverty programs had been a disaster, they said. Rather than enabling the poor to lift themselves out of poverty, they had encouraged more and more able-bodied people to accept handouts permanently and had reduced their incentives to become self-supporting. The result was a permanent underclass of single or abandoned mothers and children living on welfare at the edge of, rather than as part of, society. According to Charles Murray, a conservative social scientist, "we tried to provide more for the poor and produced more poor instead."

Another New Right concern was the apparent decline of America's strength relative to the Soviet Union. Détente had served to mask the Soviet's giant, destabilizing arms buildup, they said. While Americans were lulled by cultural exchanges, Soviet concessions on Jewish emigration, and the like, the Soviet Union had thrown enormous resources into building an all-ocean navy, expanding its nuclear missile arsenal, and pumping up its already vast army. By 1980, many conservatives claimed, the Soviet Union had come even with, or surpassed, the United States in its military might and its ability to win a war of its choosing. This new strength explained the recent Soviet adventurism in Afghanistan and in parts of Africa.

Reaganomics

Thus Reagan came to office in January 1981 backed by a determined army of activists with a bold conservative program. Even millions of Americans who were not New Right ideologues anticipated significant course corrections for the ship of state in economics, social policy, and foreign relations.

Tax Cuts

The first important item on the Reagan agenda was a major tax cut. First suggested in the mid 1970s by Representative Jack Kemp of New York and Senator William V. Roth, Jr., of Delaware (both Republicans), the deep slash was designed to remove the shackles on enterprise and stimulate the economy. Appealing not only to supply-siders, it also won support from the followers of Howard Jarvis, leader of the Proposition 13 tax revolt that had succeeded in trimming California property taxes drastically after 1978. Taking advantage of his election momentum and employing his legendary persuasive powers to good effect, the president induced Congress to pass the biggest federal tax cut in history.

The Economic Recovery Tax Act of 1981 promised to lop $750 billion off the country's tax bill over the succeeding five years, primarily by cutting individual income taxes by 25 percent in three yearly installments. Although these cuts were to be across-the-board, people in the higher income tax brackets would be the largest gainers in total taxes saved. In addition, the law chopped billions off corporation taxes for the purpose of stimulating business.

Critics attacked the cuts as likely to produce giant federal budget deficits. Since deficits had long been among the most heinous crimes in the conservative indictment of liberal Democrats, the matter required explanation. The administration had a number of ready answers. Quoting the supply-siders, it declared that the economy, once freed from the constraining effects of exorbitant taxes, would surge to new levels and increase the Treasury's revenues. The budget would be balanced without pain to anyone. When first expounded by Reagan during the Republican presidential primaries in 1980, George Bush, his chief rival, called this formula "voodoo economics," but in 1981 the public was willing to give it a chance.

The other response—and, some critics said, really the heart of the Reagan tax policy—was that deficits would be avoided by drastically cutting domestic spending programs. Some months later David Stockman, the youthful director of the budget, admitted that "the plan was to have a strategic deficit that would give you an argument for cutting back the programs that weren't desired." In effect the inevitable deficits would force the liberals to accept cuts in social spending whether they liked it or not.

Cutbacks

In fact Stockman wanted to cut more than the benefits to the poor. His goal, he later wrote, was to attack "weak claims," not "weak clients." The boondoggles for the powerful, that is, should be no more exempt from review and cutback than those for the disadvantaged. Thus subsidies for truckers, middle-class college students, and for the nuclear power industry must go; they were special privileges for a few at the expense of the many and the efficiency of the economy as a whole.

It proved harder to reduce domestic programs than the administration thought, however. The president announced that he would retain a "safety net" of welfare programs under the truly indigent, but he and his colleagues took aim at many antipoverty and other entitlement programs that dated back to the Lyndon Johnson Great Society era. In 1981, during the first flush of enthusiasm for the Reagan policies, Congress agreed to sharp cuts in such programs as food stamps, Aid to Families with Dependent Children, child nutrition, Supplemental Security Income, health block grants, and Low Income Energy Assistance. It voted to trim job-training programs, aid for college students, and public-service employment. The administration also imposed limits on unemployment insurance programs and the cost of Medicare and Medicaid health insurance. It also sought to remove benefits from farmers, cities, and favored businesses. All told, during 1982–85 the Reagan forces managed to secure cuts of approximately $175 billion in nonmilitary spending.

But this was only about half of what the president needed to avoid large deficits. In truth many of the social programs were vulnerable. Not all were effective; many were bandages on deep social wounds that really required more drastic treatment. Others were wasteful, payoffs to one group or another without any serious rationale. Yet many had powerful constituencies—their direct beneficiaries and liberal politicians—and the resistance to deep cuts proved formidable and effective. The business and farm groups were even better defended. Lobbyists, local officials, and members of Congress besieged Stockman demanding that their favorite enterprise be exempt from the tax axe. Nor were his opponents only liberal Democrats. Republican Senator Howard Baker of Tennessee defended his pet Clinch River nuclear reactor project against projected cuts. Senator Jesse Helms of North Carolina, one of the most conservative people in Congress, insisted that subsidies to tobacco farmers be retained. Another conservative Republican senator, Orrin Hatch of Utah, defended the Job Corps because, Stockman wrote, the corps had a large office in Utah. Even fellow administration officials refused to cooperate with spending cuts. Secretary of State Alexander Haig, the budget director reported, refused to consider any cuts in the State Department budget on the grounds that foreign policy should be exempt from the economy drive.

Social Security

No program was as tough to take on as social security. By the early 1980s the nation's retirees represented an awesome bloc of alert and militant voters. Over the years they had succeeded in beefing up social security retirement benefits so that by the Reagan era the elderly were no longer, as a group, among the country's most seriously disadvantaged. That distinction had passed to the young. Owing to family breakup, teenage parenting, actual cuts in social programs, and the erosion of welfare benefits by inflation, more and more young children belonged to low-income families. Yet the elderly "gray panthers" refused to see themselves as a privileged group and fought back effectively.

In 1981, in the first flush of pro-Reagan enthusiasm, Congress allowed small cuts in projected social security increases. In May 1981, pleading the need to keep the system from going bankrupt, the administration asked for deeper cuts in social security programs. Its requests fell on deaf ears. By now social security had become a sacred cow and the Senate voted 96 to 0 to reject the proposals.

The problem did not go away. The United States had an aging population, and the millions of retired people in their seventies and eighties promised to be an enormous future economic burden on a proportionately ever smaller group of working people. There were powerful actuarial reasons for either limiting retirement and medicare benefits or hiking social security taxes. But the issue proved to be such a hot political potato that neither party wanted to tackle it, and it required bipartisan action through a national commission to push through modestly scaled-down benefits and higher social security taxes.

At the end of the process the nation's seniors emerged as the most effective pressure group in sight, one that no politician with a normal sense of self-preservation cared to challenge. Some social pundits worried that the 1980s struggle over social security foreshadowed a future confrontation of the generations over how to divide up the social pie.

Reagan and Poverty

All told, if the Reagan administration intended to eliminate the welfare state as constructed by the Democrats since the 1930s, it was unsuccessful. Although many saw flaws in the other person's program, they seldom perceived any in those that benefited themselves. Too many Americans had a stake in the system, and the beneficiaries were not just the nation's outsiders.

But liberals inevitably emphasized the impact on the poor. Notwithstanding the Stockman claim, the Reagan attack, they insisted, penalized those least able to defend themselves and spared the rich and powerful. The administration's policies were helping to swell the number of Americans below the poverty line.

They were right about the number of the poor; they increased. And the poor were more visible than ever before. In the big cities, particularly, homelessness became a major problem. Americans winced when Soviet television in 1986 carried a propaganda program showing people sleeping on the streets of New York and other American cities.

But it was not clear that altered public policy was responsible for the change for the worse. Some social observers pointed the finger of blame at family collapse and rising illegitimacy and the resulting neglect of children. Still others emphasized the structural changes in the economy that traditional welfare programs simply did not

Single mothers and their children made up an increasing proportion of America's poor during the 1980s. (Black Star/Joe Rodriguez)

address. Since the 1950s, they said, the United States had become an "information society" where an ever increasing number of jobs required ability to handle words and numbers. Those who lacked the ability simply could not find work to support themselves decently. Programs that merely served up dollars would never meet the needs of such people adequately. As for the homeless, conservatives said, most of them were mentally disturbed people released from hospitals under permissive patients' rights laws. Their problem was mental illness, a condition without known cure, not poverty.

Budget Deficits

Unable to extract the large social program cuts it wanted from Congress, the administration could not avoid massive budget deficits. But the problem was made far worse by its insistence on an enormous arms buildup. Between 1980 and 1985 military spending rose almost 40 percent, the outlays going primarily to the new weapons systems that Defense Secretary Caspar Weinberger convinced Congress the military needed to keep up with the Soviet Union.

Burgeoning defense outlays, modest domestic program reductions, and multibillion-dollar tax cuts combined to produce the most immense budget deficits in the

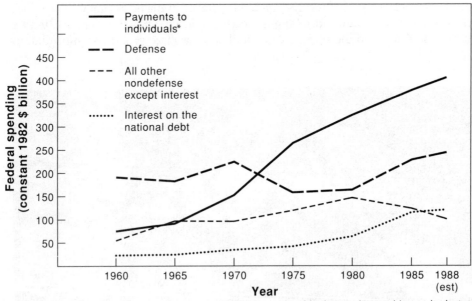

*Includes Social Security and other entitlement programs mandated by law and not subject to budgetary discretion.

Figure 15–1 The Components of Federal Spending, 1960–1988 (Constant 1982 Billion Dollars)

Sources: *Statistical Abstract of the United States, 1987* (Washington: U.S. Bureau of the Census, 1986), p. 295; *Statistical Abstract of the United States, 1988* (Washington: U.S. Bureau of the Census, 1987), p. 294; and *Budget of the United States Government, 1989* (Washington: U.S. Office of Management and Budget, 1988), pp. 6g–42.

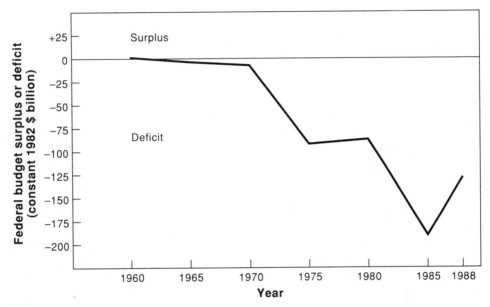

Figure 15–2 The Federal Budget, 1960–1988 (Constant 1982 Billion Dollars)

Sources: Adapted from *Statistical Abstract of the United States, 1987* (Washington: U.S. Bureau of the Census, 1987), p. 295 and *Statistical Abstract of the United States, 1988* (Washington: U.S. Bureau of the Census, 1987), pp. 291 and 294; *Budget of the United States Government, 1990*, Historical Tables (Washington: U.S. Office of Management and Budget, 1989), pp. 19–20.

country's history. (See Figures 15–1 and 15–2.) In President Carter's last year the Treasury had a shortfall of about $74 billion. In 1983, two years after the tax cut bill, it had leaped to $208 billion; in 1986 it was over $220 billion.* By the latter date the accumulated national debt was over $2 trillion, more than twice the amount of 1980. The interest on this colossal sum alone was $135 billion each year.

Each party blamed the other for the deficits. Republicans said the Democrats who controlled Congress were unwilling to cut out even useless programs. The Democrats blamed the Republican administration's military buildup and the ill-considered Republican tax cuts of 1981. Neither seemed willing to yield, and to get the budget down Congress passed the Gramm-Rudman-Hollings law in 1985, forcing modest automatic budget cuts across the board whether Congress acted or not.

The Economic Balance Sheet

Clearly this was not the result that "Reaganomics" was designed to achieve. But its effects were hidden. Economically sophisticated Americans, and some ordinary people as well, worried about the deficits and the national debt. They were a mortgage on the country's future and would be an impossible burden on its children and

---

*(These figures are in ordinary, or *current*, dollars; Figure 15–2 surveys the deficit since 1960 in *constant* 1982 dollars, which eliminate discrepancies caused by changes in the value of the dollar.)

grandchildren, people feared. But in the short run they seemed to have little effect, largely, the pundits said, because foreigners were willing to lend the United States as much as it needed to live beyond its means.

More immediately painful was the severe economic slump of the administration's first years in office. In 1979 there had been 6 million unemployed; by 1983 there were 10.7 million, representing 9.6 percent of the labor force, the highest total since the 1930s. (See Figure 14–3 in Chapter 14.) The public responded at the polls during the 1982 congressional elections by throwing out twenty-five Republican representatives, although still leaving the GOP with a Senate majority.

There was another side of the economic coin, however, one that was tied to the first. In the last Carter years, as we saw, prices had risen at a pace not seen since the Civil War era. Beginning in 1979, Paul Volcker, Carter's appointee as chairman of the Federal Reserve Board, restricted money growth sharply to counter the inflationary surge. By 1981 the prime interest rate, the amount charged the best-rated business borrowers, had leaped to over 20 percent. Such high rates discouraged consumer buying and business investment and the result was the 1981–83 slump. But another effect was to stop inflation in its tracks for the first time in almost a decade. By 1982 the rise in the consumer price index was down to 6 percent; for the next three years it averaged about 3.5 percent, among the lowest figures since the early 1960s. In effect, in cooperation with the Reagan administration, the Fed had, by policies that produced recession and high unemployment, squeezed inflation down to a manageable level.

And then the employment picture too improved. In 1983 the unemployment rate began to drop. By 1984 it was down to under 7 percent. In 1988 it fell to under 6 percent. By the time of the 1988 presidential election the Republicans could boast that under their watch millions of new jobs had been created. In many parts of the country, in fact, as the Reagan administration wound down, there were serious labor shortages, especially in entry-level positions.

How did the American people as a whole fare under Reaganomics? By the middle of Reagan's second term some of the results began to come in.

They were mixed. It was true that unemployment and inflation were down. But the Reagan era achievements in these categories just about returned the nation to where it had been in the early seventies. On the other hand GNP growth rates during the Reagan years were no better than they had been during the preceding seven mediocre years—and they were far below those of the 1960s. Another disquieting figure related to productivity growth. Between 1979 and 1986 average output per hour in private business increased by 1.4 percent a year. This was about half the average productivity gain of the period 1948–1965 and considerably lower than the productivity gains of most other industrial countries.

What about individual Americans and American families? In early 1989 House Ways and Means Committee data revealed that between the beginning of the eighties decade and 1987 American average family incomes had risen 5.6 percent. Unfortunately the gains had been highly uneven. Low-income families had *less* purchasing power in 1987 than in 1979, and upper-income families had more. The disparities were even greater for personal incomes (see Figure 15–3), revealing, according to Democrat Thomas J. Downey of New York, Chairman of the House Subcommittee on

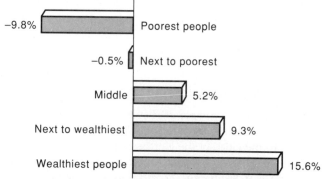

Figure 15–3 *Average Personal Income by Fifths of the Population from 1979 to 1987 (Constant 1987 Dollars)*

Source: *Adapted from chart in the* New York Times, *March 23, 1989, p. A24. Data from House of Representatives Ways and Means Committee.*

Human Resources, trends "inimical to the health of a democracy." Even the overall gains, the data indicated, were achieved only by the growing number of families with two wage earners. Indeed as other data showed, real wages had actually declined by about 2 percent between 1980 and 1987. In all fairness not all the deterioration at the bottom could be blamed on Reagan's economic policies. Much of it, as we noted was connected with family disruption, divorce, illegitimacy, and other social problems. On the other hand the Reagan administration had done virtually nothing to offset these trends, its critics noted.

Minorities and Women

The 1970s had been a time of mixed fortunes for the nation's nonwhite and non-European population. Higher birthrates and massive immigration, legal and illegal, from Asia and Latin America had increased their proportion of the total population. For the first time Asians could be found in large numbers in many American cities.

Some of these minority people had done very well. In south Florida, refugees from Castro's Cuba had prospered as businesspeople and professionals. In 1987 the mayor of Miami was Xavier Suarez, a Cuban refugee. Many of the Asians too had flourished. Chinese from Taiwan and Hong Kong as well as members of the pre–World War II Chinese-American community had made enormous strides in the sciences and the arts. An Wang, a Chinese-American from Shanghai with a Ph.D. from Harvard, founded Wang Laboratories, a leader in the computer industry. Yo-Yo Ma, another Chinese-American Harvard graduate, was one of the world's outstanding cellists. Koreans, Pakistanis, Indians, and Indochinese immigrants established many successful small businesses, following the lead of other immigrant groups in previous generations. Korean, Chinese, Japanese, Vietnamese, and Indian students regularly won a quarter or more of the National Merit scholarships and Westinghouse science talent awards. Many had gained admission to the most prestigious and selective American colleges and universities and white middle-class parents were beginning to complain that their own children were being crowded out.

Hispanic Americans

Cubans aside, people of Hispanic background had not done as well. In 1975 the average income of Hispanic families was $9,500 compared to $14,300 for Anglo whites. In the cities of the Northeast Puerto Ricans, although American citizens, were still primarily unskilled workers living in crime-ridden, run-down neighborhoods. In the West and Southwest, Mexican-Americans filled much the same uncomfortable niche in society.

Many Mexican-Americans were native-born citizens; thousands of others, however, were illegal immigrants. Such "undocumented" residents generally found it easy to get unskilled work in construction, in agriculture, and in factories. Although their wages were low, they were far better than those paid south of the border, and thousands risked arrest by American border guards to cross into the United States from Mexico and Central America.

So large was this migration that by the end of the 1970s there was a growing chorus of complaint that the nation had "lost control of its borders" and, especially in the Southwest, that Anglo culture was being swamped by an alien tidal wave. In some places Anglos fought back by resisting bilingual education or by demanding laws declaring English alone the nation's official language. In 1986 Congress passed the Simpson-Rodino Act imposing fines on employers who hired undocumented immigrants, but at the same time granting a general amnesty to all illegal immigrants who had arrived in the United States before January 1, 1982. The law required that newcomers apply for amnesty, but compliance was slow, and it was not clear whether the measure would end the fears of many Americans about unregulated immigration.

African-Americans

The seventies had been a time of slow economic progress for African-Americans. Thousands of African-American families clearly had made it into the middle class; some had even achieved wealth. During the Reagan years employment increases for blacks exceeded those for whites. Yet median black family incomes remained far behind those of whites.

Increasingly, moreover, a chasm had appeared between the top and the bottom of the African-American community. Below the successful African-American middle class was an expanding black ghetto underclass of husbandless women with their children and young black men without the skills or work habits to get and retain decent jobs. Many of these young males drifted into and out of crime; many died young from violence.

A particularly devastating aspect of ghetto life in the 1980s was the drug scourge. Drugs were not entirely a ghetto phenomenon, of course. Many young middle-class people continued to smoke marijuana. So common had it become that in many communities the authorities simply ignored the practice. Cocaine ("coke") use had spread widely among white middle-class young adults in the arts, professions, and businesses with immensely damaging results. But the use of heroin and "crack," a quick-acting form of cocaine, had come to permeate ghetto communities all over the nation. The drug plague not only ruined individual lives, it was also a source of ghetto crime and prostitution as addicts sought to find money to pay for their expensive habits. By mid-decade AIDS, a deadly blood and bodily fluid–borne disease that at first affected mostly homosexuals, had spread to addicts who injected heroin with unclean needles. AIDS further ravaged the ghettos.

The authorities did their best to combat the drug danger. The responses ranged from first lady Nancy Reagan's "Just Say No!" campaign to the federal government's attempt to oust from office General Manuel Noriega, the Panama strongman who had made his country a haven for drug dealers. Millions of dollars were spent on air and sea interdictions of drug runners and on attempts to stop drug production at its source abroad with the cooperation of foreign governments. Nothing seemed to work. By the end of the decade the drug plague was probably worse than at the beginning.

The chasm between the African-American middle-class and the underclass was physical as well as economic and social. As one social commentator observed, middle-class black families

> tend to move out of these economically and socially depressed areas to better neighborhoods where they and their children have a better opportunity to lead a better life. They leave behind the least educated and the most deprived. . . . As a result there is a concentration of misery in the very hearts of our largest cities.

One disquieting feature of the 1980s was the apparent resurgence of overt and public race prejudice. In cities around the country tribal hostilities between working-class whites and blacks erupted in acts of violence. The best publicized of these was the attack by a group of white youths on several young African-American men in Howard Beach, a lower middle-class white neighborhood in New York City. Fleeing from his tormentors, one of the black men was hit by a car and killed. Although three of the white youths were convicted of manslaughter and sentenced to long prison terms, the event produced deep resentment in the African-American community and measurably worsened race relations in New York City.

But the picture was not entirely bleak. During the seventies and the eighties African-Americans were able to harvest many of the civic fruits of the Second Reconstruction. Jim Crow was dead everywhere. Nowhere in the nation were there separate public facilities for blacks and whites. African-Americans now voted even in the South and had become a political force to be reckoned with in Dixie as never before since the post–Civil War era. In the North African-American political power had been converted into big city mayorships. As the eighties came to an end, African-American politicians were mayors in almost all of the nation's metropolises except New York, Boston, and San Francisco.

Clearly the problems that African-Americans faced were not derived from legal discrimination but from factors such as private prejudice, structural economic change, and community deterioration—all far less easy to handle. Yet black leaders blamed the Reagan administration for many of the setbacks.

The indictment was detailed. The conservative social attitudes of the president and his associates had created a climate that encouraged bolder expression of bigotry, they said. The Reagan administration had also chipped away at many of the legal gains of the recent past. The president supported efforts of segregated private schools to gain tax-exempt status. He at first had refused to endorse extension of the 1965 Voting Rights Act. The Reagan Justice Department had opposed the affirmative action programs of a number of cities, and the administration had tried to gut the Civil Rights Commission established in 1956 to investigate civil rights violations. Most important of all was the administration's drastic cuts in social programs. These had hurt African-Americans disproportionately. The Reagan administration, declared a National Urban League report in early 1984, was "almost universally regarded by blacks as the most hostile administration in the last 50 years."

The Feminist Tide Recedes

During the Reagan era the feminist political drive slowed, a process that could be tracked by the fate of the Equal Rights Amendment (ERA).

This proposed measure simply stated: "Equality of rights under the law shall not be denied or abridged by the United States or by any State on account of sex." It had first been proposed by Alice Paul's National Women's Party in the early 1920s soon after women won the vote. Although introduced into every session of Congress from 1923 on, it had made little progress during the next twenty-five years.

After World War II the ERA picked up the support of club women's groups, unions, liberal church organizations, and civil rights leaders. In 1945, 1953, and again in 1959, it passed the Senate (with amendments) but each time was defeated in the House. With the advent of the militant feminism of the late 1960s the ERA acquired new support. In October 1971 the House of Representatives approved it by a vote of 354 to 23. Five months later the Senate passed the ERA by 84 to 8.

To become the law of the land, the amendment had to be ratified by two-thirds (thirty-eight) of the state legislatures in a period of seven years. At first it charged ahead, being confirmed in thirty-two states in a little over a year. Then the process stopped.

In 1973 Phyllis Schlafly and other conservatives organized a "stop ERA" campaign. They aimed their appeal not only at conservative men but also at traditional women who resented the tone and manner of militant feminists, and although many worked, who saw their jobs as secondary to their roles as wives and mothers. The stop ERA forces declared that the amendment would deprive women of the protective labor and social legislation that had been enacted on their behalf since the early twentieth century. Women, moreover, would be forced to serve in the armed forces, even in combat roles. They would lose their advantage in custody battles involving children and would be denied alimony in divorces. The campaign was at times alarmist and silly. According to some opponents of ERA, for example, the amendment would forbid separate restrooms for men and women in public accommodations.

But whether fair or foul the campaign proved effective. By 1979 ERA had still not won the requisite number of ratifications. At this point Congress extended the ratification deadline for three and a half more years, but again the proposal could not gain the requisite number of states. In 1982 ERA was declared dead. Efforts were made during the next years to again secure congressional passage, but they failed. Although the ERA remained on the liberal agenda, in the Reagan era the public mood had changed. Feminism as a movement had begun to recede.

Reagan and the Environment

The president and his associates were clearly less sensitive to environmental concerns than their predecessors. Many Reagan appointees, including Interior Secretary James Watt, believed that efforts to safeguard the environment often hobbled economic growth and productivity. Lawsuits by public interest groups, massive environmental impact studies, excessive caution of the Food and Drug Administration in authorizing new drugs, and the like were economically harmful. Useful projects, they said, were not undertaken and jobs and profits lost; costs were pushed up; the public was denied important drugs and facilities. The nuclear power industry, they claimed, had been virtually destroyed by exaggerated fear of accidents.

Deeds matched words. Under Reagan the government cut the budget for the Consumer Product Safety Commission, the agency that administered consumer safety laws. It also cut back the Environmental Protection Agency (EPA), the chief government bureau responsible for protecting the natural environment against pollution and contamination. Reagan appointed Ann Burford, a conservative Colorado lawyer, to head EPA and administer $1.4 billion "superfund" to clean up toxic waste sites. She and her assistant Rita Lavelle soon came under fire for administering the agency to suit favored businesses and for failing to move effectively to eliminate the many lethal toxic dumps that dotted the nation. In early 1983 both resigned from their posts, and in December Lavelle was indicted for perjury for denying that she knew of her superior's deals concerning waste dumping.

Watt himself, meanwhile, came under attack for seeking to transfer federal timber, mineral, and water rights in the national forests to private businesses. A leading figure in the "sagebrush rebellion," an antienvironmentalist western movement to return control of natural resources to the communities where they were located, he had little respect for traditional conservation views. In October 1983, after having made a coarse remark that insulted African-Americans, Jews, women, and the handicapped all at the same time, he resigned and was replaced by William Clark. Clark was at least more circumspect in his environmental policies.

Reagan's Foreign Policy

If Reagan's domestic agenda required the scaling down of government programs, his foreign agenda required the exact opposite. Ronald Reagan had campaigned as the candidate of the most committed Cold War element in American political life. In office, Reagan and Secretary of Defense Caspar Weinberger extracted from Congress the funds for a massive buildup in the American armed forces. In 1980, the last Carter year, the Defense Department budget was $136 billion. By 1986 it had soared to $273 billion.

The military buildup was designed to offset Soviet strength and provide the United States with the clout to achieve its international goals. Yet at times these goals seemed to translate primarily into verbal bluster. Reagan was quick to attack the Soviet Union when the occasion seemed ripe. The Soviet Union, he stated in a speech to a group of Christian evangelists in Orlando, Florida, had "the aggressive impulses of an evil empire." In late August 1983, when a South Korean airliner strayed into Soviet airspace in Siberia and was shot down, the president denounced the Soviet Union as "barbarous" and "uncivilized," although he probably knew that the incident was a stupid Soviet blunder rather than a calculated slaughter of innocent civilians.

Reagan clearly shared a naive but spontaneous belligerent foreign policy mood with many Americans. Borrowing an image from the Sylvester Stallone movies about a one-man anti-Communist scourge, critics accused the president of displaying a Rambo-like attitude toward foreign affairs. In fact his record of action was strangely mixed. He sent marines to Lebanon in 1983 to help pacify that chaotic land, and when 241 were killed by a bomb set off by a fanatical Islamic fundamentalist, he withdrew them hurriedly. Soon after, as if to make up for this fiasco, he sent 10,000 American paratroopers to invade the tiny island of Grenada to overturn a Marxist regime that the administration believed was making the country a base for Castro's Cuba.

Central America

Reagan's willingness to project American power abroad was most vigorously pursued in Central America. The region was poor, socially volatile, and inclined to be anti-Yankee. It seemed ripe for authoritarian, pro-Soviet revolutions of the sort that had brought Castro to power in Cuba. Such changes, the Reaganites felt, would further Soviet ends and threaten American interests in Latin America. In El Salvador the United States sought with some success to prop up with infusions of money and military advice conservative-to-moderate governments under attack by leftists. By the last years of the Reagan administration El Salvador no longer seemed a serious trouble spot.

Nicaragua was a thornier problem. There a Marxist regime, the Sandinistas, had overturned the authoritarian government of Anastasio Somoza, a traditional Latin American strongman, and taken control in 1979. The Sandinistas, like other left-wing Latin American movements, promised to relieve the poverty of the peasantry, but they also banned domestic political opposition and provided aid to leftist guerrillas in El Salvador. The administration soon began to explore ways to topple them from power.

In 1984 the CIA began to mine Nicaraguan ports to prevent delivery of Soviet and Cuban arms. The Sandinistas succeeded in getting the World Court to condemn the American blockade effort. The American government also began to supply arms, food, uniforms, and advice to a group of anti-Sandinista guerrillas called the Contras, who hoped to overturn the regime they accused of being as authoritarian as that of Somoza.

The presence of another Marxist government in the Western Hemisphere disturbed many ordinary Americans. But a majority of citizens still remembered the Vietnam War and feared becoming involved in another endless military morass. For that reason and also because many thought the Contras unworthy of support, Congress vacillated in its response to administration requests to provide funds for them. In early 1983 the Democratic-controlled House of Representatives refused Contra military aid, but that June it agreed to provide $27 million for "humanitarian aid"—supplies, medicines, clothing, and the like. News of CIA involvement in mining Nicaraguan harbors outraged a majority of Congress. The Democratic speaker of the house, Tip O'Neill, called the Contras "butchers" and insisted they be abandoned by the United States. Congress at this point, over the president's loud protest, passed the Boland Amendment requiring the chief executive to consult Congress before spending any more money to support the anti-Sandinista war. Then after Sandinista leader Daniel Ortega visited Moscow, Congress relented and again voted $27 million in humanitarian aid to the Contras. The tug-of-war between the administration and a liberal Congress would have wide repercussions in other areas of foreign policy.

The Authoritarian versus Totalitarian Distinction

The Carter administration had made human rights violations a measure of international virtue, although it had not always applied the yardstick equally to all parties. Reagan would have none of this. He and his advisers found UN Ambassador Jeane Kirkpatrick's formula for distinguishing between "authoritarian" and "totalitarian" regimes more persuasive. The first were traditional tyrannies run by strong leaders, usually corrupt but not dangerous internationally. The second were like the Nazis and Communists: they imposed total ideological conformity on their society and were usually expansionist. The United States could afford to tolerate the former and in fact, although reluctantly, might be compelled to aid them if threatened. The latter were inveterate enemies who had to be stopped.

The theory justified bolstering tyrants such as Jean-Claude ("Baby Doc") Duvalier in Haiti and Ferdinand Marcos in the Philippines, although it did not preclude abandoning them when they lost all popular support, as both eventually did. It also excused continued relations with the repressive white regime in South Africa that denied elementary civil rights and civil liberties to its large black majority. The administration's tolerance of South African *apartheid* brought criticism from African-Americans and students as well as liberals. On scores of campuses during the 1980s protest demonstrations against South Africa, demands that American corporations and universities divest themselves of economic holdings in the country and that the United States join in imposing sanctions on the racist nation became the new version of the civil rights movement. Despite the protests the administration, fearing to precipitate social collapse from which African radicals and the Soviet Union might profit, refused to take overtly hostile steps against the regime in Pretoria. Rather, the president said, the United States must seek "constructive engagement" with the South African government to gradually move it toward racial justice without producing a catastrophic breakdown. Nevertheless Congress eventually voted sanctions.

The Middle East

In the Middle East the United States played an ambiguous role. The Reagan administration was an even better friend of Israel than its predecessors. Israel, in fact, became an unofficial ally of the United States. This connection made America the target of the most militant Arab nationalists, such as Libyan Muammar Qaddafi and Syria's Hafiz Assad, as well as of Islamic fundamentalists like Iran's Ayatollah Khomeini. The United States did not lose all its friends in the Arab world, however. The more moderate Arab nations, especially Egypt, Saudi Arabia, and the oil sheikdoms of the Persian Gulf region, loathed the extreme nationalists and the Islamic fundamentalists and looked to the United States for support.

The United States had several simultaneous objectives in the Middle East. It wished to protect the oil supply of the Western nations and avoid repeating the energy crisis of the 1970s. It also hoped to exclude the Soviet Union from a major role in the region. The key to stabilizing the region was to find some way of ending the continuing hostility toward Israel of all of its Arab neighbors except Egypt. This hostility, in turn, was clearly exacerbated by the forty-year-long problem of the Palestinians, who ever since Israeli independence had been refugees wanted by no one, not even their fellow Arabs. Many of the Palestinians supported the Palestine Liberation Organization (PLO), a group hostile to Israel's existence and dedicated to carving out some sort of independent Palestinian state from Israeli territory, by violence and terrorism if necessary.

For much of Reagan's first term the Middle East cockpit was Lebanon, a small Arab-speaking state with a large Christian population. In 1982 Israel, some said with United States approval, invaded Lebanon to expel the PLO and, the Israelis claimed, protect Lebanese Christians against their Muslim rivals. The Israelis rooted out the PLO, but the invasion soon turned into the Israeli equivalent of Vietnam, and the Israeli army gradually withdrew. Lebanon quickly collapsed into chaos. Christians fought Muslims, and Shiite Muslims under Khomeini's influence fought Sunni Muslims. Thousands died in the almost daily bombings and shellings, with neither side giving quarter. The Syrians introduced troops to fill the power vacuum left by the Israeli expulsion of the PLO, but they only added another element of disorder.

In 1983, as mentioned, the United States sent marines to the troubled nation as part of an international peacekeeping force. The effort to impose order offended the more militant Lebanese elements, especially the Party of God, a Khomeini-sponsored Shiite group. They soon made the United States a major target of their hatred. In April 1983 a car bomb exploded near the U.S. Embassy in Beirut killing fifty people. In October a bomb-laden vehicle driven by a fanatical anti-American crashed into the marine barracks in Beirut killing 241 U.S. servicemen.

Even after the United States withdrew its forces, the hostility of Islamic militants to America continued. During the months that followed, U.S. airlines, U.S. airline passengers in Europe and the Middle East, and U.S. service personnel in Europe became the targets of hijackings and terrorist attacks mounted by extremist groups, some apparently in the pay of Libya's Qaddafi, Syria's Assad, or Iran's Khomeini.

In Lebanon itself American reporters, businessmen, officials, and professors at the American University in Beirut were seized as hostages to coerce the United States into abandoning what the militants perceived as a pro-Israel, anti-Arab policy. The media played up the suffering of the hostages' families and, already sensitized to hostage taking by the Teheran embassy incident of 1979–81, the American public became emotionally caught up in the plight of the captives.

Despite their sympathies Americans had no reason to believe that the president would ever deal with terrorists who attacked innocent civilians. Reagan projected a tough image against international blackmailers. As he had announced during his debate with Carter in October 1980: "there will be no negotiation with terrorists of any kind." Surely he would not yield to terrorist blackmail.

Reagan's Reelection and Second Term

Reagan had made mistakes during his first term. He had promised to balance the budget, but deficits had soared out of sight. He had promised to make Americans once more respected in the world, but American civilians and service people were under attack all over Europe, and many American tourists were afraid to travel in the Mediterranean area. He had promised prosperity, but by early 1983 unemployment rates had reached forty-year records. One of the president's more disconcerting qualities was his weak grasp of detail. He often made statements that proved untrue. At one point, for example, he claimed that American submarines did not carry nuclear weapons. Of course they did. At another he announced that "growing and decaying vegetation" were "responsible for 93 percent of the oxides of nitrogen" that polluted the atmosphere. They were not. This tendency to misstate facts proved so embarrassing that his advisers began to steer him away from press conferences where he had to respond spontaneously to questions posed by reporters.

Yet as his first term wound down, the public continued to give him high marks. In early 1984 his approval rating was 54 percent according to a Gallup poll. In part this was because a sharp upturn in the economy finally began to push unemployment down. Inflation too had been tamed. But it was also because the white, middle-class American public could not find it in its collective heart to dislike Reagan. He seemed so "nice," such a good guy. The public particularly admired his bravery and good humor in those hours and days in 1981 after an obsessed young man tried to assassinate him in Washington. As he was brought into the hospital for chest surgery to remove the bullet, Reagan quipped to the doctors, "I hope you're Republicans," and "I forgot to duck." Critics ruefully called him "the Teflon president"; nothing distasteful stuck to his skin.

The renomination of the Reagan-Bush ticket in 1984 was a foregone conclusion. The battle to head the Democratic ticket, however, was hard fought. Front-runner from the outset was Walter Mondale, a former U.S. Senator from Minnesota, Carter's vice president, and a protégé of Hubert Humphrey. Mondale successfully cultivated many of the elements of the old New Deal coalition: the industrial trade unions, teachers, Catholics, racial minorities. His party rivals included Senator John Glenn of Ohio, the former astronaut; Jesse Jackson, a civil rights associate of Martin Luther King; and Gary Hart, the young, Kennedyesque senator from Colorado.

Glenn, a wooden speaker, quickly fell by the wayside. Jackson, an eloquent African-American minister, surprised everyone by making himself a credible candidate of a "Rainbow Coalition" of blacks, other racial minorities, poor whites, and left-liberals demanding a return to positive government on behalf of the nation's outsiders. Unfortunately Jackson made some antisemitic remarks that damaged him with many Democratic voters. Hart was the candidate of the "Atari Democrats," the well-educated young men and women of the baby boom generation who were sufficiently liberal to remain in the Democratic party but wanted to get away from the traditional focus on minorities and the poor. For a time Hart gave the Mondale forces a bad scare, but by the time of the Democratic convention the former vice president had the nomination sewed up.

The convention in San Francisco seemed to heal most of the party's wounds from the nomination campaign. Jackson delivered a speech in which he apologized for his unwise remarks. The keynote speaker was Governor Mario Cuomo of New York, who eloquently recounted his parents' rise from immigrant status to middle-class success. The Democrats, he said, were like a happy and compassionate family that provided help to all its members. Mondale himself, hoping to capitalize on a supposed "gender gap" between men and women in their support of Reagan, chose as his running mate Congresswoman Geraldine Ferraro of New York, the first woman on a major party presidential ticket. He also impressed observers with his courage when he declared in his acceptance speech that as president he would ask Congress for a major tax increase to bring down the runaway budget deficit. For a time after the convention the polls showed Mondale running neck-and-neck with Reagan.

Walter Mondale and Geraldine Ferraro at the 1984 Democratic National Convention.
(UPI/Bettmann Newsphotos)

The polls quickly turned around. Taking advantage of the American public's distaste for taxes, Reagan denounced Mondale's tax promise. "Democrats," he declared, "see an America where every day is April 15th." For Republicans, on the other hand, "everyday is the Fourth of July." The Democrats were their own worst enemies. Mondale lost whatever chance he had of winning in the South by first choosing Bert Lance, a Georgian and former aide to Jimmy Carter, to head the Democratic National Committee and then, when faced with criticism, withdrawing his name. Ferraro was not the asset she promised to be. Questions were raised about the tax returns she filed jointly with her husband, and her explanations suggested to many people that something fishy was involved. Mondale did well against the president in the first of two debates, but Reagan recouped in the second, and soon forged far ahead in the polls. By the end of September it was clear that the president would win and win big.

And he did. The Reagan-Bush ticket took every state in the union except Mondale's own Minnesota and won 59 percent of the popular vote. The president had won by large majorities in almost every voter category: the elderly, the young, women, Catholics, Protestants. Jews gave him larger percentages than they gave most Republicans; even union households, usually Democratic bastions, gave him almost half their votes. The president's coattails proved short, however. The Republicans gained only 14 seats in the House and lost two in the Senate.

Few presidents have ever been as successful in their second term as in their first. By the time they complete their fourth year in office, their opponents have become bolder and more adept at frustrating them; dissensions have appeared among their supporters; they often have enacted their legislative programs and have little new to offer. In Reagan's case the second term problem was exacerbated by his age. Born in 1911, by the time of his second inaugural Reagan was seventy-five, the oldest president ever to hold office. Although well preserved for a man of his years, age compounded by surgery for colon cancer and prostate problems had taken its toll. Never an attentive administrator he increasingly allowed the day-to-day running of his office to be handled by former Secretary of the Treasury Donald Regan, who in 1984 had exchanged places with James Baker to become White House chief of staff.

The Iran-Contra Affair

The president's inattention caused the administration grave difficulties in foreign affairs and resulted in an appalling loss in public standing.

Easily touched by individual suffering, Reagan was concerned about the Lebanon hostages and sensitive to their families' accusations that the administration was remiss in its efforts to recover them. Although he feared making the hostages a public issue and a test of administration capacity, when presented with a scheme to trade American arms for the hostages' release he went along despite all his talk of not dealing with terrorists.

The plan was concocted by CIA Director William Casey, National Security Council head Admiral John Poindexter, and Marine Corps Lieutenant Colonel Oliver North, Poindexter's aide. It seemed, in North's later words, to be "a neat idea." The Iranians had been fighting a desperate war against Iraq, a Persian Gulf neighbor, since 1980. Ever since their break with the United States following the shah's overthrow, they had been short of planes, guns, and ammunition and had been forced to throw waves of young, untrained men against their well-armed enemy, suffering horrendous losses in the process. They were eager to buy arms, but other nations disliked their fanaticism and most refused to sell up-to-date weapons to them. Their desperate need for modern weapons might be used, Casey and his colleagues felt, to get the Iranians to secure the hostages' release.

And there were other possibilities in such a secret arrangement. The United States had no reason to favor permanent enmity with Iran; that only helped the Soviet Union. The three men believed there were moderate elements in Teheran who, after the aged Ayatollah's death, might wish to reestablish relations with the United States and who might be attracted by an offer of arms. In fact it was this part of the deal that they emphasized when presenting their scheme to the president.

And there was still another likely bonus: some of the profits from arms sales to Iran could be used to finance the Contras. Because Congress was unwilling to provide money for the Nicaraguan "freedom fighters," aid would have to come from other sources or communism would continue to grow in the Western Hemisphere. North had been secretly soliciting private contributions for the Contras from rich Americans for some time. He had even secured a contribution from the sultan of Brunei, a pro-American, oil-rich Asian ruler. But far better would be a secret diversion of profits to the Contras from an Iranian arms deal. One of our major enemies would, unknowingly, be contributing to our fight against another of our enemies! The fact that these machinations ignored the Boland Amendment, made a mockery of American no-deals-with-terrorists principles, and were based on ignorance of Iranian politics did not deter the plotters.

In May 1986 Robert McFarlane, former national security adviser, led a secret American arms sale delegation to Iran carrying a cake and a Bible as gifts for their Iranian contacts. The Americans were treated rather offhandedly by these low-level officials, which suggested strongly that the anticipated diplomatic gains were probably illusory. Yet the Americans persisted. In all the Americans negotiated five arms deals with the Iranians, a process that yielded several million dollars, some portion of which was shunted to the Contras by North and Poindexter. The hostage yield proved disappointing, however. Only three Americans were released and, in fact, several more were kidnapped after the first hostages were let go.

The Scandal Breaks

In November 1986 a Lebanese newspaper published an account of the arms for hostages deal with Iran, and a tidal wave of criticism crashed over Reagan and his advisers. Within the administration itself Secretary of State George Shultz and Secretary of Defense Weinberger had objected to the arrangement when it was first discussed, but the president himself had been unwilling to see the scheme for what it was—a violation of his own resolve not to pay international blackmail. His first public response to the stories was that while we had sold "small amounts of weapons and spare parts" to Iran our only purpose had been to make contact with Iranian moderates.

At the end of November, while disclaiming full knowledge of the Iran-Contra scheme, he fired North and announced Poindexter's resignation. The following day he promised to appoint a special committee headed by former Senator John Tower of Texas to investigate the matter. Soon after, he appointed a special Watergate-type prosecutor to flush out any illegal acts. Meanwhile, a perfunctory investigation had been launched by Attorney General Edwin Meese that seemed aimed, critics would later say, at allowing the conspirators time to cover their tracks rather than finding out what had really happened.

The Iran-Contra affair finally peeled off the president's Teflon skin. The public had given Reagan credit for courage and boldness. Just the previous April he had ordered American air strikes against Libyan cities to teach Qaddafi, the suspected sponsor of much of the anti-Western terrorism, a lesson. Qaddafi had been squelched. Now the president had made a deal with the Iranians, another Mideast terrorist sponsor! Reagan was not acting like Rambo; he was acting like Casper Milquetoast. What anti-terrorist credibility could the United States now have in the world?

The administration's reputation soon suffered further blows. In February the Tower Commission absolved the president of direct knowledge of the diversion of funds to the Contras but reported that he had been confused and unaware of what his subordinates were planning. His "management style," the report said, was deeply flawed. The commission blamed White House Chief of Staff Regan for failing to prevent "the chaos that descended upon the White House." Regan tried to hold on to his office, but by this time Nancy Reagan, always protective of her husband's reputation, had turned against him and he was forced to resign. Replacing him was Howard Baker, a respected former Republican senator from Tennessee.

During the next few months, while a joint House-Senate congressional committee prepared to hold public hearings on the scandal, the president gradually conceded he had made mistakes. On March 4 he accepted "full responsibility" for the arms sales to Iran. But two weeks later he denied knowledge of the diversion of arms profits to the Contras. The televised congressional hearings began on May 5, and for the next three months scores of high federal officials appeared before the committee to describe their part in the complex affair. CIA Director Casey, who almost certainly was deeply implicated in the fiasco, died of a brain tumor in early May and was spared the ordeal. But Poindexter and North, especially, were severely grilled by the investigators, who charged that they had conducted a rogue operation—in effect a private manipulation of foreign policy—that ignored constituted authority and violated constitutional safeguards.

North was a well-spoken, clean-cut young marine officer who tried, with some success, to turn the attack against his attackers. Playing the role of an unashamed American patriot, he made the Iran-Contra scheme seem a bold attempt to counter the spineless Central American policies of the doves in Congress. The young officer made such a good first impression that many Americans watching the hearings forgot that he was defending a series of moves that were not only illegal but also, in the end, damaging to America's image as a bold defender of the Free World. For a time the country was seized by "Olliemania," a conviction, as one reporter wrote, that the colonel "somehow embodied Jimmy Stewart, Gary Cooper, and John Wayne in one bemedaled uniform."

The November 1987 report of the House-Senate Iran-Contra Committee blasted the plotters.

> The common ingredients of the Iran and contra policies were secrecy, deception, and disdain for law. A small group of senior officials believed that they alone knew what was right. . . . When exposure was threatened, they destroyed official documents and lied to cabinet officers, to the public, and to elected representatives in Congress.

Later Independent Counsel Lawrence Walsh obtained criminal indictments against a number of the participants.

Reagan and Soviet-American Relations

For a time the president's weakening grip affected Soviet-American relations. During his first term, as discussed, Reagan fired off regular volleys against the "evil empire." Soviet-American antagonism did not cease after 1984. In fact, in 1986 it took on new intensity as the United States and the Soviet Union became involved in a war of spies. When the United States arrested Soviet agent Gannady Zakharov, the Soviets responded by arresting *U.S. News & World Report* Moscow correspondent Nicholas Daniloff. Eventually one was traded for the other.

During Reagan's first term, Soviet-American relations were seriously impaired by the American arms buildup. Reagan sought to base a new class of intermediate range Pershing missiles in Europe to counter a Soviet buildup of equivalent missiles. The move mobilized a coalition of antiwar, antinuclear, and anti-American groups in Europe and America to march in protest. Despite the opposition the missiles were delivered and put in place on the soil of European NATO countries in the last months of 1983.

Star Wars

More disturbing to some groups was the president's strategic defense initiative (SDI) plan, soon labeled "Star Wars" by its opponents and the media. First announced in March 1983, the theory behind SDI was that a system could be built that would intercept and destroy en route any Soviet nuclear missiles fired at the United States. As such it would offer an alternative to nuclear retaliation. Fear of such retaliation, it was assumed, would serve as a deterrent to any attack. If either of the superpowers launched nuclear warheads at the other, it might destroy its opponent but would be certain to be destroyed in turn. The desire to avoid such mutually assured destruction (MAD) had prevented nuclear war for almost forty years, and there were many knowledgeable observers who believed that it was still the only effective defense against a humanity-destroying nuclear exchange.

SDI immediately came under attack from politicians, scientists, and academics. The indictment was broad ranging: it was impractical; no matter how sophisticated the technology, some attacking missiles would get through and cause untold destruction. It was not technically feasible; computers fail, rockets misfire, electrical circuits short. And there would be no way to test the Star Wars equipment; it would have to work the first time. Moreover there was the cost; it would absorb as much as a trillion dollars in the decade ahead. And Star Wars would only escalate the Cold War further. The Soviets were certain to try to find ways to equal it or counter it.

The criticism seemed compelling to many. Congress appropriated funds for preliminary research into Star Wars technology, but refused to make a full commitment. Yet whatever the misgivings of Americans and however the administration denied that it was merely a bargaining chip, SDI did probably goad the Soviet Union into major arms concessions.

Gorbachev

During most of Reagan's first term Russia was undergoing a rapid turnover of leadership. In 1982 the sixty-eight-year-old Yuri Andropov succeeded Leonid Brezhnev as Kremlin ruler. Less than two years later he died and was succeeded by the sickly Konstantin Chernenko. Chernenko lasted little more than a year and was followed in March 1985 by Mikhail Gorbachev. A healthy man of fifty-four, Gorbachev promised continuity in Soviet leadership for the first time in a generation.

He also promised a new era in Soviet life. Well-traveled, open in personal manner, impressed with the need to shake Soviet society out of its doldrums, Gorbachhev favored *glasnot* (intellectual openness) and *perestroika* (economic restructuring) to make the Soviet Union—left far behind economically and technologically by Western Europe, Japan, and America—competitive in the world. At home Gorbachev permitted greater freedom of expression. He allowed a number of prominent dissenters, long refused visas, to leave the Soviet Union. He sought to reform the production system by introducing quasi-capitalist incentives and greater local autonomy to factory managers. He tried to discourage widespread Soviet alcoholism by making vodka more expensive. He had no intention of turning the Soviet Union into a Western democracy or surrendering the ultimate tight control of the Communist party, but he saw that the rigid, old bureaucratic system inevitably consigned his country to second-class status in competition with the industrialized democracies and must be changed.

Essential to Gorbachev's reform program was détente with the United States. The Soviets could not now afford to begin another major arms race with America, especially one involving advanced computer technology. Soviet science was simply not the equal to the West's in this area and, short of extraordinary efforts, could not compete. SDI thus posed a major threat to Gorbachev's plans for a revitalized Soviet Union, as did the arms race generally. The competition must be stopped.

Arms Negotiations

In late 1983, in protest against the Pershing missiles Soviet negotiators walked out of the nuclear disarmament talks with the United States long underway in Geneva. But in January 1985 the two superpowers agreed to resume the Geneva talks with SDI included on the discussion agenda. Soon after Reagan declared that his ultimate goal was "the complete elimination of nuclear weapons" from the world. The statement and American willingness to discuss Star Wars suggested that SDI was mostly a bargaining chip to be surrendered in exchange for major Soviet arms concessions.

The new Soviet-American arms talks began in Geneva in March 1985. Gorbachev announced that the Soviet Union would cease to deploy intermediate range nuclear missiles and called on the United States to do the same. He also asked for a summit meeting with the American president to consider the arms race question.

The Geneva meeting between Reagan and Gorbachev in November 1985 was a disappointment to the friends of arms reduction. The two nations signed some minor agreements on scientific and cultural exchanges and authorized the resumption of direct air flights between the two nations that had been suspended at the time of the Soviet invasion of Afghanistan, but they achieved little on the disarmament issue. Nevertheless Reagan said, "We are headed in the right direction."

In October of the following year the two superpower leaders met again, this time in Reykjavík, Iceland, to consider once more the arms limitation issue. The Americans were ill-prepared. At one point Reagan promised that the United States would surrender *all* its nuclear armaments if the Soviets did the same—and if the Soviets accepted continued Star Wars research and development. The president had not consulted America's NATO allies, had not, apparently, checked with his advisers, and did not seem to know really what he was offering. In fact, since the Warsaw Pact countries far outstripped NATO in conventional arms, the arrangement would have handed the Soviet Union an enormous military advantage. Fortunately Gorbachev did not take the offer seriously. Instead he insisted that Star Wars be stopped, and when Reagan refused, the Iceland summit meeting broke up on a sour note.

The INF Agreement

Despite the abortive Iceland meeting, neither side allowed the arms reduction issue to rest. Gorbachev continued to need a major reduction in military expenditures to improve the ability of the Soviet economy to provide consumer goods for civilians. After the Iran-Contra scandal Reagan needed some major triumph if he was to rescue his administration's reputation and finish his presidency in a burst of glory. Not everyone looked forward to arms reductions. In both the Soviet Union and the United States hawks and Cold Warriors perceived arms reduction as a trick of the other side to gain a military advantage. American conservatives such as Senator Jesse Helms of North Carolina and the journalist George Will criticized the propensity of well-intentioned Americans to believe *any* arms reduction agreement a victory.

Yet the arms reduction process continued. In February 1987 Gorbachev offered to sign "without delay" an agreement to eliminate all Soviet and American intermediate range nuclear forces (INF), those weapons that NATO had deployed just a few years before. A whole class of nuclear weapons would be junked, and he would not ask that Star Wars be abandoned.

In the United States critics of arms reduction denounced the proposal. The American NATO commander in Europe said that it would expose NATO troops to the far more numerous Warsaw Pact conventional forces without the nuclear deterrent they formerly wielded to offset the imbalance. Although the administration insisted that Soviet compliance with any arms reduction treaty would be subject to strict verification procedures, critics continued to express doubts of Soviet trustworthiness.

Despite the doubts, the two parties were able to come to an agreement in time for a major summit meeting in Washington in early December 1987. The occasion became a major media event with the administration pulling out all the stops to make the biggest splash possible. Gorbachev was going to be used to restore a flagging administration's popularity and prestige. The Soviet leader had no objection. For his part he would use the event to consolidate his standing among his colleagues in the Kremlin.

The Gorbachevs arrived in Washington and were treated as visiting royalty. Raisa Gorbachev, like her husband, seemed a different sort of Soviet person, well-dressed, articulate, and sprightly. The Russians pulled out all the stops to charm the American public. Gorbachev told jokes and smiled a lot. He held a meeting in the Soviet Embassy for a contingent of American intellectuals and entertainment figures and flattered them by suggesting that they could help construct "interrelatedness, global peace, democratization." On the way to a White House bargaining session he ordered his chauffeur to stop on the Washington street so he could shake hands with startled pedestrians.

Reagan hoped he could induce Gorbachev to open the emigration doors for Soviet dissenters and announce a date for Soviet withdrawal from Afghanistan. The Soviet leader refused to do either, and Reagan had to be content with the INF elimination treaty. The two men did agree to meet in Moscow during the summer of 1988 to sign, if possible, an arms reduction agreement dealing with strategic, long range nuclear missiles. Many observers doubted, correctly as it turned out, that such a treaty would be ready in time.

Although he did not get all he had wanted, Reagan was immensely pleased with the results. He had been deeply impressed by Gorbachev and concluded that at long last the Soviets had abandoned their quest for world domination. His response appalled some on the far right who now declared that the president had become an unwitting tool of the communists. To almost everyone's surprise a majority of the announced 1988 Republican presidential candidates declared they opposed Senate ratification of the treaty as signed, and some observers predicted that it would have a hard time getting through the Senate confirmation process unscathed.

The predictions were wrong. Just before Reagan arrived in Moscow for his final summit with the Soviet leader in June 1988, the Senate ratified the treaty. Actually the Moscow summit turned out to be largely a public relations gesture; nothing further was accomplished in the arms reduction process, although the Soviets did announce a timetable for leaving Afghanistan. Yet taken as a whole, the summits had achieved one important administration end: by summer of 1988 Reagan had regained most of his lost popularity. The Iran-Contra affair appeared to have blown over. The Teflon principle was once more alive and well.

Continuing Economic Concerns

As Reagan's second term opened in 1985, the country's economic performance continued to present a mixed picture. Unemployment and the inflation rate remained low. But other measures of the nation's economic well-being were less positive.

Agriculture was seriously depressed during the Reagan years. Once more farmers were caught in a squeeze. During the inflation of the 1970s and early 1980s farm prices had been high and moving constantly higher. As usual in such circumstances farmers had borrowed money and bought new equipment to increase output. Then the government got a tight grip on inflation. In May 1985 farm prices were more than 10 percent below those of a year before and farmers were in trouble.

The administration tinkered with the situation. Reagan lifted the wheat export embargo that his predecessor had imposed on the Soviet Union after Afghanistan but rejected as "budget busting" a congressional measure to provide farmers with debt relief. The administration, moreover, in line with its deregulatory urge, pushed through a new farm bill that reduced federal supports for farm prices. In 1986 the farm belt was seething with discontent against the Republican administration it had so enthusiastically endorsed five or six years before.

More Deficits

During Reagan's second term, the budget deficit continued to soar, reaching over $220 billion in 1986. Even worse American exports continued to fall further behind imports. In 1984 the American trade deficit had reached $107 billion. In 1987 it leaped to $170 billion, the highest in history by far.

For over a century the United States had had a trade surplus; ever since World War I, seventy years before, it had been a creditor nation. By the mid-1980s Americans were buying far more from other nations than they were selling to them, and paying for the excess by going into debt. By 1990 by one estimate Americans would have to pay out over $100 billion each year in interest to foreigners who had lent the United States money. Meanwhile foreigners were exchanging their IOUs for American real estate, factories, and stocks and bonds. Some perceptive observers feared the United States was fast becoming an economic colony of Japan and Western Europe.

There were several common explanations for the increasing inability of the United States to compete in the international economy. One was the high price of American dollars relative to other currencies. This made all American goods expensive in yen, marks, francs, and pounds. The high value of the dollar, in turn, resulted from the high interest rates of the Volcker years at the Federal Reserve Board.

Competition in Technology

But there were other reasons as well, ones that promised to hurt American exports even after the dollar began to fall, as it did in late 1987 and early 1988. American goods, it was said, were no longer as desirable as those of its major industrial competitors.

Automobiles imported from Japan line a New Jersey dock. (JeanPierre Laffont /Sygma)

The charge had much substance. Compared to the Japanese and the West Europeans, and with the exception of aircraft and computers, the United States often produced products that were inferior to its competitors'. Americans may have pioneered the video cassette recorder, the pocket calculator, the long-playing record, and other consumer electronics, but the Japanese had learned to make them cheaper and better and had swept American-made items off the shelves. At one time the United States sold thousands of American automobiles abroad; by the 1980s the big three American car manufacturers were finding it difficult to hold on to even their markets at home.

A tragic event of 1986 underscored America's technological weakness. Ever since the last manned moon expedition in 1974, the National Aeronautics and Space Administration had come to rely on the reusable space shuttle as the chief vehicle for its activities. The shuttle was supposed to pay its way in a time of reduced budgets for space exploration by carrying commercial payloads into orbit. On January 28, 1986, an unusually cold day in south Florida, the shuttle *Challenger* exploded in a ball of flame shortly after lift off from Cape Kennedy. Seven crew members, including Christa McAuliffe, a Concord, New Hampshire, school teacher who was chosen to publicize the shuttle program among school children, died in the blast.

An investigation determined that the cold weather had damaged the shuttle O-ring seals, allowing combustible gases to be released. For two years the American space program virtually shut down while the flaws were repaired. Having neglected to develop other rocket launching systems, during this period American communications firms turned to other nations for needed launch services, thus depriving the United States of millions of dollars. Meanwhile the Soviets continued to widen the space program gap that the United States had allowed to open. Although the shuttle launch program resumed in 1988, by that time America had clearly lost its lead in space. Many experts wondered if it could ever regain it.

There was another side of the picture that was not so unfavorable to American ingenuity and innovation. Several of America's major international competitors imposed barriers on foreign goods. Japan, for example, in order to protect its farmers, refused to import American rice and beef, although they were both cheaper than the domestic product. The Japanese, in fact, refused to buy very much of anything from abroad, despite efforts of their own government to increase consumption. At the same time, American firms insisted, they often resorted to industrial espionage to steal American technology or turned to "dumping" products in the United States at a loss in order to undercut American manufacturers and gain control of the American market. In March 1987 President Reagan responded to alleged Japanese dumping of semiconductor chips with high duties on a wide range of Japanese electronics products.

Many Americans deeply resented "unfair" Japanese trade practices. In Detroit automobile workers and their spokespeople demanded high tariffs on Japanese cars. At one point, to dramatize their displeasure, autoworkers publicly destroyed a Japanese automobile with sledge hammers. The government resisted strong protectionist moves as likely to set off an international trade war and seriously weaken the free world economy. It imposed a quota system on Japanese car imports, but made it temporary. Most economists endorsed the administration's restraint, but in the 1988 presidential nominating campaign at least one Democratic candidate, Congressman Richard Gephardt, of Missouri, made protectionism the keystone of his platform.

The Stock Market

One of the more buoyant features of the economy in 1986–87 was the tremendous stock market surge. Fueled by foreign stock buyers seeking outlets for their dollars and by Americans swept up in a speculative frenzy, the Dow-Jones industrial stock averages leaped to over 2700 by the late summer of 1987. The surge created hundreds of billions of dollars of paper wealth and produced a feeling of euphoria in financial circles.

The 1980s bull market, like its 1920s predecessor, was sustained by a mood of unrestrained materialism. Thousands of the brightest young Americans made becoming millionaires before the age of thirty their fondest goal. Enrollments in Masters of Business Administration programs soared; so did law school applications. The new class of *yuppies* (young upwardly mobile urban professionals) worked hard in finance, the media, and corporate law, and seemed to avoid personal commitment to families and spouses. Players in the fast track, many were drawn to alcohol, marijuana, and cocaine to relieve the tensions in their lives. In 1984 Jay McInerny's novel *Bright Lights, Big City* told their story through the misadventures of a young man in New York just after college who cannot pull his personal life together and wanders in a daze of "coke" and despair.

The bull market was also pumped up by the take-over game. By the early 1980s clever financiers like Michael Milken and Ivan Boesky had discovered that many large corporations were worth more as separate pieces than as a whole. If they could win control of such companies they could sell off the valuable parts and make immense profits. To achieve control the "corporate raiders" needed capital to buy up the firms' stock. Their device was the "junk bond," a high-interest security. These were sold to provide the raiders with cash for the buy-out or exchanged for the stock of the target corporation. The take-overs often made millions for the promoters, but left many firms with enormous fixed debts that threatened their solvency.

None of this manipulation was illegal in itself, but at times the take-overs were accompanied by criminal use of insider information. In 1987 the Justice Department indicted Boesky and lesser raiders for picking up millions through insider information.

On October 9, 1987, the stock bubble burst. After several weeks of moderate decline the Dow-Jones averages plummeted 500 points on *Black Monday,* the largest one-day drop in the history of Wall Street. Wall Street's collapse shook the foreign stock exchanges; several lost an even larger proportion of their value overnight. Over the next few months all the exchanges proved volatile before settling down.

For a time experts feared that the 1987–88 market downturn would mark the beginning of a long international economic slide. Holding American budget deficits responsible, they insisted that the government take drastic steps to cut them. The jolt of Black Monday brought Congress and the president together to try to break the long-standing budget deadlock, but the two sides could only agree on minor tax changes and increases in the spending cuts mandated by the Gramm-Rudman-Hollings law.

The major difficulty, as in the past, was the impasse over new taxes versus spending cuts and social programs versus defense. Part of the problem, however, was the Tax Reform Act of 1986. This measure made the federal tax system fairer by scaling back tax deductions for interest payments and some kinds of real estate taxes and reducing the amounts deductible for business entertainment and other expenses largely incurred by upper-income people. In exchange for such concessions, it lowered the maximum income tax rates from 50 to 28 percent. It also dropped millions of lower-income people from the income tax rolls. To raise taxes promised to violate the many bargains made to get the reform bill through Congress.

Fortunately the worst did not happen. There was some good news for the American economy in early 1988. In the last weeks of 1987 the American dollar began to fall against the major foreign currencies. The effect was to make American exports cheaper and foreign imports more expensive. The 1988 trade deficit was 137 billion, down significantly from 1987. No one could tell whether the trend would continue; no one could tell whether America had once again become competitive in the world's markets.

End-of-Term Issues

Reagan and the Supreme Court

As the Reagan administration approached its end, the desire of the president and other conservatives to entrench their principles in the Supreme Court grew more compelling. By the midpoint of his second term Reagan had been able to appoint two conservative justices, Sandra Day O'Connor and Antonin Scalia, to the highest federal court. After Chief Justice Warren Burger decided to step down, he was able as well to elevate associate justice William Rehnquist, a conservative, to his place. Yet the moderates and liberals continued to get their way on many social issues that came before the court. Then in 1987 Justice Lewis Powell, a political moderate who had often been a swing vote on key issues, resigned for reasons of health. Reagan now had a chance to truly tip the balance to the political right and quickly nominated federal appeals court Judge Robert Bork for Powell's slot.

The Bork nomination became a battle royal between liberals and conservatives. Liberals claimed that Bork had no regard for the right of privacy, that his view that the Supreme Court must always be guided by the "original intent" of congress was seriously outdated and reactionary, and that he was hostile to civil rights. Conservatives claimed that he was a brilliant and thoughtful traditionalist who would turn the Court away from the disruptive "judicial activism" of the recent past and return it to a more appropriate role. In the end the Senate by a wide margin rejected the nomination.

The chagrined president now hastily nominated another conservative federal judge, Douglas Ginsburg. But Ginsburg admitted that he had smoked marijuana as a law school professor and soon withdrew his name. Finally Reagan nominated Judge Anthony Kennedy. Although a conservative, Kennedy seemed a reasonable man and was confirmed without a serious fight. It now looked as if, no matter what the fate of the political right at the polls, one of the three branches of government would be firmly locked up for the conservatives for many years to come.

Nicaragua Again

As the Reagan administration wound down, Nicaragua once more became a major issue. Most Americans still shied away from a major military involvement in Central America. A poll in early 1986 showed 62 percent of the voters opposed to giving aid to the Contras. Even among Reagan supporters only 35 percent favored contra military aid. Yet the administration continued to press for the overthrow of the Sandinistas and continued to demand that Congress provide military supplies for the freedom fighters.

In late 1987 it began to look as if a peaceful solution to the Nicaraguan problem might be achieved. In early 1987 the five Central American presidents, led by Oscar Arias Sanchez of Costa Rica, proposed a peace plan to bring the Contras and

Sandinistas together in face-to-face negotiations, restore democratic rights in Nicaragua, and end the threat of American intervention. The Arias plan aroused enthusiasm around the world and won the Nobel Peace Prize for the Costa Rican president.

At home most Democrats and many moderates approved the scheme. The right, including the administration, remained skeptical. Although Sandinista President Ortega agreed to meet directly with his Contra enemies and restored some civil liberties to the country, Reagan continued to denounce his regime and demand further funding for the Contras. At one point Speaker of the House James Wright declared that he believed the president would only be content with a military victory and that he did not want a peaceful solution. By the early months of 1988 it remained unclear whether Nicaragua would continue to be a festering sore or whether the healing process had begun.

The 1988 Presidential Election

For a whole generation now the presidential election process had become longer, more expensive, and more distracting. By the 1980s campaigning for the major party nominations began almost two years before election day and involved a half-dozen or more serious candidates in each party hurtling from coast to coast to collect delegates from the thirty or so caucuses and primaries that were held early in the election year.

For 1988, the year that marked the end of the Reagan administration, both parties were seeking presidential candidates. In the Republican camp the two leading contenders were Vice President George Bush and Senate Minority Leader Bob Dole of Kansas. Both men were approximately in the Republican center. There was no Republican left anymore; it had virtually disappeared since Reagan's advent.

The Democrats started with eight serious candidates: former Colorado senator Gary Hart; Governor Michael Dukakis of Massachusetts; Senator Paul Simon of Illinois; Congressman Richard Gephardt of Missouri; former governor Bruce Babbitt of Arizona; Senator Joseph Biden of Delaware; and the Reverend Jesse Jackson, like Hart, a major contender from 1984. Hart was the frontrunner at the beginning, but in the summer of 1987 he destroyed his chances by involving himself with a young woman who was not his wife and then denying their relationship. Many Americans took this as a sign of poor judgment if not dubious personal morals. Hart resigned from the race. In December 1987 he decided to return, but did poorly thereafter and ceased to be a serious contender. By this time Senator Biden, having been caught plagiarizing other men's speeches and inventing a law school record for himself, also withdrew.

By late spring George Bush had far outstripped Dole and sewed up the Republican nomination. The Democratic race lasted longer with Jesse Jackson, representing the party's most liberal wing, running closely behind Dukakis in the primaries. Jackson's appeal to African-American voters resembled John Kennedy's to Catholics in 1960: he was one of them and he symbolized their hopes for full political acceptance. But many white Democrats perceived him as too radical; others simply would not vote for a black man. In the end Jackson fell behind Dukakis.

At the Atlanta convention in July Dukakis easily won the Democratic nomination. Jackson's supporters demanded that he be given second place. But Dukakis and the party leaders, fearing that a Dukakis-Jackson ticket could not win, refused. Instead, the Massachusetts governor chose as his running mate Lloyd Bentsen, a conservative senator from Texas who balanced the ticket ideologically and gave the Democrats a fighting chance to win the big Texas electoral vote. Jackson promised to campaign for the party candidates in the fall.

By the time the Republicans assembled in New Orleans to confirm Bush's nomination, the Democrats were ahead in the opinion polls. Bush hoped to don the mantle of the still popular Reagan and identify himself with Republican prosperity and other administration accomplishments. But initially many voters perceived him as a rich Yale "preppie" who lacked the common touch. Party leaders worried that he could not attract the "Reagan Democrats," blue-collar Democratic voters who had defected to Ronald Reagan in 1980 and 1984. He also seemed stiff and uncaring, qualities that seemed to repel women voters especially.

Bush succeeded in allaying some of these feelings in an effective acceptance speech following his formal nomination in New Orleans. But he wounded himself by choosing as his running mate the forty-one-year-old senator from Indiana, Dan Quayle. Soon after Quayle's selection it became known that in 1969 he had joined the Indiana National Guard to avoid active service in Vietnam. Critics said that he had used his family's money and influence to enter the guard at a time when there were few openings and most other men could not choose that option. To the skeptics Quayle seemed a draft-evader and the son of privileged wealth.

Despite Quayle, Bush quickly took the lead. The Republican managers went on the attack with a negative campaign that depicted Dukakis as an extreme liberal who endorsed abortion on demand, had freed on parole a dangerous black criminal, and would saddle the American people with new taxes for expensive social programs. At the same time, to distinguish himself modestly from his predecessor, Bush talked of a "kinder, gentler nation" and "a thousand points of light" representing voluntary private efforts to improve the lot of the nation's underprivileged. He also repeated over and over again the promise: "no new taxes."

Dukakis tried to fend off the Republican attacks. He warned that America's world economic lead would dwindle further if steps were not taken to reverse its decline and said the economy was as full of holes as Swiss cheese. He emphasized his "competence" to handle the difficult tasks of governing. But many people found him too passionless, too cerebral. The Republicans, moreover, could claim that the country was prosperous and at peace. Long before November Dukakis was running far behind.

The election was a resounding Bush-Quayle victory. The Republican ticket was elected by a popular majority of 48.8 million to 41.8 million. In the electoral college Bush received 426 electoral votes to his opponent's 111. The Dukakis-Bentsen vote was concentrated in the Northeast, the upper midwest, and the Pacific Northwest, the more liberal regions of the country. The new Republican regional coalition of the South and West had held fast.

And yet there was no sign of a mandate such as Reagan had received in 1980. Indeed, the Democrats increased their majorities slightly in congress. For the first time since 1960 the party winning the presidency had actually lost congressional seats.

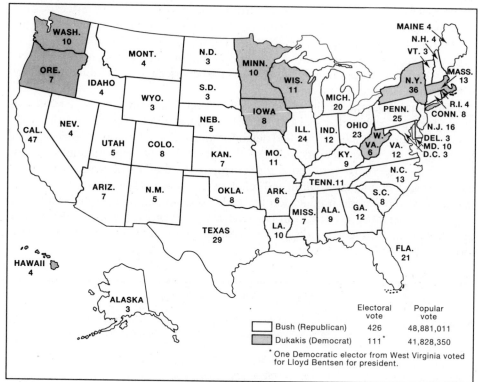

Figure 15–4 The 1988 Presidential Election

The End of the Reagan Era

Ronald Reagan left office on January 20, 1989. His administration had spanned eight eventful years. But what did they mean?

The public mandate of 1980, confirmed in 1984, had been an experiment to see if less government would work better than the system that had evolved under the New Deal–Fair Deal–Great Society programs and had been consolidated, if not extended, under Republican presidents. Reagan had helped to stop the growth of government and had returned economic responsibility to individuals. But he had not succeeded in dismantling the social service state he had inherited from his predecessors. In the end he had proven to be as pragmatic as president of the United States as he had been as governor of California. In foreign affairs too he had revealed himself as a practical man. Having labeled the Soviet Union the evil empire, in his last months he negotiated the most sweeping nuclear arms reduction in U.S. history. Like Dwight Eisenhower and Richard Nixon before him, he had, whatever his intentions, legitimized the role of government in America that the Democrats had bequeathed.

As the nation approached the 1990s immense problems remained. The United States faced the prospect of relative economic decline in the face of powerful challenges from abroad. These were not from its adversaries in the Marxist camp, but from its fellow capitalist nations. Could the United States compete with Japan and the Pacific rim? Could it compete with the West Europeans? In 1992 Europe was due to become a single economic unit, one with 320 million consumers and a total GNP greater than that of the United States. Would the American giant be able to keep up with the new European colossus?

And what about the quality of American life? Could something be done to elevate the sodden underclass that mocked the nation's ideals? Could crime and drugs be eliminated from the cities' streets and neighborhoods? Could the natural environment be rescued from steady deterioration and the natural beauty of the mountains, lakes, beaches, and forests be restored and maintained? Could the country's antagonistic cultural, racial, ethnic, ideological, and religious components live together in relative harmony? Could American education be made equal to that of any other nation on earth and Americans rescued from the ignorance and provinciality that threatened their leadership? These were the challenges of the 1990s and would probably remain those of the twenty-first century.

FOR FURTHER READING

Reagan's background is brilliantly analyzed in Garry Wills, *Reagan's America* (1988). Robert Dallek in *Ronald Reagan and the Politics of Symbolism* (1984) seeks to psychoanalyze the Reagan movement.

The story of the political New Right has been told in the following skeptical or hostile works: Alan Crawford, *Thunder on the Right: The "New Right" and the Politics of Resentment* (1980); Thomas Ferguson and Joel Rogers, *Right Turn: The Decline of the Democrats and the Future of American Politics* (1986); Sidney Blumenthal, *The Rise of the Counter-Establishment: From Conservative Ideology to Political Power* (1986). A less partisan treatment is Paul Gottfried and Thomas Fleming, *The Conservative Movement* (1988). For the neoconservatives see Peter Steinfels, *The Neo-Conservatives: The Men Who Are Changing America's Politics* (1979). The New Right states its own case in Robert W. Whitaker (ed.), *The New Right Papers* (1982); Martin Anderson, *Revolution* (1988); and Richard Viguerie, *The Establishment vs. the People: Is a New Populist Revolt on the Way?* (1983).

For the Christian right see the rather overwrought Flo Conway and Jim Siegeleman, *Holy Terror: The Fundamentalist War on America's Freedoms in Religion, Politics, and Our Lives* (1984). More judicious studies include, Erling Jorstad, *The Politics of Moralism: The New Christian Right in American Life* (1981); Robert C. Liebman and Robert Wuthnow (eds.), *The New Christian Right: Mobilization and Legitimation* (1983); and Richard John Neuhaus and John Cromartie (eds.), *Piety and Politics: Evangelicals and Fundamentalists Confront the World* (1987).

Two works by conservative preachers convey the views of the new Christian right: Tim LaHaye, *The Battle for the Mind* (1980) and Jerry Falwell, *The Fundamentalist Phenomenon: The Resurgence of Conservative Christianity* (1986).

The televangelist phenomenon is described by Larry Martz, *Ministry of Greed: The Inside Story of the Televangelists and their Holy Wars* (1988) and Jeffrey K. Hadden and Charles E. Swann, *Prime Time Preachers: The Rising Power of Televangelism* (1981).

The conservative economic views of Reagan's supporters can be followed in Jude Wanniski, *The Way the World Works: How Economies Fail—and Succeed* (1978); Alan S. Blinder, *Hard Heads, Soft Hearts: Tough-Minded Economics for a Just Society* (1987); and Paul Craig Roberts, *The Supply-Side Revolution* (1984). Also see George Gilder, *Wealth and Poverty* (1981). For the views of the man who helped engineer the Reagan tax cuts see David Stockman's *The Triumph of Politics: The Inside Story of the Reagan Revolution* (1986).

Critical appraisals of Reaganomics include Robert Lekachman, *Vision and Nightmares: America After Reagan* (1988); Barry Bluestone and Bennett Harrison, *The Deindustrialization of America* (1982); and Benjamin M. Friedman, *Day of Reckoning: The Consequences of American Economic Policy under Reagan and After* (1988). Also see Martha Derthick and Paul Quirk, *The Politics of Deregulation* (1985).

Reaganite social policies were influenced by works such as Charles Murray, *Losing Ground: American Social Policy, 1950–1980* (1984).

A vivid, if biased, compendium of what Americans were thinking about in the Reagan years is Studs Terkel's *The Great Divide: Second Thoughts on the American Dream* (1988). For the yuppie phenomenon of the seventies and eighties see Paul C. Light, *Baby Boomers* (1988).

Reagan's ability to manipulate the media is described in Mark Hertsgaard, *On Bended Knee: The Press and the Reagan Presidency* (1988).

One good place to begin any consideration of Soviet-American policy during the Reagan period is Mikhail Gorbachev, *Perestroika: New Thinking for Our Country and the World* (1987). Also see, however, Alexander Haig, *Caveat* (1984) and Strobe Talbott, *Deadly Gambits* (1984).

For the best account of the Iran-Contra affair see William S. Cohen and George J. Mitchell, *Men of Zeal: A Candid Inside Story of the Iran-Contra Hearings* (1988). Also see *The Tower Commission Report* (1987). How the Iran-Contra fiasco immobilized the Reagan administration is described in Jane Mayer and Doyle McManus, *Landslide: The Unmaking of the President, 1984–1988* (1988).

As the Reagan administration wound down former members wrote *kiss-and-tell* books that revealed interesting details on how the government was run during the 1980s. Some of these are Donald T. Regan, *For the Record: From Wall Street to Washington* (1988); Larry Speakes, *Speaking Out: Inside the Reagan White House* (1988); and Michael K. Deaver, *Behind the Scenes* (1987).

Index